THE NEW PERSPECTIVE ON PAUL

The New Perspective on Paul

Revised Edition

James D. G. Dunn

WILLIAM B. EERDMANS PUBLISHING COMPANY

GRAND RAPIDS, MICHIGAN / CAMBRIDGE, U.K.

Originally published 2005 in Germany
as part of the Wissenschaftliche Untersuchungen zum Neuen Testament series by
Mohr Siebeck Tübingen

Revised edition published 2008 in the United States of America by
Wm. B. Eerdmans Publishing Co.
2140 Oak Industrial Drive N.E., Grand Rapids, Michigan 49505 /
P.O. Box 163, Cambridge CB3 9PU U.K.
www.eerdmans.com

Printed in the United States of America

12 11 10 09 08   7 6 5 4 3 2 1

ISBN 978-0-8028-4562-7

Note: Chapter One has been modified and expanded from its original publication.

To
Tom Wright

φίλος,
συνεργὸς καὶ συστρατιώτης
ἐπίσκοπος

Contents

Preface

Choosing a title for a book is always a hazardous business. It has to be a title which is informative, but which also attracts attention, rather than being dully or merely descriptive. And yet the more it attracts attention, the more likely it is to cause misunderstanding or to be misrepresented. So I choose this title, *The New Perspective on Paul*, with some misgivings.

I do so, in the first place, since my article of the same title (reprinted as ch. 2 below) is regularly regarded as signalling a new phase in Pauline studies or a fresh way of looking at Paul's gospel and theology (or at his teaching on justification by faith in particular). Since the volume largely consists of a collection of this and twenty-one other essays which in one way or another speak to or try to advance this 'new perspective', the title could have been *'The New Perspective on Paul' and Other Essays*. But that would not make sufficiently clear that the large first essay (ch. 1) is entirely new and written for the volume, and it is this new essay, 'The New Perspective on Paul: whence, what and whither?', to which I particularly want to draw interested readers' attention. The final essay, on Phil. 3.2-14, also is written for this volume to indicate a renewed appreciation of just how effective is this summary of the full-roundedness of Paul's theology on the controverted subjects.

More to the point, the title 'the New Perspective' seems to have struck a chord with many, and to have become established as the most obvious referent for this different or fresh way of looking at Paul, particularly among those who are critical of 'the new perspective' (as the bibliography attests). So the reference is eminently recognizable; those for whom the volume has been put together will know almost at once what the content of the volume is likely to be. And given the controversy which 'the new perspective on Paul' has generated, it will easily be recognized that the volume is intended as my attempt to respond to the debate on the 'new perspective', as well as providing a resource for any who might find it helpful to have ready access to the full range of my developing thoughts/insights on the subject.

All that being so, I need to add at once that the title should not be read as '*the* new perspective on Paul', as though that was the *only* 'new perspective' possible or accessible to students of Paul; given the brief history of the title, it would have been more misleading to entitle the volume 'A New Perspective on Paul'. Nor should it be read as 'the *new* perspective on Paul', as implying that any and every *old* perspective is thereby rendered passé or condemned to the dustbin; quite the contrary, as the opening essay should make clear. Nor should it be read as a claim to provide a definitive statement of 'The New Perspective on Paul'; in the pages that follow, I speak only for myself, not as representative of some kind of 'school'. Nor, perhaps I should add, is 'the new perspective' some kind of 'dogma' which is somehow binding on its 'adherents'; that is not how properly critical (including self-critical) exegesis and historical scholarship goes about its task.

The title simply indicates my continuing belief that 'the new perspective' has provided fresh and valuable insights into Paul's theology and continues to contribute to a more rounded appreciation of the mission and theology of Saul the Pharisee become Paul the Christian apostle. As the opening essay should make clear, I have mostly found the discussion generated by and round 'the new perspective' stimulating and informative, sometimes correcting, but always clarifying and sharpening my own appreciation of Paul. The volume, then, is not a passionate defence of 'the new perspective', as though 'the new perspective' was an item of faith to die for, or as though every criticism of whatever I had written earlier had, as a matter of honour, to be resolutely rebuffed. My aim in all my writing is always to offer a contribution to a collegial and developing appreciation of what is, of course, a much richer and fuller theology than any one person can formulate or single essay, or volume, can encapsulate. So, in this case, the opening essay attempts to explain how I came to 'the new perspective', to clarify what I understand it to be, and to take the discussion further. And the final essay attempts to demonstrate the richness and fullness of Paul's understanding of God's saving righteousness as illustrated by the single passage, Phil. 3.2-14.

I am grateful, then, to Jörg Frey, editor of WUNT, for the original suggestion that I should put together my essays on 'the new perspective', and for encouraging me to provide the opening essay. I am grateful also to the editors and publishers of the original articles for permission to reprint them, and to Henning Ziebritzki, of Mohr Siebeck, who undertook to reprint articles from the pre-computer phase of my research on the subject. I owe a considerable debt of gratitude to Friedrich Avemarie, John Barclay, Kevin Bywater, Don Garlington, Michael Gorman, Terry Halewood, Peter O'Brien and Michael Thompson for help with bibliography; and to Henning Ziebritzki for letting me see an early proof copy of the second volume of Carson, O'Brien & Seifrid, *Justification and Variegated Nomism*. Mark Mattison's Paul Page on the web (www.thepaulpage.com) is an excellent resource for those interested in the ongoing debate.

But my main thanks are due to those with whom I was able to discuss some or all of the subject matter of the first chapter, or who read earlier drafts of parts or the whole of the first chapter, and who contributed often valuable comment and advice — Friedrich Avemarie, John Barclay, Phillip Esler, Don

Garlington, Simon Gathercole, Bruce Longenecker, Stephen Taylor, Mark Seifrid, Peter Stuhlmacher, Francis Watson and Tom Wright. I have not always followed the advice proffered, but I benefited greatly from the exchanges and made many changes to the text, very much with the hope that the resulting reformulations make for a more irenic and positive impact of the whole. As I try to make clear in the first chapter, I do not regard 'the new perspective' as refuting or replacing some or any 'old perspective', but as complementing other perspectives and as contributing to a fuller and richer understanding of the gospel and theology of the first and greatest Christian theologian. If this volume advances that objective I shall count its publication worthwhile.

JAMES D.G. DUNN
Hogmanay, 2004

Chapter 1

The New Perspective: whence, what and whither?

1. A personal account

As I indicated in the Preface to my *Theology of Paul the Apostle*,[1] my interest in Paul goes back to my 6th form (13th grade) school days, when I ran a lunchtime series for my younger fellow-pupils on Paul's missionary journeys. That interest deepened appreciably in the course of my student days and became a fascination during my research at Cambridge in the mid-1960s. So I was not dismayed when in my first university lecturing post, at Nottingham starting in 1970, I found the expectation to be that I should put on a course on Paul's letter to the Romans. And when, a year later, I was able to substitute a more ambitious course on 'the Beginnings of Christianity', Paul's theology naturally featured prominently from the first.

A question soon arose for me, which became a nagging puzzle during the rest of the '70s. I naturally lapped up Paul's teaching on justification by faith, or *through* faith, as I soon began to correct myself. It was so fundamental to the gospel, and so central within the Reformed and Evangelical traditions within which my own theological awakening and early development had taken place. But it was obvious from any study of the key Pauline passages that in his teaching on justification through faith Paul was reacting against some other teaching — 'by faith *apart from works of the law*' (Rom. 3.28), 'from faith in Christ and *not from works of the law*' (Gal. 2.16). What was Paul reacting against? What were these 'works of the law'? The textbooks and commentators provided a fairly standard answer: Paul was reacting against the typical Jewish teaching that justification was by works of achievement — that is, against the characteristic Jewish assertion that God's acceptance had to be earned by the self-effort of merit-winning good behaviour.[2]

---

[1] *The Theology of Paul the Apostle* (Grand Rapids: Eerdmans/Edinburgh: T&T Clark, 1998).

[2] As H. B. P. Mijoga, *The Pauline Notion of Deeds of the Law* (San Francisco: International Scholars Publications, 1999) documents, the dominant tradition has regarded 'works of the law' as indicating 'a legalistic works righteousness' (5-21). A recent example is R. N. Longenecker, *Galatians* (WBC 41; Dallas: Word, 1990): 'a catch phrase to signal the whole legalistic complex of ideas having to do with winning God's favour by a merit-amassing observance of Torah' (86).

Not untypical of my early reading was the commentary on Rom. 4.6ff. by Franz Leenhardt, who notes 'that the juridical mentality of the rabbis (and in this they resembled all men of all times) thought of the believer's relations with God as an account showing debit and credit. The important point was that on the credit side should be listed more good works than there were bad works on the debit side'.[3] In a footnote he quotes J. Bonsirven's observation (*Jud. Palest.* II 58-9) that it was such an attitude which 'earned for the Pharisees their nickname as calculators'. Also, W. Bousset: 'Life thus became a game of reckoning, a constant inspection of the account which the pious man has in the divine bank' (*Rel. Jud.* 3rd ed. 1926, 393). Influential was Emil Schürer's characterisation of Judaism at the time of Jesus in terms of 'external formalism . . . very far removed from true piety'.[4] To similar effect was Matthew Black's description of Pharisaism as 'the immediate ancestor of . . . the largely arid religion of the Jews after the fall of Jerusalem', 'a sterile religion of codified tradition, regulating every part of life by a halachah . . .'.[5] My reaction was understandable: no wonder Paul found his conversion liberating from such a religion (Rom. 8.2; Gal. 5.1)!

All that seemed to be taken for granted and to go largely unquestioned in my early reading on Paul and his gospel. But the puzzle which quickly began to nag emerged from my initial probing into one of the key phrases in Paul's justification teaching — the phrase, '*the righteousness of God*'. How could one not seek to unpack that phrase when confronted with the thematic statement of Rom. 1.16-17? — 'the gospel is the power of God for salvation to all who believe, Jew first and also Greek, for in it is revealed the righteousness of God from faith to faith, as it is written, "The righteous by faith shall live" (Hab. 2.4)'. I found the articles on the subject by Elizabeth and Paul Achtemeier in *Interpreter's Dictionary of the Bible* highly illuminating — but puzzle-provoking.[6] For the Achtemeiers brought home to me that Paul's central phrase was drawn directly from the Old Testament, and resonated through and through with characteristic Jewish emphases. 'Righteousness' was a rela-

---

[3] F. J. Leenhardt, *The Epistle to the Romans* (1957; ET London: Lutterworth, 1961) 115-6.

[4] E. Schürer, *The History of the Jewish People in the Time of Jesus Christ* (ET Edinburgh: T&T Clark, 5 vols. 1886-90): 'when even prayer itself, that centre of the religious life, was bound in the fetters of a rigid mechanism, vital piety could scarcely be any longer spoken of' (2/2.115). Characteristic also was Rudolf Bultmann's *Primitive Christianity in its Contemporary Setting* (London: Thames & Hudson, 1956) in which the main description of 'Judaism' has the heading 'Jewish Legalism' (59-71). F. Watson, *Paul and the Hermeneutics of Faith* (London: T&T Clark International, 2004) is probably fair when he notes: 'It is made unambiguously clear that Bultmann personally dislikes the historical phenomenon he is writing about, and that he intends to communicate that dislike to his readers' (7).

[5] M. Black, 'Pharisees', *IDB* 3 (1962) 774-81 (here 81).

[6] E. R. Achtemeier, 'Righteousness in the Old Testament' and P. J. Achtemeier, 'Righteousness in the New Testament', *IDB* 4 (1962) 80-5, 91-9.

tional concept, and was to be understood 'as meeting the demands of a relationship'. The same applied to 'the righteousness of God': it presupposed the covenant relationship made with man at God's initiative; God was righteous when he met the demands of that covenant relationship.[7] Hence the (to me) surprising talk (particularly in Second Isaiah and the Psalms) of God's *righteousness* as denoting his *saving action* towards his people, his *redemption* and *vindication* even of an erring people.[8] Hence also the realisation that the righteousness of God could include the thought of God's *faithfulness* to his covenant promises (Rom. 3.3-5).[9]

The puzzle is obvious, though at that stage (the '70s) it was still only nagging. If 'the righteousness of God' refers to God's justifying action, then how does it correlate with the traditional view that Paul was reacting against a view which taught that justification had to be earned? If 'the righteousness of God' presupposed divine election of and expressed divine faithfulness to and upholding of a faithless people, then where did the thought of justification to be *earned* by works come into the picture? If Paul was able to draw on the characteristic OT emphasis on the graciousness of God's righteousness as a statement of his own gospel, how could he also imply that the characteristic Jew understood justification as a status to be earned? Something had gone wrong somewhere, but where?

The puzzle was only deepened when I first noted the now famous hymn at the end of the Community Rule of Qumran (1QS 11.11-15):[10]

---

[7] I did not appreciate at that time the importance of the earlier work of H. Cremer, *Die paulinische Rechtfertigungslehre im Zusammenhange ihrer geschichtlichen Voraussetzungen* (Gütersloh: Bertelsmann, 1899, ²1900) 34-8, but found the insight confirmed by the then dominant OT theologies of W. Eichrodt, *Theology of the Old Testament Vol. 1* (⁶1959; London: SCM, 1961) 239-49, and G. von Rad, *Old Testament Theology Vol. 1* (1957; Edinburgh: Oliver & Boyd, 1962) 370-6. So now e.g. F. Hahn, *Theologie des Neuen Testaments* (Tübingen: Mohr Siebeck, 2002) 1.247-8; J. Roloff, 'Die lutherische Rechtfertigungslehre und ihre biblische Grundlage', in W. Kraus & K.-W. Niebuhr, hg., *Frühjudentum und Neues Testament im Horizont Biblischer Theologie* (WUNT 162; Tübingen: Mohr Siebeck, 2003) 275-300: 'God's righteousness did not come new into the world first with Christ; it was already effective previously in Israel' (290); J. M. Bassler, *Navigating Paul* (Louisville: Westminster John Knox, 2007) ch. 5.

[8] So I could empathise with Luther's experience as I had first encountered it in R. Bainton, *Here I Stand* (London: Hodder & Stoughton, 1951) 65, and as cited in 'The Justice of God: A Renewed Perspective on Justification by Faith', *JTS* 43 (1992) 1-22 (here 1) reprinted below ch. 7 (here 193).

[9] These became crucial insights in my commentary on *Romans* (WBC 38; Dallas: Word, 1988) 41-2, 132-4.

[10] It was K. Kertelge, *"Rechtfertigung" bei Paulus: Studien zur Struktur und zum Bedeutungsgehalt des paulinischen Rechtfertigungsbegriffs* (Münster: Aschendorff, 1967) 29-33, who first drew my attention to this text. Similarly 1QH 12(= 4).29-37; 13(= 5).5-6; 15(= 7).16-19; 1QM 11.3-4; not to mention Ps. 103.10 and Dan. 9.16-18, and even 4 Ezra 8.34-36.

As for me, if [12]I stumble, the mercies of God shall be my eternal salvation. If I stagger because of the sin of flesh, my justification *(mshpti)* shall be by the righteousness of God which endures for ever. [13]. . . He will draw me near by his grace, and by his mercy will he bring [14]my justification *(mshpti)*. He will judge me in the righteousness of his truth and in the greatness of his goodness he will pardon *(ykpr)* all my sins. Through his righteousness he will cleanse me of the uncleanness of [15]man and of the sins of the children of men (Vermes).[11]

Here was a text which spoke feelingly of God's grace, mercy and righteousness as the only ground of hope, of the assurance of sins forgiven.[12] The text was so *Pauline* in character and emphasis![13] And yet this very document (1QS) was also being held up as an example of the sort of narrow, sectarian legalism which, it was generally assumed, must have characterised the 'Judaism' of Paul's day (Gal. 1.13-14), or at least have been very like the Pharisaism with which Paul was most familiar.[14] How to reconcile the traditional view of Jewish merit-earning legalism with both the OT teaching on God's righteousness and the Qumran hymn's apparently total reliance on the grace of God for a favourable judgment? What was Paul reacting against in his own so OT-ish, so Qumranish(!) teaching on justification by grace through faith?

In my initial work for my commentary of Romans I had identified the incident at Antioch (Gal. 2.11-14) as a key which might well unlock some of the puzzles. And my examination both of that episode and of the relations between Paul and Jerusalem in the first two years of the '80s helped clarify the tensions in Paul's missionary work, arising particularly from his vocation and

---

[11] Of more recently published scrolls see particularly 4Q507 and 4Q511 frag. 28+29. See further H. Lichtenberger, *Studien zum Menschenbild in Texten der Qumrangemeinde* (Göttingen: Vandenhoeck & Ruprecht, 1980) 73-93.

[12] Note that 1QH 12 (= 4).29-31 and 17 (= 9).14-15 echo Ps. 143.2, on which Paul also builds his doctrine of justification (Rom. 3.20; Gal. 2.16). J. C. R. de Roo, *'Works of the Law' at Qumran and in Paul* (NTM 13; Sheffield Phoenix, 2007) draws attention to 1QH 9.35-36: 'O righteous men, put away iniquity! Hold fast [to the covenant], all you perfect of way' (27) — righteousness as a status relationship not broken by iniquity, because the covenant made provision to cover iniquity.

[13] The parallel was early on noted by David Flusser, 'The Dead Sea Sect and Pre-Pauline Christianity' (1958), *Judaism and the Origins of Christianity* (Jerusalem: Hebrew University, 1988) 23-74 (here 33-5). As N. Dahl, 'The Doctrine of Justification: Its Social Function and Implications' (1964), *Studies in Paul* (Minneapolis: Augsburg, 1977) 95-120 observed: 'Some of the Scrolls from Qumran speak of the sin of man and of God's righteousness in a manner that sounds strikingly Pauline, not to say Lutheran. . . . the beliefs voiced by members of the Qumran community correspond to a number of the classical formulations of the doctrine of justification. . . . the terminology of justification . . . has a positive connection to a religious language still existing in Judaism. . . . The similarity with Paul's doctrine of justification through the saving righteousness of God is truly remarkable' (97, 99-100).

[14] The influential study by J. Jeremias, *Jerusalem at the Time of Jesus* ([3]1967; London: SCM, 1969) had drawn on CD to fill out his understanding of 'patterns of community life like those of Pharisaic rule' (259-60).

commitment to Gentile mission.[15] But how these insights could feed into any resolution of the puzzle was not yet evident. However, that period also gave me opportunity to study closely the recently published work by E. P. Sanders on *Paul and Palestinian Judaism*.[16] And it was here that the puzzle became a question which I could no longer push to one side. It had to be answered: what was it that Paul was reacting against?

Sanders in effect gave NT scholarship *a new perspective on Second Temple Judaism*. He objected in forthright polemical fashion that the traditional perspective on Judaism from the side of Christian scholarship was simply wrong. He pointed out that Jewish scholars had long been puzzled at what seemed to them a caricature of the Judaism they were familiar with; how could Paul the Pharisee characterise the Judaism of his day so misleadingly (they were, it should be said, reading Paul in the traditional terms of Christian scholarship)?[17] Sanders also noted that scholars from the Christian side, like George Foot Moore and James Parkes,[18] had long protested against the traditional characterisation of Paul's Judaism as narrowly and coldly legalistic. Sadly, however, their protests had not been heard.[19] Sanders was determined that his protest would not be ignored.[20]

---

[15] J. D. G. Dunn, 'The Incident at Antioch (Gal. 2.11-18)', *JSNT* 18 (1983) 3-57 (the lecture was first delivered in 1980); also 'The Relationship between Paul and Jerusalem according to Galatians 1 and 2', *NTS* 28 (1982) 461-78; both republished in my *Jesus, Paul and the Law: Studies in Mark and Galatians* (London: SPCK, 1990) 129-74, 108-26 (both with additional notes). The former has also been reprinted in M. D. Nanos, ed., *The Galatians Debate* (Peabody, MA: Hendrickson, 2002) 199-234. The latter is well received by R. Schäfer, *Paulus bis zum Apostelkonzil* (WUNT 2.179; Tübingen: Mohr Siebeck, 2004) 123-49, 175-80, 201-21.

[16] Subtitled *A Comparison of Patterns of Religion* (London: SCM, 1977).

[17] 'Reading Schechter and Montefiore, one wonders what Paul found in Judaism to attack' (Sanders, *Paul and Palestinian Judaism* 12), referring back to his quotation (p. 6) from S. Schechter, *Aspects of Rabbinic Theology* (New York, 1961 = 1909): 'Either the theology of the Rabbis must be wrong, its conceptions of God debasing, its leading motives materialistic and coarse, and its teachers lacking in enthusiasm and spirituality, or the Apostle to the Gentiles is quite unintelligible' (18). See further J. G. Gager, *Reinventing Paul* (New York: Oxford University, 2000) ch. 1; S. Westerholm, *Perspectives Old and New on Paul: The "Lutheran" Paul and His Critics* (Grand Rapids: Eerdmans, 2004) on C. G. Montefiore and H. J. Schoeps (118-28).

[18] Sanders, *Paul and Palestinian Judaism* 6, quotes J. Parkes, *Jesus, Paul and the Jews* (London, 1936): '. . . if Paul was really attacking "Rabbinic Judaism", then much of his argument is irrelevant, his abuse unmerited, and his conception of that which he was attacking inaccurate' (120).

[19] See further Sanders, *Paul and Palestinian Judaism* 33-59. Cf. the criticism of F. Weber by P. S. Alexander, 'Torah and Salvation in Tannaitic Literature', in D. A. Carson, et al. eds., *Justification and Variegated Nomism. Vol. 1: The Complexities of Second Temple Judaism* (WUNT 2.140; Tübingen: Mohr Siebeck, 2001) 261-301: 'his account is permeated by an anti-Jewish animus which is determined to depict Judaism as nothing more than a dry, legalistic works-righteousness' (271).

[20] In private conversation, Sanders observed to me that Moore's protest had been hidden in his great work on *Judaism in the First Centuries of the Christian Era: The Age of the*

Sanders' basic point was that Judaism was not obsessed with works righteousness as a way to secure a divine favour previously unknown. On the contrary, Israel's theology of salvation began from the initiative of God and the givenness of God's favour. God had chosen Israel to be his people; he had made his covenant with them. Members of the covenant therefore did not need to gain his favour before they could properly count themselves acceptable to God; they *started* from that position.[21] At the same time, members of the covenant were expected to obey the law; obedience was necessary if they were to *maintain* their membership of the covenant. In a famous distinction, obedience was required, but to 'stay in', not to 'get in': 'obedience maintains one's position in the covenant, but it does not earn God's grace as such', was Sanders' summary of the consistent emphasis of the rabbinic and second temple literature which he surveyed.[22]

Crucial to Sanders' new perspective on Judaism was the recognition that in this 'pattern of religion' God did not require perfection, but allowed for failure, by providing means of atonement and forgiveness for those who repented of their sin. Hence the overall balance of this new perspective summed up in the most famous of Sanders' phrases, which he himself clearly regarded as the key formula — 'covenantal nomism' *(Bundesnomismus, nomisme d'Alliance)* — indicating the inter-relationship between divine initiative ('covenant') and human response ('nomism') which he saw to be so characteristic of Judaism: 'covenantal nomism is the view that one's place in God's plan is established on the basis of the covenant and that the covenant requires as the proper response of man his obedience to its commandments, while providing means of atonement for transgression'.[23]

I took Sanders to have made his case, and was more than ordinarily grateful

---

Tannaim (Cambridge, Mass. 1927-30) and had only been explicit in his 'Christian Writers on Judaism', *HTR* 15 (1922) 41-61 — with the consequence that Moore's *Judaism* was often cited in support of the traditional denigration of Judaism, something which would have horrified Moore. It was this which made Sanders determined that his own polemical protest would be 'up-front' and unmistakeable. This observation also provides a response to the critique and puzzlement of M. Silva, 'The Law and Christianity: Dunn's New Synthesis', *WTJ* 53 (1991) 339-53 (here 348).

[21] T. R. Schreiner, *Paul Apostle of God's Glory in Christ: A Pauline Theology* (Downers Grove, IL: IVP, 2001): 'First God redeems Israel from Egypt, *and then* he gives the law, so obedience to the law is a response to God's grace, not an attempt to gain righteousness by works (see Ex 19–20)' (117-8).

[22] *Paul and Palestinian Judaism* 420; 'Paul is in agreement with Palestinian Judaism. . . . salvation is by grace but judgment is according to works; works are the condition of remaining "in", but they do not earn salvation' (543). Cf. already Moore: ' "a lot in the World to Come" . . . in rabbinical Judaism . . . is ultimately assured to every Israelite on the ground of the original election of the people by the free grace of God, prompted not by its merits, collective or individual, but solely by God's love. . . . These facts are ignored when Judaism is set in antithesis to Christianity. . . . If the one is grace, so is the other' (*Judaism* 2.94-5).

[23] *Paul and Palestinian Judaism* 75; see also 236, 420, 544; in 'The New Perspective on Paul', *BJRL* 65 (1983) 95-122, reprinted in *Jesus, Paul and the Law* 183-214 (reprinted below

for the correction he had provided to the traditionally more negative view of Judaism.[24] Unfortunately, however, his treatment of Paul failed to answer my own key question. In fact, in setting the record straight so far as the Judaism confronted by Paul was concerned, Sanders only increased the puzzle. If the Judaism of Paul's day also gave such a place to divine election, atonement and forgiveness, then what was Paul objecting to?[25] Sanders did not help me to make sense of Paul against this background. And his own solution in terms of Paul's inconsistency did not seem to me a satisfactory resolution of the puzzle.[26] Moreover, as became clear to me later, Sanders' characterisation of Paul's soteriology in terms of 'from solution to plight'[27] continued to pose the issues too much in terms of the traditional Protestant view of Paul to which he was objecting. To be sure, he was reacting against the tradition which in effect took Paul's exposition of the gospel in Romans 1–3 as a reflection of Paul's own experience ('from plight to solution'). But did not Sanders' own new perspective on Palestinian Judaism require a more substantial reconfiguring of the issue which crystallised Paul's exposition of the gospel?

---

ch. 2), I note that, though criticising Sanders' methodology, J. Neusner accepted Sanders' representation of rabbinic Judaism at this point as a 'wholly sound and . . . self-evident proposition' (204 n. 16; below 103 n. 16); noted also by C. Strecker, 'Paulus aus einer "neuen Perspektive": der Paradigmenwechsel in der jüngeren Paulusforschung', *Kirche und Israel* 11 (1996) 3-18 (here 7); see further my *The Theology of Paul* 338 n. 15. D. Garlington, *'The Obedience of Faith': A Pauline Phrase in Historical Context* (WUNT 2.38; Tübingen: Mohr Siebeck, 1991) demonstrated the persistence of the covenantal nomism paradigm through the apocrypha. R. Bergmeier, 'Das Gesetz im Römerbrief', *Das Gesetz im Römerbrief und andere Studien zum Neuen Testament* (WUNT 121; Tübingen: Mohr Siebeck, 2000) 31-90 has taken Sanders' point (44-8).

[24] N. T. Wright, 'The Paul of History and the Apostle of Faith', *TynBul* 29 (1978) 61-88, was the first to recognise the significance of Sanders' work and to offer 'a new way of looking at Paul . . . (and) a new perspective on . . . Pauline problems' (64, 77-84). K. Stendahl, *Paul Among Jews and Gentiles* (London: SCM, 1976) earlier spoke of 'a new perspective' (for systematic theology and practical theology) opened up by his own insight into the springs of Paul's theology (see n. 31 below).

[25] Morna Hooker posed the problem afresh: 'In many ways, the pattern which Sanders insists is the basis of Palestinian Judaism fits exactly the Pauline pattern of Christian experience: God's saving grace evokes man's answering obedience' ('Paul and "Covenantal Nomism"' [1982], *From Adam to Christ: Essays on Paul* [Cambridge: Cambridge University, 1990] 155-64 [here 157]).

[26] See 'New Perspective' 186-8 (below 103-5). H. Räisänen's atomistic reading of the Pauline texts to find an alienated Paul in his *Paul and the Law* (WUNT 29; Tübingen: Mohr, 1983), appearing at about the same time as Sanders' second volume, *Paul, the Law and the Jewish People* (Philadelphia: Fortress, 1983), seemed to me equally unsatisfactory (*Jesus, Paul and the Law* 215; below 121). Gager attempts to resolve the seeming inconsistencies by inferring that when Paul talks in negative terms about the law he is talking about the law and Gentiles; 'Paul had no argument against the Jewish law in relation to Israel and the Jews'; when Paul says 'no one *(anthrōpos)* is justified by works of the law', he refers only to Gentiles — 'no one = Gentile' (*Reinventing Paul* 52, 57-8, 86-8); but see n. 208 below.

[27] *Paul and Palestinian Judaism* 474-5, 497

My T. W. Manson Lecture on 'The New Perspective on Paul' (1983) was a first attempt to find a better answer.[28] I found it in the context occasioning Paul's first use of the key term, 'works of the law', in Gal 2.16.[29] The context makes it clear enough that 'works of the law' was the phrase used to characterise the insistence of Jewish believers that obedience of law ('nomism') was reason necessary and sufficient for them to 'separate' (2.12) from other believers and was essential to their being 'counted righteous' (2.16). The 'works of the law' in view were evidently the circumcision which 'the false brothers' in effect tried to 'compel' Gentile believers to observe (2.3-4), and the food laws which Peter and the other Jewish believers tried to 'compel' Gentile believers to obey if table-fellowship was to be maintained (2.14).

In 1984, in dialogue with Heikki Räisänen, I broadened the argument by seeking an explanation for the problematic Gal. 3.10 in the *'social function'* of the law: that the law served to mark off, 'separate' Israel from the nations; that, as Gal. 2.1-16 had demonstrated, works of the law could function as boundary markers, rituals and practices which distinguished Israel from the nations.[30] Might that provide the key to Paul's objection? — that in speaking of 'works of the law' Paul had in mind this boundary-marking, separating function of the law? That would certainly fit with the observation made some time earlier by Krister Stendahl, that the 'doctrine of justification by faith was hammered out by Paul for the very specific and limited purpose of defending the rights of Gentile converts to be full and genuine heirs to the promises of the God of Israel'.[31] And it fitted very closely with the role attributed to the law in the Letter of Aristeas 139-142:

---

[28] Below ch. 2. As Henri Blocher puts it: 'The new perspective on Paul was born of a new perspective on Second Temple Judaism' — 'Justification of the Ungodly *(Sola Fide):* Theological Reflections', in D. A. Carson, et al., eds., *Justification and Variegated Nomism. Vol. 2: The Paradoxes of Paul* (Tübingen: Mohr Siebeck, 2004) 465-500 (here 469).

[29] 'New Perspective' 188-9 (below 105-6).

[30] 'Works of the Law and the Curse of the Law (Gal. 3.10-14)', *NTS* 31 (1985) 523-42, reprinted in *Jesus, Paul and the Law* 215-41; and below ch. 3. Räisänen had also characterised 'works of the law' as 'something that separates the Jew from the Gentile' (*Paul and the Law* 171; further references to Sanders and Neusner on 124-5 below). I was late in noting that in the same year that 'The New Perspective' was published, R. Heiligenthal, *Werke als Zeichen* (WUNT 2.9; Tübingen: Mohr, 1983), drew attention to the socially delimiting function of 'works' in Gal. 2 — 'works of the law as signs of group membership' (127-34); 'When Paul speaks of the "works of the law", he thinks concretely of the food laws and circumcision' (133).

[31] Stendahl, *Paul Among Jews and Gentiles* 2, taking up one of the key themes of his famous essay, 'The Apostle Paul and the Introspective Conscience of the West', *HTR* 56 (1963) 199-215, reprinted in the same volume (78-96): 'it was his grappling with the question about the place of the Gentiles in the Church and in the plan of God . . . which had driven him [Paul] to that interpretation of the Law which was to become his in a unique way' (84). Similarly N. T. Wright, *Paul: Fresh Perspectives* (London: SPCK, 2005): 'every time Paul discusses justification he seems simultaneously to be talking about Gentile inclusion' (36).

[139]In his wisdom the legislator [i.e. Moses] . . . surrounded us with unbroken palisades and iron walls to prevent our mixing with any of the other peoples in any matter, being thus kept pure in body and soul. . . . [142]To prevent our being perverted by contact with others or by mixing with bad influences, he hedged us in on all sides with strict observances connected with meat and drink and touch and hearing and sight, after the manner of the Law (Charlesworth).

Observances of the law as boundary markers indeed![32]

My ongoing work on Romans seemed to indicate that I was on the right lines.[33] The 'boasting' of the 'Jew' in Rom. 2.17-23 is certainly to be understood as a boasting in covenant privilege over against the less-favoured, or rather passed-over Gentiles:[34] 'boasting' in God/in the law (2.17, 23) is filled out in terms of the confidence of the 'Jew' that he is 'a guide to the blind, a light for those in darkness, an instructor of the foolish, a teacher of the young, having the embodiment of knowledge and of truth in the law' (19-20). A 'boasting' of self-confidence and self-reliance,[35] 'boasting' in self-achieved

---

[32] As Sanders also observed: 'There is something which is common to circumcision, Sabbath, and food laws, and which sets them off from other laws: they created a social distinction between Jews and other races in the Greco-Roman world. Further, they were aspects of Judaism which drew criticism and ridicule from pagan authors' (*Paul, the Law and the Jewish People* 102). See further 'Works of the Law' 216-9 (below 122-5), with Neusner's similar observation (232 n. 16; below 125 n. 16); also 'The New Perspective on Paul: Paul and the Law', in my *Romans* lxvii-lxxi, reprinted below ch. 4 (here 144-9); also 'What was the Issue between Paul and "Those of the Circumcision"?', in M. Hengel & U. Heckel, eds., *Paulus und das antike Judentum* (WUNT 58; Tübingen: Mohr Siebeck, 1991) 295-312 (here 298-305), reprinted below ch. 5 (here 155-63); and 'The Theology of Galatians: The Issue of Covenantal Nomism', in J. M. Bassler, ed., *Pauline Theology Volume I: Thessalonians, Philippians, Galatians, Philemon* (Minneapolis: Fortress, 1991) 125-46 (here 125-8) (below ch. 6, here 173-76).

[33] Already reflected in my 'Works of the Law' (221-5; below 128-32). As well as my commentary on Romans (above n. 9) I have in mind my 'Yet Once More — "The Works of the Law"', *JSNT* 46 (1992) 99-117 (here 104-14) (reprinted below ch. 8, here 217-8).

[34] Sanders, *Paul, the Law and the Jewish People* 33; similarly Wright, 'History' 82; also 'The Letter to the Romans', *NIB* 10 (2002) 446. See further my *Romans* 110-1, 115; I develop the argument in 'What was the Issue' 305-13 (below 163-71). The citation of *Pss. Sol.* 17.1 and *2 Bar.* 48.22-24 ('We shall always be blessed; at least, we did not mingle with the nations. For we are all a people of the Name') catch the mood well (U. Wilckens, *Der Brief an die Römer* vol. 1 [EKK; Zürich: Benziger, 1978] 147-8; E. Lohse, *Der Brief an die Römer* [KEK; Göttingen: Vandenhoeck & Ruprecht, 2003] 109-10). S. K. Stowers, *A Rereading of Romans* (New Haven: Yale University, 1994) critiques this reading of Rom. 2, but fails to note the strong echoes of both the Psalms of Solomon and the Wisdom of Solomon in the attitude which Paul critiques in 2.1-6 (cf. particularly Wisd. 15.1-4 with Rom. 2.4; see my *Theology of Paul* 116-7; and below ch. 5 #V), though Stowers does recognise a (selective) comparison between Wisd. 14 and Rom. 1.18–2.15 (92).

[35] R. Bultmann, *kauchaomai*, *TDNT* 3.648-9; also *Theology of the New Testament* (London: SCM, 1952) 242-3: 'The self-reliant attitude of the man who puts his trust in his own strength and in that which is controllable by him' (240); H. Hübner, *Law in Paul's Thought* (Edinburgh: T&T Clark, 1984) 113-24; R. H. Bell, *No One Seeks for God: An Exegetical and Theological Study of Romans 1.18–3.20* (WUNT 106; Tübingen: Mohr Siebeck, 1998) de-

righteousness (which I had previously assumed),[36] is remote from the context.[37] Likewise, in 3.27-30 the sequence clearly implies that to boast on the ground of, or as encouraged by the law of works is equivalent to affirming that God is God of Jews only; works of the law somehow function to reinforce Israel's exclusive claim on God.[38] The verses indicate two alternative/opposed logical sequences:

---

fends Bultmann's view (186-8, 193). For further bibliography see de Roo, *Works of the Law'* *at Qumran* 43-5 and n. 4.

[36] C. E. B. Cranfield, *Romans* (ICC; Edinburgh: T&T Clark, vol. 1 1975), commenting also on 3.27: 'the act of asserting a claim on God on the ground of one's works, of claiming to have put God in one's debt' (165).

[37] Cf. N. T. Wright, 'The Law in Romans 2', in J. D. G. Dunn, ed., *Paul and the Mosaic Law* (Grand Rapids: Eerdmans, 2001) 131-50 (here 139-43): 'this Torah-base, upon which she [Israel] 'rests (v. 17), is not the legalist's ladder of merit. It is Israel's national charter'. D. Moo, *The Epistle to the Romans* (NICNT; Grand Rapids: Eerdmans, 1996): 'Thus, the Jews' "boasting in God" is not wrong in itself — an instance of human pride and arrogance — but a legitimate pride and joy in the God who had given to Israel so many good things' (160); contrast, however, his treatment of 3.27 — 'the pride in accomplishments, the tendency for the Jew to think that his obedience to the law constituted some kind of claim on God' (247). C. G. Kruse, *Paul, the Law and Justification* (Leicester: Apollos, 1996): 'The boast of the Jews which Paul condemned was not that they had earned their salvation by observance of the law, but rather a presumption that they are better off in God's sight than the Gentiles because they are Jews and because they have the law (2:17-20)' (191-2). T. R. Schreiner, *Romans* (BECNT; Grand Rapids: Baker, 1998): 'In this context boasting is not censured' (130). T. Eskola, *Theodicy and Predestination in Pauline Soteriology* (WUNT 2.100; Tübingen: Mohr Siebeck, 1998): 'This kind of boasting/glorying cannot be identified with legalistic self-confidence' (231). Similarly K. Haacker, *Der Brief des Paulus an die Römer* (ThHK 6; Leipzig: Evangelische, 1999) 68.

[38] See further my *Romans* 184-5, 190-1; Wilckens, *Römer* 1.244-5; M. A. Seifrid, *Justification by Faith: The Origin and Development of a Central Pauline Theme* (SuppNovT 68; Leiden: Brill, 1992): 'the *kauchesis* of Rom 3:27 signifies Jewish privileges' (35-6); Mijoga, *Deeds of the Law:* 'Paul is attacking the self-confidence of the Jew as a Jew and as a member of God's chosen people' (151); L. Thurén, *Derhetorizing Paul: A Dynamic Perspective on Pauline Theology and the Law* (WUNT 124; Tübingen: Mohr Siebeck, 2000): 'in Rom 3,27-30 he [Paul] excludes Jewish boasting of the status conferred on them by the law' (169); S. J. Gathercole, *Where is Boasting? Early Jewish Soteriology and Paul's Response in Romans 1–5* (Grand Rapids: Eerdmans, 2002): 'the boasting in 3:27 most logically points back to 2:17-24' (225); R. K. Rapa, *The Meaning of "Works of the Law" in Galatians and Romans* (New York: Peter Lang, 2001) 249-51; Wright, 'Romans' 480; Bassler, *Navigating Paul:* 'Jewish boasting in their privileged status as God's covenant people' (62); cf. Haacker, *Römer* 92-3. Schreiner is misleading when he claims that the particle *ē* which opens v. 29 indicates 'that a fresh argument is being introduced' (*Romans* 205). The particle simply denotes the carrying forward of the same argument by reference to scripture (as in Rom. 11.2; 1 Cor. 6.16), or to an accepted conviction (as in Rom. 6.3; 1 Cor. 6.9, 19), or as here to the fundamental Jewish creed *(Shema)*. And even if more of a break between vv. 28 and 29 is to be recognised (D. J. Moo, 'Israel and the Law in Romans 5–11: Interaction with the New Perspective', in Carson, et al., *Justification and Variegated Nomism Vol. 2* 185-216 [206]), the point of 3.29-30 remains: justification by faith is a way of saying that God is not God of Jews only but also of Gentiles, since he justifies *both* by faith apart from the works of the law (3.28) that are possible only for Jews.

not: of works → justification from works → God of Jews only
boasting
excluded by law
    but: of faith → justification through faith → God also of Gentiles →
    establishes law

And similarly in 9.30–10.4, the sequence of thought links Israel's failure in misplacing emphasis on works of the law (9.32)[39] with Paul's fellow-Jews' mistaken 'zeal' (10.2) and assumption that righteousness was to be 'established' as 'their own', that is (exclusively) their own, theirs and not others' (10.3).[40] Again the perspective is primarily of a status (covenant) given exclusively to Israel, setting Israel apart from and privileging Israel over against the (other) nations,[41] a status affirmed and maintained by the works of the law which demonstrated and constituted Israel's set-apartness to God; Paul now saw this attitude as a failure to grasp the character and 'to all-ness' of faith.

Similarly my ongoing study of Galatians helped fill out the increasingly coherent picture of Paul's theology of justification and its rationale. In my work

---

[39] For the possibility that the metaphor of 'pursuit' is sustained through 9.30–10.4 see J. A. Fitzmyer, *Romans* (AB 33; New York: Doubleday, 1992) 584; but the critique of works is not directed against 'human effort' (Moo, 'Israel and the Law 210-11) since pursuit 'from faith' is regarded positively.

[40] See further my *Romans* 582-3, 587-8; Wright, 'Romans' 649, 654-5; K. Kuula, *The Law, the Covenant and God's Plan: Vol. 2. Paul's Treatment of the Law and Israel in Romans* (Göttingen: Vandenhoeck & Ruprecht, 2003) 309-12. Cf. B. Byrne, 'The Problem of *Nomos* and the Relationship with Judaism in Romans', *CBQ* 62 (2000) 294-309: 'In the light of what Paul has established earlier in the letter (chaps. 3-4), "their own righteousness" . . . can only mean the righteousness of Israel as holy people separate from the sinful rest of humankind, the righteousness that the "law of works" sought to foster and preserve' (302); D. Marguerat, 'Paul et la Loi: le retournement (Philippiens 3,2–4,1)', in A. Dettwiler, et al., eds., *Paul, une théologie en construction* (Genève: Labor et Fides, 2004) 251-75 (here 272-3). I owed the exegetical insight into the significance of *idios* to G. E. Howard, 'Christ the End of the Law: The Meaning of Romans 10:4', *JBL* 88 (1969) 331-7 (here 336), who also persuaded B. C. Wintle, 'Justification in Pauline Thought', in D. A. Carson, ed., *Right With God: Justification in the Bible and the World* (Carlisle: Paternoster, 1992) 51-68 (262 n. 31); Moo discusses the interpretation (*Romans* 634-5), with further bibliography (n. 22). I confess to some disappointment that so few have noted the parallel (in the use of 'establish') between the standpoint criticised in 10.2-3 and that so powerfully expounded in 1 Macc. 2.27 (Haacker, *Römer* 204-5 is the exception; Eskola, *Theodicy and Predestination* 237 n. 7 thinks that I overinterpret 'established', but ignores the link in the context to 'zeal' and 'their own'; Gathercole, *Where is Boasting?* 228-9 notes the parallel but plays down the Maccabean link between 'zeal' and 'establishing' what is distinctive to Israel). Contrast, e.g., the earlier R. H. Gundry, 'Grace, Works, and Staying Saved in Paul', *Biblica* 66 (1985) 1-38 (here 17-19).

[41] Sanders, *Paul, the Law and the Jewish People* 38; Wright, 'Romans' 654. Wright coined the phrase ' "national righteousness", the belief that fleshly descent guarantees membership of God's true covenant people' ('History' 65, 71, 82-3; and below 114 n. 36). B. N. Longenecker, *Eschatology and the Covenant: A Comparison of 4 Ezra and Romans 1–11* (JSNTS 57; Sheffield: Sheffield Academic, 1991) preferred the term 'ethnocentric covenantalism'. M. F. Bird, *The Saving Righteousness of God* (Milton Keynes: Paternoster, 2007) prefers 'ethnocentric nomism' (116-7).

on Rom. 10.2 I had become aware of the tradition of 'zeal' within Israel, as *a dedication to maintain Israel's set-apartness to God* — exemplified by the stories of Simeon and Levi, Phinehas, Elijah and the Maccabees[42] — such dedication as warranted the use of force against fellow Israelites deemed to be threatening that holy set-apartness.[43] Such 'zeal', after all, was the counterpart of God's 'jealousy' (the same word!) (Ex. 20.5; 34.14; Num. 25.11-13; Deut. 4.24; 5.9; etc); indeed, in Num. 11.29 Phinehas' zeal is understood as a direct reflection of Yahweh's.[44] God's 'zeal' that Israel should keep herself for God alone was directly mirrored in the 'zeal' which defended and reinforced the boundaries separating Israel from the (other) nations. This seemed to me to make best sense of the fact that Paul ascribes his own violent persecution of 'the church of God' to this same 'zeal' (Phil. 3.6; Gal. 1.13-14). Paul's persecuting zeal was not simply zeal to be the best that he could be (zeal for the law),[45] but a grim determination to maintain Israel's holiness by attacking — 'seeking to destroy'! (Gal. 1.13, 23) — those Jews who (in his view) were beginning to breach Israel's boundaries.[46] Not only so, but the fact that Paul describes his conversion in terms of a calling to preach Christ among the nations (Gal. 1.15-16) implies fairly clearly that Paul was indeed converted: he turned right

---

[42] Simeon and Levi — Gen. 34; Jdt 9.2-4; *Jub.* 30.

Phinehas — Num. 25.6-13; Sir. 45.23-24; 1 Macc. 2.54; *4 Macc.* 18.12.

Elijah — 1 Kgs 18 (note 18.40); Sir. 48.2-3; 1 Macc. 2.58.

The Maccabees — 1 Macc. 2.23-27; Josephus, *Ant.* 12.271; cf. 2 Macc. 4.2.
See further below 360-1.

[43] *Romans* 586-7; noted also by J. L. Martyn, *Galatians* (AB 33A; New York: Doubleday, 1997) 155 (briefly) and 161-3 (but ignoring the rationale of Phinehas-type zeal).

[44] 'Like Joshua's zeal on behalf of Moses (Nu. 11:29), Phinehas's zeal on behalf of Yahweh realises Yahweh's own jealousy . . . which otherwise would have consumed all Israel' (E. Reuter, *qn'*, *TDOT* 13.56). A. Stumpff had already observed (*TDNT* 2.879), that the term ('zeal') is linked with 'anger' (Deut. 29.20) and 'wrath' (Num. 25.11; Ezek. 16.38, 42; 36.6; 38.19). See further below ch. 22 n. 35.

[45] Gathercole is misleading when he affirms that 'Paul does not see the "zeal" of his own past as Jewish piety' (*Where is Boasting?* 208); 'not as *Christian* piety' would make better sense.

[46] J. Becker, *Paul: Apostle to the Gentiles* (Louisville: John Knox, 1993): 'Can anyone in Paul's time speak at all of so similar a zeal without evoking the spirit of Phinehas?' (68). T. Holland, *Contours of Pauline Theology* (Fearn, Ross-shire: Mentor, 2004) mistakenly infers from such references to Paul's zeal (indeed a self-styled 'zealot' — Gal. 1.14; Acts 22.3) that I regard the pre-Christian Paul as a 'Zealot', that is, that I associate him with the political revolutionaries who led the revolt against Rome in 66 (188-92), apparently unaware that the term 'zealot' only took on such political and titular significance 25-30 years after Paul's conversion (see my *Jesus Remembered* [Grand Rapids: Eerdmans, 2003] 272-3). Holland also thinks Paul's acceptance of his role as an evangelist to the Gentiles was 'the most natural of changes' (190)! He justifiably asks whether a Gentile mission had begun before Paul's conversion (195), though he ignores both Acts 11.19-21 and the question whether Luke has delayed his account of the Hellenist breakthrough at Antioch in order to insert the story of Paul's conversion (Acts 9) and to give priority to Peter's conversion of Cornelius (Acts 10–11).

round, one hundred and eighty degrees, and committed himself to a gospel for the Gentiles which he had so violently persecuted.[47]

My investigation of 'Pharisees, Sinners, and Jesus', published in the same year as my Romans commentary, in response to Sanders' interpretation of the term 'sinners' in the ministry of Jesus,[48] had also brought me to recognise that the term ('sinners') could be and was used in a strongly *factional* sense.[49] The term of course denotes those who disregard the law, law-breakers, the wicked. But for those 'within the law', that also included those 'outside the law'; Gentiles by definition were 'out-laws', 'sinners'.[50] And for those who insisted that obedience of the law required acceptance of their particular interpretation of the law, the *Jews* who failed to follow that interpretation were equally law-breakers, 'sinners'.[51] This again brought a flood of light on Gal. 2.15: 'we are Jews by nature and not "Gentile sinners"'. Here was the same typically Jewish attitude to Gentiles. Paul evidently saw the Jewish believers treating the Gentile believers in Antioch in the same condemnatory spirit ('sinners'), indeed, displaying the very sectarian spirit against which Jesus himself had protested, and on the same issue of table-fellowship (Matt. 11.19; Mark 2.17).[52]

---

[47] I set out the case most fully in my contribution to the Peter Stuhlmacher Festschrift: 'Paul's Conversion — A Light to Twentieth Century Disputes', in *Evangelium — Schriftauslegung — Kirche*, ed. J. Ådna et al. (Göttingen: Vandenhoeck & Ruprecht, 1997) 77-93; reprinted below ch. 15. Roloff's position is close to mine: 'The certainty that he had been especially entrusted with the proclamation of Jesus among the Gentiles was for him the decisive realization of the Damascus event' ('lutherische Rechtfertigungslehre' 283-4). Seifrid rightly asserts that 'Paul's conversion involved the reevaluation of the role of Torah and of Israel's privileges in the divine granting of righteousness' (*Justification* 37), but misses the significance of 'zeal' in his attempt to 'reconstruct' Paul's conversion from his self-references (136-46, 255-7). J. Taylor, 'Why did Paul persecute the church?, in G. N. Stanton & G. Stroumsa, eds., *Tolerance and Intolerance in Early Judaism and Christianity* (Cambridge: University Press, 1998) 99-120, is also oblivious to the light shed on his question by the 'zeal' motif. U. Schnelle, *Apostle Paul: His Life and Theology* (Grand Rapids: Baker Academic, 2005) is vulnerable to similar criticism (85-6).

[48] E. P. Sanders, *Jesus and Judaism* (London: SCM, 1985) ch. 6.

[49] 'Pharisees, Sinners, and Jesus', in *The Social World of Formative Christianity and Judaism*, H. C. Kee FS, ed. J. Neusner, et al. (Philadelphia: Fortress, 1988) 264-89, reprinted in *Jesus, Paul and the Law* 61-86.

[50] Ps. 9.17; Tob. 13.6; *Jub.* 33.23-24; *Pss. Sol.* 1.1; 2.1-2; Matt 5.47/Luke 6.33; Gal. 2.15.

[51] 'Pharisees, Sinners, and Jesus' 73-7; also *The Partings of the Ways between Christianity and Judaism* (London: SCM/Philadelphia: TPI, 1991) 103-6; where I refer to 1 Macc. 1.34; 2.44, 48; *1 Enoch* 1.1, 7-9; 5.6-7; 82.4-7; 1QpHab 5.5; 1QH 10(= 2).10, 12, 24; 12(= 4).34; *Pss. Sol.* 1.8; 2.3; 7.2; 8.12-13; 17.5-8, 23. The most obvious example is the calendrical dispute which racked Second Temple Judaism in the two centuries before Paul: to observe a feast according to the wrong calendar was to *fail* to observe the feast, or to observe the feast of Gentiles (*Jub.* 6.32-35; *1 En.* 82.4-7); see my 'Echoes of Intra-Jewish Polemic in Paul's Letter to the Galatians', *JBL* 112 (1993) 457-77 (here 470-3) (reprinted below ch. 9, here 238-41). And further M. A. Elliott, *The Survivors of Israel: A Reconsideration of the Theology of Pre-Christian Judaism* (Grand Rapids: Eerdmans, 2000) 144-62.

[52] Cf. Seifrid: 'sources which display some form of polemical stance against other Jews are

And it follows that use of the same word 'sinners' two verses later (Gal. 2.17) constitutes a protest against the same sectarian spirit: to sit light to the hard interpretation of the food laws demanded by Peter, as Paul did, was to call upon oneself the condemnatory epithet 'sinner', and to make Christ, who accepts sinners, the servant of sin (2.17)![53]

Taking up from my earlier 1984 article (above), the 'new perspective' had suggested to me that 'all who are from the works of the law' (Gal. 3.10) was best taken as a reference to those who insisted on a full-scale covenantal nomism (rather than on earning salvation by works righteousness), such as had provoked the crises in Jerusalem and Antioch, and now again in Galatia.[54] In addition I began to see that the force of Lev. 18.5 (Gal. 3.12) had probably been misunderstood: it served to indicate how the covenant life should be lived ('He who does these things shall live by them'), life within the covenant, and not just life after death.[55] Which also shed light on Gal. 3.21: the law was provided not to *give* life (only God or his Spirit could do that), but to order the life of the covenant people.[56] And the earlier insight, that the boasting which Paul condemned had more to do with pride in ethnic privilege than with pride in self-achievement, seemed to be further strengthened by Gal. 6.12-13: the Jewish missionaries would boast in the flesh of *the Galatians,* when they persuaded the Galatians to be circumcised in the flesh, to conform their uncircumcised identity to the circumcised identity of the covenant people (Gen. 17.9-14).[57]

---

the proper point of departure for a comparison with Paul' (*Justification* 62). In *Theology of Paul* I suggest that Paul was aware of the tradition of Jesus eating with 'sinners' (191-2).

[53] See further my *The Epistle to the Galatians* (London: A. & C. Black, 1993) 132-4, 141-2; also 'Echoes of Intra-Jewish Polemic' 460-70 (below 238-48). 'A typical Jewish-Christian interjection' (Becker, *Paul* 96). See also E. H. Kok, *The Truth of the Gospel: A Study in Galatians 2:15-21* (Hong Kong: Alliance Bible Seminary, 2000); Schäfer, *Paulus bis zum Apostelkonzil* 265-8; and cf. Martyn, *Galatians* 254-5; and the more elaborate thesis of M. Winninge, *Sinners and the Righteous: A Comparative Study of the Psalms of Solomon and Paul's Letters* (CBNTS 26; Stockholm: Almqvist & Wiksell, 1995) here 253. Otherwise J. Lambrecht, 'Paul's Reasoning in Galatians 2:11-21', in Dunn, ed., *Paul and the Mosaic Law* 53-74 (here 56-8). A. A. Das, *Paul, the Law, and the Covenant* (Peabody, MA: Hendrickson, 2001) also misses the factional overtones of 'sinner' here (169-70).

[54] *Galatians* 170-4, even though the relation of 10a to 10b remains unclear. Martyn translates 'those whose identity is derived from observance of the Law' (*Galatians* 308). See further my 'Theology of Galatians' (below ch. 6).

[55] See further below #4.2(10).

[56] *Galatians* 175-6, 192-3. Cf. Westerholm, *Perspectives:* 'no law requiring dikaios deeds (this *is* what laws do) can resuscitate the dead' (282); 'the law's function is more limited' (319); 'The law was given to regulate, not transform, this life of sin' (380). Martyn seems to miss the distinction between giving life (3.21) and ordering life (3.12) (*Galatians* 359-60), but he is hardly untypical in this.

[57] *Galatians* 336, 339-40; I develop the point in my '"Neither Circumcision nor Uncircumcision, but . . ." (Gal. 5.2-12; 6.12-16; cf. 1 Cor. 7.17-20)', in A. Vanhoye, ed., *La foi agissant par l'Amour (Galates 4,12–6,16)* (Rome: Abbaye de S. Paul, 1996) 79-110 (here 88-92), reprinted below ch. 13; cf. Martyn, *Galatians* 561-2.

A year later, in 1994, I was much heartened by the (at last!) publication of the sectarian text from Qumran, 4QMMT.[58] I had known of the text for some time and was naturally intrigued by the report that it used the phrase 'the works of the law'. But when I first saw it at the SBL meeting that November, 1994, I was stunned by the astonishing parallel which it provided with Galatians.[59] Particularly striking were the three parallels. (i) 'Works of the law' are used in reference to various halakhoth described earlier in the letter (cf. Gal. 2.16); clearly implicit is the claim that the law was only properly observed at these points when the Qumran interpretations of the law were followed.[60] (ii) The conviction that the law had to be observed in just this way, that these works of the law had to be performed, was ground necessary and sufficient for the Qumran sect to 'separate' (that word again) from the rest of the people (cf. Gal. 2.12).[61] (iii) The letter's conclusion clearly implies that righteousness will be reckoned (echoing Gen. 15.6) only to those who perform these works of the law (cf. Gal. 2.16).[62] Here was an astonishing parallel with the situation which confronted Paul in Antioch and which led to his first recorded formulation of his key slogan: justification by faith and not by works of the law. The believing Jews in Antioch, including Peter, were in effect insisting that Gentiles must 'judaize' (2.14), that is, must observe certain requirements, certain works of the law;[63] they were thus, in Paul's view, making these works a requirement addi-

---

[58] E. Qimron & J. Strugnell, *Miqsat Ma'ase Ha-Torah* (DJD 10.5; Oxford: Clarendon, 1994).

[59] '4QMMT and Galatians', *NTS* 43 (1997) 147-53, reprinted below ch. 14. M. G. Abegg, '4QMMT C 27, 31 and "Works Righteousness"', *DSD* 6 (1999) 139-47 has drawn similar conclusions. I had been familiar with other related phrases in the DSS which expressed the same concerns — particularly 1QS 5.21, 23; 6.18 and 4Q174 1.7 (*Romans* 154); on 4Q174 1.7 reading 'works of the law' rather than 'works of thanksgiving', see now de Roo, *'Works of the Law' at Qumran* 11-15.

[60] Bell, *No One Seeks for God* 230-3, is typical of those who miss the factional context of MMT's use of the phrase. B. Witherington, *Grace in Galatia: A Commentary on Paul's Letter to the Galatians* (Edinburgh: T&T Clark, 1998) 176-8, 353-4 seems to miss the obvious logic: that if all works of the law are required then those referred to in particular cannot be dispensed with. See further below.

[61] Elliott describes them as 'defining laws', or 'identity issues', which 'serve effectively to identify, or point out, the elect' (*Survivors of Israel* 174-8). See further Bergmeier, *Gesetz* 38-9; and cf. N. T. Wright, '4QMMT and Paul: Justification, "Works", and Eschatology', in S.-W. Son, ed., *History and Exegesis*, E.E. Ellis FS (New York: T&T Clark, 2006) 104-32.

[62]

4QMMT		Galatians
MMT C26-27	Works of the law focusing the general requirement to obey the law on certain specific issues.	Gal. 2.16
MMT C7-8	Insistence on these works of the law as sufficient and necessary to require separation from the people.	Gal. 2.12
MMT C31	Confidence that works of the law, as represented by those indicated, will result in justification	Gal. 2.16

[63] For the meaning of 'judaize' in the first century see my *Galatians* 15 n. 1 and 129. P. F. Esler, *Galatians* (London: Routledge, 1998) ignores this evidence and argues that 'judaize' must include the requirement to be circumcised (137-9). Martyn's observation is sounder:

tional to faith. Hence Paul's expostulation: 'No one is justified by works of the law, but only through faith' (2.16).[64]

This is what I meant and still mean when I speak of 'the new perspective on Paul', as I attempted to work it out in fuller detail some years later in my *Theology of Paul*.[65] In summary:

1. It builds on Sanders' new perspective on Second Temple Judaism, and Sanders' reassertion of the basic graciousness expressed in Judaism's understanding and practice of covenantal nomism.
2. It observes that a social function of the law was an integral aspect of Israel's covenantal nomism, where separateness *to* God (holiness) was understood to require separateness *from* the (other) nations as two sides of the one coin, and that the law was understood as the means to maintaining both.
3. It notes that Paul's own teaching on justification focuses largely if not principally on the need to overcome the barrier which the law was seen to interpose between Jew and Gentile, so that the 'all' of 'to all who believe' (Rom. 1.17) signifies, in the first place, Gentile as well as Jew.
4. It suggests that 'works of law' became a key slogan in Paul's exposition of his justification gospel because so many of Paul's fellow Jewish believers were insisting on certain works as indispensable to their own (and others?) standing within the covenant, and therefore as indispensable to salvation.
5. It protests that failure to recognise this major dimension of Paul's doctrine of justification by faith may have ignored or excluded a vital factor in com-

---

'We can be sure that the message [of the messengers from James] did not directly and explicitly rescind the formula of the Jerusalem conference with its acknowledgment of the Antioch church's circumcision-free mission. Had it done so, Paul would certainly have pointed that out. . . . The issue of circumcision was not reopened' (*Galatians* 233). As in his earlier 'Making and Breaking an Agreement Mediterranean Style: A New Reading of Galatians 2:1-14', *BibInt* 3 (1995) 285-314, Esler assumes that a social-science appreciation of possible honour-shame considerations gives him license to interpret the episode in a way wholly discreditable to Peter and Barnabas. For James' motivation see further M. Bockmuehl, 'Antioch and James the Just', in B. Chilton & C. A. Evans, ed., *James the Just and Christian Origins* (NovTSup 98; Leiden: Brill, 1999) 155-98.

[64] Martyn characterises well how Paul allowed 'his speech to Peter to become without notice a speech addressed to the Teachers in Galatia. . . . Verses 15 and 16 constitute an overlap between the once-upon-a-time remark to Peter and the contemporary speech to the Teachers' (*Galatians* 230); similarly my *Galatians* 132.

[65] *Theology of Paul* #14, especially 338-40, 354-66. At about the same time I wrote 'Paul and Justification by Faith', in R. N. Longenecker, *The Road to Damascus: The Impact of Paul's Conversion on His Life, Thought, and Ministry* (Grand Rapids: Eerdmans, 1997) 85-101, reprinted below ch. 16. Strecker's 'Paulus aus einer "neuen Perspektive"' includes one of the best attempts to summarise my views (11-13); and see now particularly M. Bachmann, 'J. D. G. Dunn und die Neue Paulusperspektive', *TZ* 63 (2007) 25-43; also the sympathetic but critical appraisals of O. Wischmeyer, ed., *Paulus* (Tübingen: Francke, 2006) 35-43, and Bassler, *Navigating Paul* 13-17.

bating the nationalism and racialism which has so distorted and diminished Christianity past and present.

2. Clarifying confusions and misunderstandings

It did not take long for criticisms of this new perspective to be forthcoming.[66] Four are worth trying to respond to at once, since they should help clarify issues and possibly prevent further discussion becoming too preoccupied with particular formulations or with the overtones which some ears pick up, fairly or unfairly. It is perhaps worth saying at once that the discussion should focus on the central thrust of the case and not allow itself to be distracted by phrases which might have been chosen more carefully, or by specifically directed comments taken out of context. The criticisms are as follows: (1) The new perspective was set up in antithesis to and as a repudiation of the traditional Reformation doctrine of justification by faith.[67] (2) I had reduced 'works of the law' to a few 'boundary markers';[68] (3) I had re-

---

[66] For recent reviews of the debate regarding the new perspective, see particularly S. Westerholm, 'The "New Perspective" at Twenty-Five', in Carson et al., *Justification and Variegated Nomism Vol. 2* 1-38.

[67] Particularly in a paper read to the Tyndale Fellowship, Cambridge, in 2000, by Carl Trueman, 'A Man More Sinned Against than Sinning? The Portrait of Martin Luther in Contemporary New Testament Scholarship: Some Casual Observations of a Mere Historian', accessible on the Paul Page on the internet; also Lee Gatiss, 'Justified Hesitation? J. D. G. Dunn vs. The Protestant Doctrine of Justification', in the e-journal *The Theologian* (2001) and in *Churchman,* number 115/1 (2001) 29-48. Similarly B. Corley, 'Interpreting Paul's Conversion — Then and Now', in Longenecker, *The Road to Damascus* 1-17 — 'a frontal assault on the Augustinian-Lutheran paradigm, arguing that that earlier understanding was a drastic misreading of both Judaism and Paul' (3). 'Pauline scholars working inside the "new perspective" have usually rejected several of the great themes of Paul's theology. This concerns especially the teaching about justification' (Eskola, *Theodicy and Predestination* 274). P. F. M. Zahl, 'Mistakes of the New Perspective on Paul', *Themelios* 27/1 (Autumn 2001) 5-11: 'rejection of the Reformation . . . is a big plank of the New Perspective' (7). S. Kim, *Paul and the New Perspective: Second Thoughts on the Origin of Paul's Gospel* (WUNT 140; Tübingen: Mohr Siebeck/Grand Rapids: Eerdmans, 2002): 'the New Perspective School is in many respects overturning the Reformation interpretation of Paul's gospel' (xiv). D. Macleod, 'The New Perspective: Paul, Luther and Judaism', *Scottish Bulletin of Evangelical Theology* 22.1 (2004) 4-31: 'If Stendahl, Dunn and Wright are correct, Luther and Calvin were profoundly wrong' (4-5). D. Garlington, 'The New Perspective on Paul: An Appraisal Two Decades Later', *Criswell Theological Review* 2.2 (2005) 17-38 responds to similar criticisms of the new perspective (26-32).

[68] C. E. B. Cranfield, '"The Works of the Law" in the Epistle to the Romans', *JSNT* 43 (1991) 89-101, reprinted in Cranfield, *On Romans and Other New Testament Essays* (Edinburgh: T&T Clark, 1998) 1-14 — 'a special restricted sense' (4); T. R. Schreiner, '"Works of Law" in Paul', *NovT* 33 (1991) 217-44 (here 225-31); Fitzmyer, *Romans* 338; O. Hofius, 'Zur Auslegung von Römer 9,30-33' (1993), *Paulusstudien II* (WUNT 143; Tübingen: Mohr Siebeck, 2002) 155-66 (here 158-9 n. 26); Lohse, *Römer* 126-7.

duced Paul's objection to the law to merely a (Jewish) 'attitude' to the law (or attitude to others as a result of the law);[69] (4) I had delayed Paul's formulation of the doctrine of justification until his response to the Antioch incident and thereby denied its fundamental importance to Paul's gospel and reduced it to the status of a pragmatic solution to a problem of relationships among Christians.[70]

Let me say at once that there is some justification for these critical comments since my early formulations were not sufficiently refined. So at least some restatement is called for.

2.1 Anti-Lutheran?

The criticism that my work on the 'new perspective' constitutes a fundamental repudiation of the central Protestant affirmation of justification by faith draws principally on my own essay, 'The Justice of God: A Renewed Perspective on Justification by Faith'.[71] At the heart of the criticism is the charge that I attack Martin Luther but show no firsthand knowledge of Luther's writings. Now, I freely admit that I am no expert on Luther and that my direct familiarity with his writings is limited — particularly his commentaries on *Romans* and *Galatians,* and John Dillenberger's *Martin Luther: Selections from his Writings.*[72] Otherwise my knowledge consists of quotations and references in biographies, histories and theological studies referring to Luther in greater or less detail.[73] In 'The Justice of God' essay I draw only on Roland Bainton's *Here I Stand,*[74] which greatly influenced me in my student days, and M. Saperstein, *Moments of Crisis in Jewish-Christian Relations,*[75] who quotes directly from *Luther's Works.* So had I been intent on critiquing Luther directly (or engaging in a study of Reformation theology) I would certainly be open to criticism; whereas my primary concern is with the way Luther has been perceived and

---

[69] H. Räisänen, 'Galatians 2.16 and Paul's Break with Judaism', *Jesus, Paul and Torah: Collected Essays* (JSNTS 43; Sheffield: Sheffield Academic, 1992) 112-26 (here 122); and his pupil, K. Kuula, *The Law, the Covenant and God's Plan: Vol. 1. Paul's Polemical Treatment of the Law in Galatians* (Göttingen: Vandenhoeck & Ruprecht, 1999): 'for Paul the problem of the law was not that it was *misinterpreted* in a sectarian, exclusive way. It is not a misinterpretation of the law that the apostle contests here but the law itself' (59 n. 3, 76-7).

[70] Particularly Kim, *Paul and the New Perspective* 45-53.

[71] *JTS* 43 (1992) 1-22; reprinted below ch. 7.

[72] Anchor Books; New York: Doubleday, 1961. See my *The Theology of Paul's Letter to the Galatians* (Cambridge: Cambridge University, 1993) 140-3.

[73] Most recently D. K. McKim, ed., *The Cambridge Companion to Martin Luther* (Cambridge: Cambridge University, 2003), though, somewhat surprisingly, it does not provide a sustained treatment of 'justification by faith'.

[74] London: Hodder & Stoughton, 1951.

[75] London: SCM, 1989; I draw on Saperstein's quotations from Luther's *Table Talk* again in *Theology of Paul* 337 n. 7.

used in the modern period.[76] In fact, in the 'Justice of God' essay I criticise Luther directly at only one point — in regard to his notorious tract *On the Jews and their Lies,* which I trust no one would wish to defend today[77] — though I confess to much looser (too loose) language in writing at a more popular level elsewhere.[78]

A further relevant factor which probably deserves mention is that as a Presbyterian, trained for ministry in the Church of Scotland, the main 16th century influence shaping me in my early theologising was that of John Calvin and the Reformed rather than the Lutheran tradition. For example, from the Westminster Confession I early on learned that there is a single 'covenant of grace' running through both Testaments — 'not two covenants of grace differing in substance, but one and the same under various dispensations' — and that 'the justification of believers under the Old Testament was . . . one and the same

---

[76] Contrary to Trueman (Gatiss makes the same charge more moderately), I do not attribute to Luther the view that the 'I' of Romans 7 refers to Paul's pre-Christian state. Trueman is evidently unaware of my earlier 'Rom. 7.14-25 in the Theology of Paul', *TZ* 31 (1975) 257-73, and *Jesus and the Spirit* (London: SCM, 1975) 314, 444 n. 57, in which I explicitly indicate that I am following in the footsteps of Luther and Calvin in interpreting Rom. 7.14-25 as a description of Paul's continuing experience as a believer. In the 'Justice of God' essay the criticisms took up those which W. G. Kümmel, *Römer 7 und die Bekehrung des Paulus* (Leipzig: Hinrichs, 1929) directed against what had become the strong Protestant interpretation of Romans 7 as a piece of pre-Christian autobiography, and particularly Stendahl's criticism of the way he perceived Luther's conversion to have been interpreted within his own Lutheran tradition. The exegetical criticism which I offer is directed not at Luther himself, but against those who regarded Luther's conversion as paradigmatic and as a key to understanding Paul's conversion (see also below n. 89). As W. Wrede, *Paul* (London: Philip Green, 1907) had earlier noted: 'the soul strivings of Luther have stood as model for the portrait of Paul' (146). Similarly V. Stolle, *Luther und Paulus: Die exegetischen und hermeneutischen Grundlagen der lutherischen Rechtfertigungslehre im Paulinismus Luthers* (Leipzig: Evangelische, 2002), ch. 2: 'Luther's autobiographical conception of himself as "Paul": 1. Luther's self-understanding as a Paul of his time'. Likewise the criticism that I charged Luther with 'thinking of justification in distinctly individualistic terms' fails to appreciate that the reference is to the way Luther's conversion was understood — I do not say by Luther himself. My main target, in fact, was Bultmann's highly influential existentialist reading of Paul; note also Dahl's observation that 'a certain narrowing occurred. . . . The focus of the doctrine became the individual's relationship to God' ('Doctrine of Justification' 118). 'Individualistic' was simply a way of pointing out that the dimension of peoples and not just individuals is bound up in Paul's key slogan — 'to Jew first but also Gentile' ('Gentiles' = 'nations') (see again below #2.3). My overall concern is echoed by Roloff, 'Die lutherische Rechtfertigungslehre und ihre biblische Grundlage' 277-82: 'In the case of the teaching on justification, which according to its self-understanding should express in an exemplary way the *understanding of scripture* as the *norma normans,* it has actually established *the teaching of the Church* as the *norma normans*' (278).

[77] Presumably it is this writing which Stephen Westerholm has in mind in his observation that 'when he (Luther) writes polemically, his terms and tone are often monumentally lamentable' ('The "New Perspective" at Twenty-Five' 38).

[78] With Alan Suggate, *The Justice of God: A Fresh Look at the Old Doctrine of Justification by Faith* (Carlisle: Paternoster/Grand Rapids: Eerdmans, 1993) 13-14.

with the justification of believers under the New Testament'.[79] And in my early reflection on the theology of baptism I was much impressed by Calvin's insistence on the continuity between the Testaments and on the very complete resemblance between circumcision and baptism as to promise and effect.[80] I suppose this background may help explain what may have become an almost instinctive reaction on my part against too great stress on the *dis*continuities between the native religion of Jesus, himself 'a servant of circumcision' (Rom. 15.8), and Christianity.

Carl Trueman, however, maintains that the new perspective is not just a rejection of Lutheran teaching on justification but amounts to a charge 'that the whole of Christian tradition is basically wrongheaded over salvation, [and] that the Reformers were more guilty than most in the perversion of the gospel'. Insofar as the criticism is directed against me personally, I simply have to say that I recognise none of what he asserts.[81] I am totally astonished by such statements and wonder whether Trueman has been reading what I wrote. It is all the more puzzling since I took pains to emphasise at the beginning of the 'Justice of God' essay that *the central affirmation of the doctrine of justification by grace through faith is and remains absolutely fundamental for Christian faith* — a point reasserted once again in the conclusion.[82] So, insofar as my essay on 'The Justice of God' can be regarded as representative of the new perspective,

---

[79] The Westminster Confession #7.3-6; #11.6.

[80] *Institutes* 4.16.10-16. See further F. Wendel, *Calvin: The Origins and Development of his Religious Thought* (1950; ET London: Collins Fontana, 1965) 208-14, 325-6.

[81] I am equally astonished at the even more virulent attacks directed against N. T. Wright, *What Saint Paul Really Said* (Grand Rapids: Eerdmans, 1997), to the same effect, particularly in the Presbyterian Church of America Web Magazine, PCANews.com. G. P. Waters, *Justification and the New Perspectives on Paul* (Phillipsburg, NJ: Presbyterian & Reformed, 2004) sets out 'to illustrate the ways in which the NPP (the new perspective on Paul) deviates from the doctrines set forth in the Westminster Standards' (x); 'the soteriological sympathies of the NPP, to the degree that these sympathies exist, are not with Protestantism, but with Roman Catholicism' (xi; similarly 190). Chapter 7 is devoted to a vituperative review of Wright which beggars belief: 'We have, in Wright's thought, an inherent bias against doctrinal formulations . . . a predisposition against conceiving of the relationship of God and man in *vertical* terms' (121); 'we have in Wright an aversion to conducting theology in the way that the church has classically conceived theology' (192); 'his writings have proven a Trojan horse to the church' (198). Contrast Bird's more eirenic assessment of Wright's relation to 'Reformed Orthodoxy' (*Saving Righteousness* 183-93).

[82] 'Justice of God' 1-2, 21; below 194, 211. Similarly *The Justice of God* 8-9, 10-13; and earlier *Romans* lxv. Westerholm fully recognises this; also that my critique of the 'Lutheran' interpretation is directed to its 'shortcomings' and the fact that it 'obscured' the *point d'appui* (my term) of Paul's initial statement of the doctrine (*Perspectives* 184 and n. 8). Equally eirenic is Bird in his insistence that the vertical dimension of Paul's teaching on justification must be held together with the horizontal dimension, the latter having been too much ignored by Reformed exegetes and too much emphasised by the new perspective (*Saving Righteousness* e.g. 29-34, 153, 182).

I fail to see how it can be used to sustain Trueman's indictment of the new perspective.[83]

From the first, my concern has been not to attack or deny the classic Christian doctrine of justification by faith. My concern has always been that the doctrine of justification, as rediscovered (or reasserted) by Luther[84] and as consistently expounded within Protestantism, has neglected important aspects particularly of Paul's original formulation in the context of his mission.[85] In the 'Justice of God' essay I protest against the corollary of the traditional exposition, that Paul affirmed his doctrine against a degenerate Jewish legalism.[86] I note that Paul's teaching on justification is an expression of his mission to the Gentiles, that it embodies a protest against national or ethnic presumption and disdain for the (other) nations; hence the initial, indeed the primary emphasis of Romans, that the gospel is 'for *all* who believe, Jew first *but also* Greek' (Rom. 1.16). And I argue that an integral aspect of 'works of the law' was the concern to maintain Israel's distinctiveness and separateness from the (other) nations, and that this aspect has been but should not be ignored in our attempts to explicate Paul's key formulation, 'a person is justified by faith

---

[83] In a pleasant e-mail exchange (February 2004) Dr Trueman graciously acknowledged that his paper misrepresented my views and expressed his regret that it had found its way (unauthorised) on to the internet; my fuller response is also available on the Paul Page of the internet. Unfortunately, the original paper continues to be referred to, most recently by T. George, 'Modernizing Luther, Domesticating Paul: Another Perspective', in Carson et al., *Justification and Variegated Nomism Vol. 2* 437-63 (here 439 n. 7).

[84] Perhaps it should be made clear that I fully recognise that 'justification by faith' had by no means been lost to sight in the centuries prior to Luther; see A. McGrath, *Iustitia Dei: A History of the Christian Doctrine of Justification* (Cambridge: Cambridge University, 1986, ²1998) chs. 2-5; T. C. Oden, *The Justification Reader* (Grand Rapids: Eerdmans, 2002).

[85] It is this missing dimension to which I referred in attributing to the Lutheran theology of justification 'a significant misunderstanding of Paul' ('Justice of God' 2). That was a misleading and unnecessarily provocative way of introducing my point (to make the audience sit up and take notice) which I regret. A more appropriate target for criticism at this point would appear to be Francis Watson in his earlier thesis, *Paul, Judaism and the Gentiles* (SNTSMS 56; Cambridge: Cambridge University, 1986), who argues explicitly from the outset that 'the Reformation tradition's approach to Paul is fundamentally wrong' (1) and sums up the then current trend in some Pauline scholarship as 'the process of "delutheranizing Paul"' (18). But Watson has publicly repented of his more youthful exuberance and criticised the new perspective with equal fervour in a paper at the British New Testament Conference, Manchester, September 2001, 'Not the New Perspective', also available on the Paul Page on the web. N. Elliott, *The Rhetoric of Romans: Argumentative Constraint and Strategy and Paul's Dialogue with Judaism* (JSNTS 45; Sheffield: Sheffield Academic, 1990) speaks of the 'Lutheran captivity' of Romans, but acknowledges that this is a tendentious description (292-3). McGrath also notes that 'the "doctrine of justification" has come to bear a meaning within dogmatic theology which is quite independent of its Pauline origins' (*Iustitia Dei* 2-3).

[86] Gatiss's response at this point does not give enough weight to the denigration of Judaism which has been such a feature of Christian theology in the modern period; the bibliography in 'The Justice of God' 5-6 nn. 11-15 (below 197 nn. 11-15) should provide sufficient documentation.

apart from works of the law' (Rom. 3.28).[87] The problem, if I may put it so, is that Luther's fundamental distinction between gospel and law[88] was too completely focused on the danger of self-achieved works-righteousness and too quickly transposed into an antithesis between Christianity and Judaism.[89]

Perhaps I should repeat the point, since the belief that the new perspective repudiates the foundational character of justification by faith and denies the gospel appears to be widespread particularly in some North American and Lutheran circles.[90] I affirm as a central point of Christian faith that God's accep-

---

[87] 'Justice of God' 5-15; below 197-205. The fourth section of the essay (15-21; below 206-10), has not been taken up, but is directly relevant to the discussion below (##4.2-3).

[88] As noted, for example, by H. M. Müller, '"Evangelium latuit in lege": Luthers Kreuzespredigt als Schlüssel seiner Bibelhermeneutik', in *Jesus Christus als die Mitte der Schrift*, O. Hofius FS, ed. C. Landmesser, et al. (BZNW 86; Berlin: de Gruyter, 1997) 101-26: 'the distinction between law and gospel grew out of Luther's exegetical work in his conversation with the apostle . . . the distinction between law and gospel as basis for the teaching of justification by faith.' 'Only he who takes up this distinction and lets his thinking be led by it is, according to Luther, a good theologian' (101-2; also 107-9). See further Bergmeier, *Gesetz* 31-5, who notes, *inter alia*, Harnack's observation that 'The whole sphere of the law belongs religiously according to Luther "to an outdated stage; whoever does not recognize this must remain a Jew"' (34). But note also the caution of B. Wannenwetsch, 'Luther's Moral Theology', in McKim, ed., *Martin Luther* 120-35: 'Luther's theology of law cannot be equated with the infamous law and gospel antinomy' (124-6). And see now V. Stolle, 'Nomos zwischen Tora und Lex', in M. Bachmann, *Lutherische und Neue Paulusperspektive* (WUNT; Tübingen: Mohr Siebeck, 2005) 41-67, who shows that the classic gospel/law antithesis has to be qualified and that for Luther himself the contrast between the Lutheran perspective and the new perspective may have been overdrawn; it is important not least to grasp the fact that for Luther the law continues to have a function in the life of the Christian (52, 56).

[89] Cf. E. Lohse, *Paulus* (München: C. H. Beck, 1996): 'It is justified to point out, however, that one may not conclude from Luther's sharp confrontation against mediaeval works righteousness to a correspondingly dark background of the Judaism of Paul's time, as has happened not seldom in the older discussion' (285); P. Stuhlmacher, *Revisiting Paul's Doctrine of Justification: A Challenge to the New Perspective* (Downers Grove, IL: IVP, 2001): 'Luther saw the Jewish and Jewish-Christian adversaries of Paul as one with the Catholic theologians of his time, while he and his followers appeared in the role of Paul and his pupils. This blurring of the distinction between historical and dogmatic perspectives remains a factor in German Pauline scholarship to this day' (35).

[90] For the perception among responsible scholars that the new perspective set out to distance Paul from the 'Lutheran' Paul — 'the "de-lutheranizing" of the Apostle' (Strecker, 'Paulus aus einer "neuen Perspektive"' 3-4) — see e.g. R. B. Matlock, 'Almost Cultural Studies? Reflections on the "New Perspective" on Paul', in J. C. Exum & S. D. Moore, eds., *Biblical Studies/Cultural Studies: The Third Sheffield Colloquium* (JSOTS 266; Sheffield: Sheffield Academic, 1998) 433-59: 'the new perspective defines itself polemically over against what it typically identifies as the 'Lutheran' reading of Paul, this negative self-definition providing the real unity for what is otherwise an internally divided and still developing set of views' (436); B. Byrne, 'Interpreting Romans Theologically in a Post-"New Perspective" Perspective', *HTR* 94 (2001) 227-41 (here 228, 230); Lohse, *Römer* 140; the new perspective thinks 'it necessary to rescue Paul from the clutches of Luther if we are to understand him aright' (George, 'Modernizing Luther' 441); Blocher speaks of the new perspective as 'to a great extent an anti-Lutheran perspective' ('Justification of the Ungodly' 473). T. L. Donaldson's review of my *Theology of Paul* in *CRBR* 1998, is entitled 'In Search of a

tance of any and every person is by his grace alone and through faith alone; I would have hoped that my chapter on 'Justification by Faith' (particularly #14.7) in my *Theology of Paul* would have made that clear enough. For my own part, even though it is not the language of the Reformed tradition,[91] I have no particular problem in affirming that the doctrine of justification (in its fully orbed expression) is *articulus stantis et cadentis ecclesiae;* I am astonished by and repudiate entirely the charge that 'the new perspective on Paul' constitutes an attack on and denial of that Lutheran fundamental. Anyone who reads that from my writing is reading in what he wants to see, not reading out what is there. The point I am trying to make is simply that there is another dimension (or other dimensions) of the biblical doctrine of God's justice and of Paul's teaching on justification which have been overlooked and neglected, and that it is important to recover these aspects and to think them through afresh in the changing circumstances of today's world. In a word, I seek *not* to diminish let alone repudiate the doctrine of justification *(mē genoito),* but to bring more fully to light its still greater riches.

2.2 Works of the Law

It has been a matter of regret to me that my initial formulation of the case I was making (regarding 'works of the law') allowed it to be so readily dismissed.[92] Let me make it quite clear, then: I have no doubt that 'works of the law' refer to what the law requires, the conduct prescribed by the Torah;[93]

Paul Neither Lutheran nor Idiosyncratic'; the subtitle of Westerholm's *Perspectives Old and New on Paul* is *The "Lutheran" Paul and His Critics;* and the volume edited by M. Bachmann, *Lutherische und Neue Paulusperspektive,* initially had as a possible title, *Lutherische oder Neue Paulusperspektive.* On the other hand, Sanders' protest, that to interpret Paul by setting the Reformation *sola gratia/sola fide* in antithesis to an alleged Jewish 'works-righteousness' is hardly likely to grasp the intention of the Pauline statements, is steadily gaining a hearing within German NT scholarship, as indicated by K.-W. Niebuhr, 'Die paulinische Rechtfertigungslehre in der gegenwärtigen exegetischen Diskussion', in T. Söding, ed., *Worum geht es in der Rechtfertigungslehre: das biblische Fundament der "Gemeinsamen Erklärung" von katholischer Kirche und lutherischem Weltbund* (Freiburg: Herder, 1999) 106-30 (here 118-21); and in several of the contributions in the Bachmann volume, particularly by K. Haacker, 'Verdienste und Grenzen der "neuern Perspektive" der Paulus-Auslegung' (1-15), H. Frankemölle, 'Völker-Verheissung (Gen 12-18) und Sinai-Tora im Römerbrief' (275-307), and W. Krauss, 'Gottes Gerechtigkeit und Gottes Volk' (329-47, especially 330-6 and 344); also K. Haacker, 'Merits and Limits of the "New Perspective on the Apostle Paul"', in S.-W. Son, ed., *History and Exegesis,* E. E. Ellis FS (New York: T&T Clark, 2006) 275-89.

[91] See McGrath, *Iustitia Dei* 188, 225-6.

[92] Particularly 'New Perspective' 201-2 (below 118-9). Watson justifiably chides me at this point (*Hermeneutics of Faith* 334-5 n. 41).

[93] M. Bachmann, 'Rechtfertigung und Gesetzeswerke bei Paulus', *TZ* 49 (1993) 1-33, and '4QMMT und Galaterbrief, *ma'ase hatorah* und *ERGA NOMOU'*, *ZNW* 89 (1998) 91-113, both reprinted in *Antijudaismus im Galaterbrief: Exegetische Studien zu einem polemischen*

whatever the law requires to be done can be described as 'doing' the law, as a work of the law.[94] As I hope I have made clear in subsequent contributions, the

Schreiben und zur Theologie des Apostels Paulus (NTOA 40; Freiburg: Universitätsverlag, 1999) 1-31, 33-56, argues that the phrase refers only to the law's precepts or halakhic rulings (further 'Keil oder Mikroskop?'), a rendering which avoids the Lutheran antithesis between 'faith' and 'works' ('Neue Paulusperspektive' 40-1). Whereas J. C. R. de Roo, 'The Concept of "Works of the Law" in Jewish and Christian Literature', in S. E. Porter & B. W. R. Pearson, eds., *Christian-Jewish Relations Through the Centuries* (JSNTS 192; Sheffield: Sheffield Academic, 2000) 116-47, followed by A. A. Das, *Paul and the Jews* (Peabody, MA; Hendrickson, 2003) 40-41, insists with equal vehemence that the phrase refers only to 'deeds' as distinct from 'precepts'. The distinction in both cases is forced. See further Bergmeier, *Gesetz* 40-2; and 'Vom Tun der Tora', in Bachmann, ed., *Lutherische und Neue Paulusperspektive* 161-81 (here 161-4); also my 'Noch einmal "Works of the Law": The Dialogue Continues', in I. Dunderberg & C. Tuckett, eds., *Fair Play: Diversity and Conflicts in Early Christianity,* H. Räisänen FS (Leiden: Brill, 2002) 273-90, reprinted below ch. 19 (in revised form), here #II (below 418-22), and my response in Bachmann, ed., *Lutherische und Neue Paulusperspektive* 397-401; also to Bergmeier (402-4). De Roo seems to think that I agree with Bachmann in regarding *erga nomou* as referring only to 'precepts', and continues to insist on 'a clear distinction between "works performed" and "works prescribed"' (*'Works of the Law' at Qumran* 82-5, 92, and further ch. 4 as a whole) in order to press for the meaning of the former as 'opposed to' *(sic!)* the latter. My point to both Bachmann and de Roo is that the phrase includes *both* meanings, as one today might use a phrase like 'payment of taxes' to refer both to the requirement and, of course, also its performance. 4QMMT C26, with its clear reference back to the rulings of section B seems precisely to cover that range (*pace* de Roo 90-4).

[94] The point is properly emphasised by Cranfield, 'Works of the Law' 5; also by others, e.g., T. R. Schreiner, *The Law and its Fulfilment: A Pauline Theology of Law* (Grand Rapids: Baker, 1993) 51-4; D. Flusser, 'Die Gesetzeswerke in Qumran und bei Paulus', in P. Schäfer, ed., *Geschichte — Tradition — Reflexion, Band I Judentum,* M. Hengel FS (Tübingen: Mohr Siebeck, 1996) 395-403; Eskola, *Theodicy and Predestination* 208-20; Bell, *No One Seeks for God* 228-35; Mijoga, *Deeds of the Law* 2, 158-9 (also 65-7, 74-7); F. Avemarie, 'Die Werke des Gesetzes im Spiegel des Jakobusbriefs: A Very Old Perspective on Paul', *ZTK* 98 (2001) 282-309; Gathercole, *Where is Boasting?* 92-6, 238-40, 249; see also Martyn, *Galatians* 260-3. Reference can be made to Ex. 18.20 (e.g. my '4QMMT and Galatians' 150 n. 19, below 342 n. 18; 'Noch einmal' 280-1, below 419-20). Bergmeier also refers to Josephus, *Ap.* 2.169, 172 (*Gesetz* 37 and n. 41); see further 39-41. Rapa's main argument in *Meaning* is that Paul went beyond the identity marking function of 'works of the law' to focus on their soteriological implications, something I do not dispute. I already clarified my view in my 1985 essay 'Works of the Law' 220 and 223 (below 127 and 130), as Kuula, *Law* 2.116-7 notes, and reinforced the point in my responses to P. Stuhlmacher (*Jesus, Paul and the Law* 210) and to Cranfield ('Yet Once More'; below ch. 8). Esler missed this clarification (*Galatians* 182-3), but Westerholm again recognises it in summarising my contribution (*Perspectives* 189; 'The "New Perspective" at Twenty-Five' 12-13). I do not accept T. Laato's claim that I have modified my position considerably — T. Laato, 'Paul's Anthropological Considerations: Two Problems', in Carson, et al., *Justification and Variegated Nomism Vol. 2* 343-59 (here 356 n. 71). The discussion by P. T. O'Brien, 'Was Paul a Covenantal Nomist?', in Carson, et al., *Justification and Variegated Nomism Vol. 2* 249-96 is mostly derivative and fails to grapple with the key evidence (277-82). H.-J. Eckstein, *Verheissung und Gesetz: Eine exegetische Untersuchung zu Galater 2,15–4,7* (WUNT 86; Tübingen: Mohr Siebeck, 1996) 21-6 emphasises that the phrase denotes 'being under the law' (4.21) and 'doing the whole law' (5.3), but without reference to my work or to 4QMMT. Waters' attempt to push Wright and myself into saying that 'the works of the law . . . are exclusively concerned with *identity* and not at all with *activity*' (*Justification* 195) is too ridiculous for words.

phrase 'works of the law' is a way of describing the law observance required of all covenant members,[95] and could be regarded as an appropriate way of filling out the second half of the Sanders' formula — 'covenantal *nomism*'.[96] Putting the point from Paul's perspective, Paul was clear that justification is by faith alone: to regard any 'works of the law' as essential (in addition to faith) undermines 'faith alone'. The gospel principle is clear: 'no one is justified by works of the law, but only *(ean mē)*[97] through faith in Jesus Christ' (Gal. 2.16).[98]

At same time, the context occasioning the first enunciation of that principle (Gal. 2.1-16) reminds us that the general principle can be put to test by particular works of the law.[99] Evidently some believing Jews wanted to insist that

---

[95] Contra L. Gaston, 'Paul and the Torah', *Paul and the Torah* (Vancouver: University of British Columbia, 1987) 15-34, who mistakenly believes that the phrase 'works of the law' appears in no Jewish writing and must refer to 'the adoption of selected Jewish practices on the part of Gentiles' (25, also 69-70); followed uncritically by Stowers, *Rereading Romans* 187, and Gager: '"works of the law" is a Pauline tag for Gentiles' (*Reinventing Paul* 121). D. E. Aune, 'Recent Readings of Paul Relating to Justification by Faith', in D. E. Aune, ed., *Rereading Paul Together* (Grand Rapids: Baker Academic, 2006) gives a useful summary of the 'New View' of Paul espoused by Gaston and Gager in particular (219-23).

[96] Hence the emphasis in e.g. 'What was the Issue' and 'The Theology of Galatians' (below chs. 5 and 6), that Paul's argument in Romans 2 and Galatians as a whole can properly be described as directed against twin misperceptions of covenantal nomism — in effect that the 'nomism' part of the formula had *not* been given *sufficient* emphasis (Romans 2), or had been given *too much* emphasis (Galatians)! Gundry, 'Grace, Works, and Staying Saved in Paul', had already pointed out that the issue in Galatians is not 'getting in' but 'staying in' (8-12 — using Sanders' terms).

[97] See below n. 153.

[98] Witherington seriously misrepresents (or misunderstands) my view of Paul: 'Dunn's theory that Paul will argue for faith in Christ plus observance of major tenants (*sic* — read 'tenets') of the Law relieved of its restrictive and ritualistic aspects' (*Grace in Galatia* 162 — 'making Paul sound more like his opponents than like himself'). Paul's teaching *is* clear at this point, whatever qualifications that he himself introduces at other points (see further below ##4.2(10) and 4.3(11)).

[99] Stuhlmacher ignores the context out of which Gal. 2.16 emerged and which determined its formulation and fails to note that 'the works of the law' in 4QMMT C were the grounds for Qumran's separation from 'the multitude of the people' (*Revisiting* 42-4). Similarly, Fitzmyer (*Romans* 338) and Bird (*Saving Righteousness* 98) fail to note that the point of comparison with 4QMMT is not the 'restricted' reference of the phrase, but the fact that specified requirements of the law/halakhoth (on ritual purity, temple cult and marriage laws) were being set forth as test-cases of others' acceptability to God; to separate from others on halakhic grounds is to regard these others as unacceptable to God, is to treat these rulings as a boundary requiring such separation (cf. Mijoga, *Deeds of the Law* 110-3; but also 121-2, 140-5); see also above n. 60 and further 'Noch einmal' 284-7 (below 426-9). Surprisingly, Wright too misses the fact that the point of comparison is not what constituted the boundary, but the boundary-drawing attitude itself, excluding the other, whether other Jew or Gentile ('Romans' 460; '4QMMT and Paul' 110, 129-30). F. Watson, 'Constructing an Antithesis: Pauline and Other Jewish Perspectives on Divine and Human Agency', in J. M. G. Barclay & S. Gathercole, eds., *Divine and Human Agency in Paul and his Cultural Environment* (LNTS 335; London: T&T Clark, 2006) 99-116 also questions whether the 'works of the law' in 4QMMT are understood as defining a boundary, on the grounds that 'the aim of the letter is

circumcision was necessary for those who believed in Messiah Jesus (under-standably, in view of Gen. 17.9-14); that challenge was successfully resisted (Gal. 2.1-10). But then the bulk of believing Jews, Peter and Barnabas in-cluded, acted on the belief that it was still necessary for Jews to eat separately from Gentiles; the laws on clean and unclean were still essential (2.11-14).[100]

precisely that the "boundary" created by aberrant practice should be removed' (107 n. 20); but he fails to appreciate that for a sect like Qumran to classify halakhic interpretations of Torah different from their own as 'aberrant' was indeed to mark out a boundary between the sect and other Jews. Lohse likewise misses the point: the Qumran confidence in divine righ-teousness was, of course, not over against *Gentiles* (*Römer* 144), but it was *over against* other Jews! I made this point already in 'Yet Once More' 103-4 (below 216-7), in 'Echoes of Intra-Jewish Polemic' (below 234-5) and in '4QMMT and Galatians' 150-1 (below 342-3); also 'Paul et la Torah: le rôle et la fonction de la Loi dans la théologie de Paul l'apôtre', in A.Dettwiler, J.-D. Kaestli & D. Marguerat, eds., *Paul, une théologie en construction* (Genève: Labor et Fides, 2004) 227-49 (below ch. 21), here 243-5 (below 462-4). In contrast, C. Burchard, 'Nicht aus Werken des Gesetzes gerecht, sondern aus Glauben an Jesus Christus — seit wann?', in H. Lichtenberger, ed., *Geschichte — Tradition — Reflexion, Band III: Frühes Christentum,* M. Hengel FS (Tübingen: Mohr Siebeck, 1996) 405-15 (here 410-1), K. L. Yinger, *Paul, Judaism and Judgment According to Deeds* (SNTSMS 105; Cambridge: Cambridge University, 1999) 169-74, Rapa, *Meaning* 54, 143-4, 172 n. 11, 173 n. 21 and 264 (with qualifications), and de Roo, *'The Works of the Law'* at Qumran 94-5 have taken the point. 'The distinctive food purity laws practiced by the Qumran sectarians served as bound-ary markers distinguishing them from Gentiles and also other Jewish groups' ('The Role of Food as Related to Covenant in Qumran Literature', in S. E. Porter & J. C. R. de Roo, eds., *The Concept of the Covenant in the Second Temple Period* [SSJSup 71; Leiden: Brill, 2003] 129-64, here 163). M. G. Abegg, 'Paul and James on the Law in Light of the Dead Sea Scrolls', in J. J. Collins & C. A. Evans, eds., *Christian Beginnings and the Dead Sea Scrolls* (Grand Rapids: Baker Academic, 2006) 63-74, rightly observes that 'the interpretation of the law, which had been revealed by God, is the focus of the phrase "works of the law"'; 'it was a par-ticular set of "works of the law" that defined Qumran Judaism for what it was'; '"obeying the law" was *in accordance with the correct interpretation*' (71-3, also 66-8). The point is ex-pressed well by F. Vouga, *An die Galater* (HNT 10; Tübingen: Mohr Siebeck, 1998): 'circum-cision and the laws of clean and unclean as signs of election and holiness are symbols of the whole law and of belonging to the people of the covenant' (58). As also by R. B. Hays, *The HarperCollins Study Bible,* ed. W. A. Meeks, et al. [New York: HarperCollins, 1993] 2185: '"works of the law" refer primarily to practices commanded by the law (circumcision, dietary laws, Sabbath observance) that distinctively mark Jewish ethnic identity; *these symbolize comprehensive obedience to the law's covenant obligations*' (as cited by D. Garlington, *In De-fense of the New Perspective on Paul* [Eugene, OR: Wipf & Stock, 2005] 39). In 'Yet Once More' 101 (below 214-5), I note that often in Christianity's history a larger principle can come to focus in particular issues, where e.g. the infallibility of the Pope, maleness of the priesthood, believer's baptism, inerrancy of the Bible, can all be matters which are added to faith in Christ as essential for mutual recognition and cooperation.

[100] In 'The Incident at Antioch' I tried to allow for all the factors which motivated Peter to 'separate' from mixed Jew/Gentile table fellowship; for a more recent statement see my *Galatians* 119-24; and further Lohse, *Paulus* 92-3; Martyn, *Galatians* 241-3; Schäfer, *Paulus bis zum Apostelkonzil* 236-8. Rapa sums up the attitude which provoked Paul's rebuke, though he refers it to the 'judaizers' in Galatia: 'The "works of the law" were the nomistic observances re-lated to the Jewish law that these judaizers argued were part and parcel of what it meant to be "Christian"' (138-9). I summarise a more complex situation by reference to 'the laws of clean and unclean', since they seem to provide the basic motivation (see further below #2.3).

In Paul's eyes such action was a breach of the basic principle: to insist that the laws of clean and unclean were still binding on believing Jews was to require works of the law in addition to faith in Christ. As Nils Dahl puts it: 'For Paul, the behaviour of Peter and Barnabas constitutes their rejection of the doctrine of justification by faith'.[101] In contrast, the primary concern of Peter and the others, we may deduce, was not so much in terms of their earning merit by such obedience. It was more the conviction that these rules in particular were still binding on all Jews, that to be faithful to God they had to remain faithful to the contract made by God with his people, including the laws of clean and unclean.[102]

Alternatively, if the focus on circumcision and food laws still seems to be too narrow for some, we could observe a third element in the equation — 'living like a Jew/judaizing' (*ioudaizein* — 2.14). In Paul's eyes, Peter and the other believing Jews were in effect insisting that believing Gentiles should observe the food laws = judaize = do works of the law. In other words, 'works of the law' are not only a way of describing what members of the covenant are obligated to do by virtue of their covenant membership ('covenantal nomism').[103] 'Works of the law' also denote the Jewish way of life, including the distinctively Jewish way of life (hence also Paul's objection in 5.3).[104] To 'live jewishly' (*ioudaikōs zēn* — 2.14) is to live according to the law, to do what the law

---

[101] Dahl, 'Doctrine of Justification' 109; 'with v. 16 Paul makes clear what momentous consequences must result from the renouncing of table-fellowship' (Lohse, *Paulus* 94).

[102] See further my *Theology of Galatians* 75-9; also *Theology of Paul* 360 n. 104. Kim insists on reading 'works of the law' as 'human achievements or as good works done to earn God's favour' (*Paul and the New Perspective* 59-60), which hardly does justice to the concerns which must have weighed with Peter in the Antioch incident. Contrast the more sympathetic treatment of I.-G. Hong, *The Law in Galatians* (JSNTSupp 81; Sheffield: JSOT Press, 1993) 133-48, and Kruse, *Paul* 41-2, 186. Schnelle thinks that such differentiations (between the law generally and certain laws in particular) are simply not found in Paul (*Paul* 281 n. 52); what then of 1 Cor. 7.19?

[103] Cf. Westerholm, *Perspectives* 367-70: 'For the Jewish Christian advocates of circumcision, then, the Jewish covenant and laws still provided the framework within which God's people must live' (368).

[104] Cf. J. B. Tyson, '"Works of Law" in Galatians', *JBL* 92 (1973) 423-31; Eskola: '... "works of the law" denotes obedience and service to the whole law of Moses. This was a central part of Jewish identity' (*Theodicy and Predestination* 220). F. J. Matera, 'Galatians in Perspective', *Interpretation* 54 (2000) 233-45, expresses my point well: 'In Galatians, it ["works of the law"] refers to certain specific works of the law that would, if adopted, identify the Galatians as having embraced a Jewish way of life' (237). Watson repeats his earlier observation that 'works of the law' stands for 'the way of life of the Jewish people, those who are within God's covenant with Israel' (*Hermeneutics of Faith* 69 n. 79). That a function of the law was its role in marking out the people of God was generally recognised in the Symposium on *Paul and the Mosaic Law* (330); e.g. R. B. Hays, 'Three Dramatic Roles: The Law in Romans 3–4': 'The law defines the identity of the Jewish people' (151-4). To suggest that my observations about Gal. 2.16 set in its pre-context is equivalent to 'replacing "the law" in Galatians 3:21 by "ceremonial regulations"' (Blocher, 'Justification of the Ungodly' 487) is as 'absurd' as the suggestion itself.

commands (works of the law).[105] It should occasion no surprise, then, that the more profound principle (faith and not works) should be triggered by the question of Jew and Gentile eating together.[106]

In short, then, I do not want to narrow 'the works of the law' to boundary issues.[107] But it is fairly obvious that any view which insists that *all* works of the law are to be observed will naturally insist that *any* works of the law which are at all contentious *must* therefore and nevertheless be observed. And the fact remains that the issue which caused the first recorded statement of the great principle of justification by faith alone were the works of the law by which Judaism distinguished itself and kept itself separate from the (other) nations.[108] Which brings us nicely to the third point of clarification.

---

[105] '. . . "works of the law" are equivalent to "living like a Jew" '; 'doing what the law demands is a sign of adopting the Jewish way of life . . . "the works of the law", that is, maintaining a Jewish life-style'; 'Paul opposes "the works of the law" in Galatians because they represent imposing a Jewish life-style . . . on his Gentile converts' (J. M. G. Barclay, *Obeying the Truth: A Study of Paul's Ethics in Galatians* [Edinburgh: T&T Clark, 1988] 78, 82, 239); '*ioudaizein* [means] a Jewish way of life . . . , so *ioudaikōs zēn*, a Jewish way of life, whose *notae iusti* define themselves *ex ergōn nomou*' (Bergmeier, *Gesetz* 42). Similarly R. Liebers, *Das Gesetz als Evangelium: Untersuchingen zur Gesetzeskritik des Paulus* (Zürich: Theologischer, 1989) 54; M. Bachmann, *Sünder oder Übertreter: Studien zur Argumentation in Gal 2,15ff.* (WUNT 59; Tübingen: Mohr Siebeck, 1992) 93-4. See my earlier formulation in *Partings* 133.

[106] At this point I find myself pleasingly close to Westerholm, *Perspectives* 383-4: 'Paul was not addressing the Pelagian or sixteenth-century disputes over works. But he responded to the insistence that Gentiles be circumcised by taking up the fundamental issue of how human beings, in spite of their sin, can experience life in God's favor' (384; see further his final chapter 440-5).

[107] I used various terms in 'The New Perspective' — 'identity markers', 'badges of covenant membership' (192), as well as 'defining boundaries' and (193) 'boundary markers' (192-4; below 113-5) — but did not bring out clearly enough the wider reference in these early essays. Wright used the same imagery of circumcision 'as badge of national identity' ('History' 65) and develops it in the same way in *The Climax of the Covenant: Christ and the Law in Pauline Theology* (Edinburgh: T&T Clark, 1991) 240-4; similarly *What Saint Paul Really Said* 130-2. So also W. S. Campbell, *Paul's Gospel in an Intercultural Context* (Frankfurt: Peter Lang, 1991) 126-7. In reading 'boundary markers' as though the characterisation was simply a re-run of the old 'ceremonial law' versus 'moral law' issue, Zahl ('Mistakes' 9-10) totally fails to reckon with the social and ethnic dimension highlighted by the term (see further #2.3 below). And to characterise circumcision as a kind of 'body-piercing' (George, 'Modernizing Luther' 457, following Zahl 9) displays a lamentable ignorance of the function of circumcision as the most crucial identity marker of Israel (*hē peritomē* = the Jews).

[108] The critique of M. A. Seifrid, 'Blind Alleys in the Controversy over the Paul of History', *TynBul* 45 (1994) 73-95 (here 77-85) is much more nuanced than the others (n. 94 above): 'The *erga (nomou)* which the circumcised were to perform marked the difference between the righteous and the ungodly. . . . in rejecting *erga nomou* as a guarantee of salvation, Paul rejects a moral superiority gained by obedience' (84-5). Such a formulation constitutes a helpful middle way ('both-and') which could provide a basis for a richer synthesis. Byrne also comes eirenically closer to my reformulation ('The Problem of Nomos' 299-301); as also, for the most part, M. Silva, 'Faith Versus Works of Law in Galatians', in Carson, et al., *Justification and Variegated Nomism Vol. 2* 217-48 (here 221-2); and see Haacker, 'Merits and

2.3 A wrong attitude/a misunderstanding?

To what extent was Jewish 'attitude' to Gentiles at the heart of the problem?[109] Does it not trivialise Paul's teaching on justification and on the curse of the law to see the crucial doctrine of justification as (simply!) about good race relations?[110] Have I not reduced the Pauline teaching on justification to 'the concept of a new missionary strategy',[111] or to a merely sociological category?[112] Have I not over-emphasised the social and national dynamic behind

---

Limits' 284-5. In contrast, V. M. Smiles, *The Gospel and the Law in Galatia: Paul's Response to Jewish-Christian Separatism and the Threat of Galatian Apostasy* (Collegeville: Liturgical, Glazier, 1998) simply confuses the issue when he insists that 'it is the law's claims upon the *entire world* that Paul must contest . . . the law's own fundamental claim to determine for *all humanity* the basis of the divine-human relationship that Paul must expose' (126-8).

[109] Räisänen (n. 69 above) was picking up my language in 'Works of the Law' 231 (below 139-40) — the attitude to the law as requiring those observances/works which marked out Jews in distinction from Gentiles and which required separation from Gentiles. In highlighting the importance of the inclusion of Gentiles for Paul's gospel, Stendahl is effectively the father of the new perspective (above n. 31).

[110] R. Y. K. Fung, *Galatians* (NICNT; Grand Rapids: Eerdmans, 1988), comments on one of my less happy phrases ('the curse of a wrong understanding of the law' — 'Works of the Law' 229; below 137) as 'ill-suited to the idea of Christ as the bearer of the curse' (148 n. 60) — earlier response in *Jesus, Paul and the Law* 237. Cranfield similarly finds the thought that Rom. 3.21-26 goes on 'merely to draw out the consequences for the self-understanding of the Jewish people' to be 'an intolerable anticlimax'; Dunn's view 'actually reduces Paul's argument to polemic against a misunderstanding' ('Works of the Law' 8-9, 13). Similarly Das, *Paul, the Law and the Covenant* 160 ('deliverance from a mere nationalistic misunderstanding'), and Kim, *Paul and the New Perspective* 133-4. Even more critical is Westerholm, *Perspectives* 317-9: 'So limited a view of the atonement would have astonished even the most dogmatic TULIP theologian' (317-8). R. B. Matlock, 'Sins of the Flesh and Suspicious Minds: Dunn's New Theology of Paul', *JSNT* 72 (1998) 67-90, makes far too much play of the term 'misunderstanding' in his critique of my *Theology of Paul;* I respond in 'Whatever Happened to Exegesis? In Response to the Reviews by R. B. Matlock and D. A. Campbell', *JSNT* 72 (1998) 113-20 (here 115-6).

[111] E. Lohse, 'Theologie der Rechtfertigung im kritischen Disput: zu einigen neueren Perspektiven in der Interpretation der Theologie des Apostels Paulus', *Göttingische Gelehrte Anzeigen* 249 (1997) 66-81 (here 76); also *Römer* 140-5; echoed by F. W. Horn and R. Penna, in Bachmann, ed., *Lutherische und Neue Perspektive* 37-8, and 268-9; I respond in 394-5 and 410-2. Schreiner draws on J. G. Machen's observation, 'that the reason Paul was devoted to justification by faith was not because it made possible the Gentile mission but because it was true' (*Paul* 195); but the two are hardly mutually exclusive alternatives. See also n. 156 below.

[112] R. S. Smith, *Justification and Eschatology: A dialogue with 'The New Perspective on Paul'*, *Reformed Theological Review* Supplement Series #1 (2001), attributes to me the view that justification is 'not so much a theological doctrine (i.e., a question of how a person stands in God's presence) as a sociological doctrine (i.e., how Jews and Gentiles stand in each other's presence)' (9). No! the issue was whether and on what terms *Gentiles* could stand *with* Jews in *God's* presence. The misperception highlights the danger of setting 'social' and 'theological' interpretations in antithesis, a danger to which several succumb (Smiles, *The Gospel and the Law* 125-8; Thurén, *Derhetorizing Paul* 139-40, cf. 150 n. 57; Marguerat, 'Paul et la Loi' 265, 270-1). But Smith subsequently acknowledges the concerns of the 'new

Paul's language and seriously underplayed Paul's analysis of the radical helplessness of the human situation and his concern for the salvation of the individual?[113] For my own part, I have *no* desire to diminish the seriousness of the
charges which Paul levels against humankind, particularly in the devastating
analysis of Rom. 1.18–3.20, as I hope my earlier work has made clear.[114] And
though I recognise a danger of overreacting to what could be a too-narrowly
individualistic emphasis, an emphasis which, I suppose, could be encouraged
equally by Rudolf Bultmann's existentialism and by Billy Graham's evangelism, I certainly do not want to downplay in any way such intensely personal
passages as Rom. 5.1-5 and Gal. 2.19-20.[115] All I want to do is to remind those
interested that there is *also* a social and ethnic dimension to Paul's own understanding and expression of the gospel.

It remains the case that Paul formulated his statements of justification by
faith and not works of the law with a view to his mission as apostle to the
Gentiles, and as a result of his understanding of the gospel being challenged by
fellow Jews (Gal. 2.2-4; Acts 15.1, 5). The issue of whether and how Gentiles
can be accepted by God is at the heart of Paul's theology, the conviction that
the gospel of God's righteousness is for *all* who believe, Gentile as well as Jew
(Rom. 1.16-17).[116] The issue arose, no doubt, because Israel had been taught to
keep itself separate from Gentiles, that Gentiles were a threat to Israel's holiness, that for Israel to be set apart *to* God it had to be set apart *from* the
(other) nations.[117] No OT passage makes this clearer than Lev. 20.22-26: the

---

perspective' in recognising 'that Paul's teaching on justification by faith functions both as an
attack upon national (Jewish) restrictiveness and as a rebuke to Jewish (Christian) separateness' (89-90).

[113] Silva, 'The Law and Christianity: Dunn's New Synthesis', 351-2; Moo, 'Israel and the
Law' 192-5; Byrne, 'Interpreting Romans Theologically' 231-2. S. Westerholm, 'Paul and the
Law in Romans 9–11', in J. D. G. Dunn ed., *Paul and the Mosaic Law* (WUNT 89; Tübingen:
J. C. B. Mohr, 1996; Grand Rapids: Eerdmans, 2001) 215-37: 'To deny Paul's contrast between
"faith" and "works", or to confine its scope to a polemic against Jewish particularism, is thus
to fail to appreciate both the theocentric focus of Paul's religious view and the radicalness
with which he views the human dilemma and the divine redemption' (236). 'When one
catches the power of Paul's vision of the human plight (as Luther was able to do), one can
hardly imagine that it was eclipsed by the Jew-Gentile issue' (Blocher, 'Justification of the
Ungodly' 485-8). S. J. Gathercole, 'Justified by Faith, Justified by his Blood: The Evidence of
Romans 3:21–4:25', in Carson, et al., *Justification and Variegated Nomism Vol. 2* 147-84, criticises those who 'attribute too much importance to the doctrine of justification as it relates to
the inclusion of Gentiles' (148).

[114] See particularly my *Theology of Paul* 79-127 (##4 and 5).

[115] But I am baffled by Blocher's insistence that Gal. 2.20 'should be understood of juridical representation, not of vital union' ('Justification of the Ungodly' 499).

[116] Niebuhr, 'paulinische Rechtfertigungslehre' 124-6. Bird goes so far as to say 'that confronting legalistic opponents was not the most explosive issue that Paul dealt with. Rather,
the most pressing issue of Paul's ministry was trying to get Gentiles accepted *as* Gentiles into
fellowship *by* Jewish Christians' (*Saving Righteousness* 108).

[117] The oracle of Balaam was influential at this point — Israel as 'a people dwelling alone,

laws distinguishing clean from unclean were given as a sign of Israel's separation from the nations, and as a way of reinforcing that separation (insisted on even more strongly in *Jub.* 22.16).[118] *This was evidently the theological rationale behind Peter's 'separation' from the Gentiles of Antioch* (Gal. 2.12).[119]

Similarly it was precisely the recognition that the theology of clean and unclean should no longer prevail which is at the heart of Luke's account of Peter's breakthrough to the Gentile centurion Cornelius in Acts 10–11. According to Luke, Peter had never previously questioned the laws of clean and unclean (10.14; 11.8); they were simply part of the Jewish mind-set. But he learned a crucial lesson from the vision calling on him to eat unclean flesh (10.11-16; 11.5-10). The lesson was that henceforth he must not only change his eating habits, but that he should no longer call any *person* common or unclean (10.28). Luke's account shows us what Paul was up against, and what caused him to take his stand against the same Peter(!) at Antioch. As the sequence of Gal. 2.15-17 clearly implies, *Jewish 'attitude' to Gentile 'sinners' was a make or break issue for the gospel, the gospel of justification by faith.*[120]

It was this characteristically Jewish 'attitude' to the law, or to Gentiles on the

---

and not reckoning itself among the nations' (Num. 23.9) — as Philo expounds: the people 'which shall dwell alone, not reckoned among other nations' cannot be harmed 'because in virtue of the distinction of their peculiar customs they do not mix with others to depart from the way of their fathers' (*Mos.* 1.278). Eskola, *Theodicy and Predestination* 218, misses the link between divine jealousy (keeping Israel for himself) and the zeal (of a Phinehas) which prevents Israel from becoming mixed up with other, idolatrous nations (see above n. 42). See further F. Avemarie, *Tora und Leben: Untersuchungen zur Heilsbedeutung der Tora in der frühen rabbinischen Literatur* (Tübingen: Mohr Siebeck, 1996) 501-10. I do not understand why Watson thinks that 'the social function of the law in establishing Israel's separation', which I identify, is 'a secondary corruption of the original concept of holiness' (*Hermeneutics of Faith* 328-9). He is presumably confusing the sequence of analysis with a sequence of purpose or outcome. My point is that holiness, separation *to* God, inevitably involved also separation *from* others — two sides of the same coin.

[118] Hong refers to Deut. 7.1-11 and Ezra 10.11 (*Law in Galatians* 147). For the importance of Lev. 20.26 in rabbinic tradition see Avemarie, *Tora und Leben* 193-5, 446-7, 449-50, 503, 510-11.

[119] The point is recognised by I. H. Marshall, *New Testament Theology* (Downers Grove, IL: InterVarsity, 2004) 211. See further my '4QMMT and Galatians' 147-8 (below 339-40). Whatever the precise terms on which Peter and the other Christian Jews had eaten with Gentile believers at Antioch — see now J. G. Crossley, *The Date of Mark's Gospel: Insight from the Law in Earliest Christianity* (JSNTS 266; London: T&T Clark International, 2004) 141-54 — it was clearly the logic of Israel's 'set-apartness' which weighed decisively with the Christian Jews. It is evident from such passages as Rom. 14.14, Juvenal, *Satires* 14.96-106 and Tacitus, *Hist.* 5.5.2 that diaspora Jews (many or typically) believed it necessary to observe the laws of clean/unclean outside the land of Israel.

[120] On the disparagement of Gentiles *per se* as 'sinners' see above nn. 49, 50. H. Merklein, '"Nicht aus Werken des Gesetzes . . .": Eine Auslegung von Gal 2,15-21', *Studien zu Jesus und Paulus II* (WUNT 105; Tübingen: Mohr Siebeck, 1998) 303-15: 'They [Jewish Christians] are "by nature Jews" and therefore — as a matter of course — *not* sinners like the gentiles' (304).

basis of the law,[121] that Paul found it essential to challenge in order to maintain
the gospel of justification by faith.[122] In Paul's view, this was indeed a 'misunderstanding', not of the law's role when only Israel was in view, 'before the
coming of faith' (Gal. 3.23), but *of its role now that faith had come,* now that the
gospel was to be seen as for Gentiles as well as Jews.[123] The misunderstanding
was that the works, which could quite properly be expected of Jews as such,
should be demanded of Gentiles as well, as a condition of their being reckoned
acceptable to God — thus exposing the basic mistake of requiring anything in
addition to faith.[124]

Pauline scholarship simply must not diminish the importance for Paul of
the gospel as the power of God in breaking down barriers (not least of the
law) between Jew and Gentile. It was central and essential for him that the
gospel enables and expects such diverse peoples to sit and eat at the same table; 'the truth of the gospel' was at stake (Gal. 2.11-21).[125] What was it that
roused Paul's anger at Antioch? What was it that he saw as such a threat to
the fundamental truth of justification by faith? — precisely the refusal of
one group of Christians fully to accept another group of Christians! The
statement of justification which Paul formulated in the wake of the Antioch
episode (2.16) at the very least includes the message that justification means
fully accepting the other believer who is different from you, who disagrees

---

[121] For Jewish 'attitudes' to Gentiles see e.g. my 'Pharisees, Sinners, and Jesus' 73-4; also
'Incident at Antioch' 142; H. D. Betz, *Galatians* (Hermeneia; Philadelphia: Fortress, 1979)
115; Longenecker, *Galatians* 83. The fact that Paul attributes the crisis to fear of 'those of the
circumcision' (Gal. 2.12), that is, those who 'derive their basic identity from their ethnic (Jewish) heritage' (Martyn, *Galatians* 234), underscores the centrality of the Jew/Gentile divide.
It should not be forgotten that circumcision was also a marker of separateness: according to
Josephus, God commanded Abraham to practise circumcision 'to the intent that his posterity
should be kept from mixing with others' (*Ant.* 1.192); see also *Jub.* 15.26, 34; Tacitus, *Hist.*
5.5.2; and further 'Neither Circumcision' 82-92 (below 315-23).

[122] Gager (*Reinventing Paul* 49) and Kim (*Paul and the New Perspective* 61 n. 212) think
that the new perspective replaces one distorted picture of Judaism (as soulless legalism) with
an equally distorted caricature of Judaism as a racist, nationalist religion. But the problem
that Paul encountered was precisely that a messianic sect of a nationalist religion (Judaism =
the religion of the Judeans) had become a missionary sect seeking to convert into and to fully
accept non-Jews within a non-nationalistic version of Israel's traditional religion.

[123] See further my *Theology of Paul* 137-50; 'Noch einmal' 277-9 (below 417-8). Note that
Paul saw the two crises, in Jerusalem over Titus, and in Antioch over table-fellowship, as of a
piece: in both cases 'the truth of the gospel' (2.5, 14) was being imperilled by Jewish attempts
to 'compel' (2.3, 14) Gentiles to conform with Jewish distinctives. Cf. G. Strecker, *Theology*
of the New Testament (New York: de Gruyter, 2000): 'to establish the Torah of Judaism within
the Christian community by means of the circumcision commandment and to reestablish
Jewish national unity that had been called in question by the apostle's preaching' (141).

[124] Westerholm's dictum, 'It is the law that demands deeds, not the law as misconstrued by
Jews, that is at issue in Paul's references to its works' (*Perspectives* 315), therefore poses as an
'either-or' what he would have better presented as a 'both-and'.

[125] See further my *Theology of Paul's Letter to the Galatians* 25-8, where I note also the
apocalyptic dimensions of the issue (46-52); see also below n. 128.

with you.[126] Evidently the two dimensions are inextricably interlocked — the vertical and the horizontal, acceptance by God with acceptance of others. It is not possible to be right with God while refusing to respect and accept what Jonathan Sacks has described as 'the dignity of difference'.[127]

So, it is hardly a coincidence that Paul's greatest letter, to the Romans, rounds off with a discussion of this very theme (Rom. 14.1–15.6), summed up in the exhortation to 'welcome one another, just as Christ has welcomed you' (15.7). Nor that the letter climaxes in the vision attested by law, prophet and psalmist of Gentiles worshipping and glorifying God together with God's ancient people (15.9-12), a vision being fulfilled through Paul's own mission. Nor should we forget that Paul counted this as the great 'mystery' which had been hidden from the ages and the generations but which had now been revealed in the gospel: that God's purpose from of old had been to include the Gentiles with his people.[128] In Ephesians particularly this is the climactic mystery of the ages, to reveal and implement which Paul had been commissioned: that 'the Gentiles have become fellow heirs, members of the same body' (Eph. 3.6). Christ died to break down the wall, the law with its commandments and ordinances, the wall that divided Jew from Gentile (2.14-16).[129] In him the two have become one,

---

[126] Smith puts the argument of Gal. 2.11-17 into reverse when he concludes on the basis of Gal. 4.21-31 that 'For Paul, those who have been justified by faith cannot have fellowship with those who seek to be justified on some other basis' (*Justification and Eschatology* 131).

[127] J. Sacks, *The Dignity of Difference* (London: Continuum, 2002). Sadly, the problem confronted by Paul is still alive today among those Israelis (and Christians) who use the promise of land to Abraham (Gen. 13.15; 17.8; etc.) as the justification for a policy of settlement in Palestinian territory which in effect seeks to repeat the occupation of the promised land by expelling the native people, through expropriation of land, destruction of olive groves and property, control of water supplies and crushing restrictions on daily living. Conveniently forgotten is that some forms of the covenant with the patriarchs (including the sacred moment of covenant ratification) promise them the 'land from the river of Egypt to the great river, the river Euphrates' (15.18; Deut. 1.7-8; 11.24; Josh. 1.3-4); for the extension of the promise to embrace the whole earth(!) see Rom. 4.13 and my *Romans* 213.

[128] Rom. 11.25; (16.25-27); Eph. 1.9-10; 3.3-6; Col. 1.26-27; 2.2; 4.3. I am baffled by the charge of R. W. Yarbrough, 'Paul and Salvation History', in Carson, et al., *Justification and Variegated Nomism Vol. 2* 297-342, that I am hostile to, 'marginalize' or 'debunk' a salvation-historical perspective on Paul (307-8, 324, 342), especially when Yarbrough defines 'salvation history' as 'the personal redemptive activity of God within human history to effect his eternal saving intentions' (297). On the contrary, I see the very point of Romans and Galatians to be the argument that the gospel to the Gentiles is the fulfilment and climax of God's saving purpose. I am more accustomed to being criticised for stressing the *continuities* between Paul and God's revelation to and through Israel! Contrast the more subtle critique of Carson ('Mystery and Fulfilment' 434-5), with much of which I resonate. I deal with the tension between salvation-history and apocalyptic in Paul most fully in my 'How New was Paul's Gospel? The Problem of Continuity and Discontinuity', in L. A. Jervis & P. Richardson, eds., *Gospel in Paul: Studies on Corinthians, Galatians and Romans,* R. N. Longenecker FS (JSNTS 108; Sheffield: Sheffield Academic, 1994) 367-88, reprinted below ch. 10; and further 'Neither Circumcision' 104-6 (below 333-4).

[129] The reference may well be to the barrier within the Temple complex in Jerusalem

and the church is presented precisely as existing to be *the place where the separated peoples come together as one* (2.17-22).[130] The surmounting of these ancient hostilities was not merely a by-product of the gospel, far less a distraction from the true meaning of the gospel, but *the climactic achievement of the gospel,* the completion of God's purposes from the beginning of time.[131]

Such 'attitudes', and 'misunderstandings', which maintain barriers between peoples and races, which demean others and treat them as of lesser importance before God, which refuse respect for others who see things differently, would not only have undermined the teaching of justification by faith, but would have crippled, indeed destroyed Christianity if they had not been thus challenged. And Christians today should not hesitate to draw the same lessons from Paul's teaching in confronting the same challenges to the gospel: to see others as essentially a threat to my own or my people's status (or rights/privileges), will always cripple and destroy mutual acceptance and community; to insist that others can be respected and accepted only if they share the same tribal loyalty, only if they formulate their faith in the words that we recognise, only if they act in ways that we approve, narrows the grace of God and the truth of the gospel in ways that would cause Paul the same anguish and anger as he experienced in Antioch. At one end of the scale we have the same refusal of some Christians to eat at the same table (the *Lord's* table!) with other Christians,[132] the same insis-

---

which excluded Gentiles from the inner courts on pain of death; see e.g. those listed by R. Schnackenburg, *Der Brief an die Epheser* (EKKNT 10; Zürich: Benziger, 1982) 113-4. For the imagery cf. *Ep. Arist.* 139, 142 cited above (18).

[130] Paul's concerns in all this are not adequately summed up in terms of 'universalism', though J. M. G. Barclay, '"Neither Jew Nor Greek": Multiculturalism and the New Perspective on Paul', in M. G. Brett, ed., *Ethnicity and the Bible* (Leiden: Brill, 1996) 197-214, warns legitimately of echoes in the new perspective of Baur's antithesis between 'Christian universalism' and 'Jewish particularism' (197, 200, 202, 204), and his reflections on 'Paul and multiculturalism', in dialogue with D. Boyarin, *A Radical Jew: Paul and the Politics of Identity* (Berkeley: University of California, 1994), are both insightful and of considerable valuable (209-14). See also my 'Was Judaism Particularist or Universalist?', in ed. J. Neusner & A. J. Avery-Peck, *Judaism in Late Antiquity,* Part III: *Where We Stand: Issues and Debates in Ancient Judaism,* Vol. 2 (Handbuch der Orientalisk; Leiden: Brill, 1999) 57-73.

[131] So I continue to resonate with Stendahl in his response to Käsemann's criticism of his 'Introspective Conscience' essay ('Justification and Salvation History', *Perspectives on Paul* [London: SCM, 1971] 60-78), when he suggests 'that in Paul the very argument about justification by faith functions within his reflection on God's plan for the world' (*Paul* 131). It is a major feature of Wright's contributions on this subject that he puts so much weight on the narrative context of Paul's theologising, in this case the story of God's purposes for and dealings with his world. I accept the perspective, though with caution; see my 'The Narrative Approach to Paul: Whose Story?', in B. W. Longenecker, ed., *Narrative Dynamics in Paul: A Critical Assessment* (Louisville/London: Westminster John Knox, 2002) 217-30.

[132] See my 'Should Paul Once Again Oppose Peter to his Face?', *The Heythrop Journal* 34 (1993) 58-65. Wright makes the same point and plea: Justification 'is the basis for that unity of the church, across racial barriers, for which Paul fought so hard' ('Romans and the Theology of Paul', in D. M. Hay & E. E. Johnson, eds., *Pauline Theology, Volume III: Romans* [Min-

tence by some Christians to refuse recognition and cooperation with other Christians because justification by faith in Christ alone is an *insufficient* statement of the gospel! Ironically, even the very insistence on the doctrine of 'justification by faith and not works' can itself become an added 'work' by which the gospel of justification by faith alone is compromised and corrupted![133] At the other end of the scale we need only instance examples of apartheid, or racial segregation in the southern states of the USA, or the community tensions in Northern Ireland, or the massacres of Tutsis in Rwanda, or the internecine hostilities in former Yugoslavia — all involving Christians![134] Not to mention the tragic 'turning of the tables' when Judaism's separateness was horrifically overtaken by Christianity's supersessionism and anti-semitism.[135] Justification by faith speaks against all such fundamentalism which uses biblical texts to justify unjust treatment of others, which narrows the grace of God to some sectarian formulation, which insists on the God-givenness of any policy or practice which demeans the 'Gentile', or which demands as a condition of Christian acceptance more than the faith which works through love (Gal. 5.6).[136]

The point, I repeat, if the new perspective is to be properly appreciated, is to recognise that the way by which such 'attitudes', such 'misunderstandings' of God's concern for the 'other', the 'outsider', were challenged was by means of Paul's gospel of justification, of God's acceptance, for *all* who believe, and on

---

neapolis: Fortress, 1995] 30-67 [here 66]); 'the doctrine of justification is in fact the great *ecumenical* doctrine' (*What Saint Paul Really Said* 158-9).

[133] Tom Wright refers me to Richard Hooker's observation that one is not justified by faith by believing in justification by faith, but that one is justified by faith by believing in Jesus Christ.

[134] Timothy George both takes the point and misses it: 'Racism of any brand in any culture is incompatible with the truth of the gospel, not because it leads to social exclusivism, but because it stands in opposition to the "new creation" God is bringing into being: the body of Christ based not on caste, color, gender, or social condition but on grace alone' ('Modernizing Luther' 458). My point is that 'social exclusivism' denies the 'new creation' and the gospel of 'grace alone'; that is why Paul protested so vigorously against it.

[135] Barry Matlock perceptively notes that 'we moderns are not typically concerned so much about sin and guilt as we are about notions of community, so that our theological climate is reflected here' and wonders 'whether Luther's Paul comes to grief more for his failure to fit the twentieth century than the first' ('Almost Cultural Studies?' 439, 443); cf. Barclay, 'Neither Jew Nor Greek' 204-6. I readily recognise that the 'new perspective' Paul speaks to 20th and 21st century concerns, just as the 'Lutheran' Paul spoke to 16th century concerns. My point would be rather that the concerns of both periods made readers of Paul more sensitive to dimensions of Paul's teaching on justification which had been neglected or misperceived.

[136] At this point I find myself often reflecting on F. W. Faber's great hymn, 'There's a wideness in God's mercy', especially the fifth verse:

'But we make his love too narrow
By false limits of our own;
And we magnify his strictness
With a zeal he will not own'.

no other condition — not ethnicity, not colour, not race, not class, not creed, not denomination. It is crucial to the health of the churches that this aspect of Paul's doctrine of justification by faith alone be not neglected — as it has been frequently neglected in the history of Christianity, and still today in many parts of the 'Christian West'. There is something ironic in the fact that in pushing so hard to the more fundamental need of humankind before God, so many commentators ignore or play down the seriousness of the issue which actually brought the more fundamental point to such vital and all-consuming relevance for Paul.

This I say once again is what the 'new perspective' is all about for me. It does *not* set this understanding of justification by faith in antithesis to the justification of the individual by faith. It is *not* opposed to the classic Reformed doctrine of justification. It simply observes that a social and ethnic dimension was part of the doctrine from its first formulation, was indeed integral to the first recorded exposition and defence of the doctrine — 'Jew first but also Greek'. These are the slogans which we should use to summarise Paul's gospel — 'to all who believe, Jew first but also Greek', 'no distinction between Jew and Greek . . . to all who call upon him' (Rom. 1.16; 10.12) — not the dogmatically logical 'from plight to solution', still less Sanders' somewhat contrived antithesis, 'from solution to plight'.[137] This is the lost theological dimension of the doctrine which needs to be brought afresh into the light, *not* to diminish the traditional doctrine, but to enrich the doctrine from its biblical roots and to recover the wholeness of Paul's teaching on the subject.[138]

2.4 A late development?

Do I argue or imply (as Kim claims)[139] that Paul came to the doctrine of justification through faith and not works only at Antioch, that is, many years after his conversion and at least some years after he began his missionary and evangelistic work? Here again there may be at least some misunderstanding to clear up.

The question is whether there was any development in Paul's understanding and expression of justification by faith up to and including his response to the Antioch incident in Gal. 2.15ff. In brief, my response is that Paul's understanding of justification from faith was probably clear and firm from the first, but the antithetical *formulation*, 'from faith *and not from works of the law*', was probably the outcome of his confrontation with his fellow believing Jews in Jerusalem and Antioch (Gal. 2.1-16). I do *not* think that it took the Galatian cri-

---

[137] Zahl thinks that 'solution to plight' is 'a lynchpin of the New Perspective' ('Mistakes' 6, 10), but it does not feature in my version of 'the new perspective'.

[138] I carry forward my response to the charges indicated in n. 110 above in ##3.1-3 below.

[139] See n. 70 above.

sis to bring Paul to the conclusion that God accepted *all* those who believed the gospel.[140] My reasoning is still the same. So far as I can see, Paul's understanding of God's righteousness as a saving righteousness was part of his Jewish/scriptural inheritance, as Rom. 1.16-17 implies. What was primarily at issue was whether that gracious outreach extended to Gentiles as well — to all, Gentile as well as Jew (Rom. 1.16-17). Paul's pre-Christian 'zeal' was directed to maintaining Jewish 'blamelessness', including a holiness unblemished by contact with other nations, and to persecuting those who threatened that holy set-apartness (Phil. 3.4-6).[141] He recalled his conversion as the opening of his eyes to recognise that Gentiles too were the objects of God's saving grace, through his Son, Jesus Christ (Gal. 1.12-16). I assume that *from his first evangelistic outreach* as a Christian, whenever that was,[142] he preached the good news that God's saving righteousness was for all, Jew first but also Gentile — that is, Gentiles as Gentiles, without requiring them to become proselytes.[143]

---

[140] *Pace* Strecker: 'Paul's message of justification was occasioned for the first time by the Galatian crisis and developed in his letter to the Galatians' (*Theology* 139); Schnelle, *Paul* 135-7, 278-9: 'In Gal. 2:16 Paul takes a decisive step beyond the agreement made at the apostolic council and the disputed issue at the Antioch incident' (278); also, to some extent, Martyn, who sees Paul's formulation in Gal. 2.16 as Paul's interpretation of the common gospel of justification in polemical response to the nomistic interpretation of that gospel brought by the other missionaries ('the Teachers' in Martyn's terminology) to the Galatians (*Galatians* 268-75); and, to the same extent, even Westerholm: 'It was when his Galatian converts were told to get circumcised and submit to the Mosaic law that Paul first clarified the relationship between Israel's law and the church's faith' (*Perspectives* 442).

[141] See above #1 at n. 42; and further #2.3.

[142] Did Paul preach already in Arabia (Gal. 1.17), as, e.g., Kim deduces (*Paul and the New Perspective* 46)? See e.g. the brief discussion in my *Galatians* 69-70; M. Hengel & A. M. Schwemer, *Paul Between Damascus and Antioch* (London: SCM, 1997) 106-13. Whatever the correct deduction from Gal. 1.17, the key point is that Paul's evangelistic work began well before the Antioch incident (Gal. 1.21-23; 2.7-9). On the unlikely suggestion that Gal. 5.11 indicates a period of Paul's (Christian) mission when he did 'preach circumcision' see T. L. Donaldson, *Paul and the Gentiles: Remapping the Apostle's Convictional World* (Minneapolis: Fortress, 1997) 278-84; Martyn, *Galatians* 166-8.

[143] Kim cites Hengel & Schwemer, *Paul Between Damascus and Antioch* 95-8 in his support (*Paul and the New Perspective* 52), on the whole fairly, though Hengel's own position seems to be rather more nuanced than Kim's: 'I shall not attempt here to put back to the time of Paul's conversion his doctrine of salvation wholly by grace or the justification of the sinner by faith alone as he developed it conceptually, fully and in so many aspects. We can only guess when and how he developed individual formulas' (101; similarly 105). Hengel's briefer essay omits the nuance — 'The Attitude of Paul to the Law in the Unknown Years between Damascus and Antioch', in J. D. G. Dunn, ed., *Paul and the Mosaic Law* (Grand Rapids: Eerdmans, 2001) 25-51 (here 33-5, 46-7, 50) = 'The Stance of the Apostle Paul Toward the Law in the Unknown Years Between Damascus and Antioch', in Carson, et al., *Justification and Variegated Nomism Vol. 2* 75-103 (here 84-6, 98, 102). To describe Gal. 2.16 as formulated 'more or less incidentally/accidentally (zufällig)' (34, 85), however, is surely to diminish unjustifiably the importance of the confrontation with Peter. Lohse suggests that Paul brought the gospel he preached to 'a concise (knappen) expression' (*Paulus* 94; further 209-14); and Hahn allows that Paul's justification teaching came to 'further explication' but not

The course of the earliest preaching to Gentiles raises an interesting and intriguing question. If Paul, and the others, did not demand circumcision from the first, why did the issue of circumcision not arise till the late 40s, to be raised and resolved formally for the first time at the Jerusalem 'council' (Gal. 2.1-10; Acts 15)? I have attempted to suggest answers to this before,[144] but the suggestions have cut little ice with Kim. To repeat my argument in outline. My guess is that the believing Gentiles were initially regarded as in the same ambiguous situation as Gentile God-fearers, that is, Gentiles who were adherents of the local synagogue and had adopted some Jewish beliefs and customs, but had not accepted circumcision.[145] It was only when the number of Gentile converts began to outnumber the believing Jews that alarm bells began to ring. The exception (uncircumcised God-fearers) was becoming the rule (believing Gentiles). This was the issue tackled at Jerusalem and resolved satisfactorily for Paul's mission (Gal. 2.1-10). But evidently the further issue of the level of Torah obedience expected for believing Jews, especially in their relationships with these believing Gentiles, was not yet fully recognised, or was left unresolved or ambiguous at Jerusalem.[146] Hence the incident at Antioch, when believing Jews insisted on maintaining a (higher) level of Torah observance which rendered table fellowship with the believing Gentiles impossible (2.11-14).

Kim scoffs at this attempt at historical reconstruction as 'incredible':[147] incredible that Paul should not have perceived the issues of circumcision and food laws for his Gentile converts for such a lengthy period; incredible that a former Pharisee, so zealous for the law, could have failed to see the issue from the first and to resolve the issue from the beginning of his missionary work. In reacting so dismissively, Kim fails to acknowledge that there is an important question here: why the issues of circumcision and then of table-fellowship did not arise for so many years and then in the way they did. He ignores the fact that the questions about circumcision and laws of clean and unclean were raised not by Paul but *by his fellow Jewish believers*. Part of the answer pre-

---

'change' (Wandlung) or 'development' (Entwicklung) (*Theologie* 1.245-6). See further the discussion in Burchard, 'Nicht aus Werken des Gesetzes gerecht'.

[144] See my *Partings* 124-35; also 'The Theology of Galatians' (125-46; = ch. 6 below); also, briefly, 'In Search of Common Ground', in Dunn ed., *Paul and the Mosaic Law* 309-34 (here 315-7), reprinted below ch. 12 (here 290-3).

[145] Sufficient detail can be found in my *Romans* xlvii-xlviii, and *Partings* 125. See further F. W. Horn, 'Der Verzicht auf die Beschneidung im frühen Christentum', *NTS* 42 (1996) 479-505; and on 'Godfearers', B. Wander, *Gottesfürchtige und Sympathisanten: Studien zum heidnischen Umfeld von Diasporasynagogen* (WUNT 104; Tübingen: Mohr Siebeck, 1998).

[146] 'The Law is not mentioned because its continuing validity is taken for granted' (Martyn, *Galatians* 267-8). See also C. K. Barrett, 'Christocentricity at Antioch', *On Paul: Essays on His Life, Work and Influence in the Early Church* (London: T&T Clark, 2003) 37-54 (here 49-53).

[147] The word ('incredible') is used repeatedly by Kim, *Paul and the New Perspective* 13-35.

sumably is that whereas for Saul the persecutor breaches of the boundary of circumcision had been an issue, for Paul the apostle they were *not;* that is what he had been converted *from.* My point simply put is that it was the posing of the issues which seems to have provoked the expression of the theological rationale. As Mark Seifrid observes: 'It is scarcely imaginable that Paul's companion in Gentile mission, Barnabas, would have wavered at Antioch if earlier he had been exposed to the full force of the polemic [I might add 'and of the theology'] Paul employs in the letter to Galatia'.[148] It was because Paul was so challenged that he was forced to make explicit formulation of what his gospel involved for Jewish as well as Gentile believers.[149]

The point is nicely illustrated by Peter's conduct at Antioch: for Peter too there had been no issue; it only became so with the arrival of the 'men from James' (Gal. 2.12).[150] In 'The New Perspective' I observed from the obvious reading of Gal. 2.15-16 ('we Jews know . . .') that Paul evidently understood his gospel of justification through faith in Christ to be common ground with his fellow Jewish believers.[151] And I argued furthermore that the *ean mē* of Gal. 2.16 indicates an appeal to the attitude of Peter, in view of the fact that Peter was evidently able to hold *both* that justification was by faith in Christ *and* that it was still necessary for believing Jews to observe works of the law (food laws in the case in point).[152] Despite criticism, and whatever the precise force of *ean mē* ('except', or 'but'),[153] the key point remains firm: at Antioch Peter acted in

---

[148] *Justification* 180.

[149] I should perhaps again add that I have not developed the hypothesis because of some imagined antipathy to the fundamental character of Paul's teaching on justification but only as an attempt to make the best sense of the data of the text, that is, as an act of responsible exegesis.

[150] S. J. Gathercole, 'The Petrine and Pauline *Sola Fide* in Galatians 2', in Bachmann, ed., *Lutherische und Neue Paulusperspektive* 309-27, argues most implausibly that the issue of table-fellowship must have been recognised and already resolved in the Jerusalem consultation (315, 319); but see my response in Bachmann 417-22.

[151] 'A consensus statement of Antiochene theology' (Becker, *Paul* 96); 'an important doctrine held to by Paul and Cephas alike' (Kruse, *Paul* 109-10); 'a standard Jewish view' (Westerholm, *Perspectives* 370); see further M. Theobald, 'Der Kanon von der Rechtfertigung (Gal 2,16; Röm 3,28)', *Studien zum Römerbrief* (WUNT 136; Tübingen: Mohr Siebeck, 2001)164-225 (here 182-92); Schäfer, *Paulus bis zum Apostelkonzil* 253-65.

[152] 'New Perspective' 189-91 and n. 25, 195-8 (below 106-8 and n. 25, 112-5). 'Probably many Jewish Christians did not see their turning to the Messiah Jesus as a soteriological alternative to the principle of the works of the law' (Merklein, '"Nicht aus Werken"' 306). See further Martyn, *Galatians* 264-8. Silva, surprisingly, finds this a 'curious interpretation' ('Faith Versus Works' 217 n. 3).

[153] I respond to earlier criticism in the 'Additional Notes' to 'The New Perspective' (207-9, 212). A. A. Das, 'Another Look at *ean mē* in Galatians 2:16', *JBL* 119 (2000) 529-39, comes to my support (the formula is deliberately ambiguous; also his *Paul and the Jews* 31-2), though he needs to bear in mind that the belief described in 2.16a seems to be the belief put into practice at Antioch by Peter and the other Christian Jews. In a paper on 'Galatians 2:15-16' at the British New Testament Conference in Edinburgh (September 2004), M. C. de Boer

a way which implied that it was still necessary for (Jewish) believers to observe (certain key) works of the law, even though he already agreed that justification was by faith in Christ.[154] Peter's action made it clear (to Paul) that there was a critical issue for the gospel at stake at this point, and he formulated Gal. 2.16 accordingly, and probably with an antithetical sharpness — *not* faith plus, *not* both faith and works, but *only* through faith.[155]

In short then, the issue of faith *versus works* as such does not seem to have emerged for some time after the Gentile mission had begun. It was evidently the success of that mission which brought to the surface the question whether justification by faith in Christ Jesus was in any way or degree dependent on observance of the law, on doing the works of the law, on adopting a characteristically Jewish way of life.[156] The development which I see attested in the text is that it was the insistence by traditionalist Jewish believers that at least some key laws were still binding which forced the issue to be faced. The circumcision question was resolved with a fair degree of amicableness.[157] But it was the in-

---

gave a preview of his forthcoming New Testament Library commentary on Galatians (Westminster John Knox), in which he similarly argues that 2.15-16a is a *captatio benevolentiae* intended by Paul to win the sympathy of those who disagreed with him by use of the ambiguous *ean mē*. Eckstein in effect limits the force of the *captatio,* the rhetorical *concessio,* to 2.15 (*Verheissung* 7-9).

[154] To quote again F. Mussner, *Der Galaterbrief* (HTKNT 9; Freiburg: Herder, ³1977): 'The Jew would not let the pauline antithesis "faith"/"works of the law" pass; for him it makes no sense' (170).

[155] It is Paul who adds *ex ergōn nomou* to his allusive use of Ps. 143 (LXX 142).2 (Gal. 2.16; Rom. 3.20; see further my *Romans* 153-4), a text which was probably common ground between Paul and Peter ('we know . . .'); for Paul the narrower focus *(ex ergōn nomou)* was an inescapable corollary of the common and more fundamental principle. See also Schäfer, *Paulus bis zum Apostelkonzil* 253-65, 483-4.

[156] I would therefore qualify the way Stendahl posed his challenge, as even more the earlier views of Wrede and Schweitzer on justification, summed up by P. Stuhlmacher as 'simply a polemical doctrine formulated against Judaizers' (Stuhlmacher, *Revisiting* 10); Paul's formulation grew out of his Gentile mission, but its relevance was not limited to that mission. In fact, I agree with Stuhlmacher's own formulation: 'It is clear from Galatians and Philippians that the Jewish and Jewish-Christian opponents of the apostle did in fact play a role in the formation of Paul's doctrine of justification' (29). The description of the new perspective's view as advocating that 'justification by faith is not the center of Paul's theology but instead represents a pragmatic tactic to facilitate the Gentile mission', by D. A. Hagner, 'Paul and Judaism: Testing the New Perspective', in Stuhlmacher, *Revisiting* 75-105 (here 77), is also tendentious and unsatisfactory as a description of what I have been saying on the subject. O'Brien criticises me in similar terms: 'justification by faith is effectively pushed to the periphery of Paul's teaching, despite Dunn's claims regarding its centrality' ('Was Paul a Covenantal Nomist?' 274, 282). It would be more accurate, in my view, to say that controversy over Paul's Gentile mission brought home to Paul more clearly/sharply the centrality and character of justification by faith. See further #2.3 above.

[157] Although not for 'the false brothers' of Gal. 2.4 and the trouble-making missionaries attacked in Galatians; Paul saw 'the truth of the gospel' (2.5, 14) as expressed in 'the gospel for the circumcised' — that is, as not requiring or dependent upon Gentiles 'living like Jews' (2.14), that is, here in effect, becoming proselytes.

sistence on the laws of clean and unclean at Antioch which raised the issue whether faith needed to be complemented by works of the law, any works of the law. In other words, Paul's formulation in Gal. 2.16 was, as the context suggests, formulated in response to the crisis at Antioch. The belief that justification was from faith in Christ Jesus was the common ground. The events at Antioch showed Paul that the teaching had to be sharpened — faith *and not works*.[158]

3. Taking the debate forward

Other criticisms of the new perspective raise substantive issues of exegesis which call for further reflection and not simply restatement. In this section, then, I acknowledge the benefit of the scholarly dialogue of the past decade and that, hopefully, it has brought me to a sharper and more nuanced appreciation of what was at stake for Paul. There are a further four issues which call for comment. (5) My exegesis of Gal. 3.10-14 has been put in serious question.[159] (6) Whatever may be said about Gal. 2.16 in context, Rom 3.20, 4.4-5 and 9.11-12 show that 'works-righteousness' *was* still the fundamental issue.[160] (7) I have failed to take with sufficient seriousness Paul's break with the law.[161] (8) The later Paulines, particularly Eph. 2.8-10, but also 2 Tim. 1.9-10 and Tit. 3.5-6, demonstrate that the traditional interpretation of Paul's teaching on justification was the interpretation intended by Paul.[162]

3.1 (5) Back to Galatians

I do not particularly want to defend all my exegetical suggestions on Gal. 3.10-14 at this point, though the key to interpreting 3.10 still seems to me to lie in resolving the tension between a phrase which seems to describe those who *do* the law ('those who are of works of the law') and the charge that such people *fail to do* everything written in the book of the law.[163] My own sense of what Paul was con-

---

[158] Similarly Niebuhr, 'paulinische Rechtfertigungslehre' 113-4, 128; cf. Martyn's complete argument (*Galatians* 263-75), and Theobald's thesis in 'Kanon'.

[159] 'Tortuous and improbable', according to Wright, *Climax of the Covenant* 153; B. W. Longenecker, *The Triumph of Abraham's God* (Edinburgh: T&T Clark, 1998) 136.

[160] Cranfield, 'Works of the Law' 5-14; Moo, *Romans* 211-7, 581-2; Waters, *Justification* 161-2.

[161] 'Paul's critique of the law is much more radical than Dunn allows and . . . we should not shrink from speaking of his "break" with Judaism' (Räisänen, 'Galatians 2.16' 114-5).

[162] See particularly I. H. Marshall, 'Salvation, Grace and Works in the Later Writings in the Pauline Corpus', *NTS* 42 (1996) 339-58; also *New Testament Theology* 447-8.

[163] See ch.3, 225-6 and 'Noch einmal' 282-3 (below 421-2). Cf. Stuhlmacher: 'sin for Paul consisted not only of individual transgressions of the commandments but could also include

fronting still suggests that the most fruitful resolution of the tension is in terms of a people (or group/faction) whose whole way of life was determined by the law, who identified themselves by their nomistic life-style (living jewishly — 2.14),[164] but who nevertheless were missing what Paul regarded as vital — that justification was by faith (alone). If I may put it so, 'those of works of the law' took their religious identity too narrowly from the 'life' *(zēsetai)* of Lev. 18.5 (Gal. 3.12), whereas 'those of (Abraham's) faith' took their religious identity from the 'life' *(zēsetai)* of Hab. 2.4 (Gal. 3.11).[165] If I am right, this feeds into the argument of the second half of Galatians 3, that in this connection the law's role was limited to the period when it served as *paidagōgos* to Israel, prior to the coming of Christ, after which the possibility of faith in Christ was no longer restricted to ethnic Israel (3.23-29).[166] 'Those of the works of the law' were simply 'behind the times' (4.1-10). But to defend and develop the exegesis offered in my *Galatians* commentary in regard to the larger argument would take too much space here.[167]

---

pious zeal for those commandments' *(Revisiting* 25). Watson objects to my protest against putting too much emphasis on 'doing' the law *(Hermeneutics of Faith* 329), without apparently realising that my protest was directed against the commentators mentioned in my *Galatians* 176 ('doing' as self-achievement). For his own view of Gal. 3.10 see *Hermeneutics of Faith* 434.

[164] 'Those whose identity is derived from observance of the Law' (Martyn, *Galatians* 307); J. R. Wisdom, *Blessing for the Nations and the Curse of the Law: Paul's Citation of Genesis and Deuteronomy in Gal. 3.8-10* (WUNT 2.133; Tübingen: Mohr Siebeck, 2001) 160-4; Silva, 'Faith Versus Works' 223-6; see also above n. 105. Laato continues to interpret Gal. 3.10 in the light of 5.3 as indicating Paul's view that 'everyone who relies on the works of the law must fulfil all the commandments (without exception!) down to the smallest detail'. But the argument that 'the whole law' *(holos ho nomos)* (5.3) refers to 'the sum of individual commands and prohibitions' which the Jew is obligated to do (an impossibility), and is different from 'the whole law' *(ho pas nomos)* which the Christian is capable of fulfilling (5.14) ('Paul's Anthropological Considerations' 356-8), ignores the fact that in Matthew's version of the love command (to which 5.14 refers) it sums up 'the whole law' *(holos ho nomos)*. See below n. 216 and further my *Galatians* 170-2, 265-7, 288-91. See also M. Cranford, 'The Possibility of Perfect Obedience: Paul and an Implied Premise in Galatians 3:10 and 5:3', *NovT* 36 (1994) 242-58.

[165] Of course, for Paul's opponents the *zēsetai* in each case would be the same; it is Paul who pulls them apart.

[166] In commenting on Rom. 9.30ff., Gathercole criticises the new perspective for attributing to Paul 'an *ad hoc* theology based on God changing his mind about part of the Torah because Israel had abused it' *(Where is Boasting?* 229), but he ignores the clarity of the divine plan proposed by Paul in Gal. 3.

[167] But see *Theology of Paul's Letter to the Galatians* 83-92; and for a more recent statement, 'Paul et la Torah' 231-6 (below 451-5). I remain unpersuaded by the attempt by Kuula, building on one of Martyn's principal theses in *Galatians*, to argue that Paul's christological and apocalyptic perspectives have swamped any lingering salvation-historical point of view *(Law* 1 ch. 3). Continuity of 'promise', 'seed of Abraham' and 'inheritance' were clearly more important elements of Paul's gospel than as *ad hominem* arguments with his Galatian opponents (3.29–4.7); were they not so, it would have been more sensible for him to place his complete emphasis on the work of Christ and the gift of the Spirit and to ignore all such language completely. See also n. 128 above and n. 382 below.

The point I simply want to make now is that Gal. 3.10-14 has to be read in its context, that is, as part of an argument which runs through the first half of the chapter (3.1-14).[168] The passage is clearly structured to reinforce the fact, and its significance, that the Galatian Gentile believers had already been accepted by God, as evidenced by their reception of the Spirit 'from hearing with faith' and not 'from works of the law' (3.2, 5, 14). The key claim, for the larger argument, is that the Gentile believers are 'sons of Abraham' by virtue of their believing as he did (3.6-9).[169] But what links the final paragraph of the section (3.10-14) to the argument is the play on blessing (3.8, 14) and curse (3.10, 13) – the blessing promised to Abraham (Gen. 12.3; 18.18) and the curses which climax Deuteronomy's covenantal nomism (Deut. 27–28).[170] Paul's concern was to assure his readers that in receiving the Spirit they had already experienced the blessing promised to or through Abraham (Gal. 3.8-9, 14). From the train of argument, that evidently involved or depended on the removal of the curses threatened in Deuteronomy, which Christ accomplished on the cross (3.13).[171] The implication lies close to hand, therefore, that the curses of covenantal nomism (I am using shorthand) were what prevented the blessing coming to the Gentiles.[172]

---

[168] Something ignored, for example, by Kim, *Paul and the New Perspective* 20-1.

[169] So far as Galatians is concerned, it is this opening exposition of Gen. 15.6 in 3.6-9 which surely demonstrates the weakness of the *pistis Christou* = 'the faith of Christ' argument, currently so popular in North America and elsewhere. Here at least it should be clear that the 'faith' *(pistis)* spoken of in 3.7-9 is to be understood in terms of Abraham's believing *(episteusen)* in the headline text (3.6); similarly Schreiner, *Paul* 212-6. That conclusion naturally carries weight with the subsequent *pistis* references in the subsequent verses. For the debate see R. B. Hays, 'PISTIS and Pauline Christology: What is at Stake?' and J. D. G. Dunn, 'Once More, PISTIS CHRISTOU', in E. E. Johnson & D. M. Hay, eds., *Pauline Theology. Vol. IV: Looking Back, Pressing On* (Atlanta: Georgia, 1997) 35-60, 61-81 respectively, reprinted in R. B. Hays, *The Faith of Jesus Christ: The Narrative Substructure of Galatians 3:1–4:11* (Grand Rapids: Eerdmans, ²2002) 272-97 and 249-71 respectively. See also my 'In Search of Common Ground' 316-8 (below 292-4); and my contribution to the Richard Hays FS, *'EK PISTEŌS: A Key to the Meaning of PISTIS CHRISTOU'* (forthcoming). The discussion by Moisés Silva is a cool draft of good sense ('Faith Versus Works' 227-34; also 234-6); for the phrase in Romans, see Watson, *Hermeneutics of Faith* 73-6; and see now the most recent and full treatment by K. F. Ulrichs, *Christusglaube: Studien zum Syntagma* pistis Christou *und zum paulinischen Verständnis von Glaube und Rechtfertigung* (WUNT 2.227; Tübingen: Mohr Siebeck, 2007).

[170] See esp. Wisdom, *Blessing for the Nations;* and Watson, *Hermeneutics of Faith* 185-93.

[171] Gal. 3.10-13 'serves as a bridge between 3.8, which contains the promise of the Gentiles' sharing in the blessing of Abraham by faith, and 3.14, which speaks of its fulfilment in the gift of the Spirit. In other words, the passage explains how the blessing of Abraham, namely justification by faith, has come to the Gentiles' (Hong, *Law in Galatians* 133, referring to Sanders, *Paul, the Law and the Jewish People* 22). My own suggestion regarding Gal. 3.13 (*Galatians* 176-8) has not cut much ice in the debate; but see now Schäfer, *Paulus bis zum Apostelkonzil* 116-20.

[172] Cf. T. L. Donaldson, 'The "Curse of the Law" and the Inclusion of the Gentiles: Galatians 3.13-14', *NTS* 32 (1986) 94-112.

Is it too much, then, to make the further deduction that the covenantal nomism of Paul the zealous persecutor, of the 'false brothers' of 2.4, and of the Jewish missionaries so disturbing the Galatian churches, itself was the main obstacle to the blessing of Abraham extending to Gentiles, as the Antioch incident had illustrated and the other missionaries now demonstrated?[173] If not, perhaps we could go a step further, to observe that Paul's argument seems to imply that a continued insistence on the doing of the law by believing Jews ('those of the works of the law') was tantamount to invoking the curse of the law on all law-breakers, including the Gentile out-laws (Paul's logic in 2.17 re-expressed in terms of the law's 'curse' on the 'sinner'). That, of course, would feed back into my original suggestion that insistence on 'the works of the law' was itself failure to observe *all* that is written in the Torah (notably the Genesis promise of blessing to the nations).

However, without claiming to be able to solve all the exegetical conundrums of these verses, my basic point here remains: that the main thrust of Paul's first elaboration of the principle enunciated in 2.16 is in terms of how *Gentile* believers have rightly received the promised blessing of justification without having to adopt a *Jewish* way of life (works of the law).

3.2 (6) Understanding Romans

Even if it could be accepted that the works of the law in Gal. 2.16 seem to refer in particular to the boundary issues of circumcision and food laws, few are persuaded that the equivalent initial reference to works of the law in Rom. 3.20 and the subsequent reference in 9.11-12 in particular can be so restricted in scope. And for most, the obvious reference of 4.4-5 is to a works-righteousness, to an understanding of righteousness as earned by work.[174] Here again I do not question the fundamental statement of principle which Paul enunciates in these passages. But again I wonder if the conclusion that Paul is attacking a works-righteousness attitude, an attitude embraced by Jews of his time, is quite so soundly based as most think, and whether Paul's attack is again somewhat broader.

On 3.19-20 it still seems to me to be too little recognised that Paul's indictment is addressed 'to those who are under the law' and is the climax of his attempt to demonstrate that *all,* Jews as well as Greeks, are under the power of sin (3.9).[175] It was his fellow Jews in particular who needed to hear that no one is justified by

---

[173] I have already indicated that I see Galatians as Paul's own critique of the agitators' 'covenantal nomism' (above n. 96); similarly Kruse, *Paul* 111-2.

[174] Particularly S. Westerholm, *Israel's Law and the Church's Faith* (Grand Rapids: Eerdmans, 1988), to whom I already responded in *Jesus, Paul and the Law* 237-40; T. Laato, *Paulus und das Judentum: Anthropologische Erwägungen* (Abo 1991) — 'egocentric legalism' (248).

[175] Gager argues that 3.19 is directed exclusively to Gentiles (*Reinventing Paul* 119-20),

works of the law.[176] And what were these works of the law? If there is any looking back to Paul's earlier indictment, in what appears at any rate to be a summary and climax of that indictment, then what was Paul summarising by referring to 'works of the law'?[177] It cannot be the catalogue of breaches of the law in
2.21-24, referred to also in 2.25, 27; *breaches* of the law could never be described
as 'works of the law', as doing what the law demands.[178] Nor, presumably and for
the same reason, can the reference be to Israel's unfaithfulness and wickedness
(3.3-5), or to the catalogue of sin in 3.10-18.[179] The only obvious reference is to
the critique of Israel's boasting in 2.17-20, 23: that they know and therefore can
do God's will; that the law instructs them as to what really counts with God, and
circumcision expresses their commitment to obeying it (2.25).[180] That this was

---

but 'those (with)in the law' can hardly refer to anyone other than those who defined themselves by reference to the Torah, who relied on the Torah, who claimed they had the embodiment of knowledge and truth in the law, and who boasted in it (2.17, 20, 23); see further below n. 208.

[176] 'Yet Once More' 105-9 (below 217-21). 'For Paul the term *ex ergōn nomou* is specifically for those *en nomō* (3.19; cf. 2.12)' (Bergmeier, *Gesetz* 55-6). Rapa (*Meaning* 243-5),
Gathercole (*Where is Boasting?* 213-4; 'Justified by Faith' 150), and Watson (*Hermeneutics of
Faith* 65-6) agree. 'Paul's fellow Jews were not proto-Pelagians, attempting to pull themselves
up by their moral shoelaces. They were, rather, responding out of gratitude to the God who
had chosen and called Israel to be the covenant people and who had given Israel the law
both as a sign of that covenant membership and as the means of making it real' (Wright,
'Romans' 459-61).

[177] Cranfield's initial response at this point curiously ignores that the issue is what Paul
could have been referring to by speaking so summarily of 'works of the law' in 3.20 ('Works
of the Law' 5-6). He goes on to identify the phrase with 'the work [singular] of the law' in
2.15 and the doing of the law envisaged in 2.13, 14, 25, 26 ('Works of the Law' 6-7), without
attempting to resolve the consequent confusion with 3.20 (according to 2.13 such 'doers of
the law' will be justified!). Gathercole also, in properly emphasising Paul's condemnation of
sin in Rom. 2, fails to give adequate explanation for the sudden reference to 'works of the
law' in 3.20 (*Where is Boasting?* 203-5).

[178] Several commentators seem to identify the 'works of the law' referred to in 3.20 with
the *disobedience* of the law which makes the 'Jew' liable to judgment — Bell, *No One Seeks
for God* 228-35: works of the law in 3.20 refer to a doing of the law which no one does (see
n. 368 below). Das: 'the "works of the law" (so to speak) that Paul identifies are the moral
failures on the part of the Jews' (*Paul, the Law and the Covenant* 190); Schreiner: 'People are
condemned through works of the law because they fail to keep the law' (*Paul* 113);
Westerholm: 'The "works of the law" that do not justify are the demands of the law that are
not met'; 'the "works of the law" that do not lead to righteousness are the deeds of righteousness *not* done by sinners' (*Perspectives* 316, 445 — my emphasis). No! the works of the law
are (by definition!) *'doing'* what the law demands, but failing to realise that acceptance by
God is not dependent on that doing. Herewith I respond to Matlock's criticism ('Sins' 78, referred to by Westerholm, *Perspectives* 314 n. 49).

[179] Of course, I do not dispute that the gravamen of Paul's indictment is directed against
Israel's failure to obey the law ('Yet Once More' 106; below 218-9); the issue here, however,
is the reference of 'works of the law'. It was a point of agreement at the Symposium on *Paul
and the Mosaic Law* that Paul's indictment in Rom. 2 embraced both the sense of privilege
and the actual law-breaking of 'the Jew' ('In Search of Common Ground' 320-1; below 297).

[180] M. A. Seifrid, 'Unrighteous by Faith: Apostolic Proclamation in Romans 1:18–3:20', in

what Paul had in mind by his introduction of the term 'works' is confirmed, I think, by the fact that Paul reverts to the theme (3.27) as soon as he has completed his brief statement of what God's justifying righteousness is about (3.21-26). The exposition of God's righteousness is what decisively undercuts Jewish boasting. Which is also to say that the works which do not prevent boasting (3.27), but rather might seem to give ground for boasting (4.2), must at least include a reference to that which gave ground for boasting in 2.17-29.[181]

In short, I have no desire to question the theological weight which has properly been placed upon Rom. 3.20: '*no flesh* shall be justified before God by works of law'. But it still seems important to me not to lose sight of the specific situation which gave rise to this crucial theologoumenon: that it was motivated by and included reference to Israel's pride in its privileged status, a status attested and maintained over against the (other) nations by its works of the law.[182] Paul's response is terse: ensuring (final) justification is not what the law

---

Carson, et al., *Justification and Variegated Nomism Vol. 2* 106-45, criticises the new perspective at this point (130-2, 135), but acknowledges that the problem in view is 'the false assumption that they (the Jews) possessed a special knowledge of the divine demands' (124), 'a certain Jewish understanding of privilege and exclusivity' (127-8), 'a claim to a present and perceptible advantage', an advantage 'contingent upon its [Israel's] possession of the Law' (134), regarding circumcision 'as a guarantee of a salvation mediated by the Law' (135). I do not place great value on the term 'ethnocentrism', which evidently jars with Seifrid; so far as I am concerned, Paul's critique was directed against Jewish *presumption* (the chief thrust of Romans 2), not against Jewish privilege (141) but *abuse* of that privilege (Seifrid seems to misunderstand the 'new perspective' at this point). I am entirely happy when Seifrid continues: Paul 'only denies the false security which supposes that the Law transmits wisdom and righteousness to the human being'; the term 'works' in 3.27 'is associated with "boasting", the very language Paul uses in reference to the Law in Romans 2:17, 23 . . . "works of the law" were deeds of obedience to the Law's demands which were thought to secure or confirm divine favor' (141). S. Grindheim, *The Crux of Election: Paul's Critique of the Jewish Confidence in the Election of Israel* (WUNT 2.202; Tübingen: Mohr Siebeck, 2005) attempts to distance himself from 'the new perspective' (198-200), but his own position is very close: 'Paul's critique [is] of any confidence in election as conferring a visible religious advantage'; 'When visible status claims, such as pedigree and membership in the Jewish people, were seen as evidence of one's right standing with God, Paul rebuked this attitude with prophetic intensity'; for Paul 'God's election is consistently understood as manifesting a reversal of values' (195-7; see also n. 384 below); Grindheim also brings 2 Cor. 11.18 into play on the theme — boasting 'according to the flesh' (particularly 105-8).

[181] 'Yet Once More' 110-1 (below 221-2); see also above n. 38. Cf. Westerholm: 'That the issue of boundary markers compelled Paul to formulate the thesis that one is declared righteous by faith in Jesus Christ, not by the works of the law, is the entirely appropriate emphasis of recent scholarship'; 'being uniquely in possession of the law easily leads to a belief that one is uniquely positioned to please God by obeying the law's commands' (*Perspectives* 389, 391 n. 112).

[182] So also Wright, 'Romans' 461. 'In a deliberately provocative manner, he [Paul] is seeking to destabilize an entrenched position that associates the Law with the privileged status of the elect Jewish people' (Hays, 'Three Dramatic Roles' 157-8). The point is also recognised by Haacker, *Römer* 83-4, and Byrne, 'The Problem of Nomos' 302, though the latter criticises me for putting too much stress on the 'national pride' aspect of 'Israel's sinfulness'.

is about; the relevant function of the law at this point is its role in making aware of sin.

On Rom. 4.4-5 I still find myself asking whether Paul intended these verses as an accusation against his fellow Jews or as an appeal to a principle they would be the first to acknowledge (as in 3.30).[183] For one thing, Paul makes the assertion as his first step in expounding his key text, Gen. 15.6 — 'Abraham believed God and it was reckoned to him for righteousness' (Rom. 4.3). Now we know how that verse was interpreted at the time of Paul: 1 Macc. 2.52 and Jas. 2.23 are clear and sufficient evidence on that point.[184] It was taken as a reference to Abraham's *faithfulness* in obeying God's commands (even if that meant sacrificing his son Isaac);[185] no one familiar with Jewish thought would have been in any doubt that by 'works' Paul was referring briefly to 'works of the law' just mentioned (3.27-28).[186] The typically Jewish thought was in terms not of Abraham *earning justification,* but of Abraham *remaining faithful* to the God who had called him; in the terms used by Sanders, the thought was not of 'getting in' but of 'staying in'.[187] The issue for *Paul* at this point, however, was Abraham's *initial* acceptance by God, the fact that he was *already* reckoned righteous at the stage in his story marked by Gen. 15.6, that is, prior to his subsequent circumcision (Gen. 17), as Rom. 4.9-11 makes clear. To include consideration of Abraham's subsequent obedience (Gen. 26.5), as Jewish tradition

---

[183] 'In Search of Common Ground' 311-3; also *Theology of Paul* 366-7; see also the earlier 'Yet Once More' 112-3 (below 223-4); cf. Yinger, *Paul, Judaism and Judgment* 182-7. 'When Paul in Romans 4 is stressing the principle of grace over against merit . . . , can we take it for granted that he is trying to introduce a new idea? Isn't it much more plausible that he appeals to an established conviction — both of early Christianity and of ancient Judaism?' (Haacker, 'Merits and Limits' 282). O. Hofius, '"Rechtfertigung des Gottlosen" als Thema biblischer Theologie', *Paulusstudien* (WUNT 51; Tübingen: Mohr Siebeck, 1989, ²1994) 121-47, demonstrates that *iustificatio impii* as a theme in Paul's theology is deeply rooted in the Old Testament.

[184] See my *Romans* 200-2.

[185] See further B. Ego, 'Abraham als Urbild der Toratreue Israels. Traditionsgeschichtliche Überlegungen zu einem Aspekt des biblischen Abrahambildes', in F. Avemarie & H. Lichtenberger, eds., *Bund und Tora: Zur theologischen Begriffsgeschichte in alttestamentlicher, frühjüdischer und urchristlicher Tradition* (WUNT 92; Tübingen: Mohr Siebeck, 1996) 25-40; Gathercole, *Where is Boasting?* 235-8, 242-3; Watson, *Hermeneutics of Faith* ch. 5. In a private communication, Kevin Bywater notes that Gathercole presses T. Abr. 10.13 too hard as talking of 'Abraham's perfection in all his deeds' (238), since 9.3 and 14.11-14, which talk of Abraham's sin and of his being forgiven, have also to be taken into account.

[186] Rapa, *Meaning* 252; *pace* Schreiner, *Romans* 217-8, despite his recognition of the traditions referred to in n. 184 (215-7). Just as the talk of 'works' in 4QMMT B1-2 (cf. 1QH 9(= 1).26; 12(= 4).31; and Jas 2.14-26) would, of course, have been understood as action taken in obedience to God's will expressed in the Torah.

[187] G. W. Hansen, *Abraham in Galatians: Epistolary and Rhetorical Contexts* (JSNTS 29; Sheffield: Sheffield Academic, 1989), concludes his review of 'Abraham in Jewish Literature' (175-99): 'in Jewish literature Abraham is portrayed in the context of covenantal nomism' (199).

did, was to confuse the key issue so central to the key question of whether Gentiles could be regarded as also and equally acceptable to God. The factors to be taken into consideration in regards to *final* justification are not in view here.[188]

The recognition of the interpretation of Gen. 15.6 challenged by Paul helps make sense of the first step in Paul's counter-interpretation of Gen. 15.6. For evidently, Rom. 4.4-5 are intended as an exposition of the verb 'reckoning';[189] it is the image of the owner or steward reckoning payment on the basis of hours worked which is in view, in contrast to a free gift of grace which does not calculate faithfulness and piety.[190] So it is that kind of 'reckoning/calculating' which is excluded.[191] If there is reference to the way in which Abraham's faithfulness was regarded within Jewish tradition, as a not to be ignored factor in his being counted righteousness,[192] then Paul's point is to deny that that was a factor in Abraham's initial justification. It is not the first part of the dictum (v. 4) which applies to Gen. 15.6, but the latter part (v. 5). It was not faithful Abraham to whom God gave the promise, but Abraham the type of the ungodly-idolater-become-proselyte.[193] The Jewish interlocutor might well have replied that

---

[188] It is a major thrust of Gathercole's critique of the new perspective in *Where is Boasting?* that the new perspective ignores Second Temple Judaism's theology of the final vindication of God's people on the basis of their obedience (below #4.2(10)). Paul could be said to be ignoring it too, or rather excluding it from consideration at this point, in his single-minded focus on Gen. 15.6 as showing how Abraham was initially justified solely on the basis of accepting God's promise; see further below #4.2(10).

[189] *Romans* 197-8, 202-5; cf. Moo, *Romans* 263.

[190] Cf. of course Matt. 20.1-16!

[191] M. Cranford, 'Abraham in Romans 4: The Father of All Who Believe', *NTS* 41 (1995) 71-88, particularly 76-83: 'Paul draws on the workman imagery for the specific purpose of explaining the term *logizesthai*, not the term *erga*, as traditional interpreters typically assume. . . . The key issue is not faith versus works, but reckoning according to obligation versus reckoning according to favour. . . . The workman metaphor in v. 4 only becomes evidence for the Lutheran position when the faith/works antithesis is already presupposed' (80-1).

[192] Gathercole, *Where is Boasting?* 244-6. De Roo argues that Paul was reacting against reliance by others on Abraham's good deeds for justification, Abraham's 'works of the law' as vicarious, Abraham as a redeemer figure (*'Works of the Law' at Qumran* ch. 6; also 'God's Covenant with the Forefathers', in S. E. Porter & J. C. R. de Roo, eds., *The Concept of the Covenant in the Second Temple Period* (SSJSup 71; Leiden: Brill, 2003) 191-202), but the evidence is too slight to support the weight she gives, and the motif has to be read into Paul's exposition.

[193] Gathercole, *Where is Boasting?* 245, ignores the other strand of Jewish interpretation of the Abraham story which lies behind Paul's exposition, that Abraham was regarded as the type of the proselyte, the Gentile who turns away from idolatry to the one true God (*Jub.* 12.1-21; Josephus, *Ant.* 1.155; *Apoc. Abr.* 1–8; see further my *Romans* lxix-lxx and 204-5; N. Calvert-Koyzis, *Paul, Monotheism and the People of God: The Significance of Abraham Traditions for Early Judaism and Christianity* [JSNTSupp 273; London: T&T Clark International, 2004] 123-36; cf. de Roo, *'Works of the Law' at Qumran,* 69, 142-4, who thinks that Paul emphasises Abraham's sinfulness). So the question of how Abraham received that initial acceptance by God was critical to Paul's theology of justification and mission.

Paul was separating initial justification from final justification in an unrealistic way, and that is an issue to which we shall have to return (#4.2(10)). But at this point the focus is on the question of how Abraham initially became recipient of the promise of God and was at that time already counted righteous — this being Paul's way of explaining how any one, ungodly Gentile as well as Jew (Rom. 3.30), comes to be accepted by God.

Here again I have no intention of denying the profound gospel truth enshrined in these verses.[194] But I do wonder how many Jews, even those numbered with Paul's interlocutors, would have denied v. 4 in relation to God's choice of Abraham and of Israel, given not least that the classical statement of covenantal nomism indicated so clearly that the covenant with Israel was an act of divine grace and not at all of their achieving (Deut. 4.32-40; 6.10-12, 20-23; 7.6-8; 8.17-18; etc).[195] Just as I wonder whether the thrust against faithfulness, which was motivated in part at least by regarding non-Jews as 'the ungodly', has been given sufficient recognition.[196] But I fully recognise that there is an issue here which requires more discussion — the relation between initial justification and final justification.[197]

Similarly with Rom. 4.6-8. The point again is that the key verb 'reckoned'

---

[194] 'In Search of Common Ground' 327, 331-2 (below 303, 308-9).

[195] As Grindheim notes, 'Election is predicated of Israel as a people at the lowest point in their history, when they are enslaved in Egypt. . . . The reason for Israel's election is not to be found in her instrinsic value, but in the Lord himself, in his love and his faithfulness to his own promise' (*Crux of Election* 33). For a particularly fine expression of Israel's confidence in election see 1 Chron. 16.14-22 = Ps. 105.7-15.

[196] The argument that 'works' in 4.2 has nothing to do with 'boundary markers' (Schreiner, *Romans* 218-9; also *Paul* 112; similarly Watson, *Hermeneutics of Faith* 181-2 n. 20) has a superficial attraction, but forgets that the exposition of Gen. 15.6 follows from Rom. 3.29-30, cites Abraham as '*our* forefather', and already presupposes the issue of circumcision; the argument again ignores the fact that Abraham was celebrated in Second Temple Judaism as the archetype of the proselyte who rejects idolatry for monotheism (Calvert-Koyzis, *Paul, Monotheism* 125, 127, 129, 134-5; see above n. 193). P. T. O'Brien, 'Was Paul Converted?', in Carson et al., *Justification and Variegated Nomism Vol. 2* 361-91, wants to divide Paul's argument into two distinct sections — soteriological (3.27-28; 4.1-8) and salvation-historical (3.29-30; 4.9-18), with the inclusion of the Gentiles not yet in view till the latter in each case (378 n. 57; following Gathercole, *Where is Boasting?* 230-2, 245-7; also 'Justified by Faith', especially 155-6, 160); but the reference to 'boasting' (3.27) and to Abraham as 'our forefather' suggests that the two issues are too tightly wrapped up in Paul's thought to be so simply distinguished; as Cranford observes, Paul draws on the figure of Abraham in Romans 4 as an integral part of his argument that it was always God's intention to include Gentiles among his people ('Abraham in Romans 4'); see further n. 198 below. To recognise that 'ungodly' can refer to those outside the covenant hardly means denying that 'ungodly' denotes 'a sinner before God' (*pace* Waters, *Justification* 174); and how Waters can argue that I define 'faith' as 'faithfulness' (188) baffles me.

[197] Gathercole's final comment (*Where is Boasting?* 265-6) shows his awareness of the need for further discussion on 'the relationship between final justification (Rom. 2.13) and present-past justification (Rom. 4.3)', but he has not sufficiently reflected on that relationship in his exposition of Rom. 4.1-5.

(logizesthai) was used of David's justification in a context where final vindication was not in view, and quite 'apart from works'. David's law observance was
not a factor in his sin not being reckoned to him; the implications for the
uncircumcised (4.9-12) and those not 'from the law' (4.13-16) were obvious to
Paul.[198]

Rom. 9.11-12 is also highly relevant here: 'When they [Jacob and Esau] were
not yet born nor had done anything good or evil, in order that the purpose of
God should stand in terms of election, not from works but from him who
calls . . .'. An obvious interpretation of the passage is that the two negative
phrases ('not yet . . . had done anything good or evil', 'not from works') are synonymous, the point repeated in equivalent terms for emphasis.[199] But again I
have to ask whether that interpretation is as obvious as it at first appears. At the
very least the equivalence is called into question by the talk of 'doing good or
evil', since, so far as I am aware, no definition of 'works' includes the thought that
an evil work could be merit-earning.[200] A more obvious interpretation is that the
two negatives are complementary rather than synonymous. The first denies that
election had anything to do with the status or accomplishments of those elected
— just as Deuteronomy repeatedly insisted (the passages cited two paragraphs
earlier), and as Paul had reaffirmed in 4.4-5 and again in 9.16. The second denies
that the divine call anticipated or depended on the sort of obedience and way of
life envisaged by 'covenantal nomism' ('living jewishly' — Gal. 2.14).[201] Paul, in

---

[198] See further my *Romans* 205-7. Gathercole is somewhat disingenuous when he observes that 'the sins of David obviously had nothing to do with boundary markers or the excluding of Gentiles from the promise' (*Where is Boasting?* 247; 'Justified by Faith' 159, 161),
since the thrust of the argument is so much determined by the contrast between the circumcised and the uncircumcised, 'those of the law' and 'those of (Abraham's) faith'. Similarly his
italicised comment 'that David although circumcised, sabbatarian, and kosher, is described
as without works because of his disobedience' (247) is misleading. David *had* works (246),
just as Abraham had (n. 185 above); but they did not count in this case of him being forgiven,
reckoned righteous — *chōris ergōn*, 'apart from works', rather than 'without works' (4.6).
Schreiner simply confuses the issue by identifying David's 'works' with the sins referred to in
4.7-8 (*Romans* 219).

[199] See n. 160 above. Westerholm, 'Paul and the Law in Romans 9–11': 'What is emphatically excluded is consideration of any human "work" in the granting of divine favour (9:12):
an exclusion which naturally includes the particular "works" enjoined by Moses' (228); also
Perspectives 320; Moo, 'Israel and the Law' 208-10.

[200] Schreiner, however, concludes from 9.11-12 that 'works can be defined as the performance of deeds, both good and evil' (*The Law and its Fulfilment* 52). It is worth noting that
elsewhere 'doing good or evil' is a critical criterion in final judgment (John 5.29; cf. Rom. 2.6-
10), including also judgment of Christians (2 Cor. 5.10). See also n. 178 above.

[201] See further my *Romans* 543-4. Moo rejects the assumption that Paul uses 'works' here
as a shorthand for 'works of the law' (*Romans* 581-2), presumably forgetting that Paul also
uses the shorthand in 4.2 where it is clear that 'works of the law' are in view (see e.g. Bell, *No
One Seeks for God* 229, 264; and above n. 186); Mijoga takes it as self-evident that *erga* in
Rom. 3.27, 4.2, 6 and 9.12, 32 is simply an 'abbreviated form' of the fuller formula *erga
nomou* (3.20, 28; Gal. 2.16; 3.2, 5, 10) (*Deeds of the Law* 1, 53, 146, 153, 155, 157).

other words, closes off *both* alternatives which might diminish the sovereign 'arbitrariness' of divine election: dependent *neither* on any human activity of good or evil, *nor* on the demonstration of covenant faithfulness. Similarly in Rom. 11.6: the continuing loyalty of the 'remnant' is a proof of the effectiveness of 'the election of grace'; were it dependent on their 'works', then 'grace would no longer be grace'.[202]

In all this, all I am looking for in the discussion of these passages is some recognition that when Paul talks of works of the law he was thinking primarily, with his Jewish interlocutors, of doing what the law requires, of living within the covenant of God's election in accordance with the rules laid down by God at Sinai (and before). The thought of *earning* 'the election of grace' by the 'works' (to be subsequently) performed by the elect people is far from the thought. The challenge to Paul's mission was rather that those who accept the gospel and receive the Spirit ought therefore to do the works of the covenant's law, and that failure to do these works amounts to a refusal to accept the terms of God's covenanted favour.[203] That is what was at issue, and that is what Paul denied: God's acceptance was by grace through faith alone. There are further issues to be discussed which go beyond these texts (see below #4.2(10)). The point here, however, is that the texts under discussion were all, may I note once again, primarily concerned with the issue of how it was that non-judaizing (not living jewishly) Gentiles could be counted acceptable to God and members of the church of God here and now.

3.3 (7) Did Paul 'break' with the law?

I have attempted to confront this issue repeatedly in the last ten years, so here I will simply summarise the fuller treatments already offered. In my contribution to the Lars Hartman Festschrift I dealt only with Galatians and Romans.[204] In *The Theology of Paul* I wrestled with the complexity of Paul's treatment of the law; even to begin to do justice to that complexity I found it necessary to treat the theme extensively in three different chapters (##6, 14, 23). And most recently I have again worked in sequence through the individual texts (Galatians, Corinthians, Romans), attempting further to clarify and

---

[202] See again my *Romans* 639; cf. Kuula, *Law* 2.159.

[203] In 'In Search of Common Ground' 319 (below 295), and more fully 'Did Paul have a Covenant Theology? Reflections on Romans 9.4 and 11.27', in S. E. Porter & J. C. R. de Roo, eds., *The Concept of the Covenant in the Second Temple Period* (Leiden: Brill, 2003) 287-307 (reprinted below ch. 20), I note that 'covenant' was not a central or major category within Paul's own theologising (somewhat against the thrust of Wright's *Climax of the Covenant*).

[204] 'Was Paul against the Law? The Law in Galatians and Romans: A Test-Case of Text in Context' in *Texts and Contexts: Biblical Texts in Their Textual and Situational Contexts*, L. Hartman FS, ed. T. Fornberg & D. Hellholm (Oslo: Scandinavian University Press, 1995) 455-75; reprinted below ch. 11; see also 'In Search of Common Ground' 328-33 (below 305-9).

develop my understanding of Paul on this contentious subject.[205] In the light
of these investigations I cannot accept that talk of a 'break' with the law, as a
summary of Paul's overall attitude to the law, is justified.[206]

But what about the most negative-sounding references to the law, the sharpest of Paul's strictures on the law?

In Galatians Paul affirms that 'I through the law have died to the law' (Gal.
2.19). In context, however, the thought is connected with being designated a
'sinner' by those confident that their interpretation and doing of the law attested them as 'righteous' (2.17),[207] and is contrasted with the alternative of
him embracing again the zealous nomistic life-style he had followed prior to
his conversion (2.18). So Paul is presumably referring in 2.19 to his own abrupt
rejection of that way of life in his conversion; the death in view is death to a life
determined from top to bottom by Torah (or a sequence of halakhic rulings
derived from Torah). Christ has replaced Torah as the principal motivation
and referent for his living.

In contrast to many, I remain convinced that the way to read Paul's answer
to the question, 'Why then the law?' (Gal. 3.19), is as affirming an essentially
positive role for the law as a kind of guardian angel for Israel prior to the coming of Christ (3.19-22). It is his fellow Jews' failure to recognise that that role is
now complete (3.23-25; 4.1-5) which caused him to liken their continued sub-
ordination to the law with slavery to the elemental spirits of the world (4.3, 8-
10).[208] This does not mean that we should play down, far less deny the sharpness of Paul's analysis of the role of the law as effectively an enslaving power
(4.9, 24; 5.1), from which the coming of faith and of the Spirit has brought freedom (3.25-26; 4.4-7, 28-29; 5.13-26). But it does remind us that Paul's analysis
arises from, and indeed focuses all the time on the Galatian troublemakers' in-

---

[205] 'Paul et la Torah' (below ch. 21), in which I draw attention to the flexible way in which
Paul used *nomos*.

[206] See also Hahn, *Theologie* 1.234-42, 289-92. Witherington criticises me for 'limiting the
scope of what Paul means by certain key terms in the debate' (*Grace in Galatia* 351-5), but
his own brief discussion is limited to only one strand of Paul's discussion of the law and ignores the nuances which a fuller exposition of all that Paul has to say on the subject would
call for and which I attempt to outline in this section; cf. e.g. his implausible suggestion that
'keeping God's commandments' in 1 Cor. 7.19 refers to 'commandments'(!) 'that are part of
the Law of Christ, not simply [*sic!*] those found in the Mosaic Law' (370 n. 36).

[207] See above at n. 53.

[208] See further 'Was Paul against the Law?' 457-65 (below 267-75), and 'Paul et la Torah'
231-6 (below 451-5); cf. Esler, *Galatians* 194-203. D. A. Carson, 'Mystery and Fulfilment: Towards a More Comprehensive Paradigm of Paul's Understanding of the Old and the New', in
Carson et al., *Justification and Variegated Nomism Vol. 2* 393-436: 'Paul's salvation-historical
argument in Galatians 3 responds not primarily to appeals to the law's boundary markers,
but to a wrong estimate of its place and function in God's sweeping salvific purposes' (412,
435). My point is simply that it was the insistence (by Peter and other believing Jews) on
maintaining such boundary markers which probably brought home to Paul that the role of
the law vis-à-vis Israel was now ended (Gal. 3.25).

sistence that the way of life (the covenantal nomism) required of Israel by the Torah was still binding on believing Jews and on all Gentiles who wanted to be united with them in a community of faith in Messiah Jesus.[209]

The reference to the law as 'the power of sin' in 1 Cor. 15.56 presumably has in mind both the law's effect in stimulating sin ('the law of sin' — Rom. 7.23, 25; 8.2) and its role in condemning sin to death (as in Rom. 1.32); the theology subsequently worked out in Romans was already well thought through by Paul.[210] And in 2 Cor. 3 more weight needs to be given to the fact that Paul speaks of *gramma* and not Torah; so the thrust of his very negative remarks (the *gramma* as death-dealing — 3.6) is directed against the law too narrowly conceived, not the Torah as such.[211]

In Romans the law forms an important sub-theme of Paul's main exposition. He makes clear that it has, and still has(!) a twofold role. First, the law serves as a measure of sin, defines sin, makes sinners conscious of their sin, and provides a yardstick by which sin will be judged; the repetition of the same point shows that this was axiomatic for Paul (Rom. 3.20; 4.15; 5.13; 7.13). That is why the portrayal of judgment in terms of the law in 2.12-16 cannot be regarded as an aberration or a reference to a role now passé for Paul.[212] Nor should the *chōris nomou* of Rom. 3.21 be taken to imply the elimination or total exclusion of the law from the whole process.[213] On the contrary, 'Paul understands with Judaism the law of Moses as the valid expression of God's will for justice'.[214]

---

[209] Gager attempts to maintain the almost impossible position (exegetically) that Paul's treatment of the law in Galatians has in view only Gentiles, not Jews (*Reinventing Paul* 88-92; following Gaston, *Paul and the Torah*). But how anyone can refer the following verses to Gentiles beats me: Gal. 3.10 ('all who rely on works of the law'), 3.19 (the law [of Sinai] 'was added [to the promise to Abraham] for the sake of transgressions'), 3.23 ('held in custody under the law'), 4.4-5 (Christ 'born under the law in order that he might redeem those under the law'); in 4.21, to be 'under the law' is obviously a reference to the status 'wanted' by those considering circumcision; and in treating 4.21–5.1 Gager (93-7) completely ignores Paul's explicit link between Hagar and 'the present Jerusalem' (4.25). This is simply poor exegesis. It is also incredible that Jesus as Messiah (of Israel!) should for Paul be irrelevant to Israel's salvation; cf. A. J. M. Wedderburn, 'Eine neuere Paulusperspektive?', in E.-M. Becker & P. Pilhofer, eds., *Biographie und Persönlichkeit des Paulus* (WUNT 187; Tübingen: Mohr Siebeck, 2006) 46-64 (here 54-5).

[210] See further 'Paul et la Torah' 228 n. 5 (below 448 n. 5).

[211] See further 'Paul et la Torah' 236-7 (below 455-6). See also the discussion in S. J. Hafemann, *Paul, Moses, and the History of Israel* (WUNT 81; Tübingen: Mohr Siebeck, 1995) 156-86.

[212] See further 'Was Paul against the Law?' 466 (below 276); 'Paul et la Torah' 238-9 (below 457-8).

[213] Bergmeier, *Gesetz* 37.

[214] Bergmeier, *Gesetz* 55, citing F. Lang, 'Erwägungen zu Gesetz und Verheissung in Römer 10,4-13', in C. Landmesser, et al. eds., *Jesus Christus als die Mitte der Schrift*, O. Hofius FS (BZNW 86; Berlin: de Gruyter, 1997) 579-602 (here 582). See also the earlier essay, dedicated to Friedrich Lang, by O. Hofius, 'Das Gesetz des Mose und das Gesetz Christi', *Paulusstudien* (WUNT 51; Tübingen: Mohr Siebeck, 1989, ²1994) 50-74, here 56-63.

Second, however, Paul seems to imply that the law is as dangerous and as negative a power as are sin and death (Rom. 5.20; 7.5).[215] Yet here again it quickly becomes clear that Paul poses this possible implication only to *deny* it emphatically: the law is *not* to be identified with sin (7.7). Romans 7 is misunderstood, then, if it is not recognised to be, as a major part of Paul's intention, a *defence* of the law;[216] the real culprit is *sin,* using and abusing the law to incite desire/lust and to produce what is contrary to God's will (7.7-25).

What becomes clear from all this is that Paul's attitude to and treatment of the law was much more carefully nuanced than the straight law/gospel antithesis allows. And when we add the positive role which Paul evidently continued to attribute to the law (Rom. 3.27-31; 8.1-4; 13.8-10; etc.),[217] it becomes evident that the antithesis can become seriously misleading. Perhaps this can be regarded as a further pointer to the need to recognise that Paul's reaction to his native Judaism was not one of wholesale denunciation but was targeted against the misconception of the role of works in the process of salvation, the

---

[215] See particularly Hübner, *Law* 26-36.

[216] The point was made repeatedly by Kümmel, *Römer 7*. It was a point of agreement at the Symposium on *Paul and the Mosaic Law* 322-3 (below 298-9). See also my 'Was Paul against the Law?' 467-9 (below 277-9); *Theology of Paul* 156-9; Moo, *Romans* 423. Seifrid objects: in Rom. 7 Paul is not defending the law but 'attempting to persuade his audience of the validity of [his] exclusion of the Law from God's saving purpose' (*Justification* 227).

[217] See further my 'Was Paul against the Law?' 469-73 (below 279-83); also *Theology of Paul* #23; also Das, *Paul and the Jews* 155-80. Hofius ('Gesetz des Mose' 66-9) denies that Paul has any concept of a *tertius usus legis,* a continuing ethical use of the Mosaic law for Christians; but he acknowledges that in Paul's view Christian conduct should 'correspond' to Torah requirements (Rom. 13.8-10), and he hardly explains why, if he (Hofius) is right, Paul should insist on the importance of 'keeping the commandments' (1 Cor. 7.19) rather than simply obeying Christ or following Christ's example (as in Rom. 15.5). Kuula insists on reading Paul's treatment of the law in Galatians as entirely negative, but his arguments at this point (*Law* 1.182-5) ignore the continuities of Paul's language of 'fulfilling the whole law' (Gal. 5.14) with Matthew's presentation of Jesus as 'fulfilling' the law and calling for a full obedience to it, and as summing up 'the whole law' in the love command (Matt. 5.17-20; 22.40). Similarly, P. F. Esler continues to maintain the view of his *Galatians* 203-4, that 'fulfilment' of the law (Gal. 5.14) means the consummation of the will of God quite apart from the law ('the moral standards or norms of the law . . . have no further purpose for those who believe in Christ'), in his more recent *Conflict and Identity in Romans: The Social Setting of Paul's Letter* (Minneapolis: Fortress, 2003) in reference to Rom. 13.8-10 (333-5); but he lightly passes over the fact that the same formula is expanded in 8.4, where what is 'fulfilled' is 'the righteous requirement of the law' (244); see further n. 327 below. For all Westerholm's somewhat tortuous argument (*Perspectives* 321-30), the most obvious reading of 3.27-31, 9.32 and 10.6-10, not to mention 8.4, Gal. 5.6 etc., is that 'the law of faith' is an acceptable shorthand for Paul's claim that what the law requires is (only) fulfilled by/from faith (see further 'Paul et la Torah' 240-2 [below 450, 459-60], and below #4.3(11)). His deduction from Phil. 3.9 and Rom. 10.3-5 'that the righteousness of God's law is opposed to that of God' (329) exaggerates Paul's critique of 'the righteousness which is from the law' (the phrase actually used by these texts). In particular, Paul's continuing abhorrence of idolatry and sexual license can only be explained by the continuing influence of the law on his theology and conduct (see again my *Theology of Paul* 690-2, 703-4); see n. 362 below.

covenantal nomism which effectively excluded Gentiles from that process. No passage may signal this more clearly than 1 Cor. 7.19, where Paul both regards circumcision with indifference and, in the same breath, insists on the importance of keeping God's commandments (knowing full well, of course, that his Jewish contemporaries would regard circumcision as one of these commandments).[218] *Only someone who differentiated between requirements of the law,* for some good reason, could write like this.[219] Evidently, Paul's reaction against the law was targeted against that aspect of the law which circumcision so visibly expressed — acceptance by God as coterminous with the people of God circumcised in the flesh.[220]

3.4 (8) The later Paul

It is a fair comment that too little attention has been paid to the later writings of the Pauline corpus in the early days of the new perspective,[221] presumably on the usual grounds that an attempt to grasp Paul's teachings should focus on the letters whose authorship by Paul is undisputed. For however the question of authorship of Ephesians and the Pastorals is to be resolved, these letters do attest what may simply be described as an ongoing Pauline tradition, and at the very least can be regarded as the earliest interpretations of the earlier Pauline tradition, that is of the tradition which has absorbed our attention thus far.[222]

The key text is Eph. 2.8-10: 'For by grace you have been saved through faith, and that not of yourselves, but as the gift of God, not of works, lest anyone should boast. For we are his making, created in Christ Jesus for good works, which God prepared beforehand that we should walk in them'. Here we have the essential elements of Paul's doctrine of justification — grace and faith, set in antithesis to works and boasting. Is not this just the same point and antithesis that Paul was making in passages like Romans 4.2-5 and 11.6?

However, two features of the passage give cause for pause. (a) Salvation is spoken of here as a completed act ('you have been saved'), whereas the earlier

---

[218] See further my 'Neither Circumcision' 106-10; below 335-7.

[219] 'Paul et la Torah' 237-8 (below 456-7).

[220] P. J. Tomson, 'Paul's Jewish Background in View of His Law Teaching in 1 Cor 7', in Dunn, ed., *Paul and the Mosaic Law* 251-70, observes that the images of 'foreskin' and 'circumcision' are metonymies for being Gentile or Jewish, and that in Antiquity, which knew of no 'secularized Jews', this either meant being non-Jewish or an observant Jew. So he paraphrases 1 Cor. 7.19: 'being a law-abiding Jew or living as a gentile mean nothing, but keeping God's commandments' (267).

[221] Marshall, 'Salvation, Grace and Works' 341 and n. 9.

[222] In what follows I partly pick up and partly take further my 'Whatever Happened to "Works of the Law"?', in *Epitoayto:* P. Pokorny FS (Prague: Mlyn, 1998) 107-20; reprinted below ch. 17.

Paul spoke of salvation as future (Rom. 5.9-10; 13.11; 1 Cor. 3.15), and of Christians as 'those who are being saved' (1 Cor. 1.18; 2 Cor. 2.15). There the metaphor of 'salvation' covered the whole process of renewal and final redemption (Rom. 8.23); here the thought is of the decisive character of the beginning of that process. Paul, of course, had spoken on occasion with almost equal emphasis of 'having been justified from faith' (Rom. 5.1), but had never elsewhere used the metaphor of salvation in such an 'already realised' way; the equally important 'not yet' emphasis of his soteriology was too much wrapped up in the salvation metaphor.[223] This suggests at least a different or shifting perspective behind the writing of Ephesians.

(b) The earlier talk of 'works' was almost always of 'the works *of the law*', that which was obligatory upon Jews as members of Israel, the covenant people.[224] The primary question was whether these works were obligatory (also) for Gentile believers. Paul's response had been clear: only faith was necessary; to require works of the law in addition to faith was to subvert the gospel of justification by faith alone (Rom. 3.28; 9.30-32; Gal. 2.15-16). Here the thought seems to have broadened out to refer to human effort in general as inadequate to the demands of salvation; salvation could be accomplished only by grace alone through faith alone.[225] At the very least this implies that the Reformation understanding of Paul's theology of justification was already shared by the first Christian commentator on that theology.

The matter, however, is a little more complex. For as we have seen, the more profound theologoumenon, that no individual or people can achieve acceptance by God by his/her/its own efforts, is clearly asserted in Rom. 4.4-5; 9.11, 16; 11.6 (see #3.2(6) above). This is the theological reasoning which underpins the more specific assertion that works of the law should not be required as essential for justification. My point above was that this more profound understanding of God's ways with humankind was already well understood within Jewish tradition, and a fundamental credo within its primary textbook of covenantal nomism, 'the book of the law' Deuteronomy.[226] That is why Paul could appeal to it (he did not need to argue for it) in dealing with the more specific threat that works of the law were a threat to that fundamental principle.

My reading of the situation confronted by Ephesians 2 is therefore some-

---

[223] Rom. 8.24-25 is not an exception; see my *Romans* 475-6.

[224] Although Paul speaks of 'works' without adding 'of the law' in Rom. 4.2, 6; 9.12, 32; 11.6, the implication is that he is using shorthand for the fuller phrase, as Marshall recognises ('Salvation, Grace and Works' 345). See also n. 201 above.

[225] A. T. Lincoln (with A. J. M. Wedderburn), *The Theology of the Later Pauline Letters* (Cambridge: Cambridge University, 1993) 135-6. 'Long before Augustine and Luther, the author of Ephesians already interpreted the Pauline phrases "works of the law" and "works" in terms of general human accomplishment' (Das, *Paul, the Law and the Covenant* 272).

[226] As again Marshall recognises ('Salvation, Grace and Works' 350-2, 357).

what different. The issue of Gentile believers' acceptability within a community of salvation which still saw the world through the traditional lens of Jewish privilege (2.11-12)[227] was no longer being posed in terms of 'works of the law'. It was seen more bluntly in terms of 'the barrier of the wall that separates', 'the law with its commandments and ordinances', whose effect was to create hostility between Jew and Gentile. This barrier had now been broken down by Christ, thus creating a new corporate embodiment of the community of salvation and making peace (2.14-16). That in effect was the same issue which Paul had confronted when he insisted that justification was by faith apart from works. But in moving it beyond the narrower issue of specific works of the law like circumcision and the laws of clean and unclean, which were the issues which had provoked Paul to write so fiercely to the Galatians, the author to the Ephesians sharpens and thus clarifies the issue as one of Jewish privilege misguidedly protected by the law, and thus in danger of maintaining a state of hostility between Jew and Gentile, when in Christ there could now be peace.

Which also means that the other profound issue, of one's total inability to achieve salvation by one's own effort, could be stated boldly and bluntly (2.8-10), without any danger of becoming confused with the issue of works of the law in particular.[228] Just as the author could go on to insist that good works are expected of 'the saved', without any fear that the works in view might be confused with the now passé demand of earlier Jewish believers that works of the law were still necessary for (final) salvation.

In short, the debate surrounding the new perspective should be very grateful to Ephesians. For the letter pulls apart into two separate theologoumena the two issues (justification by grace and not human achievement, justification by faith and not by becoming a proselyte) which have become confused as a result of Paul's formulation (as the situation in Galatia required of him) in terms of 'works of the law'. Ephesians shows that the challenge of the new perspective on Paul's soteriology is not best posed as 'Lutheran *or* New Perspective' but better as 'Lutheran *and* New Perspective'.

The two passages in the Pastorals cited by Marshall, in the event do not add much to the clarification made possible by Ephesians 2.[229]

2 Tim. 1.9-10: God 'who saved us and called us with a holy calling, not in accor-

---

[227] See further T. L. Yee, *Jews, Gentiles and Ethnic Reconciliation: Paul's Jewish Identity and Ephesians* (SNTSMS 130; Cambridge: Cambridge University, 2005), particularly ch. 3.

[228] The same is true of the critique of 'boasting' (2.9), which can revert to the more fundamental critique of boasting in 1 Cor. 1.29, 31 without becoming confused with the more distinctively Jewish boasting in the privilege of election (as in Rom. 2.17-23).

[229] See further my 'Whatever Happened?' 113-6; below 389-92.

dance with our works but in accordance with his own purpose and grace, which was given to us in Christ Jesus before times eternal'.

Tit. 3.5-7: God 'saved us not because of works in righteousness which we had done, but in accordance with his mercy . . . so that having been justified by his grace we might become heirs in accordance with the hope of eternal life'.

The contrast is more or less the same, between grace and works, and emphasises the point made so explicitly in Eph. 2.8-9. What is lacking is any sense in the near context of these passages, and indeed in the Pastorals as a whole, that the issues which had provoked the writing of Galatians and still heavily influenced Romans were still alive and threatening. Even the concerns of Eph. 2.11-22 are no longer evident. Such threat as there is that can be described in any distinctive sense as 'Jewish' is almost lost in the more wide-ranging warnings with only echoes of old disputes now distant. And the call for 'good works' can be made with a regularity which suggests that the possibility of confusing them with 'works of the law' belonged similarly to that distant past.[230] In a word, the Pastorals add little or nothing to our quest for clarification of Paul's affirmation that 'by works of the law shall no flesh be justified before God' (Rom. 3.20).

All these clarifications and further reflections are an attempt to restate what might be called the Jew/Gentile dimension so integral to Paul's doctrine of justification, and to call attention once again to the amount of light which a 'new perspective' reading of 'works of the law' seems to shed on Paul's expositions of the doctrine of initial justification in both Galatians and Romans. I do so, I repeat once more, not to offer an *alternative* to the emphases of the classic doctrine of justification, far less in *opposition* to them, but to plead for recognition of that dimension in our own twenty-first century restatements of that doctrine, with awareness of its ramifications for social, international and ecumenical relationships. It is the total graciousness of God's action in justifying anyone and everyone which rules out all pride, not only boasting in self-achievement but also boasting in ethnic identity and religious tradition.

4. More substantive issues

My hope is that the debate occasioned by the new perspective can now move forward. If we can move beyond the confusions and misunderstandings, the

---

[230] See further my contributions on the Deutero-Paulines in C. A. Evans & D. A. Hagner, eds., *Anti-Semitism and Early Christianity: Issues of Polemic and Faith* (Minneapolis: Fortress, 1993) 151-65 (here 160-4); and in J. Barclay & J. Sweet, eds., *Early Christian Thought in its Jewish Context* (Cambridge: Cambridge University, 1996) 130-44 (here 140-3).

false polarisations which are the meat and drink of polemic, and the debates over particular texts which will probably be never-ending, it should be possible to engage in a more fruitful discussion of the main issues which have emerged from quarter a century's reflection on Sanders' new perspective on Second Temple Judaism. In this way the debate may help to achieve a richer and fuller understanding of Paul's teaching on justification and on its implications for Christian living.

There seem to me to be four major issues which have emerged. (9) Has Sanders exaggerated the 'covenant' aspect/strand of a soteriology which is much less consistent?[231] (10) Has sufficient recognition been given to the aspect/strand of Second Temple Judaism's soteriology which makes (eschatological) salvation dependent on obedience to the law?[232] On the other hand, have the objections to the new perspective given enough weight to Paul's own teaching on 'the obedience of faith' and that Christians too will be judged according to their works?[233] (11) Is the obedience which Paul expected of Christians different in kind or character (Spirit-enabled) from the obedience demanded of Israel?[234] (12) In many ways most critical of all: if Second Temple Judaism and Pauline soteriology may equally be defined in terms of 'covenantal nomism', then what need of Christ? Does the new perspective give enough weight to the need for and the work of Christ (Rom 8.33-34)?[235]

---

[231] The central thesis of Avemarie's *Tora und Leben* is that within rabbinic thinking the Torah and active obedience were of much higher (and indeed immediate) 'soteriological' importance than Sanders was ready to admit (see especially 38-44, 291-4, 582-4; but see also n. 252 below); affirmed by Stuhlmacher, *Revisiting* 40-1; Alexander, 'Torah and Salvation' 273. For criticism of Sanders see also particularly Westerholm, *Perspectives* 341-51; also Waters, *Justification* 35-58, 152-3; Bird, *Saving Righteousness* 93-4 n. 14. Frankemölle describes 'covenantal nomism' as an 'ideal abstraction' ('Völker-Verheissung' 302); my response is in the same volume (415-6).

[232] Particularly Gathercole, *Where is Boasting?*: 'the evidence for a final judgment according to works in Second Temple Judaism is overwhelming, and the denial of, or lack of emphasis on, this doctrine on the part of the New Perspective scholars is unwarranted' (223).

[233] K. P. Donfried, 'Justification and Last Judgment in Paul', *ZNW* 67 (1976) 90-110, reprinted in his *Paul, Thessalonica and Early Christianity* (London: T&T Clark, 2002) 253-78, with further reflection, 'Justification and Last Judgment in Paul — Twenty-Five Years Later' (279-92); K. R. Snodgrass, 'Justification by Grace — to the Doers: An Analysis of the Place of Romans 2 in the Theology of Paul', *NTS* 32 (1986) 72-93; Yinger, *Paul, Judaism and Judgment*; C. VanLandingham, *Judgment and Justification in Early Judaism and the Apostle Paul* (Peabody, MA: Hendrickson, 2006) chs. 2-3.

[234] See for example, C. H. Talbert, 'Paul, Judaism, and the Revisionists', *CBQ* 63 (2001) 1-22.

[235] P. Stuhlmacher, 'Christus Jesus ist hier, der gestorben ist, ja vielmehr, der auch auferweckt ist, der zur Rechten Gottes ist und uns vertritt', in F. Avemarie & H. Lichtenberger, eds., *Auferstehung — Resurrection* (WUNT 135; Tübingen: Mohr Siebeck, 2001) 351-61; my 'Response to Peter Stuhlmacher' (below n. 294) is to the sequence of questions he poses to the new perspective. Das, while acknowledging the strengths and value of the new perspective, calls for a 'newer perspective': 'Paul nullifies the gracious framework of covenant, elec-

These are major issues which invite a much more extended debate. At this point I can only indicate the ways in which my own understanding and appreciation of Paul is steadily developing as a result of the debate already under way.

4.1 (9) The question of consistency

I agree with Avemarie that Sanders is open to criticism on this score. But three points can be made in at least partial defence.

(a) It needs to be recalled that Sanders was correcting an imbalance prevalent at the time in NT scholarship's perception of Second Temple Judaism. I can attest from my own studies as a student that the dominant view of Judaism within Christian circles was very negative. I have referred above (#1) to the salutary impact of the opening pages of Sanders' *Paul and Palestinian Judaism;* a later generation which did not experience the currents of anti-Judaism still flowing in 1950s and 1960s should not underestimate the importance of Sanders' protest. My own oft-repeated illustration is the use of the term *Spätjudentum* to refer to Second Temple Judaism. How could first-century Judaism be *late* Judaism? Apart from anything else, Judaism still flourishes twenty centuries later! But the logic of the term 'late Judaism' is clear. It is rooted in the belief that Judaism's only reason for existence was to prepare the way for Christ and for Christianity. Once Christ came, once Christianity emerged, there was no further need or role for Judaism in the divine scheme of things. So first-century Judaism was *late* Judaism because it was the *last* Judaism, the *end* of divinely authorised Judaism![236] The point I want to make is simply that such a highly restrictive, but also denigrating and negative view of Judaism, was current in German textbooks as late as the end of the twentieth century. Sanders' protest was necessary.

(b) Sanders' key formula, 'covenantal nomism', has come under particularly heavy criticism (hence the length of this section). But in my view the formula

---

tion, and sacrifice, in favour of a very different framework centred on Christ' (*Paul, the Law and the Covenant* 268-71).

[236] Niebuhr, 'paulinische Rechtfertigungslehre' 117-8.

[237] 'Sanders belongs to a line of interpreters of Tannaitic Judaism who have tended, often in conscious rejection of Weber, to stress its "liberal" side' (Alexander, 'Torah and Salvation' 271; further 272-3). But Sanders' stress, for example, that 'Israel's situation in the covenant required the law to be obeyed as fully and completely as possible', and that it was possible for individuals to behave in such a way as to exclude themselves from the covenant (*Paul and Palestinian Judaism* 81, 266), hardly justified Elliott's dismissive comment that for Sanders 'keeping the law is *merely* a way of . . . "staying in" the covenant' (*Survivors of Israel* 53 my emphasis). Sanders was also well aware of the tensions in rabbinic Judaism on the subject (87-101): 'The Rabbis did not have the Pauline/Lutheran problem of "works-righteousness", and so felt no embarrassment at saying that the exodus was earned' (100).

should also be given more credit than it has so far received. For, as already noted, it implies a necessary inter-relationship, as Sanders clearly saw, between divine initiative and grace (covenant) and human obedience of the law (nomism). Now it may well be the case, no doubt is the case, that some of Sanders' statements are imbalanced in that they overstate the covenant side of the inter-relationship.[237] When a previous imbalance (a) is being corrected, that will often happen, particularly if previous attempts to correct the imbalance were largely ignored.[238] My point, however, is that Sanders' own key formula, 'covenantal nomism', already indicated both that the *two* sides of the inter-relationship needed to be recognised and the broad terms of that inter-relationship: covenant as presupposition for nomism;[239] but covenant as still in an important sense dependent on nomism. As Avemarie observes, 'To speak of the Torah means to speak of the Torah of Israel: not to men generally is the Torah given, but to the one people of God. . . . The Torah is God's gift to and claim upon Israel'.[240]

Andrew Das has gone a long way to recognise this inter-relationship in early Judaism,[241] though he needs to acknowledge both an element of eulogy and hagiography in references to heroes of the past, and that those entering Israel (proselytes) or a sect like Qumran were naturally expected to make a whole-hearted (100%) commitment. The volume edited by Don Carson, Peter O'Brien and Mark Seifrid sets out to examine the inter-relationship in much finer detail (as Sanders' work warranted), and its findings largely concur: that such an inter-relationship does need to be recognised, even if Sanders did not state it adequately at various points. Indeed, my impression after reading the volume was that instead of its present title, *Justification and Variegated Nomism*, it would more appropriately have been entitled *Justification and Variegated Covenantal Nomism!*[242] In view of which, Carson's conclusion at the

---

[238] See above n. 20. In an early critique of Sanders, D. A. Carson, *Divine Sovereignty and Human Responsibility* (Atlanta, GA: John Knox, 1981) recognises the point (89), and while anticipating the large scale critique reviewed below (e.g. 106), he compliments Sanders on his 'otherwise excellent work' with whose thrust he agrees (121).

[239] Westerholm has taken the point: 'the fundamental truth that Judaism, described in its own terms, knew and depended on God's grace and did not promote a self-righteous pursuit of salvation by works' (*Perspectives* 444).

[240] Avemarie, *Tora und Leben* 446, 448; and further 530-76. See also Avemarie, 'Erwählung und Vergeltung. Zur optionalen Struktur rabbinischer Soteriologie', *NTS* 45 (1999) 108-26, who emphasises that in rabbinic theology both election (Erwählung) and reward (Vergeltung) are criteria of equal value for participation in the world to come, even though they seem to be contrary principles, and that they often appear to be independent of each other.

[241] Das, *Paul, the Law, and the Covenant* 12-44; but the subsequent argument, that 'the increased focus on the law's rigorous demand is a *natural outgrowth* of the compromise of the • careful balance maintained between grace and demand in pre–70 C.E. Jewish writings' (69 my emphasis), implies less a balance and more a latent legalism in Second Temple Judaism.

[242] For example, with various qualifications appropriate to 'variegated covenantal

end of the volume, on the basis of the findings by contributors to the volume, that Sanders' category of 'covenantal nomism' is 'reductionist', 'misleading' and at times 'mistaken'[243] is unjustifiably harsh and unduly dismissive.[244]

On the other hand, in what is otherwise a strong study, Westerholm largely misses the point by assuming that he is responding to a position which posed 'belonging to a covenant' and 'doing what one ought' as somehow alternatives, sidestepping the obvious implication that 'righteousness' for Israel of course meant fulfilling the obligations consequent on covenant membership, and that the measure of that righteousness was the law.[245] And Francis Watson criticises Sanders for 'dogmatically' assuming that Palestinian Judaism gave priority to divine grace and for assuming that in the formula 'covenantal nomism', 'covenant' always takes precedence over 'nomism'.[246] But he ignores (at this point) the frequency with which the divine 'promise' is cited as the motivating factor in God's dealings with Israel in his principal texts (particularly Deuteronomy), an odd fact in view of his own emphasis on the point;[247] and he ig-

---

nomism', P. Enns finds Sanders' understanding of Second Temple Judaism supported by 1 Esdras (75), the Additions to Daniel (79-80), pseudo-Philo (92) and *Jubilees* (97); R. Bauckham finds the same in regard to *1 Enoch* (148) and the *Apocalypse of Zephaniah* (158-60); R. A. Kugler the same in regard to the *Testaments of the Twelve Patriarchs* (190); D. E. Gowan the same in regard to the Wisdom literature (238-9); M. Bockmuehl the same with qualifications in regard to 1QS (412-4) — Seifrid (435-8) simply repeats his previous exegesis of 1QS 11.2-3, an exegesis crucial to his argument, despite the penetrating critique of that earlier exegesis by Bockmuehl (398-9 n. 60). Alexander aligns himself closely with Avemarie, but urges caution on how this inconsistency should be interpreted: 'Avemarie correctly stresses the inconsistency of the rabbinic texts. . . . I suspect that what lies behind it is simply fidelity to Scripture, which is just as inconsistent as the rabbis are on this point' ('Torah and Salvation' 273); note also his comments on 'legalism and the burden of the law' (279-83), and on 'God as Merciful: Repentance and Atonement' and 'Torah and Salvation in the Tannaitic Midrashim' (286-97); 'Tannaitic Judaism aligns itself closely with the theological thought of the Deuteronomistic school. Broadly speaking, if there was a theology in early post-biblical Judaism it was the theology of Deuteronomy' (299). See also E. M. Cook, 'Covenantal Nomism in the Psalms Targum', in S. E. Porter & J. C. R. de Roo, eds., *The Concept of the Covenant in the Second Temple Period* (SSJSup 71; Leiden: Brill, 2003) 203-20; Aune, *Rereading Paul Together* 215-7.

[243] 'Summaries and Conclusions' 543-6; followed by O'Brien, 'Was Paul a Covenantal Nomist' 252-5. It is curious that Carson finds it necessary to describe the characterisation of Second Temple religion in terms of 'covenantal nomism' as 'doctrinaire' (548) and as exercising 'hegemonic control' over the reading of Paul ('Mystery and Fulfilment' 394-5), language which may reflect more his own mind-set than that of the new perspective; cf. Kim's talk of 'the New Perspective School' with its 'dogma' *(sic)* of covenantal nomism (*Paul and the New Perspective* 83, 294-5).

[244] Cf. the brief critique by Das, *Paul and the Jews* 11-12 n. 22.

[245] Westerholm, *Perspectives* 287-9 (for some reason he introduces the unJewish category of 'virtue' — 290); similarly he fails to appreciate that in terms of 'covenantal nomism' Gentiles are inevitably 'sinners' (Gal. 2.15 — in contrast to 'Jews by nature'), simply because being outside the covenant they do not observe the law of the covenant (290-1).

[246] Watson, *Hermeneutics of Faith* 7-13, 323-8.

[247] Watson, *Hermeneutics of Faith* 15 n. 28.

nores the extent to which 'staying in' equalled doing all that the law commands (nomism) as the condition for the enjoyment of life.[248]

Seifrid is one who reacts strongly to the renewed stress on the covenant
which Sanders' work precipitated in the new perspective.[249] He recognises that
in the Hebrew Bible there are 'four times the number of occurrences of a "saving righteousness" of God [64] than . . . those involving a punitive divine justice [15]', but argues that more attention should be given to the latter. This
involves criticising the emphasis on righteousness having to do with 'relationships', which, he maintains, does not give enough weight to righteousness understood as measured by a 'norm', 'right order' or 'that which is morally right'.
Unfortunately, he presses his argument too hard. Recognition of a 'covenant
context' surely does not depend on the appearance of the term 'covenant';
Sanders' claim that 'it is the fundamental nature of the covenant conception
which largely accounts for the relative scarcity of the term "covenant"'[250]
should have been given more weight;[251] on this point Avemarie is much closer
to Sanders than those who call on the former in order to criticise the latter
seem to appreciate.[252] And the language of 'norm' is quite justified (God-

---

[248] C. L. Quarles, 'The New Perspective and Means of Atonement in Jewish Literature of
the Second Temple Period', *Criswell Theological Review* 2.2 (2005) 39-56, justifiably observes that Jews who were distant from or who had abandoned the temple 'sought atonement for sin through personal acts of righteousness rather than temple sacrifice' (55); but
while qualifying the 'covenantal' element in 'covenantal nomism', the observation does not
affect the basic balance implied in the dual phrase.

[249] M. A. Seifrid, 'Righteousness Language in the Hebrew Scriptures and Early Judaism',
in Carson, et al., *Justification and Variegated Nomism Vol. 1* 415-42 (references to 416, 428);
followed by O'Brien, 'Was Paul a Covenantal Nomist?' 275-6, 287.

[250] Sanders, *Paul and Palestinian Judaism* 420-1; Sanders is referring to Rabbinic literature
at this point, but the observation is of much wider application in Second Temple Jewish literature.

[251] Cf. D. A. Carson's discussion of 'the imputation of Christ's righteousness' — 'The Vindication of Imputation', in M. Husbands & D. J. Trier, eds., *Justification: What's at Stake in the
Current Debates* (Downers Grive, IL: InterVarsity Press, 2004) 46-78. Seifrid accepts the
point; his argument is simply that righteousness language itself does not derive from the
sphere of covenantal ideas, even though it comes into contact with covenantal language (private correspondence).

[252] See F. Avemarie, 'Bund als Gabe und Recht: Semantische Überlegungen zu *b^erît* in der
rabbinischen Literatur', in F. Avemarie & H. Lichtenberger, eds., *Bund und Tora: Zur
theologischen Begriffsgeschichte in alttestamentlicher, frühjüdischer und urchristlicher Tradition* (Tübingen: Mohr Siebeck, 1996) 163-216, where he concludes: 'The profile of rabbinic
soteriology which E. P. Sanders in *Paul and Palestinian Judaism* has drawn, gains through the
results of our overview a surprisingly far-reaching confirmation. Surprising because it appears at first as though the strong conceptual significance with which Sanders views the category of covenant is not confirmed by the rabbinic use of *b^erît*. But it has turned out here that
the rabbinic talk of "covenant" actually helps to bring to expression several of the elemen-
tary conceptions which Sanders has summed up under the label "covenantal nomism": Israel's election, its destiny for eschatological salvation, its obligation to fulfil the Torah, and
God's absolute faithfulness to his people. . . . In reference to what the rabbis thought and said

determined right), so long as the norm is not seen as some abstract ideal (which is what those who have made play with the language of 'relationship' were objecting to),[253] but rather as a norm concretised in a relation (God and creation, God and Israel, relationships within the covenant people),[254] where the particularities of the relationship may result in an action being judged 'righteous', even when it appears to break a norm governing society (the case in point being Judah and Tamar in Gen. 38.24, 26).[255]

Seifrid summarises his argument and elaborates its relevance in the follow-up article in volume 2 of *Justification and Variegated Nomism*.[256] His warning against *reducing* the Hebrew concept of 'righteousness' to 'covenant faithfulness' or 'salvation' is fair.[257] That God's 'righteousness' towards the peoples he

---

about the promise to the fathers, circumcision, the Sinai revelation, eschatological salvation and the whole changing history of Israel with God, it is entirely appropriate to speak of a rabbinic "covenant theology"' (213-5). Similarly *Tora und Leben* 584 n. 40.

[253] Eichrodt, *Theology* 1.240-1; von Rad, *Theology* 1.371.

[254] 'The long-standing debate over whether the basic meaning of the root *sdq* is "conformity to a norm" or "mutual fulfilment of claims arising from a particular relationship" may be bypassed if we agree with Ziesler that the "norm" in question is the demands that stem from God's relationship with his people in the covenant' (Moo, *Romans* 79-80, referring to J. A. Ziesler, *The Meaning of Righteousness in Paul* [SNTSMS 20; Cambridge: Cambridge University, 1972] 36-9). Garlington subjects Seifrid's essay to stringent review, and criticises his 'myopic conception of righteousness' (*Defense* 66-95).

[255] Seifrid, 'Righteousness Language' 420. On the Judah/Tamar episode see von Rad, *Theology* 1.374. VanLandingham argues that *dikaiosynē* is not a forensic term and never means salvation or justification, but denotes 'a concrete, objective reality of qualitative righteousness' (*Judgment and Justification* 246, 252), and that the verb *(dikaioō)* does not mean 'acquit' but 'make righteous' (ch. 4). But he makes hard work of passages like Ps. 143.2, Isa. 43.9, 26 and *Pss. Sol.* 8.23, 9.2, and in the NT, Matt. 12.37, Luke 18.14 and Jas. 2.21. He can certainly point to Rom. 5.19 (the many 'made righteous'), but it is significant in regard to his thesis that Paul does *not* use *dikaioō* at that point. And the argument that *dikaioō* means 'made righteous' (that is, really, qualitatively righteous, in VanLandingham's interpretation) (303, 308) is at best forced (as he effectively acknowledges — 320) and makes nonsense of one of his own key texts (Rom. 2.13), which on his view says in effect that the righteous will be made righteous. Most striking of all, he pays little attention to Rom. 4.4-5, where the forensic background is clear in the allusion to the legal impropriety of a judge 'justifying the ungodly' (see e.g. my *Romans* 204), and where again the thought is entirely of attributing a righteous status to one who is unrighteous.

[256] M. A. Seifrid, 'Paul's Use of Righteousness Language Against its Hellenistic Background', in Carson et al., *Justification and Variegated Nomism Vol. 2* 39-74 (here 40-4); 'righteousness language in the Hebrew Scriptures . . . (is) largely built around the establishment of saving justice for the oppressed' (45).

[257] See also Seifrid, 'Paul's Use of Righteousness Language' 51-2; followed by Schreiner, *Paul* 199. Seifrid's primary target is Wright, who in his 'Romans and the Theology of Paul' repeatedly defines divine righteousness as 'the covenant faithfulness of God' (33, 38-9, 43, 56, 65); also *What Saint Paul Really Said* ch.6; also *Paul: Fresh Perspectives* 25, 30, 32 etc. Influential also has been S. K. Williams, 'The "Righteousness of God" in Romans', *JBL* 99 (1980) 241-90 (here 265-71). In my *Theology of Paul* I talk of overlapping terms — God's 'righteousness' overlapping with God's 'faithfulness' (342-4). See also Bird's critique of Seifrid (*Saving Righteousness* 36-9).

has created includes wrath and judgment as well as faithfulness and salvation is clearly implicit in the sequences Rom. 1.16-18 and 3.3-6.[258] But apart from that I do not regard the 'covenantal nomism' thesis to be much disturbed by Seifrid's arguments.[259]

M. A. Elliott comes at Sanders' 'covenantal nomism' from a different angle. His goal in a too discursive and prolix treatment is to reconsider and challenge what he calls 'the conventional nationalistic view of election theology'. He does so by concentrating on the sectarianism evident in the writings of Second Temple Judaism, which 'represented a profound reaction to the idea of a national identity that focused on ethnic Israel' ('a protest movement that expressed itself in *nonnationalistic* terms'), and which 'far from evidencing an unconditional or unilateral covenant theology . . . pointed to a highly individualistic and conditional view of covenant'.[260] But if Elliott intended his characterisation of 'an unconditional or unilateral covenant theology' as a description of Sanders, it misses the target, since, as we have seen, Sanders saw the possibility of exclusion from the covenant people to be a very real one.

Moreover, Elliott seems to misjudge the sectarian mentality or 'factionalism' (my term), which I agree is very prominent in Second Temple Jewish literature.[261] It is not best described as an abandoning of nationalistic theology for 'a highly individualistic view of the covenant'. On the contrary, it is better grasped as *a focusing of the national hope on the devout of Israel.* The thought is not of the righteous giving up on Israel, but of unfaithful Israelites apostatising from Israel and only the righteous inheriting the promises of the covenant: we alone faithful to Israel's covenant are alone 'Israel'.[262] For example, the Qumran community thought of itself as 'the congregation of Israel' (1Q28a/QSa 1.1). Even less is the thought of individuals from *any* people establishing

---

[258] See further my *Romans* 42, 132-5; Seifrid, 'Paul's Use of Righteousness Language' 58-9. Blocher justifiably notes the emphasis on 'righteous judgment' (Rom. 2.5) in the Pauline corpus ('Justification of the Ungodly' 473-6).

[259] He agrees in some degree with my own evaluation of the first volume (n. 242 above): 'a number of the essays . . . found that various corpora of Jewish writings fit nicely into the scheme of "covenantal nomism"' — having already concluded 'that the apostle Paul recognises in contemporary Judaism something like the "covenantal nomism" that Sanders describes' ('Unrighteous by Faith' 144). Curiously, however, he also maintains that the 'works of the law' of which Paul speaks were '*not* the condition of remaining "in" [the covenant] but the result of it' (143 my emphasis), despite his earlier description of 'works of the law' as 'deeds of obedience to the Law's demands which were thought to secure or confirm divine favor' (141).

[260] Elliott, *Survivors of Israel,* quotations from 113, 241, 353, 639.

[261] See my 'Pharisees, Sinners, and Jesus' 71-7; also 'Jesus and Factionalism in Early Judaism', in *Hillel and Jesus: Comparisons of Two Major Religious Leaders,* ed. J. H. Charlesworth & L. L. Johns (Minneapolis: Fortress, 1997) 156-75. Elliott refers only to my *Partings* 103-6.

[262] 'The "faithful remnant" was the true Israel which kept the law of God' (Eskola, *Theodicy and Predestination* 40). Paul of course argues in effect in an analogous way (Rom. 9.6–10.13).

themselves as 'Israel', but rather of a group *within Israel,* whose self-understanding presupposes God's election of and covenant with Israel, remaining (alone) faithful (or returning) to the covenant which in the beginning had established Israel as God's elect.[263] The scenario being worked out in the minds and practices of such factions, most obviously Qumran, is the one provided by Deut. 30,[264] which provided the basis for the pattern of sin-exile-restoration, as clearly indicated in CD 1.4-8.

Most striking is the difficulty Elliott has in coping with the evidence that even the more sectarian documents expressed the hope for national restoration. One need only think of passages like *1 Enoch* 90.34-38, *Jub.* 1.15-25 and *Pss. Sol.* 17.21-46[265] to recognise that the covenant with national Israel was not denied or disowned by the factionalists, but reaffirmed and reinforced in the hope that apostate and dispersed Israelites would return and the wholeness of the people be realised afresh. Elliott attempts to save his thesis by noting that what is in view in these passages is a 'converted' Israel. But of course! That is the implication of Deut. 30 and accords with the character of sectarianism — to assume that the group of 'righteous', 'devout', are alone faithful to the obligations of the covenant (covenantal *nomism*), and that the restoration of Israel will come about only when the apostate 'sinners' recognise that the group/faction/sect were right after all![266] In effect, for all his labours, Elliott has not made the case for a nonnationalistic soteriology among the factions of Second Temple Judaism,[267] but has simply underlined the importance of *both* elements of Sanders' summary (covenantal nomism) in the diverse yet characteristically Jewish soteriologies of the period.

The most radical challenge to Sanders is the recent study by Chris VanLandingham, *Judgment and Justification in Early Judaism and the Apostle*

---

[263] It was a further point of agreement in the Symposium on *Paul and the Mosaic Law* 'that while we can speak of salvation in individual and corporate terms in Second Temple Judaism, the question of the individual's status is derivative from membership of the covenant people' (312; below 288); see also 260 below.

[264] Recognised by Elliott, *Survivors of Israel* 278. Surprisingly Elliott pays no attention to Wright's regular claim that 'the controlling story' across the board in Second Temple Judaism's eschatology was of 'return from exile'; see particularly N. T. Wright, *The New Testament and the People of God* (London: SPCK, 1992) 268-71, 299-301.

[265] Dealt with by Elliott, *Survivors of Israel* 521-6, 533-40, 555-61; he finds the 'persistent hope for the eventual salvation of the nation' 'perhaps surprising' (573).

[266] 'The faithful remnant of the present . . . firmly believed that its message of protest and teachings about true righteousness would eventually be vindicated — especially . . . by the "elect" nation itself as it honoured the remnant and eventually joined their cause' (Elliott, *Survivors of Israel* 637). The parallel with Rom. 11.25-32 should not be ignored.

[267] The thesis applies still less to rabbinic Judaism — Alexander: 'Salvation for the Mishnah seems first and foremost to be national rather than individual. . . . The Mishnah also speaks of salvation in individual terms . . . but this individual salvation must be seen within the context of national salvation'; 'Salvation for Tannaitic Judaism is essentially national' ('Torah and Salvation' 274-5, 300).

Paul. The first two chapters are a direct challenge to Sanders' conclusions that in Palestinian Judaism neither election nor final salvation can be earned but depend on God's grace and mercy.[268] In contrast, VanLandingham insists that God's 'grace' is neither undeserved nor free,[269] and that to the extent that mercy is discussed, it simply refers to God's salvation, not the reason for it.[270] 'At the judgment, God's covenant with the Jewish people does not determine one's eternal destiny; that, rather, depends on one's behavior'.[271]

In chapter 2 VanLandingham in effect reinforces the arguments already mounted against Sanders, by highlighting the emphasis in Second Temple Judaism on the necessity of obedience if salvation is to be secured,[272] as also Elliott's case that in Second Temple Judaism only the righteous expect or can expect to be saved. Unfortunately, he falls into the same trap as Elliott in his failure to recognise the assumption of such documents that the righteous are, of course, the righteous *of Israel*, in other words, that their being part of the covenant people is the presupposition and starting point of their righteousness.[273] And as to the assertion, typical of VanLandingham's thesis, that 'it makes more sense to say the righteous are elect because of their righteousness than to say the elect are righteous because of their election',[274] the obvious rejoinder is that he poses as an either-or what is best understood as a both-and. Election and righteousness go together in Second Temple thought symbiotically — which is also why sin/unrighteousness/apostasy is so self-contradictory and disastrous for any Deuteronomist/covenantal nomist. Judgment is better

---

[268] Sanders, *Paul and Palestinian Judaism* 421-2.

[269] VanLandingham, *Judgment and Justification* 55-60.

[270] VanLandingham, *Judgment and Justification* 17, 144-5.

[271] VanLandingham, *Judgment and Justification* 17.

[272] E.g. in reference to Jubilees: 'This heavenly record-keeping [4.22-24; 30.21-24; 36.10] demonstrates that one's behaviour determines one's eternal destiny' (*Judgment and Justification* 74); 'all the blessings that God promises to bestow depend on obedience to the covenant' (79); in Daniel 'the righteous receive God's mercy because they deserve it' (85); in *1 Enoch* 1–5 'the "elect" are not predestined by God, and "righteous" is not a status granted to them apart from their behavior' (89); in reference to Qumran, 'it is obvious that the covenant is more than God's obligation to his people, but also the people's obligation to God' (85; see further 103-7) — is this telling us something new? But he has to struggle to retain 1QS 10–11 and 1QH[a] within his thesis (119-31): 'texts such as 1QS 10-11 and 1QH[a] should not receive a *central importance* in determining the sect's theology on these matters' (135). On the other hand, his criticism of Sanders that 'no evidence exists that the covenant alone is efficacious or has a guaranteed soteriological effect for any particular generation or individual' (146; though note the clarifications of 154 and 171) is essentially sound.

[273] To claim that any belief that 'a relatively small proportion of Israelites' will survive the judgment is 'incompatible with covenantal nomism' (*Judgment and Justification* 102), or that the sectarianism of the *Psalms of Solomon* is 'legalism' (139), fails to appreciate how severely the nomistic element in 'covenantal nomism' could be and was interpreted within Second Temple sectarianism. Contrast Yinger, *Paul, Judaism and Judgment* 73-8.

[274] VanLandingham, *Judgment and Justification* 94.

seen as dependent on both election and obedience, as judgment on the obedience called for by the covenant relationship.

But VanLandingham's most radical contention comes in his first chapter: 'that election (like salvation) is *not* a gift of God's grace, but a reward for proper behavior'. God chose Abraham because he was righteous; the promise of Gen. 15 follows upon Abraham's obedience, described in Gen. 12.4 and 13.17; the repeated promise of Gen. 17 is conditional upon circumcision; and the renewal of the promise in Gen. 22 is a reward for Abraham's willingness to sacrifice Isaac (22.15-18), as also in 26.4-5.[275] The pre-promise piety of Abraham VanLandingham finds emphasised in *Jub.* 12.12-21, pseudo-Philo 6 and the *Apocalypse of Abraham.*[276] The argument is repeated for the patriarchs Isaac and Jacob and for the nation of Israel.[277]

Unfortunately, as justified as VanLandingham is in drawing attention to the emphasis on Abraham's piety, he has overstated his case. In the biblical witness itself, the promise of Gen. 12.1-3 assumes no prior qualification. That Abraham should obey the accompanying command is, of course, taken for granted; but that is precisely the inter-relationship which 'covenantal nomism' asserts. Likewise the talk of 'reward' in Gen. 15.1 is prospective, and the requirement of circumcision in Gen. 17.1-14 is Abraham's response to the covenant promised to him and his descendants, his and their part of the covenant sovereignly offered (covenantal nomism). And while *Jubilees* does indeed make much of Abram's piety prior to Gen. 12.1-3,[278] the claim that in pseudo-Philo 'God established a covenant with Abraham in the first place because of recognition of Abraham's piety'[279] is read into the text of pseudo-Philo 6–8. Much more prominent, as VanLandingham recognises,[280] but without letting it modify his thesis, is pseudo-Philo's repeated confidence in the covenant promised to Abraham and the fathers (9.3-4, 7; 10.2; 11.1; 12.4; 13.10; etc.). In short, VanLandingham repeatedly confuses the obedience required to maintain the covenant with obedience as ground for the divine initiative, and he plays down the sovereign promise character of the covenant made with the fathers and the nation.[281] That they

---

[275] *Judgment and Justification* 18, 19, 20-3.

[276] *Judgment and Justification* 23-6, 28-33, 34-5; noted also by de Roo, *'Works of the Law' at Qumran* 105-7. VanLandingham also draws upon Philo and Josephus (26-8, 33-4); A. E. Cairus, 'Works-Righteousness in the Biblical Narrative of Josephus', *ExpT* 115 (2003-04) 257-9, refers to Josephus, *Ant.* 1.183, with similar effect; but to what extent do Philo and Josephus qualify as witnesses to the self-understanding of the piety of Palestinian Judaism?

[277] *Judgment and Justification* 37-9, 39-55.

[278] Watson comments on *Jubilees* and Jas. 2.21-24: 'It does not occur to either of these readers of Genesis that the primary theme of the Abraham narrative is divine action rather than human' (*Hermeneutics of Faith* 235).

[279] *Judgment and Justification* 31.

[280] *Judgment and Justification* 29.

[281] This is true also of other texts cited by VanLandingham: Sir. 44.19-21; Wis. 10.5; 1 Macc. 2.52; CD 3.1-4 (*Judgment and Justification* 36). He recognises that it is 'difficult to separate

had a responsibility to respond does not constitute a denial that the divine promise was an act of prevenient initiative.

In short, the categorisation of Judaism's soteriology in terms of 'covenantal nomism' still seems to be a fair overall summary, even if the initial statement of it by Sanders may have underemphasised the nomism side of the formula and overemphasised the unanimity of Second Temple Judaism on the subject, and despite attempts of Sanders' critics either to treat it as a rigid rule or to question its basically integrated character. After all, it is still possible, and indeed necessary, to speak of 'Judaism', even though recognising that a more accurate sociological description would require us to speak of Judaisms (plural).[282] As already indicated, when I use the term in relation to Second Temple Judaism I have in mind primarily the theology exemplified by Deuteronomy.[283] A good parallel is the widespread consensus that Paul's soteriology is characterised by an 'already/not yet' tension, even if the elements and character of the tension are not agreed. All that the phrase does is indicate *that* there was a symbiotic relationship between election (covenant) and Torah (nomism) in Second Temple Judaism's soteriology, not *what* the relationship was or *how* it was perceived by different Second Temple writers and factions. The givenness of election and the obligations resulting therefrom were two foci round which the ellipse of Second Temple Judaism's soteriology was circumscribed, but depending on the play allowed by the link between the two foci, the circumference could be drawn more tightly or more loosely. Let me repeat the point, in the hope of avoiding further misunderstanding. It is not my intention to defend Sanders' own statements regarding 'covenantal nomism'; criticisms made by Avemarie and others are justified. My point is rather that there was an inter-relationship between given election and required obedience in the soteriology of Second Temple Judaism, an inter-relationship which prior to Sanders was not sufficiently recognised, and which can now be fairly and effectively characterised in the phrase 'covenantal nomism'.

(c) The whole discussion highlights the dangers
- of systematising the statements of different writers of different time periods and in different situations, or

---

election from obligation, grace from Law, promise from obedience' (41), but still presses his argument that 'God's election of Abraham is nothing short of a reward offered in response to Abraham's righteousness. The notion that God's grace precedes human obligation is nowhere to be found' (64), despite his acknowledgement that passages like Deut. 7.7-8 and 9.4-5 'sound the note of grace' (41). Similarly Westerholm's drawing attention to rabbinic texts which treat Israel's willingness to submit to the laws of the covenant as a condition that had to be met before God would grant them the covenant in the first place (*Perspectives* 349-50) seems to confuse the *purpose* of election with the *reason* for election (as Sanders, *Paul and Palestinian Judaism* 93 had suggested).

[282] I discuss the matter at some length in *Jesus Remembered* 255-92.

[283] I refer again to Alexander's comment cited above (n. 242). See also below 156.

– of abstracting into critical juxtaposition statements from different genres and rhetorical contexts.

It stands to reason that in certain circumstances (of pride and prosperity) human dependence on the priority and gratuitousness of divine election will be the point of emphasis; I have already instanced the opening chapters of Deuteronomy. In other circumstances (of disobedience and disregard) the point of emphasis will be on the need for obedience and on the perils of failing to obey; Deuteronomy 28 is an equivalently appropriate instance. Are these inconsistent, or simply the different rhetoric appropriate to different circumstances, or even different sections of the same book?![284] I will be drawing attention below to parallels with Christian, including Pauline writing, where a similar diversity between emphasis on grace and necessity of obedience can readily be documented. Is Paul, then, as 'inconsistent' as Jewish texts, or do both simply remind us that different modes of speech are appropriate in different circumstances?

So there were those in Second Temple Judaism and in rabbinic Judaism who seem to have distorted what should be the creative tension between the two elements in Israel's covenantal nomism. What a surprise! So there were groups and factions who reinforced the nomistic obligation on Israel, who measured their standing as 'righteous' by their faithfulness to halakhoth which others disputed, and who denounced as 'sinners' those who did not accept these halakhoth.[285] Replace 'halakhoth' with such terms as 'inerrancy', 'six-day creation', 'Papal infallibility', 'Sabbath observance', 'penal substitution', 'male headship' and the same could be said of not a few factions/groups/traditionalists within Christianity. Yes indeed, in each case there is a danger that the pureness of divine grace is being compromised, that zeal for God and for God's law/word has exalted secondary issues/adiaphora, to the status of essentials/fundamentals. Sadly fundamentalists of all sorts fail to appreciate that justification by faith alone stands opposed to all such fundamentalism: *justification is by faith alone and not by reference also to factional shibboleths!* But should a fundamentalist expression

---

[284] So I question Seifrid's conclusion from Avemarie, that many rabbinic statements represent 'nomism' which stand apart from Sanders' proposed 'overarching synthesis' [covenantal nomism] (M. A. Seifrid, *Christ, our Righteousness: Paul's Theology of Justification* (Downers Grove, IL: IVP Apollos, 2000) 16. Would any rabbi insist that his emphasis on obedience was independent of God's prior choice of Israel (see Avemarie's own view of the matter cited in n. 252 above)?

[285] The claim that Paul (and Jesus) were objecting not to Judaism but to (a) factional view(s) within Second Temple Judaism has a too little noticed corollary: that Paul (and Jesus) were themselves part of an intra-Jewish dispute on how the balance of covenantal nomism should be played out. Waters comments: 'It is hard to defend a religion as gracious when at least some of its teachers on some occasions proclaim that an adherent is ultimately accepted at the bar of judgment because the sum total of his good deeds outweighs the sum total of his bad deeds' (*Justification* 57). So a religion is to be judged by *some* teaching of *some* extremists; God help us!

of a religion be seen as characteristically expressive of that religion? And are the inconsistencies between different expressions of covenantal nomism simply that ('inconsistencies'), or a demonstration that 'covenantal nomism' is inadequate as a characterisation of Second Temple Jewish soteriology (which I question), or an indication that Paul was addressing only a limited range of expressions within Second Temple Judaism? Which brings us to the next point.

4.2 (10) Final justification

On the whole question of the eschatological dimension of justification high-lighted by Stuhlmacher[286] and Gathercole[287] in particular, I again have no hesitation in acknowledging that much of the criticism is justified, even though too little recognition has been given to the fact that in *The Theology of Paul* my treatment of Paul's soteriology spreads across two chapters, entitled 'The Beginning of Salvation' and 'The Process of Salvation' (chs. 5–6), and that the discussion of 'Justification by faith' in the former (#14) is complemented by the discussion of 'The eschatological tension' in the latter (#18).[288] Here too some clarification is in order.

(a) We should recall, once again, that the focus of the early phase of the 'new perspective' was determined by the recognition that Paul's formulation of justification by faith and not works arose out of the issue of how Gentiles as Gentiles could be expected to share in the covenant blessings of Israel (Stendahl).[289] It was natural, therefore, that attention should focus on the question of how Gentiles 'get in', whether to the (new) covenant people of God or to acceptance by Israel's God. If I am right, the response of Peter and the other believing Jews at Antioch was determined in large part by concern that they themselves should 'stay in' the covenant; but the focus of the discussion, for Paul as well, was on the full *initial* acceptance of Gentiles within the communities of faith in Christ.[290] The same was true of Paul's key argumentation in reference to Abraham in both Gal. 3 and Rom. 4.[291] Paul focuses ex-

---

[286] *Revisiting* 14-16, 40-1.

[287] See n. 232 above. In his review of Gathercole, B. W. Longenecker, 'On Critiquing the "New Perspective" on Paul: A Case Study', *ZNW* 96 (2005) 263-71, rightly points out that a change of emphasis is not the same as denial (266-8). Bird also thinks that I 'minimize' final judgment 'and subordinate it beneath the application of justification to covenantal membership' (*Saving Righteousness* 101), a criticism I simply do not recognise.

[288] See particularly *Theology of Paul* 467. I set out the future tense of justification/judgment in my 'Jesus the Judge: Further Thoughts on Paul's Christology and Soteriology', in D. Kendall & S. T. Davis, eds., *The Convergence of Theology*, G. O'Collins FS (New York: Paulist, 2001) 34-54 (here 40-3) (below ch. 18, here 400-3); as previously, e.g., 97 and 326 n. 47 below.

[289] See above n. 31.

[290] See above at nn.100-102, 119-20.

[291] See above #3.2(6).

clusively on what Gen. 15.6 says about Abraham being 'reckoned righteous' there and then; hence the emphatic aorist of Rom. 5.1. Gathercole's objection to the new perspective (as neglecting final justification) might as well be directed against Paul himself! If I am right, it was the *Jewish interlocutor* who was pressing the case that justification depended (also) on faithful obedience subsequent to Gen. 15.6; and it was Paul who insisted on focusing on what we might call 'conversion justification', and principally to defend his claim that Gentile believers were *already* reckoned righteous, just as Abraham was when he believed.

We should recall equally that the traditional focus of justification by faith has also been on initial acceptance by God. 'Justification' has been typically understood in Christian theology as something which happened when one believed — justification by faith.[292] Hence the classic (albeit misunderstood) distinction between justification and sanctification.[293] Paul's own treatment provides clear precedent for treating 'justification' as the beginning of the salvation process.[294] To repeat, Romans 4 is all about Abraham being justified (reckoned righteous) near the beginning of his encounters with God, not at the end. And Paul's summary of his gospel in Rom. 5.1 quite explicitly speaks of justification by faith as something already accomplished in the lives of himself and his readers. So it is entirely understandable that the debate initiated by Sanders and the new perspective should have focused its attention on that obviously crucial aspect of the subject. To put it another way, initially the subject of *final* justification (acquittal at final judgment) was not in focus. But neither was it in dispute.[295] It is, however, entirely warranted on exegetical grounds to affirm that the Pauline doctrine of justification cannot be properly formulated without reference to final judgment.[296]

---

[292] Cf. e.g. Stuhlmacher: 'the event of baptism is the event of justification' (*Revisiting* 60; see further 62-3).

[293] Donfried, 'Justification and Last Judgment in Paul', represented the older model: 'the Christian life is a process which begins in justification, is actualised in sanctification and is consummated with salvation' (265, 267), but still gives too much the impression of a sequential process — though with some subsequent clarification (281).

[294] Hence my own setting it within chapter 5, 'The Beginning of Salvation' in *The Theology of Paul,* though I regret the misunderstandings which that decision led to in regard to Paul's teaching on judgment; in continuing his criticism of me at this point, Stuhlmacher, *Revisiting* 42, ignores the reply I had already made to him in 1999 on this and other points, 'A Response to Peter Stuhlmacher', in F. Avemarie & H. Lichtenberger, eds., *Auferstehung — Resurrection* (WUNT 135; Tübingen: Mohr Siebeck, 2001) 363-8. Stuhlmacher also emphasises that justification is a process (*Revisiting* ch. 3).

[295] I may refer to my earlier references on the point ('New Perspective' 190; below 107-8) and the additional notes in *Jesus, Paul and the Law* 208 (response to Räisänen) and 239-40 (response to Westerholm).

[296] *Contra* VanLandingham, who argues that Paul does not use the *dikai-* group of terms in reference to the Last Judgment or to indicate acquittal at the Last Judgment (*Judgment and Justification* 245, 302). But we need only to consider the use of *dikaioō* in Rom. 2.13 and

However, the balance should not be tipped too far in that direction: the inter-relationship of the two elements of 'covenantal nomism' should be maintained. Lev. 18.5 is a case in point.[297] It initially refers primarily to the way life should be lived within the covenant people, the way of ensuring maintenance of covenant status, length of days for the people in the land (Ezek. 20.5-26 'by whose observance man shall live'; cf. e.g. Deut. 4.1; 5.32-33; 6.24; 8.1; 30.15-20; Neh. 9.29; Prov. 3.1-2; 6.23; Sir. 17.11; Bar. 3.9; 4.1; *Ep. Arist.* 127; *T. Mos.* 12.10; Philo, *Cong.* 86–87; pseudo-Philo 23.10; *4 Ezra* 7.21).[298] But as thought of life continuing into the age to come evolved into the idea of eternal life, the promise element in Lev. 18.5 became more explicit.[299] This is evident already at Qumran: 1QS 4.6-8 — 'plentiful peace in a long life . . . eternal enjoyment with

---

3.4-6; here again it is hard to exclude the thought of final judgment in Rom. 3.20, given the developing argument of 3.4-6, 9, 19; and the picture conjured up in 8.33-34 is clear enough (*egkaleō* a legal technical term — LSJ; and further my *Romans* 502-3; despite VanLandingham 326-8). In the last passage there may be no explicit reference to 'justification by faith' (241), but the complete reliance on the advocacy of Christ comes to the same thing, despite the tension with the thought elsewhere of judgment according to works.

[297] In what follows I am responding to S. J. Gathercole, 'Torah, Life, and Salvation: Leviticus 18.5 in Early Judaism and the New Testament', in C. A. Evans, ed., *From Prophecy to Testament: The Function of the Old Testament in the New* (Peabody, MA: Hendrickson, 2004) 126-45. The issue was only beginning to come to the surface in the Symposium on *Paul and the Mosaic Law* (312 n. 6; below 288 n. 7). But see already W. C. Kaiser, 'Leviticus 18:5 and Paul: "Do This and You Shall Live" (Eternally?)', *JETS* 14 (1971) 19-28.

[298] I was already making this point in *Jesus, Paul and the Law* 239, in response to Westerholm. Gathercole charges me with reducing the thought of Lev. 18.5 to 'an essentially tautologous meaning' ('the one who does these things does them', or 'the one who lives by these things lives by them') ('Torah, Life and Salvation' 127-8). But the texts listed should make it clear that the thought is essentially the Deuteronomistic one: 'Choose life so that you and your descendants may live, loving the Lord your God, obeying him, and holding fast to him; for that means life to you and length of days, so that you may live in the land that the Lord swore to give to your ancestors' (Deut. 30.19-20) — obedience as the way to live and to ensure long life within and of the covenant people. It is a weakness of Gathercole's treatment that he confines discussion to passages where an echo of Lev. 18.5 may be perceived — even if understandable in an article on the use of Lev. 18.5! Watson disputes that Lev. 18.5 prescribes 'the distinctive way of life of the people of Israel', his own phrase (316): 'Leviticus 18.5 is most plausibly to be understood as a conditional promise of "life"' (*Hermeneutics of Faith* 322). But he too does not take sufficient note that the thought is the Deuteronomistic one of life lived in the land. For rabbinic use of Lev. 18.5 see Avemarie, *Tora und Leben* 104-17.

[299] Baruch A. Levine, *The JPS Torah Commentary on Leviticus* (Skokie, IL: Varda Books, 2004): 'The simple sense of the clause, "he shall live by them", is that one should live his life in accordance with God's laws and commandments and that he should obey them all his life or while he is alive. This clause has, however, stimulated other interpretations reflecting its unusual syntax and its semantic nuances. Syntax allows us to understand this clause as one of result: "that man shall perform, so that [as a result] he may acquire life by them". Performance of God's laws and commandments holds forth the reward of life, whereas their violation threatens man with death. This interpretation is the basis for the traditional understanding of our verse by later commentaries, which state that observance of the commandments is rewarded by life in the world to come' (91).

endless life'; CD 3.20 — he 'will acquire eternal life'; 7.6 — 'they shall live a thousand generations'. Similarly in the *Psalms of Solomon:*

[1]The Lord is faithful to those who truly love him,
　To those who endure his discipline,
[2]To those who live in the righteousness of his commandments,
　In the Law, which he has commanded for our life.
[3]The Lord's devout shall live by it forever;
　the Lord's paradise, the trees of life, are his devout ones.
[4]Their planting is firmly rooted forever;
　they shall not be uprooted as long as the heavens shall last.
[5]For Israel is the portion and inheritance of God.
　. . .
[10]The devout of the Lord will inherit life in happiness'
　(14.1-5, 10; see also 3.11-12; 9.5).[300]

Similarly in Wis 2.23 and 6.18 — man created for immortality, and observing the laws as confirmation *(bebaiōsis)* of immortality; is that not simply an extension of the promise of life to the obedient into a concept of immortality — 'the righteous will live for ever' (5.15)? And we should not forget the question put to Jesus by the rich young man: 'What must I do to inherit eternal life?' (Mark 10.17 pars.). Equally to the point is *Mishnah Abot* 2.7: 'if (a man) has gained for himself words of the Law he has gained for himself life in the world to come'. The point, then, once again, is that the two emphases should not be polarised: the Torah was seen both as 'the way of life and the way to life', and the twin emphases should not be played off against each other.[301] Friedrich Avemarie sums up the appropriate inter-relationship well:

Certainly the Torah leads to life when it is kept, but the early rabbis did not understand by "life" only participation in the world to come, nor did the way from obedience to life necessarily go by way of counting merits, reckoning up fulfilments and transgressions, and a concluding judgment. The attainment of eternal life could certainly be attributed to a judgment on human deeds,[302] but as regards motivation, the rabbis thought not so much of the expectation of rewards but of doing things out of obedience to God and for the sake of the Torah itself.[303]

---

[300] Gathercole insists that 'for our life' (14.2) has a 'prospective' sense 'unto' *(eis)* ('Torah, Life, and Salvation' 133); but that is an odd way to put it ('into our life [in the age to come]'); and Gathercole ignores the rest of 14.1-5.

[301] See my most recent statement in 'Paul et la Torah' 241 (below 459-60). Gathercole, *Where is Boasting?* 96-111, does not pay sufficient attention to the implication of continuity between covenant life and eternal life in the *Wirkungsgeschichte* of Lev. 18.5 — eternal life can be seen as experienced already (see further n. 313 below), or as actualised only beyond the death of this life (more typical in the NT).

[302] The German (durchaus als eine Vergeltungsfolge menschlichen Handelns verstehen) would be better rendered, '. . . certainly be understood as a recompense for human deeds'.

[303] Avemarie, *Tora und Leben* 582, cited also by H. Lichtenberger, 'The Understanding of the Torah in the Judaism of Paul's Day: A Sketch', in Dunn ed., *Paul and the Mosaic Law* 7-

On the issue of the inter-relationship between (initial) justification and final judgment, and between faith and obedience, it is also important to recognise that *NT teaching has the same or at least a very similar inter-relationship.*[304] Obedience is also required of believers (Rom. 1.5; 6.16, 19; 15.18; 1 Pet. 1.2).[305] The OT's insistence that one could not be righteous before God without acting righteously towards the neighbour (e.g. Deut. 24.10-22; Ezek. 18.5-9) remains true for the followers of Jesus (e.g. Luke 19.1-9; Rom. 14.1–15.7).[306] Paul expected his converts to 'lead a life worthy of God' (1 Thess. 2.12); he looked for 'the harvest or fruit of righteousness' in their lives (2 Cor. 9.9-10; Phil. 1.11).[307] Paul as well as Matthew looks for 'fulfilment' of the law (Matt. 5.17-20; Rom. 8.4),[308] for believers to produce 'good works' (Matt. 5.16; 2 Cor. 9.8; Col. 1.10). In speaking of the love which fulfils the law Paul evidently had very specific conduct in mind (Rom. 12.9–13.10; Gal. 5.13-15).[309] 'Keeping' the requirements of the law continued to be important for Paul (Rom. 2.26-27; 1 Cor. 7.19).[310] Final judgment will be 'according to works' (Matt. 16.27; John 5.28-29; Rom. 2.6-11;

---

23 (here 22-3). Avemarie thus sums up the first section of his ch. 6, 'Leben durch die Tora: 6.1 Die Tora als Mittel und Weg zum Leben' (376-99). Cf. Eskola: 'According to the knowledge we have from the contemporary sources of Judaism, the religion of Israel was not always eschatological. Salvation had to do more with this day ("that you might live") than the future' (*Theodicy and Predestination* 54).

[304] So already Sanders, *Paul, the Law and the Jewish People,* especially 105-13; and argued now particularly by Yinger, *Paul, Judaism and Judgment* 2-4, 286-90, and VanLandingham, *Judgment and Justification* ch. 3: e.g. 'other than making Jesus Christ the tribunal, Paul has not altered Jewish belief in the Last Judgment in any significant way' (240). Yinger reviews earlier attempts to deal with the tension, whether by concluding that Paul was completely inconsistent on the issue, or by seeking a resolution in terms of rhetoric, or by subordinating one emphasis to the other in substantial degree (6-15).

[305] 'Paul insists on the ethical corollary and consequences of God's choice and acceptance as strongly as the Deuteronomist, with the equal recognition on the part of both that the necessary obedience has to be from the heart. For Paul as much as Deuteronomy 'righteousness' in effect sums up both sides of covenantal nomism, both the saving action of God and the obligation of obedience to that righteousness (e.g. Rom. 6.18-19)' (Dunn, 'In Search of Common Ground' 328; below 304), noting also that F. Thielman, *Paul and the Law* (Downers Grove, IL: IVP, 1994) 238-41 is part of a growing consensus on this point (304 n. 52). On Rom. 6.16 see VanLandingham, *Judgment and Justification* 232-5.

[306] See further my 'Justice of God' 18-21 (below 208-10); unfortunately this aspect of the righteousness for which God looks has been neglected in the debate on the new perspective.

[307] As the theme of 2 Cor. 9 indicates, the concern reflects the characteristic OT concern for justice in human relationships. The point is recognised by Schreiner, despite his insistence that God declares righteous and does not make righteous (*Paul* 205, 209).

[308] On Rom. 8.4 see VanLandingham, *Judgment and Justification* 236-9.

[309] Bergmeier, *Gesetz* 80-2. 'Although the true Abrahamic family are free from the yoke of the law, they are not free from the obligation to *work* — to turn their faith into loving behaviour' (Barclay, *Obeying the Truth* 94).

[310] It is Tomson's thesis that Paul's practical instructions (in 1 Corinthians) have halakhic character and precedent ('Paul's Jewish Background'); summarising his earlier *Paul and the Jewish Law: Halakha in the Letters of the Apostle to the Gentiles* (CRINT III/1; Assen/Maastricht: Van Gorcum, 1990).

1 Cor. 3.8; 2 Cor. 5.10; 11.15; Col. 3.25; Rev. 20.11-15).[311] Imagery of reward for achievement or good deeds (works) is not lacking (e.g. Matt. 6.1-6; 10.41-42; 25.34-40; 1 Cor. 3.14; 9.24-25; Phil. 3.14; Col. 3.24; 2 Tim. 4.8).[312] Salvation (eternal life) is in some degree conditional on faithfulness (e.g. Mark 13.13; Rom. 8.13; 1 Cor. 15.2; Gal. 6.8; Col. 1.23).[313] Does this mean that early Christianity was as 'inconsistent' in its soteriology as Second Temple Judaism?[314] How are we to distinguish justification 'not by works' from final justification 'according to works'?[315] How could Paul say both that circumcision does not matter, but keeping the commandments does, and in the same sentence (1 Cor. 7.19)?[316]

---

[311] Recognised by Gathercole, *Where is Boasting?* 113-9, 124-31, who also notes that Jesus in Luke 10.28 seems to make eternal life dependent on 'doing' (121-4). Gathercole is remarkably unphased by all this (the chapter is headed 'Jewish Soteriology in the New Testament'), despite the possible corollary that Paul's doctrine of justification was *directed against other writers of the NT* as much as against the soteriology of Second Temple Judaism. For his solution to the tension within Paul's own thought, see #4.3(11) below. Bell simply denies that the judgment envisaged in Romans 2 applies to Christians (*No One Seeks for God* 254-6; see also below nn. 369-71). Contrast Snodgrass, who notes that 'approximately three-fourths of Paul's judgment sayings refer to the judgment of Christians' (Snodgrass, 'Justification by Grace — to the Doers' 93 n. 101). On Romans 2 and 2 Cor. 5.10 see VanLandingham, *Judgment and Justification* 215-32 and 199-202 respectively.

[312] E. Käsemann, *Commentary on Romans* (1973; ET Grand Rapids: Eerdmans, 1980), in commenting on Rom. 2.7, does not hesitate to speak in terms of 'reward': 'The goal lies transcendently outside the sphere of earthly possibilities but is the reward for constant concentration on it as indicated by *zētein* and the related prepositional phrase' (60). See further Yinger, *Paul, Judaism and Judgment* 207-15, 277-8, who notes, inter alia, that while the 'reward' in 1 Cor. 3.14-15 can be distinguished from salvation, in Col. 3.24 the reward *is* 'the inheritance' (234-5); on 'the inheritance' see e.g. my *Colossians and Philemon* (NIGTC; Grand Rapids: Eerdmans, 1996) 256-7.

[313] See my *Theology of Paul* 497-8, and below n. 353. It is important, however, to observe that as in Judaism's reflection on Lev. 18.5, for Paul and John 'life' is part of the 'already' as well as the 'not yet' (e.g. John 3.36; 5.24; 6.47-48, 53-54; 10.28; 17.2-3; Rom. 6.4; 8.2, 6, 10; 2 Cor. 4.12; 1 John 5.13).

[314] This complaint is at the heart of Räisänen's critique of Paul: '. . . it would be possible to claim that Paul actually teaches salvation (or at least reward) by works! If we (reasonably enough) refrain from such a claim, it might be wise not to apply it to Paul's Jewish contemporaries either. There is a difference of emphasis . . . ; it is not clear that the pattern itself is much different' (*Paul and the Law* 186).

[315] Hagner's response to Yinger is simply to ask, 'But if Paul saw no problem with works-righteousness, why did he repeatedly argue so strongly against it?' ('Paul and Judaism' 97 n. 69). But that simply underlines the need to clarify what it was that Paul was objecting to in Gal. 2.16; and if the new perspective does not offer any kind of help in clarifying the issue, then Hagner has to address the question of how serious Paul was when he spoke of final justification as 'according to works'. Similarly O'Brien's attempt to query Hooker's observation (n. 25 above) is rather facile ('Was Paul a Covenantal Nomist? 255-63), and his response to Yinger (263-70) does not take with sufficient seriousness the level of responsibility Paul's exhortations placed upon his converts (see 88 below).

[316] Seifrid comments on 1 Cor. 7.19: Paul's 'rejection of "works of the Law" notwithstanding, we may nicely fit Paul into "covenantal nomism"' ('Paul's Use of Righteousness Language' 65).

Does the new perspective still offer a viable or at least partial answer to such conundrums — the negative thrust directed against insistence on works of the law that discriminate and separate, the positive thrust to encourage works not tied to a narrowing of divine grace?[317]

(b) Gathercole's focus on eschatological justification is part of a larger critique of the new perspective which argues that the trouble with Judaism, in Paul's eyes, was that it was *synergistic*.[318] The response recognises the importance of the covenant in the soteriology of Judaism but argues that Judaism's insistence on obedience implied an understanding of salvation in which human cooperation (hence synergism) was essential in addition to divine grace, and in which final justification was by works of merit, Judaism as 'a covenantal nomism with an element of works-righteousness'.[319] A formulation by P. Enns sums up the position well: salvation should not be linked so closely to election, as Sanders had argued; 'it might be less confusing to say that *election* is by grace but *salvation* is by obedience'.[320] In Westerholm's terms, 'the very essence of 'Lutheranism' is that 'humans can contribute nothing to their salvation. . . . It seems fair to say that it is not to be found in Judaism as depicted by Sanders'.[321] My own Doctor-father, C. F. D. Moule, had already posed the equivalent issue in regard to Sanders' own formulation: since 'staying in' depends on observance, Moule asks 'whether "covenantal nomism" itself is so far

---

[317] Again it is perhaps worth noting the difference here from Calvin's classic appreciation (cf. Melanchthon) of 'the third use' of the law: it was the ceremonial law which had been abrogated ('not in effect but in use only'), but the moral law (the ten commandments) remained in force; obedience was still required of the Christian (*Institutes* 2.7.12-17). See further Wendel, *Calvin* 200-6.

[318] As Eskola notes: 'In principle, soteriological synergism is possible only in an eschatological theology' (*Theodicy and Predestination* 45).

[319] Kim, *Paul and the New Perspective* 83-4; see further 143-52. Gundry, 'Grace, Works, and Staying Saved in Paul' was the first to argue this case against Sanders (note particularly 36); subsequently see particularly Laato, who emphasises Judaism's 'anthropological optimism' (*Paulus und das Judentum* 83-94, 206, 210) = *Paul and Judaism: An Anthropological Approach* (Atlanta: Scholars, 1995) e.g. 150, 167; and Eskola, *Theodicy and Predestination* 44-51, 56-8, 84-93. Zahl prefers to speak of 'the "semi-Pelagianism" of Second Temple Judaism' ('Mistakes' 7-8). D. A. Hagner's critique, 'Paul and Judaism. The Jewish Matrix of Early Christianity: Issues in the Current Debate', *BBR* 3 (1993) 111-30 (here 122) is updated in 'Paul and Judaism' 84-8 (with excellent bibliography). And the argument runs through various contributions in Carson, et al., *Justification and Variegated Nomism Vol. 1*, and Gathercole, *Where is Boasting?* Part I; similarly Marguerat,'Paul et la Loi' 263-5. Mijoga, however, insists strongly that to speak of 'merit' in connection with Paul's *erga nomou* is to import 'into Paul's phrase a later western theological concept' (*Deeds of the Law* 77-88,112).

[320] P. Enns, 'Expansions of Scripture', in Carson, et al., *Justification and Variegated Nomism Vol. 1* 73-98 (here 98); Enns continues, '"Being in" is by birth; it is nationalistic. Staying in, however, is a matter of personal effort. . . . the final outcome is based on more than initial inclusion in the covenant' (98). But note again Donfried's claim that Paul's soteriology operates with effectively the same tension between 'justification' and 'salvation' (nn. 233, 293 above).

[321] Westerholm, *Perspectives* 341-51 (here 351).

from implicit "legalism"'.[322] Similarly Talbert: 'Once covenantal nomism is set in an eschatological context, it becomes legalistic nomism'.[323]

Here again it is perhaps worth reiterating that as a criticism of the new perspective, this may slightly miss the point, since, as already noted, the new perspective, like Paul in Gal. 3 and Rom. 4, has been concerned primarily with the issue of how Abraham was initially counted righteous, as a pattern for the conversion of the ungodly, Jew as well as Gentile. The criticism resonates curiously with the critique made by Jas. 2.14-26 of a 'faith without works' position. For that argument is clearly directed against the structure of argument used in Rom. 3.27–4.22.[324] In other words, James 2 provides something of a confirmation of the point just made — that the argument of the Romans passage was restricted to the initial justification of Abraham. James makes the same argument that Paul, keeping his focus narrow, was aiming to deny, so far as Abraham's initial justification and other potential proselytes' conversion was concerned.

So it is not at all clear, so far as concerns the issue on which Paul focused his exposition of justification, in Rom. 4 and Gal. 3 at any rate, that Paul was attempting to address the issue of Jewish synergism in eschatological (final justification) perspective. Presumably he would have been a good deal more cautious as regards the sort of thing he said about judgment according to works (Rom. 2.6-11; 2 Cor. 5.10), about sowing to the Spirit and reaping eternal life (Gal. 6.8), or about the prize of the upward call (Phil. 3.14), had he been so concerned about the danger of a synergistic understanding of salvation. Here again the Paul/James 'controversy' on 'faith without works' may be instructive. For the usual refutation that there was/is any conflict between Paul and James on this point stresses, quite appropriately, that Paul also believed in the importance of works and of faith working through love (Gal. 5.6).[325] So if James 2

---

[322] 'Jesus, Paul and Judaism', in G. F. Hawthorne & O. Betz, eds., *Tradition and Interpretation in the New Testament*, E. E. Ellis FS (Tübingen: Mohr Siebeck/Grand Rapids: Eerdmans, 1987) 43-52 (here 48). Similarly R. L. Reymond, *Paul: Missionary Theologian* (Fearn: Mentor, 2000), speaks of 'covenantal legalism' (461). Cf. Carson's conclusion that 'covenantal nomism as a category is not really an alternative to merit theology . . . (and) includes and baptizes a great deal of merit theology' ('Summaries and Conclusions' 544-5). Perhaps one should note in passing, that if 'covenantal nomism' is itself inherently synergistic, then the criticism that Sanders has ignored the synergism of Judaism's soteriology is unfounded!

[323] Talbert, 'Paul, Judaism and the Revisionists' 4. 'The motivation of those who thought they could be righteous by works of law involved legalism, even though they also would appeal to God's grace' (Schreiner, *The Law and its Fulfilment* 95). 'If legalism means that keeping the law affects eschatological salvation, then covenantal nomism is legalistic nomism by definition' (Eskola, *Theodicy and Predestination* 56). In my response to Cranfield I also noted that the covenantal nomistic attitude expressed by Peter and the other Christian Jews at Antioch (Gal. 2.11-16) 'is not so very far from the attitude of the merit-earner of Professor Cranfield's interpretation' (Yet Once More' 113; below 224); see also 'In Search of Common Ground' 312 (below 288).

[324] See my *Romans* 197.

[325] We should include Jesus at this point; A. P. Stanley, *Did Jesus Teach Salvation by*

can be seen as complementary with justification by faith (alone), should those who press for that complementarity be so keen to insist on the antithesis between Paul and his Jewish interlocutor in the way they do? Luther at least escapes any charge of inconsistency on that score!

The fact remains that both Judaism and Paul saw clearly that the inter-relationship between divine grace and human response had to be maintained and expressed in daily living.[326] Both recognised in their own ways that without the divine initiative there could be no hope of salvation, even of starting on the process. But both also believed that those in good standing with God had to meet the obligations of a law given them by their founder (Gal. 6.2).[327] Both evidently believed that without human response ('works') there could be no grounds for judgment ('according to works') of those at present in process of being saved. Human responsibility before God is something which both Jew and Christian recognise and affirm. Paul is the first to say that Jesus is both Saviour (Phil. 3.20) and Judge (2 Cor. 5.10).[328]

So, if it is indeed fair to characterise Jewish soteriology as synergistic, should we not in fairness read the exhortations in passages like Rom. 12.9-21, Gal. 6.1-5 and Col. 3.5–4.1 in a similar way? Was Paul's 'work of faith and labour of love' (1 Thess. 1.3) or his 'faith working through love' (Gal. 5.6) or his 'obedience of faith' (Rom. 1.5) as synergistic in its own way as Judaism's covenantal nomism?[329] Or are we to understand that for Paul there was a crucial difference between Jewish obedience and Christian obedience? The issue takes us into the next section.

Works? The Role of Works in Salvation in the Synoptic Gospels (Eugene, OR: Pickwick, 2006) answers his question: 'yes, Jesus *did* teach salvation by works — in the same way that James taught *justification by works*' (333).

[326] My far from perfect appreciation of the disputes prompted by the Reformation (reckoning righteous vs making righteous, imputing vs infusing righteousness, *tertius usus*, faith as a work, etc.) makes me wonder whether such disputes, *mutatis mutandis*, mirror the same tension between divine initiative and human respons(ibility) that we find in Judaism between election and works of the law.

[327] See e.g. Barclay, *Obeying the Truth,* who refers both Gal. 5.14 and 6.2 to the Mosaic law, but goes on to observe that 'Christians do not "observe" the law, they "fulfil" it, and they fulfil it through the one love-command and as it is redefined as "the law of Christ"' . . . ambiguity is the price Paul has to pay for his attempt to claim the law in support of his own proposals for Christian morality' (141-4); Hong, *Law in Galatians* 170-88; Longenecker, *Triumph of Abraham's God* 83-8; see also n. 217 above. 'The fulfilling of certain laws, including those stated here (Romans 13:8 "Do not commit adultery", "Do not murder", "Do not steal", "Do not covet"), entails conduct in line with those laws, even though Paul does not speak of "doing" them or "keeping" them' (Carson, 'Mystery and Fulfilment' 429).

[328] See further my 'Jesus the Judge' 46-50 (below 406-10).

[329] In a quite unexpected way, my plea to take more seriously Paul's calls for obedience on the part of his converts seems to be similar to Avemarie's criticism of Sanders that he did not give enough weight to the demands for Torah obedience within rabbinic tradition (n. 231)! Kuula begins his *Law* Vol. 2 by boldly asserting: 'Paul's own soteriology is quite legalistic and it lays much weight on human works. It is best described by the terms "synergism" or "co-operation"' (5; see also 108-10).

4.3 (11) Judgment according to works

If it is the case that Christians, members of the new covenant, no less than members of the old, are expected to be obedient, and if it is also the case that both are liable to judgment, and that eternal life is in some degree conditional on that obedience (works), where does that leave the debate?[330] Is Paul just as inconsistent as those he was criticising? He was criticising a contemporary Jewish view that eternal life was dependent on doing works of the law, but at the same time (with different dialogue partners) he was warning his fellow Christians of the same danger of failing to complete the course. Alternatively posed, if Paul's objection to Judaism was aimed at the synergism inescap-able(?) in *any* covenantal nomism formula, then does his own urging of his converts to obedience not fall under the same critique?[331] Or was his under-standing of Christian obedience different from obedience to the law?

The discussion here could rehearse the older Reformation debates about distinctions between 'justification' and 'sanctification', and between 'persever-ance' and 'preservation', not to mention predestination and free will.[332] For example, is the faith which justifies somehow different from the faith which sanctifies? That hardly appears likely, in view of passages like Gal. 3.2-4 and Rom. 3.31. Rom. 4.17-21 and 14.23 imply that faith is that complete reliance upon God without which any conduct is (liable to be) 'sin'.[333] As already noted, Paul speaks freely of 'the obedience of faith' (Rom. 1.5), and does not hesitate to speak of 'faith working through love' (Gal. 5.6).[334] Alternatively posed, is Christian righteousness never more than imputed (Protestant),[335] or

---

[330] The concerns expressed by Donfried, 'Justification and Last Judgment in Paul' 269-78, continue to be important; see further n. 233 and the texts cited on 77-8 above.

[331] Ironically Bird's attempt to express both the 'already' and the 'not yet' of justification (*Saving Righteousness* 172-8) formulates the latter in terms echoing the 'nomism' part of Sanders' 'covenantal nomism' formula: 'obedience is required for maintaining the status of justification' (177).

[332] I recognise that both in this section and in the next I am reflecting concerns expressed more from the Reformed side in these debates (McGrath, *Iustitia Dei* 219-26).

[333] See further my *Romans* 828-9; *Galatians* 270-2.

[334] Cf. D. B. Garlington, *Faith, Obedience and Perseverance* (WUNT 79; Tübingen: Mohr Siebeck, 1994) 44-71, who takes the 'doers of the law' in Rom. 2.13 to be Christians, and the 'hearers of the law' to be Israel. '"Doing the law" is not to be defined as "works-righteous-ness" or unaided human achievement; it is, rather, "the obedience of faith", i.e., continuance in the Creator/creature relationship as articulated by Paul's Christological gospel' (71). 'Jus-tification and sanctification are not successive stages in the Christian's life, but are simulta-neous' (159); 'faith, obedience, and perseverance are one and the same' (163).

[335] McGrath summarises 'the leading primary characteristics of Protestant doctrines of justification': '1. Justification is defined as the forensic *declaration* that the believer is righ-teous, rather than the process by which he is *made* righteous, involving a change in his *status* rather than his *nature*. 2. A deliberate and systematic distinction is made between *justifi-cation* (the external act by which God declares the sinner to be righteous) and *sanctification* or *regeneration* (the internal process of renewal within man). . . . 3. Justifying righteousness

is it (also) infused (Catholic)?[336] So, is faith in Christ the only fulfilment of the law possible?[337] Does all Christian conduct and obedience never amount to anything before God so far as final justification is considered?[338] Is Christ the only one who fulfils the law, so that righteousness as demanded and measured by the law can only be what Christ does in and through the believer?[339] Since

---

... is defined as the alien righteousness of Christ, external to man and imputed to him, rather than a righteousness which is inherent to him, located within him, or which in any sense may be said to belong to him' (*Iustitia Dei* 189). The question debated in the volume edited by Husbands & Trier is 'whether imputed righteousness is fictive, forensic or transformative' (*Justification* 7); and see the vigorous debate between Garlington and John Piper, on the theme of 'Imputation or Union with Christ?', in Garlington's *Defense* 107-97; Garlington justifiably insists that if justification is 'the article by which the church stands or falls', no less is christology — 'the church stands or falls with Christ' (211). E. Käsemann's famous redefinition of divine righteousness as a gift with 'the character of power' ('"The Righteousness of God" in Paul', *New Testament Questions of Today* [London: SCM, 1969] 168-82 [here 170]) was an attempt to resolve the tension between 'declare righteous' and 'make righteous' (176). Käsemann's argument is taken up by Strecker, *Theology* 152-5; its importance recognised earlier, e.g., by P. T. O'Brien, 'Justification in Paul and Some Crucial Issues in the Last Two Decades', in D. A. Carson, ed., *Right with God: Justification in the Bible and the World* (Carlisle: Paternoster, 1992) 69-95 (here 70-8). In the debate within conservative Reformed tradition, Schreiner has been persuaded that 'righteousness is forensic rather than transformative' and treats the subject differently from his *Romans* (*Paul* 192 n. 2, 203-9); and Waters insists that justification is entirely forensic and righteousness entirely imputed (*Justification* e.g. 171, 180-1, 187); I need simply refer them to Bird, *Saving Righteousness* — e.g. as in n. 383 below.

336 Characteristically Catholic is Kertelge's qualification of the Reformation 'sola fide' in summing up his discussion of 'Faith and Justification': 'In Paul faith always means obedience to the saving will of God and therefore contains an active element as a person complies with the claim of God' (225). Donfried draws attention to the balance achieved in the Lutheran-Roman Catholic *Joint Declaration on the Doctrine of Justification* (Grand Rapids: Eerdmans, 2000), as indicated in its final sentence: 'By grace alone, in faith in Christ's saving work and not because of any merit on our part, we are accepted by God and receive the Holy Spirit, *who renews our hearts while equipping and calling us to good works*' ('Justification and Last Judgment' 292 my emphasis).

337 '. . . in grasping Christ by faith, people are accounted as really having "done the law" . . . this does not mean that Christian behaviour is how the law is fulfilled' (Moo, *Romans* 483-5); 'He fulfills the law in that he *believes* in Christ' (Bergmeier, *Gesetz* 79); R. H. Gundry, 'The Nonimputation of Christ's Righteousness', in Husbands & Trier, *Justification* 17-45: 'what God counts as righteousness consists in faith' (25).

338 C. H. Cosgrove, 'Justification in Paul: A Linguistic and Theological Reflection', *JBL* 106 (1987) 653-70, attempts to resolve the dilemma by distinguishing justification *by means of* works from justification *on the basis of* works (662-4) and can even assert, 'Past justification provides neither the grounds of exemption from future wrath nor the model for such exemption' (667).

339 B. Byrne, 'Living Out the Righteousness of God: The Contribution of Rom 6:1–8:13 to an Understanding of Paul's Ethical Presuppositions', *CBQ* 43 (1981) 557-81: 'it is through living out or, rather, allowing Christ to live out this righteousness within oneself that eternal life is gained' (558); P. Stuhlmacher, *Paul's Letter to the Romans* (Louisville: Westminster John Knox, 1994) 120; 'Christ does the good works of the Christians' (Laato, *Paulus und das Judentum* 203); 'Christ — the new person — is present within faith, performing his works'

all believers continue to be sinners, should we regard final as well as initial justification as justification of the ungodly — all that the believer contributes to
his/her justification being only his/her sin? The crucial judgment would then
be only of the believer as believer, without reference to any character of faithful living.

Or in more recent terms, is the difference between Jewish and Pauline
soteriology that the former is essentially optimistic (anthropological optimism), whereas Paul is essentially pessimistic (anthropological pessimism)?
Timo Laato has placed this distinction at the centre of his thesis, and concludes
that in Judaism 'Salvation requires human cooperation. It does not rest per se
on the grace of God'. He finds 'a basic difference between the Jewish and the
Pauline structure of religion. "Staying in" rests in the first instance on the decision of man in the strength of his free will', whereas 'in Paul's case [it rests] on
the inworking of God by means of the gospel'.[340] Similarly for Timo Eskola
'the most crucial difference between Paul and his Jewish tradition is that he
radicalized his anthropology'. 'In a synergistic context a totally negative anthropology is impossible. This is why the original feature of Paul's theology is
the radicalization of the concept of sin'. 'In Paul's soteriology there is no room
for synergism'.[341] Don Hagner takes up the same theme: 'Paul abandoned the
synergism of Jewish soteriology for the monergism of total dependence upon
the grace of God in Christ'.[342]

In the current debate the principal answer to the conundrum is found in the
Spirit. In contrast to the failure of the old covenant to meet the demands of the
law, members of the new covenant are enabled or empowered to 'fulfil the requirements of the law' by the Spirit (Rom. 8.4); 'those who have the Spirit actually keep the law'.[343] In commenting on Rom. 2.7-10, Stuhlmacher speaks of
those who have been granted 'a new nature in righteousness and the spiritual
ability to do what is right'.[344] And Bergmeier comments: 'The law finds true
fulfilment first on the level of the Spirit. . . . In the mind of Paul one should
speak not of a *nova obedientia,* but of an obedience now possible for the first

---

(Seifrid, *Christ, our Righteousness* 149). Garlington continues the first passage quoted in
n. 334 above: 'It is *in Christ* that one becomes a "doer of the law"; and the Christian's loving
obedience to God is nothing other than the extension to him/her of the loving righteousness
of *Christ himself* (*Faith* 71).

[340] Laato, *Paulus und das Judentum* 190, 194, 210.

[341] Eskola, *Theodicy and Predestination* 125-8, 140, 161-4.

[342] Hagner, 'Paul and Judaism' 92. Similarly Seifrid: Paul 'no longer viewed God as coop-
erating with human effort within the framework of the covenant with Israel. Now for Paul,
God's act in Christ effected salvation in itself' (*Justification* 255).

[343] Schreiner, *Romans* 404-7; 'the Spirit, not self-effort, produces obedience'; 'the Spirit's
work in a person produces obedience to the law (Rom. 2.26-29). . . . The works that are necessary for salvation . . . are evidence of a salvation already given' (*The Law and its Fulfilment*
187-8, 203; further ch. 6); similarly *Paul* 281-2 (further ch. 12).

[344] Stuhlmacher, *Romans* 47.

time'.[345] Brendan Byrne suggests that combining Jer. 31.33 (the law written 'on their hearts') and Ezek. 36.26 (placing a new spirit within) 'makes it natural [for Paul] to speak . . . of the Spirit as "law"'.[346] Gathercole speaks of 'Paul's theology of the divine empowerment of Christians' — 'the Spirit does offer power to fulfil the Torah under the new covenant' — and thus has no qualms in concluding that 'for Paul, divine action is both the source and the continuous cause of obedience for the Christian', so that belief in final vindication on the basis of obedience' can be affirmed of Paul also.[347] Similarly Westerholm readily agrees that those granted God's Spirit 'to empower their living must express the reality of their new life in suitable behavior'; God's Spirit 'enables them to serve God in a new way. . . . With faith that is active in love, believers not under the law may in fact fulfil the righteousness that the law requires'.[348]

It would be hard to deny the central thrust of such exposition. Paul, after all, emphasises the importance of Christians 'walking by the Spirit', or 'being led by the Spirit' (Rom. 8.4; 14; Gal. 5.16, 18, 25). He implies that this is different from walking according to the flesh, the deeds of the law (Rom. 7.6; Gal. 5.18, 23). He clearly sees knowledge of God's will as more effectively given by/to the renewed mind (Rom. 12.2) than by the law (Rom. 2.18).[349] He evidently distinguishes 'faith working through love' as of a different order from 'all that the law requires' (Gal. 5.3, 6).[350] Clearly then Paul saw a fundamental role for the Spirit in Christian ethics; to that extent at least his ethics can be described as 'charismatic ethics'.

The question is, however, what difference does that make? Is the outcome looked for very different from the outcome sought by the OT prophets? It

---

[345] Bergmeier, *Gesetz* 75-6, going on to cite E. Reinmuth, *Geist und Gesetz* (ThA 44; Berlin 1985): 'Obviously it is the function of the Spirit to bring to realization the fulfilment of the law's requirements which became possible in the condemnation of sin' (70); also O. Hofius, 'Gesetz und Evangelium nach 2. Korinther 3', *Paulusstudien* (WUNT 51; Tübingen ²1994) 75-120: 'The deliverance from the Torah's judgment of death is much more at one and the same time the deliverance for that new life determined by the Spirit of God, in which, in accordance with the promise of Ezek. 36.26f., the holy will of God first of all can find and does find its fulfilment' (120); similarly Schnelle, *Paulus* 489-90, 550-1.

[346] Byrne, 'The Problem of *Nomos*' 304-6; see also his 'Interpreting Romans Theologically' 237-8.

[347] *Where is Boasting?* 132, 223, 264.

[348] Westerholm, *Perspectives* 431-4; 'The "works" which Paul discounts are those of the unredeemed "flesh"; the righteous behaviour that he requires is the "fruit" of the Spirit borne in those who have responded to God's demonstration of righteousness with faith' ('Paul and the Law in Romans 9–11' 236). Similarly Seifrid: Paul 'understands the gospel to work true obedience to the Law in those who believe' ('Unrighteous by Faith' 124-5); 'The Spirit, and the Spirit alone, effects real obedience . . . the work of the Spirit is justification (initial and final) in its outworking' (private correspondence); and Laato, *Paul and Judaism* 161-2.

[349] See my *Romans* 714-5.

[350] See further 'Neither Circumcision' 101-4 (below 331-3).

cannot mean, can it, that Paul was able simply to assume that Christians would, and did(!) live perfect or sinless lives by the power of the Spirit? The claim has indeed been made that Paul so believed and taught.[351] But Paul never made the claim for himself (cf. 1 Cor. 9.26-27; Phil. 3.12). And the fact that Paul found it necessary to exhort his fellow-Christians (e.g. Rom. 6.12-19; 8.13; Col. 3.5-10, 23-25)[352] and to warn them of the perils of moral failure (1 Cor. 3.17; 10.12; 11.27-29; 2 Cor. 12.21; 13.5; Gal. 5.4; 6.7-8; Col. 1.22-23) certainly implies that he did not assume that Christians would live blameless lives.[353] On the contrary, his understanding of the process of salvation was of a *process,* of a wasting away of the 'outward person' and renewal of the 'inward' person (2 Cor. 4.16), with completeness, maturity/perfection as the goal, not as the already accomplished fact (Gal. 3.3; Phil. 1.6; Col. 1.28; 4.12).[354] But he did ex-

---

[351] Most recently by T. Engberg-Pedersen, *Paul and the Stoics* (Edinburgh: T&T Clark, 2000) 8-9, 167-8, 171-3, 231-3. For earlier references see my *Jesus and the Spirit* (London: SCM, 1975) 317. It can be argued that the Qumran community also believed that obedience by the Spirit atoned for sin and enabled the covenanters to walk with perfection in the ways of God (1QS 3.6-12).

[352] Smith eliminates the imperatives when he interprets Rom. 8.13 and Gal. 5.16 as Paul 'emphasising that those who have the Spirit *will* put to death the deeds of the body and *will* not gratify the desires of the flesh' (*Justification and Eschatology* 81 n. 91).

[353] Cf. VanLandingham: 'Paul firmly holds the possibility that believers could be rejected at the Last Judgment on the basis of their moral failure' (*Judgment and Justification* 198, 240-1); but his unwillingness to recognise the 'already' significance of conversion (as in 1 Cor. 6.11) parallels his playing down of the covenant in Judaism's covenantal nomism (see above 73; e.g. 175-6). Bell, however, denies that such warnings are real: the *sola gratia, sola fide* simply mean that all Christians will be saved (*No One Seeks for God* 252-6). Similarly J. M. Gundry-Volf, *Paul and Perseverance: Staying In and Falling Away* (WUNT 2.37; Tübingen: Mohr Siebeck, 1990); cf. the facile brevity of de Roo, *'Works of the Law' at Qumran* 132-3. Apparently, then, the famous *m. Sanhedrin* 10.1 ('All Israelites have a share in the world to come') can be rewritten to apply to Christians without qualification! VanLandingham's criticism of Gundry-Volf seems fair: 'her investigation is improperly guided by a few key passages that serve as heuristic templates against which she excludes everything else' (185-6). See also Yinger's criticism of Gundry-Volf in *Paul, Judaism and Judgment* 252 n. 171. Schreiner seems to take a strong Calvinist stand: the eternal decree cannot be broken; defection simply demonstrates that faith was never genuine (*Paul* 276-9); but he goes on to introduce qualifications through the rest of the chapter (279-305). For Waters, 'justification is a decisive and final act at the initial stages of Christian experience . . . (and) final justification (if we may so speak) is rendered certain and unalterable by God's present justification of the believer' (*Justification* 210-1). On 1 Cor. 10.1-13 in particular, see B. J. Oropeza, *Paul and Apostasy: Eschatology, Perseverance, and Falling Away in the Corinthian Congregation* (WUNT 2.115; Tübingen: Mohr Siebeck, 2000).

[354] See further my *Theology of Paul* #18. A fresh study is required of Paul's understanding of 'perfection/maturity' in comparison with the same concept in Second Temple Judaism.

[355] Phil. 2.12-13: 'work out your own salvation with fear and trembling, for it is God who energises in you both to will and to be effective for his good pleasure'. In responding to the question whether believers contribute to their own salvation, Westerholm comments: Paul 'could not be more emphatic that anything they do even as believers remains a product of divine grace' and quotes Calvin, 'we are justified not without works yet not through works' (*Perspectives* 402 n. 143).

pect the process to produce a tested, approved character *(dokimē)* (Rom. 5.4; 2 Cor. 2.9), a metamorphosis into the image of the Creator (Rom. 12.2; 2 Cor. 3.18; Col. 3.10) as the end result. So in Paul's soteriology, faith and the Spirit do not reduce or remove the human responsibility of obedience (Rom. 1.5; 15.18; 16.19; 1 Cor. 11.16; 2 Cor. 10.5-6; Phil. 2.12;[355] 2 Thess. 3.14), and the expected outcome is not simply imputed righteousness but *transformed persons*. This need not count as a denial that for Paul the righteousness found finally acceptable in the believer at the final judgment is and always will be an 'alien righteousness',[356] but equally, such an affirmation should not be seen as a denial that the believer, the one who 'walks by the Spirit' is expected to fulfil the requirements of the law. It is not very helpful to insist that justification is entirely extrinsic and forensic,[357] if it narrows down the process of salvation to the single metaphor of justification and does not give sufficient attention to the transformation which is equally part of that process.

Moreover, it remains important to recall that the eschatological gift of the Spirit was understood in the OT as the means to ensure the desired obedience of the law (Deut. 30.6; Ezek. 36.26-27; cf. Jer. 31.31-34). Also that Paul/the first Christians regarded the gift of the Spirit as equivalent to the promised circumcision of the heart (Rom. 2.28-29; 2 Cor. 3.3, 6; Phil. 3.3). Was not the obvious implication, then, that the conduct enabled by the Spirit is the conduct which answers to the will of God in the Torah? This is certainly how Paul seems to have thought. He states explicitly that the goal of Christian conduct, as enabled by the Spirit, is the 'fulfilment' of the law (Rom. 8.4).[358] The law can be described as 'the law of faith', because faith 'establishes' the law (Rom. 3.31). Faith working through love 'fulfils' the whole law (Gal. 5.6, 14).[359] Even if circumcision can now be reckoned as of no importance in terms of God's ongoing will, keeping God's commandments remains a priority for Christians (1 Cor. 7.19).[360]

---

[356] McGrath, *Iustitia Dei* 189-90.

[357] As Waters does (*Justification* 173, 180-1).

[358] Gathercole is somewhat disingenuous when he follows Westerholm in writing: 'fulfilment of the Torah is a by-product rather than the goal of Christian obedience. The Christian believer does not set out to fulfill Torah, but the Torah is nevertheless fulfilled in him or her: "Paul is describing, not prescribing Christian behaviour" when he talks of Torah-fulfillment' (*Where is Boasting?* 128, citing Westerholm, now *Perspectives* 434). More realistic is the comment of J. Lambrecht & R. W. Thompson, *Justification by Faith: The Implications of Romans 3:27-31* (Wilmington: Glazier, 1989): 'Paul specifically draws attention to human behaviour. The just requirement of the law is only fulfilled in persons who actually obey the law' (68).

[359] 'Living faith necessarily comes to concrete expression in the actions of love' (Hahn, *Theologie* 1.289-90).

[360] See also 'Paul et la Torah' #3.2 (= 456-7 below). Westerholm indulges in special pleading when he comments on 1 Cor. 7.19 that 'the statement need mean no more than that submitting to God's will is essential' (*Perspectives* 435 n. 64); see also n. 206 above.

So the end in view is the same — keeping the commandments, obeying the will of God still expressed in and through the law. Of course, Paul understands it as the law interpreted through faith, the law of love, the law of Christ.[361] But if I am right, it is still the law. It is obviously true that certain laws had diminished in significance for Paul, circumcision in particular. But 'keeping the commandments of God' still remained important for the Christian. And however Paul regarded circumcision and the laws of clean and unclean, the laws on idolatry and illicit sexual conduct remained in full force so far as he was concerned.[362] Or in the more general terms of Rom. 2.6-11, it was still imperative that Christians persevered in doing good, in 'working the good', since for Christians also favourable judgment would be dependent on that quality of living.[363] The fact that Paul retained such a lively sense that Christians too must be judged, however Christ and the Spirit effected their conduct, should not be downplayed, for judgment implies responsibility to obey, to do, to work — and to be judged in regard to that responsibility.

What difference, then, does the coming of the eschatological Spirit make in this whole question? At the very least a more effective doing of God's will appears to be the appropriate answer. But does that make any difference to the Pauline agreement that judgment will proceed 'according to works'? Does that make any difference to the implication of a degree of conditionality in Paul's understanding of the judgment of believers? He may have been relatively relaxed about the issue in 1 Cor. 3.11-15: so long as the foundation (Jesus Christ) remains secure, salvation itself is secure.[364] But elsewhere, as already noted, there remains an uncertainty as to whether his work and the conversions he had brought about would be 'in vain' (1 Cor. 15.2; 2 Cor. 6.1; Gal. 4.11; Phil. 2.14-16; 1 Thess. 3.5).[365] Is it unfair, then, to wonder whether the difference between Jewish failure to fulfil the law and Christian success in fulfilling the law is exaggerated — on the grounds, perhaps, that there *must* be a differ-

---

[361] See further my *Theology of Paul* #23.

[362] See further my *Theology of Paul* ##2.2 and 24.7, ##5.5 and 24; cf. Tomson's thesis (above n. 310). It is worth noting that Paul does not refer to avoidance of idolatry or *porneia* (sexual license) as 'works of the law', even though such avoidance is 'doing the law'. This strengthens the suggestion that for Paul the phrase 'works of the law' is not simply to be equated with 'doing the law' but is a negative characterisation of the motivation for 'doing the law' which so conflicted with his gospel for all who believe.

[363] Cf. Bergmeier, *Gesetz* 52-4; 'these verses state Paul's personal view' (Gathercole, *Where is Boasting?* 126).

[364] Cf. F. Avemarie, 'Die Wiederkehr der Werke', *Jahrbuch für evangelikale Theologie* 19 (2005) 123-38 (here 130).

[365] See further my 'Jesus the Judge' 49-50 (= 409 below), and above at nn. 312, 353. Stuhlmacher fails to give weight to this conditional element in so many of Paul's formulations in *Revisiting* 69; but in his *Romans* he had already noted that 'for Paul no salvation was possible in the case of a believer who impugns or repudiates the gospel (Gal. 1:8; 2 Cor. 11:4, 13-15; Phil. 3:18f.)' (47).

ence between the two patterns of religion, and that so far as ethics is concerned the difference can only be found in the gift of the eschatological Spirit, and that the Spirit *must* have made a difference, otherwise the distinction/antithesis between Christianity and Judaism cannot be sustained?[366] For unless Christians are in fact notably more loving than others, and not just loving God but loving the neighbour as themselves, one cannot help wondering where and what the difference is.

And on the crucial point of dispute, what is the difference? If the finding that Judaism's soteriology was synergistic means that salvation was in at least some measure dependent on obeying the law, then we note that Paul expected believers to obey the law, and warned them that if they did not fulfil the law, in that they continued to live according to the flesh, they would die (Rom. 8.4, 13).[367] Does not *any* emphasis on human responsibility before God run the risk of being rebuked as synergistic? — an echo of the long-running argument as to whether faith itself is a human action and therefore a 'work'.[368] The difficulty which commentators have found with fitting Rom. 2.6-11 into their reconstruction of Paul's doctrine of justification by faith is telling at this point. For if, on the one hand, *no one* does any good, *no one* fits the description of 2.7 and 10, then Rom. 2.6 and 10 are a dead letter, applying to no one,[369] and it is hard to escape the inference that Paul was being frivolous in so speaking of the most solemn of all subjects.[370] But if, on the other hand, Paul is entirely serious,

---

[366] Cf. Räisänen's typically trenchant comments (*Paul and the Law* 118); and Longenecker's critique of Gathercole ('Critiquing the "New Perspective"' 269-71).

[367] The tension here cannot be resolved by categorising the works which are indispensable as 'evidential' rather than 'instrumental' (as by Smith, *Justification and Eschatology* 113). It does not give enough weight to the conditional element in Paul's paraenesis; and if such a solution is acceptable to free Paul's soteriology from perceived inconsistency, why is it not acceptable for resolving the similar tension in Judaism's covenantal nomism?

[368] Cf. Bell's argument that repentance is a 'work' (*No One Seeks for God* 183). Westerholm does not hesitate to speak of faith for both Luther and Paul as 'a living, busy, active, mighty thing' ('The "New Perspective" at Twenty-Five' 38), thinking, presumably, inter alia, of Luther's comments on Gal. 5.6 and Rom. 14.23. See further Wannenwetsch, 'Luther's Moral Theology' 128-30.

[369] Bell has no hesitation in arguing that the pious Jew and the pious Gentile envisaged in Rom. 2.12-16, 26-29 *do not exist;* (Gentile) Christians are nowhere in view in Rom. 2, neither 2.7, 2.14, nor even 2.26-29 (*No One Seeks for God* 142, 151-3, 162, 194-200, 253)! For those who regard Rom. 2 as hypothetical in whole or part, see Moo, *Romans* 140-2; VanLandingham, *Judgment and Justification* 215 n. 137; de Roo, *'Works of the Law' at Qumran* 47 n. 22; add Eskola, *Theodicy and Predestination* 133-5; Watson, *Hermeneutics of Faith* 352-3 n. 57 (though he concedes that 'within Romans 2 itself, he [Paul] certainly wishes them [his anonymous righteous Gentiles] to sound like real people'); Avemarie, 'Wiederkehr' 131. The Symposium on *Paul and the Mosaic Law* was unable to agree on the matter ('In Search of Common Ground' 321; below 297).

[370] VanLandingham quotes Räisänen's *Paul and the Law* 103-4 with effect: 'It is hard to see, however, what point there would have been in taking up such a fictitious matter at all. Above all, such an imaginary Gentile would be of no use for Paul's polemic against the Jew.

on the ground that 'everyone who does good' refers only to the Christians,[371] then Paul's theology of justification by faith alone has to be qualified as final justification by faith *and* by works accomplished by the believer in the power of the Spirit. If Paul is thus vulnerable to such a charge being levied against him, despite his insistence elsewhere that justification is by faith alone and entirely on the basis of grace, then at the very least the charges brought against Judaism's 'covenantal nomism' should be a good deal less fault-finding. And if the response is that Paul believed that acceptance by God was always and only by the grace of God, quite apart from any or all subsequent obedience of the believer, should Sanders' insistence on the primacy of the covenant within Judaism's soteriology not be given more credit than his critics have allowed?

Critics, please note: my concern is *not* to argue that Paul's understanding of salvation was synergistic; I have *no* desire to promote a Pelagian or semi-Pelagian interpretation of Paul;[372] I have no doubt that I and all other believers in Christ will be saying 'the prayer of humble access' throughout our lives and to the end.[373] My concern is rather twofold: (a) to question whether the charge of synergism should be laid so confidently at the door of Judaism when some of Paul's language seems vulnerable to the same charge; and (b) to ask proponents of Pauline 'monergism' to take more seriously and with due seri-

---

How could a non-existent Gentile "condemn" him?' (*Judgment and Justification* 216). C. K. Barrett, *The Epistle to the Romans* (BNTC; London: A. & C. Black, 1957, [2]1991) had already observed: 'Paul does not say, If Gentiles were to do ... but when, or whenever ... Gentiles do the things that the law requires' (49). 2.16 hardly suggests that Paul thought of the whole process described in 2.6-16 as unreal or as rendered passé by the event of the cross; see also Yinger, *Paul, Judaism and Judgment* 176-7, and further 150-66, 178-81.

[371] There are strong arguments in favour of reading Rom. 2.14-15 as referring to Christians — see, for example, Garlington (above n. 334), Wright, 'The Law in Romans 2' 136-9, 143-9; S. G. Gathercole, 'A Law unto Themselves: The Gentiles in Romans 2.14-15 Revisited', *JSNT* 85 (2002) 27-49; VanLandingham, *Judgment and Justification* 228-32; Bird, *Saving Righteousness* 158-72 — but the arguments can hardly avoid carrying 2.6 and 10 with them. Otherwise Räisänen, *Paul and the Law* 103-5 (Paul is speaking about Gentiles who fulfil the law outside the Christian community).

[372] The accusation is that of Waters, *Justification* 186.

[373] 'Lord, we come to your table trusting in your mercy and not in any goodness of our own. We are not worthy even to gather up the crumbs under your table, but it is your nature always to have mercy, and on that we depend'. At the same time I want to sing with Charles Wesley:

Forth in thy name, O Lord, I go,
  My daily labour to pursue,
Thee, only thee, resolved to know
  In all I think, or speak, or do.

Thee may I set at my right hand,
  Whose eyes my inmost substance see,
And labour on at thy command,
  And offer all my works to thee.

The task thy wisdom has assigned
  O let me cheerfully fulfil,
In all my works thy presence find,
  And prove thy good and perfect will.

For thee delightfully employ
  Whate'er thy bounteous grace has given,
And run my course with even joy,
  And closely walk with thee to heaven.

ousness the other Pauline teaching and exhortations referred to above.[374] In the latter connection, I have to insist that it is Paul's own teaching and urgings which force the issue upon us. According to 2 Cor. 5.10, the judgment on each will be according to what *each* has done. Even if done by (the indwelling) Christ or in the power of the Spirit, the doer is the individual and judgment will be in accordance with that doing. It is that Pauline understanding of final judgment which has to be integrated with the Pauline understanding of justification by faith. I do not for a minute suppose that Paul was not aware of the danger that too much emphasis on 'the obedience of faith', on 'putting to death the deeds of the body', and such like, could lead to reliance upon and pride in achievement. But that clearly did not prevent him from urging such responsibility upon believers. The integration here is one which both sides of the debate occasioned by the new perspective need to work hard to retain.

4.4 (12) Participation in Christ

There *is* a difference between the soteriology of Second Temple Judaism and that of Paul. And the difference is obviously summed up in Jesus Christ. The assertion is almost axiomatic and hardly needs to be argued for. But the difference is not that one placed responsibility to obey on those to whom it held out the prospect of salvation, while the other promised salvation to a passive faith in Christ. Not that one called for a moral transformation and a lived out obedience, while the other resigned itself to a life of moral failure since the saving righteousness of Christ could never be more than imputed. Not that one warned that salvation could be lost by those who failed to obey, while the other held out unconditional assurance to faith expressed in baptism in the name of Christ. What then?

This brings us to the last and most serious issue raised in criticism of the new perspective — the implications for christology. For if Second Temple Judaism and early Christianity were so similar in the inter-relationship their soteriologies maintained between divine grace and human response (#4.3(11)), then was there any need for Christ to live and die? If the old covenant was so effective, then what need of the new? — 'if it ain't broke, it don't need fixing'![375] Or if the new covenant was simply a renewal and more effective implementation of the old, then the importance of the gift of the Spirit is clear (note again Ezek. 36.26-27), but why Christ, and why his death?[376] If Judaism and Chris-

---

[374] Above 77-8, 85-8. McGrath notes that the Formula of Concord did not endorse monergism and radically modified Luther's own teaching (*Iustitia Dei* 217-9).

[375] So e.g. Eskola: 'Justification, in this context, means in no sense an inauguration of something new. . . . It is rather a confirmation of the old covenant' (*Theodicy and Predestination* 224).

[376] F. Watson, 'The Triune Divine Identity: Reflections on Pauline God Language, in Dis-

tianity both hold out not so very different versions of covenantal nomism, then Christ died to no purpose.[377]

The question is a real and important one — but not just for the new perspective. If Abraham provides a model for saving faith, then it is a faith which presumably can still be exercised in God, quite apart from Christ. If Jesus' own parable of the Prodigal Son (Luke 15) is an adequate expression of the gospel, then we should note that it lacks the role of a saviour son. The problem is an old one. It lies at the heart of 19th century liberalism and late 20th century neo-liberalism. In both cases the role of Jesus as teacher is set in contrast to Paul's gospel of cross and resurrection.[378] Does not the new perspective fall into the same trap? As the liberal and neo-liberal quests of the historical Jesus emphasise the Jewish and wisdom character of Jesus' teaching, and so open up a gulf between Jesus and the Christianity of his followers, so the new perspective by drawing attention to the Jewishness of the gospel may be running the danger of reducing or even denying its most distinctive Christian element.

Peter Stuhlmacher in particular has protested that the new perspective does not give enough weight to Rom. 8.31-34:

What therefore shall we say in view of these things? If God is for us, who is against us? He who indeed did not spare his own Son but gave him up for us all, how shall he not also with him give us all things? Who will bring charges against the elect of God? It is God who justifies. Who is there to condemn? It is Christ (Jesus) who died, rather was raised, who also is at the right hand of God, who also intercedes on our behalf.

The key point for Stuhlmacher is that the text demonstrates that final justification is wholly dependent on Christ's saving death; not just initial justification (Rom. 5.1) but final judgment. Since Paul regards no one as a doer of the law

---

agreement with J. D. G. Dunn', *JSNT* 80 (2000) 99-124, is deeply worried that I am in danger of making Paul's christology 'redundant' (109); the concern is shared by Gathercole ('Justified by Faith' 163-8); also by Carson: 'it is less clear to me that Dunn sees how radically Christocentric Paul's reading of the Old Testament really is' ('Mystery and Fulfillment' 435).

[377] Kim repeatedly accuses me of self-contradiction and of ignoring and even of adamantly refusing to acknowledge the christological insights present in the Damascus christophany (*Paul and the New Perspective* e.g. 15-19, 48-9), but his reading of most of my earlier work is so tendentious and he so consistently misses the point of my concerns (the margins of my copy of his book are covered with exclamation marks!) that it is probably better to leave the evaluations of our disagreements to others, if they can be bothered. Similarly O'Brien: 'According to Dunn, Paul did not receive new convictions about Christology or soteriology or fresh insights about the law' ('Was Paul Converted?' 367-9). I find that an astonishing misrepresentation, especially in view of the care I took on the point in my 'Paul's Conversion' 81, 83-4 (below 352, 354-5). To protest that Paul's call to become apostle to the Gentiles has not been given sufficient attention in the study of Paul's conversion, as I do, is *not* to deny that other christological and soteriological insights were given to Paul at the same time.

[378] See the critiques in my *Jesus Remembered,* particularly 48-9, 61-3; the contrast is clear in the characteristic and sustained emphases of Geza Vermes, *The Religion of Jesus the Jew* (London: SCM, 1993); also *The Authentic Gospel of Jesus* (London: Penguin, 2003).

(Rom. 3.9-18), the only chance of salvation for Jew and Gentile alike is by faith in Christ Jesus. Only when Christ speaks on their behalf before the throne of judgment can there be any hope of a verdict of acquittal. 'Since all men are sinners, they themselves cannot be recognised as righteous doers of the whole law, even if they have done some good. Without Christ and his intercession they are lost'.[379] On this interpretation, of course, the issue raised in #4.3(11) above ceases to pose a problem. For no one, no Christian, can 'fulfil' the law or keep the commandments. So far as final justification is concerned, the Spirit indwelling Christians makes no difference! Talk of Christians being presented 'pure' *(hagnos, eilikrinēs)*, 'blameless' *(amōmos, aproskopos)*, 'faultless' *(amemptos)*, 'irreproachable' *(anegklētos)* and 'mature/perfect' *(teleios)* at the coming of Christ changes nothing so far as final judgment is concerned, despite the clear implications of passages like 1 Cor. 1.8, 2 Cor. 11.2, Phil 1.6, 10, Col. 1.22, 28 and 1 Thess. 3.13; 5.23.[380] To make this point is not to question the centrality and *sine qua non* of divine grace or that the believer is totally dependent on its enabling, which are consistent features of Paul's teaching on the subject elsewhere (Rom. 6.22-23; 1 Cor. 15.10; Gal. 2.20; Phil. 2.13; 4.13). But by the same token, the outcome which Paul looked for and expected ('blameless', 'faultless', 'irreproachable' etc.) should not be sidelined.[381]

A partial answer, of course, could be that Paul envisaged the possibility in effect of Christ becoming an adversary rather than an advocate, for those who failed to retain faith in Christ (1 Cor. 15.2). Paul implies as much in Gal. 5.4, and it coheres with the warning Jesus himself had given (Luke 12.8-9 pars.). In

---

[379] Personal correspondence with Professor Stuhlmacher, in May 2003. Seifrid's exposition of Luther's understanding of justification and its restatement by Stuhlmacher is very helpful at this point ('Paul's Use of Righteousness Language' 67-74): justification 'includes within its scope deliverance at the final judgment. . . . Without in any way diminishing the reality of the righteousness at work in us, we find then the whole of that righteousness outside ourselves in Christ' (74). Similarly in Stuhlmacher's earlier essay, 'The Law as a Topic of Biblical Theology', *Reconciliation, Law and Righteousness: Essays in Biblical Theology* (Philadelphia: Fortress, 1986) 110-33: 'Paul expressly states that the promise that the crucified and risen Christ will intercede for believers in the last judgment and that they will finally be vindicated applies even if they with their actions fail in the sight of God (cf. Rom. 8:31ff.; 1 Cor. 3:11-15)' (129). Bell's refutation of 'double justification' (*No One Seeks for God* 256) is equivalent in effect: the first justification (Rom. 5.1) is decisive and final.

[380] Seifrid: 'The only point where one might wish for greater clarity is in Stuhlmacher's insistence on the *inherent connection* between "imputed" and "effective" righteousness' ('Paul's Use of Righteousness Language' 74). Cf. Donfried's earlier criticism of Stuhlmacher ('Justification and Last Judgment' 257-60). In regard to Stuhlmacher's evident concern to be faithful to what he regards as the critical insight of the Reformation, Donfried wags a reproachful finger: 'the issue is to correctly understand Paul, not the Reformation' (260).

[381] 'When Paul looks ahead to the future and asks, as well he might, what God will say on the last day, he holds up as his joy and crown, not the merits and death of Jesus, but the churches he has planted who remain faithful to the gospel' (Wright, *Paul: Fresh Perspectives* 148). Of course, Wright does not ignore Rom. 8.31-34; his point is that neither should passages like Phil. 4.1 be ignored!

which case any good done by the apostate would not count on his/her behalf, so long as faith in Christ was the decisive criterion of justification, initial or final. That would leave us, be it noted, back with the equivalent Jewish conviction that the Israelite maintained his place within the covenant by faithfulness, but lost it by apostasy; by turning to other gods, the erstwhile member of the covenant annulled the covenant so far as his own membership of the covenant was considered. In the final judgment the fact that he had been born a member of the covenant people would not count in his favour. Ironically, then, the new covenant would be understood to operate just like the old, with election *in Christ* replacing the election *of Israel*.

There is, however, a more profound answer which provides what seems to me a better expression of the inter-relationship between the divine grace and the obedience of faith, both so prominent in Paul's letters. It lies in the recognition that Paul's gospel is only partially expressed through the forensic metaphor of justification.[382] The gospel is also expressed in terms of the gift of the Spirit. But also in terms of identification with Christ.[383] The point is not simply that justifi-

---

[382] In accusing me of 'nominalism', Waters (*Justification* 114-7, 177, 192) reveals his failure to appreciate that while a metaphor is *not* literal it *is* referential (see e.g. my *Jesus Remembered* 403).

[383] Hence the three key chapters in my *Theology of Paul* ##14-16 — 'Justification by faith', 'Participation in Christ' and 'the Gift of the Spirit'; similarly Schnelle, *Paulus* 454-93. Here again I should perhaps recognise the influence of Calvin more than that of Luther (Wendel, *Calvin* 234-42; McGrath, *Iustitia Dei* 223-6). It is important at this point to avoid the polarisation of 'justification' and 'participation' encouraged by the well known assertion of A. Schweitzer, *The Mysticism of Paul the Apostle* (London: Black, 1931) — 'The doctrine of righteousness by faith is therefore a subsidiary crater, which has formed within the rim of the main crater — the mystical doctrine of redemption through being-in-Christ' (225) — and given fresh currency by Sanders, *Paul and Palestinian Judaism* 453-72, 502-8, 514, 548-9; also Kuula, *Law* 1.37-45, and *Law* 2 chs. 2–3, 9. Laato puts the point well: 'In the final analysis, they [juridical and participatory categories] are like two sides of the same medal. Separated from the juridical categories, the participatory categories threaten to generate an enthusiastic interest in one's own inner life. On the other hand, independent of the participatory categories, the juridical categories run the risk of becoming nothing more than an empty doctrine' ('Paul's Anthropological Considerations' 349). Bird prefers the term 'incorporated righteousness' (rather than 'imputed righteousness': '*at the exegetical level* union with Christ rather than imputation is the most useful way of articulating Paul's ideas about justification' (5; also ch. 4 and 182). VanLandingham, *Judgment and Justification,* is particularly vulnerable to criticism here since he gives little thought to the bearing of Paul's christology on the question and none at all to the highly significant role of the 'in Christ' motif in Paul's soteriology. D. A. Campbell, *The Quest for Paul's Gospel: A Suggested Strategy* (JSNTS 274; London: T&T Clark, 2005) makes a curiously abstract attempt to give a 'participationist' account exclusive theological hegemony: the 'JF (justification by faith) model' must be 'eliminated' and the 'SH (salvation-history) model' subordinated to the 'PPME (pneumatologically participatory martyrological eschatology) model'. But his definition of 'model' (as providing a coherent account — 32) is far from adequate; he makes no real attempt to justify 'model' as an exhaustive and exclusive explanation; and a convincing argument that the elements of PPME constitute such a single coherent model is lacking. Can the complexity of a spiritual reality which includes aspects both individual and corporate, both historical and eschatological,

cation is 'in Christ' (1 Cor. 1.30; Gal. 2.17; Phil. 3.9) — an emphasis given too little attention in the current discussion. It is more that identification with Christ is a *process* to be worked through and not simply a *status* to be accepted. It is through and by means of this strand of his theology that Paul brings out most effectively his understanding of salvation as a life-long process; in some contrast, 'justification' focuses only on the beginning and end of the process. The key element in that process is 'becoming like Christ', being conformed to Christ's image (Rom. 8.29; 1 Cor. 15.49; 2 Cor. 3.18; Phil. 3.21). It is not that believers are 'saved' there and then when they first believe; salvation is the end point of a process of transformation (Rom. 5.10; 13.11; 1 Cor. 1.18; 2 Cor. 2.15; 1 Thess. 5.8).[384] In summary, that process can be characterised as a growing conquest of or detachment from the flesh, a wasting away of the 'outward person', while the 'inner person' is renewed. It is a process of ongoing renewal by the Spirit until the whole person has been reclaimed for God, when the body also will be transformed into the vehicle of the Spirit in the resurrection, a *sōma pneumatikon,* a 'spiritual body' (Rom. 8.11, 23; 1 Cor. 15.44-50; 2 Cor. 4.16–5.5; Gal. 6.8). Above all, it is a process of sharing in Christ's death, of being conformed to his death, with a view to a full sharing in his resurrection (Rom. 6.5; 8.17; 2 Cor. 4.17-18; 13.4; Gal. 2.19).[385]

The point, then, is that Paul envisaged salvation as *a process of transformation* of the believer, not simply of the believer's *status,* but of the *believer* as such. Final judgment will be the measure of that transformation. Central to the process is the believer's moral determination and obedience. Fundamental to the process is the enabling, in motivation and doing, of the Spirit. But the transformation is 'in Christ', 'into Christ', 'with Christ', in the 'body of Christ', and into the image of Christ, the new creation.[386] If it is true that Christ alone

---

both christological and pneumatological, and in Paul is evidently capable of being metaphored in such diversity, be reduced to a single 'model' or narrow rationality?

[384] Hence the hesitation in attributing Eph. 2.8-10 to Paul himself (above #3.4(8)).

[385] At this point I refer again to my *Theology of Paul* #18, where I attempt to fill out what has been a much too neglected aspect of Paul's theology and gospel. M. J. Gorman has developed the theme in *Cruciformity: Paul's Narrative Spirituality of the Cross* (Grand Rapids: Eerdmans, 2001); and cf. Grindheim's thesis in *The Crux of Election:* 'To be elect implies being conformed to the image of Christ and his cross . . . ; the Jewish confidence in the election of Israel must be reproved because it was incompatible with the cross of Christ' (199-200). Smith recognises the importance of both 'justification' and 'participation' in Paul's soteriology, though he attempts to subordinate the latter to the former, and he misses the depth of the 'being conformed to Christ's death' motif (*Justification and Eschatology* 109-112). Despite his title, D. G. Powers, *Salvation through Participation: An Examination of the Notion of the Believers' Corporate Unity with Christ in Early Christian Soteriology* (Leuven: Peeters, 2001), is primarily concerned with the corporate implications of Paul's 'dying for' formulae (but here see ch. 5).

[386] Bird talks of the need 'to accentuate the effective nature of justification' and quotes Calvin's *Institutes* 3.16.1: 'we are justified not without works, and yet not by works, since in the participation in Christ, by which we are justified, is contained not less sanctification than justification' (*Saving Righteousness* 111)

had/has the 'native ability' to measure up to God's pattern for humanity, then it is by becoming like Christ that those 'in Christ' will satisfy the final inspection. Not by being 'in Christ' as a mystical experience or by virtue of an ecclesiastical rite. Not solely by having righteousness imputed as an 'alien righteousness'. And certainly not by Pelagian or semi-Pelagian self-effort. But by a progressive transformation into Christ's likeness (2 Cor. 3.18), whose climax and completion is the transformation/resurrection of the body (2 Cor. 4.16–5.5). 'Justification' and 'new creation' (2 Cor. 5.17; Gal. 6.15) go together.

There is a passage in which more clearly than anywhere else Paul brings two if not all three of his models of salvation into interaction — Phil. 3.8-14.[387] There it is clear that the 'blamelessness' he had enjoyed under the law as a zealous Pharisee no longer counted for anything once he had come to know Christ. The 'surpassing greatness of knowing Christ' rendered any potential advantage null and void (3.6-8). But that is only the beginning of the story of salvation. For he also wanted to be 'found in Christ', a condition which he elaborates with his chief metaphors. (a) To be 'found in Christ' means not having his own righteousness from the law, but the righteousness which is through faith in Christ, the righteousness which is from God to faith. But it means also (b) knowing the power of Christ's resurrection (we could substitute the Spirit here without changing the substance of the thought).[388] And it means also (c) sharing in Christ's sufferings and being conformed to his death, 'if perhaps/somehow' he might attain to the resurrection from the dead. It is this third strand which takes the discussion beyond the options discussed in #4.3(11) above, both justification as the all embracing model, and the further entirely appropriate addition of Spirit-enabled obedience.[389]

The element of conditionality should not be ignored ('if perhaps/somehow').[390] But here the condition of attaining to the resurrection, that is, of attaining to the climax and completion of the process of salvation, is not a blameless life or sustained obedience/faithfulness, but the conformity of the

---

[387] Not unfairly, Silva rebukes me for giving inadequate attention to Phil. 3.9 in my earlier work ('Law and Christianity' 352). But see now the essay written for the present volume, 'Philippians 3.2-14 and the New Perspective on Paul' (chap. 22 below).

[388] The equivalence and link between Rom. 6.4b = 7.6b = 8.4 is obvious.

[389] Though I am obviously close to the position of Garlington in nn. 334, 339 above. Wannenwetsch shows the possibility of fruitful rapprochement: 'Only in our being conformed to Christ, in our being made a Christ-like person, is the accusing function of the law overcome' ('Luther's Moral Theology' 126). Cf. F. Bovon, 'The New Person and the Law According to the Apostle Paul', *New Testament Traditions and Apocryphal Narratives* (Allison Park: Pickwick, 1995) 15-25: '. . . this newness which has been bestowed . . . is lived concretely, historically and ethically in the participation in the sufferings of Christ, that is to say in service which takes the shape of suffering' (22).

[390] As already noted, it is this element of conditionality which undermines the thoroughgoing monergism which, for example, Hagner (n. 342 above) advocates as the Christian answer and contrast to Jewish synergism.

believer (in character and conduct) to the total self-giving of the cross. 'Justification' and the gift of the Spirit might well mark the beginning of the process most effectively, just as final justification and resurrection by the power of the Spirit might well mark the end of the process most effectively. But it is *the transformation of the justified sinner by the power of the indwelling Spirit to become more and more like Christ, like Christ in his dying as well as his rising again, which best characterises the ongoing process of salvation.* Within this process there is more room for the human responsibility of sustained commitment, obedience and doing good — as Paul at once goes on to make clear when he re-engages the image of the dedicated athlete, conscious of how much of the race has still to be run and bending every fibre of his being to attain the goal (3.12-14).[391]

In short, if it is in fact the case that there is as much tension and (potential) inconsistency in Paul as in Judaism, between divine grace and human obedience, then the resolution of that tension and inconsistency is provided for Paul primarily by his understanding of the death and resurrection of Christ, not just as a once-for-all event, but as a divine power working steadily within and through believers individually and corporately to transform them to become more and more Christ-like, cross-like (cruciformed), and thus to complete the process of salvation, maturity, perfection, and blamelessness, at the end of which they can face the final judgment with confidence in Christ.

Where does such an exposition leave the debate on the new perspective? For one thing, it reminds us that the attempt to define the 'old perspective' simply in terms of Lutheranism ('the Lutheran Paul', *a la* Westerholm) is to neglect the Reformed contribution to the Reformation rediscovery of Pauline theology; Luther needs to be complemented by Calvin. For another, it reminds us that while the 'new perspective' was justified in highlighting the issue of Jewish pride in election and status before God as a fundamental factor explaining Paul's formulation of his teaching on justification, the still more fundamental insight that no one can stand before God in his/her own strength must not be obscured either. More important, so far as Paul's own theology and gospel is concerned, it reminds us that Paul's understanding of the process of salvation in terms of incorporation into and conformity with Christ is quite as central and important in his soteriology as his understanding of justification; the two cannot and never should be played off against each other. And as to Jewish/Christian relations, we can move on more confidently from such denigrations as equating covenant faithfulness with legalism and focus more sharply on the justification (or otherwise) of the Christian claim that in Jesus Messiah/Christ the hopes of Jewish prophet and seer have been fulfilled and that 'in Christ' the goal of 'the upward call of God' can finally be realised.

---

[391] See further 'Philippians 3.2-14' 487-9 below.

5. Conclusions

So, where do things stand as a result of 'the new perspective' on Paul, but also in the light of the debate which it has stirred up? Five points are certainly worth making.

1. There can surely be no possibility of scholarship in the Christian tradition going back to the old portrayal of Judaism, either now or in the first century, as an arid, sterile and narrowly legalistic religion. Likewise there can surely be no going back to an interpretation of Paul's doctrine of justification which depends on sharp antitheses between Judaism and Christianity, between law and grace, between obedience and faith, and which both feeds on and perpetuates the shameful tradition of Christian anti-Judaism.

2. The fact should not be marginalised that Paul's exposition of justification by faith and not works emerged in the context of his Gentile mission and as the defence of what was of fundamental importance to him: that the gospel was for all, for Gentile as well as Jew, and without requiring the Gentile to become a proselyte or to adopt a Jewish way of life. To recognise this is *not* to deny or play down the more fundamental fact that no person can stand before God except by God's forgiving, justifying grace. It *is* to recognise that justification by faith was never simply about individuals as such. Paul's theology of justification had a social and corporate dimension which was integral to it. To ignore Paul's protest against any suggestion that God's acceptance is somehow conditional on where a person was born, what nation or race that person belongs to, what culture or class that person has grown up within, or on that person adopting a particular pattern of individual or corporate living, is to lose one of the most important aspects of Paul's gospel. Super-power, chosennation, Western 'civilization' presumption needs to hear that aspect of Paul's doctrine as clearly today as ever before.

3. Justification by faith alone needs to be reasserted as strongly as ever it was by Paul or by Augustine or by Luther. To acknowledge dependence wholly on God the Creator and Redeemer, to glorify and worship him alone, to trust in him and give him thanks is the proper and only proper response of the creature before the Creator. But its full scope needs to be reappreciated. For justification by faith speaks against all attempts to add *anything* to the gospel as essential to salvation or to require *anything* additional to the gospel as the basis for believers to eat and work together — not excluding particular definitions of apostolic succession, eucharistic exclusivity, denial of women's ministry, assertions of biblical inerrancy, and such *extras*. Even the *insistence* on a particular formulation of the doctrine of 'justification by faith alone' can become one of the 'works' by which a self-perceived orthodoxy clouds the truth of the gospel! Today there are still many Peters who hold themselves 'separate' from other believers at the Lord's table or in mission by insisting on something as

essential *in addition to* the gospel of justification by faith, and who need to be confronted by Paul's understanding of the liberty and freedom of that gospel.

4. The inter-relationship has to be maintained between justification by faith and judgment according to works. Even if Second Temple Judaism can be shown to be synergistic in its understanding of salvation, it will not be an adequate understanding of Paul's response to deny that he called for obedience to God's will on the part of his converts and made final salvation in some measure dependent on believers living according to the Spirit. If Paul had expected himself and his converts to be transformed to become like Christ, then that expectation cannot be easily separated from his own rigorous self-discipline and his call for his converts to be obedient to the will of God. In pressing for a difference between Christianity and Judaism at this point there is a grave danger of distorting not only the soteriology of Judaism but also the soteriology of Paul. The tensions here have been long debated, but the present controversy over the new perspective shows that the debate has still a long way to run.

5. The significance Paul saw in Jesus Christ remains the primary difference between his gospel for all and the understanding of salvation in the scriptures and traditions of Israel. The eschatological significance of Christ put the old covenant into the past tense and signalled the opening of God's grace to *all* who *believe,* the fulfilment of God's purposes through Israel to the world. The possibility of the circumcised heart, of a life transformed to be like Christ's was now a reality. This also signifies that the profundity of Paul's understanding of God's saving grace cannot be adequately contained within the bounds of a single metaphor, not even the forensic metaphor of justification. To play off justification by faith and participation in Christ, or the gift of the Spirit, against each other, or to attempt to subsume one within the other, is to fail to recognise the richness of each and the limitation of each. Small minds may fret about how Christ can be both advocate and judge, how both Christ can be 'in us' and 'we in Christ', how he can be both elder brother in the Spirit and Lord and agent in creation, but Paul evidently felt no such inhibitions. He had experienced the light of the gospel of the glory of Christ, the image of God, as a gospel for all, giving assurance of acceptance now, sure hope of transformation even of sinful human beings into that image, and promise of final vindication — and that was sufficient for him.

Chapter 2

The New Perspective on Paul*

I

When chatting with other New Testament specialists I occasionally mention the fact that I am engaged in writing a commentary on Paul's letter to the Christians in Rome. The most frequent response is one of surprise, sometimes even amazement – "Not *another* commentary on Romans!" The underlying implication is that we have had quite sufficient commentaries on Romans, that surely there can be nothing new or novel to say on such a well-worked document, that a new commentator is bound to spend most of his time simply repeating the thoughts of his predecessors. I cannot say that I am particularly taken aback by such responses, because when I was first invited to write the commentary my own reaction was more or less the same – a rather stultifying sense that it had all been said before, that interpretation of Pauline theology had lost a lot of steam, and that the really interesting and challenging frontiers in New Testament studies were to be found elsewhere.

I do not for a moment want to suggest that a commentator should refrain from re-expressing the old truths and rich insights of former days and previous commentators on Paul. Mere novelty is not of itself a mark of merit, and novelty for its own sake should certainly not be encouraced in an interpreter or expositor of any text. As students of Paul we all would be the poorer if scholars like F.F. Bruce or Otto Kuss or Heinrich Schlier had refused to distil their lifetime's study of Paul into single volumes, simply because they did not have some revolutionary new theories to put forward.[1] Nor do I wish to imply that fresh thought on particular points of Pauline theology or lively debate on particular passages within the Pauline corpus has been lacking. If we think only in terms of the last few years, for example, there has been more than one controversial reconstruction of Pauline chronology.[2] Older emphases on the significance of Paul's conversion for his sub-

---

* The Manson Memorial Lecture delivered in the University of Manchester on 4 November 1982. Subsequently delivered in modified form as one of the Wilkinson Lectures in the Northen Baptist Theological Seminary, Illinois, under the title "Let Paul be Paul".

[1] F.F. Bruce, *Paul: Apostle of the Free Spirit* (Exeter, 1977); O. Kuss, *Paulus: die Rolle des Apostels in der theologischen Entwicklung der Urkirche* (Regensburg, 1971); H. Schlier, *Grundzüge einer paulinischen Theologie* (Freiburg/Basel/Wien, 1978).

[2] A. Suhl, *Paulus und seine Briefe: ein Beitrag zur paulinischen Chronologie* (Gütersloh,

sequent theology, and on the importance of the apocalyptic aspect of his teaching have been strongly and fruitfully revived.[3] There has been a challenging reappraisal of the way in which Paul was regarded in the ancient church.[4] Interesting new hypotheses on the development of Paul's thought between his writing of Galatians and his writing of Romans have been formulated,[5] and the posing of sociologically inspired questions has thrown up some important new insights.[6] The old introductory questions as to the occasion for and situation addressed by particular letters still provokes heated controversy,[7] and we can even say that a new subdivision of the literary criticism of the letters has recently been opened a dash, *not* a hyphen up – rhetorical criticism.[8] As a final example, perhaps I could be forgiven for hoping that one or two useful comments on Paul's religious experience, ecclesiology and christology have flowed from my own pen.[9]

In none of these cases, however, could I confidently say that I have been given (I speak personally) what amounts to a new perspective on Paul. In some cases the old pattern has been shaken up somewhat and the pieces have fallen a little differently. In other cases particular aspects of Paul's writing and thought have received fuller illumination or previous conclusions have had a question mark appended to them. In others I strongly suspect red herrings have been drawn in and wild geese chased. But none have succeeded in, to use a contemporary phrase, "breaking the mould" of Pauline studies, the mould into which descriptions of Paul's work and thought have regularly been poured for many decades now. There is, in my judgment, only one work written during the past decade or two which deserves that accolade. I refer to the volume entitled *Paul and Palestinian Judaism* by E.P. Sanders of McMaster University in Canada.[10]

1975), R. Jewett, *Dating Paul's Life* (London, 1979); G. Lüdemann, Paulus, *der Heidenapostel Band I: Studien zur Chronologie* (Göttingen, 1980).

[3] S. Kim, *The Origin of Paul's Gospel* (Tübingen, 1981); J.C. Beker, *Paul the Apostle: the Triumph of God in Life and Thought* (Philadelphia, 1980).

[4] A. Lindemann, *Paulus im ältesten Christentum* (Tübingen, 1979).

[5] J.W. Drane, *Paul: Libertine or Legalist?* (London, 1975); H.Hübner, *Das Gesetz bei Paulus* (Göttingen, 1978, ²1980).

[6] See particularly the work of G. Theissen, *Studien zur Soziologie des Urchristentums* (Tübingen, 1979), partial ET, *The Social Setting of Pauline Christianity* (Edinburgh, 1982).

[7] See e.g. K.P. Donfried, ed., *The Romans Debate* (Minneapolis, 1977); R. McL. Wilson, "Gnosis in Corinth", *Paul and Paulinism: Essays in Honour of C.K. Barrett*, ed. M.D. Hooker & S.G. Wilson (London, 1982) pp. 102–14; G. Howard, *Paul: Crisis in Galatia* (Cambridge, 1979).

[8] See particularly H.D. Betz, "The Literary Composition and Function of Paul's Letter to the Galatians", *NTS*, 21 (1974–75), 353–79; also *Galatians* (Hermeneia: Philadelphia, 1979); W. Wuellner, "Paul's Rhetoric of Argumentation in Romans", *CBQ*, 38 (1976), 330–51, reprinted in *The Romans Debate* (above n. 7), pp. 152–74; also "Greek Rhetoric and Pauline Argumentation", *Early Christian Literature and the Classical Intellectual Tradition: in honorem R.M. Grant*, ed. W.R. Schoedel & R.L. Wilken (Paris, 1979), pp. 177–88; R. Jewett, "Romans as an Ambassadorial Letter", *Interpretation*, 36 (1982), pp. 5–20.

[9] I refer particularly to *Jesus and the Spirit* (London, 1975) and *Christology in the Making* (London, 1980).

[10] E.P. Sanders, *Paul and Palestinian Judaism: a Comparison of Patterns of Religion* (Lon-

Sanders' basic claim is not so much that Paul has been misunderstood as that the picture of Judaism drawn from Paul's writings is historically false, not simply inaccurate in part but fundamentally mistaken. What is usually taken to be the Jewish alternative to Paul's gospel would have been hardly recognized as an expression of Judaism by Paul's kinsmen according to the flesh. Sanders notes that Jewish scholars and experts in early Judaism have for long enough been registering a protest at this point, contrasting rabbinic Judaism as they understand it with the parody of Judaism which Paul seems to have rejected. Thus, for example, Solomon Schechter:

Either the theology of the Rabbis must be wrong, its conception of God debasing, its leading motives materialistic and coarse, and its teachers lacking in enthusiasm and spirituality, or the Apostle to the Gentiles is quite unintelligible;

or a few lines later, James Parkes:

... if Paul was really attacking 'Rabbinic Judaism', then much of his argument is irrelevant, his abuse unmerited, and his conception of that which he was attacking inaccurate.[11]

But such protests seem to have fallen for the most part on deaf ears. For a hundred years now, as Sanders observes, the majority of New Testament scholars have maintained a fundamental antithesis between Paul and Judaism, especially rabbinic Judaism, and have seen this antithesis as a central factor, usually the central factor in understanding Paul the Jew-become-Christian.[12]

The problem focuses on the character of Judaism as a religion of salvation. For rabbinic specialists the emphasis in rabbinic Judaism on God's goodness and generosity, his encouragement of repentance and offer of forgiveness is plain. Whereas Paul seems to depict Judaism as coldly and calculatingly legalistic, a system of 'works' righteousness, where salvation is *earned* by the *merit of* good *works.* Looked at from another angle, the problem is the way in which Paul has been understood as the great exponent of the central Reformation doctrine of *justification by faith.* As Krister Stendahl warned twenty years ago, it is deceptively easy to read Paul in the light of Luther's agonized search for relief from a troubled conscience.[13] Since Paul's teaching on justification by faith seems to

---

don, 1977). Cf. the estimate of W.D. Davies in the Preface to the 4th edition of his *Paul and Rabbinic Judaism* (Philadelphia, 1981): "a work of immense learning and penetration, a major milestone in Pauline scholarship ... of potentially immense significance for the interpretation of Paul" (pp. xxix-xxx).

[11] Sanders, *Paul*, p. 6. See the fuller survey "Paul and Judaism in New Testament scholarship" on pp. 1–12.

[12] Sanders traces the dominance of this very negative evaluation of the Judaism of Paul's time back to F. Weber, *System der altsynagogalen palästinischen Theologie aus Targum, Midrasch und Talmud* (1880), revised as *Jüdische Theologie auf Grund des Talmud und verwandter Schriften* (Leipzig, 1897). For the following paragraph see also Sanders on "The persistence of the view of Rabbinic religion as one of legalistic works-righteousness" (*Paul*, pp. 33–59).

[13] K. Stendahl, "The Apostle Paul and the Introspective Conscience of the West", *HTR*, 56

speak so directly to Luther's subjective wrestlings, it was a natural corollary to see Paul's opponents in terms of the unreformed Catholicism which opposed Luther, with first century Judaism read through the 'grid' of the early 16th century Catholic system of merit. To a remarkable and indeed alarming degree, throughout this century the standard depiction of the Judaism which Paul rejected has been the reflex of Lutheran hermeneutic. How serious this is for New Testament scholarship may be seen when we recall that the two most influential New Testament scholars of the past two generations, Rudolf Bultmann and Ernst Käsemann, both read Paul through Lutheran spectacles and both made this understanding of justification by faith their central theological principle.[14] And the most recent full-scale treatment of this area of Pauline theology, on Paul and the law, still continues to work with the picture of Paul as one who rejected the perverted attempt to use the law as a means of earning righteousness by good works.[15]

Sanders, however, has built up a different presentation of Palestinian Judaism at the time of Paul. From a massive treatment of most of the relevant Jewish literature for that period, a rather different picture emerges. In particular, he has shown with sufficient weight of evidence that for the first-century Jew, Israel's covenant relation with God was basic, basic to the Jew's sense of national identity and to his understanding of his religion. So far as we can tell now, for first-century Judaism everything was an elaboration of the fundamental axiom that the one God had chosen Israel to be his peculiar people, to enjoy a special relationship under his rule. The law had been given as an expression of this covenant, to regulate and maintain the relationship established by the covenant. So, too, righteousness must be seen in terms of this relationship, as referring to conduct appropriate to this relationship, conduct in accord with the law. That is to say, obedience to the law in Judaism was never thought of as a means of *entering* the covenant, of *attaining* that special relationship with God; it was more a matter of *maintaining* the covenant relationship with God. From this Sanders draws out his key phrase to characterize first century Palestinian Judaism, "covenantal nomism". He defines it thus:

covenantal nomism is the view that one's place in God's plan is established on the basis of the covenant and that the covenant requires as the proper response of man his obedience to its commandments, while providing means of atonement for transgression ... *Obe-*

(1963), 199–215, reprinted in his *Paul Among Jews and Gentiles* (London, 1977) pp. 78–96. See also the several recent contributions by W.D. Davies in this area – "Paul and the People of Israel", *NTS*, 24 (1977–78), 4–39; also *Paul and Rabbinic Judaisml*, pp. xxvii f.; also "Paul and the Law: Reflection on Pitfalls in Interpretation", *Paul and Paulinism* (above n. 7), pp. 4–16.

[14] E.g. R. Bultmann, *Jesus Christ and Mythology* (London, 1960), "Demythologizing is the radical application of the doctrine of justification by faith to the sphere of knowledge and thought" (p. 84); E. Käsemann, *Das Neue Testament als Kanon* (Göttingen, 1970): "Die Rechtfertigung des Gottlosen ... muss als Kanon im Kanon betrachtet werden ..." (p. 405).

[15] Hübner (above n. 5).

dience maintains one's position in the covenant, but it does not earn God's grace as such ... Righteousness in Judaism is a term which implies the *maintenance of status* among the group of the elect.[16]

If Stendahl cracked the mould of 20th century reconstructions of Paul's theological context, by showing how much it had been determined by Luther's quest for a gracious God, Sanders has broken it altogether by showing how different these reconstructions are from what we know of first-century Judaism from other sources. We have all in greater or less degree been guilty of modernizing Paul. But now Sanders has given us an unrivalled opportunity to look at Paul afresh, to shift our perspective back from the 16th century to the first century, to do what all true exegetes want to do – that is, to see Paul properly within his own context, to hear Paul in terms of his own time, to let Paul be himself.

The most surprising feature of Sanders' writing, however, is that he himself has failed to take the opportunity his own mouldbreaking work offered. Instead of trying to explore how far Paul's theology could be explicated in relation to Judaism's "covenantal nomism", he remained more impressed by the *difference* between Paul's pattern of religious thought and that of first-century Judaism. He quickly, too quickly in my view, concluded that Paul's religion could be understood only as a basically different system from that of his fellow Jews. In Christianity a quite different mode of righteousness operated from that in Judaism, righteousness which is through faith in Christ, "from God" and not "from the law" (Phil. 3.9). Paul had broken with the law for the simple reason that following the law did not result in his being "in Christ". Christ was the end of the law (Rom. 10.4). It was this change of 'entire systems' which made it unnecessary for Paul to speak about repentance or the grace of God shown in the giving of the covenant.[17]

But this presentation of Paul is only a little better than the one rejected. There remains something very odd in Paul's attitude to his ancestral faith. The Lutheran Paul has been replaced by an idiosyncratic Paul who in arbitrary and irrational manner turns his face against the glory and greatness of Judaism's covenant theology and abandons Judaism simply because it is not Christianity. It may be, of course, that Paul was totally bowled over by his encounter with the risen Christ outside Damascus, and this experience gave him a jaundiced and unfairly prejudiced view of his erstwhile faith from that time on. But Paul was by

---

[16] Sanders, *Paul*, pp. 75, 420, 544. Worth noting is the fact that J. Neusner, though fiercely critical of Sanders' methodology, nevertheless accepts Sanders' understanding of Judaism in terms of "covenantal nomism" as valid. That rabbinic discussions *presupposed* the covenant and "were largely directed toward the question of how to fulfil the covenantal obligations" is to Neusner a "wholly sound and ... self-evident proposition". "So far as Sanders proposes to demonstrate the importance to all the kinds of ancient Judaism of covenantal nomism, election, atonement, and the like, his work must be, pronounced a complete success" – "Comparing Judaisms", *History of Religions*, 18 (1978–79), 177–91 (here pp. 177, 180).

[17] See particularly Sanders, *Paul*, pp. 550–2.

no means the only Jew who became a Christian and it is difficult to see such an arbitrary jump from one 'system' to another commending itself quite as much as it in the event obviously did to so many of his fellow Jews.

The critiques of Sanders which inevitably followed have also failed in greater or less measure to capitalize on the new perspective opened up by Sanders, either because they dispute the main thrust of Sanders' thesis, or because they do not know quite what to make of Paul when viewed from that perspective. Hans Hübner, for example, continues to operate largely within the classic Reformation categories, criticizing Sanders for failing to see Paul's attack on "legalistic works-righteousness" as central for Paul's theology.[18] On the other hand, Heikki Räisänen accepts Sanders' strictures on Paul: Paul *does* misrepresent and distort the Judaism of his own day. He has separated law from covenant and adopted a Gentile point of view. Having "become internally alienated from the ritual aspects of the law" over the years he has branded "the covenantal theology of his Jewish-Christian opponents as salvation by works of the law", thus attributing to the law a different role than the Jewish Christians themselves did.[19] And Morna Hooker points out the oddity of Sanders' conclusion, that the "pattern of religion" which emerges from Sanders' study of Palestinian Judaism bears a striking similarity to what is commonly believed to be the religion of Paul, but then struggles with only little more success than Sanders to explain why it was in that case that Paul felt the need to distance himself from that Judaism.[20]

Sanders himself has returned to the subject in a monograph entitled *Paul, the Law and the Jewish People*, the manuscript of which he has kindly permitted me to read. In it he broadens out the perspective on Paul from the narrower question of "getting in and staying in" the covenant, which was the preoccupation of *Paul and Palestinian Judaism*, and restates his position in more detail. The picture of Judaism which emerges from this fuller study of Paul does correspond to Judaism as revealed in its own literature. Paul attacks covenantal nomism, the view that accepting and living by the law is a sign and condition of favoured status. It was never God's intention, so Paul argues, that one should accept the law in order to become one of the elect. "His real attack on Judaism is against the idea of the covenant ... What is wrong with the law, and thus with Judaism, is that it does not provide for God's ultimate purpose, that of saving the entire world through faith in Christ ...".[21] But he still speaks of Paul breaking with the law, he still has Paul making an arbitrary jump from one system to another and posing an antithesis between faith in Christ and his Jewish heritage in such

---

[18] H. Hübner, "Pauli Theologiae Proprium", *NTS*, 26 (1979–80), 445–73.

[19] H. Räisänen, "Legalism and Salvation by the Law", in *Die Paulinische Literatur und Theologie*, hrsg. S. Pedersen (Göttingen, 1980), pp. 63–83.

[20] M. Hooker, "Paul and Covenantal Nomism", *Paul and Paulinism* (above n. 7), pp. 47–56.

[21] Sanders, *Paul, the Law and the Jewish People*, p. 47.

sharp, black- and white-terms, that Paul's occasional defence of Jewish prerogative (as in Rom. 9.4–6) seems equally arbitrary and bewildering, his treatment of
the law and of its place in God's purpose becomes inconsistent and illogical, and
we are left with an abrupt discontinuity between the new movement centred in
Jesus and the religion of Israel which makes little sense in particular of Paul's
olive tree allegory in Rom. 11.[22]

I must confess that I find Sanders' Paul little more convincing (and much less
attractive) than the Lutheran Paul. I am not convinced that we have yet been
given the proper reading of Paul from the new perspective of first-century Palestinian Judaism opened up so helpfully by Sanders himself. On the contrary, I believe that the new perspective on Paul does make better sense of Paul than
either Sanders or his critics have so far realized. And, if I may, I would like in
what follows to make a beginning to an exegesis and description of Paul's theology from this perspective.

II

Let me attempt to demonstrate my case by focusing particularly on one verse
and attempting to set it as fully as possible into its historical context. I refer to
Gal. 2.16. This is the most obvious place to start any attempt to take a fresh look
at Paul from our new perspective. It is probably the first time in the letters of
Paul that his major theme of justification by faith is sounded. As such, the way in
which it is formulated may well tell us much, not only about the theme itself, but
about why it meant so much to Paul. We are encouraged in this hope by the fact
that this first statement seems to grow out of Paul's attempt to define and defend
his own understanding of justification, over against whatever view was held by
his fellow Jewish Christians from Jerusalem and Antioch; and also that it seems
to form the basic statement of his gospel on which he builds his plea to his Galatian converts to hold steadfast to the gospel as he first proclaimed it to them.

It will perhaps be helpful if I sketch out the immediate preceding context of
this important verse more fully. Paul has been recalling the unhappy incident at
Antioch some time previously. At Antioch Gentiles had been accepted fully
into the circle of those Jews who believed that Jesus was God's Anointed and
that, though rejected by the leaders of his own people, God had raised him from
the dead. The leading apostles at Jerusalem had already agreed that such Gentiles need not be circumcised in order to be counted as fellow believers (Gal.
2.1–10). At Antioch the custom was for all those who had been baptized in this
faith in Jesus the Christ to share a meal in common when they met – Jews
together with Gentiles. But then "certain individuals" had arrived from James in

---

[22] Cf. H. Räisänen, "Paul's Theological Difficulties with the Law", *Studia Biblica 1978*, vol.
III, ed. E. A. Livingstone (*JSNT*, Supp. 3: Sheffield, 1980), pp. 301–20.

Jerusalem (2.11), and evidently they had found it unacceptable that the Jewish Christians should act in such disregard for the food laws laid down by Moses – the laws on clean and unclean foods, the laws on the proper slaughter of animals for meat, and probably also the various regulations governing tithing, ritual purity and avoidance of idol food already current among the more devout Jews. Whatever the men from James said or however they acted, it had an effect. Peter and all the other Jewish believers, including even Paul's associate Barnabas, withdrew from the fellowship meals, presumably in order to demonstrate their continuing loyalty to their ancestral faith – that believing in Jesus did not make them any the less devout Jews (2.12–13). But Paul had confronted Peter and accused him of hypocrisy, of not following the straight path of the gospel. In front of the whole community of believers he appealed to Peter: "If you, a Jew, live like a Gentile and not like a Jew, how can you compel the Gentiles to judaize?"- that is, to observe the food laws and table regulations drawn out from the law by the devout Jews (2.14).[23] Then Paul goes on, probably not repeating the precise words he used to Peter at Antioch, but probably echoing the line of argument which he tried to develop on that occasion,[24] "We who are Jews by nature and not Gentile sinners, know that a man is not justified by works of law except through faith in Christ Jesus. And we have believed in Christ Jesus, in order that we might be justified by faith in Christ and not by works of law, because by works of law shall no flesh be justified" (2.15–16) – the last clause echoing Ps. 143.2.

What precisely was Paul arguing here? What were the nuances and overtones which his fellow Jewish Christians would have recognized and appreciated? A careful analysis may well yield fruitful results.

a) First, then, how did Paul mean to be understood by his sudden and repeated talk of *"being justified"*? – "Knowing that a man is not justified by works of law ... in order that we might be justified by faith in Christ ... by works of law shall no flesh be justified". The format of his words shows that he is appealing to an accepted view of Jewish Christians: "we who are Jews ... know ...".[25] Indeed, as already noted, Paul is probably at this point still recalling (if not actually repeating) what it was he said to Peter at Antioch. Not only so, but his wording shows that he is actually appealing to Jewish sensibilities, we may say even to

---

[23] See J.D.G. Dunn, "The Incident at Antioch (Gal. 2.11–18)", in *JSNT* 18 (1983) pp. 3–57.

[24] "Incident at Antioch", p. 54 n. 116.

[25] It is unlikely that Paul wrote εἰδότες δέ. (1) δέ is omitted by P^{46} as well as by other important manuscripts, and was probably introduced by a scribe who misread the flow of Paul's thought and assumed that an adversative particle should be added. (2) Had Paul wished to give adversative force he would have more probably written ἡμεῖς ἐσμέν φύσει Ἰουδαῖοι ... οἴδαμεν δέ ... (contrast Rom. 6.9 and 2 Cor. 4.14 with Rom. 8.28). In fact what he wrote is "We Jews by nature ... knowing that ..." (cf. H. Schlier, *Galater* [Göttingen ⁴1965], p. 89). If he did not follow the construction through consistently, that is hardly untypical of Paul. (3) The ἐὰν μή confirms that v. 16a is intended to express the *Jewish* (Christian) understanding of justification through faith (see below p. 116).

Jewish prejudices – "we are Jews by nature and not sinners of the Gentiles". This understanding of "being justified" is thus, evidently, something Jewish, something which belongs to Jews "by nature", something which distinguishes them from "Gentile sinners".[26] But this is covenant language, the language of those conscious that they have been chosen as a people by God, and separated from the surrounding nations. Moreover, those from whom the covenant people are thus separated are described not only as Gentiles, but as "sinners". Here, too, we have the language which stems from Israel's consciousness of election. The Gentiles are "sinners" precisely insofar as they neither know nor keep the law given by God to Israel.[27] Paul therefore prefaces his first mention of "being justified" with a deliberate appeal to the standard Jewish belief, shared also by his fellow Jewish Christians, that the Jews as a race are God's covenant people. Almost certainly, then, his concept of righteousness, both noun and verb (to be made or counted righteous, to be justified), is thoroughly Jewish too, with the same strong covenant overtones – the sort of usage we find particularly in the Psalms and Second Isaiah, where God's righteousness is precisely God's covenant faithfulness, his saving power and love for his people Israel.[28] God's justification is God's recognition of Israel as his people, his verdict in favour of Israel on grounds of his covenant with Israel.

Two clarificatory corollaries immediately follow.

1) In talking of "being justified" here Paul is not thinking of a distinctively *initiatory* act of God. God's justification is not his act in first *making his* covenant with Israel, or in initially accepting someone into the covenant people. God's justification is rather God's acknowledgement that someone is in the covenan – whether that is an *initial* acknowledgment, or a *repeated* action of God (God's saving acts), or his *final* vindication of his people. So in Gal. 2.16 we are not surprized when the second reference to being justified has a future implication ("we have believed in Christ Jesus in order that we might be justified ..."), and the third reference is in the future tense ("by works of law no flesh shall be justified"). We might mention also Gal. 5.5, where Paul speaks of "awaiting the hope of righteousness". "To be justified" in Paul cannot, therefore, be treated simply as an entry or intiation formula;[29] nor is it possible to draw a clear line of distinc-

---

[26] Clem. Hom. 11.16 – "The Jew believes God and keeps the law ... But he who keeps not the law is manifestly a deserter through not believing God; and thus; is no Jew, but a sinner ..." Cf. K. Kertelge, "Zur Deutung des Rechtfertigungsbegriffs im Galaterbrief", *BZ*, 12 (1968), 213; U. Wilckens, "Was heisst bei Paulus: 'Aus Werken des Gezetzes wird kein Mensch gerecht'?", (1969), *Rechtfertigung als Freiheit: Paulusstudien* (Neukirchen, 1974), pp. 87–8; F. Mussner, *Galaterbrief* (Freiburg/Basel/Wien, [3]1977), pp. 167–9.

[27] See Dunn, "Incident at Antioch" (above n. 23), §4.1c (pp. 27–8).

[28] See particularly S.K. Williams , "The "Righteousness of God" in Romans", *JBL*, 99 (1980), 260f. For references to the Dead Sea scrolls see Mussner, *Galaterbrief, pp.* 168f.

[29] Sanders repeatedly emphasizes that "to be righteoused" (*sic*) in Paul is "transfer terminology".

tion between Paul's usage and the typically Jewish covenant usage. Already, we may observe, Paul appears a good deal less idiosyncratic and arbitrary than Sanders alleges.

2) Perhaps even more striking is the fact which also begins to emerge, that at this point Paul is wholly at one with his fellow Jews in asserting that justification is *by faith*. That is to say, integral to the idea of the covenant itself, and of God's continued action to maintain it, is the profound recognition of God's initiative and grace in first establishing and then maintaining the covenant. Justification by faith is not a distinctively Christian teaching. Paul's appeal here is not to *Christians* who happen also to be Jews, but to *Jews* whose Christian faith is but an extension of their Jewish faith in a graciously electing and sustaining God. We must return to this point shortly, but for the moment we may simply note that to ignore this fundamental feature of Israel's understanding of its covenant status is to put in jeopardy the possibility of a properly historical exegesis. Far worse, to start our exegesis here from the Reformation presupposition that Paul was attacking the idea of *earning* God's acquittal, the idea of meritorious works, is to set the whole exegetical endeavour off on the wrong track. If Paul was not an idiosyncratic Jew, neither was he a straightforward prototype of Luther.

b) What then is Paul attacking when he dismisses the idea of being justified "*by works of the law*"? – as he does, again, no less than three times in this one verse: "... not by works of law ... not by works of law ... not by works of law ...". The answer which suggests itself from what has already been said is that he was thinking of *covenant* works, works related to the covenant, works done in obedience to the law of the covenant. This is both confirmed and clarified by both the immediate and the broader contexts.

As to the immediate context, the most relevant factor is that Gal. 2.16 follows immediately upon the debates, indeed the crises at Jerusalem and at Antioch, which focused on two issues: at Jerusalem, circumcision; at Antioch, the Jewish food laws with the whole question of ritual purity unstated but clearly implied. Paul's forceful denial of justification from works of law is his response to these two issues. His denial that justification is from works of law is, more precisely, a denial that justification depends on circumcision or on observation of the Jewish purity and food taboos. We may justifiably deduce therefore that by "works of law" Paul intended his readers to think of *particular observances of the law like circumcision and the food laws*. His Galatian readership might well think also of the one other area of law observance to which Paul refers disapprovingly later in the same letter – their observance of special days and feasts (Gal. 4.10). But why these particular "works of the law"? The broader context suggests a reason.

From the broader context, provided for us by Greco-Roman literature of the period, we know that just *these observances were widely regarded as characteristically and distinctively Jewish*. Writers like Petronius, Plutarch, Tacitus and Juvenal took it for granted that, in particular, circumcision, abstention from pork, and the sabbath, were observances which marked out the practitioners as Jews, or as people who were very attracted to Jewish ways.[30] These, of course, were not all exclusively Jewish practices – for example, not only Jews practised circumcision. But this makes it all the more striking that these practices were nevertheless widely regarded as both characteristic and distinctive of the Jews as a race – a fact which tells us much about the influence of diaspora Judaism in the Greco-Roman world. It is clear, in other words, that just these observances in particular functioned as identity markers, they served to identify their practitioners as Jewish in the eyes of the wider public, they were the peculiar rites which marked out the Jews as that peculiar people.

When we set this alongside the Palestinian Judaism illuminated by Sanders, the reason for this becomes clearer, we can see why just these observances were regarded as so distinctively Jewish. The Jews regarded them in the same way! This strong impression of Greco-Roman authors, as to what religious practices characterize the Jews, was simply a reflection of the typical, the dominant attitude of the Jews themselves. These identity markers identified Jewishness because they were seen by the Jews themselves as fundamental observances of the covenant. They functioned as badges of covenant membership. A member of the covenant people was, by definition, one who observed these practices in particular. How could it be otherwise since precisely these practices belong so clearly to the basic ground rules of the covenant?

If we think of circumcision, no loyal Jew could ignore the explicit stipulations of Gen. 17:

And God said to Abraham, "As for you, you shall keep my covenant, you and your descendants after you throughout their generations. This is my covenant, which you shall keep, between me and you and your descendants after you: Every male among you shall be circumcised. You shall be circumcised in the flesh of your foreskins, and it shall be a sign of the covenant between me and you ... So shall my covenant be in your flesh an everlasting covenant. Any uncircumcised male who is not circumcised in the flesh of his foreskin shall be cut off from his people; he has broken my covenant" (Gen. 17.9–14).

What could be clearer than that? There are some indications that a few diaspora Jews avoided the literal force of this command by spiritualizing it,[31] but they are noteworthy precisely as being so exceptional. Circumcision remained an identification marker of Jewishness, of membership of the Jewish people, in the eyes both of the Gentiles and of the Jews themselves.

The laws on clean and unclean foods do not hold such a central place in the Torah (Lev. 11.1–23; Deut. 14.3–21). But we know that at least from the time of the Maccabees they had assumed increasing importance in Jewish folklore and

---

[30] Full details in M. Stern, ed., *Greek and Latin Authors on Jews and Judaism* (Israel Academy of Sciences and Humanities: Jerusalem, Vol. I, 1976, Vol. II, 1980), §§. 195, 258, 281, 301.

[31] See Philo, *Migr.*, 89–93; cf. *Qu. Ex.*, II. 2.

Jewish selfunderstanding. The Maccabean martyrs were remembered precisely as those who "stood firm and were resolved in their hearts not to eat unclean food" and who "chose to die rather than to be defiled by food or to profane the holy covenant" (I Macc. 1.62–63). And the heroes of the popular tales beloved by several generations of Jews, Daniel, Tobit and Judith, had all shown their faithfulness to God precisely by their refusal to eat "the food of Gentiles" (Dan. 1.8–16; Tob. 1.10–13; Judith 10.5; 12.1–20). Without question, then, the devout Jew of Paul's day would regard observance of the laws on clean and unclean foods as a basic expression of covenant loyalty. Moreover, from what we now know of the Pharisees at the time of Paul, not to mention also the Essenes at Qumran, the maintenance of ritual purity, particularly the ritual purity of the meal table, was a primary concern and major preoccupation.[32] No wonder then that the men from James were so upset by the slackness of Peter and the other Jewish Christians at Antioch on these matters. And no wonder that Peter and Barnabas could not resist this strong appeal to national identity and covenant faithfulness precisely with regard to these items of the law, these practices of the covenant.

As to the observance of special days, particularly the sabbath, we need only recall that the Jewish scriptures treat the sabbath as a fundamental law of creation (Gen. 2.3), that the sabbath was the only feast day to be stipulated in the decalogue (Ex. 20.8–11; Deut. 5.12–15), and that it was explicitly linked by Isaiah with the covenant as a determinative expression of covenant loyalty which would provide the basis on which Gentiles would unite with Jews in the last days in a common worship of the one God (Isa. 56.6–8). Here, too, was a work of the law which had the same basic character of defining the boundaries of the covenant people, one of these minimal observances without which one could hardly claim to be a good Jew, loyal to the covenant given by God's grace to Israel.

Given this almost axiomatic tie-up between these particular regulations of the law and covenant membership, it is no exaggeration to say that for the typical Jew of the first century A.D., particularly the Palestinian Jew, *it would be virtually impossible to conceive of participation in God's covenant, and so in God's covenant righteousness, apart from these observances, these works of the law.* If it helps, some may like to compare the role of the sacraments (baptism and the Lord's Supper) in Christianity today. These have very much the same fundamental role in Christian selfunderstanding as circumcision, table regulation and sabbath had in the Jewish self-understanding of Paul's day. Even though we acknowledge Quakers and Salvation Army as Christian bodies, even so any attempt to define the boundary markers which identify and distinguish Christians as Christians will almost certainly give a primary place to baptism and the Lord's

---

[32] See particularly J. Neusner, *From Politics to Piety* (Englewood Cliffs, 1973), pp. 80, 83–90.

Supper. If an unbaptized Christian is for most of us a contradiction in terms, even more so was a Jew who did not practise the works of the law, circumcision, table regulations and sabbath.

The conclusion follows very strongly that when Paul denied the possibility of "being justified by works of the law" it is precisely this basic Jewish self-understanding which Paul is attacking[33] – the idea that God's acknowledgment of covenant status is bound up with, even dependent upon, observance of these particular regulations – the idea that God's verdict of acquittal hangs to any extent on the individual's having declared his membership of the covenant people by embracing these distinctively Jewish rites.

Two clarificatory corollaries again follow.

1) "Works of law", "works of the law" are nowhere understood here, either by his Jewish interlocutors or by Paul himself, as works which *earn* God's favour, as merit-amassing observances. They are rather seen as *badges*: they are simply what membership of the covenant people involves, what mark out the Jews as God's people; given by God for precisely that reason, they serve to demonstrate covenant status. They are the proper response to God's covenant grace, the minimal commitment for members of God's people. In other words, Paul has in view precisely what Sanders calls "covenantal nomism". And what Paul denies is that God's justification depends on "covenantal nomism", that God's grace extends only to those who wear the badge of the covenant. This is a historical conclusion of some importance since it begins to clarify with more precision what were the continuities and discontinuities between Paul, his fellow Jewish Christians and his own Pharisaic past, so far as justification and grace, covenant and law are concerned.

2) More important for Reformation exegesis is the corollary that "works of the law" do *not* mean "good works" in general, "good works" in the sense disparaged by the heirs of Luther, works in the sense of self-achievement, "man's self-powered striving to undergird his own existence in forgetfulness of his creaturely existence" (to quote a famous definition from Bultmann).[34] The phrase "works of the law" in Gal. 2.16 is, in fact, a fairly restricted one: it refers precisely to these same identity markers described above, *covenant* works – those regulations prescribed by the law which any good Jew would simply take for granted to describe what a good Jew did. To be a Jew, was to be a member of the covenant, was to observe circumcision, food laws and sabbath. In short, once again Paul seems much less a man of 16th century Europe and much more firmly in touch with the reality of first-century Judaism than many have thought.

---

[33] Kertelge (n. 26 above): "Die *erga nomou* in v. 16 sind also der Ausdruck des jüdischen Selbstbewusstseins von v. 15" (p. 215).

[34] R. Bultmann, *Theology of the New Testament*, 1 (ET, London, 1952), 254. Cf. e.g. H. Ridderbos, *Paul: an Outline of his Theology* (1966; ET, London, 1977), p. 139: E. Käsemann, *Romans* (HNT, 1973; ET, London, 1980) pp. 93, 102, 284; Hübner, *Gesetz* p. 102; Beker, *Paul* p. 247.

c) In contrast to righteousness understood in terms of works of the law, Paul speaks of righteousness *through faith in Jesus Christ* – not just faith as such, but faith in Jesus Christ, Jesus Messiah. We are at once reminded that this is an internal Christian debate – between Paul and Peter, two Jews, but Jews who are also believers in Jesus. Paul appeals to what was obviously the common foundation belief of the new movement. What distinguishes Peter, Paul and the others from their fellow Jews is their belief in Jesus as Messiah.

But here we must be sure of what we are saying. Is it in fact this faith in *Jesus*(as) Messiah which marks them off from their fellow Jews, or is it their belief in justification by *faith*, as has so often been assumed? In the light of Sanders' findings, as we have already noted, it is much less obvious than once appeared that the typical first-century Jew would have denied justification by faith. The emphasis on God's electing grace, bis covenantal mercy and loving kindness, the very fact that one of Paul's key terms, "the righteousness of God", is drawn directly from the Old Testament in form and content – all this raises the question, *What is the point at issue here?* If not "justification by faith" as God's initiative in declaring in favour of men, if not "works of law" as merit-earning good works, then what? What precisely is involved in Paul's contrast between being justified by works of law and being justified by faith in Jesus Messiah?

Our verse suggests one answer: Paul's point is precisely that these two *are* alternatives – justification by works of law and justification by faith in Jesus are *antithetical opposites*. To say that God's favourable action towards anyone is dependent in any degree on works of the law is to *contradict* the claim that God's favour depends on faith, faith in Jesus Christ. Indeed it is quite likely that Gal. 2.16 reflects the step by which Paul's thinking hardened these two propositions into a clear-cut antithesis. Let me try to explain how I reach this conclusion.

According to v.16a the common ground (between Peter and Paul) is that "a man is not justified from works of law *except* through faith in Jesus Christ". Notice how he expresses the last phrase – "except through faith in Jesus Messiah". According to the most obvious grammatical sense, in this clause faith in Jesus is described as a *qualification* to justification by works of law, not (yet) as an antithetical alternative. Seen from the perspective of Jewish Christianity at that time, the most obvious meaning is that *the only restriction on justification from works of law is faith in Jesus as Messiah.* The only restriction, that is, to covenantal nomism is faith in Christ. *But,* in this first clause, covenantal nomism itself is not challenged or called in question – restricted, qualified, more precisely defined in relation to Jesus as Messiah, but not denied. Given that in Jewish self-understanding covenantal nomism is *not* antithetical to faith,[35] then at this point the only change which the new movement calls for is that the traditional Jewish

---

[35] Mussner, *Galaterbrief.* "Der Jude lässt die pln. Antithetik "Glaube" – "Werke des Gesetzes" – nicht gelten, ja sie ist ihm unverständlich" (p. 170).

faith be more precisely defined as faith in Jesus Messiah. This is evidently the accepted view of Jewish Christians to which Paul appeals.

The point, then, is that the common ground from which Paul's argument moves out need not be understood as setting covenantal nomism and faith in Christ in antithesis. As Peter's conduct and the conduct of the rest of the Jewish believers at Antioch made abundantly clear, so far as the Jewish Christian was concerned, belief in Jesus as Messiah did not require him to abandon his Jewishness, to give up the badges of his national religion, to call in question works of the law as the still necessary response of the Jew to God's covenant grace. And why not? Why should a Jewish belief in a Jewish Messiah make any difference to these long established Jewish distinctives?

But Paul followed a different logic – the logic of justification by faith: what is of grace through faith cannot depend in any sense, in any degree on a particular ritual response. If God's verdict in favour of an individual comes to effect through his faith, then it is dependent on nothing more than that. So, in repeating the contrast between justification from works of law and justification through faith in Jesus Christ, Paul alters it significantly: what were initially juxtaposed as complementary, are now posed as straight alternatives – "... knowing that a man is not justified from works of law *except* through faith in Jesus Christ, we have believed in Christ Jesus in order that we might be justified from faith in Christ, and *not* from works of law ...". Moreover, in describing justification by faith in Christ, Paul varies the formula slightly: we are justified not only *through* faith in Christ but also *from* faith in Christ – the implication quite probably being that in Paul's view faith in Christ is the only necessary and sufficient response that God looks for in justifying anyone.

In other words, in v. 16 Paul pushes what began as a qualification on covenantal nomism into an outright antithesis. If we have been accepted by God on the basis of faith, then it is on the basis of faith that we are acceptable, and *not* on the basis of works. Perhaps, then, for the first time, in this verse faith in Jesus Messiah begins to emerge not simply as a *narrower* definition of the elect of God, but as an *alternative* definition of the elect of God. From being *one* identity marker for the Jewish Christian alongside the other identity markers (circumcision, food laws, sabbath), faith in Jesus as Christ becomes the primary identity marker which renders the others superfluous.

This line of exposition can be re-expressed in a slightly different way, with more emphasis on the salvation-history significance of Christ. The question Paul was in effect grappling with at this point is this: How do we Jewish believers relate our covenantal nomism, our works of law, our obligations under the covenant to our new faith in Jesus as the Christ? Or. in slightly broader terms: What difference does the coming of Jesus the Messiah make to our traditional understanding of the covenant? The answer of many Jerusalem believers seems to have been, None; no difference; it is still God's covenant with Israel into which

Gentiles can be received on the recognized and well-established conditions. Others, including the leading apostles, were willing to dispense Gentile believers from the need to be circumcised as an entry requirement, but when it came to the 'crunch' they still in effect expected the Gentile believers to live as those within the covenant in traditional terms, to maintain covenant status by, in particular, conforming with the food and purity regulations which governed the meal table – even Peter and Barnabas (2.12–14). Their answer to the question was in effect: Christ's coming has made some difference, but in the day-to-day event not much; the people of God are still to be defined in essentially and distinctively Jewish terms. But at precisely this point Paul begins to develop a different answer.

In brief, Paul's new answer is that the advent of Christ had introduced the time of fulfilment, including the fulfilment of his purpose regarding the covenant. From the beginning, God's eschatological purpose in making the covenant had been the blessing of the nations: the gospel was already proclaimed when God promised Abraham, "In you shall all the nations be blessed" (Gal. 3.8; Gen. 12.3; 18.18). So, now that the time of fulfilment had come, the covenant should no longer be conceived in nationalistic or racial terms. No longer is it an exclusively Jewish *qua* Jewish privilege. The covenant is not thereby abandoned. Rather it is broadened out as God had originally intended – with the grace of God which it expressed separated from its national restriction and freely bestowed without respect to race or work, as it had been bestowed in the beginning. This is roughly the argument of Gal. 3–4, as also developed later in Rom. 3–4.

The decisive corollary which Paul saw and which he did not hesitate to draw, was that the covenant is no longer to be identified or characterized by such distinctively Jewish observances as circumcision, food laws and sabbath. *Covenant* works had become too closely identified as *Jewish* observances, *covenant* righteousness as *national* righteousness.[36] But to maintain such identifications was to ignore both the way the covenant began and the purpose it had been intended to fulfil in the end. To continue to insist on such works of the law was to ignore the central fact for Christians, that with Christ's coming God's covenant purpose had reached its intended final stage in which the more fundamental identity marker (Abraham's faith) reasserts its primacy over against the too narrowly nationalistic identity markers of circumcision, food laws and sabbath.

If this understanding of Gal. 2.16 is correct, then we in fact are being given the unique privilege in this verse of witnessing a very crucial development for the history of Christianity taking place, before our very eyes, as it were. For in this

---

[36] A phrase I owe to N.T. Wright; see his Oxford D. Phil. thesis: *The Messiah and the People of God: a study in Pauline Theology with particular reference to the argument of the Epistle to the Romans* (1980), pp. 89f.

verse we are seeing the transition from a basically Jewish self-understanding of Christ's significance to a distinctively different understanding, the transition indeed from a form of Jewish Messianism to a faith which sooner or later must break away from Judaism to exist in its own terms.

Once again two clarificatory corollaries.

1) We should not let our grasp of Paul's reasoning slip back into the old distinction between faith and works in general, between faith and 'good works'. Paul is not arguing here for a concept of faith which is totally passive because it fears to become a 'work'. It is the demand for a *particular* work as the necessary expression of faith which he denies. As he puts it later in the same letter, "In Christ Jesus neither circumcision nor uncircumcision is of any avail, but faith working through love" (5.6).

2) Nor should we press Paul's distinction between faith and works into a dichotomy between faith and ritual, simply because the works of the law which he has in mind belong to what has often been called the ritual or ceremonial law. There *is* a distinction between outward and inward, between ritual and spiritual, but no necessary antithesis. Paul has no intention here of denying a ritual expression of faith, as in baptism or the Lord's Supper. Here again we should keep the precise limitations of Paul's distinction between faith in Christ and works of law before us. What he is concerned to exclude is the *racial* not the *ritual* expression of faith; it is *nationalism* which he denies not *activism*. Whatever their basis in the scriptures, these works of the law had become identified as indices of Jewishness, as badges betokening race and nation – inevitably so when race and religion are so inextricably intertwined as they were, and are, in Judaism. What Jesus has done by his death and resurrection, in Paul's understanding, is to free the grace of God in justifying from its nationalistically restrictive clamps for a broader experience (beyond the circumcised Jew) and a fuller expression (beyond concern for ritual purity).

d) Finally, we should take note of the last clause of our verse where Paul probably alludes to Ps. 143.2.[37] Our thesis also helps explain why Paul should use the Psalm in the way he does, why he both modifies and adds to the Psalmist's words. In Ps. 143.2 we read the plea:

Enter not into judgment with your servant;
for no man living is righteous before you.

Paul does two things to the second half of the Psalm verse: he adds "from works of law", and he substitutes "all flesh" for "all living". Where the Psalmist said

"no living (being) will be justified before you",

---

[37] Despite Mussner's misgivings (*Galaterbrief*, pp. 174f.), Paul probably did intend an allusion to the psalm, as the parallel with Rom. 3.20 confirms, since the allusion is clearer there.

Paul rephrases thus,

"by *works of law* no *flesh will* be justified".[38]

How can he justify restricting the more general statement by adding "from
works of law"? The simplest answer is probably given in the substitution of "all
flesh" for "all living" . "All flesh" is a quite acceptable synonym for "all living".
But it has the merit, for Paul, of focusing the unacceptability of man in his fleshli-
ness. By that, of course, Paul will not intend a dualism between spirit and matter,
however dualistic his antithesis between spirit and flesh may seem later on in
chapter 5. He certainly has in mind man's weakness, his corruptibility, his dependence on the satisfaction of merely human appetites (4.13–14; 5.16–17; 6.8).
But the word "flesh" also embraces the thought of a merely human relationship,
of a heritage determined by physical descent, as in the allegory of chapter 4
(4.23,29).[39] That is to say, in speaking of "all flesh" Paul has in view primarily and
precisely those who think their acceptability to God and standing before God
does depend on their physical descent from Abraham, their national identity as
Jews. It is precisely this attitude, which puts too much stress on fleshly relationships and fleshly rites, precisely this attitude which Paul excoriates in his parting
shot in 6.12–13 "they want to make a good showing in the flesh ... they want to
glory in your flesh".

With the Psalm reference thus more sharply defined in terms of physical and
national identity, the addition of "from works of law" becomes merely clarificatory. It does not narrow the Psalmist's assertion any further; rather it ties into
and emphasizes more clearly the "all flesh". For works of the law, epitomized in
this letter by circumcision, are precisely acts of the flesh. To insist on circumcision is to give a primacy to the physical level of relationship which Paul can no
longer accept. "Works of the *law*", because they put such an emphasis on such
marks of racial identity, are, ironically, no different from "works of the flesh"
(5.19), so far as acceptability before God is concerned – precisely because these
works of the law in effect imprison God's righteousness within a racial and national, that is, fleshly framework. Whereas those who belong to Christ, from
Paul's perspective, have passed through a different starting point (the gift of the
Spirit – 3.3), have crucified the flesh (5.24), and the life they now lead in the flesh
they live not in terms of fleshly rites or fleshly relationships but by faith in the
Son of God (2.20). God's purposes and God's people have now expanded beyond Israel according to the flesh, and so God's righteousness can no longer be
restricted in terms of works of the law which emphasize kinship at the level of
the flesh.

---

[38] The omission of "before you" from Ps. 143.2 in Gal. 2.16 has no significance, as the *reten-
tion* of the phrase in the Rom. 3.20 allusion to the same passage makes clear.

[39] See J.D.G. Dunn, "Jesus-Flesh and Spirit: an Exposition of Romans 1.3–4", *JTS*, 24
(1973), 43–9.

Two final corollaries by way of clarification.

1) Yet once more we must note that it is *works* of the law that Paul disparages, not the law itself or law-keeping in general. In his latest contribution to the discussion Sanders recognizes the nationalistic significance of circumcision, food laws and sabbath,[40] but he keeps taking the phrase "works of the law" as though it was simply a fuller synonym for "law". So far as Sanders is concerned, no man shall be justified by works of law" is just the same as saying, "no man shall be justified by the law".[41] But Paul is as little opposed to the law *per se* as he is to good works *per se*. It is the law understood in terms of *works*, as a Jewish prerogative and national monopoly, to which he takes exception. The law understood in terms of the command to "love your neighbour as yourself" is another matter (Gal. 5.14).

2) So, too, lest the point still be confused, I repeat, Paul here is not disparaging works in general or pressing a dichotomy between outward ritual done in the flesh and inward grace operative in the spirit. Once again we must observe the limited target he has in his sights. It is works which betoken racial prerogative to which he objects, acts done in the flesh because faith in Christ is reckoned insufficient as the badge of covenant membership which he denounces. Over against Peter and the other Jewish Christians Paul insists that God's verdict in favour of believers comes to realisation through faith, from start to finish, and in no way depends on observing the works of law which hitherto had characterized and distinguished the Jews as God's people.

III

So much for Gal. 2.16. Time does not permit me to follow the development of the same line of argument through the rest of the letter, though I believe that it helps resolve more than one crux in subsequent chapters. Likewise, Paul's later letter to the Roman Christians gains considerably in coherence when viewed from the same perspective. For example, when Paul affirms that boasting is excluded in 3.27, he is not thinking of boasting in self-achievement or boasting at one's good deeds.[42] It is the boasting of the Jew which he has in mind – the boasting in Israel's special relationship with God through election, the boasting in the law as the mark of God's favour, in circumcision as the badge of belonging to God (Rom. 2.17–29). Among other things, this means that there is no significant development in Paul's thought on this particular point at least between Ga-

---

[40] See below n. 46.

[41] See also E.P. Sanders, "On the Question of Fulfilfing the Law in Paul and Rabbinic Judaism", *Donum Gentilicum: New Testament Studies in Honour of David Daube*, ed. C.K. Barrett, E. Bammel & W.D. Davies (Oxford, 1978), pp. 103–26.

[42] Contrast those cited above in n. 34.

latians and Romans. However, further exposition will have to await the commentary on Romans which I mentioned at the beginning, and which, as you may appreciate, I am now a good deal more enthusiastic about writing than I was when first asked.

It would also be premature, of course, to build extensive conclusions on the basis of just one verse. Nevertheless, there is some obligation at the end of a lecture like this to attempt some summing up, and at least to sketch out the preliminary results which seem to follow so far from this new perspective on Paul, but which must naturally be subjected to further testing.

a) In Gal. 2.16 Paul actually addresses Judaism as we know it to have been in the first century – a system of religion conscious of its special relationship with God and sensitive to its peculiar obligations within that relationship. The criticisms of Paul for his misunderstanding of Judaism therefore involve a double failure of perspective. What Jewish scholars rejected as *Paul's* misunderstanding of Judaism is *itself* a misunderstanding of Paul, based on the standard Protestant (mis)reading of Paul through Reformation spectacles. When we take these Reformation spectacles off, Paul does not appear to be so out of touch with his first-century context as even Sanders thinks. Sanders in effect freed Pauline exegesis from its 16th century blinkers, but he has still left us with a Paul who could have made little sense to his fellow Jews and whose stated willingness to observe the law elsewhere (I Cor. 9.19–23) must have sounded like the most blatant self-contradiction.

b) The major exegetical flaw of Sanders' reconstruction of Paul's view of the law (and of course not only his)[43] is his failure to perceive the significance of the little phrase "works of the law". He recognizes rightly that in disparaging "works of the law" Paul is not disparaging good works in general, far less is he thinking of good works as earning merit. But by taking "works of law" as equivalent to "doing the law" in general (the normal exegesis), he is led to the false conclusion that in disparaging "works of the law" Paul is disparaging law as such, has broken with Judaism as a whole. To be fair, the mistake is a natural one, since Judaism had itself invested so much significance in these particular works, so that the test of loyalty to covenant and law was precisely the observance of circumcision, food laws and sabbath.[44] But it is these works in particular which

---

[43] It is unfair to pick out Sanders since this is the common view of the matter, usually the result of basing exegesis primarily on Gal. 3.11 and of reading 3.10 in the light of it without sufficient reference to the initial emphatic statement of 2.16. See e.g. N.A. Dahl, *Studies in Paul* (Minneapolis, 1977), pp. 106, 170; U. Wilckens, "Zur Entwicklung des paulinischen Gesetzverständnis", *NTS*, 28 (1982), 166–9; Mussner, *Galaterbrief:* "Nur eine naive Exegese könnte ... 'die Werke des Gesetzes' auf die rituellen Vorschriften des Judentums beschranken" (p. 170). But see n. 45 below.

[44] We may compare the way in which in fundamentalist circles doctrines of substitutionary atonement and inerrancy of scripture have been regarded as touchstones of orthodoxy, even when several other doctrines are acknowledged to be of equal or greater importance.

he has in mind, and he has them in mind precisely because they had become the expression of a too narrowly nationalistic and racial conception of the covenant, because they had become a badge not of Abraham's faith but of Israel's boast.[45] Sanders glimpses this point quite clearly on more than one occasion,[46] but his failure to distinguish "works of the law" from "doing the law" prevents him from developing the insight properly.[47]

This failure has had serious consequences for Sanders' larger thesis. For had he delimited more precisely the force of Paul's negative thrust against works of the law, he would have been able to give a more adequate account of Paul's more positive attitude to the law elsewhere. In particular, he would not have had to press so hard the distinction between "getting in" (not by doing the law) and "staying in" (by keeping the law), a distinction which seems very odd precisely at Gal. 2.16, where the issue at Antioch was the day-to-day conduct of those who had already believed (2.14), and where Paul's concern regarding the Galatians is over their ending rather than their beginning (3.3).[48] In consequence also he would not have had to argue for such an arbitrary and abrupt discontinuity be-

---

[45] The same point applies to the distinction between the ritual and the moral law frequently attributed to Paul. The point is that Paul does not presuppose or develop that distinction as such. His more negative attitude to the ritual prescriptions of the law arise from the fact that it is precisely in and by these rituals as such that his Jewish kinsmen had most clearly marked themselves out as God's people the Jews – and been identified by others as "that peculiar people" (see above n. 30).

[46] See e.g. his *Paul, the Law and the Jewish People*, p. 33 – "Boasting" in Rom. 3.27 refers to "the assumption of special status on the part of the Jews" (also p. 35); his recognition of the significance of circumcision, sabbath and food laws (pp. 101–2) – "the most obvious common denominator to these laws is the fact that they distinguish Jews from Gentiles" (p. 114); and his quotation from Gaston ("Israel as a whole interpreted the righteousness of God as establishing the status of righteousness for Israel alone, excluding the Gentiles") and Howard ("Their own righteousness" is their "collective righteousness to the exclusion of the Gentiles") in his notes (p. 61, n. 107). The earlier article by J.B. Tyson, "'Works of Law' in Galatians", *JBL*, 92 (1973), 423–31, shares similar strengths and weaknesses.

[47] E.g. "The explanation of 'not by faith but by works', then, is 'they did not believe in Christ' ... Israel's failure is not that they do not obey the law in the correct way, but that they do not have faith in Christ" (p. 37) – where I would rather say, "they relied on their covenant status, as attested by the works of the law, rather than on Christ"; "His criticism of his own former life is not that he was guilty of the attitudinal sin of self-righteousness, but that he put confidence in something other than faith in Jesus Christ" (pp. 44f.) – *Tertium datur!*, ... guilty of putting his confidence in his being a Jew and in his zeal as a devout Jew; "The only thing that is wrong with the old righteousness seems to be that it is not the new one" (p. 140 – No! that it was too narrowly and nationalistically Jewish"; "In Pauline theory, Jews who enter the Christian movement renounce nothing" (p. 176) – except their claim to a Jewish monopoly in divine righteousness.

[48] Sanders tries to grapple with this point in his first main section of *Paul, the Law and the Jewish People* (p. 52 n. 20), and in effect acknowledges that the issue is "being in" (what covenant membership involves) rather than a distinction between getting in and staying in as such. The Jewish Christians and Judaizers wanted not simply a one-off action from the Gentile believers, but a continuing life-style in accordance with the Torah.

tween Paul's gospel and his Jewish past, according to which Sanders' Paul hardly seems to be addressing Sanders' Judaism. Whereas, if Paul was really speaking against the too narrow understanding of God's covenant promise and of the law in nationalist and racial terms, as I have argued, a much more coherent and consistent reconstruction of the continuities and discontinuities between Paul and Palestinian Judaism becomes possible.

c) All this confirms the earlier important thesis of Stendahl, that Paul's doctrine of justification by faith should not be understood primarily as an exposition of the individual's relation to God, but primarily in the context of Paul the Jew wrestling with the question of how Jews and Gentiles stand in relation to each other within the covenant purpose of God now reached its climax in Jesus Christ.[49] It is precisely the degree to which Israel had come to regard the covenant and the law as coterminous with Israel, as Israel's special prerogative, wherein the problem lay. Paul's solution does not require him to deny the covenant, or indeed the law as God's law, but only the covenant and the law as 'taken over' by Israel. The models of the man of faith are for Paul the founding fathers, Abraham, Isaac and Jacob, where covenant membership was neither determined by physical descent (racial consanguinity) nor dependent on works of law (Rom. 4; 9.6–13). This certainly involved something of an arbitrary hermeneutical procedure, whereby the example of Abraham in particular was treated not only as typical and normative, but also as relativizing those subsequent scriptures which emphasize Israel's special place within God's affections. But it is a procedure which Paul is more than willing to argue for and defend rather than simply to state in a take it or leave it, black and white way.

Once again, however, we are beginning to push too far beyond the proper limits of the present essay, and I must desist. But hopefully I have said enough to show how valuable the new perspective on Paul may be in giving us a clearer insight into and appreciation of Paul and his theology.

---

[49] Cf. Stendahl, *Paul among Jews and Gentiles, passim* – e.g. "... a doctrine of faith was hammered out by Paul for the very specific and limited purpose of defending the rights of Gentile converts to be full and genuine heirs to the promises of God to Israel" (p. 2).

Chapter 3

Works of the Law and the curse of the Law

(Galatians 3.10–14)*

The two most recent studies of Paul and the law both show a large measure of agreement in criticizing Paul's treatment of the law as inconsistent and self-contradictory. E.P. Sanders argues that Paul's 'break' with the law gave rise to different questions and problems, and that his 'diverse answers, when set alongside one another, do not form a logical whole'.[1] So, in particular, Paul's 'treatment of the law in chapter 2 (of Romans) cannot be harmonized with any of the diverse things which Paul says about the law elsewhere'; in Romans 2 'Paul goes beyond inconsistency or variety of argument and explanation to true self-contradiction'.[2] More thoroughgoing is H. Räisänen, who can see only one way to handle what Paul says: 'contradictions and tensions have to be *accepted* as *constant* features of Paul's theology of the law'.[3] Again and again he finds himself driven to the conclusion that Paul contradicts himself. So, for example, with Rom 13.8–10: 'Paul seems here simply to have forgotten what he wrote in ch. 7 or in 10.4'; '(Romans) 2.14–15,26–27 stand in flat contradiction to the main thesis of the section'; Paul puts forward 'artificial and conflicting theories about the law'.[4] The artificiality and tension is evident not least in Gal 3.10–12 where Räisänen finds the argument of 3.10 to be at odds with the argument of 3.11–12.[5]

Speaking personally, I find such explanations of the text very unsatisfying. They are not to be ruled out in principle, of course; but as a way of making sense of the text they must rank as hypotheses of last resort, second only to speculative emendation of the text as disagreeable to good exegesis. Basic to good exegesis is respect for the integrity of the text and, in the case of someone like Paul, respect for his intellectual calibre and theological competence. Such respect includes a constant bearing in mind the possibility or indeed likelihood that the situations confronting Paul were more complex than we can now be aware of, or include important aspects which are now invisible to us. Before I resorted to

---

* Delivered as a seminar paper (in briefer form) to the 'Paul and Israel' Seminar at the SNTS Conference in Basel, August 1984.

[1] E.P. Sanders, *Paul, the Law and the Jewish People* (Philadelphia: Fortress, 1983) 3–4.

[2] Sanders, *Law* 123,147.

[3] H. Räisänen, *Paul and the Law* (WUNT 29; Tübingen: Mohr, 1983) 10–11 (his emphasis).

[4] Räisänen, *Paul* 65, 103, 154.

[5] Räisänen, *Paul* 94–6, 109.

such conclusions therefore I would want to be fully convinced that I had entered as far as possible into the mind and context of Paul's writings. And this is where I suggest both Sanders and Räisänen have fallen short. Despite the labour they have devoted to the subject, despite the illumination which Sanders has brought to our understanding of Palestinian Judaism in relation to Paul, and despite the impressive thoroughness of Räisänen's debate with the secondary literature on the subject, they have both failed to get sufficiently inside the social situation of which 'Paul and the law' were a part. For all that they have turned their backs, quite rightly, on an individualizing exegesis of Paul's theology of justification, they have still failed to grasp the full significance of *the social function of the law* at the time of Paul and how that determines and influences both the issues confronting Paul and Paul's responses.

The social function of the Law

Anthropologists and sociologists have made us aware of the fact that any social grouping will inevitably have various features and characteristics which provide the group's self-definition (consciously or unconsciously) and mark it off from other groups. Members of the group will tend naturally to think of the group and of their membership of the group in terms of these features and characteristics, including any distinctive practices and beliefs. Two key words here are *identity* and *boundary*. In particular, ritual (a wide variety of ritual) plays an important part in providing group cohesion and maintaining identity. Thus Hans Mol:

Rites articulate and reiterate a system of meaning, and prevent it being lost from sight ... They restore, reinforce, or redirect identity. They maximize order by strengthening the place of the individual in the group, or society, and vice-versa by strengthening the bonds of a society *vis-a-vis* the individual. They unify, integrate and sacralize.[6]

Similarly Mary Douglas in her influential study, *Purity and Danger*, speaks of 'ritual as an attempt to create and maintain a particular culture'.

The rituals enact the form of social relations and in giving these relations visible expression they enable people to know their own society.[7]

The concept of 'boundary' is closely linked with that of 'identity'. As Mol points out, 'It is precisely the boundary ... which provides the sense of identity'.[8] In particular, the more a group or society feels itself under threat, the more it will tend to emphasize its boundaries. Mary Douglas has noted that 'the body is a model

---

[6] H. Mol, *Identity and the Sacred* (Oxford: Blackwell, 1976) 233.

[7] M. Douglas, *Purity and Danger* (London: Routledge & Kegan Paul, 1966) 128; see also earlier 62–5.

[8] Mol, *Identity* 57–8.

which can stand for any bounded system'. So it is no surprise when anxiety about the purity of the body and of what passes into and out of the body is emphasized at times of danger to the group. She suggests that

> when rituals express anxiety about the body's orifices the sociological counterpart of this anxiety is a care to protect the political and cultural unity of a minority group ... The anxiety about bodily margins expresses danger to group survivai.[9]

It must immediately be evident how well this analysis fits the Judaism of Paul's day. Douglas herself exemplifies her point by referring to the history of the Israelites in general, since they were always 'a hard pressed minority'.[10] But it is particularly in the post-exilic period and not least in the Maccabean period that the point becomes most clear. For the threat of Syrian assimilation in the second century BCE focused with particular intensity precisely on those bodily rituals which gave Judaism its distinctive identity and marked out its boundaries.

> According to the decree (of Antiochus), they put to death the women who had their children circumcised, and their families and those who circumcised them; and they hung the infants from their mothers' necks. But many in Israel stood firm and were resolved in their hearts not to eat unclean food. They chose to die rather than to be defiled by food or to profane the holy covenant; and they did die (1 Macc 1.60–63).

Here the identity and boundary markers are clear – circumcision and the laws of clean and unclean food. It is hardly surprising then that the two main issues with which Paul deals in Galatians are precisely the same two areas of concern – circumcision and food laws (Gal 2.1–14). For ever since the Maccabean period these two sets of legal requirement had been fundamental to the devout Jew's identity as a Jew, as member of the people whom God had chosen for himself and made covenant with; these two ritual enactments had a central role in marking Israel off from the surrounding nations. And the events described in Gal 2 took place at a time of renewed and mounting threat to Judaism's national and religious identity – following as they did the attempt of Caligula to defile the Temple (AD 40) and the deteriorating situation in Palestine.[11] Of course, for the devout Jew it was primarily a matter of remaining faithful to the covenant obligations clearly laid down in the Torah (particularly Gen 17.9–14; Lev. 11.1–23; Deut. 14.3–21). But from a social anthropological perspective it is clear also that what was at stake was a people's identity and self-understanding, and that these rituals were important not least because they served as such clear boundary markers. This is borne out by various comments of Greco-Roman authors of the period which indicate that from the outsider's perspective two of the clearest

---

[9] Douglas, *Purity* 124.
[10] Douglas, *Purity* 124.
[11] See further my 'The Incident at Antioch (Gal 2.11–18)', *JSNT* 18 (1983) 7–11.

distinguishing marks of the Jewish race were circumcision and the dietary laws.[12]
Wayne Meeks appositely cites Philo in the same connection:

Israel cannot be harmed by its opponents so long as it is 'a people dwelling alone' (Num
23.9), 'because in virtue of the distinction of their peculiar customs they do not mix with
others to depart from the way of their fathers' (*Mos.* 1.278);

and cites the most important of the 'peculiar customs' as circumcision, *kashrut*,
sabbath observance, and avoidance of civic rituals which implied recognition of
pagan gods.[13] Sanders recognizes the same point when he notes that circumcision, Sabbath and food laws 'created a social distinction between Jews and other
races in the Greco-Roman world'; similarly Räisänen – 'works of tile law are
something that *separates* the Jew from the Gentile'.[14] But neither of them follow
the insight through far enough.

We should also observe, since it will have bearing on the later discussion, that
it was not simply particular rituals as such which had this identityaffirming,
boundary-marking function. The law itself fulfilled this role.[15] After all, had not
the law been given to Israel as Israel's special prerogative, given to the chosen
people as a mark of God's favour and thus to distinguish them from the other nations? A good expression of this sense of privilege is Baruch's claim that divine
Wisdom whom nobody else knows has been given to Israel:

> She is the book of the commandments of God,
>   and the law which endures for ever.
> All who hold her fast will live,
>   and those who forsake her will die.
> Turn, O Jacob, and take her;
>   walk toward the shining of her light.
> Do not give your glory to another,
>   or your advantages to an alien people.
> Happy are we, O Israel,
>   for we know what is pleasing to God (Bar 4.1–4).

And the boundary function of the law is nowhere more clearly stated than in
Aristeas 139, 142:

---

[12] Full details in M. Stern ed., *Greek and Latin Authors on Jews and Judaism* (Jerusalem: Israel Academy of Sciences and Humanities, Vol. 1 1974, Vol. 2 1980) – circumcision: Timagenes,
Horace, Persius, Petronius, Martial, Tacitus, Juvenal, Suetonius (##81, 129, 190, 194–5, 240–1,
281, 301, 320); food laws: Erotianus, Epietetus, Plutarch, Tacitus, Juvenal, Sextus Empiricus
(##196, 253, 258, 281, 298, 334).

[13] W.A. Meeks, *The First Urban Christians* (Yale, 1983) 97.

[14] Sanders, *Law* 102; Räisänen, *Paul* 171–2.

[15] In the ancient world, of course, respect for their ancestral customs (τὰ πάτρια) was a widespread feature of social and national groups; see LSJ πάτριος; R. MacMullen, *Paganism in the
Roman Empire* (Yale, 1981) 2–3.

[Moses] fenced us round with impregnable ramparts and walls of iron, that we might not mingle at all with any of the other nations, but remain pure in body and soul ... he hedged us round on all sides by rules of purity, affecting alike what we eat, or drink, or touch, or hear, or see.

The same attitude of course was a prominent feature of two of the main sub-groups within Judaism, the Pharisees and the Essenes, since it can be fairly said of them that they both sought to affirm and strengthen the identity of the people of God precisely by emphasizing the law's distinguishing rituals and boundary character.[16]

In short, then, the particular regulations of circumcision and food laws were important not in themselves, but because they *focused* Israel's distinctiveness, made visible Israel's claims to be a people set apart, and were the clearest points which differentiated the Jews from the nations. The law was part and parcel of Israel's identity, both as a nation and as a religion. The law was coterminous with Judaism. It was impossible at the time of Paul to conceive of Judaism without the law, scarcely possible for a Jew to conceive of membership of the covenant people apart from the law. All this would have been largely taken for granted by most Jews, so much was it part of the presuppositional attitude of Jewish self-understanding. As soon as this point has been grasped, it at once becomes apparent that Paul's teaching on the law and circumcision must have posed a severe threat to most of his kinsmen's self-understanding and identity, not as individuals, but as Jews, as members of the people marked out as God's by the law. Unless this social, we may even say national and racial dimension of the issues confronting Paul is clearly grasped, it will be well nigh impossible to achieve an exegesis of Paul's treatment of the law which pays proper respect to historical context.

Works of the Law

What I have been pleading for in effect is a shift in perspective – from one dominated by the categories of the Reformation debates, to one properly set within the horizons of the social world of first century Judaism. When such a shift is car-

---

[16] 'What marks ancient Israel as distinctive perennially is its preoccupation with defining itself. In one way or another Israel sought means of declaring itself distinct from its neighbours. ... The persistent stress on differentiation, yielding a preoccupation with self-definition ... The Torah literature ... raised high those walls of separation ...' 'These laws formed a protective boundary, keeping in those who were in, keeping out those who were not' (J. Neusner, *Judaism: The Evidence of the Mishnah* [University of Chicago, 1981] 69–75). Hence the Pharisees' stress on ritual purity, to which Neusner has drawn particular attention *(From Politics to Piety* [Englewood Cliffs: Prentice-Hall, 1973, 80, 83–90; also *Judaism* 49–52) and the intensifying of ritual norms at Qumran (e.g. 1 QS 3.8–12; 5. 8; CD 10.14–11.18; see further J. Riches, *Jesus and the Transformation of Judaism* [London: Darton, 1980 122–8).

ried through it releases a flood of fresh light on the issues confronting Paul and on his response to them. A key example is the phrase τὰ ἔργα τοῦ νόμου, 'the works of the law'. The fact that Paul uses it only in the context of his argument with other Jewish Christians (or Jews) is usually recognized by commentators.[17] But sooner or later (usually sooner) the perspective slips and the assumption begins to dominate the exegesis that by 'works of the law' Paul means the attempt to win God's favour by human achievement, or some such paraphrase. Even Sanders and Räisänen who consciously distance themselves from Reformation categories, and who show much greater sensitivity to the considerations posed above than has generally been the case, in the end they too fall back into further variations on the classic Reformation antithesis: ἐξ ἔργων τοῦ νόμου refers to 'entry' requirements, says Sanders, applying his much overworked distinction between 'getting in' and 'staying in'; and Räisänen, referring to the same phrase, argues that Paul misrepresents Judaism 'by suggesting that, within it, salvation is by works ...'.[18]

In my view, however, 'works of the law' is precisely the phrase chosen by Paul (as either already familiar to his readers or self-evident to them in its significance), by which Paul denotes those obligations prescribed by the law which show the individual concerned to belong to the law, which mark out the practitioner as a member of the people of the law, the covenant people, the Jewish nation. I gave a first version of this argument in the 1982 Manson Memorial Lecture.[19] This paper constitutes an attempt to broaden and deepen that argument.

a) For one thing the genitive construction, 'works of the law' has been too little considered and its significance too much taken for granted. But as E. Lohmeyer argued, the phrase ἔργα νόμου is best taken in the sense 'service of the law', 'Dienst des Gesetzes', or in J.B. Tyson's rendering 'nomistic service'.[20] That is to say, service not so much in the sense of particular actions already accomplished, but in the sense of obligations set by the law, the religious system determined by the law. The phrase refers not to an individual's striving for moral improvement, but to a religious mode of existence, a mode of existence marked out in its distinctiveness as determined by the law, the religious practices which demonstrate the individual's 'belongingness' to the people of the law.

---

[17] See e.g. Räisänen, *Paul* 187 (also below n. 54), with other references in his n. 121. The dispute as to whether Paul in these passages is attacking Judaisin or Jewish Christians is important, but not entirely to the point here, since it is the *Jewish* attitude of the Jewish Christians which he confronts.

[18] Sanders, *Law* 105, 147 (though elsewhere he treats the phrase in a less restrictive way – pp. 46, 158–9); Räisänen, *Paul* 188–9. Cf. also U. Wilckens, 'Zur Entwicklung des paulinischen Gesetzverständnis', *NTS* 28 (1982) 154–90.

[19] 'The New Perspective on Paul', *BJRL* 65 (1983) 95–122 [= ch. 2 above]. See also K. Kertelge, 'Gesetz und Freiheit im Galaterbrief', *NTS* 30 (1984) 382–94, especially 391.

[20] E. Lohmeyer, *Probleme paulinischer Theologie* (Stuttgart: Kohlhammer, n.d.) 33–74 (here 67); J.B. Tyson, '"Works of Law" in Galatians', *JBL* 92 (1973) 423–31 (here 424–5).

Lohmeyer's insight is borne out by the way in which the equivalent phrase is used in the Qumran writings – מעשי תורה, 'deeds of the law'. For it was precisely by reference to his 'deeds', his 'observance of the law' as understood within the community in the day to day, year by year life of the community, that an individual's membership of the covenant was tested (1 QS 5.21, 23; 6.18). Likewise מעשי תורה was what marked out the community of the end days in its distinctiveness from the outsiders and enemies (4 QFlor. 1.1–7).

In terms introduced by Sanders, 'works of the law' then is another way of saying 'covenantal nomism' – that which characterizes 'being in' the covenant and not simply 'getting into' the covenant (as Sanders himself put it).[21] And in terms of the preceding analysis, 'works of the law' are Paul's way of describing in particular the identity and boundary markers which Paul's Jewish (-Christian) opponents thought, and rightly thought, were put under threat by Paul's understanding of the gospel.

b) As I noted in the Manson Lecture, this understanding of 'works of the law' makes best sense of the phrase's use in the contexts in which Paul introduces it. In Gal 2.16, where he introduces it for the first time (in his extant writings), and uses it no less than three times, ἔργα νόμου most obviously refers back to the issues at the centre of the preceding controversies – circumcision and food laws.[22] That is what was at issue – whether to be justified by faith in Jesus Christ requires also observance of these 'works', whether, as the subsequent discussion makes clear, it is possible to conceive of a membership of the covenant people which is not characterized by precisely these works. The Jerusalem Christians having conceded the argument about circumcision, so far as 'getting in' was concerned, drew the line at the food laws: a membership of the chosen people which did not include faithfulness to the food laws and purity rituals of the meal table was for them too much a contradition in terms. And Peter, Barnabas and the other Jewish Christians in Antioch evidently agreed, however reluctantly or not – the threat to Jewish identity was too great to be ignored.[23]

So too in Romans. Paul introduces the phrase, somewhat oddly, at the conclusion to the first main part of the exposition (3.19–20); again the implication must be that its meaning or reference was either well known or self-evident. Since the second half of the preceding discussion was a refutation of Jewish presumption in their favoured status as the people of the law, the 'works of the law' must be a shorthand way of referring to that in which the typical Jew placed his confidence, the law-observance which documented his membership of the covenant, his righteousness as a loyal member of the covenant. This is confirmed by the way in

---

[21] Above n. 18. Note also Sanders' attempt to clarify his earlier formulation in *Law* 165–6 n. 38.

[22] So correctly Räisänen, *Paul* 259.

[23] Cf. K. Kertelge, 'Zur Deutung des Rechtfertigungsbegriffs im Galaterbrief', *BZ* 12 (1968) 215.

which in the following paragraphs 'works of the law' are associated with 'boasting' (3.27–8; 4.2), thus explicitly recalling the earlier passage where Paul specifically attacked his own people's presumption as being the people of the law (2. 17–20,23), with circumcision once again serving as the distinguishing mark of 'the Jew' (2.25–9).

c) The same point emerges from the other prepositional phrases which Paul uses when speaking of the law. In Rom 2.12 the antithesis ἐν νόμῳ / ἀνόμως clearly has the force 'within the law', 'inside the law' and 'without the law', 'outside the law'. This is borne out by the fact that in v. 14 Paul goes on to define the Gentiles equivalently as 'those not having the law'. In other words, the law and the Jewish people are coterminous; the law identifies the Jew as Jew and constitutes the boundary which separates him from the Gentiles. Similarly in Rom 3.19–21 we find the distinction ἐν τῷ νόμῳ and χωρὶς νόμου: the law marks out those inside its boundaries and their whole religion and life-style (works of the law), that is, marks them off from those outside the law.

The phrase ὑπὸ νόμον has the same force, particularly in 1 Cor 9.20 and Gal 4. 5, where Paul speaks of the Jews as οἱ ὑπὸ νόμον, 'those under the law', those whose lives as a people are characterized by the authority of the law, by 'works of the law', nomistic service – the law as a banner, loyalty to which gives them their national identity and unity, the law as marking out the extent and boundaries of the covenant people. So in 1 Cor 9.20–21 we are not surprised to see the same distinction between Jews and Gentiles defined as between οἱ ὑπὸ νόμου and οἱ ἄνομοι, those under the law and the law-less.[24]

Thus it becomes clearer that the contrast between οἱ ἐκ νόμου and οἱ ἐκ πίστεως in Rom 4.14,16 is also a sociological as well as theological distinction. A distinction not between two sets of random individuals, one set who think their relation with God depends on human achievement and the other who are justified by faith. But a distinction between what amounts to two definitions of how the offspring, the people promised to Abraham are to be characterized. The question confronting Paul is this: Are the heirs of Abraham no more and no less than the people marked out by the law, the people whose whole existence as God's people arises out of the law, whose whole national identity comes from the law? Or are they marked out simply by faith, identified simply by faith?

In all these cases a failure to appreciate the social dimensions and national ramifications of what Paul is attacking and what he is affirming will inevitably result in a misconception of his teaching on the law.

---

[24] See also Gal 4. 4 – Jesus was 'born under the law', that is, a Jew; 4.21 – (some of) the Galatians wish to be 'under the law', that is, in effect, to become Jews. I am not persuaded by L. Gaston, 'Taul and the Torah', *Antisemitism and the Foundations of Christianity*, ed. A.T. Davies (New York: Paulist, 1979) 48–71, who argues that Paul uses the phrase 'under the law' 'to designate the gentile situation' (62–4).

d) To complete this sketch of the language matrix to which the phrase 'works of the law' belongs, we should note also the ideas associated with it. I will refer to four in particular.

(i) As noted above (b), Paul associates 'works of the law' with the 'boasting' of his Jewish interlocutor in Romans (3.27–28; 4.2), clearly recalling the boasting of the 'Jew' in 2.17,23. Bultmann's influential treatment of the theme understood this in very individualistic terms as a boasting of 'self-confidence'; and Käsemann has continued the line of interpretation by depicting the boasting Jew as the classic type of the pious individual who relies on self-achievement.[25] But clearly what Paul has in mind is the confidence of the Jew as Jew, as member of the people whom God has chosen as his own and to whom he has given the law. He boasts in the law as the long established mark of divine favour to his own.[26]

(ii) So too the Phrase ἐν τῷ φανερῷ, used to describe 'the Jew'and circumcision in Rom 2.28, has often been interpreted in individualistic terms without reference to social context, simply as the outward opposed to the inward. But what Paul has in mind is the Jew visibly marked out as such, circumcision as the public ritual act which gives the individual place within the people so marked out. It is the social function of ritual which is in view, circumcision as a badge of Jewish identity. Precisely because it is an outward visible mark, circumcision serves very effectively as a boundary marker between Jew and Gentile. So too when Paul speaks of the law as γράμμα, what he has in view is precisely the law as the visible definition of the covenant people (Rom 2.27,29; 7.6; 2 Cor 3.6–7).

(iii) Similarly the phrase ἐν σαρκί used in the same passage (Rom 2.28) denotes not merely the physical as opposed to the spiritual, but also the people of Israel in terms of physical identity and racial kinship.[27] Likewise, 'not of the flesh' stands in parallel to 'not of works' in 9.8,11, precisely because the works of the law demonstrate national identity, constitute national righteousness, the righteousness of those who hold true to the customs given by Moses to Israel. And in Gal 6.13 the boasting in the flesh which Paul attacks is the boasting of people whose pride in their national identity has been enhanced by the desire of other races to submerge their social and religious distinctiveness in that identity.

(iv) Finally we might note Paul's other criticism of his own people – that 'they sought to establish their own righteousness' (Rom 10.3). Here too 'their own' is usually taken in the sense, 'their own' as achieved by them, 'a righteous status of

---

[25] R. Bultmann, *TDNT* 3.648–9; also *New Testament Theology* (London: SCM, Vol. 1 1952) 242–3; E. Käsemann, *Commentary on Romans* (London: SCM, 1980) 102; Bultmann's position is defended by H. Hübner, *Das Gesetz bei Paulus* (Göttingen: Vandenhoeck, ²1980), especially 102.

[26] Cf. particularly, Sanders, *Law* 33, 155–7.

[27] See further J.D.G. Dunn, 'Jesus – Flesh and Spirit: an Exposition of Romans 1.3–4', *JTS* 24 (1973) 44–9.

their own earning'.[28] But the ἴδιος has more the sense of 'belonging to them, peculiar to them'. That is to say, what is in view is a righteousness which is *theirs and not anybody else's*, 'collective righteousness, to the exclusion of the Gentiles',[29] covenant righteousness, the righteousness of being God's people. They seek to '*establish*' their righteousness, not to create it or achieve it, but to confirm and make secure (στῆσαι) what is already theirs. Here is a good expression of 'covenantal nomism', the claim to a special relationship with God secure for all who remain loyal to the covenant. Not surprisingly, the phrase ἐξ ἔργων νόμου appears once again in the same context (9.32) as an equivalent way of describing their mistake; so that once again it becomes evident that 'works of the law' are what Jews do to demonstrate and maintain their standing with God as something peculiar to Israel.

To sum up, the phrase τὰ ἔργα τοῦ νόμου belongs to a complex of ideas in which the social function of the law is prominent. The law serves both to identify Israel as the people of the covenant and to mark them off as distinct from the (other) nations. 'Works of the law' denote all that the law requires of the devout Jew, but precisely because it is the law as identity and boundary marker which is in view, the law as Israel's law focuses on these rites which express Jewish distinctiveness most clearly. The conclusion of the previous section is thus confirmed: 'works of the law' refer not exclusively but particularly to those requirements which bring to sharp focus the distinctiveness of Israel's identity. It is because they have such a crucial role in defining 'Jewishness', membership of the covenant people, that circumcision and food laws feature so prominently in discussion of works of the law and righteousness. What lies behind so much of the debate is the identity crisis which Paul's work among the Gentiles precipitated for his fellow Jewish Christians.[30]

Further confirmation that we are on the right lines is provided by the way in which this perspective helps to 'iron out' two of the puzzling wrinkles in Paul's treatment of the law to which Räisänen in particular has drawn attention.[31]

---

[28] C.E.B. Cranfield, *Romans* (ICC; Edinburgh: T. & T. Clark, Vol. 2 1979) 515.

[29] G. Howard, 'Christ the End of the Law: the Meaning of Romans 10.4', *JBL* 88 (1969) 331–7 (here 336); similarly Gaston 66; Sanders, *Law* 38.

[30] A useful parallel is provided from 20th century Christianity. In classical Pentecostalism it would generally be agreed that speaking in tongues and the Pentecostal understanding of Spirit baptism are *not* the most important elements of their faith. But in fact most apologetic writing and most discussion of Pentecostalism has given considerable prominence to these two Pentecostal teachings. The reason is also the reason for the prominence of circumcision and food laws in Gal 2: in both cases we are dealing with the distinctive features of the group – what marks them off from other even closely related groups. For anyone wishing to identify himself with classical Pentecostalism in the first half of the 20th century, the make or break issue was speaking in tongues.

[31] My criticisms in 'The New Perspective' focused principally on Sanders (particularly 201–2; = 118–20 above).

1) The tension in Paul's language between the law as a negative factor and his continuing positive assessment of the law (contrast in particular Rom 2.13–15; 3.27,31; 7.12; 8.4; 9.31–32; 13.8–10).[32] The solution suggested by the above analysis is that it is the law in its social function which draws a large part of Paul's critique.[33] The law as fixing a particular social identity, as encouraging a sense of national superiority and presumption of divine favour by virtue of membership of a particular people – that is what Paul is attacking in the passages mentioned above. Divorced from that perspective, as the law understood in terms of faith rather than in terms of works, it can continue to serve in a positive role. The self-contradictions which Sanders and Räisänen have found are the result of a too blinkered perspective on their part rather than Paul's.

2) The puzzle of why other explanations which propose distinctions within the law (moral and ceremonial law, inward and outward law, core law and law *in toto*) seem to provide partial but only partial resolutions of the tension between Paul's various pronouncement.[34] They are incomplete precisely because they have missed the social function of the law, and the way in which this function focuses on particular ritual requirements. Paul does *not* defend his position by dividing up the law into acceptable and unacceptable elements. For what he is attacking is a particular *attitude* to the law as such, the law as a *whole* in its social function as distinguishing Jew from Gentile. Viewed from a *different* angle, the point of the law as a whole will come into focus in other ways, particularly in faith ('the law of faith' – Rom 3.28; 9.31–32) and love of neighbour (Rom 13.10). And, just as important, the requirements which obscure that point will become of secondary relevance as *adiaphora*.

From this perspective the coherence of even such passages as 2 Cor 3 and Rom 2 within Paul's theology of the law becomes clearer. When Paul speaks of the 'letter' killing he is not thinking of the law as such, or even of the law understood literally, but of the law as defining the covenant people with the physical visible rite of circumcision (as in Rom 2.29). It is the law understood in this way which is so destructive of the life of the Spirit.[35] And in Rom 2 what Paul has in view when he speaks of Gentiles doing the law is not some core law as such. His object is rather to undermine Jewish confidence that by *having* the law, by staying *within* the law, their position before God in the final judgment is secure. The fact that there can be a real doing of the law, a real engagement with what the law is about on the part of the Gentiles (2.14–15,26–27), reveals that confidence to

---

[32] Räisänen, *Paul* 62–73, 101–18.

[33] It should be noted that I say 'a large part of his critique'; in this essay I do not attempt to deal with other aspects of the law's function in Paul's thought (particularly Rom 5.20; 7.7–11).

[34] See particularly Räisänen's discussion (*Paul* 23–8).

[35] Räisänen's critique at this point is directed against the equally inadequate view that 'γράμμα means Jewish legalism rather than the Torah', but he has missed the social function of the Torah as a whole (*Paul* 44–6).

be false and misplaced. Or put the other way round, Jewish boasting in the law should be well and truly punctured by the fact that there are Jews who blatantly disobey some of the law's requirements (2.21–23 – *not* the boundary-defining 'works of the law'), while still Jews and still (presumably) maintaining their covenant identity.[36]

In short, a recognition of the social function of the law, and of 'works of the law' as a summary expression of the law's function as seen from within Judaism, goes a long way towards removing and resolving the contradictions and tensions which have loomed so large for Sanders and Räisänen.

Gal 3.10–14 – A test case

In 'The New Perspective on Paul' I was conscious that my argument amounted to little more than an exegesis of Gal 2. 16.[37] Several respondents observed that if my thesis were to gain in credibility it would have to make sense of Gal 3.10–14. Gal 3.10–14 does indeed provide a substantial test case, and to it we now turn.

In the preceding paragraphs Paul has reminded his readers of how they began as Christians. He emphasized again the contrast between 'works of law' and 'faith'. They knew well that they received the Spirit and entered upon the continuing experience of the Spirit ἐξ ἀκοῆς πίστεως and not ἐξ ἔργων νόμου, that is, by a response of faith which was not tied to or expressed by the (ritual) observances which characterize Judaism (Gal 3.2,5). The warning is clear: as they began, so they should continue (3.3). That is to say, their *continued* life in the Spirit should not be thought to depend on nomistic service, on covenantal nomism, any more than their beginning. Here too, implicit in the argument is the association of 'works of the law' with 'flesh' (ἐξ ἔργων νόμου vv. 2,5 parallel to σαρκί v. 3). And, once again, neither of these should be reduced to an individualistic striving for self-achievement. On the contrary, as we have now learned to expect, both terms have in view the nationalism of the typical Jewish understanding of God's covenant promise – the Spirit as given to the children of Abraham, understood naturally as the national entity Israel, marked out as God's heirs by law and circumcision of the flesh. Whereas Paul's Gentile readers knew from their own experience that their enjoyment of that promise had not

---

[36] Sanders' discussion misses the point and thus undermines his own critique (*Law* 123–32). Similarly Räisänen (*Paul* 98–101); Paul attacks typical Jewish presumption that having the law, being within the law, is what gives assurance of justification (as Räisänen recognizes later – 170); it is that attitude which Paul indicts in Rom 2.17–24, not 'every individual Jew without exception' (*Paul* 100).

[37] 'New Perspective' 200–1 (above 117–8).

depended and did not depend on their aligning themselves visibly and physically with the native Jew by embracing the ancestral customs of the Jews.

The testimony of their own experience is confirmed by scripture, which ties together Abraham's faith with the promise to Abraham, the promise which showed that God purposed to bless the Gentiles from the beginning of his covenant relationship with Abraham. As Abraham's faith was what established the covenant in the first place, so οἱ ἐκ πίστεως can quite properly regard themselves as children of Abraham, and in receiving the Spirit ἐκ πίστεως they can know that this is the blessing God purposed from the first when he accepted Abraham in covenant relationship (3.6–9). But if faith is the mark of the people of the promise, what about the law? And what about those who have always taken for granted that it is the law and works of the law which mark out the people of God's covenant? That is the issue to which Paul begins to address himself in Gal 3.10–14.

v. 10 'For as many as are ἐξ ἔργων νόμου are under a curse; for it is written, "Cursed is everyone who does not remain within everything that is written in the book of the law to do the same"' (Deut 27.26). The basic logic of the text is clear: all who are ἐξ ἔργων νόμου are under a curse, *because* they fail to abide by everything that is written in the law. This at once tells us something about οἱ ἐξ ἔργων νόμου in Paul's perspective: (1) to be ἐξ ἔργων νόμου is not the same as remaining in the law; (2) to be ἐξ ἔργων νόμου is something which *falls short* of abiding by everything written in the law.

What can Paul mean? The usual answer runs along the following lines: ὅσοι ἐξ ἔργων νόμου refers to those who seek to achieve their own righteousness before God; and in quoting Deut 27. 26 Paul presupposes that it is impossible to fulfil all that the law requires.[38] That is to say, Paul indicts his fellow Jews/Jewish Christians[39] for thinking they could make a claim upon God by keeping the law, something which is simply not possible. This exegesis however is undercut by several factors. (a) The first clause can no longer be read as an attack on self-achievement. ὅσοι ἐξ ἔργων νόμου are Jews as a whole, precisely insofar as they understand themselves in terms of the law, see their lives as members of God's covenant people characterized by the service which the law prescribes.[40] (b) The idea

---

[38] See among recent discussions, H. Hübner, 'Gal. 3.10 und die Herkunft des Paulus', *KuD* 19 (1973) 215–31; also *Gesetz* 19–20; A. Oepke/J. Rohde, *Galater* (THNT; Berlin: Evangelische, 1973) 105; H. Mussner, *Galaterbrief* (Freiburg: Herder, [3]1977) 225–6; J. Becker, *Galater* (NTD Göttingen: Vandenhoeck, 1976) 36–7; R. Smend & U. Luz, *Gesetz* (Stuttgart: Kohlhammer, 1981) 94–5; D. Hill, 'Gal. 3.10–14: Freedom and Acceptance', *ExpT* 93 (1981–2) 197; F.F. Bruce, *Galatians* (NIGTC; Exeter: Paternoster, 1982) 157–60; Räisänen, *Paul* 94. Earlier references in J. Eckert, *Die urchristliche Verkündigung im Streit zwischen Paulus und seinen Gegnern nach dem Galaterbrief* (Regensburg: Pustet, 1971) 77 n. 3.

[39] See above n. 17.

[40] See above p. 128. Mussner rightly notes recent research's recognition 'wie sehr man gerade im Frühjudentum Bund und Gesetz zusammengedacht hat' (*Galaterbrief* 229 n. 85, referring to Jaubert and Limbeck; add now particularly Sanders).

that Paul in quoting Deut 27.26 presupposes the impossibility of fulfilling the law is hardly self-evident and has to be read into the argument.[41] (c) The exegesis becomes even more precarious when we realize that it runs at cross purposes with what Paul says elsewhere – with vv. 11–12, says Räisänen;[42] and certainly with 5.14, where Paul clearly implies that 'the whole law' *can* be 'fulfilled' by loving one's neighbour as oneself.[43]

The more promising route to the proper exegesis of v. 10 is to recognize that Paul is deliberately denying what his fellow countrymen (and the Judaizers) would take for granted, setting at odds what they equated. That is to say, most Jews of Paul's day would simply assume that to be ἐξ ἔργων νόμου is to remain within all that the Torah lays down, *is* to do what the law requires.[44] But Paul denies that equation. To be of the works of the law is *not* the same as fulfilling the law, is *less* than what the law requires and so falls under the law's own curse. Why so? The answer is given by our previous exposition of 'works of the law'. Those who are ἐξ ἔργων νόμου are those who have understood the scope of God's covenant people as Israel *per se*, as that people who are defined by the law and marked out by its distinctive requirements.[45] Such an understanding of the covenant and of the law inevitably puts too much weight on physical and national factors, on outward and visible enactments, and gives too little weight to the Spirit, to faith and love from the heart. Such an understanding of the people of God inevitably results in a false set of priorities. On such an understanding of the law, fulfilment of the law will inevitably be judged in terms of these priorities. As Paul well knew from his own past, it was all too possible for the devout and loyal Jew to think of himself as 'blameless' (Phil 3.6), precisely because he was a devout and loyal Jew, precisely because he was zealous in his observance of the ancestral customs (Gal 1.14). But Paul now sees all too clearly that such an understanding of the law is *not* all that the law requires. Freed from the nationalistic presuppositions which had previously coloured his own self-understanding and

---

[41] Cf. H. Schlier, *Galater* (KEK: Göttingen: Vandenhoeck, [13]1965) 132; H. Betz, *Galatians* (Hermeneia; Philadelphia: Fortress, 1979) 145; and Sanders' highly individual argument (*Law* 20–25).

[42] See n. 5 above.

[43] See also Betz's review of the options usually canvassed for v. 10 (*Galatians* 145–6). Betz's own reconstruction of Paul's reasoning (the law was given in order to be broken and to generate sin) is hardly obvious from the text (even allowing for 3.19). It would hardly cut much ice with his readers, and on this point Paul could hardly simply assume that his readers shared his presuppositions (cf. Betz's own observation on p. 141). Moreover, as Hübner points out, such a theology attributes a very perverse motive on the part of God in giving the law (*Gesetz* 27); it is hard to think that Paul would be unaware of such a corollary or would willingly embrace it.

[44] As Sanders has argued, it is precisely the concern to 'remain within' the framework of the covenant which is at the heart of 'covenantal nomism'.

[45] Sanders' failure to appreciate the full force of the phrase ὅσοι ἐξ ἔργων νόμου is mirrored in the weak summary he gives: 'in 3.10 Paul means that those who *accept* the law are cursed' (*Law* 22, my emphasis).

which still coloured the self-understanding of the bulk of his own people, Paul could now see that fulfilment of the law has to be understood in different terms, as something which Gentiles can do without any reference to whether they are inside the law or outside the law (cf. Rom 2.14–16,26–29). To cling defiantly to the older view was to diminish the law, to distort the covenant and effectively to destroy its promise. To thus misunderstand the law by giving primacy to matters of at best secondary importance was to fall short of what the law required and thus to fall under the law's own curse (Deut 27.26). Paul could assume that his readers would recognize his train of thought, precisely because what we now call 'the social function of the law' would be part of the framework of perception for any reasonably well-informed individual of Paul's day when he encountered Judaism, precisely because the restrictiveness of being ἐξ ἔργων νόμου in nationalist and visible terms was well known in Jew/Gentile relationships. That restrictiveness had come into focus with regard to circumcision at Jerusalem (Gal 2.1–10) and with regard to the food laws at Antioch (2.11–18). In the context of the Galatian situation, the train of thought from Gal 2.16 to 3.10 would not be too difficult to follow.[46]

vv. 11–12 'And that no one ἐν νόμῳ is justified with God is plain, because "The righteous ἐκ πίστεως shall live" (Hab 2.4). And the law is not ἐκ πίστεως, but "he who does the same will live ἐν αὐτοῖς"' (Lev 18.5).

Once again Paul sets in antithesis what most of his fellow Jews would regard as equivalent:

ἐν νόμῳ	ἐκ πίστεως
ἐκ πίστεως	ἐν αὐτοῖς

In Jewish self-understanding, to be ἐν νόμῳ is to live ἐκ πίστεως (by faithfulness)[47] – in both cases the man who is righteous before God being in view, his righteousness being defined and documented precisely by the two phrases (ἐν νόμῳ, ἐκ πίστεως).[48] To do what the law specifies for the covenant people is to live ἐν αὐτοῖς, to live ἐκ πίστεως. And once again the exegetical key is the recognition of the restrictiveness implied in the two ἐν phrases. Whether they are translated 'in' or 'by' or more vaguely 'in terms of', the point is the same: Paul is referring to the typical Jewish self-understanding of the people of God as cir-

---

[46] G. Howard, *Paul: Crisis in Galatia* (SNTSMS 35; Cambridge, 1979) recognizes the narrowness of Paul's focus in his talk of 'works of the law', and Paul's concern that the law divides Jew from Gentile (especially 53, 62), but he weakens his exposition by arguing that 'being under the law' could be said of Gentiles as well as Jews (60–1); in contrast see p. 128 above.

[47] The usual understanding of Hab 2.4 MT – '... will live by his faithfulness'. It is not necessary to the discussion here to resolve the question of whether Paul intended the ἐκ πίστεως to go with ὁ δίκαιος or ζήσεται. See e.g. the discussion by H.C.C. Cavallin, 'The Righteous Shall Live by Faith', *St. Th.* 32 (1978) 33–43.

[48] That ἐν νόμῳ (v. 11) is equivalent to ἐξ ἔργων νόμου (v. 10) is plain (Bruce, *Galatians* 161), as also the parallel between 3.11 and 2.16 confirms.

cumscribed and defined by the law, as characterized by practice of the law's distinctive features.[49]

Paul however sets ἐκ πίστεως in contrast to the two ἐν phrases. He thus frees it from functioning simply as a way of defining life ἐν νόμῳ, and gives it independent significance as faith, as trust in and openness to God brought about by the word of preaching, without any reference to the law or its works. Paul need say no more either about 'faith' or about its independence from the social function of the law because his readers had experienced both for themselves in rich measure (3.2–5).[50]

In setting faith and law in such contrast here[51] Paul would not want them to be understood as mutually exclusive; nor would he want to disparage the idea of 'doing the law' as such (cf. Rom 2.13 and 2.26–27 with Gal 5.14 and 6.2).[52] Once again it is a question of priorities. For his Jewish kinsmen the law was the more dominant of the two concepts and determined the meaning of πίστις as 'faithfulness', faithfulness in observing the works of the law. But for Paul faith is the primary category and determinative factor (as the Galatians' own experience confirmed). To subordinate it once again to the dictates of covenantal nomism would be to deny their own experience, as confirmed by scripture. The life of nomistic service validated by Lev 18.5 has been superseded by the eschatological life of faith as antitypically foreshadowed by Hab 2.4.

vv. 13–14 'Christ has redeemed us from the curse of the law, having become a curse on our behalf – as it is written, "Cursed is everyone who hangs on a tree" (Deut 21.23 with 27.26) – in order that the blessing of Abraham might come in Christ Jesus to the Gentiles, in order that we might receive the promise of the Spirit through faith'.

---

[49] See above p. 128. Lev 18.5 'contains one of the fundamental doctrines of the Old Testament and of Judaism' (Betz, *Galatians* 148). By ὁ νόμος in v. 12 Paul means the law understood in this way, as Lev 18.5 indicates. The term should not be enlarged to mean 'the law' on any and every understanding of the law. The whole argument here clearly relates to a quite specific understanding of the law. In fact the *same* contrast can be posed subsequently by Paul as between 'the law of faith' and 'the law of works' (Rom 3.27; cf. 9.31–32), precisely because νόμος here is shorthand for ἔργα νόμου (see also above n. 48).

[50] In the context of 3.1–9 πίστις must refer primarily to faith exercised by man, rather than God's faithfulness (against Howard, *Paul* 63–4), though a secondary allusion to the latter cannot be entirely ruled out in view of the LXX of Hab 2. 4. That Paul refers Hab 2.4 to *Christ* (R.B. Hays, *The Faith of Jesus Christ* [SBL Dissertation 56; Chico: Scholars, 1983] 150–7) is still less likely: 3.10–12 is an exposition of the contrast between οἱ ἐκ πίστεως (v. 9) and ὅσοι ἐξ ἔργων νόμου (V. 10).

[51] A christological interpretation of 3.12 (Lev 18.5 was fulfilled through Christ) ignores the contrast clearly intended here and reads too much into the text (K. Barth, *CD* 11/2 245; R. Bring, *Galatians* [Philadelphia: Muhlenberg, 1961] 128–42; Cranfield, *Romans*, 522 n. 2).

[52] Against Schlier, *Galater* 132–5. As U. Luz and others have noted, it is not the *doing*, but the *not* doing which falls under the law's curse (*Das Geschichtsverständnis des Paulus* [München: Kaiser, 1968] 149).

The thought clearly refers back to v. 10, as the formulation of the scriptural passage to align it with the scripture quoted in v. 10 confirms.[53] Paul must intend 'the curse of the law' to be understood in the light of v. 10. That is to say, the curse of the law is not simply the condemnation which falls on any transgression and on all who fall short of the law's requirements. Paul has in mind the specific short-fall of his typical Jewish contemporary, the curse which falls on all who restrict the grace and promise of God in nationalistic terms, who treat the law as a boundary to mark the people of God off from the Gentiles, who give a false priority to ritual markers. The curse of the law here has to do primarily with that attitude which confines the covenant promise to Jews as Jews: it falls on those who live within the law in such a way as to exclude the Gentile as Gentile from the promise. This is confirmed by the second half of Paul's formulation in vv. 13–14: the purpose of Christ's redemption from the curse of the law is precisely what we would (now) expect – viz. the extension of the covenant blessing to the Gentiles.[54] The curse which was removed therefore by Christ's death was the curse which had previously prevented that blessing from reaching the Gentiles, the curse of a wrong understanding of the law. It was a curse which fell primarily on the Jew (3.10; 4.5), but Gentiles were affected by it so long as that misunderstanding of the covenant and the law remained dominant.[55] It was that curse which Jesus had brought deliverance from by his death.

This may seem at first a surprisingly narrow understanding of the redemptive effect of Christ's death, especially when a systematized theology of the atonement tends to stress deliverance from the power of sin (and the condemnation of transgression). But Paul's meaning and intention here is in fact quite narrow and specific. (1) He has already taken Deut 27.26 in a quite specific and narrow sense (v. 10). And the original reference of Deut 21.23 is very narrow and particular. It is simply because both speak of a curse and both do so in reference to covenant

---

[53] Cf. M. Wilcox, '"Upon the Tree" – Deut. 21.22–23 in the New Testament', *JBL* 96 (1977) 87.

[54] 'The summary in 3.14 shows where the emphasis of the argument in 3.1–13 falls' (Sanders, *Law* 22). The weakness of Räisänen's atomistic exegesis is illustrated by the weakness of his treatment of 3.13 which ignores the connection between vv. 13 and 14 (*Paul* 59–61, 249–51). This despite the fact that he later notes: 'It is striking how often the polemics against the law as the way to salvation are found in a context where the question of the *inclusion of the Gentiles* is the most important problem (Gal. 2–3, Rom. 3–4, Rom. 9–10)' (*Paul* 176; similarly 187).

[55] Commentators are divided on whether ἡμᾶς should be referred only to Jewish Christians (e.g. Betz, *Galatians* 148) or to Gentiles as well (e.g. B. Byrne, *'Sons of God' – 'Seed of Abraham'* [AnBib 83; Rome: Biblical Institute, 1979] 153). Paul could of course mean that the Gentiles were under the law's curse quite apart from the curse on Jewish restrictiveness, since Gentiles also fall short of all that the law requires in their own way (cf. Rom 1.18–31). But such a thought is not to the forefront of Paul's mind here (though cf. Gal 4.8–10). Nevertheless, the baleful effect of Jewish misunderstanding of the law on the Gentiles could be included without too much inexactness in the single thought of both Jew and Gentile requiring deliverance from the curse of the law falsely seen to exclude Gentile *qua* Gentile. To speak of an 'oscillating concept of the law' at this point (Räisänen, *Paul* 19–20) is therefore unwarranted.

inheritance (Deut 21.23; 27–28), that he no doubt felt justified in bringing them together as a way of understanding Jesus' death: Jesus' crucifixion could properly have Deut 21.23 referred to it, as his Jewish contemporaries would agree,[56] and therefore be seen as falling under God's curse, and therefore be related to the curse of Deut 27.26.[57]

(2) The parallel with Gal 4.4–5 clearly confirms that Paul's thought in both passages is moving along such specific and quite narrowly circumscribed lines:

Christ became a curse	Christ became under the law
to redeem from the law's curse	to redeem those under the law
that we might receive the Spirit.	that we might receive the adoption.[58]

As soon as we recall that 'those under the law' are under the curse of the law (v. 10), the purpose of Christ's redemptive work can be specified quite properly as the removal of *that* curse, as the deliverance of the heirs of the covenant promise from the ill effects of the too narrow understanding of covenant and law held by most of Paul's Jewish contemporaries, so that both Jew and Gentile can enter into the fuller scope of the covenant promise. It will be recalled that Eph 2.13–16 spells out this understanding of the cross in quite explicit terms – a confirmation from one who treasured the Pauline tradition most dearly (or from Paul himself) that this very specific doctrine of the cross was one of the principal elements in Paul's theology.

(3) We should also note how well this accords with what Paul himself states to have been the dominant impact of his conversion – the conviction that he should preach Christ among the Gentiles. Contrary to much speculation, Paul's train of thought does not seem to have been: God raised Jesus from the dead; therefore he could not have deserved to die; therefore the law which condemned him is self-condemned and his death frees those who believe in him from any obligation to obey the law.[59] Of such a train of thought Paul's writings give no evidence.[60] He himself gives central place to the conviction that in Christ God's promise was now open to the Gentiles (Gal 1.15–16). This suggests that his train of thought was rather: Christ in his death had put himself under the curse and

---

[56] See 4QpNah 1.7–8; 11QTempleScroll 64.6–13, and the careful discussion of J.A. Fitzmyer, 'Crucifixion in Ancient Palestine, Qumran Literature and the New Testament', *CBQ* 40 (1978) 493–513, reprinted in *To Advance the Gospel* (New York: Crossroad, 1981) 125–46, especially 129–35, 138–9, with references to earlier literature.

[57] See Bruce, *Galatians* 164; also 'Curse of the Law' 31.

[58] Cf. D.R. Schwartz, 'Two Pauline Allusions to the Redemptive Mechanism of the Crucifixion', *JBL* 102 (1983) 260–3. There is no 'discrepancy' between 4.4–5 and 3.13 as Betz asserts (*Galatians* 144 n. 57); both are directed primarily to the soteriological effect of Christ's death (see J.D.G. Dunn, *Christology in the Making* [London: SCM, 1980] 41–2). Cf. further Hays, *Faith* chap. III.

[59] So e.g. the most recent study by H. Weder, *Das Kreuz Jesu bei Paulus* (Göttingen: Vandenhoeck, 1981) 187–93.

[60] Cf. particularly Sanders, *Law* 25–6; Räisänen, *Paul* 249–51 (but see also above n. 54).

outside the covenant blessing (cf. Deut 11.26; 30.19–20) – that is, put himself in the place of the Gentile! Yet God vindicated him! Therefore, God is *for* the Gentiles; and consequently the law could no longer serve as a boundary dividing Jew from Gentile. In short, Christ in his death had effectively abolished this disqualification, by himself being disqualified. It is the outworking of this train of thought which we see unfolding in the incidents described in Gal 2, and climaxing in 2.21: 'If righteousness comes through the law, then Christ died in vain'. Christ's death was effective, in Paul's view, precisely because it broke through the restrictiveness of the typical Jewish understanding of God's righteousness, and demonstrated that the grace of God was now to be experienced apart from the law.[61]

To sum up, then, Gal 3.10–14 does not run counter to the thesis elaborated in the first two sections of this paper. On the contrary, the thesis enables us to grasp the point and the connection of thought in Gal 3.10–14 better than other current alternatives, and shows that the tensions perceived by Räisänen in the passage result from the blinkeredness of his perspective rather than from Paul's own thought.

Conclusion

1. Any attempt to enter sympathetically into the context of Paul's teaching on the law must take into account the social function of the law at that time. That the law served to *identify* the Jewish people as the people chosen by the one God for himself, and as a *boundary* to mark them off from all (other) nations, would have been a basic assumption of Jewish self-understanding. From such a sociological perspective it also becomes self-evident that Jews (including Jewish Christians) would be particularly sensitive at the points where the boundary seemed to be threatened and consequently their own identity challenged. It is no surprise then that in Galatians 2 it is precisely in circumcision and food laws, two of the most obvious boundary markers, that the larger controversy comes to focus.

2. Within this context 'works of the law' would be understood not simply as 'good works' in general, but as those observances of the law which brought this understanding of the law to expression, nomistic service, covenantal nomism, the observances of the law which ought to characterize the good Jew and set him apart from the Gentile, which show him to be 'within the law', 'under the law', his whole existence determined 'from the law'. It is this attitude which Paul attacks in criticizing Jewish 'boasting', their misplaced emphasis on the outward

---

[61] Contrast the artificiality of Räisänen's reconstruction of Paul's reasoning: Paul's 'point of departure is the conviction that the law *must not* be fulfilled outside of the Christian community, for otherwise Christ would have died in vain' (*Paul* 118).

and physical, their claim to an exclusively Jewish righteousness. It is this attitude which Paul sees as a stunted and distorted understanding of what the law requires, and therefore as falling under the curse of the law (Gal 3.10). It is an attitude which is at odds with the faith of Abraham and the faith through which the Galatians entered into the blessing promised to Abraham (Gal 3.11–12).

3. The recognition that what Paul is attacking is a particular and restrictive understanding of the law provides the key to many of the tensions perceived in Paul's writing on the law. Freed from that too narrow understanding of the law, the Jewish Christian (and Gentile) is able to recognize that the law has a continuing positive role, to be fulfilled in love of neighbour. And with the law seen to commend and confirm the right priorities, of faith in God (and his Christ) and love of neighbour, the other priorities which emphasize national distinctiveness can be seen to be false priorities, and the ritual practices involved set on one side as matters of indifference which no one who exercises Abraham's faith and rejoices in the promise given to Abraham should be required to observe.

4. Not least in significance is the way in which our exegesis confirms the dominance of the Jew/Gentile issue in Paul's whole thinking. In his earliest extant teaching on the death of Jesus he asserts that the whole point of Jesus' death on the cross was to remove the boundary of the law and its consequent curse, to liberate the blessing promised to Abraham for all to enjoy (Gal 2.21; 3.13–14). Just as we now recognize that Paul's teaching on justification by faith was directed to the specific issue of how the righteousness of God might be known by Gentile as well as Jew, however justified later systematic reflection on the doctrine was in enlarging and extending it;[62] so now we need to recognize that his initial teaching on the cross was also specifically directed to the same problem, however justified later Christian reflection was in enlarging and extending the doctrine of the atonement. As Gal 1.15–16 indicates, the leading edge of Paul's theological thinking was the conviction that God's purpose embraced Gentile as well as Jew, not the question of how a guilty man might find a gracious God. It was round this conviction and as an expression of it that the other central emphases of Paul's theology first took shape.[63]

---

[62] I refer particularly to K. Stendahl's justly famous essay, 'The Apostle Paul and the Introspective Conscience of the West', *HTR* 56 (1963) 199–215, reprinted in his *Paul Among Jews and Gentiles* (London: SCM, 1977) 78–96; cf. also N.A. Dahl, 'The Doctrine of Justification: its Social Function and Implications', *Studies in Paul* (Minneapolis: Augsburg, 1977) 95–120; W.D. Davies, 'Paul and the People of Israel', NTS 24 (1977–78) 4–39, reprinted in his *Jewish and Pauline Studies* (London: SPCK, 1984) 123–52 (here particularly 128); also his review of Betz's commentary, reprinted in the same collection 172–88; Gaston (as n. 24); and, of course, E.P. Sanders, *Paul and Palestinian Judaism* (London: SCM, 1977).

[63] For critique; Donaldson, 'Curse', see *Jesus, Paul and the Law* 236 n.66.

Chapter 4

The New Perspective on Paul: Paul and the Law

1. Introduction

A fresh assessment of Paul and of Romans in particular has been made possible and necessary by the new perspective on Paul provided by E.P. Sanders.[1] Sanders has been successful in getting across a point which others had made before him,[2] but which had been too little 'heard' within the community of NT scholarship. The point is that Protestant exegesis has for too long allowed a typically Lutheran emphasis on justification by faith to impose a hermeneutical grid on the text of Romans.[3] The emphasis is important, that God is the one who justifies the ungodly (Rom. 4.5), and understandably this insight has become an integrating focus in Lutheran theology with tremendous power. The problem, however, lay in what that emphasis was set in opposition to. The antithesis to 'justification by faith' – what Paul speaks of as 'justification by works' – was understood in terms of a system whereby salvation is *earned* through the *merit of good works*. This was based partly on the comparison suggested in the same passage (4.4–5), and partly on the Reformation rejection of a system where indulgences could be bought and merits accumulated. The latter protest was certainly necessary and justified, and of lasting importance, but the hermeneutical mistake was made of reading this antithesis back into the NT period, of assuming that Paul was protesting against in Pharisaic Judaism precisely what Luther protested against in the pre-Reformation church – the mistake, in other words, of assuming that the

---

[1] *Paul and Palestinian Judaism* (London: SCM, 1977) 1–12 and part 1. The earlier critique of the negative depiction of the law in OT and 'intertestamental' scholarship by M. Limbeck, *Die Ordnung des Heils: Untersuchungen zum Gesetzesverständnis des Frühjudentums* (Düsseldorf: Patmos, 1971) should also be mentioned. See also particularly L. Gaston, 'Paul and the Torah', in A.T. Davies, ed., *Antisemitism and the Foundations of Christianity* (New York: Paulist Press, 1979) 48–71 (here 48–54); and F. Watson, *Paul, Judaism and the Gentiles* (SNTSMS 56; Cambridge: University Press, 1986) 2–18. For examples of discussion in terms of older categories see O. Kuss, 'Nomos bei Paulus', *MTZ* 17 (1966) 173–226; and H. Hübner, *Law in Paul's Thought* (Edinburgh: T & T Clark, 1984).

[2] K. Stendahl, 'The Apostle Paul and the Introspective Conscience of the West', *HTR* 56 (1963) 199–215, reprinted in *Paul among Jews and Gentiles* (London: SCM, 1977) 78–96; N.A. Dahl, 'The Doctrine of Justification: Its Social Function and Implications', *Studies in Paul* (Minneapolis: Augsburg, 1977) 95–120.

[3] See e.g. the way in which G. Bornkamm, *Paul* (London: Hodder & Stoughton, 1971) sets up his discussion of the subject (137).

Judaism of Paul's day was coldly legalistic, teaching a system of earning salvation by the merit of good works, with little or no room for the free forgiveness and grace of God ('the imaginary Rabbinic Judaism, created by Christian scholars in order to form a suitably lurid background for the Epistles of St. Paul').[4]

It was this depiction of first-century Judaism which Sanders showed up for what it was – a gross caricature, which, regrettably, has played its part in feeding an evil strain of Christian anti-Semitism. On the contrary, however, as Sanders demonstrated clearly enough, Judaism's whole religious self-understanding was based on the premise of grace – that God had freely chosen Israel and made his covenant with Israel to be their God and they his people. This covenant relationship was regulated by the law, not as a way of entering the covenant, or of gaining merit, but as the way of living *within* the covenant; and that included the provision of sacrifice and atonement for those who confessed their sins and thus repented. Paul himself indicates the attitude clearly in his citation of Lev. 18.5 in Rom. 10.5 – 'the person who does these things [what the law requires] shall live by them'. This attitude Sanders characterized by the now well-known phrase 'covenantal nomism' – that is, 'the maintenance of status' among the chosen people of God by observing the law given by God as part of that covenant relationship.[5] Sanders' review had not encompassed all the available Jewish literature of the period, but it has been confirmed by the work of one of my own postgraduates, Don Garlington, who has demonstrated the consistency of the 'covenantal nomism' pattern throughout the Jewish writings contained in 'the Apocrypha'.[6]

Unfortunately Sanders did not follow through this insight far enough or with sufficient consistency. Instead of setting Paul more fully against and within this context of Judaism so understood, he advanced the thesis that Paul had jumped in arbitrary fashion (as a result of his Damascus road encounter) from one system (covenantal nomism) into another (Christianity),[7] leaving his theology, par-

---

[4] C.-G. Montefiore, *Judaism and St. Paul* (1914; reproduced New York: Arno, 1973) 65. In addition to the examples cited by Sanders, *Paul*, and Watson, *Paul*, see e.g. F.J. Leenhardt, *Romans* (CNT 1957; ET London: Lutterworth, 1961) passim, and H.Ridderbos, *Paul: An Outline of his Theology* (Grand Rapids: Eerdmans, 1975) 130–35.

[5] Sanders, *Paul* 544; see further J.D.G. Dunn, 'The New Perspective on Paul', *BJRL* 65 (1983) 95–122 [= ch. 2 above]; similarly Limbeck, *Ordnung* 29–35; cf. J.A. Ziesler, *The Meaning of Righteousness in Paul* (SNTSMS 20; Cambridge: University Press, 1972) 95.

[6] *'The Obedience of Faith': A Pauline Phrase in Historical Context* (WUNT 2.38; Tübingen: Mohr Siebeck, 1991). See also J.J. Collins, *Between Athens and Jerusalem: Jewish identity in the Hellenistic Diaspora* (New York: Crossroad, 1983), who, however, notes that the pattern is not so consistent through all diaspora literature (14–15, 29, 48, 77, 141, 167, 178–81, 236–7). For the importance of the covenant in Judaism leading up to and at the time of Paul, see also particularly A. Jaubert, *La notion d'alliance dans le Judaisme* (Editions du Seuil, 1963).

[7] Sanders, *Paul* 550–2.

ticularly in reference to the law, incoherent and contradictory.[8] On this last point he has been given strong support by Heikki Räisänen,[9] who also argues that Paul 'intended to portray Judaism as a religion of merit and achievement',[10] and that he thus 'gives a totally distorted picture of the Jewish religion'.[11] Just as puzzling from a different angle is the fact that the 'covenantal nomism' of Palestinian Judaism as described by Sanders bears a striking similarity to what has been commonly understood as the religion of Paul himself (good works as the fruit of God's prior acceptance by grace).[12] What, then, can it be to which Paul is objecting?

2. Exegetical Questions

The exegetical questions exposed here focus very largely on the issue of Paul and the law.[13] This is important since the law actually forms a major secondary theme of the letter, to an extent not usually appreciated.[14] Rather striking is the way in which Paul regularly in Romans develops part of his discussion before bringing in the law (2.12ff.; 3.27ff.; 4.13ff.; 5.20; ch. 7), while in other key sections it is the role of the law which provides a crucial hinge in the argument (3.19–21; 8.2–4; 9.31–10.5). Since these references taken together span the complete argument of chs. 1–11 in all its stages, there can be little doubt that the tension between his gospel and the law and his concern to resolve that tension provide one of Paul's chief motivations in penning the letter.

Moreover, it is hardly a coincidence that several of the most recalcitrant exegetical problems in Romans are bound up with this central secondary theme of the letter. Thus it is significant once again that Sanders and Räisänen are unable to integrate Paul's treatment of the law in ch. 2 into the rest of his theology.[15] The

---

[8] E.P. Sanders, *Paul, the Law and the Jewish People* (Philadelphia: Fortress, 1983).

[9] H. Räisänen, *Paul and the Law* (WUNT 29; Tübingen: Mohr Siebeck, 1983).

[10] 'Paul's Conversion and the Developments of his View of the Law', *NTS* 33 (1987) 404–19.

[11] 'Legalism and Salvation by the Law: Paul's Portrayal of the Jewish Religion as a Historical and Theological Problem', in S. Pedersen, ed., *Die Paulinische Literatur und Theologie* (Aarhus: Aros/Göttingen: Vandenhoeck & Ruprecht, 1980) 63–83 (here 72), reprinted in *The Torah and Christ* (Helsinki: Finnish Exegetical Society, 1096) 25–54; in agreement with H.J. Schoeps, *Paul: the Theology of the Apostle in the Light of Jewish Religious History* (London: Lutterworth, 1961) 200; though with an important concession in Räisänen, *Torah* 183.

[12] M.D. Hooker, 'Paul and "Covenantal Nomism"', in M.D. Hooker & S.G. Wilson, eds., *Paul and Paulinism*, C.K. Barrett FS (London: SPCK, 1982) 47–56.

[13] Hence, not surprisingly, the titles of the books by Sanders (n. 8) and Räisänen (n. 9), as also by Hübner (n. 1).

[14] F. Hahn, 'Das Gesetzesverständnis im Römer- und Galaterbrief', *ZNW* 67 (1976) 29–63: 'an indispensable accompanying motif' (30).

[15] Sanders, *Law* 147 – 'true self-contradiction'; Räisänen, 'Paul's Theological Difficulties with the Law', in E.A. Livingstone, ed., *Studia Biblica 1978*, Vol. III (JSNTSup 3; Sheffield:

use of *nomos* in 3.27–31 has caused unending puzzlement: should we take *nomos* in v.27 as a reference to the law or translate 'principle'? And how can Paul claim in v.31 to be 'establishing the law'? The centrality of the law in ch. 7 has been recognized, but how and whether that insight facilitates the exegesis of 7.14–25 in particular is a matter of unresolved controversy, with the meaning of *nomos* in 7.23 and 8.2 disputed in the same way as in 3.27. In the obviously crucial resumptive section, 9.30–10.4, there is equal controversy over the meaning of *nomos dikaiosynēs*, 'law of righteousness' (9.31), and *telos nomou*, 'end of the law' (10.4). And in the paraenetic section the claim that love of neighbour is a fulfilment of the law (13.8–10) causes further puzzlement to those who think that Paul has turned his back on Judaism and its law. As Räisänen's withering critique has underlined,[16] the problem of holding together in an integrated whole both the positive and the negative statements regarding the law in Romans has not reached a satisfactory solution; though Räisänen's own atomistic treatment of the texts is itself a hindrance to an integrated and coherent overview of the theme.

Clearly, then, this major secondary motif in the letter presents problems of central importance for our understanding of the letter. It may be, indeed, that they all hang together, and a correct solution of one may carry with it resolution of the others. At all events it will be necessary to gain a clearer view of the role of the law in first-century Judaism before we venture into the letter itself. Only when we can take for granted what Paul and his readers took for granted with regard to the law and its function will we be able to hear the allusions he was making and understand the arguments he was offering. The confusion and disagreement still remaining with regard to the passages listed above strongly suggest that the role of the law, both within the Judaism against which Paul was reacting, and within the new perspective on Paul, has not as yet been properly perceived. In what follows I will therefore attempt briefly to 'set the scene' for an understanding of this important integrating strand of the letter.

3. Nomos as Equivalent of Torah

First of all, we should clarify a point that has occasioned some misunderstanding and confusion, namely, the appropriateness of *nomos*/law as the translation equivalent or 'meaning' of *torah*/Torah. Since S. Schechter[17] and C.H. Dodd,[18] it has frequently been claimed that *torah* does not mean *nomos* or 'law'; rather,

---

JSOT Press, 1980) 301–20 (reprinted in *Torah* 3–24) – 'contradictory lines of thought' 307; also *Law*.

[16] *Law* 23–28, 42–83.

[17] *Aspects of Rabbinic Theology* (1909; New York: Schocken, 1961).

[18] 'The Law', *The Bible and the Greeks* (London: Hodder & Stoughton, 1935) 25–41.

torah means simply 'instruction' or 'teaching', and *the* Torah (the Pentateuch, or indeed the whole of the scriptures) includes more than law. According to an influential body of opinion, this equation of *torah*/Torah with (the) law as given by the LXX translation of *torah* using the narrower word *nomos*, subsequently contributed to Paul's 'distorted' understanding of his ancestral faith, and lies at the root of the modern characterization of Judaism as 'legalistic'.[19] However, Stephen Westerholm has now shown clearly (1) that *nomos* can be an appropriate rendering of *torah* (e.g. Gen. 26.5; Exod. 12.49; Lev. 26.46); (2) that the technical use of '*torah* to refer to a collection which spells out Israel's covenantal obligations' goes back to Deuteronomy, which provides the basis for Torah = *nomos* = law as an appropriate title for the Pentateuch (e.g. Deut. 4.8; 30.10; 32.46); and (3) that Paul's use of *nomos* to sum up Israel's obligations as set out by Moses is 'fully in line with Hebrew usage of *torah*' (cf. e.g. Rom. 2.12, 17–18; 7.12 and 10.5, with 1 Kings 2.3; Ezra 7.6, 10, 12, 14, 26; Neh. 8.14; 9.14, 34; and Jer. 32.23).

In particular, the basic understanding of 'covenantal nomism' is more or less self-evident in the central foundation act of Israel as a nation – the exodus from Egypt and the giving of the law at Sinai. As quintessentially expressed in Exod. 20 and Deut. 5, the law (here the ten commandments – cf. Deut. 4.8 with 5.1) follows upon the prior act of divine initiative ('I am the Lord your God, who brought you out of the land of Egypt ...'); obedience to this law is Israel's response to divine grace, not an attempt to gain God's favour conceived as grudgingly given and calculatingly dispensed. As already implied, the fullest and most sustained expression of this basic Jewish theologoumenon is Deuteronomy, the classic statement of Israel's covenant theology: the statutes and ordinances of the law (chs. 5–28) set out explicitly as God's covenant made with Israel (5.2–3; 29.1); the promise (and warning) repeatedly reaffirmed in numerous variations, 'This do and live' (e.g. 4.1, 10, 40; 5.29–33; 6.1–2, 18, 24; 7.12–13; etc.).[20] Not surprisingly, in Romans Paul interacts more frequently with Deuteronomy than with any other section of the Pentateuch; and his exposition of Deut. 30.12–14 is at the centre of his attempt to expound the continuing and wider significance of the law in a way which retrieves the law from a too narrowly defined understanding of 'This do and live' (10.5–13).

It is unnecessary to enter into the debate about how deeply rooted this understanding of covenant and law was in pre-exilic Israelite religion.[21] Whatever the

---

[19] E.g. Dodd, 'Law' 34; Schoeps, *Paul* 29; S. Sandmel, *The Genius of Paul* (1958; Philadelphia: Fortress, 1979) 47–8; cited by S. Westerholm, '*Torah, Nomos* and *Law*: A Question of Meaning', *SR* 15 (1986) 327–36 (here 330–1); also P. Lapide & P. Stuhlmacher, *Paul: Rabbi and Apostle* (Minneapolis: Augsburg, 1984) 39.

[20] See also my *Romans* (WBC 38; Dallas: Word, 1988) on 2.13 and 10.5.

[21] See e.g. E. W. Nicholson, *God and his People: Covenant and Theology in the Old Testament* (Oxford: Clarendon, 1986).

actual facts in that case, the attitude of covenantal nomism was certainly given determinative shape by Ezra's reforms in the post-exilic period, with their deliberate policy of national and cultic segregation as dictated by the law (Ezra 9–10). This trend was massively reinforced by the Maccabean crisis, where it was precisely Israel's identity as the covenant people, the people of the law, which was at stake (1 Macc. 1.57; 2.27, 50; 2 Macc. 1.2–4; 2.21–22; 5.15; 13.14), and where 'zeal for the law' became the watchword of national resistance (1 Macc. 2.26–27, 50, 58; 2 Macc. 4.2; 7.2, 9, 11, 37; 8.21; 13.14).[22] So, too, in the period following the Maccabean crisis the tie-in between election, covenant and law remains a fundamental and persistent theme of Jewish self-understanding, as illustrated by ben Sira,[23] *Jubilees*,[24] the Damascus document,[25] and pseudo-Philo.[26] In particular we may note the outworking of all this in two of the main groups in Palestinian Judaism at the time of Jesus and Paul. The Qumran community defined membership of the covenant of grace in terms of observing God's precepts and clinging to God's commandments (1QS 1.7–8; 5.1–3), and commitment to the law had to be total and to be examined every year, with any breach severely punished (1QS 5.24; 8.16–9.2). And the Pharisees were known for their *akribeia*, 'strictness', in observing the law,[27] and evidently also for their concern to maintain a level of purity in their daily lives which the law required only for the temple cult itself.[28] For rabbinic traditions on Israel's special relationship with the law we may confine ourselves to two quotations provided by Schoeps: *Sifre Deut*. 53b-75b – God addresses Israel in the words 'Let it be clear from the keeping of the commandments that you are a people holy to me'; and *Mek. Exod*. 20.6 – 'By covenant is meant nothing other than the Torah'.[29]

3.1   The law thus became a basic expression of Israel's *distinctiveness* as the people specially chosen by (the one) God to be his people. In sociological terms the law functioned as an 'identity marker' and 'boundary', reinforcing Israel's sense of distinctiveness and distinguishing Israel from the surrounding nations.[30] This sense of separateness was deeply rooted in Israel's national con-

---

[22] See further my *Romans* on 10.2.

[23] Sir. 17.11–17; 24.23; 28.7; 39.8; 42.2; 44.19–20; 45.5, 7, 15, 17, 24–25.

[24] *Jub*. 1.4–5, 9–10, 12, 14, 29; 2.21; 6.4–16; 14.17–20; 15.4–16, 19–21, 25–29, 34; 16.14; 19.29; 20.3; etc.

[25] CD 1.4–5, 15–18, 20; 3.2–4, 10–16; 4.7–10; 6.2–5; etc.

[26] *LAB* 4.5, 11; 7.4; 8.3; 9.3–4, 7–8, 13, 15; 10.2; 11.1–5; etc.

[27] See my *Romans* xl.

[28] See again my *Romans* on 14.14.

[29] Schoeps, *Paul* 195, 216; see further Str-B 3.126–33.

[30] J. Neusner, *Judaism: The Evidence of the Mishnah* (Chicago: University Press, 1981) 72–5; W. A. Meeks, *The First Urban Christians: The Social World of the Apostle Paul* (New Haven: Yale University, 1983) 97; J.D.G. Dunn, 'Works of the Law and the Curse of the Law (Galatians 3.10–14)', *NTS* 31 (1985) 523–42 (524–7) [= ch. 3 above (122–5)].

sciousness (e.g. Lev. 20.24–26; Ezra 10.11; Neh. 13.3; *Pss. Sol.* 17.28; *3 Macc.* 3.4) and comes to powerful expression in *Jub.* 22.16:

> Separate yourself from the Gentiles,
>   and do not eat with them,
>   and do not perform deeds like theirs.
> And do not become associates of theirs.
> Because their deeds are defiled,
>   and all of their ways are contaminated,
>   and despicable, and abominable.

The letter of *Aristeas* 139–142 expresses the same conviction in terms which reinforce the sociological insight:

> [139]In his wisdom the legislator [i.e. Moses] ... surrounded us with unbroken palisades and iron walls to prevent our mixing with any of the other peoples in any matter, ... [142]So, to prevent our being perverted by contact with others or by mixing with bad influences, he hedged us in on all sides with strict observances connected with meat and drink and touch and hearing and sight, after the manner of the Law.

Similarly Philo, Mos. 1.278: Israel will be a people

> which shall dwell alone, not reckoned among other nations ... because in virtue of the distinction of their peculiar customs they do not mix with others to depart from the ways of their fathers.

And a funerary inscription from Italy praises a woman 'who lived a gracious life inside Judaism (*kalōs biōsasa en tō Ioudaismō*) – Judaism understood as 'a sort of fenced off area in which Jewish lives are led'.[31]

Consistent with this is the characterization of Gentiles as *anomos* and their works as *anomia*: by definition they were 'without the law, outside the law', that is, outside the area (Israel) coterminous with the law, marked out by the law; so already in the Psalms,[32] in 1 Maccabees,[33] and in the self-evident equation, Gentile = 'sinner'.[34] Not surprisingly this desire to live within the law and to be marked off from the lawless and sinner became a dominant concern in the factionalism which was a feature of Judaism in the period from the Maccabeans to the emergence of rabbinic Judaism as the most powerful faction within post-CE 70 Judaism. It was expressed in the frequent complaints of 'the righteous' and 'devout' over against those (within Israel) whom they characterized as 'sinners'.[35]

---

[31] Y. Amir, 'The Term *Ioudaismos*: A Study in Jewish-Hellenistic Self-Definition', *Immanuel* 14 (1982) 34–41 (here 35–6, 39–40).

[32] Pss. 28.3; 37.28; 55.3; 73.3; 92.7; 104.35; 125.3.

[33] 1 Macc. 3.5–6; 7.5; 9.23, 58, 69; 11.25; 14.14.

[34] As in Tob. 13.6[LXX 8]; *Jub.* 23.23–24; *Pss. Sol.* 1.1; 2.1–2; 17.22–25; Matt. 5.47/Luke 6.33; Gal. 2.15.

[35] As in Wisd. Sol. 2–5; *Jub.* 6.32–35; 23.16, 26; *1 Enoch* 1.1, 7–9; 5.6–7; 82.4–7; 1QS 2.4–5;

3.2 A natural and more or less inevitable converse of this sense of distinctive-ness was the sense of *privilege*, precisely in being the nation specially chosen by the one God and favoured by gift of covenant and law. This comes out particu-larly clearly in writings which could not simply ignore and dismiss Gentiles as sinners, but which had to attempt some sort of apologetic for the claims of Israel in the face of a much more powerful Gentile world. Thus both Philo ad Josephus speak with understandable if exaggerated pride of the widespread desire among Greeks and barbarians to adopt Jewish customs and laws. Phil, *Mos.* 2.17–25:

> they attract and win the attention of all ... the sanctity of our legislation has been a source of wonder not only to Jews and to all others also.

Josephus, *Ap.* 2.277–286:

> The masses have long since shown a keen desire to adopt our religious observances ... Were we not ourselves aware of the excellence of our laws, assuredly we should have been impelled to pride [*mega phronein*] ourselves upon them by the multitude of their ad-mirers.

Expressive of the same pride in the law of Moses is what seems to have been a fairly sustained attempt in Jewish apologetic to present Moses as 'the first wise man', who was teacher of Orpheus and from whose writings Plato and Pytha-goras learned much of their wisdom.[36]

Pride in the law as the mark of God's special favour to Israel is also well illus-trated in the identification of divine Wisdom with the law, the assertion that the universally desirable Wisdom, immanent within creation but hidden from human eyes, is embodied within 'the book of the covenant of the Most High God, the law which Moses commanded us as an inheritance for the congrega-tions of Jacob' (Sir. 24.23). The same claim is expressed more forcefully in Bar. 3.36–4.4:

> [36] ... (He) gave her to Jacob his servant and to Israel whom he loved
>
> . . . . . .
>
> [1]She is the book of the commandments of God,
>   and the law which endures for ever.
> All who hold her fast will live,
>   but those who forsake her will die.
> [2]Turn, O Jacob, and take her;
>   walk towards the shining of her light.
> [3]Do not give your glory (*tēn doxan sou*) to another;
>   or your advantages (*ta sympheronta*) to an alien people.

1QH 10[=2].8–19; CD 1.13–21; *Pss. Sol.* 3.3–12; 4.8; 13.5–12; 15.1–13; 'Pharisees' probably = 'separated ones'; see also my *Romans* on 3.7, 4.5, 7–8 and 9.6.

[36] Eupolemus, frag. 1; Artapanus, frag. 3; Aristobulus, frag. 3–4; from Eusebius, *Praep. Evang.* 9.26.1; 9.27.3–6; 13.12.1–4; texts in J.H. Charlesworth, ed., *The Old Testament Pseudepi-grapha*, Vol. 2 (London: Darton, Longman and Todd, 1985).

[4]Blessed are we, O Israel,
  for what is pleasing to God is known (*gnōsta*) to us.

For those confronted by the crushing of Rome within Palestine this sense of privilege was difficult to maintain. *Psalms of Solomon* found a solution in pressing the older distinction between discipline and punishment (particularly *Pss. Sol.* 3, 10 and 13) – thus 13.6–11:

> The destruction of the sinner is terrible
>   but nothing shall harm the righteous, of all these things,
> For the discipline of the righteous (for things done) in ignorance
>   is not the same as the destruction of the sinners
>   . . . .
> For the Lord will spare his devout,
>   and he will wipe away their mistakes with discipline.
> For the life of the righteous (goes on) for ever,
>   but sinners shall be taken away to destruction . . .

Less easy to satisfy was the writer of *4 Ezra*, who in common with his fellow Jews saw the law given to Israel as a mark of divine favour (3.19; 9.31), but who could not understand how God could spare the sinful nations and yet allow his law-keeping people to be so harshly treated (3.28–36; 4.23–24; 5.23–30; 6.55–59).

3.3 A sociological perspective also helps us to see how the conviction of privileged election and the practice of covenantal nomism almost inevitably come to expression in focal points of distinctiveness, particular laws and especially ritual practices which reinforced the sense of distinctive identity and marked Israel off most clearly from the other nations. In this case three of Israel's laws gained particular prominence as being especially distinctive – circumcision, food laws and Sabbath.[37] These were not the only beliefs and practices which marked out Jews, but from the Maccabean period onward they gained increasing significance for their boundary-defining character and were widely recognized both within and without Judaism as particularly and distinctively characteristic of Jews. Not that they were intrinsically more important than other laws, simply that they had become points of particular sensitivity in Jewish national understanding and were test cases of covenant loyalty. Since I provide sufficient documentation elsewhere I need say no more here.[38]

---

[37] Cf. Limbeck, *Ordnung* 34; Meeks, *First Urban Christians* 36–7, 97; Sanders, *Law* 102.
[38] See my *Romans*, on 2.25 and 14.2, 5.

4. Paul and the Law in Romans

This, then, is the context within which and against which we must set Paul's treatment of the law in Romans. The Jews, proselytes and God-worshipping Gentiles among his readership would read what Paul says about the law in the light of this close interconnection in Jewish theology of Israel's election, covenant and law. They would, I believe, recognize that what Paul was concerned about was the fact that covenant promise and law had become too inextricably identified with ethnic Israel as such, with the Jewish people marked out in their national distinctiveness by the practices of circumcision, food laws and Sabbath in particular.[39] They would recognize that what Paul was endeavouring to do was to free both promise and law for a wider range of recipients, freed from the ethnic constraints which he saw to be narrowing the grace of God and diverting the saving purpose of God out of its main channel – Christ.

Not least in importance, by setting Paul's treatment of the law into this matrix we are enabled to offer a solution to the sequence of exegetical problems and disputes outline above (#2). Thus it should occasion no surprise that Rom. 2 turns out to be a developing critique of precisely these features of Jewish covenant theology which were sketched out above (#3) – the law as dividing Jew from non-Jew, the haves from the have-nots, those within from those without (2.12–14); the law as a source of ethnic pride for the typical devout Jew (2.17–23); and circumcision as the focal point for this sense of privileged distinctiveness (2.25–29).[40] Paul regularly warns against 'the works of the law', not as 'good works' in general or as any attempt by the individual to amass merit for himself, but rather as that pattern of obedience by which 'the righteous' maintain their status within the people of the covenant, as evidenced not least by their dedication on such sensitive 'test' issues as Sabbath and food laws.[41]

Likewise I argue that an important hermeneutical key to such crucial passages as 3.27–31, 7.14–25 and 9.30–10.4 is precisely the recognition that Paul's negative thrust against the law is against the law taken over too completely by Israel, the law misunderstood by a misplaced emphasis on boundary-marking ritual, the law become a tool of sin in its too close identification with matters of the flesh, the law side-tracked into a focus for nationalistic zeal. Freed from that too narrowly Jewish perspective, the law still has an important part to play in 'the obedience of faith'. And the paraenetic section (12.1–15.6) can then be seen as Paul's attempt to provide a basic guideline for social living, the law redefined for

---

[39] N.T. Wright, *The Messiah and the People of God* (D.Phil dissertation, University of Oxford, 1980) ch. 2 appropriately coins the phrase 'national righteousness'.

[40] L. Hartman, 'Bundesideologie in und hinter einigen paulinischen Texten', in Pedersen, ed., *Paulinische Literatur und Theologie* (n. 11 above) 103–18, draws attention to the consistent strand of 'covenant theology' in and behind these chapters.

[41] See further my *Romans*, on 3.20 and 14.2, 5.

the eschatological people of God in place of the law misunderstood in too distinctively Jewish terms, with the climax understandably focused on a treatment of the two older test-cases, food laws and Sabbath (14.1–15.6). It is my contention that only with such an understanding can we do adequate justice to both the positive and the negative thrusts of Paul's treatment of the law in Romans, and that failure to appreciate 'the social function' of the law (as outlined above) is a fatal weakness both of alternative attempts[42] and of Räisänen's critique.

In short, properly understood, Paul's treatment of the law, which has seemed so confused and incoherent to many commentators, actually becomes one of the chief integrating strands which binds the whole letter into a cohesive and powerful treatment of Jewish covenant theology in the light of Christ.

---

[42] E.g. C.E.B. Cranfield, 'Paul and the Law', *SJT* 17 (1964) 43–68; Hahn (n. 14 above); Hübner (n. 1 above).

Chapter 5

What was the Issue between Paul and "Those of the Circumcision"?

I

"Those of the circumcision" (οἱ ἐκ περιτομῆς) appear in the NT as a group or body of people who were deeply suspicious of the developing mission to the Gentiles and who were opposed to Paul in particular.

Acts 11:2 – When Peter went up to Jerusalem (after preaching to and baptizing the Gentile centurion, Cornelius) those of the circumcision took issue with him (διεκρίνοντο πρὸς αὐτὸν οἱ ἐκ περιτομῆς), saying. "Why did you go to uncircumcised men and eat with them"?

Gal 2:12 – Before certain men came from James he (Cephas/Peter) ate with the Gentiles: but when they came he withdrew and separated himself, fearing those of the circumcision (τοὺς ἐκ περιτομῆς).

Tit 1:10 – There are many insubordinate men, idle talkers and deceivers especially those of the circumcision (οἱ ἐκ τῆς περιτομῆς).

It is also clear that "those of the circumcision" is a way of designating Jews. Whether we should speak more precisely of Jews in their suspicion and opposition, or of Jews in general, whether of believing (Christian) Jews and/or unbelieving Jews[1], are questions we need not go into for the moment.

The question for us is: Why were those of the circumcision so suspicious and hostile? What was the issue? What was at stake? One answer, if not a large part of the complete answer, naturally focuses on circumcision itself. They are described as "those of the circumcision" in part at least because circumcision was the issue, or was the key to the suspicion and opposition. This is sufficiently obvious from those letters and passages in which Paul confronts most sharply what we may call for the moment "the Jew/Gentile issue". The issue was bound up with the meaning and value of circumcision (Rom 2:25 – 3:1). The desirability and/or necessity of circumcision for Gentile converts was at the heart of the matter (Gal 2:3; 5:2–12). "Who are the circumcision?" was a question Paul felt able and thought necessary to contest (Phil 3:3). But that information only provides a first step towards answering our main question; it simply serves to focus the question more sharply on circumcision itself. Why was circumcision so import-

---

[1] See e.g. commentaries on Gal 2:12.

ant? Why was it such a focal point of dispute, of apologetic and polemic? What was at issue? What was at stake in all this?

I need hardly remind you of the classic Reformation answer to the question: Paul contested the necessity of circumcision because it was a prime example of meritorious works, of self-achieved salvation, an impossibility for the creature and sinner before the Creator and Saviour God; Paul was confronted by a legalistic Judaism which he contested as the advocate of justification by faith. Nor need I remind you that such a reading of Jewish opinion, or particularly of Judaism as a whole, has been radically questioned – initially by Jewish scholars who found this reading of Paul both baffling and offensive, and latterly by Christians[2]. Nor will I attempt here to follow up that debate, in which I have been involved elsewhere[3], and which has already been the subject of several reviews[4].

Clearly however something of a fresh look at the old question is necessary – especially a fresh look which sets the question firmly within the context of the Judaism (or Judaisms)[5] of the period. Too many expositions of Paul at this point have been content to follow a logic which they see in his argument, without sufficiently rooting it within or checking it against the fuller picture we now have of first century Judaism. Citation of Jewish sources has often been much too heavily dependent on a lopsided view and use of rabbinic traditions and/or on selective proof-texting (4 Ezra particularly). The resulting strains and contradictions

---

[2] Most recently by M. LIMBECK, *Die Ordnung des Heils: Untersuchungen zum Gesetzesverständnis des Frühjudentums* (Düsseldorf: Patmos, 1971) and most decisively and influentially, in English-speaking scholarship at any rate, by E.P. SANDERS, *Paul and Palestinian Judaism* (London: SCM, 1977). See also particularly L. GASTON, "Paul and the Torah" (1979), *Paul and the Torah* (Vancouver: University of British Columbia, 1987) 15–34; F. WATSON, *Paul, Judaism and the Gentiles* (SNTSMS 56; Cambridge University, 1986) 2–18. For examples of discussion in the more traditional categories see O. KUSS "Nomos bei Paulus", *MTZ* 17 (1966) 173–226, and H. HÜBNER, *Law in Paul's Thought* (Edinburgh: T & T. Clark, 1984).

[3] See particularly J.D.G. DUNN, "The New Perspective on Paul", *BJRL* 65 (1983) 95–122 [= ch. 2 above], and "Works of the Law and the Curse of the Law (Galatians 3:10–14)", *NTS* 31 (1985) 523–42 [= ch. 3 above], both reprinted in DUNN, *Jesus, Paul and the Law* (London: SPCK/Philadelphia: Westminster, 1990), with further responses and contributions to the debate which should make clear both my indebtedness to SANDERS in particular, but also the extent of my disagreement with him.

[4] See e.g. J.M.G. BARCLAY, "Paul and the Law: Observations on Some Recent Debates", *Themelios* 12.1 (1986) 5–15; F.F. BRUCE, "Paul and the law in recent research", *Law and Religion. Essays on the Place of the Law in Israel and Early Christianity*, ed. B. LINDARS (Cambridge: James Clarke, 1988) 115–25; G. KLEIN, "Ein Sturmzentrum der Paulusforschung", *VuF* 33 (1988) 40–56; J. LAMBRECHT, "Gesetzesverständnis bei Paulus", *Das Gesetz im Neuen Testament*, hrsg. K. KERTELGE (Freiburg: Herder, 1986), 88–127; D.J. MOO, "Paul and the Law in the Last Ten Years", *SJT* 40 (1987) 287–307; A.J.M. WEDDERBURN, "Paul and the Law", *SJT* 38 (1985) 613–22; S. WESTERHOLM, *Israel's Faith and the Church's Faith. Paul and His Recent Interpreters* (Grand Rapids: Eerdmans, 1988).

[5] As J. NEUSNER has often pointed out, the plural may be the more accurate description of the historical reality.

within the exposition of Pauline theology (as well as with other Jewish source material) has been well presented by H. Räisänen[6].

In a single paper it is obviously impossible to give an adequate overview of the Judaism of Paul's period and of the significance of circumcision therein. But it may be possible to sketch in the main outlines of the more detailed picture, with sufficient documentation to demonstrate its authenticity. This more modest, but still ambitious task I will attempt, drawing mainly on the so-called "intertestamental" literature (including the DSS), which has best claim to speak for at least some of the Judaisms of Paul's period.

To understand the significance of circumcision for the bulk of Paul's Jewish comtemporaries it is of course necessary to set it within its own context. This will necessitate a brief consideration of two of its most immediate correlates – "covenant" and "law". The full extent of the correlation will become apparent later. For the moment it is enough to note that circumcision first emerged in Jewish tradition in connection with the covenant made with Abraham (Gen 17), and that the tie-in between covenant and circumcision is central to Paul's discussion (Gal 3–4; Rom 4)[7]. Circumcision equally could be seen as a key expression of the law: the parallel formulation of Rom 4:12 and 16 is sufficient indication that οἱ ἐκ περιτομῆς and οἱ ἐκ τοῦ νόμου are near synonyms, at least in Paul's perspective. It was in fact, as we shall see, the double relation of circumcision to covenant and law which lay at the heart of the problem confronting Paul. Nor is it insignificant that E. P. Sanders has been able to sum up the dominant Jewish attitude of the period as "covenantal nomism" – the concern to maintain covenant status by observing the torah[8]; within that perspective bodily circumcision was the first act of torah-observance (of covenantal nomism) for both native born Jew and proselyte[9]. Here too, as again we shall see, it was the, to most Jews, self-evident correlation between covenant and law as epitomized in circumcision which was at the heart of the problem for Paul.

Consequently we will need to begin with a brief sketch of Jewish self-understanding of covenant and law and of "covenantal nomism".

II

Without entering into the tradition-history lying behind the several redactions of the Pentateuch and their influence on the rest of the Jewish scriptures, it is suf-

---

[6] *Paul and the Law* (WUNT 29; Tübingen: Mohr, 1983).

[7] Rom 4 is a reminder that a discussion of "covenant theology" does not depend on or require the use of the word "covenant" itself. See further below.

[8] SANDERS, *PPJ*. e.g. 544; similarly LIMBECK (n. 2) 29–35.

[9] Cf. P. BORGEN, "Debates on Circumcision in Philo and Paul", *Paul Preaches Circumcision and Please Men* (Trondheim: Tapir, 1983) 18.

ficiently clear that the Deuteronomic model stamped a fundamental and lasting
character on Jewish self-understanding[10]. In this model the tie-in between covenant and law is central, and the pattern of covenantal nomism is clear. The heart
of the book (Deut 5–28) is set out as a restatement of the covenant made at
Horeb/Sinai (5:2–3); 29:1 sums up the whole of the block of teaching – "These
are the words of the covenant which the Lord commanded Moses to make with
the people of Israel in the land of Moab, besides the covenant which he had
made with them at Horeb". And throughout the book the emphasis of covenantal nomism is sustained and reinforced in numerous restatements of the promise
(and warning): "This do and live" (4:1, 10, 40; 5:29–33; 6:1–2, 18, 24; 7:12–13;
etc). Deuteronomy thus provides the classic statement of Jewish covenant theology.

In view of the often repeated observation that תּוֹרָה is a much broader category than νόμος, and that the LXX rendering of the former by the latter distorted Jewish thought and gave unjustified foundation to the perception of Jewish "legalism"[11], it is important to realize that the equation *Torah* = law is firmly
rooted in Deuteronomy itself. In Deuteronomy תּוֹרָה denotes the collection of
ordinances/commandments/statutes which spell out Israel's covenantal obligations – "all this law" כָּל הַתּוֹרָה (4:8), "all the words of this law" (כָּל דִּבְרֵי הַתּוֹרָה
(32:46); and the basis oi the equation, *Torah* = Pentateuch, is already firmly established (30:10 – "this book of the law"). This does *not* support the further unjustified association of νόμος with legalism – another outworking of the traditional denigration of "late Judaism". But it does mean that Paul's use of νόμος to
sum up Israel's obligations as set out by Moses cannot be dismissed as a Hellenistic Jew's Septuagintal distortion of his heritage, and that Paul's theological argument was interacting with a very important strand of Jewish thought and
life[12].

Without attempting to trace the course of theological development following
the appearance of Deuteronomy, or to evaluate the impact of the exile and the
Ezra reforms, it is sufficient for us to note that the Deuteronomic pattern was
massively reinforced by the Maccabean crisis. In that crisis it was precisely Israel's identity as the covenant people, the people of the law, which was at stake
(1. Macc 1: 57; 2:27, 50; 2. Macc 1: 2–4; 2:21–22; 5:15; 13:14). And the response to
that crisis was expressed in terms of "zeal for the law" as the watchword of na-

---

[10] See particularly E.W. NICHOLSON, *God and His People: Covenant and Theology in the Old
Testament* (Oxford: Clarendon, 1986).

[11] See S. SCHECHTER, *Aspects of Rabbinic Theology* (1909) (New York: Schocken, 1961) 117;
C.H. DODD, "The Law", *The Bible and the Greeks* (London: Hodder, 1935) 25–41; H.-J.
SCHOEPS, *Paul: The Theology of the Apostle in the Light of Jewish Religious History* (London:
Lutterworth, 1961) ch. 5.

[12] See particularly S. WESTERHOLM, "Torah, Nomos, and Law: A Question of 'Meaning'",
Studies in Religion 15 (1986) 327–36.

tional resistance (1. Macc 2:26–27, 50, 58; 2. Macc 4:2; 7:2, 9, 11, 37; 8:21; 13:14). From these passages it becomes clear that in the piety crystallized and cherished among the Maccabees and their successors, zeal for the law, devotion to the covenant and loyalty to the nation had become inextricably interwoven.

So too in the period following the Maccabean crisis the tie-in between election, covenant and law remains a fundamental and persistent theme of Jewish self-understanding. Ben Sira, for example, echoes Deuteronomy's assumption both of Yahweh's universal sovereignty and of his special covenant choice of Israel (Deut 32:8–9; Sir 17:11–17). And Ben Sira is the first clearly to identify universal divine wisdom with "the book of the covenant of the Most High God, the law which Moses commanded us as an inheritance for the congregations of Jacob" (24:23). Elsewhere he speaks naturally of the law and the covenant in a single breath – "the law of the covenant" (39:8; see also 28:7; 42:2; 44:19–20; 45:5). Jubilees is another classic expression of covenantal nomism, with its repeated emphases on the covenants made by Yahweh, the statutory obligations which follow from them, and his special choice of Israel from among the nations (e. g. 1:4–5; 2:21; 6:4–16; 15; 22:15–16; 23:19 – "the law and the covenant"). Similarly with the Oumran community, membership of the covenant was understood precisely in terms of observing God's precepts and holding fast to his commandments (e.g. CD 1:15–18, 20; 3:10–16; 1 QS 1:7–8; 5:1–3). No different is Pseudo-Philo, for whom the link between covenant and law, or, which is the same thing, (Israel's) election and commandments, is equally axiomatic (9:7–8; 23:10; 30:2; 35:2–3). So when PsSol 10:4 speaks of "the law of the eternal covenant", or when we read in MekhExod 20:6, "By covenant is meant nothing other than the Torah", we can be sure we are in touch with one of the most basic strands of Jewish self-understanding.

Despite the variety of Judaism(s) represented in the above literature, then, and with surprisingly few exceptions, we can speak of a common pattern of "covenantal nomism" as characteristic of the Judaism of Paul's day[13]. That is to say, it was part of the basic framework of reference, taken for granted by many or most Jews, that God had made a special covenant with Israel to be his own,

---

[13] For the importance of the covenant within "intertestamental" Judaism see particularly A. JAUBERT, *La notion d'alliance dans le Judaisme* (Editions du Seuil, 1963). The dominance of the pattern of "covenantal nomism" has been established by SANDERS, *PPJ*, though his work has to be supplemented by D. GARLINGTON, *"The Obedience of Faith": A Pauline Phrase in Historical Context* (WUNT 2.38; Tübingen: Mohr Siebeck, 1991), who has demonstrated the presence of the pattern throughout the whole of "the Apocrypha", and J.J. COLLINS, *Between Athens and Jerusalem: Jewish Identity in the Hellenistic Diaspora* (New York: Crossroad, 1983), who notes, however, that the pattern is not quite so consistent through all the diaspora literature. "Intertestamental" literature may not be the only witness to the Judaism(s) of Paul's day, but it is certainly a primary witness, and in any description of first century Judaism the consistency of that witness should not be discounted by contrasting it with pre-exilic or rabbinic literature.

and as integral to that covenant had given Israel the law to provide Israel with the means of living within that covenant.

III

Several corollaries followed from this basic axiom of covenantal nomism. Two of them fill out the outline of the characteristic Jewish self-understanding of the period and deserve fuller note, as of particular relevance to our overarching question.

The first is that the law so understood became a basic expression of Israel's *distinctiveness* as the people specially chosen by the one God to be his people. In sociological terms the law functioned as an "identity marker" and "boundary", reinforcing Israel's assumption of distinctiveness and distinguishing Israel from the surrounding nations[14]. This sense of separateness was deeply rooted in Israel's national-consciousness (Lev 20:24–6; Ezek 44:9; Joel 3:17; PsSol 17:28); it was brought to pointed and practical expression in the enforced divorces of the Ezra reforms (Ezra 10: 11; Neh 13:3), reinforced by the example of the heroes and heroines of the period (Dan 1:3–16; 10:3; Tob 1:10–12; Jud 12:2, 19; AddEsth 14:17; JosAs 7:1; 8:5; 3 Macc 3:4), and comes to powerful expression particularly in Jub 22:16:

Separate yourself from the Gentiles,
    and do not eat with them,
    and do not perform deeds like theirs.
And do not become associates of theirs.
Because their deeds are defiled,
    and all of their ways are contaminated,
    and despicable, and abominable.

The letter of Aristeas expresses the same conviction in terms which reinforce the sociological insight.

In his wisdom the legislator ... surrounded us with unbroken
palisades and iron walls to prevent our mixing with any of the other
peoples in any matter... So, to prevent our being perverted by
contact with others or by mixing with bad influences, he hedged us
in on all sides with strict observances connected with meat and drink
and touch and hearing and sight, after the manner of the Law (Arist 139, 142).

Similarly Philo *VitMos* 1:278: Israel will be a people "which shall dwell alone, not reckoned among other nations ... because in virtue of the distinction of their

---

[14] J. NEUSNER, *Judaism: The Evidence of the Mishnah* (University of Chicago, 1981) 72–75; W. A. MEEKS, *The First Urban Christians: The Social World of the Apostle Paul* (Yale University, 1983) 97; DUNN, "Works of Law" (n.3) 524–7 (above 122–5).

peculiar customs they do not mix with others to depart from the ways of their fathers". And a funerary inscription from Italy praises a woman "who lived a gracious life inside Judaism (καλῶς βιώσασα ἐν τῷ Ἰουδαϊσμῷ)" – Judaism understood as "a sort of fenced off area in which Jewish lives are led"[15]. This characteristic of Jewish self-understanding and social practice did not go unnoticed by others and formed part of the antiJewish polemic of Roman intellectuals, most emphatically expressed by Tacitus, *Hist* particularly 5.5.2.

Consistent with this is the characterization of Gentiles as ἄνομος and their works as ἀνομία: by definition they were "without the law, outside the law", that is, outside the area (Israel) coterminous with the law, marked out by the law; so already in the Psalms (28:3; 37:28; 55:3; 73:3; 92:7; 104:35; 125:3), in 1 Maccabees (Gentiles and apostates – 3:5–6; 7:5; 9:23, 58, 69; 11: 25; 14:14), and in the self-evident equation, Gentile = "sinner" (as in 1 Macc 2:44, 48; Tob 13:6 [LXX 8]; Jub 23:23–4; PsSol 1:1; 2:1–2; 17:22–5; Matt 5:47/Luke 6:33; Gal 2:15). Not surprisingly this desire to live within the law and marked off from the lawless and sinner became a dominant concern in the factionalism which was a feature of Judaism in the period from the Maccabeans to the emergence of rabbinic Judaism as the most powerful faction within post CE 70 Judaism – expressed in the frequent complaints of "the righteous" and "devout" over against those (within Israel) whom they characterized as "sinners" (as in WisdSol 2–5; Jub 6:32–5; 23:16, 26; 1 Enoch 1:1, 7–9; 5:6–7; 82:4–7; 1QS 2:4–5; 1QH 10[=2].8–19; CD 1:13–21; PsSol 3:3–12; 4:8; 13:5–12; 15:1–13; Pharisees probably = "separated ones")[16].

A second, natural and more or less inevitable converse of this sense of distinctiveness was the sense of *privilege*, privilege precisely in being the nation specially chosen by the one God and favoured by gift of covenant and law. This comes out particularly clearly in writings which could not simply ignore and dismiss Gentiles as sinners, but which had to attempt some sort of apologetic for the claims of Israel in the face of a much more powerful Gentile world. Thus both Philo and Josephus speak with understandable if exaggerated pride of the widespread desire among Greek and barbarian to adopt Jewish customs and laws (Philo, *VitMos* 2:17–25 – "they attract and win the attention of all ... the sanctity of our legislation has been a source of wonder not only to Jews but to all others also"; Josephus, *Ap* 2:277–86 – "The masses have long since shown a keen desire to adopt our religious observances ... Were we not ourselves aware of the excellence of our laws, assuredly we should have been impelled to pride [μέγα φρονεῖν] ourselves upon them by the multitude of their admirers"). Expressive of the same pride in the law of Moses is what seems to have been a fairly sus-

---

[15] Y. Amir, "The Term Ἰουδαϊσμός: A study in Jewish-Hellenistic Self-Identification", *Immanuel* 14 (1982) 35–6, 39–40.

[16] See further J.D.G. Dunn, "Pharisees, Sinners and Jesus", *The Social World of Formative Christianity and Judaism*, FS H.C. Kee, ed. P. Borgen et al. (Philadelphia: Fortress, 1988), reprinted in *Jesus, Paul and the Law* (n. 3) ch. 3.

tained attempt in Jewish apologetic to present Moses as "the first wise man", who was teacher of Orpheus and from whose writings Plato and Pythagoras learned much of their wisdom (Eupolemus, *frag.* 1; Artapanus, *frag.* 3; Aristobulus, *frag.* 3–4; from Eusebius, *Praeparatio Evangelica* 9.26.1; 9.27.3–6 and 13.12.1–4)[17].

Pride in the law as the mark of God's special favour to Israel is also well illustrated in the identification of divine Wisdom with the Torah, the assertion that the universally desirable Wisdom, immanent within creation but hidden from human eyes, is embodied precisely in the law and nowhere else so completely or so clearly – as already in Sir 24:23 cited above. The same claim is expressed more forcefully in Bar 3:36–4:4:

... (He) gave her to Jacob his servant
 and to Israel whom he loved.
...
She is the book of the commandments of God,
 and the law which endures for ever.
All who hold her fast will live,
 but those who forsake her will die.
Turn, O Jacob, and take her:
 walk towards the shining of her light.
Do not give your glory (τὴν δόξαν σου) to another,
 or your advantages (τὰ συμφέροντα) to an alien people.
Blessed are we, O Israel,
 for what is pleasing to God is known (γνωστά) to us.

For those confronted by the crushing power of Rome within Palestine this sense of privilege was difficult to maintain. PssSol found a solution in pressing the older distinction between discipline and punishment (particularly PssSol 3, 10 and 13) – thus 13:6–11.

The destruction of the sinner is terrible
 but nothing shall harm the righteous, of all these things.
For the discipline of the righteous (for things done) in ignorance
 is not the same as the destruction of the sinners.

 ...

For the Lord will spare his devout,
 and he will wipe away their mistakes with discipline.
For the life of the righteous (goes on) for ever,
 but sinners shall be taken away to destruction ...

---

[17] Texts in J.H. CHARLESWORTH, ed. *The Old Testament Pseudepigrapha*, Vol. 2 (London: Darton, 1985). See also J.G. GAGER, *Moses in Greco-Roman Paganism*, SBLMS 16 (Nashville: Abingdon, 1972) ch. 1.

Less easy to satisfy was 4 Ezra, who in common with his fellow Jews saw the law given to Israel as a mark of divine favour (3:19; 9:31), but who could not understand how God could spare the sinful nations and yet allow his law-keeping people to be so harshly treated (3:28–36; 4:23–4; 5:23–30; 6:55–9).

In short, characteristic of early Judaism was the sense of Israel's distinctiveness and privilege as the people chosen by God and marked out from the other nations by this covenant relation and by the Torah practice of those loyal to this covenant (and thus to God). It is not necessary to document such conviction from every strand of Judaism; it is enough to say that a broad spread within early Judaism shared these convictions, as integral to their self-understanding and as fundamental to their perception of their social world.

IV

Within this mind-set and world-view circumcision played a vital role; indeed we cannot hope to "get inside" that mind-set and world-view without understanding the central role of circumcision within Judaism.

This was rooted in the clear statement of Gen 17 – the constitutional document of circumcision within the covenant. There (Gen 17:9–14) the covenant made with Abraham and his descendants is expressed exclusively in terms of circumcision in words of God – "This is my covenant which you shall keep, between me and you and your descendants after you: Every male among you shall be circumcised". Circumcision is described as "a sign of the covenant between me and you". God continues: "So shall my covenant be in your flesh an everlasting covenant. Any circumcised male who is not circumcised in the flesh of his foreskin shall be cut off from his people; he has broken the covenant. " Here in explicit terms circumcision is presented as a central and fundamental factor in the covenant and in the identity of Abraham's descendants as God's people; from this early on, that is, from the time this tradition became established in Gen 17, circumcision was perceived to mark out the boundary distinguishing those within the covenant from those outside.

That this was how Gen 17 was read within Judaism in the time prior to Paul is clearly indicated by Jub 15:25–34, which follows Gen 17 fairly closely, but which does not hesitate to reinforce the point: "Everyone who is born, the flesh of whose foreskin in not circumcised on the eighth day, belongs not to the children of the covenant which the Lord made with Abraham, but to the children of destruction". 1QH 14[=6].20–21 likewise identifies the "uncircumcised" with the "unclean or violent", equally outside the covenant and unacceptable to God. And Pseudo-Philo, in assuming quite understandably that Moses was circumcised from the first, can describe the covenant both as "the covenant of God" and "the covenant of the flesh" (9:13, 15); so much was circumcision of the essence of the covenant. "The covenant with Abraham, circumcision, determined the identity of the Jewish people."[18]

As with other features of Israel's covenant theology, the Maccabean crisis helped to cement the association between covenant and circumcision, circumcision *par excellence* as expressing covenant identity and marking out covenant boundary. Thus the crisis became acute because some Jewish youths "removed the marks of circumcision and abandoned the holy covenant. They joined with the Gentiles ..." (1 Macc 1:15). Gen 17 was taken with utmost seriousness by the Maccabean patriots: to remove circumcision was to cease to be a member of the covenant; that meant ceasing to be a member of the covenant people, ceasing to be a Jew, and becoming a Gentile, and *ipso facto* outside the boundary of God's election favour. So circumcision became the test of covenant loyalty, as Antiochus tried to prevent circumcision (1 Macc 1:48, 60–61; 2. Macc 6:10), and the Maccabees insisted with equal ferocity that all boys within the borders of Israel must be circumcised (1 Macc 2:46). So too when the Hasmonaeans extended their borders it was taken for granted that those whom they had conquered and incorporated into their territory must be circumcised; they could not belong to the people of the covenant, the people of the land, without being circumcised (Josephus, *Ant* 13:257–8, 318)[19].

This self-perception of most Jews of the time is reflected in the various comments on the topic of circumcision made by Greco-Roman writers, who also took it for granted that it was a distinctively Jewish rite. Even though it was well enough known that other peoples practised circumcision (Samaritans, Arabs, Egyptians – cf. Jer 9:25–26; Philo, *SpecLeg* 1:2), circumcision was nevertheless regarded as a rite which marked out the Jews. So for example Tacitus, *Hist* 5.5.2 – the Jews "adopted circumcision to distinguish themselves from other peoples by this difference" (circumcidere genitalia instituerunt, ut diversitate noscantur)[20]. In sociological terms, circumcision clearly functioned as a primary and effective identity and boundary marker, particularly for the Jewish minorities in the cities

---

[18] L.H. SCHIFFMAN, "The Rabbinic Understanding of Covenant", *RevExp* 84 (1987) 289–98; here 297, with reference to the Mishnah. He notes also that "sons of the covenant" = Israelites is a usage found throughout the entire rabbinic corpus with absolutely no change of meaning.

[19] It is true that questions regarding the necessity of circumcision were raised in a few, probably untypical cases (Philo, *Migr* 92; Jos, *Ant* 20:38–42); but in each case the answer given was that the rite of circumcision was too fundamental to be dispensed with (Philo, *Migr* 93–4; Jos, *Ant* 20:43–8). At all events, the evidence in the text above must be regarded as providing a broader and more representative picture of early Judaism. See further J. NOLLAND. "Uncircumcised Proselytes?" *JSJ* 12 (1981) 173–94; E. SCHÜRER. *The History of the Jewish People in the Age of Jesus Christ*, Vol. 3 rev. and ed. G. VERMES et al. (Edinburgh: T. & T. Clark, 1986) 169; against N.J. MCELENEY, "Conversion, Circumcision and the Law", *NTS* 20 (1973–74) 319–41.

[20] Text in M. STERN, *Greek and Latin Authors on Jews and Judaism*, 3 vols. (Jerusalem: Israel Academy of Sciences and Humanities, 1976, 1980, 1984) § 281. Other examples include Petronius, *Sat* 102:14, *Frag* 37, and Juvenal, *Sat* 14:99 (texts in Stern §§ 194, 195, 301).

of the diaspora. It was not the only such marker[21], but because circumcision was such a distinctive feature within a Hellenistic environment, because it had been so integrally tied into the covenant from the first, and because it had become such a test-case for national loyalty for all who regarded themselves as heirs of the Maccabean inheritance, it was bound to be *the* mark of the covenant people for most Jews of Paul's time.

Of course there was much more to covenantal nomism than circumcision. But within a more complex system some features usually stand out as particularly distinctive, as test-cases for the system as a whole. In such cases the whole system can be seen to come to focus in one or other specific feature, and attitudes to that system can be measured by the attitude to that feature. The system as a whole can be thought to stand or fall in terms of that one feature. Such seems to have been the case with circumcision within Judaism. So much so that most Jews would simply have taken it for granted: "no circumcision, no covenant". It would not have been a point of disagreement or dispute in almost every case. As the Lord was one God, as Israel was his people, so circumcision was the sign and seal of the covenant bond between God and his people. As slavery would be taken for granted as part of the economic and social world of the day, so the starting point for any description or definition of the first century Jew would assume that every male Jew had been circumcised. Covenant, law, Jewish ethnic identity, circumcision were mutually interdependent categories, each inconceivable without the other.

V

It is against this background that we have to set our principal question. Given the self-understanding of early Judaism illustrated above, and given the fundamental role of circumcision within it, what was the issue between Paul and "those of the circumcision"?

It might be assumed that the answer would come to clearest expression in the passages where Paul deals most explicitly with the questions of covenant and circumcision, particularly Rom 4, and perhaps also Gal 3. And indeed the answer is to be found in these passages. But it would be a mistake to turn to them immediately. For both chapters comprise very specific arguments, which can be easily taken out of context, and which need to be understood within the sequence of Paul's train of thought. Only in the light of Rom 2 (not to mention Rom 3) can we hope fully to understand Rom 4. Somewhat surprisingly in fact the clearest pointers to the answer are to be found in Rom 2. By way of contrast, we may

---

[21] The other most prominent such markers were the sabbath and food-laws; see further LIMBECK (n. 2) 34; MEEKS (n. 14) 36–7, 97: E. P. SANDERS, *Paul, the Law, and the Jewish People* (Philadelphia: Fortress, 1983) 102; DUNN (n. 3).

make bold to suggest, the difficulty which this passage has always posed to the classical doctrine of "justification by faith"[22], and the confusion in which the most polemical responses to that doctrine have left Rom 2[23], is a further indication that the history of exegesis of Paul has been remarkably unsuccessful in its attempts to understand Paul's line of thought and his argument with "those of the circumcision" within its historical context.

What is particularly striking for us is the way in which Rom 2 in effect matches the phases of the exposition offered above[24].

a) In 2:1–11 Paul takes up the theology of covenantal nomism in a positive way, but in so doing he puts a substantial question-mark at one of the main assumptions underlying the typical Jewish understanding of covenantal nomism.

Thus, on the one hand, he takes as equally axiomatic for himself two fundamental axioms in Jewish understanding of God's dealings with humankind. 2:6: "God will render to each according to his works" (Ps 62:12; Prov 24:12). This is not "a rabbinic works theology"[25], but a recognition that God is judge and a straightforward doctrine of judgment, which is shared equally by Jew[26] and Christian[27]. 2:11 – "There is no partiality with God". This pivotal statement in Paul's argument[28] is also a Jewish theologoumenon, wherein God is consistently presented as a model of impartiality[29]. It is important to realize that Paul stands fully within the biblical and Jewish tradition at this point. The Creator God expects his creatures to obey him. The covenant God expect his people to obey him (covenantal nomism). God the final Judge will take just and impartial account of human good and evil.

At the same time, however, there is more than a hint that Paul is citing these Jewish axioms against his own people, or, more precisely, against an assumption which most of them shared that such judgement will naturally work in favour of God's people Israel. The implication that Paul is actually debating the signific-

---

[22] See e.g. the recent attempt to resolve the old dilemma (with reference to earlier literature) by K.R. SNODGRASS, "Justification by Grace – to the Doers: An Analysis of the Place of Romans 2 in the Theology of Paul", *NTS* 32 (1986) 72–93.

[23] I refer particularly to SANDERS (n. 21) 123–35, and RÄISÄNEN (n. 6) 101–9.

[24] This was something which emerged in the course of preparing the present paper. As my *Romans*, Word Biblical Commentary 38 (Dallas: Word, 1988) lxix–lxxi shows, I had already noted that the typical Jewish self-understanding of covenant, law and circumcision fell naturally into the pattern of analysis offered also above, before I realized quite how close the match was with Rom 2. For fuller exposition of Rom 2 see my *Romans* ad loc.

[25] As E. SYNOFZIK, *Die Gerichts- und Vergeltungsaussagen bei Paulus* (Göttingen: Vandenhoeck, 1977) 81.

[26] See also Job 34:11; Jer 17:10; Hos 12:2; Sir 16:12–14; 1 Enoch 100:7; JosAs 28:3; PsPhilo 3:10.

[27] Cf. Matt 16:27; 2 Cor 5:10; Col 3:25; 2 Tim 4:14; 1 Pet 1:17; Rev 2:23.

[28] J.M. BASSLER, *Divine Impartiality: Paul and a Theological Axiom*, SBLDS 59 (Chico: Scholars Press, 1982).

[29] Deut 10: 17; 2 Chron 19:7; Sir 35:12–13; Jub 5:16; 21:4; 30:16; 33:18; PsSol 2:18; 2 Bar 13:8; 44:4; 1 Enoch 63:8; Ps-Philo 20:4.

ance of these theologoumena (not questioning them) is there in the very style Paul uses – the diatribe denoting the in-house, school debate[30], in this case an intra-Jewish debate. But it comes to clearest expression in what is probably a deliberate echo of WisdSol 15:1ff. in 2:4[31]. In WisdSol 15:1–6 the assumption is made that God's people are free of the grosser gentile sins and that any Jewish sin is insufficient to disturb Israel's favoured status as the people chosen by God[32]. It is just that assumption which would have been strengthened by the typically Hellenistic Jewish polemic against gentile idolatry in Rom 1:18–32 and which the interlocutor in ch. 2 is presumed to share (2:1–3).

In consequence we should probably recognize that in 2:6 Paul had in view a (probably widespread) Jewish assumption that their works, their practice of the law (covenantal nomism) would be acknowledged by God the Judge as that which he had demanded of his people (cf. particularly Tob 4:9–11; PsSol 9:3–5). Likewise some Jewish affirmations of God's impartiality could easily be read wholly within the context of covenantal nomism (e. g. Deut 10: 17–19; Jub 5:17–18; 33:16–20), and PsSol 2:18 seems to be an expression of covenant confidence that God will not fail to recompense the nations for their despoiling of Jerusalem (2:18ff.; cf. 8:25–32).

Rom 2:1–11 therefore has something of the character of a "double-take" indictment – designed to maintain the assent of the one under indictment, while little by little bringing him to conscious awareness that his own assumption of security is false[33].

b) In 2:12–16 Paul introduces the law. Where so much exegesis has missed the way and allowed itself to be sidetracked is the failure to recognize that Paul's argument is determined entirely by the boundary function of the law. The paragraph is not a discussion of works-righteousness or an exposition of natural law as such. It revolves wholly around the Jewish assumption that the law is a bound-

---

[30] S.K. Stowers. *The Diatribe and Paul's Letter to the Romans*, SBLDS 57 (Chico: Scholars, 1981), 75–8.

[31] That Paul frequently echoes this section of WisdSol in Rom 1–2 is widely recognized among commentators.

[32] WisdSol 15:1–6 –
But you, our God, are kind and true (χρηστὸς καὶ ἀληθής),
    patient (μακρόθυμος) and in mercy governing all things.
For even if we sin, we are yours, knowing your power;
    but we will not sin, knowing that we are reckoned yours.
For to know you is complete righteousness,
    and to know your power is the root of immortality.
For neither has the evil intent of human art misled us,
    nor the fruitless toil of painters ...

[33] This observation of course strengthens the majority, but by no means unanimous view that Paul has a specifically Jewish interlocutor in view in ch. 2 from the first (even when he expresses himself in terms which are more open).

ary which marks off those inside from those outside, and that this fact is decisive in the final judgment.

Thus he starts with a distinction which he immediately questions (2:12) – the distinction between being "in/within the law" (ἐν νόμῳ) and "without/outside the law" (ἀνόμως), between those who have the law and those who do not have the law (2:14). The boundary function of the law, as marking off Jew (inside the boundary of the law, having the law) from Gentile (outside the law, not having the law), could hardly be expressed more clearly. His point is not simply to re-place this distinction with the distinction between *doing* the law and *hearing* the law: emphasis on the need to *do* the law is again characteristically Jewish[34] and exhortations to the same effect can readily be documented from Jewish sources[35]. Paul's point is rather that the assumption cannot be made that "having" the law and "doing" the law amount to the same thing. There are those outside the law, not having the law, who "do the things of the law" (2:14).

Here again exegesis needs to avoid being sidetracked into questions of which Gentiles Paul had in mind (only Christians?). He may not have had any specific Gentiles in mind; his argument does not depend on the identification of any particular law-keeping Gentile. His point is simply that if there are any Gentiles who do what the law requires (however such law-keeping may come about), that fact is sufficient to call in question the significance of the boundary function of the law so far as the final judgment is concerned. The interlocutor cannot assume that only those within the law (Jews) can or do keep the law. He cannot assume that being within the law is a necessary presupposition to a doing of the law which God will vindicate. Living as a Jew (within the law) is not synonymous with doing the law. A Gentile, even while still a Gentile (not having the law), can be acceptable to God[36].

c) In 2:17–24 Paul takes up the theme of Jewish privilege. As 2:12–16 presupposes a Jewish sense of distinctiveness determined by the Jewish law, so 2:17–24 presupposes a Jewish sense of privilege in Israel's election and particularly in the law. So the interlocutor is identified for the first time explicitly as a Jew (2:17) – that is, a Jew as distinct from a Gentile[37]. And there then follows a sequence of phrases which catch well what may properly be described as a typically Jewish assumption that God's choice of Israel and gift of the law to Israel has given the Jew a position of advantage over the less fortunate Gentile. He "rests on the

---

[34] E.g. Deut 4:1,5–6, 13–14; 30:11–14; 1 Macc 2:67; 13:48; 1QpHab 7:11; 12:4–5.

[35] E.g. Philo, *Cong* 70; *Praem* 79; Jos, *Ant* 20:44; *mAbot* 1:17; 5:14.

[36] The suggestion of N. Dahl is attractive that in 2:15 Paul is countering a Jewish claim that the law and its commands would provide Israel with special advocates to witness for (or against) them in the final judgment; so Gentiles will have the advocacy of conscience and thoughts (taken up by Bassler [n. 28] 148).

[37] Is should be recalled that Ἰουδαϊσμός emerged in the Maccabean period (first in 2 Macc 2:21; 8:1; 14:38) as a designation for the national religion of the Jews in its self-conscious distinc-tiveness and fierce loyalty to the law and the traditional customs.

law" (2:17). This is not to be regarded as an "illusory" boast or confused with a concept of merit[38]. It simply characterizes Jewish confidence that their possession of the law, marking Israel off from the nations, is a sure mark of God's favour – an attitude well exemplified in 2 Bar 48:22–24. He "boasts in God" (2:17)[39] – that is, by clear implication, in God as Israel's God, the one God whose choice of Israel has marked Israel out from the rest – an exclusiveness (our God and not theirs) which Paul calls more sharply in question in 3:27–9 and 10:3. By virtue of his regular instruction in the law he knows God's will (2:18; cf. Bar 4:4; WisdSol 15:2–3; 4 Ezra 8:12), knows what really matters. He is confident that the privilege of the law gives him sight, so that he is in a position to act as guide of the not so privileged Gentile (2:19)[40], gives him light, so that he himself can provide light to those outside the limits of the law's illumination (2:19)[41]; and so on. It is not hard to see that in all this Paul catches the authentic tone of Jewish conviction of covenant privilege.

It is this assumption which Paul proceeds to attack. The list of challenges which follows ("Do you steal? ... Do you commit adultery? ... Do you commit sacrilege?") has often been misunderstood, as though Paul was making wild accusations against all Jews, or was using a few isolated incidents to condemn the whole people[42]. But such charges are simply part of the rhetoric of moral exhortation[43], and as such appear in both prophetic and rabbinic tradition[44]. Note particularly the parallels in Ps 50:16–21, PsSol 8:8–14, Philo, *Conf* 163, TLevi 14:4–8 and CD 6:16–17. So too the attempt to interpret the passage along the lines of Matt 5:21–48 misses the point[45]. For Paul's target is not any Jews in particular or all Jews as individuals. Rather his aim is the typical Jew's confidence that he stands in a position of ethical privilege and superiority by virtue of having the law. The fact that there are some who bear the name "Jew", who belong to the covenant people, who "have the law", and who yet steal, commit adultery or rob temples[46], is sufficient to call in question the assumption that being a member of

---

[38] As typically by HÜBNER (n. 2) 113.

[39] Cf. Deut 10:21; Pss 5:11; 89:17; Jer 9:23–4; Sir 50:20; PsSol 7:1.

[40] Cf. Isa 42:7; 1 Enoch 105:1; Sib Or 3:195; Jos, *Ap* 2:291 – 5; Philo, *Abr* 98.

[41] Cf. Isa 42:6–7; 49:6; Ps 119:105; WisdSol 18:4; Sir 24:27; 45:17; TLevi 14:4 1QSb 4:27; Ps-Philo 23:10.

[42] Cf. e.g. RÄISÄNEN (n. 6) 100 – "a piece of propagandist denigration" (101); É. TROCMÉ, "The Jews as Seen by Paul and Luke", *"To See Ourselves As Others See Us": Christians, Jews, "Others" in Late Antiquity*, ed. J. NEUSNER et al. (Chico: Scholars, 1985) 153.

[43] A. FRIDRICHSEN, "Der wahre Jude und sein Lob: Röm 2:28f.", *Symbolae Arctoae* 1 (1927) 39–49, notes similar challenges in Epictetus to those who call themselves Stoics (2.19.19–28; 3.7.17; 3.24.40); almost "a classic example of indictment of the pretentious philosopher" (STOWERS [n. 30] 96–7).

[44] E.g. Isa 3:14–15; Jer 7:8–11; Ezek 22:6–12; Mal 3:5; (H.L. Strack –) P. BILLERBECK, *Kommentar zum Neuen Testament aus Talmud und Midrasch*, München 1926, 3:105–11.

[45] C.K. BARRETT, *Romans* (London: Black, 1957) *ad loc.*

[46] Paul's Roman readers would probably still be able to recall the notorious case, narrated by

the covenant people, having the law, puts "the Jew" in a privileged position. It is the typical Jewish "boasting in the law" (2:23), the climax of the indictment, which Paul is seeking to undermine – that is, the pride in covenantal nomism, that by living within the law, maintaining covenant identity (Jewish distinctiveness), individual sins notwithstanding, the Jewish privileged position before God will be preserved.

d) For those who have followed the drift of Paul's argument (or indeed of the above exposition), it would occasion no suprise when Paul in the final paragraph turned his attention to circumcision in particular (2:25–9). For, as we have seen, the typical Jewish sense of distinctiveness and privilege came to particular focus in the rite of circumcision. The point comes out in the language itself, in the fact that "circumcision/uncircumcision" can be used as fully equivalent to "Jew/Gentile" (2:26; also 3:30; 4:9; Gal 2:7–9; Phil 3:3; Col 3:11). Clearly then this was the chief point of differentiation, the most distinctive identity marker. The distinction between Jew and Gentile could be boiled down to or summed up in the one fact of Jewish circumcision – both as physical rite and because of all the national and religious significance that rite embodied. It may even be that περιτομή and ἀκροβυστία were nicknames used by different factions for their opponents[47], the antagonists seizing, as so often, on the most prominent distinguishing feature of the other. In this case it would be a Jewish choice of nicknames, focusing their self-characterization on the single mark of identification which symbolized their whole claim to be God's people, and characterizing the Gentiles by the *absence* of that mark.

The argument of 2:25–9 fully confirms the line of exegesis developed above. For what is clearly under attack in 2:25–7 is the assumption that circumcision *per se* gives the circumcised person a position of advantage over the uncircumcised. Again the point should not be misconstrued. Paul is not attacking circumcision itself: "circumcision is of benefit ..." (2:25). His target is the boundary function of circumcision and the assumption that those who are within that boundary (as betokened by the fact of their circumcision) are thereby in a position of acceptability to God denied to those outside that boundary. The point comes to expression in 2:28–9 in Paul's designation of circumcision with the phrases ἐν τῷ φανερῷ, ἐν σαρκί and ἐν γράμματι. Once again this is not to be misconstrued as an attack on literalism, or on ritual as such. What is in view is rather the function of circumcision as a visible outward mark thereby providing a clear division between different sets of people (circumcised and uncircumcised), circumcision as an identification that the flesh so circumcised is *Jewish* flesh, circumcision and

---

Jos, *Ant* 18:81–4, of a Jew in Rome misappropriating funds and gifts intended for the temple, a scandal which resulted in the expulsion of the Jewish community from Rome in CE 19.

[47] So argued by J. Marcus, "The Circumcision and the Uncircumcision in Rome" *NTS* 35 (1989) 67–81. In a similar way the nicknames "weak" and "strong" in 14:1–15:6 betray a more Gentile perspective.

the written code summed up in the rite of circumcision as denoting ethnic distinctiveness and privilege. Paul's target is the identification of covenant and law too narrowly with *Judaism*, the understanding of Judaism as *essentially* a national religion. The definition of "Jew", one praised by God (2:19), cannot be so constricted, and should not be so perverted.

In Rom 2, therefore, it becomes progressively clearer that Paul is seeking to undermine a Jewish assumption of national distinctiveness and privilege, such as was documented in the earlier sections above. The presumption lying behind the typical Jewish understanding and practice of covenantal nomism and expressed most clearly in the crucial significance of circumcision he regards as equally "under the power of sin" (3:9) and subject to God's wrath (1:18) as the other sins of creaturely presumption usually associated (by Jews) with the Gentiles (2:1–11). Before the power of sin and the judgment of God, possession of the law is no safeguard (2:12–16), covenant status is no security (2:17–24), circumcision provides no guarantee (2:25–9).

This line of exegesis is clearly confirmed by Rom 3. Paul's critique immediately raises the question, "What then is the advantage of the Jew, or what is the value of circumcision?" (3:1). Obviously then it is precisely the advantage of being a Jew, the value of circumcision as the most distinctive and visible mark of Jewishness, which Paul has called in question. The assumption is that God's covenant has been with "the Jew", with "the circumcised", so that Paul's indictment seems to call God's covenant faithfulness in question (3:3). Paul's response is that God's faithfulness is not at all at issue; his indictment rather indicates that Jewish restriction of the covenant in narrowly national and ethnic terms is to be designated *un*faithfulness (rather than as covenant loyalty)[48].

Had we time and space we could go on to demonstrate how Paul carries forward his debate with the most characteristic Jewish self-understanding of his time. We would see how use of the concept "works of the law" has its meaning wholly within this context – works of the law as more or less equivalent to "covenantal nomism" (Rom 3–4)[49]. And we could explore the delicate balance Paul strives to attain in Rom 9–11 between reaffirmation of God's covenant faithfulness to Israel and denial that the covenant has to be understood in explicitly ethnic terms and righteousness as national righteousness, the righteousness of Jew as Jew over against Gentile as Gentile (10:3). Not to mention Galatians. But the above will have to suffice.

---

[48] Israel's ἀπιστία should not be construed in terms of unbelief (in Jesus Messiah), as most recently by C.E.B. CRANFIELD, *Romans*, ICC vol. 1 (Edinburgh: T. & T. Clark, 1975) *ad loc.*; H. RÄISÄNEN, "Zum Verständnis von Röm 3:1–8", *The Torah and Christ* (Helsinki: Finnish Exegetical Society, 1986) 185–205; C.H. COSGROVE, "What If Some Have Not Believed? The Occasion and Thrust of Romans 3:1–8", *ZNW* 78 (1987) 90–105. The thought of 3:1ff. is still clearly determined by the argument of ch. 2, as 3:1 confirms beyond reasonable dispute.

[49] See further DUNN (n. 3).

VI

So what was the issue between Paul and "those of the circumcision"? The answer hopefully has already been made clear. The very description of the group denotes the mind-set Paul has indicted in Rom 2. οἱ ἐκ περιτομῆς, like its near synonym, οἱ ἐκ τοῦ νόμου, defines a social entity marked out and bounded by law and circumcision in particular. These are phrases denoting ethnic identity; the group's self-identity arises out of (ἐκ) their practice of the law and fact of circumcision (covenantal nomism). But this also means a group who regard covenant grace as restricted to that ethnic unit, dependent on being within the boundaries of the law denoted above all by circumcision. It is this to which Paul objects. The response of faith to electing grace cannot be so restricted and determined by national and ethnic boundaries. That insight does not call Israel's election into question; rather it shows how election works. It is Israel's failure to understand this and consequent abuse of its covenant privilege which Paul seeks to expose. Whether God's grace is *to* Israel exclusive of Greek or is rather *through* Israel with Greek also in view, whether the law is to be understood as a boundary confining that grace within Israel or is rather to be understood as co-ordinated with faith, whether the chief effective significance of circumcision is to distinguish Jew from Gentile. That is the issue between Paul and "those of the circumcision".

Postscript

There are clearly several points, both of misunderstanding and of disagreement, between those English-speaking scholars who approach Paul from what we might call the post-Sanders "New Perspective"[50] and their German colleagues. Let me say, then, as straightforwardly as possible: to analyse the issue confronting Paul, or between Paul and "those of the circumcision", in the terms used in the above essay, is *not* to deny that there are other, and indeed deeper dimensions involved – not least Paul's theology of the cross, his whole analysis of the human race in Adamic terms, and the emphases which have characterized the best expositions of "faith and works" from the Reformation onwards. My concern is rather to affirm that the issue as expounded above is a *fundamental* part of the larger or fuller issue, and one which has been too much lost sight of in the more traditional expositions of Paul. I have attempted to point this up precisely by fixing attention on Rom 2, a passage which has caused so many problems for such traditional expositions. By attempting to understand Rom 2 without immediate recourse to Rom 3:21ff. or 4:4–5 or 5–8, I do not of course seek a com-

---

[50] See further my *Jesus, Paul and the Law* (n.3).

plete exposition of Paul's gospel or deny the central importance of these passages in a fuller exposition of Paul's gospel. Rather I wish to draw attention to the significance of the fact that Paul introduces the issue confronting him and brings it to focus in terms which match so well with what we found in other strands of early Judaism. The importance of recognizing this point is that the issue in these terms remains a matter of central concern for Paul, as Rom 9–11 (the theological climax of the argument of Romans) shows, not least by reverting to the questions of 3:1–8, the questions, that is to say, raised precisely by the indictment of Rom 2. It is my conviction that only when Rom 2 is understood in the terms outlined above, are we able to integrate that otherwise difficult chapter and chapters 9–11 properly into our understanding of Paul's theology – both as a historical description of what he was trying to say and in our ongoing appropriation of that theology.

Chapter 6

The Theology of Galatians
The Issue of Covenantal Nomism

My thesis is that Galatians is Paul's first sustained attempt to deal with the issue of covenantal nomism. His argument is basically (1) that the outworking of God's saving power will be consistent with its initial decisive expression, (2) that that initial expression of God's covenant purpose was in terms of promise and faith and always had the Gentiles in view from the first, and (3) that the law, where it is understood in a way which conflicts with that initial expression, has been given a distorted role.

I will begin by recalling what "covenantal nomism" means and why it was so important at the time of Paul. Then I will attempt to demonstrate exegetically that covenantal nomism is the issue underlying Paul's argument in Galatians and how Paul deals with it in what I see to be his three-stranded argument. Finally, I will try to indicate why I think that Galatians is Paul's first full-scale attempt to deal with this issue. In all this I take it for granted that, however else we may want to speak of "the theology of Galatians," we must at least start by asking what Paul was saying within the context of his times and of his mission and in relation to the specific situation in Galatia, and what he wanted his Galatian readership and audience to hear and to understand in what he wrote. In the spirit of the seminar I will confine my discussion to Galatians itself and not attempt to underpin or develop the main part of the thesis by reference to any other Pauline text.[1]

I

"Covenantal nomism" as coined by E. P. Sanders, is a phrase well fitted to characterize Jewish self-understanding or, more precisely, the understanding of the relation between God and his people Israel as it comes to expression consist-

---

[1] This is a reworked version of the paper delivered to the Pauline Theology Group of the SBL at its Chicago meeting in 1988. I wish to express my appreciation to members of the group for a most valuable discussion of the first draft, particularly to J. Louis Martyn, the chief respondent. The revision, I hope, reflects something of the benefit I derived from that discussion. A fuller version appears in *Jesus, Paul and the Law* (London: SPCK; Philadelphia: Westminster, 1990).

ently (though not uniformly) within Jewish literature, particularly from Deute-ronomy on.[2] Fundamental to Judaism's sense of identity was the conviction that God had made a special *covenant* with the patriarchs, the central feature of which was the choice of Israel to be God's peculiar people (e.g., Deut 4:31; 2 Macc 8:15; *Pss. Sol.* 9:10; CD 6:2; 8:18), and had given the *law* as an integral part of the covenant both to show Israel how to live within that covenant ("This do and you shall live" [Deut 4:1, 10, 40; 5:29–33; 6:1–2, 18, 24; etc.]) and to make it possible for them to do so (the system of atonement).[3] Thus in the phrase "cove-nantal nomism" the former word emphasizes God's prevenient grace, and the latter cannot and should not be confused with legalism or with any idea of "earn-ing" salvation.

The typical mind-set of covenantal nomism included a strong sense of special privilege and prerogative over against other peoples (e.g., Bar 3:36–4:4; *Pss. Sol.* 13:6–11; Philo, *Vit. Mos.* 2.17–25; Josephus, *Ag. Ap.* 2.38 §§ 277–86). But it also and inevitably meant a reinforcing of the sense of national identity and separate-ness from other nations (e.g., *Jub.* 22:16; *Ep. Arist.* 139, 142; Philo, *Vit. Mos.* 1.278).[4] This was evidently a major motivating factor in the reconstitution of Judea after the exile (Ezra 9–10), and the same sense of a basic need to remain loyal to the covenant obligations was obviously one of the most powerful factors in the Maccabean attempt to restore national integrity and to retain national identity. At that time, the obligations of covenantal nomism focused on those features of national and religious life which marked out the distinctiveness of the jewish people – circumcision and food laws (1 Macc 1:60–63). This was be-cause these demands of the law had become a principal target of Syrian persecu-tion – and for the same reason, namely, that they prevented assimilation and in-tegration into a larger international and religious whole. At the same time "Ju-daism" first appears in our literature precisely as a protest against such h:leniz-ing pressure (2 Macc 2:21; 8:1; 14:38), that is, as a way of marking off the entity of Jewish self-identity from a Hellenism that had swamped and threatened to ob-literate such national distinctives. The verb "to judaize" is coined to indicate those Gentiles who chose to live their lives in accord with the ancestral customs and practices distinctive of the Jewish nation (Esth 8:17 LXX; Josephus, *J.W.* 2.17.10 § 454; 2.18.2 §§ 462–63).[5]

Equally it is evident that these concerns shaped so clearly by the Maccabean national crisis continued to be a dominant factor in the following period. All the

---

[2] E.P. Sanders, *Paul and Palestinian Judaism* (Philadelphia: Fortress, 1977) 75, 420, 544; J.J. Collins, *Between Athens and Jerusalem: Jewish Identity in the Hellenistic Diaspora* (New York: Crossroad, 1983); see index, under "covenantal nomism"

[3] Rightly emphasized by Sanders (*Paul and Palestinian Judaism*, 422).

[4] See further my *Romans* (WBC 38; Dallas: Word, 1988) lxvii–lxxi. [= 144–9 above]

[5] Texts cited in my "Incident at Antioch (Gal 2.11–18)," *JSNT* 18 (1983) 26–27, reprinted in my *Jesus, Paul and the Law*, chap. 6.

literature from then on through the next two centuries bears testimony to a concern to assert, define, and defend the boundaries of the covenant, as different groups claimed that *their* understanding and practice were the *proper* covenantal nomism, that they (alone) were the "righteous" and "devout," and that the other nonpractitioners were "sinners," disloyal to the covenant – if not apostates – by their failure to keep the law as it should be kept (e.g., Wisdom of Solomon 2–5; *Jub.* 6:32–35; 1 *Enoch* 1:1, 7–9; 1QS 2:4–5; *Pss. Sol.* 3:3–12; 13:5–12).[6] In this period circumcision and food laws, together with other specific commandments like sabbath and festivals, remained the clearest identity and boundary markers of Judaism as a whole, as indicated by evidence both within and without the corpus of Jewish writings.[7]

All this is more or less noncontroversial: the evidence is clear and consistent. I emphasize it by way of introduction to the particular study of Galatians for the obvious reason that the thrust of Paul's argument regarding these same two features, covenant and law, is unlikely to be understood without an adequate grasp of *the taken-for-granted nature of covenantal nomism within Jewish circles.* The extent to which Paul is actually addressing covenantal nomism has, of course, yet to be established, but where such a fundamental mind-set was involved, any discussion of covenant and law in relation to Judaism was bound to be influenced in greater rather than lesser degree by that mind-set and its taken-for-granteds.

More controversial, I suppose, may be two specific claims that I have already advanced elsewhere, even though they seem to me to follow inevitably from the above.[8] The first claim is that covenantal nomism was so tightly bound up with a sense of national or ethnic identity that the law became coterminous with Israel, marking out the Jews in their distinctiveness as God's people and in their distinctiveness from others (Gentiles = not God's people).[9] That is to say, however universal the claims made for the law might have been,[10] it never ceased to be the Jewish law; its religious appeal (evident in the many God-fearers who at-

---

[6] See further my "Pharisees, Sinners and Jesus," in *The Social World of Formative Christianity and Judaism: Essays in Tribute to Howard Clark Kee* (ed. J. Neusner et al.; Philadelphia: Fortress, 1988) 264–89, reprinted in *Jesus, Paul and the Law*, chap. 3.

[7] See, e.g., the texts cited in my "New Perspective on Paul," *BJRL* 65 (1983) 107–10, reprinted in *Jesus, Paul and the Law*, chap. 7 [=ch. 2 above, here 108–11].

[8] "New Perspective" and "Works of the Law and the Curse of the Law (Galatians 3:10–14)," *NTS* 31 (1985) 523–42, reprinted in *Jesus, Paul and the Law*, chap. 8 [=ch. 3 above]. The points have been well grasped by J.M.G. Barclay, *Obeying the Truth: A Study of Paul's Ethics in Galatians* (Studies of the New Testament and Its World; Edinburgh: T. & T. Clark, 1988) 78, 82.

[9] See also T.D. Gordon, "The Problem at Galatia," *Int* 41 (1987) 32–43, esp. p. 38, and those cited by him; and P. Alexander, "Jewish Law in the Time of Jesus: Towards a Clarification of the Problem," in *Law and Religion: Essays on the Place of the Law in Israel and Early Christianity* (ed. B. Lindars; Cambridge: James Clarke, 1988). Alexander notes that "the centrality of the Torah of Moses to Judaism was the centrality of a national flag" (p. 56).

[10] See N.A. Dahl, "The One God of Jews and Gentiles," in *Studies in Paul* (Minneapolis: Augsburg, 1977) 178–91.

tached themselves in differing degrees to the diaspora synagogues)[11] was never such as could be divorced from its national function as the civil and criminal code of the Jews as a distinct ethnic entity. This "social function of the law" I believe to be important for our fuller understanding of the mind-set with which Paul is engaging in Galatians.

The second claim is that the phrase "works of the law" was a way of describing the same covenantal-nomistic mind-set; that is, "works of the law" refers to the praxis which the law of the covenant laid upon the covenant member. This is borne out by the use of an equivalent phrase, "deeds of the law" in the Dead Sea Scrolls, where it describes the obligations laid upon the sectarian by his membership in the Qumran community (1QS 5:21, 23; 6:18; 4QFlor 1:1–7; and an unpublished text from Cave 4), though whether it was of wider currency or simply a natural way of expressing covenantal obligations we cannot say. In particular, such a sense of obligation probably came to particular expression in those commandments that focused on the distinctiveness of the claim to be a people set apart by the one God. In the Maccabean crisis that meant specifically circumcision and the food laws, and there are sufficient indications thereafter that wherever Jewish identity came into question the issue of covenantal nomism would focus on these same commandments and on any others that reinforced Jewish distinctiveness. Such deeds/works of the law became the test cases for Jewish faithfulness.[12]

With one of our key terms thus clarified, we can now turn to Galatians and attempt to explicate the line of argument and emphases Paul employs to meet the challenge confronting his understanding of the gospel among his Galatian converts.[13]

II

Paul was concerned with the issue of covenantal nomism as it was affecting his converts in Galatia. This becomes clear in Paul's consistent focus on what we might call the "second phase." It is most explicit in 3:3: what follows from the beginning they have made? How do they think the completion of God's saving work will be achieved? The same concern lies behind almost every paragraph of the letter, in a whole sequence of variations. What follows from the gospel and its acceptance (1:6–7; 2:14)? What is the outworking of the grace of God (1:6)?

---

[11] For details, see my "Incident at Antioch," 21–23; see also my *Romans*, xlvii–xlviii.

[12] Note the clarification of my earliest statement of this conclusion in *Jesus, Paul and the Law*, particularly chap. 7, Additional Note 6.

[13] This is not to say that Paul accepted his Galatian opponents' frame of reference (a criticism made of the first draft of this paper by J.L. Martyn at the SBL seminar in Chicago), but simply to say that the teaching in Galatians had set an agenda and posed an issue to which Paul had to respond; see section III below.

For Paul it was apostleship to the Gentiles (1:16; 2:9); for those he opposed it was evidently the law (2:21; 5:4). If the issue of circumcision for Gentiles had been settled (2:1–10), what about the issue of continuing life-style, as focused (as also with the Pharisees)[14] in table fellowship (2:11–14)?

Most persistent of all is the argument regarding the relation of faith and the law. How is (the initial expression of) faith to be correlated with "works of the law"? The implication of the ἐὰν μή of 2:16a, especially in its context as referring back to the issue of food laws at Antioch (2:11–14), is that Jewish Christians thought works of the law (like observance of the dietary laws) were quite compatible with faith in Christ and still a necessary (covenantal) obligation for Jewish believers in Messiah Jesus.[15] But Paul drives that distinction (faith in Christ and works of law) into an outright antithesis (2:16bc;[16] 3:2, 5, 10–12): to regard the law (covenantal nomism) as the outworking of faith is retrogressive, a stepping back from the freedom of the children of God into immature childhood and slavery (3:23–4:11; 4:21–31). The outworking of faith has to be conceived in different terms from works of the law (circumcision, etc.): that is, in terms of the Spirit as against works of the flesh (5:16–26; 6:7–9), a focusing on physical features which would include a nationalistic evaluation of circumcision (3:3; 4:21–31; 6:12–13). This outworking may be conceived in terms of the law, but not the law focused in such Jewish distinctives as circumcision, but focused rather in love of neighbor (5:6, 13–14) as exemplified by Christ (6:1–4).[17]

The issue underlying all this is covenantal nomism, that is, the issue of whether those Gentiles who had come to faith in the Messiah of the Jews and who thus claimed a share in the benefits of God's covenant with Israel needed to live in accordance with the law of Israel – either by following Jewish customs ("to judaize") or by becoming proselytes – in order to sustain that claim.[18] That this is the issue has been obscured by several factors. One is the fact that covenantal nomism was such a taken-for-granted for the typical Jewish mind-set that it did not need to be spelled out any more clearly than it is.[19] A second is that "works of the law" have for too long been understood as "good works by which individuals try to gain acceptance by God." This fundamental misunderstanding has skewed the whole exegesis of the letter, distorting or concealing the Jewish (as

---

[14] J. Neusner, *From Politics to Piety* (Englewood Cliffs, NJ: Prentice Hall, 1973); see also his *Judaism, The Evidence of the Mishnah* (Chicago: University of Chicago Press, 1981).

[15] See my clarification of the exposition of Gal 2:16 in *Jesus, Paul and the Law*, chap. 7, Additional Note 9.

[16] See further below; see also *Jesus, Paul and the Law*, chap. 7, Additional Note 3.

[17] See particularly Barclay, *Obeying*, 125–42.

[18] I had formulated this thesis before reading C.K. Barrett, *Freedom and Obligation: A Study of the Epistle to the Galatians* (Philadelphia: Westminster, 1985) 10: The theology of the judaizers "seems to me to tally in some remarkable ways (though not in every way) with the covenantal nomism of E.P. Sanders."

[19] See pp. 173–5 above.

well as Christian) recognition of the priority of God's grace and losing sight of the corporate dimension of the discussion in its focus on an individualistic doctrine of justification by faith.[20] Third, Sanders' own rebuttal of that misplaced emphasis in turn clouded the issue by making too sharp a distinction between entry into the covenant and continuance or maintenance of status within it. "Justification" (being "righteoused") was classified as "transfer terminology,"[21] with the implication that that was also where Paul's emphasis on faith belonged, that is, only with the question of entry and not with that of continuance. (Yet Gal 5:4–5 indicates that justification has much to do with continuance and final outcome!) Consequently, *the issue of the continuum between faith and its outworking corollary was obscured:* Does (covenant) faith (necessarily, inevitably?) come to expression in (covenant) works of the law or continue to be the basis of continuance as well as of entry, or what?[22] This last confusion has been the more plausible since so much of the issue in Galatians focuses on circumcision, which seems to reinforce a distinction between "entry into covenant" and "maintenance of status." But the issue of works of the law first comes to expression as a result of the Antioch incident (2:11–16), where the concern was clearly the maintenance of covenant status on the part of the Jewish Christians in Antioch through faithful observance of the food laws. Moreover, it was not merely circumcision which the Galatian converts were being exhorted to undergo, but circumcision as the beginning of that law observance which was expected of all devout covenant members (4:10; 5:3). At this point it is well to recall that circumcision was not typically thought of within Judaism as a rite of entry into the covenant but as one of the commandments by obeying which one expressed one's status as a Jew (or proselyte)[23] –the first act, we may say, of covenantal nomism.

III

The main thrust of Paul's argument against covenantal nomism has three strands. (1) *The expression of life within the covenant should be consistent with its beginning.* This is evident from Paul's initial appeal to his readers: what they are doing is abandoning the grace of God, which first brought them to faith, in favor of a different gospel (1:6–9). The appeal is regularly repeated throughout the

---

[20] See further *Jesus, Paul and the Law*, chap. 7 [=ch. 2 above].

[21] E.P. Sanders, *Paul, the Law, and the Jewish People* (Philadelphia: Fortress, 1983).

[22] See further *Jesus, Paul and the Law*, chap. 7, Additional Note 8.

[23] P. Borgen, "Observations on the Theme 'Paul and Philo,'" in *Die paulinische Literatur und Theologie* (ed. S. Pedersen; Teologiske Studier 7; Aarhus: Aros, 1980) 85–102. Borgen notes that "Philo's and Hillel's understanding has thus been that bodily circumcision was not the requirement for entering the Jewish community, but was one of the commandments which they had to obey upon receiving status as a Jew" (p. 88).

rest of the letter (3:1–5; 4:8–11; 5:1–12). It was by faith that they became participants in the promises of God; their continuing status as such would be maintained in the same way. Paul sees his own experience of being commissioned
with the gospel in the same light (1:11–2:10; 2:18–20). Whatever his relationship
with Jerusalem after his conversion, and whatever may have passed between
himself and the pillar apostles on his two visits there, the crucial fact is that they
added nothing to him but gave full recognition to the grace of God which was
the manifest proof of his original commissioning (2:6–9). Similarly, he is concerned to make it clear that to have resumed a full-scale observance of the food
laws in table fellowship would have been equivalent to his building again what
Christ's death and commissioning had pulled down for him (2:14–21). The same
point is found at the heart of his argument in chap. 3: the law neither annuls nor
alters the terms of the original covenant promise to Abraham (3:15–20). That is
to say, the original promise to Abraham, as given to faith, continues to characterize the covenant and the relationship with God which it sustains; to insist that
covenantal nomism with its now traditional checkpoints was the only way to live
for heirs of the promise was to make the promise void. It is still, of course,
necessary to know how faith will work out in practice. Guidance on life-style and
praxis is still necessary: hence the final exhortation in 5:13–6: 10. There Paul
clearly shows that he sees the law as still having a function. He still believes in a
kind of "covenantal nomism"! But it has markers different from the ancestral
customs of the Jews – love and Spirit, not circumcision.[24]

Paul's argument is thus clear. *Ongoing praxis must be a continuing expression
of the faith by which his readers first began to function within God's covenant
promise and purpose* – a beginning whose divinely given character was self-evident both to Paul and to his readers. Stated thus, the argument is certainly open
to sharp criticism: The law was also given by God; why should works of the law
be regarded as an antithesis to faith? We hardly need Jas 2:18–26 to spell this line
of criticism out for us. But at least Paul's logic is clear, and it is only part of the
complete argument.

(2) The second strand of Paul's argument is that *God's promise always had the
Gentiles in view from the beginning*. This is obviously the point of 3:6–9, where
the gospel is focused in the original promise to Abraham, "In you shall all the nations be blessed" (3:8 LXX).[25] The point is clear: the promise is to be offered to
those originally in view in it and on the original terms – to the Gentiles, by faith.
The covenant promise was not intended solely for Jews.[26]

---

[24] See particularly the central thesis of Barclay, *Obeying:* that Paul addresses both the issue of
identity and that of behavioral patterns, that "a major ingredient in the Galatian dispute is the
question of how the members of God's people should live," and that the exhortation of 5:13–6:10
"develops out of and concludes his earlier arguments" (p. 216). See also my *Romans,* 705–6.

[25] See F.F. Bruce, *Galatians* (NIGTC; Exeter: Paternoster, 1982) 156–57.

[26] J.L. Martyn, in his response to the Chicago version of this paper, largely ignored and in-

The verses that follow (3:10–14) have been much disputed and much misunderstood, but they are most obviously to be taken as speaking of a curse on
lawlessness, and therefore as a curse which the law has interposed between the
Gentiles (lawless) and their share in the promise. Thus the whole thrust of the
paragraph is the opening up of the blessing of Abraham to the Gentiles which
Christ achieved by removing that curse in his death (3:13–14). Therefore, whatever else is in view, Paul almost certainly has in mind the law's function in brand-
ing the Gentile per se as "sinner" (2:15) – outside Israel, outside the law, therefore sinner and transgressor, and under a curse. *The curse of the law on the Gentile as Gentile is precisely that corollary of covenantal nomism as it had come to be
understood in the nationalistic presumption* (we are the "righteous"; they the
"sinners") *and ethnic restrictiveness* (inheritance is limited to the Jews and proselytes – οἱ ἐξ ἔργων νόμου) *which Paul now contests.*[27]

We see a similar pattern in the argument about Christ as Abraham's "seed"
according to the promise (3:16). The whole point of this argument is to enable
Paul to make the claim that Gentiles have become partakers of the promise "in
Christ" (3:14, 28–29),[28] through the Spirit (3:14). Paul evidently does not need to
debate more fundamental issues of christology. The centrality of Christ and his
death for the gospel (1:4; 2:19–21; 3:1; 4:4–5; 6:12) and the necessity for faith in
him (2:16; 3:22–24, 26) were emphases he shared with his readers and indeed
with the "judaizers."[29] What Paul needed to emphasize was what we might call
the Gentile dimension of his christology and his gospel (1:15–16; 2:2–5, 7–8,
15–17; 3:8, 13–14, 16, 27–29; 5:6, 11; 6:14–15), that faith in Christ *continues* to be
the means through which *continued* participation in the promise and inheritance
of Abraham is maintained. What Paul was concerned about was that the gospel
which they took as their common starting point was actually distorted in its fun-
damentals if these emphases, which were outworkings of the gospel and christology, were not followed through. For the Galatian believers to accept the covenantal nomism which reclaimed the Jewish Christians at Antioch (2:12–14)
would be to lose the gospel and Christ (1:6–9; 5:4).

---

deed discounted this horizontal *Heilsgeschichte* dimension of the whole discussion. Contrast
B.R. Gaventa, "The Singularity of the Gospel: A Reading of Galatians" and R.B. Hays, "Crucified with Christ: A Synthesis of the Theology of 1 and 2 Thessalonians, Philemon, Philippians,
and Galatians" in Bassler, ed., *Pauline Theology Vol I*. 159 and 231–4 respectively; see also the
essays by R. Scroggs and D.J. Lull in the same volume.

[27] For a fuller exposition, see *Jesus, Paul and the Law*, chap. 8 and Additional Note 1. See also
the main thesis of G. Howard, *Paul: Crisis in Galatia* (SNTSMS 35; Cambridge: Cambridge
University Press, 1979), though I disagree with several subsidiary aspects of Howard's argument.

[28] See J.C. Beker, *Paul the Apostle: The Triumph of God in Life and Thought* (Philadelphia:
Fortress, 1980) 50–52, 96; J.L. Martyn, "Paul and His Jewish-Christian Interpreters," *USQR* 42
(1987–88) 3–4.

[29] R.B. Hays rightly notes that in Galatians christology is "not the issue" ("Christology and
Ethics in Galatians: The Law of Christ," *CBQ* 49 [1987] 276).

So too Paul evidently felt no need to justify the assumption that the gift of the Spirit was the fulfillment of the promise to Abraham. This must be because the gift of the Spirit to Gentiles was both recognized among the first Christians and acknowledged as the sure indication of God's acceptance/justifying act (so Gal 3:2–5; 4:6, 29; 5:5; see also Acts 10:44–48; 11:15–18; Rom 8:9, 14).[30] "This reception of the 'Spirit' is the primary datum of the Christian churches in Galatia."[31] Here too what Paul needed to emphasize was the gift and continued experience of the Spirit as operating independently of the law and ethnic (fleshly) considerations (3:2–5; 4:3–7, 29; 5:5–6, 18; 6:8).[32] In both cases, the christology and pneumatology of the letter presuppose a richer and fuller theology as fundamental, but in the letter itself Paul develops only those aspects of immediate importance to the situation of the readers.

We might simply note also how much of Paul's own self-understanding of his commission (that is, of his whole existence as a Christian) was bound up with the conviction that it was now time to reach out to and bring in the Gentiles on equal terms with the Jews (that is, without their ceasing to be "Greeks" as distinct from "Jews"). Hence he emphasized in his description of his conversion and calling that he was "called ... to preach God's Son among the Gentiles" (1:15–16).[33] Clearly, his conviction that he had been called from the first to go to the uncircumcision was bound up with his understanding that the Gentiles were in view from the first expression of the covenant promise. Which of these two came first and gave rise to the other it is not possible now to say.

(3) What then was *the purpose of the law?* The question arises inevitably from the line of argument outlined above. The fact that it also arises in 3:19 and 21 may be taken as at least some confirmation that our analysis of Paul's argument so far is on the right lines. The question arises, obviously, because Paul's treatment of the law as so far outlined has had strongly pejorative features. "Works of

---

[30] See further my *Baptism in the Holy Spirit: A Reexamination of the New Testament Teaching on the Gift of the Spirit in Relation to Pentecostalism Today* (SBT 2/15; London: SCM, 1970).

[31] H.D. Betz, "Spirit, Freedom, and Law: Paul's Message to the Galatian Churches," *SEÅ* 39 (1974) 145. See also D. J. Lull, *The Spirit in Galatia: Paul's Interpretation of Pneuma as Divine Power* (SBLDS 49; Chico, CA: Scholars Press, 1980); S.K. Williams, "Justification and the Spirit in Galatians," *JSNT* 29 (1987) 91–100; idem, "*Promise* in Galatians: A Reading of Paul's Reading of Scripture," *JBL* 107 (1988) 709–20. Williams argues that the promise to Abraham is the promise of the Spirit.

[32] See now Barclay, *Obeying*, particularly chap. 4, "The Sufficiency of the Spirit."

[33] See further my "'A Light to the Gentiles': The Significance of the Damascus Road Christophany for Paul," in *The Glory of Christ in the New Testament: Studies in Christology in Memory of G.B. Caird* (ed. L.D. Hurst and N.T. Wright; Oxford: Clarendon, 1987) 251–66, reprinted in *Jesus, Paul and the Law*, chap. 4. See also Gordon, "Problem at Galatia," 35. A corollary of this is that Paul's principal concern in Galatians 1–2 was not to defend his apostleship or apostolic authority as such (so still G. Lüdemann, *Paulus, der Heidenapostel: Band II, Antipaulinismus in frühen Christentum* [Göttingen: Vandenhoeck & Ruprecht, 1983] 145); see B.R. Gaventa, "Galatians 1 and 2: Autobiography as Paradigm," *NovT* 28 (1986) 309–26; and B. Lategan, "Is Paul Defending his Apostleship in Galatians?" *NTS* 34 (1988) 411–30.

the law" he regards in a very negative light (2:16; 3:2, 5, 10). It is the law which is understood to condemn Gentiles as "sinners" (2:15), to place a curse on the lawless which prevents them from participating in the covenant promise (3:10–14). But he does see a positive role for the law, at least in that he speaks of love of neighbor as fulfilling the whole law (5:14). What then is Paul objecting to so strongly?

The answer has already been suggested in the treatment of the curse of the law: Paul objects to covenantal nomism understood as it then was consistently throughout Judaism – covenantal nomism as restricting the covenant to those within the boundaries marked by the law, that is, to Jews and proselytes.[34] This is confirmed by his emphasis on another word used with strong negative overtones – "flesh" (3:3; 5:19, 24; 6:8). "Flesh" also marks out a misunderstood relationship with Abraham, or rather a relationship with Abraham in which the emphasis has been misplaced. Hence the allegory of 4:21–31: there is a line of descent from Abraham understood in terms of the flesh – a racial or ethnic or national identity – and that is not the line of promise.[35] To limit participation in the promise to a relationship κατὰ σάρκα is to misunderstand the promise.[36] Hence too the point of 6:12–13: the glorying in the flesh which Paul condemns is a glorying not in human exertion or in ritual action, but in ethnic identity.[37] To insist that Gentiles must be circumcised is to assume that God's purpose means the triumph of Israel as a nation state, whose supremacy is acknowledged by those who seek to become part of it by crossing the ritual boundaries which divide Gentile from Jew.[38]

---

[34] See also Paul's argument in 2:21: If righteousness was still in terms of the law and still included a covenantal nomistic "us and them" distinction between Jews and Gentiles, then Christ's death was "in vain" since it had not ended the covenantal nomistic function of the law as a dividing line that excluded Gentiles as such from the blessings of the covenant promise.

[35] The fact that Paul speaks of *two* covenants in Gal 4:21–31 is an interesting variation on the continuity/discontinuity Paul sees in salvation history. Strictly speaking, the "covenantal nomism" to which Paul objects refers only to the covenant of slavery; the correlative of the covenant of promise is the freedom of the Spirit (3:2–5; etc.).

[36] See particularly J.L. Martyn, "A Law-Observant Mission to Gentiles: The Background of Galatians," *Michigan Quarterly Review* 22 (1983) 221–36, esp. pp. 231–32; reprinted in *SJT* 38 (1985) 307–24, esp. pp. 318–20; idem, "Apocalyptic Antinomies in Paul's Letter to the Galatians," *NTS* 31 (1985) 410–24. My exegesis does not exclude the possibility that Paul was reacting to his "opponents" at this point (so advocated by Martyn, Barclay [*Obeying*, 91], and earlier by C.K. Barrett ["The Allegory of Abraham, Sarah, and Hagar in the Argument of Galatians," in *Essays on Paul* (London: SPCK, 1982) 154–70]). Barrett appositely cites *Jub.* 16:17–18 as an indication of the sort of exposition they would probably have used (note also 1 Macc 2:16). See now particularly G. Bouwman, "Die Hagar- und Sara-Perikope (Gal 4:21–31)," *ANRW* 11.25.4 (1987) 3135–55; and more generally J.M.G. Barclay, "Mirror-Reading a Polemical Letter: Galatians as a Test Case," *JSNT* 31 (1987) 73–93.

[37] W. Schmithals's threadbare hypothesis falls apart here in his argument that the "glorying in the flesh" is expressed in a gnostic "contempt for the flesh" ("The Heretics in Galatia," in *Paul and the Gnostics* [Nashville: Abingdon, 1972] 55). Not gnostic but ethnic identity is the issue at this point.

[38] This false evaluation of circumcision and flesh means also a failure to recognize the proper

I suspect this also provides the key to the puzzling statement in 3:19: the law was given through angels ("in hand of mediator" is probably in apposition to "ordained through angels," in the light of the next clause). Anyone familiar with the Jewish understanding of the one God's ordering of his creation and of the nations within it would be familiar also with the idea of God having appointed guardian angels for each state (Deut 32:8–9; Sir 17:17; *Jub.* 15:31–32; *1 Enoch* 20:5; *Tg. Ps.-J.* Gen 11:7–8).[39] The usual corollary in Jewish thought was that God, having appointed angels over other nations, kept Israel for himself, with no mediator interposing. The point Paul is probably making is that to treat the law in such an exclusive, restrictive way is equivalent to treating the law as though it was given through Israel's guardian angels or, indeed, as though the law itself was Israel's guardian angel (the implication of 4:8–10, coming as it does at the end of 3:23–4:10; hence also the definition of the characteristic state of the Jews as "under the law" as a ruling power [3:23; 4:4–5, 21; 5:18]).[40] To thus regard the law as a national identity marker, as a boundary dividing Jew from Gentile, is in effect to deny the oneness of God.

Even this treatment of the law is not unreservedly negative. There was a positive side to this giving of the law to Israel. It gave the covenant people a way of dealing with sin in the period of time prior to the coming of Christ (3:19).[41] The

---

function of the law (3:19; 4:8–10) and so also to keep it (3:10; 6:13; see also Rom 2:17–29). See also *Jesus, Paul and the Law*, chap. 8 [= ch. 3 above] and Additional Note 1.

[39] R. Meyer, "λαός," *TDNT* 4. 39–41. See also T. Callan, "Pauline Midrash: The Exegetical Background for Gal 3:19b," *JBL* 99 (1980) 549–67.

[40] Here I dispute such views as those of J. W. Drane that 3:19 amounts to "a categorical denial of the divine origin of the Torah" (*Paul: Libertine or Legalist?: A Study in the Theology of the Major Pauline Epistles* [London: SPCK, 1975] 34) or of H. Hübner that 3:19 means that the law "is the product of demonic angelic powers" (*Law in Paul's Thought* [Edinburgh: T. & T. Clark, 1984] 24–36), both of whom read too much into the text and ignore the context of Jewish thought, where the association of angels in the giving of the law was quite familiar and unthreatening (Deut 33:2 LXX; *Jub.* 1:29ff.; Philo, *Somn.* 1.143; Josephus, *Ant.* 15.5.3 § 136; see also Acts 7:38, 53; Heb 2:2); see also S. Westerholm, *Israel's Law and the Church's Faith: Paul and His Recent Interpreters* (Grand Rapids: Eerdmans, 1988) 176–79. A.J.M. Wedderburn chides me for denying that Paul is opposed to the law *per se*, referring to Gal 3:19, which he thinks does "seem to express opposition to the law per se," though without further explanation ("Paul and the Law," *SJT* 38 [1985] 618 n. 11). So too I must register my dissent with Howard (*Paul*, 60–61) and L. Gaston ("Paul and the Torah," in *Antisemitism and the Foundations of Christianity* [ed. A.T. Davies; New York: Paulist, 1979] 62–64), who maintain that "under the law" could include, or even specifically designate, the Gentile situation, and with Martyn, who maintained in the Chicago seminar that the phrase "to be under" meant to be "under the tyrannical power of something." But see n. 42 below.

[41] I see no grounds within this phase of Paul's argument to interpret 3:19 ("the law was added for the sake of transgressions") in terms of *multiplying* transgressions (so, e.g., Barrett, *Freedom*, 33; Westerholm, *Israel's Law*, 178, 182). That reads Gal 3:19 too much through the differently slanted and more careful argument of Rom 5:20. Here Paul is explaining the positive side of covenantal nomism in the period before Christ (see further below n. 42). Likewise, the point of 3:21 is not totally to dismiss the law; the mistake Paul objects to is the assumption that the law

law (guardian angel) served to direct, govern, and protect Israel until the promise could be fulfilled in Christ (3:23–4:7).[42] But now that Christ has come, the promise is open to Gentile as well as Jew on the original conditions. Consequently, to return under the oversight of the law in its role as guardian of national rights and prerogatives is to return to childish subserviency and servility and to deny the fullness of the promise. The upshot is that Paul is able to pose a different alternative from that usually posed by Judaism. Judaism asserted: within the law = within the covenant. Paul in contrast asserted: within Christ = within the covenant; within the law = outside Christ (5:4).[43]

In short, Paul's attitude to the law in Galatians has regularly been misperceived as more unyieldingly negative than it is. The misunderstanding has been based on a misperception of "works of the law" as "good works" and of 3:10 as requiring perfect compliance with the law.[44] But once the point has been grasped that Paul's chief target is a covenantal nomism understood in restrictively nationalistic terms – "works of the law" as maintaining Jewish identity, "the curse of the law" as falling on the lawless so as to exclude Gentiles as such from the covenant promise – then it becomes clear that Paul's negative remarks had a more limited thrust and that so long as the law is not similarly misunderstood as defining and defending the prerogatives of a particular group, it still has a positive role to play in the expression of God's purpose and will.[45]

---

fulfills the role of the promise (*giving* life) as well as its own role (*regulating* life within the covenant [2:12], particularly in the period before Christ).

[42] See particularly D.J. Lull, "'The Law Was Our Pedagogue': A Study in Galatians 3:19–25," *JBL* 105 (1986) 481–98; N.H. Young, "*Paidagogos:* The Social Setting of a Pauline Metaphor," *NovT* 29 (1987) 150–76; T.D. Gordon, "A Note on ΠΑΙΔΑΓΩΓΟΣ in Galatians 3:24–25," *NTS* 35 (1989) 150–54. Young sees the emphasis of 3:23–24 as falling "on the confining and restrictive rather than either the corrective or protective functions of a pedagogue" (p. 171). He concludes: "Thus the law is 'our pedagogue' in the sense that the restrictive regulations which separated Jew and Gentile, which Sinai epitomized, were only temporary. Just as a pedagogue's guardian role finished when the child arrived at maturity, so the legal separation of Jew and Gentile ended with the coming of the new age in Christ" (p. 176). Gordon sees the *paidagogos's* function as guarding and protecting Israel "from the defiling idolatry of the Gentiles, preserving a community which propagated faith in the God of Abraham until the promise made to Abraham became historical reality" (p. 154).

[43] See J.H. Neyrey, "Bewitched in Galatia: Paul and Cultural Anthropology," *CBQ* 50 (1988) 72–100, esp. pp. 80–83.

[44] This is the nub of Hübner's consistent misinterpretation of Paul's treatment of the law in Galatians. His insistence that 3:10 has in view "the primarily *quantitative* demand of the law that all ... its stipulations be followed out, so that whoever transgresses against even a single one of these stipulations is accursed" (*Law*, 38) ignores the facts that "doing what the law requires" includes the provision of atonement for failure (see above n. 3), and that Paul equally expects "the whole law" to be "fulfilled" by believers (5:14). See also Barclay's critique of Hübner at this point (*Obeying*, 136–37). Hübner's, of course, is a variant of the normal interpretation of 3:10 (see *Jesus, Paul and the Law*, chap. 8 n. 38).

[45] F. Watson turns Paul's concerns upside down. Far from objecting to a covenantal nomism which inevitably means a reinforcement of the boundary between Jew(ish Christian) and Gentile (Christian), Watson thinks Paul's objective was that "the church should separate from the

IV

The last main part of my thesis is the claim that *Galatians is Paul's first sustained attempt to deal with the issue of covenantal nomism within the new movement we call Christianity*. The main ground for the claim is that covenantal nomism does not seem to have been an issue before the Antioch incident (2:11–14). Here the relation between 2:1–10 and 2:11–14 is important. What had been settled at Jerusalem (2:1–10) was the issue of circumcision. What emerged at Antioch (2:11–14) was a different issue – food laws. Just how different these issues were lay at the heart of the disagreement.

If we assume that the "certain individuals from James" (2:12) had accepted the Jerusalem agreement not to require circumcision of Gentile converts (however unwillingly, perhaps), then it follows that they must have regarded the agreement as permitting a concession rather than as conceding a principle. They may well have regarded it as simply extending the degree of hospitality to God-fearers which diaspora Judaism had hitherto regularly practiced (not least in Syria; see Josephus, *J.W.* 2.18.2 §§ 462–63; 7.3.3 §§ 50–51). That they did not think the principle of covenantal nomism had thereby been conceded is probably indicated by 2:10: almsgiving was such a fundamental expression of covenantal righteousness (Dan 4:27; Sir 29:12; 40:24; Tob 4:10; 12:9; 14:10–11)[46] that Paul's ready agreement to maintain the practice could easily be read as an expression of his own readiness to maintain the principle of covenantal nomism. Moreover, since the tradition of Gentile sympathizers willingly embracing the ancestral customs of the Jews ("judaizing") was so well established,[47] the men from James may well have assumed that the table fellowship in Antioch was on a judaizing

---

Jewish community" (*Paul, Judaism and the Gentiles: A Sociological Approach* [SNTSMS 56; Cambridge: Cambridge University Press, 1986] 64). This thesis recognizes only the discontinuities in Paul's view of *Heilsgeschichte* (promise/law, two covenants) and fails to recognize the continuity of Abraham's seed, of the "we" which includes Jew and Gentile (3:14; 4:5), of a sonship coming to maturity (3:23–4:5), and of the law fulfilled with faith and in love (5:6, 14). The other major flaw in Watson's thesis is that he uses "Jewish community" in a too undifferentiated and all-inclusive sense. There were Jews for whom Paul's argument and gospel would mean total separation, but there were others – Jewish Christians still functioning as Jews in synagogue service – who would go along with Paul (himself a Jewish Christian). And there were no doubt still others, Jews and Jewish Christians, with ambivalent views in between. It was not a case of Paul accepting the boundaries (circumcision, food laws, etc.) as immovable and simply stepping outside of them (contrast 1 Cor 9:20–21); he was attempting to redraw the boundaries with Gentile Christians inside! See also my critique of Watson in *Romans*, see index, under "Watson"; also my responses to P.F. Esler and H. Räisänen in *Jesus, Paul and the Law*, chap. 6, Additional Note 10, and chap. 7, Additional Note 4, respectively.

[46] See further K. Berger, "Almosen für Israel: Zum historischen Kontext der paulinischen Kollekte," *NTS* 23 (1976–77) 180–204.

[47] See n. 5 above.

basis. This would be sufficient to explain why the issue did not emerge earlier from the Jerusalem side.[48]

On Paul's side, the agreement at Jerusalem was probably taken as a point of principle. Paul understood circumcision in what we would now call covenantal nomistic terms: it was not simply a rite of entry, but the first act of a continuing compliance with the law. The agreement in Jerusalem would be understood by him as providing a precedent for playing down other boundary-defining, Gentile-excluding commandments. If, however, 2:10 is once again anything to go by, the issue was not yet so clearly defined for him. He warmly agreed to a continuing emphasis on almsgiving without seeing it as a qualification of the agreement on circumcision. Perhaps the relief at winning the day on his principal objective made him eager to assent to this one request (requirement?) without sufficient thought for how it would be understood in Jerusalem. Or perhaps the connection between covenantal nomism and Jewish ethnic identity had not yet become sharply focused for him; after all, any almsgiving by Gentile to Jew could be readily understood within such a mind-set as part of Gentile acknowledgment of Jewish hegemony (Isa 45:14; 60:5–17; 61:6; Mic 4:13; Tob 13:11; 1QM 12:13–15).

Whatever the precise facts on either side, and whatever the shared or differing understandings of the Jerusalem agreement,[49] the Antioch incident itself seems to have come as a surprise to both sides – the men from James surprised at Jewish Christians' disregard of the food laws to such an extent, and Paul surprised that there still was an issue here. In any event, the Antioch incident seems to have been the first major dispute on the issue of food laws or, in more general terms, on the issue of whether covenantal nomism as hitherto understood was still binding on Jewish Christians.

Gal 2:14–16 does look as though Paul is marking out a step beyond a previously agreed position. To be more precise, in these verses Paul seems to be making explicit a theological logic which he may well previously have taken for granted (and so not previously formulated), but which others (even close associates) had not recognized or agreed to, as the Antioch incident demonstrated. What he now saw with clarity was that the gospel relativized the nationalistic expression of covenantal nomism, and it is this which he (quite possibly for the first time) expressed at Antioch to Peter. Since Peter and the other Jewish Christians

---

[48] For the pressures leading to the demand of the men from James, see my "Incident at Antioch," § 2.2, with particular reference to R. Jewett, "The Agitators and the Galatian Congregation," *NTS* 17 (1970–71) 204–6.

[49] I question whether it is right to speak of a "unilateral reversal of the earlier agreement" on the part of James (so P.J. Achtemeier, *The Quest for Unity in the New Testament Church* [Philadelphia: Fortress, 1987] 54; see also Watson, *Paul*, 53–56). Barrett's formulation is probably nearer the mark: "What agreement there was had probably been inadequately thought through" (*Freedom*, 12).

at Antioch probably did not accept Paul's argument at that time,[50] Paul uses the opportunity of this letter to Galatia to restate, and presumably to strengthen, the argument used then.

The issue is clearly posed in ethnic terms – Jew and Gentile, "living like Gentiles" "judaizing" (2:14). Here the traditional parameters of covenantal nomism are in view: they can be defined simply as "not living like the Gentiles" (see, e.g., *Jub.* 6:35; 15:34; *Pss. Sol.* 8:13). Likewise, the traditional life-style of the God-fearer – "judaizing" – is evident. The assumption of the men from James and of Peter and the other Jewish Christians is clearly implied: in order for the Jew(ish Christians) to continue to practice their covenantal nomism, the Gentile God-fearers/Christians should be prepared to judaize, to live like Jews. What Paul cannot stomach, however, is that this should be made a requirement for faith. The use of the same verb in 2:3 and 2:14 ("compel") is not accidental. What Paul objects to is that the agreement made in Jerusalem is being set at naught by the de facto compulsion of the Jewish Christians' behavior in regard to table fellowship at Antioch.

The sense of ethnic boundary and distinctiveness is again to the fore in v. 15 – "Jews by nature," "Gentile sinners." And since "sinner" indicates the lawless person (see e.g., Ps 27:2; 54:3; 1 Macc 1:34; 2:44), again the implication is clear that the issue focuses on the function of the law as defining the Gentile per se as "sinner" (Ps 9:17; 1 Macc 2:48; *Pss. Sol.* 1:1; 2:1–2; Luke 6:33/Matt 5:47).[51] To be noted is the fact that Paul expresses himself in traditionally Jewish terms ("we are Jews by nature"). *He speaks as one who is consciously within Judaism* and conscious of his distinctiveness from the Gentile; he speaks as one within the law, who has traditionally seen the Gentile as outside the bounds marked out by the law – and so by definition a "sinner." Since it is this very distinction that he will be going on to question, it must be that Paul is trying to argue from an agreed position and perspective within Judaism to a new position and perspective. It is probable also that the movement in self-understanding which he is thereby trying to encourage was a reflection of his own changed self-understanding. But he remains a Jew; *it is still an inner-Jewish dispute.*[52] He is still able

---

[50] That Paul's plea to Peter was unsuccessful is now accepted by most commentators. See, e.g., Achtemeier, *Quest*, 59 and those cited by him in nn. 8–9; and see further below.

[51] A. Suhl completely ignores this whole dimension of the historical context when he attempts to defend the paraphrase, "We, of course Jews by nature and not stemming from the Gentiles, are nevertheless sinners (as much as them)" ("Der Galaterbrief – Situation und Argumentation," *ANRW* II.25.4 [1987] 3102–6).

[52] See further K. Haacker, "Paulus und das Judentum im Galaterbrief," *Gottes Augapfel: Beiträge zur Erneuerung des Verhältnisses von Christen und Juden* (ed. E. Brocke and J. Sein; Neukirchen-Vluyn: Neukirchener Verlag, 1986) 95–111; and W.D. Davies's critical review of H.D. Betz, *Galatians: A Commentary on Paul's Letter to the Churches in Galatia* (Hermeneia; Philadelphia: Fortress, 1979) in *Jewish and Pauline Studies* (London: SPCK, 1984) 172–88.

to identify himself with the older mind-set, which suggests that the full implications of his own changed perspective are still only becoming clear to him.

This sheds light on the much misunderstood opening to 2:16, which I still think has to be read as follows: "We are Jews by nature ... knowing that someone is not justified by works of law except [*or*, but only] through faith in Jesus Christ ..."[53] Paul continues to locate himself within the Jewish mind-set, but now the traditional Jewish perspective is qualified by giving "faith in Christ" the decisive role.[54] *What is expressed here is the viewpoint of Peter and the other Jewish Christians at Antioch.* They are all at one so far as the gospel's call for faith in Jesus Christ is concerned. The Jewish Christian understanding is that although this is a fundamental redefinition of covenantal nomism, the life of righteousness *within* the covenant is still defined by works of the law. But that, the Jewish Christians now believe, is not decisive for acceptance by God and final acquittal. Faith in God's Messiah is the primary necessity. "No one is justified by works of law unless they also believe in Messiah Jesus."

This is Paul's starting point, as his own Jewish identity was in v. 15, but he goes on from that to underline the equally evident fact that faith in Christ Jesus has been exercised and has been fully effective *without* works of the law. Experience has demonstrated that God's acceptance is not conditional on covenantal nomism, certainly as that is usually understood. Experience of grace has given sufficient proof that "no one will be justified before God" (Ps 143:2), and that must include all who depend on their Jewish status and praxis for justification or who think of themselves as righteous because they live in accordance with the ancestral customs. Jewish Christians and Galatians should carry this basic insight through in their continuing life together and not return to questions of ethnic ("flesh") and religious ("sinners") distinctions.

---

[53] See further my "New Perspective," in *Jesus, Paul and the Law*, with Additional Notes 3 and 9; and Watson, *Paul*, 197 n. 73.

[54] I remain quite unconvinced by the now renewedly popular argument that "the faith of Christ" means "Christ's faith" rather than "faith in Christ" The latter is wholly in line with the sustained thrust of the letter, including the fundamental distinction between (human) faith and (human) works, whereas the former introduces a quite different tack. R.B. Hays, for example, in the fullest recent treatment, finds himself drawn into arguing that effectively all the key πίστις references in Gal 3:1–14 denote the faithfulness of Christ (*The Faith of Jesus Christ* [SBLDS 56; Chico, CA: Scholars Press, 1983] chap. 4). But the relevant πίστις references of 3:7–9 are bracketed by talk of Abraham's believing and Abraham's πίστις (vv. 6, 9) and are more naturally understood as carrying the same sense of πίστις. Further, 3:14 is more naturally understood to speak of the mode of *receiving* ("through faith") than of the mode of bestowing. The problem with "the faith of Christ" interpretation is that to be sustainable it must draw in most other πίστις references, leaving the verbal reference to human believing without a noun counterpart at important points in the argument, the mode of human reception thus unspecified, and references like Gal 5:5–6 in some confusion. The debate on this phrase was postponed at the Chicago meeting till the Pauline Theology Group reaches Romans. But see also now Barclay, *Obeying*, 78 n. 8; and Westerholm, *Israel's Law*, 111–12 n. 12.

Here again, therefore, the very structure of the argument seems to indicate a transition in Paul's own thinking and perspective. We seem to see Paul working through the implications of his understanding of the gospel, Paul forced by the turn of events in Antioch to bring to clear expression consequences and corollaries which he had previously practiced without having had to spell out their full theological rationale.

A further indication that there has been some development in Paul's own position, or at least in his articulation of it as it related to more traditional Jewish perspectives, is the change in Paul's attitude toward the Jerusalem apostles as it becomes evident in 2:1–10. In this passage the tension between a readiness to accept their authority and a clear distancing of himself from them is quite evident.[55]

On the one hand, he readily acknowledges that their reception of his understanding of the gospel would determine whether his work had been or was in vain (2:2). He expresses himself with great care when he describes the actual encounter in Jerusalem (2:3ff.), but the implication of v. 3 is that Paul recognized the Jerusalem authorities' right to require circumcision, if they so chose. His relief that they did not "compel" Titus to be circumcised is fairly evident, as is his relief that they "added nothing to him" (2:6) so far as his understanding and preaching of the gospel was concerned. But the implication is the same: he acknowledged thereby that they had a right to make such stipulations. Indeed, this may lie behind his readiness to accept the obligation that was actually laid down in v. 10, to remember the poor. There is even an implication that he recognized the pillar apostles' authority to confirm his mission to the Gentiles. Such, at any rate, seems to be the significance of the right hand of fellowship given in order that Barnabas and Paul should go to the Gentiles, just as Peter and the others should go to the circumcised (2:9).

At the same time, Paul also clearly wants to distance himself from the Jerusalem authorities. He describes them as "those reputed to be of some account" "those regarded as pillars" (2:6, 9), phrases neatly chosen to indicate that they were highly esteemed, but not necessarily by him. In v. 10 he coyly omits the verb that would have been most appropriate to describe the obligation laid upon him by the pillar apostles, lest, presumably, it seem that he had agreed to an element of traditional covenantal nomism at their behest. Clearest of all is the parenthesis inserted into v. 6: "what they [the pillar apostles] once were matters nothing to me; God takes no account of human evaluation of status." Here Paul is almost explicit in his implication that he had once accorded the Jerusalem apostles

---

[55] In the following paragraphs I draw on my "Relationship between Paul and Jerusalem according to Galatians 1 and 2," *NTS* 28 (1982) 461–78, reprinted in *Jesus, Paul and the Law*, chap. 5.

an authority which he no longer recognized and to which he was no longer willing to submit.

The best way to explain the tension between these rather different attitudes to the Jerusalem authorities is that they reflect different stages in Paul's own career and mission. There was a period when he acknowledged and would have been ready to defer to the authority of Peter and the others. Presumably this was the period when he was active as a member of the church in Antioch, that is to say, during his time both as a teacher in Antioch (if we follow Acts 13:1), and as a missionary commissioned by Antioch (Acts 13:2–3).[56] The decisive factor here, presumably, would be that Antioch saw itself as a daughter church of Jerusalem. Consequently, Paul probably attended the Jerusalem consultation (Gal 2:1–10) as a delegate from Antioch. All during this period, and immediately thereafter, he recognized and operated within the terms of Jerusalem's authority. The degree of mutual acceptance implies that covenantal nomism as such had not yet become an issue.

That issue only came to the surface in the Antioch incident (2:11–14). Whether it would have exploded into outright disagreement at Jerusalem if the pillar apostles had after all tried to "compel" Titus to be circumcised we cannot tell. Quite likely the answer is yes. Paul was sufficiently clearheaded on the circumcision issue to fight his corner with the utmost resolution (2:5). *But the acceptance of his argument at that time was probably enough to prevent the issue emerging in terms of mutually exclusive possibilities: either* covenantal nomism *or* faith. What is clear enough is that when such compulsion was exerted by the men from James, and when Peter and the other Jewish Christians acquiesced to what they demanded, at that point Paul drew the line (2:14ff.). His rejection of the demands of covenantal nomism as they affected the Gentile Christians was at the same time a rejection of the Jerusalem authority which laid them down. Here again, therefore, is sufficient indication that the Antioch incident was a decisive factor in the development of Paul's understanding of the gospel, both of how it related to covenantal nomism and what that meant for Gentile believers in relation to the hitherto unquestioned assumption that covenant membership was bound up with Jewish ethnic identity.[57]

---

[56] I take "apostles" in Acts 14:4, 14 in the sense of emissaries or missionaries of Antioch (see 2 Cor 8:23; Phil 2:25), since according to Acts 1:21–22 neither Paul nor Barnabas could be accounted apostles in the sense of witnesses of Christ's resurrection (as claimed by Paul for himself in 1 Cor 9:1; 15:7–11).

[57] Watson argues that the Gentile mission began as a response to the failure of the Jewish Christian congregation of Antioch in its preaching among the Jews and that it "involved a more or less complete separation from the Jewish community" (*Paul*, 31–32, 36–38). This ignores the evidence of Gal 2:9 that there was a conjoint mission to Jews and Gentiles and of Gal 2:12a that there was at least initially in Antioch a continuum of Jew, Jewish-Christian, and Gentile Christian. It also treats 1 Cor 9:21–22 (present tense) and 2 Cor 11:24 in a highly tendentious way, not to mention the primary thrust of Romans 9–11. The implication is that Paul continued to oper-

To complete the argument I include a brief response to those who claim that Paul's attitude to the law (and so also to covenantal nomism) was a more or less immediate consequence of his Damascus road conversion.[58]

In the first place, I find no evidence to indicate that the Hellenists had already "abandoned" the law. The only material that explicitly claims to express Hellenist views (Acts 7) is directed against the temple and not against the law. In Acts 7 the attitude to the law is positive (7:38, 53). That temple and law were tightly bound together is, of course, true (the laws of sacrifice, etc.), and hence the accusation against Stephen in Acts 6:14 is formulated in terms of both. But it requires no argument to claim that the law could be held in high esteem even when the temple was heavily criticized or, subsequently, when the temple ceased to be a factor in the life and praxis of Judaism. We cannot assume therefore that what Paul was converted to was a Hellenist rejection of the law.

Paul's persecution of the church was certainly an expression of his zeal for the law (Gal 1:13–14; Phil 3:6). This should not be taken as implying a wholesale rejection of the law by the Hellenists who were being persecuted. The key word here is "zeal." It indicates the attitude of a zealot, one who wanted to define the boundaries around the covenant more sharply, to mark off the righteous more clearly from the sinner. It expresses an attitude evident in such writings as *1 Enoch* 1–5, the *Psalms of Solomon*, and the Dead Sea Scrolls, and also, it would appear, among the Pharisees – a factional or even sectarian attitude that was prepared to condemn and even to persecute fellow Jews whose loyalty to the ancestral traditions was not so firm and whose practice seemed to question and so to threaten these more tightly drawn boundaries.[59] Thus we should probably envisage a persecution by Paul of Jews who *in their own reckoning* were being properly observant of what the law required – a condemnation of fellow Jews equivalent to that of the Pharisees by the Qumran covenanters, or of the Sadducees by the *Psalms of Solomon*, or subsequently of the fainthearted by the Zealots.[60]

Paul's own view of his conversion is not of a *conversion* as such – not a conversion in his attitude to the law and far less a conversion from Judaism – but of a

---

ate within the context of the synagogue so far as possible and sought to maintain the continuum. See also n. 45 above.

[58] Particularly S. Kim, *The Origin of Paul's Gospel* (WUNT 2/4; Tübingen: Mohr [Siebeck], 1981); and C. Dietzfelbinger, *Die Berufung des Paulus als Ursprung seiner Theologie* (WMANT 58; Neukirchen-Vluyn: Neukirchener Verlag, 1985). What follows supplements the discussion of *Jesus, Paul and the Law*, chap. 4.

[59] See Haacker, "Paulus und das Judentum," 104–7; my *Romans*, 586–87; and *Jesus, Paul and the Law*, chap. 4, Additional Note 1. Despite Sanders's rejection of the claim that Paul's persecution of the church was tied up with his convictions as a Pharisee, it must be significant to the contrary that Paul uses the same word, "zeal," to characterize both his commitment to the ancestral customs of his people (that is, as a Pharisee [Gal 1:14]) and his energy in persecution (Phil 3:6).

[60] See also *Jesus, Paul and the Law*, chap. 3.

comissioning to go to the Gentiles (Gal 1:15–16).[61] His acknowledgment of the crucified as Lord did not lead him at once to the conclusion that the law which counted the crucified as accursed was wholly discredited and disowned by God. Such a line of reasoning appears nowhere in Paul's writings. The theological logic focuses rather on the relation between the curse of the law and the Gentile. For Christ to have died as one cursed by the law meant that he had been put outside the covenant, had become, in effect, like a Gentile. For God to have vindicated this Christ therefore meant that that boundary line between Gentile and Jew no longer counted with God. God accepted the outsider; his promise could now be accepted by the Gentiles without their coming within the boundary of the law (3:13–14).[62] The seed and principle of Paul's full-blown theology of justification was thus given him from the first, which is why he puts so much emphasis on the "revelation of Christ" (1:12) in the letter. But evidently the full implications of it were not worked out and did not become clear in these early years, presumably because the ambiguity of God-fearers and proselytes both believing in Jesus *and* willing to judaize to some extent (as they had done before they heard about Jesus) meant that the issue had not yet come into focus. Certainly it is hard to believe that Jew and Gentile believers in Messiah Jesus had completely abandoned the law in Antioch for a decade or more before it came to the attention of the more conservative brothers in Judea or caused any kind of surprise or comment.[63]

In short, the evidence of Galatians seems to indicate that an evolving situation in Antioch and a double confrontation with what had hitherto usually been regarded as central in covenantal nomism brought home to Paul what he now saw always to have been implicit in his initial commissioning to the Gentiles. It is this implication for covenantal nomism which he works out, probably for the first time in such detail, in his letter to his converts in Galatia.

---

[61] Ibid., chap. 4 n. 1.

[62] See the fuller exposition in *Jesus, Paul and the Law*, chap. 4 and chap. 8 n. 56a.

[63] Ibid., chap. 6, Additional Note 1.

Chapter 7

The Justice of God

A renewed perspective on justification by faith

I

IT was sometime in 1515 or 1516 that Martin Luther made the great discovery from which the Reformation sprang and which has been central to Protestant, particularly Lutheran theology ever since. He discovered 'justification by faith'. That epochal moment is recalled in Luther's own words.[1]

> I greatly longed to understand Paul's Epistle to the Romans and nothing stood in the way but that one expression, 'the justice of God', because I took it to mean that justice whereby God is just and deals justly in punishing the unjust. My situation was that, although an impeccable monk, I stood before God as a sinner troubled in conscience, and I had no confidence that my merit would please him. Therefore I did not love a just and angry God, but rather hated and murmured against him. Yet I clung to the dear Paul and had a great yearning to know what he meant.
>
> Night and day I pondered until I saw the connection between the justice of God and the statement that 'the just shall live by faith' [Rom. 1:17]. Then I grasped that the justice of God is that righteousness by which through grace and sheer mercy God justifies us through faith. Thereupon I felt myself to be reborn and to have gone through open doors into paradise. The whole of Scripture took on a new meaning, and whereas before the 'justice of God' had filled me with hate, now it became to me inexpressibly sweet in greater love. This passage of Paul became to me a gate of heaven ...

That was the moment, we may say, when the pre-Reformation belief in the 'justice of God' gave way to the Reformation belief in 'justification by faith'.

The insight into divine human relationships thus crystallized by Luther's conversion experience is fundamental and far reaching: that God's grace is always prior, the only ground on which we can stand before him; that for any human creatures to think to make a claim upon God by virtue of what they possess or control or do is a presumption of absolute folly; that religion can all too quickly be perverted into a system which sustains a self-deluding pride in piety. 'Justification by faith' thus understood and propounded has been a sharp-edged sword cutting through all such self-deception and misapplied principle, a powerful

---

[1] The citation is from Roland Bainton's *Here I Stand* (London: Hodder & Stoughton, 1951), 65, slightly adapted.

shibboleth to distinguish right-thinking theology and the spirituality which God acknowledges from every counterfeit. We need only recall how in this century Rudolf Bultmann launched his progromme of demythologizing on its basis,[2] and how Ernst Käsemann and others have defended 'justification by faith' as the 'canon within the canon', the primary test by which we may discern the spirits and recognize the word of God today.[3]

At the same time, however, the transition from 'the justice of God' to 'justification by faith' was not wholly positive. Luther's conversion experience and the insight which it gave him also began a tradition in biblical interpretation, which has resulted for many in the loss or neglect of other crucial bibilical insights related to the same theme of divine justice. And particularly in the case of Paul, Luther's discovery of 'justification by faith' and the theological impetus which it gave especially to Lutheran theology has involved a significant misunderstanding of Paul, not least in relation to 'justification by faith' itself. To develop and defend this claim is the main purpose of the present paper.

Before entering fully upon our theme, I should perhaps emphasize that what I say is not and should not be conceived as an attack on the Protestant doctrine of justification. Such an inference would be wholly unjustified. The Protestant doctrine of justification has been a restatement of central biblical insights of incalculable influence and priceless value. In drawing attention to aspects of a larger, still richer doctrine I do not mean to detract from or diminish the aspect which has been so prominent in Reformation-inspired exegesis and teaching. It is important, however, that these other aspects be brought more fully into the light so that in turn their value may once again be appreciated and their influence felt to fuller effect.

II

The more negative influence of Luther's conversion and rediscovery of justification by faith can be characterized in four ways – all of them effects of the reflection backwards of Luther's experience on to Paul, as indeed in some measure of Augustine's conversion more than eleven centuries earlier. That there should have been such reflection backwards is not surprising. For it had been Paul who had given Luther the key for which he had so long struggled and searched. And

---

[2] R. Bultmann, *Kerygma and Myth*, ed. H.W. Bartsch (London: SPCK, 1957), 210–11; id. *Jesus Christ and Mythology* (London: SCM, 1960), 70.

[3] E. Käsemann, *Das Neue Testament als Kanon* (Göttingen: Vandenhoeck, 1970), 405. Similarly with ecclesiology: 'Paul's doctrine of the charismata is to be understood as the projection into ecclesiology of the doctrine of justification by faith' and rules out a purely individualistic interpretation of justification ('Ministry and Community in the New Testament'. *Essays on New Testament Themes* [London: SCM, 1964], 75–6).

it was clearly one of Paul's own primary categories, 'justification by faith', which had been the key. No wonder then that Paul's own conversion should be read in the light of Luther's. And no wonder that Luther and those who joined him should assume that Luther's discovery had first been Paul's.

1. What this meant, first of all, was that Paul's conversion was understood as *the climax to a long, inward, spiritual struggle*, during which Paul had wrestled with the pangs of a troubled conscience – just like Luther. Vivid pictures of Paul's inner turmoil following the lynching of Stephen, of his shutting his ears to the voice of conscience by pursuing his role as persecutor ever more fiercely, of his kicking against the goads (Acts 26: 14), could be painted in bold colours by exegete and preacher. The cries of self-perplexed anguish in Rom. 7:14–25, 'I do not do what I want, but I do the very thing I hate' (7:15), 'Who will deliver me from this body of death?' 7:24), could be drawn in as the self-confession of the pre-Christian Paul. Like Luther and Augustine before him,[4] it could be assumed that Paul had found justification by faith to be the answer to his own spiritual torment, the peace with God which follows from the recognition that God's acceptance is not dependent on human effort.

The trouble was that in passages where Paul speaks explicitly about his pre-conversion experience there is no hint whatsoever of any such agony of conscience. In Gal. 1:13–14 he recalls, still with an echo of his previous confidence, how 'I advanced in Judaism beyond many of my own age among my people, so extremely zealous was I for the traditions of my fathers'. And, even more striking, in Phil. 3:6 he notes that prior to his encounter with Christ on the Damascus road, and 'as regards righteousness under the law' he had been 'blameless'. Not much of a troubled conscience is evident here. But it was not until the end of the third decade of this century that Werner Kümmel effectively undermined the more traditional interpretation of Rom. 7 and prevented it from being used as a piece of pre-Christian autobiography.[5] And even so it has only been in the last decade or so that Krister Stendahl's critique, 'The Apostle Paul and the Introspective Conscience of the West', first published in 1963, has been given the hearing and the weight it deserves.[6]

However we understand Paul's conversion, therefore, it was not a conversion like Luther's. Consequently, it follows that an interpretation of Paul's teaching

---

[4] Augustine's *Confessions* 8:5 is the classic example of reading pre-conversion experience in the light of Rom. 7.

[5] W.G. Kümmel, *Römer 7 und die Bekehrung des Paulus* (Leipzig: Hinrichs, 1929).

[6] K. Stendahl, 'The Apostle Paul and the Introspective Conscience of the West', *HTR* 56 (1963), 199–215; repr. *Paul among Jews and Gentiles* (Philadelphia: Fortress/London: SCM, 1977), 78–96; e.g. 'Paul never urges Jews to find in Christ the answer to the anguish of a plagued conscience'; 'The famous formula "simul iustus et peccator" ... cannot be substantiated as the centre of Paul's conscious attitude towards his personal sins' (pp. 81–2).

on justification by faith should not be predicated on the assumption that it was.

2. A second corollary to the juxtaposition of Paul's conversion and Luther's was the understanding of justification by faith in *distinctively individualistic terms*. Justification was all about the individual finding peace with God, just like Luther – and Paul. Of course the gospel was for each one, for every person in his or her own individuality. An impression reinforced, quite understandably, by the fact that the individual Abraham is presented by Paul as the great archetype of justification by faith (Gal. 3 and Rom. 4), and by the highly personal language in an archetypal passage like Rom. 5:1 – 'Therefore, since we are justified by faith, we have peace with God through our Lord Jesus Christ.'

There were attempts, earlier in this century, to shift the focus of the traditional teaching on justification. William Wrede called it 'the *polemical doctrine* of Paul (which) is only made intelligible by the struggle of his life, his controversy with Judaism and Jewish Christianity, and is only intended for this'.[7] And Albert Schweitzer maintained that the doctrine of righteousness by faith was only a subsidiary element within the more fundamental mystical doctrine of being in Christ.[8] But such protests were swamped by the tremendous influence of Bultmann's extistentialist interpretation of Paul, reinforcing as it did the more traditional, individualistic reading, and giving rise to powerful restatements of the classic Lutheran doctrine within the Bultmann school.[9] One might also note its outworking in the individualism and privatization of religion which was such a feature of the political philosophy which dominated the 1980s in this country.

Here again it has been Krister Stendahl, another Lutheran, whose initially lone protest, indicated in the same article, but elaborated in lectures published in 1977, has slowly gained a hearing. There he contends 'that the main lines of Pauline interpretation ... have for many centuries been out of touch with one of the most basic of the questions and concerns that shaped Paul's thinking in the first place: the relation between Jews and Gentiles'. In particular, the 'doctrine of justification by faith was hammered out by Paul for the very specific and limited purpose of defending the rights of Gentile converts to be full and genuine heirs to the promises of God to Israel'.[10] Stendahl's protest has gained in strength as, in the wake of the Holocaust, Jewish/Christian relations began to climb once again to the top of the theological agenda.

---

[7] W. Wrede, *Paul* (London: Philip Green, 1907), 122–8; his emphasis.

[8] A. Schweitzer, *The Mysticism of Paul the Apostle* (London: Black, 1931), 219–26.

[9] See below nn. 30 and 31.

[10] Stendahl, *Paul Among Jews and Gentiles*, 1–2: cf. the earlier article: 'Where Paul was concerned about the possibility for Gentiles to be included in the messianic community, his statements are now read as answers to the quest for assurance about man's salvation out of a common human predicament' (p. 86).

3. Thirdly, bound up with Luther's understanding of Paul's conversion was the idea that it was a conversion *from Judaism* – as indeed a passage like Gal. 1: 13–14 could imply (where Paul speaks of his previous way of life 'within Judaism'). Unfortunately, however, the further corollary was drawn: that Judaism was the antithesis of Christianity, what Paul had been saved from. Such a view, of course, had been prominent in Christianity at least since the Epistle of Barnabas, and fitted well with the strong strand of anti-semitism which so disfigured Christianity's attitude to Jews and Judaism in the Middle Ages, an attitude which Luther himself expressed in characteristic forthrightness in his infamous *On the Jews and Their Lies*.[11] Tragically, however, it reinforced Christian suspicion, not to say hatred of Judaism, which was to reach its horrific outworking in the Holocaust. In scholarly circles the idea that Judaism was the antithesis of Christianity was expressed well through the middle of this century in the depiction of Judaism as simply the precursor of Christianity: so that *pre*-Christian Judaism was simply '*late* Judaism'[12] (where this left the Judaism of the next nineteen centuries was a question not even considered). And still today there are German scholars who speak of Judaism as something done away with by Jesus.[13] Even Jurgen Moltmann, for all the sensitivity of his response to the Holocaust,[14] is not immune from criticism at this point.[15] And E.P. Sanders, for all that he has undermined other pejorative stereotypes, as we shall see, has not helped at this point by characterizing Christianity and Judaism as distinct forms or patterns of religion.[16]

Now at last, however, a point which had been made by several is beginning to sink home in its wider implications: that Paul himself never saw what happened to him on the Damascus road as a *conversion*; and certainly not as a conversion *from* Judaism, the religion of his fathers. For him it was a *calling*, like that of Jeremiah of old (cf. Gal. 1: 15 with Jer. 1:5), a commissioning to fulfil the role of the servant of Yahweh in taking the gospel to the Gentiles (Isa. 49:1–6), an opening

---

[11] See e.g. M. Saperstein, *Moments of Crisis in Jewish-Christian Relations* (London: SCM/Philadelphia: TPI, 1989), 33–5.

[12] Examples in C. Klein, *Anti-Judaism in Christian Theology* (London: SPCK/Philadelphia: Fortress, 1978), ch. 2.

[13] I echo the words of W. Pannenberg, *Jesus: God and Man* (Philadelphia: Westminster/London: SCM, 1968), 255; see the critiques of R.J. Neuhaus, 'Introduction' to Pannenberg's *Theology and the Kingdom of God* (Philadelphia: Westminster, 1969), 35–6; and J.T. Pawlikowski, *Christ in the Light of the Christian-Jewish Dialogue* (New York: Paulist, 1982) 37–42. Similarly M. Noth, *The History of Israel* (London: Black, ²1960), 432, cited by Klein p. 26; L. Goppelt, *Theology of the New Testament, Vol. 1. The Ministry of Jesus in its Theological Significance* (1975; Grand Rapids: Eerdmans, 1981), 97.

[14] *The Crucified God* (New York: Harper & Row/London: SCM, 1974).

[15] See Pawlikowski, pp. 42–7; and further I. Wollaston, *Comparative Study of Jewish and Christian Responses to the Holocaust* (Durham University Ph.D. 1989).

[16] E.P. Sanders, *Paul and Palestinian Judaism. A Comparison of Patterns of Religion* (London: SCM, 1977).

out of the promise to Abraham of blessing to the nations as had always been
God's intention (Gen. 12:3 etc).[17] As Alan Segal argues, we may still speak
properly, in psychological or sociological terms, of a 'conversion of Paul', but not
of a conversion *from* Judaism; if anything rather of a conversion *within* Judaism.[18] The full implications of all this for our appreciation of Paul's post-conversion relationship with second Temple Judaism, and for any restatement of
justification by faith, are still matters of debate within the community of specialists in this area.

4. Finally, and most insidious of all, was the way this reading of Paul's teaching
on justification by faith in the light of Luther's experience reinforced the impression that Judaism, and not least the Judaism of Paul's time, was a *degenerate
religion*. Luther had striven to please God by his acts of penitence and good
works. The Church of his day taught that salvation could be gained by merit, the
merit of the saints, that the time spent in purgatory could be diminished by the
purchase of indulgences. That was what the discovery of justification by faith
had freed him from. It was all too easy to read Paul's experience through the
same grid. What Luther had been delivered from was also what Paul had been
delivered from. As the medieval church taught salvation by merit and good
works, so must the Judaism of Paul's day.[19] It was a degenerate religion precisely
because it was legalistic, dependent on human effort, and self-satisfied with the
results. And the Pharisees were the worst of all – narrow-minded, legalistic bi-
gots.[20]

In vain might Jewish scholars protest: this was not the Judaism they knew.[21]
Possibly another form of early Judaism of which no trace now remains – in the
diaspora, from where Paul came, perhaps. But not traditional Judaism, with its
emphasis precisely on repentance (a category strikingly absent from Paul) and
atonement – that is, on God's provision for sin. For a Jew like Solomon Schechter the apostle to the Gentiles was unintelligible – or should we say, the Protestant Paul. Still in 1969 Samuel Sandmel had to protest against the article on the

---

[17] The basic point was noted by such as J. Knox, *Chapters in a Life of Paul* (London: Black,
1954) p.117 (others in my *Jesus, Paul and the Law* [London: SPCK/Louisville, Westminster,
1990] p.101 n.1), but its broader implications and full significance were not fully appreciated.
On this point too Stendahl was once again the most important and influential exception (*Paul*,
pp.7–11, 84–5).

[18] A. Segal, *Paul the Convert: The Apostolate and Apostasy of Saul the Pharisee* (New Haven:
Yale, 1990).

[19] Luther himself made the explicit link: the Church was tarnished with 'Jewish legalism'; the
Catholics' 'rules and regulations remind me of the Jews, and actually very much was borrowed
from the Jews'; the Catholic understanding of the sacraments is essentially the same as the Jewish view of circumcision; on faith and works, the doctrine of the church was a variation of the
Jewish error that mere acts can win favour in God's sight (Saperstein, p.30).

[20] See further Klein chs.3 and 4.

[21] I take the following examples, referring to C.G. Montefiore, H.J. Schoeps, and S. Schechter from Sanders, *Paul and Palestinian Judaism* (London: SCM, 1977), 4–8.

'Pharisees' in *Interpreter's Dictionary of the Bible*, which characterized Pharisaism as 'the immediate ancestor of Rabbinical (or normative) Judaism, the arid and sterile religion of the Jews after the fall of Jerusalem'.[22]

On the non-Jewish side the protest had long been echoed by G.F. Moore, R.T. Herford and James Parkes.[23] But only with the publication of E.P. Sanders's *Paul and Palestinian Judaism*[24] has the message got through at last to English-speaking New Testament scholarship: that Judaism is first and foremost a religion of grace, with human obedience always understood as response to that grace. The covenant was given by divine initiative, and the law provides the framework for life within the covenant, the means of living within the covenant, *not* a means of getting accepted into the covenant in the first place. It is no accident that the Ten Commandments are preceded by the words: 'I am the Lord your God, who brought you out of the land of Egypt, out of the house of bondage.' Somewhat surprisingly, the picture which Sanders painted of what he called 'covenantal nomism' is remarkably like the classic Reformation theology of works – that good works are the consequence and outworking of divine grace, not the means by which that grace is first attained.[25]

That such a conclusion can be drawn is, of course, a remarkable outcome. The wheel of scholarly perception of first century Judaism has turned through a complete 180° arc, to a point precisely opposite from where it began. The Judaism of what Sanders christened as 'covenantal nomism' can now be seen to preach good Protestant doctrine: that grace is always prior; that human effort is ever the response to divine inititive; that good works are the fruit and not the root of salvation. But if that is so, where does that leave Paul? And where does it leave justification by faith? In formulating his own teaching on the theme, what was it that Paul was protesting against?

III

The chief clue had already been picked up by Wrede and Stendahl: that Paul's discussion of the theme of justification by faith is confined to two of Paul's principal letters – Galatians and Romans. Each is dominated by the issue of Jew/

---

[22] S. Sandmel, *The First Christian Century in Judaism and Christianity. Certainties and Uncertainties* (New York: Oxford University, 1969), 101, referring to the article by M. Black.

[23] G.F. Moore, 'Christian Writers on Judaism', *HTR* 14 (1922), 197–254; R.T. Herford, *Judaism in the New Testament Period* (London: Lindsey, 1928); J. Parkes, *The Conflict of the Church and the Synagogue. A Study in the Origins of Antisemitism* (Jewish Publication Society of America, 1934).

[24] Sanders, *Paul*; see not least his critique of the persistent view that rabbinic Judaism is a religion of legalistic works-righteousness (pp. 33–59).

[25] Cf. M.D. Hooker, 'Paul and "Covenantal Nomism"', *Paul and Paulinism. Essays in Honour of C.K. Barrett*, ed. M.D. Hooker and S.G. Wilson (London: SPCK, 1982), 47–56.

Gentile relationships. In each case Paul is dealing above all with the question: How is it that Gentiles can be acceptable to God equally as Jews? Paul's teaching on justification by faith is formulated precisely as an answer to that question. The presupposition, of course, was that Israel is God's chosen people, the one nation among all the nations which he chose for himself;[26] that Gentiles were, in the words of Ephesians, 'alienated from the commonwealth of Israel, strangers to the convenants of promise, having no hope and without God in the world' (Eph. 2:12). Paul's claim is presicely that that line of demarcation has been removed, 'the barrier formed by the dividing wall' between Jew and Gentile has been broken down (Eph. 2:14).[27] On this point there is no distinction: God's justifying grace is for Gentiles as well as Jews, since it is received by faith, which Gentile as well as Jew can exercise.

Of course exegesis within the mainstream Reformation tradition recognized this dimension in Paul's teaching, but its significance was too quickly and too often lost sight of. When Paul emphasized the universal sweep of God's saving grace – 'for all who believe' (Rom. 3:22; 4:11; 10:4), 'to all Abraham's descendants' (Rom. 4:16), 'you are all God's sons' (Gal. 3:26) – the 'all' was too quickly transposed into 'every single individual'; whereas for Paul, the 'all' meant primarily 'all, that is, Gentiles as well as Jews'. Not that the 'all, meaning every individual' is a wrong interpretation. Far from it. Nevertheless, by abstracting Paul's teaching on justification for all from its historical context an important dimension of that teaching was lost sight of. Let me further illustrate and document the point by citing three motifs which could have alerted us to the missing dimension but whose significance was equally lost sight of and inadequately interpreted.

1. In the two passages where Paul describes his own past before his conversion-commissioning, he speaks of his *'zeal'*. Gal. 1:14 – 'I advanced in Judaism beyond many of my own age among my people, so extremely zealous was I for the traditions of my fathers.' Phil. 3:5–6 – 'as to the law a Pharisee, as to zeal a persecutor of the church ...'. In Rom. 10:3 he uses the same word in giving testimony on behalf of his people – 'they have a zeal for God' (Rom. 10:3) – where presumably there is also something of a self-testimony reflecting his own pre-Christian past.

Now 'zeal' we know to have been characteristic of Jewish piety,[28] as evidenced by an overwhelming concern to do the will of God. It corresponded to the 'zeal' or 'jealousy' of God, that is, the exclusiveness of God's claim upon and relationship with Israel: you shall have no other gods, for I am a jealous/zealous God (Exod. 20:4–5; 34:12–16; Deut. 4:23–4; 5:8–9; 6: 14–15; Josh. 24:19–20). Conse-

---

[26] e.g. Deut. 32:8–9; Sir. 17:17; Jub. 15:30–2.

[27] See particularly M. Barth, *Ephesians* (*Anchor Bible* 34; New York: Doubleday, 1974), 282–91.

[28] A. Stumpff, *TDNT* 2. 878.

quently it was the word used with greatest approval for those who demonstrated such divine zeal by fighting to defend that exclusiveness, by maintaining Israel's distinctiveness as God's own people over against the other nations, the Gentiles. In particular, there are several heroes of Israel's past, remembered within the tradition precisely for their zeal in this respect.

Thus Judith (9:4) and Jubilees (30:5–20) both commend the zeal of Simeon and Levi in maintaining the purity and holiness of Israel's relation with the Lord, by killing the Schechemites who defiled their sister Dinah (Gen. 34). Ben Sira and 1 Maccabees hold up both Phinehas (Sir. 45:23–4; 1 Macc. 2:54) and Elijah (Sir. 48.2; 1 Macc. 2:58) as models of zeal for God, 'zeal for the law', because they forceably defended the set-apartness of Israel – Phinehas by killing the Israelite who brought a Midianite woman to his tent (Num. 25:10–13), and Elijah by putting to death all the prophets of Baal after his victory in the contest on Mount Carmel (1 Kgs. 18:40). And both 1 Maccabees and Josephus recall the rallying cry of Mattathias, the initial leader of the Maccabean revolt – 'Let everyone who is zealous for the law and would establish the covenant come out after me' (1 Macc. 2:27; Josephus, *Ant.* 12:271) – after he, burning with zeal like Phinehas of old, had killed the Jew who was about to offer sacrifice on the Syrian altar (1 Macc. 2:23–6). The Mishnah also recalls that

If a man stole a sacred vessel ... or made an Aramean woman his paramour, the zealots may fall on him. If a priest served [at the altar] in a state of uncleanness ... the young men among the priests took him outside the Temple court and split open his brain with clubs (*m. Sanh.* 9. 6)

It is not difficult to recognize that Paul saw himself as standing in that tradition of holy zeal: 'as regards zeal, a persecutor of the church' (Phil. 3:6); 'I persecuted the church of God violently and tried to destroy it ... so extremely zealous was I for the traditions of my fathers' (Gal. 1:13–14). As the Zealots after him,[29] so Paul had been fired by the zeal of Phinehas and had been ready to use violent means to defend Israel's prerogative as holy to the Lord, separated from the nations. The opening up of the gospel to the Gentiles by the Hellenist evangelists was evidently understood by the pre-Christian Paul as a threat to Israel's distinctiveness as God's own chosen people, as a dilution of Israel's holy set-apartness, as a dangerous breach of what the Epistle of Aristeas calls the 'palisades and iron walls' formed by the strict laws to prevent Israel from mixing with other nations (Ep. Aristeas 139, 142).

It is this fact which also goes a long way to explaining why it is that Paul regarded what we call his conversion primarily as a calling – and precisely as a calling to take the gospel to the Gentiles. Thus consistently in the three Acts accounts of his conversion (Acts 9:15; 22:14–15; 26:16–18). And thus, in his own

---

[29] See particularly M. Hengel, *The Zealots* (²1976; Edinburgh: T. & T. Clark, 1989), 149–77.

self-testimony in Galatians: 'It pleased God, who set me apart from my mother's womb and called me through his grace, to reveal his Son in me *in order that I might preach him among the Gentiles*' (Gal. 1:15–16). Not surprisingly, that which Paul was converted to was what he had attacked so violently as a persecutor. For Paul, justification by faith had to do as much, if not more with the breaking down of the racial and national exclusiveness of Israel's covenant claims, than with his own personal experience of grace as persecutor of the Church of God.

2. A second motif in Paul's letters whose full significance was lost sight of is that of *boasting*. The point is important, since it is precisely 'boasting' which Paul says has been excluded by a right understanding of justification by faith (Rom. 3:27; 4:2). Bultmann in particular seized upon the word as pointing to the heart of Paul's message. 'For Paul καυχᾶσθαι discloses the basic attitude of the Jew to be one of self-confidence which seeks glory before God and which relies upon itself', 'sinful self-reliance'.[30] And Käsemann in his commentary at this point universalized the godly Jew as the classic type of that piety which boasts in its own achievements.[31] In such restatements of classic Protestant theology Paul's theology of justification is understood as a weapon directed precisely against the religion of self-reliance and self-achievement.

More recent exegesis, however, has paid more attention to the context in which Paul speaks of boasting. For one thing the verse towards the end of Rom. 3 clearly recalls the double reference to Jewish boasting in chapter 2. There, the one who calls himself a Jew is characterized as 'boasting in God' and as 'boasting in the law' (2:17, 23). From the flow of argument in chapter 2 we can see what it is Paul had in mind: viz. the confidence of those conscious of their privilege in 'having the law' (2:12, 14), and thus being in a position of advantage over against others – knowing the will of God, able to discern what is important, a guide to the blind, a light to those in darkness, an instructor of the foolish, etc. (2:17–20). In other words, the boast is not the boast of *self*-confidence, but of *Jewish* confidence, the boast of one conscious of his privilege as a member of the people of Israel.

And for another, the argument which Paul immediately employs in recalling the theme of boasting in 3:27 underlines the same point. The logical corollary of such boasting is to affirm that God is God of the Jews only, and not also of the Gentiles. 'No', says Paul, 'God of the Gentiles also', otherwise the basic Jewish

---

[30] R. Bultmann, TDNT 3. 648–9; also *Theology of the New Testament* (London: SCM, 1952), 1. 242–3.

[31] E. Käsemann, *Romans* (Grand Rapids: Eerdmans/London: SCM, 1980), 102. Similarly G. Bornkamm, *Paul* (London: Hodder, 1971): 'In a way the Jew symbolizes man in his highest potentialities; he represents "the religious man" ...' (p. 95). So also e.g. F.J. Leenhardt, *Romans* (London: Lutterworth, 1961), 108–9; G.E. Ladd, A *Theology of the New Testament* (London: Lutterworth, 1974), 447.

credo, 'God is one', could not be maintained; other gods, of the Gentiles, would have to be assumed. But if God is one, then, deduces Paul, it must mean that he justifies both circumcised and uncircumcised in the same way – from, or through faith (3:29–30). In other words, justification by faith is a corollary of Jewish monotheism, directed primarily against the exclusiveness of Israel's own claim upon that one God.

A similar confusion has resulted from reading Rom. 10:3 with what we might call Reformation spectacles: 'Israel was unaware of God's rightousness and sought to establish their own righteousness ...'. Not surprisingly, Paul's talk of 'their own righteousness' triggered off the familiar Reformation polemic. Thus again Bultmann transposes the phrase into 'righteousness which man exerts himself to achieve'.[32] And Charles Cranfield similarly – 'a righteous status of their own earning'.[33] But the Greek, ἴδιος, is not well fitted to express the sense, 'mine, as achieved by me'. Rather it denotes 'mine' as belonging to me, in contrast to what someone else can claim as belonging to him, 'mine' as 'peculiar to me'.[34] In other words, it again expresses Israel's covenant consciousness, its assumption of a special relationship with God, of a righteousness which is peculiarly theirs, to the exclusion of the Gentiles. Moreover, Paul's talk of Israel seeking 'to establish righteousness as theirs alone' probably echoes the rallying cry of Mattathias, already referred to: 'Let everyone who is zealous for the law and would establish the covenant come out after me' (1 Macc. 2:27).[35] Once again the belief against which justification by faith is directed is the belief that Israel's privilege and prerogative as God's elect people had to be established and defended against Gentile encroachment.[36]

3. Finally, we might note the need to reasses Paul's polemic against *'works of the law'*. This is a crucial element in the discussion, since, of course, it is precisely the antithesis between justification through faith and justification through works which characterizes Paul's major treatments of the theme: 'knowing that no human being as justified from works of the law, but only through faith in Jesus Christ' (Gal. 2:16); 'for we reckon that someone is justified by faith, without works of the law' (Rom. 3:28). On this point the traditional Protestant exegesis is consistent: 'works of the law' can be glossed as 'good works', the ex-

---

[32] Bultmann, *Theology*, 1, 285.

[33] C.E.B. Cranfield, *Romans* (ICC, Edinburgh: T. & T. Clark, 2 vols. 1975, 1979), 515.

[34] BAGD, ἴδιος.

[35] See further my *Romans* (WBC 38; Dallas: Word, 1988), 587–8.

[36] The similiar sounding contrast of Phil. 3:9 ('not having my own righteousness which is from the law, but that which is through faith in Christ, the righteousness from God to faith') is usually taken as aimed polemically against self-achieved righteousness (e.g. G.F. Hawthorne, *Philippians* (WBC 43; Waco: Word, 1983, 141). But the idea of self-*achievement* is read into the text; 'my own righteousness from the law' is quite open to other interpretations, along the lines ideed of Rom. 10:3, or in continuity with Phil. 3:4ff., in terms of confidence in 'my righteousncss' as a Jcw (or Pharisee).

pression of 'man's arrogant striving after self-righteousness',[37] the ground on which self-achieved righteousness makes its boast. But we have already seen reason enough to question such an interpretation. If the idea of self-achieved righteousness has to give way to the more soundly based exegesis of a Jewish or national righteousness, then the phrase 'works of the law' has to be reassessed also.

The nearest parallel to Paul's phrase comes in fact in the Qumran writings – 'deeds of the law' (מעשי תורה). In 4QFlor. 1:1–7 'deeds of the law' are what marked out the Qumran community in its distinctiveness from outsiders and enemies. In 1QS 5:20–4 and 6:18; 'deeds in reference to the Torah' are what the community member has to be tested on every year. And the so far unpublished 4Q *Miqṣat Ma'aseh Ha-Torah* (4QMMT) consists in a sequence of sectarian halakhic regulations.[38] In other words, 'deeds of the law' denote the interpretations of the Torah which marked out the Qumran community as distinctive, the obligations which members took upon themselves as members and by which they maintained their membership.

This also fits well with Paul's usage. For the first time he uses the phrase, in Gal. 2:16, it obviously has reference to the issues raised by the immediately preceding episodes at Jerusalem and Antioch: the question of 'works of the law' is typified by the issues of whether Titus the Gentile should be circumcised (Gal. 2:1–10), and whether Gentile Christians should be expected to observe the Jewish food laws (Gal. 2:11–15). The question whether Gentile Christians should be circumcised and should observe the food laws evidently brought the issue of 'works of the law' into sharp focus, and probably made 'works of the law' an issue in a way they had not been previously. This is precisely what we would expect where there were Christian Jews who looked back to the Maccabean revolt with pride; for it was precisely these two issues, circumcision and foods laws, which became the test-cases of covenant and national loyalty then (1 Macc. 1: 60–3). That is to say, 'deeds, or works of the law' was a way of characterizing the same intense concern shared by so many Jews of the period to maintain the distinctiveness of their relationship with God as over against the Gentiles. It was by doing 'the works of the law' that a devout Jew maintained covenant status and marked out the set-apartness of Israel from the other nations. The Qumran understanding of 'deeds of the law' was simply a sectarian and more particularist expression of the widespread Jewish conviction that 'works of the law' were what marked off Jews from 'Gentile sinners' (Gal. 2:15).

It is not practicable to develop the point more thoroughly within the scope of this paper, so I must hope that the evidence adduced has been sufficient for the

---

[37] G. Bertram, *TDNT* 2. 651; Bultmann, *Theology*, 263–4.

[38] See L.H. Schiffman, 'The Temple Scroll and the Systems of Jewish Law of the Second Temple Period', *Temple Scroll Studies*, ed. G.H. Brooke (Sheffield: JSOT, 1989), 239–55, here pp. 245–50.

purpose,[39] and that the point itself is clear. When Paul said in effect, 'All are justified by faith and not by works', he meant *not* 'Every individual must cease from his own efforts and simply trust in God's acceptance', however legitimate and important an interpretation of his words that is. What he meant was, 'Justification is not confined to Jews as marked out by their distinctive works; it is open to all, to Gentile as well as Jew, through faith.'

In short, a major weakness of the classic Protestant understanding of justicification, seen as the mirror reflection of Luther's own discovery of it, is that it has missed or downplayed what was probably the most important aspect of the doctrine for Paul himself. It has missed, in other words, the fundamental critique of Israel's tendency to nationalist presumption, not so say racial pride – a critique already made from within Jewish tradition by such as Jonah, Amos (9:7) and John the Baptist (Matt. 3:9), not to mention Jesus himself (Matt. 8:10–12). For Paul justification means that God accepts persons without reference to whether they have been born into a particular race, or not (Rom 9:6–8); without reference to whether they have maintained the traditional and distinguishing customs of that race, or not (Rom. 9:9–11; 11:6). Justification is by faith alone (Rom. 3:28; 9:30–2).

One cannot help wondering whether European history over the last century might not have been radically different, particularly if Lutheran Germany had been able to keep more fully alive that understanding of justification by faith. And an invaluable weapon against apartheid has also been too much lost sight of in South Africa, another country which prides itself in its biblical heritage and its Reformation roots. Not that Anglo-Saxon Britain and north America can afford to strike judgmental postures on this subject, given the tendency of so many churches in affluent countries to identify Christian civilization with, for example, Victorian culture or the American way of life. Justification by faith is a banner raised by Paul against any and all such presumption of privileged status before God by virtue of race, culture or nationality, against any and all attempts to preserve such spurious distinctions by practices that exclude and divide.

---

[39] See further my *Romans*, 153–5; also *Jesus, Paul and the Law* (London: SPCK/Louisville: Westminster, 1990), chs. 7–8 [= ch. 2 and 3 above]; also *The Partings of the Ways* (London: SCM, 1991), ch. 7. There I note that the phrase 'works of the law' in Rom. 3:20 similarly summarizes and looks back to the confidence in the law and in circumcision in particular which Paul had critiqued in 2:17ff. I also pointed out that Rom. 4:4–5 is the first step in an attempt to define the force of 'reckoned' (Gen. 15:6), and that it does so simply by contrasting human contractual arrangements with the astonishing generosity of God. Despite the general assumption to the contrary, there is *no* implication in Rom. 4:4–5 that Paul's Jewish contemporaries thought of their covenant relation with God as though it was a contract between human employer and employee.

IV

There is, however, one further dimension which needs equally to be brought to the fore. So far we have attempted to step backwards behind the classic Protestant doctrine of 'justification by faith' into the shoes, or at least into the context of Paul's own treatment of the theme. Now we need to take one further step backwards – into the resources of insight, language, and tradition on which Paul himself drew. From Luther to Paul; and now from Paul to the Old Testament.

It is natural, of course, that the discussion so far should have been almost exclusively at the level of the New Testament and of Paul in particular, since the Christian doctrine of justification by faith has been so heavily dependent on Paul. What has been too quickly forgotten, or left neglected in the background, is the fact that Paul's own teaching was based on the Old Testament, or more precisely, the Jewish scriptures; and that, even though it is common knowledge that Paul's teaching depends completely on his exposition of key texts such as Gen. 15:6 and Hab. 2:4. What must be particularly surprising for anyone brought up in a tradition which posed Christianity and Judaism in antithesis, or indeed the New Testament and the Old in contrast, is the degree to which Paul's understanding of justification is Jewish and Old Testament through and through. Two points are especially worthy of attention.

1. First, in Old Testament thinking 'righteousness' is a relational concept. To appreciate the force of this point we of the European tradition need to make a conscious step beyond or behind the Graeco-Roman thought which is still so basic to our way of thinking. In Graeco-Roman tradition 'righteousness' and 'justice' were ideal concepts or absolute ethical norms against which particular claims and duties could be measured.[40] Failure to measure up to this standard involved ethical or criminal liability. Justice functioned as a quasi-divine principle which had to be sustained and appeased lest disorder and anarchy prevail. We today still echo such a view when we say things like, 'The demands of justice must be satisfied'.

But since the important study by H. Cremer, at the turn of the century,[41] the recognition has steadily gained ground that in Hebrew thought righteousness is a concept of *relation*. Righteousness is not something which an individual has on his or her own, independently of anyone else, as could be the case in the Graeco-Roman concept – 'righteous' as meeting the standard set by the ideal of 'justice'. In Hebrew thought, however, righteousness is something one has precisely in one's relationships as a social being. People are righteous when they meet the claims which others have on them by virtue of their relationship.[42] In particular,

---

[40] See e.g. G. von Rad, *Old Testament Theology* (Edinburgh: Ioliver & Boyd, 1962), 1. 370–1.

[41] H. Cremer, *Die paulinische Rechtfertigungslehre im Zusammenhange ihrer geschichtlichen Voraussetzungen* (Gütersloh: Bertelsmann, ²1900).

[42] Cremer, 34–8.

the responsibility of the judge is to recognize what these various obligations are within the people and to judge them accordingly, clearing the innocent and not deferring to the great (e.g. Exod. 23:7–8; Lev. 19: 15; Isa. 5:23).[43] And Saul confesses that David is more righteous then he, because David had remained faithful to his responsibility towards Saul as God's anointed, whereas Saul had abused the responsibility of his superior status and power (1 Sam. 24:17).

The same is true of God's righteousness. In this case the relationship is the covenant into which God entered with Israel when he chose them to be his people. That is to say, God is righteous not because he satisfies some ideal of justice external to himself. Rather, God is righteous when he fulfils the obligations he took upon himself to be Israel's God. That means, in rescuing Israel and in punishing Israel's enemies (e.g. Exod. 9:27; 1 Sam. 12:7; Dan. 9:16; Mic. 6:5). Not to be missed is the important fact that divine righteousness is seen here wholly in terms of grace – God freely entering into a covenant with Israel and freely assuming responsibilities to those he has thus freely chosen. The 'prevenience' of grace is at the very heart of Jewish self-understanding, as again illustrated by the beginning of the decalogue: 'I am the Lord your God, who brought you out of the land of Egypt, out of the house of bondage' (Exod. 20:2; Deut. 5:6). And particularly in the Psalms and in Second Isaiah, the logic of covenant grace is followed through, with the result that righteousness and salvation become virtually synonymous: the righteousness of God as God's action to restore his own and to sustain them within the covenant despite their repeated failures (e.g. Ps. 31:1; 35:24; 71:15; 143:11; Isa. 45:21; 51:5, 6, 8; 62:1–2).[44]

It is clearly this sense of the righteousness of God which Paul took over in his own discussion of justification by faith – the righteousness of God which is God's saving power to faith (Rom. 1:16–17). All the more regretable, then, that this dependence of Paul on the thoroughly Old Testament, that is Jewish category of righteousness and theology of justification has not been more fully appreciated in this century, despite the impact of Cremer's study on Old Testament scholarship. Apart from anything else, it would have short-circuited the old Reformation disputes, which still linger on: Is 'the righteousness of God' subjective genitive or objective genitive, an attitude of God or something he does?[45] and does the equivalent verb, 'to justsify', mean 'to *make* righteous' or 'to *count* righteous'? – the classic subject of dispute between Catholic and Protestant.[46] For once we recognize that righteousness and justification are the language of relationship it becomes evident that both disputes push unjustifiably for an either-or answer. In reality, the relationship envisaged is something dynamic and presup-

---

[43] See also W. Eichrodt, *Theology of the Old Testament* (London: SCM, 1961), 1. 240–1.

[44] See further my *Romans*, 41.

[45] See e.g. Cranfield, *Romans*, 92–9.

[46] See e.g. J. Reumann, *Righteousness in the New Testament* (Philadelphia: Fortress/New York: Paulist, 1982).

poses that the divine partner acts on behalf of, in and with the defective human partners, drawing them into the relationship, sustaining them within it, and acquitting them in the final judgement.

The other side of this is, of course, the obligations which the human covenant partners took upon themselves in accepting the covenant – the obligation to do the law, to walk in the statutes and ordinances of God. The one Lord God who had chosen Israel to be his people had given them the law precisely in order to show them how to live as his people. Hence again the form of the ten commandments: 'I am the Lord your God, who brought you out of the land of Egypt, ... (Therefore) you shall have no other gods before me'; and so on (Exod. 20:2ff.; Deut. 5:6ff.). Hence too the classic expression of covenant theology and obligation in Deuteronomy, saying in effect: here is how you must live in the light of the covenant Yahweh has made with you; do this and live. This is precisely what Sanders meant when he coined the phrase 'covenantal nomism' – the law understood as governing life within the covenant people, obedience to the law understood as the proper expression of covenant membership. Any thought of using the law to gain access to that covenant relationship with God is wholly lacking and wholly antithetical to the spirit of the covenant theology classically set out in Deuteronomy. No one would think to accuse a law-abiding citizen today of trying to curry favour with the authorities or to gain citizenship. No more should the covenantal nomist of past or present be accused of seeking to earn God's favour.

Once again, then, the degree to which Jewish covenantal theology parallels classic Protestant doctrines of perseverance and good works is plain. And hopefully I need not elaborate the point further. The important point to underline here is that these doctrines follow as directly from Jewish covenantal theology as they do from classic Protestant theology of justification by faith. The reason why Christianity and rabbinic Judaism went their separate ways was not because of any dispute over the fundamental principles of grace and faith and human obedience; dispute about the particulars and outworkings of these principles, no doubt, but not about the principles themselves. To characterize Judaism *per se* as a religion of self-achievement is not only scurrilous, it is simply bad exegesis.

2. This brings us to a second point which arises directly out of the typical Old Testament emphases on the theme of righteousness and which deserves to be given more attention than it has received of late. For just as the recipients of divine righteousness were expected to respond appropriately towards God, so they were expected to respond towards their neighbour. The vertical dimension of righteousness (the obligation of covenant members towards God) was closely bound up with the horizontal dimension of righteousness (the obligation of covenant members towards each other). Responsibility towards one's neighbour arose directly out of Israel's covenant relation with God. That is to say, one could not be righteous towards God without also being righteous towards one's

neighbour; obligation towards God was incomplete when obligation towards the neighbour was deficient.

The point, worthy of repetition, is that the two responsibilities go together – the vertical and the horizontal. The two tables of the decalogue are interdependent – a right relation with God, and a right relation with one's neighbour. The biblical writers are at one in insisting that it is not possible to have one without the other. Hence the fierceness of the prophet's denunciation of those who thought they could be acceptable before God while at the same time disregarding their obligations to the poor. The two go together. The point is made with memorable prose in such passages as Isa. 58, Amos 5 and Mic. 3. One of the best examples is Ezek. 18:5–9.

If a man is righteous and does what is lawful and right – if he does not eat upon the mountains or lift up his eyes to the idols of the house of Israel, does not defile his neighbour's wife or approach a woman in her time of impurity, does not oppress any one, but restores to the debtor his pledge, commits no robbery, gives his bread to the hungry and covers the naked with a garment, does not lend at interest or take any increase, withholds his hand from iniquity, executes true justice between man and man, walks in my statutes, and is careful to observe my ordinances – he is righteous, he shall surely live, says the Lord God.

Particularly notable in all this is the strong sense that the obligation towards God and the neighbour includes especially responsibility towards the disadvantaged – characteristically towards the widow, the orphan, the stranger and the poor. So, for example, in Zech. 7:9–10:

Thus says the Lord of hosts, Render true judgments, show kindness and mercy each to his brother, do not oppress the widow, the fatherless, the sojourner, or the poor; and let none of you devise evil against his brother in your heart.

This concern for the disadvantaged should not be confused with a purely individualistic charity; it was enshrined in civil law, recognized as a responsibility of society. The classic expression is Deuteronomy, particularly Deut 24:10–22. Note particularly the practicalness of the rulings given.

When you make your neighbour a loan of any sort, you shall not go into his house to fetch his pledge ... And if he is a poor man, you shall not sleep in his pledge; when the sun goes down, you shall restore to him the pledge that he may sleep in his cloak and bless you; and it shall be righteousness to you before the Lord your God.

You shall not oppress a hired servant who is poor and needy, whether he is one of the sojourners who are in your land within your towns; you shall give him his hire on the day he earns it, before the sun goes down ...

You shall not pervert the justice due to the sojourner or to the fatherless, or take a widow's garment in pledge; but you shall remember that you were a slave in Egypt and the Lord your God redeemed you from there; therefore I command you to do this.

When you reap your harvest in your field, and have forgotten a sheaf in the field, you shall not go back to get it; it shall be for the sojourner, the fatherless, and the widow; that the Lord your God may bless you in all the work of your hands. When you beat your olive trees, you shall not go over the boughs again; it shall be for the sojourner, the fatherless, and the widow ... You shall remember that you were a slave in the land of Egypt; therefore I command you to do this.

Significant also is the familial imagery used in both Deuteronomy and Zechariah – the poor, not simply as neighbour, but as brother (Deut. 15:11; Zech. 7:9–10). Israel's self-unterstanding as son to God as Father was interdependent on recognition of the fellow covenant member, and particularly the disadvantaged covenant member, as brother. But it is equally significant to remember that the obligation to the neighbour embraces not only the fellow citizen, but also the sojourner, the resident alien (Lev. 19:18, 34). And, we might add, Christians dare not forget that Jesus also named the enemy as neighbour (Matt. 5:43–8).

All this is part and parcel of the Old Testament understanding of righteousness – and so also part and parcel of the Old Testament background on which Paul drew in formulating his teaching on justification by faith. The relative absence of these fuller social dimensions in Paul's teaching (but cf. Rom. 12: 9–21; 14:1–15:9; 2 Cor. 9.6–12) should not blind us to that fact. Nor the ease with which we translate Paul's teaching on justification into individualistic or pietistic terms. The more fully we recognize that Paul's teaching on divine righteousness is Old Testament through and through, the more we must also recognize the character of that righteousness as calling for a righteousness in response which is social in character and gives highest priority to sustaining the disadvantaged in society. Unless these two aspects of Old Testament thought are firmly grasped, the concept of righteousness is bound to become distorted: righteousness as essentially involving relationships, arising out of relationships, expressed in relationships; and righteousness as both horizontal and vertical, as involving responsibility to the neighbour as part and parcel of one's responsibility towards God. In Hebrew thought it would not be possible for someone to be righteous apart from, without reference to that individual's responsibility to others; it would not be possible to be righteous before God while remaining involved in unjust relationships with fellow humans. And central in this understanding of righteousness was the recognition of society's responsibility towards the disadvantaged and the concern to conform social relationships to the model of the caring family.

In short, this discovery of the horizontal and social dimension of justification by faith indicates that such social concerns lie at the heart of this so characteristic and fundamental Christian and Protestant doctrine. Which is also to say that the obligation to such social and political concern lies at the heart of our faith.

V

In the light of all that has been said, the conclusion is obvious. Having worked our way backwards, from Luther to Paul, and from Paul back into the Old Testament, we are now in a position to move forward once again and to restate a more rounded and richer and more biblical doctrine of justification. In doing so there is no call to set aside the often penetrating insights of Reformation and Protestant restatements of the doctrine. But we do need to complement them with a firm reassertion of the corporate and social implications of the full doctrine – in terms both of what it says about nationalist and racialist presumption, and of what it says about civic and political responsibility for the disadvantaged in a society which cherishes its biblical heritage.

As one leitmotiv or integrating concept in such a restatement I offer the title of this paper – the justice of God. Of course that theme is far larger and more demanding than I could hope to deal with, here or elsewhere. My concern is simply to indicate that Luther's movement from the 'justice of God' to 'justification by faith' needs now to be reversed in some measure. Nor do I suggest that 'justice' should (wholly) replace 'justification' as the leading motif. Apart from anything else, 'justice' serves no better to bring out the relational character of the theme. But at least it avoids the fatal disjunction of terminology which has been the consequence of English having to translate what in Hebrew and Greek are integrated concepts – justify, righteous, righteousness, justice.[47] It also avoids the too technical language of 'justify' and 'righteousness' which no longer has much resonance outside Protestant theology.

And above all it highlights some of the key conclusions and issues raised by the above treatment. First, that this fundamental Protestant and fundamental Pauline category is also a fundamentally Jewish category. Secondly, that a central issue for both Jew and Christian is the correlation of the recognition of the justice and the faithfulness of God with the recognition that the one Creator God is God of Gentile as well as of Jew (the central problem of Paul's letter to the Romans). And thirdly, that acceptability before the just and gracious God is inseparable from a lived out responsibility for the disadvantaged neighbour and the enemy. With such a restatement the doctrine of justification by faith could re-emerge once again in its full power as a means to salvation for both individual and community.

---

[47] In Hebrew principally the צדק root, especially where it begins to overlap with the concept of משפט; in Greek the διχ root.

Chapter 8

Yet Once More – 'The Works of the Law'

A Response

My near neighbour in Durham, Charles Cranfield, has done me the honour of devoting a recent essay to the rebuttal of my exegesis of ἔργα νόμου.[1] I am grateful for his kindly remarks and robust critique. In fact, some of the points he makes have already been responded to in the Additional Notes to the reissue of the two essays he cites.[2] And I have also attempted something of a restatement of my position even since then.[3] However, Professor Cranfield's critique is so detailed that it would be unjust to ignore it, although in the space available I will have to confine myself to the chief points he raises and to refer to my earlier treatments for more thorough demonstration of particular claims. At the same time it may be appropriate to continue the dialogue with one or two others who have already responded to the clarification of my initial statements (n.2),[4] since I invited such response and am eager to pursue any dialogue which offers hope of clarifying the subject matter and my own understanding of it.

1. ERGA NOMOU

1.1 One of the clarifications provided by my earlier responses is that 'works of the law' are not to be understood as restricted to circumcision, food laws and

---

[1] C.E.B. Cranfield, '"The Works of the Law" in the Epistle to the Romans', *JSNT* 43 (1991) pp. 89–101. He is responding particularly to my commentary on *Romans* (WBC 38; Dallas: Word, 1988); see also n. 2 below. Cf. also the more nuanced but in the end similar critiques of R.N. Longenecker, *Galatians* (WBC 41; Dallas: Word, 1990) pp. 85–6, and D. Moo, *Romans 1–8* (Wycliffe Exegetical Commentary; Chicago: Moody, 1991) pp. 210–11, 214–15.

[2] 'The New Perspective on Paul', *BJRL* 65 (1983) pp. 95–122 [= ch. 2 above]; 'Works of the Law and the Curse of the Law (Galatians 3.10–14)', *NTS* 31 (1985) pp. 523–42 [= ch. 3 above]; reprinted with additional notes in *Jesus, Paul and the Law. Studies in Mark and Galatians* (London: SPCK/Louisville: Westminster, 1990) 183–214 and 215–41 respectively.

[3] *The Partings of the Ways between Christianity and Judaism* (London: SCM/ Philadelphia: TPI, 1991) ch. 7.

[4] Particularly T.R. Schreiner, '"Works of Law" in Paul', *NovT* 33 (1991) pp. 217–44; Schreiner's critique of my position comes in pp. 225–31. M. Silva has also kindly drawn my attention to his review article of my *Jesus, Paul and the Law* – 'The Law and Christianity: Dunn's New Synthesis', *Westminster Theological Journal* 53 (1991) pp. 339–53.

sabbath issues. Unfortunately, most of Professor Cranfield's critique is actually based on this misreading of my earlier presentations. I do not, however, advocate 'a special restricted sense'[5] for the phrase. On the contrary, as I understand the usage, 'works of the law' characterize the whole mindset of 'covenantal nomism' – that is, the conviction that status within the covenant (= righteousness) is maintained by doing what the law requires ('works of the law').[6] Circumcision and food laws in particular come into play simply(!) because they provided the key test cases for most Jews of Paul's time. So far as the 'false brothers' of Gal. 2.4 were concerned, one simply could not be reckoned a member of the covenant people without circumcision. And as for James and the Christian Jews in Antioch, faithfulness to covenant obligation, and so righteousness, simply could not be maintained without continued observance of the food laws (Gal. 2.11–14). This is surely what is primarily in view in Paul's first mention of 'works of the law' (Gal. 2.16). Whatever else he might have been attacking, he was certainly attacking an attitude to the law (prevalent among Christian Jews in Jerusalem and Antioch) which focused in the requirement of the law to practise circumcision and/or food laws. So, *not* a special restricted sense, but a general sense given particular point by certain crucial issues and disputes.

I confess to being a little surprized by the difficulty apparently experienced by some respondents in recognizing how ἔργα νόμου can denote what the law requires, but with special reference to such crucial issues. In general terms the point is that within a larger set of beliefs or convictions (regarding conduct, worship and so forth) it often happens that circumstances force certain items within that set into prominence. Such items may not be fundamental in the sense of providing a foundation for the rest of the beliefs and convictions. But circumstances force them to become fundamental in the sense of epitomising or crystalizing the distinctiveness of the group which espouses them. Examples are easy

---

[5] Cranfield pp. 91, 92. This is Cranfield's summary phrase for the fuller exposition he provides for the earlier form of my argument: 'By "the works of the law" ... Paul did not mean obedience to the law generally, but specifically, he [Dunn] thinks, adherance to those practices prescribed by the law which most obviously distinguished Jews from their Gentile neighbours, in particular circumcision, keeping the sabbath and observance of the food laws; and, when Paul declared that no flesh will be justified before God by the works of the law, he did not mean that no one will be justified on the ground of his having obeyed the law since fallen men and women come nowhere near such true obedience, but was polemicizing against his Jewish contemporaries' complacent reliance on their privileged status as God's covenant people and their exclusiveness towards the Gentiles' (pp. 89–90). This is offered as a summary of my *Romans* pp. 153–55, 158–59, but hardly reflects the nuance of the exegesis at that point – Rom. 3.20 (we return to the meaning of Rom. 3.20 in §2 below).

[6] In the final chapter of *Jesus, Paul and the Law* (so also ch. 6 above) I argue that the whole letter to Galatians was Paul's first sustained attempt to deal with the issue of 'covenantal nomism' – the inelegant but usefully descriptive phrase which E. P. Sanders introduced into the reassessment of Judaism at the time of Paul for which his (Sanders') work called.

to cite: the infallibility of the Pope for Roman Catholics;[7] the maleness of the priesthood for many anglo-Catholics; believers' baptism for Baptists; speaking in tongues as 'the initial evidence' of Spirit baptism for classic Pentecostals; 'inerrancy' for Protestant fundamentalists. Such beliefs/convictions become crucial for these denominations/groups because they mark out these denominations'/groups' distinctive identity; they are boundary markers, distinguishing these denominations/groups from others; they are the shibboleths which tell at once where the speakers come from; they are the vital test-cases, the make or break issues which are sufficient of themselves to demonstrate either loyalty to or apostasy from the group (at least in the eyes of those members of the denomination/group who patrol the denomination's/group's boundaries with diligence and zeal to ensure that the boundary markers are retained in place and maintained in effect). My claim is simply that circumcision and food laws in particular so functioned in the controversies reflected particularly in Gal. 2.1–14.

I repeat: this is not to say that ἔργα νόμου reduces or is to be 'restricted' in meaning to these particular requirements. ἔργα νόμου continues to denote what is required of the members of the covenant people, those to whom the law has been given to show them how to live as God's people, those who have been redeemed by him from 'the house of bondage'. But the circumstances of the Maccabean crisis in particular brought the larger issue of what is required of the loyal Jew to sharp focus in the specific issues of circumcision and food laws (as 1 Macc. 1.60–63 indicates so vividly). And from that period onwards, whenever the need to maintain Israel's distinctive identity became an issue in relation to Gentile encroachments, *it was inevitable that circumcision and food laws would re-emerge as crucial test cases on which Israel's identity as the people of God was seen to hang.*

1.2 To put the same point another way, Professor Cranfield appears to ignore, more or less completely, the social context and ramifications of such a view of the law and its requirements. This dimension of the law's function becomes apparent in the same context in Galatians in the use of the disparaging description, 'Gentile sinners' (Gal. 2.15). The attitude which came to expression in an insistence on 'works of the law' was an attitude which regarded Gentiles *ipso facto* as 'sinners', that is, ignorant of and outside the law, and therefore outside the realm of righteousness.[8] For Christian Jews to ignore the food laws, as they had been doing at Antioch, clearly rendered them 'sinners' in the eyes of 'the men from James', that is, effectively placed them in the same status before God as 'Gentile

---

[7] Recently reiterated in the Holy See's unyielding response to the report of the Anglican Roman Catholic International Commission (ARCIC).

[8] See my fuller treatment, once again, in *Jesus, Paul and the Law* ch. 3; with further restatement in *Partings* chs. 6–7.

sinners' (hence 2.17). It is this view which Paul contests so vigorously by pressing the logic of 'justification by faith' (2.16ff.); it is this barrier, between Jew and Gentile, which has been broken by the grace of God in Christ's death (2.19–21; 3.13–14) – a logic which Eph. 2.11–22 saw and expressed so clearly.

Too little appreciated in all this has been the significance of the fact that Paul can describe Jews in general as '(the) circumcision' and Gentiles in general as '(the) uncircumcision' – *not* 'the circumcised' and 'the uncircumcised' (Rom. 2.26; 3.30; 4.9; Gal. 2.7–9) – ἡ περιτομή, *not* οἱ περιτετμημένοι. How is it that the noun denoting a particular ritual act can come to stand for a whole people? The answer is obvious: because that ritual act was understood to sum up that people, to distinguish them most clearly as a people. Again parallels from the history of Christianity are obvious, where a particular belief or act so characterizes a group that the group can be named and defined by that belief or act – *Roman* Catholics, (Ana)baptists, Quakers, and so on. To be noted also is the fact that these nicknames ('the circumcision', 'the uncircumcision') betray a Jewish perspective: it is those who regard circumcision highly who designate those lacking it as 'the uncircumcision'. These very nicknames, therefore, are proof in themselves of the degree to which all the differences between Jews and Gentiles could come to focus in the specific ritual act of circumcision, *the degree to which all the works of the law could be epitomised by this one requirement of the law.*

1.3　Perhaps most surprising of all is Professor Cranfield's rather cavalier dismissal of the evidence of the Qumran texts.[9] This is surely unwise when these references (particularly 4QFlor. 1.1–7) constitute the only close parallel to Paul's phrase in the usage of the period. What is most significant in that usage is that it seems clearly to express a very similar sectarian attitude to that attacked by Paul: only those to be counted as faithful members of the covenant who observe the 'deeds of the law'.

The point is this: מעשׂי התררה ('deeds of the law') were, of course, understood by the Qumran covenanters to mean all that the law required of the loyal covenanter. But 'all that the law required of the loyal covenanter' really meant in practice Qumran's sectarian understanding of what the law required. In other words, *'deeds of the law' denoted precisely that understanding of the law's requirements which distinguished the Qumran covenanters from their fellow Jews.* This is confirmed by the soon to be published Dead Sea scroll, 4QMMT, a document which takes its name from this very phrase (4Q *Miqsat Ma'aseh Ha-Torah*), and which makes it clear that מעשׂי התררה come to focus in particular halakhic disputes – those points of halakhic dispute where the Qumran covenanters differed

---

[9] 'The passages in the Qumran texts, to which he [Dunn] appeals ... do not seem to us to offer very clear support" (Cranfield p. 92 n. 4).

from other Jews, including particularly, it would appear, the Pharisees,[10] else-where in the Scrolls probably referred to as 'those who seek smooth things'.

Of course, circumcision was not a boundary issue for a dispute *within* the boundaries of Israel, between different factions within second Temple Judaism; in contrast, the purity laws affecting the meal table did provide a number of internal boundaries between the different αἱρέσεις (sects) of second Temple Judaism as well as an external boundary marking off Jew from Gentile. But the attitude is the same in each case. And we need simply transpose the attitude expressed in the Qumran use of מעשׂי התררה from an internal Jewish dispute regarding particular halakhic rulings to one where the boundary ran between Jew and Gentile to find ourselves with ἔργα νόμου focusing in circumcision in particular. In short, in the current dispute the point needs to be pressed, rather than played down, that in the Qumran talk of 'deeds of the law' we have a very close parallel to Paul's talk of 'works of the law'.

1.4 May one hope that this further clarification of my understanding of 'works of the law' will discourage future dialogue partners from basing any critique on the earlier formulations of that understanding.

2. The function of ἔργα νόμου in Rom. 3.20ff.

2.1 A major point of Professor Cranfield's critique is that in my exposition of Rom. 3.20 I 'have lost sight of Paul's argument'. 3.20 sums up the whole indictment from 1.18 onwards, not just from 2.1 onwards; it sums up a universal indictment ('all human beings are sinners' – 3.23), not just an indictment of Jews in particular.[11]

I confess to being slightly puzzled by this criticism; for in no way do I wish to deny that Rom. 3.20 sums up the universality of the indictment of 1.18–32. The point which Professor Cranfield ignores, however, is the way Paul goes about drawing up this universal indictment. He does so, first, by indicting humanity as a whole (1.18–32), but in terms characteristic of Jewish polemic against Gentile idolatry and sexuality in particular. From that point on, however, his primary concern is to demonstrate that the 'Jew' falls under the same indictment; *Jews are not exempt from the condemnation they see as falling on Gentiles*. This is clearly the thrust from 2.1 onwards, when the interlocutor who thinks he is free of God's condemnation is steadily revealed to be the 'Jew'. Hence the puzzlement of 3.1 ('What then is the advantage of the Jew?'). Hence too the catena of

---

[10] The halakhic regulations in 4QMMT are conveniently summarized by L.H. Schiffman, 'The Temple Scroll and the Systems of Jewish Law of the Second Temple Period', *Temple Scroll Studies*, ed. G.J. Brooke (JSPS 7; Sheffield: Sheffield Academic, 1989) pp. 239–55, here 245–50.

[11] Cranfield p. 93.

texts in 3.10–18, where Paul takes a sequence of verses in which the righteous (Israel) plead against the wicked (Gentiles) and uses them to sum up his universal indictment; universal, precisely because they apply to Jews *as well as* to everyone else.[12]

Clearest and most significant of all is the way in which Paul introduces 3.20. This summary indictment (in terms of 'works of the law') is addressed *particularly to Jews:* 'we know that whatever the law says it says to those within the law, in order that every mouth might be stopped . . .' (3.19). *The whole point of the second stage of the indictment is to ensure that Jews recognize themselves to be included within the universal indictment* – that is, Jew as well as Gentile, or, in terms of a thematic phrase in these chapters, 'Jew first, but also Gentile'. And that is what is summed up here.

So too with 3.20 itself. When Paul speaks of 'justification by works of the law' *he can have only one people in mind* – Israel, the Jews in general.[13] The only law in view is the Jewish law.[14] Only the Jews (in general) cherished this law; only they thought in terms of 'works of the law' and of 'justification' in terms of the law. When, therefore, Paul speaks of 'no flesh' as being justified by works of the law, he clearly means to ensure that his fellow Jews recognize that they *specifically* are *not* exempt. The emphasis on 'flesh' is apposite, since it should remind the 'Jew' of his particular trust in the flesh (2.28–29; cf. Phil. 3.4).

In short, then, I do not at all disagree that the indictment of 1.18–3.20 is universal. It should be apparent, however, that in order to make his indictment universal Paul has to demonstrate that the 'Jew' in general is included, that his trust in flesh and in works of the law is misplaced if he thinks that he thereby escapes from that universal indictment.

2.2   But what does the indictment of the 'Jew' in Rom. 2 actually amount to? Here I grant that some clarification of my earlier attempts to explain Paul's train of thought is necessary, and I am grateful to the critique of Dr Schreiner in particular for alerting me to this. Let me say at once, then, that Paul is clearly talking about actual disobedience, actual breach of the law in Rom. 2, particularly 2.21–27. He is not criticizing his fellow Jews simply for their attitude to the law. Dr Schreiner puts the critique more sharply: 'Nothing is said here [Rom. 3.20] about a wrong attitude or an exclusive spirit; the problem is disobedience'.[15] But

---

[12] For details see my *Romans* (WBC 38; Dallas: Word, 1988) pp. 149–51, 157.

[13] Cf. J. Ziesler, *Romans* (London: SCM/Philadelphia: TPI, 1989) pp. 105–6.

[14] I assume from his own comments on these verses that Cranfield agrees; see his *Romans* (ICC; Edinburgh: T. & T. Clark, vol.1 1975) pp. 158, 195. Rom 2.15 is too complex to exegete here; see my *Romans* pp. 98–100; against Cranfield's own implausible exegesis of 2.14 (*Romans* particularly pp. 156–7). But since I do not dispute that 'work(s) of the law' mean 'work(s) required by the law' Cranfield's criticism (p. 94) loses its point anyway.

[15] Schreiner p. 228; similarly Moo p. 215.

in my judgment it would be more accurate to conclude that Paul is condemning both – both the actual disobedience and the typical Jewish attitude to the law. Let me explain.

In Rom. 2 Paul has in view both actual disobedience *and the assumption of the 'Jew' that such disobedience is not so serious as the lawlessness of the non-Jew.* This comes out particularly in the first section of Rom. 2. One may note in passing that a major reason for the difficulties experienced by so many exegetes in handling Rom. 2 is their failure to integrate all the sections of Rom. 2, their failure to follow the movement of thought through Rom. 2. I have already attempted a fuller exposition in my *Romans*, somewhat refined in a subsequent paper.[16] Here I need simply note the following points.

a) The assumption under attack in the opening verses of Rom. 2 is clearly that held by the interlocutor that he[17] 'escapes the judgment of God' (2.3). That the 'Jew' is already in view is widely recognized and fairly obvious from two features in particular. (i) From the degree to which the indictment of 1.18ff. echoes typical hellenistic Jewish condemnation of Gentile religion and conduct. Anyone aware of the strong parallels between 1.18ff. and Wisd. Sol. 11–15 in particular would also recognize that Paul was 'playing to a Jewish gallery' in 1.18ff. and that 2.1 is the point at which Paul swings round to address that gallery. (ii) From the echoes of Pss. Sol. 15.8 and Wisd. Sol. 15.1ff. in Rom. 2.3–4.[18] The same assumption is still in view: that Jews are different from Gentiles; that they are not 'sinners' like the Gentiles; that they do not sin like the Gentiles, or if they do, their sin is not so serious. Thus, Israel is disciplined, but others are punished; Israel is chastised, but others are scourged; Israel is tested, but the ungodly condemned; Israel expects mercy, but their opponents can look only for wrath (Pss. Sol. e.g. 3.4–16; 7.1–10; 8.27–40; 13.4–11; Wisd. Sol. 11.9–10; 12.22; 16.9–10). This is the attitude which Paul labels 'impenitence' and 'hardness of heart' (Rom. 2.5); *the (Jewish) interlocutor has been failing to take sin seriously enough.*

Paul's target in Rom. 2.1ff., therefore, is the 'Jew' who thinks he is safe from God's condemnation. That is, the interlocutor's assumption is *not* that he never sins, but rather that since he is within the covenant and people of God he will be treated more favourably by God. Even if he sins like the Gentiles his place within the covenant means that his sin will be discounted (not least because sacrifice will make atonement for his sins). This attitude comes to repeated expression in the Psalms of Solomon – e.g. 3.9; 5.7–9; 9.11–15; 13.4, 6, 9; 16.11–15. In other words, there is an insider/outsider distinction in view here: the insider is chastised, the outsider is condemned. We need not assume that Paul had the

---

[16] 'What was the Issue between Paul and "Those of the Circumcision"?', *Paulus und das antike Judentum*, ed. M. Hengel & U. Heckel (WUNT; Tübingen: Mohr, 1991) pp. 295–317 [=ch. 5 above].

[17] I follow the Greek in using masculine pronouns, without implying gender specificity.

[18] Cf. also particularly Pss. Sol. 8.27–35 with Rom. 3.3–4.

Psalms of Solomon as such in view. But it certainly seems most likely that he was attacking the same attitude as also expressed in the Psalms of Solomon.

b) Rom 2.12–16 confirm that the issue is the attitude of the insider to the outsider. Now Paul elaborates it in terms of the law. The distinction is between those 'within the law' and those without (2.12), between those who 'have the law' and those who do not (2.14). The assumption under attack once again is that having the law makes a difference. On the contrary, Paul insists, those inside the law will be judged just as surely as those outside; being a member of the people of the law will not give the 'Jew' a favoured position in the judgment; the measure of 'doing the law' will be common to both Jew and Gentile.

c) That it is *the Jewish sense of privilege and advantage over others which is in the centre of Paul's view* is clear beyond dispute in Rom. 2.17–24. But, responds Paul, since the 'Jew' does things which are as bad as any Gentile he cannot assume that his privileged position will save him.

d) The same implication is clear in 2.25–29: what is in view in part at least is the Jewish sense that circumcision gives the 'Jew' a place of privilege in relation to others before God. Since Paul commends the 'uncircumcised' who keep the law, over the 'circumcised' who fail to keep the law, he must have in mind the 'Jew' as one who assumes that his circumcision is a prophylactic against serious sin. It certainly cannot mean that he was thinking of the 'Jew' as one who boasts simply of his law-keeping (as merit earning); rather of the 'Jew' as one who boasts of his righteous status (documented and maintained, to be sure, by his 'works of the law') which ensures that any failure to keep the law is not regarded as sufficient to disturb that status.[19]

In short, we cannot say that Paul is attacking only a false attitude to the law in Rom 2–3.[20] But neither can we say that he is indicting only disobedience of the law. He has in mind *both*. He has to convince his Jewish interlocutor that Jewish failure to obey the law is as serious as Gentile sin. The problem is that the law is preventing the 'Jew' from recognizing the seriousness of his sin. To that degree the primary problem *is* the Jewish attitude to the law, simply because the sense of difference and of privilege which it inculcates dulls the sense of sin's seriousness.

It is this which Paul evidently has in mind when he sums up his indictment in 3.20 in terms of ἔργα νόμου. The attitude of confidence expressed in 'works of the law' is the assumption of the 'Jew' that he will be acquitted at the final judgment, while others (Gentiles) will be condemned. It is *not* an assumption of sinlessness, of perfect keeping of the law; it *is* the assumption that his status within the covenant people, as attested by his 'works of the law', will ensure his final ac-

---

[19] See again the Psalms of Solomon references cited above.

[20] I hope I have not said this anywhere, but if I have been so understood I am glad to have the opportunity to set the record straight.

quittal. It is *not* the assumption that his 'works of the law' earn him salvation or outweigh his sins;[21] it *is* the assumption that whatever his sins they will not be serious enough to debar him from the life of the age to come, that his obedience to the requirements of the covenant ('works of the law'), not least his observance of the sacrificial cult, will cover his sins, and that therefore there is no need for anything more radical in the way of repentance. In pointed and almost explicit contrast Paul states that the role of the law is to bring consciousness of sin, not to dull that consciousness (3.20b).[22]

In short, there is no dispute, I think, that ἔργα νόμου in Rom. 3.20 sum up the indictment of 1.18–3.20. But what is so badly misunderstood by many exegetes is the thrust of that indictment. When it is read against the background of Jewish polemic against Gentile religiosity and 'Gentile' as 'sinner', as I believe it must, it should become clear that 'works of the law' do not denote any attempt to earn favour with God. There is nothing of that in the indictment. What we *do* see, and see in plenty, is a Jewish assumption of 'favoured nation' status, and the corollary assumption that even when Jews sin it is not so serious as Gentile sin. It is *this* attitude and misapprehension which Paul sums up as the confidence of justification by works of the law. The clear implication being that *it is his 'works of the law'* (since they maintain his covenant status and document his distinctiveness from Gentile sinners) *which give the 'Jew' his false confidence and which cloak the seriousness of his sin.*

2.3 This line of exegesis, or something very like it, is surely confirmed by Rom. 3.27ff. For the brief central section of the argument (3.21–26) is bracketed by sections dealing with the implications of Paul's gospel for Jews (2.1–3.20 and 3.27–4.25). And 3.27ff. is clearly intended by Paul as the most immediate corollary to be drawn from that central section. Here again I must confess to being very surprised at Professor Cranfield's attempt to argue otherwise.[23] To describe Paul's concern for the outworking of his gospel for his own people's understanding of the law and of God as 'an intolerable anticlimax' shows a striking lack of sympathy with the depth of Paul's concern on just this point (cf. 9.1–3), and a striking lack of understanding of just how central to Paul's whole exposition the position of his fellow Jews was. As a Jew he had no problem with the thought

---

[21] So still among recent commentaries, W. Schmithals, *Der Römerbrief* (Gütersloh: Gütersloher, 1988) p. 114.

[22] Hence the 'for' which introduces 3.20b, and which Cranfield rebukes me for ignoring (p. 93).

[23] Dunn's exegesis is 'a quite unjustified limiting of Paul's concern. How could Paul, immediately after vv. 21–26 ... go on merely to draw out the consequences for the self-understanding of the Jewish people? At this particular point anything less than a drawing-out of the consequences for the self-understanding of human beings as such would be an intolerable anticlimax. It is not just Jewish boasting which is here excluded ... but all human boasting before God' (Cranfield p. 96).

that Gentiles were 'sinners' in need of salvation (cf. again Gal. 2.15); it was his fellow Jews who needed to be convinced that their need was as great; it was Jewish presumption to the contrary which had to be deflated; so to do must, almost inevitably, have been a central objective in Paul's exposition of the gospel.

Hence the immediate conclusion to be drawn from 3.21–26 relates to boasting. Despite Professor Cranfield, this *must* be Jewish boasting. (i) It is boasting which relates to 'works of the law' (the same phrase, the same law, as in 3.19–20); (ii) it thus clearly echoes the boasting of 2.17 and 23 ('boasting in the law'), the only boasting previously mentioned in the letter, (iii) as is confirmed by the resumption in 3.27 of the diatribe style which Paul uses in these chapters in his debate with the Jewish interlocutor. We might indeed justifiably paraphrase 3.27: 'Where then is that boasting (ἡ καύχησις not καύχησις)', that is the boasting spoken of in 2.17 and 23?[24] It is surely very hard to avoid the obvious conclusion: that *it is precisely Jewish boasting in the law which is ruled out by the gospel stated in 3.21–26;* that is, Jewish assumption of privileged status over against the Gentile, Jewish assumption that the law provided an effective safeguard, for those within its bounds and doing its works, against the very sins which would result in Gentile condemnation and destruction.[25]

And this conclusion is surely confirmed by 3.29–30 ('Is he the God of Jews only?'). The false assumption bound up in the boasting of 3.27 is that God is God of the Jewish people alone. The assumption is well known to us (Deut. 32.8–9; Sir. 17.17; *Jub.* 15.31–32). It is that false assumption which, evidently, Paul's argument from 3.19 (or perhaps better, from 2.1) has been designed to undermine. *Whatever else it might be aimed at, Paul's gospel of justification by faith is clearly aimed at Jewish assumption of privileged status before God.*

The real dispute between Professor Cranfield and myself therefore reduces to the question, Where do 'works of the law' fit in? He claims in effect that 'works of the law' denote a privileged status *earned* by obedience to the law;[26] I am convinced that 'works of the law' denote privileged status as *attested* and *maintained* by obedience to the law. Since nothing has been said thus far in Romans about earning this privilege, and since the boasting of 2.17–20 is *all* in terms of privileged status provided by the law, I would have to claim that flow of argument and context strongly support the latter alternative.

2.4 The flow of argument, of course, runs on into Rom. 4. For those aware of the typical Jewish exaltation of Abraham at that time, as perhaps the pre-eminent model of Jewish piety, there should be no difficulty in understanding why

---

[24] As most recognize; see now e.g. Schmithals p. 129.

[25] 'The boasting is of those who think they have a special status because they are Jews' (Ziesler p. 117).

[26] Cranfield p. 96.

Paul should turn to Abraham and to Gen. 15.6 in particular.[27] Only those who are unwilling to see Paul's exposition of Gen. 15.6 as directed against the prevailing interpretation of Gen. 15.6 (reflected also in James 2.23!) could fail to recognize that Jewish spirituality was well able to portray Abraham as one who performed 'works of the law', in the sense of doing what the law required and thus testifying to his covenant faithfulness.[28] Hence the main line of argument in the second half of Rom. 4: that Abraham's 'believing' should be understood *not* as (covenant) faithfulness (as in Sir. 44.20; 1 Macc. 2.52; *Jub.* 17.15–18; 18.16; 19.8), but as sheer, naked faith (Rom. 4.18–22).

The only point at which this line of exegesis really comes into question is Rom. 4.4–5. And here it would appear that my exegesis is most vulnerable. For does the passage not speak of working for pay? And since it opposes that model of 'reckoning' to the forgiveness of divine grace, is not the implication that Paul is thus opposing his gospel of justification by grace through faith to a Jewish doctrine of justification as reward for works? So most deduce, with the corollary that any attempt to deny that Paul was attacking a doctrine of salvation earned by good works must therefore fail.[29]

This conclusion and corollary, however, is, in my opinion, reached too hastily and too casually. For one thing, the illustration of working for pay was prompted not simply by the talk of works/working; rather it is drawn in for the primary purpose of demonstrating the meaning of λογίζεσθαι. It was almost certainly the occurrence of this particular word in Gen. 15.6, a word well known as a technical term in commercial dealings, which suggested the business illustration. In normal usage that word denoted the reckoning of recompense for services provided; but that is a sense which Paul deems inappropriate to divine-human relations. It is *that* against which Paul is reacting – that is, the normal business meaning of the word. In order to make sense of the illustration within the argument it is unnecessary to read further overtones into the illustration. In particular, it by no means necessarily follows that the 'Jew' (Paul's diatribe partner) saw God's relations with Israel on the model of human business relationships or so exegeted Gen. 15.6 – at least, not in terms of understanding salvation as something which could be bought.

For another, we should not quickly assume that ἐργάζεσθαι in 4.4–5 is wholly equivalent to ἔργα νόμου. By no means is that so. The verb in Paul is uniformly

---

[27] May I simply refer to my *Romans* pp. 198–202 for full documentation.

[28] The basis for presenting Abraham as the model covenant law-keeper was already given in Gen. 26.5!

[29] So e.g. Schreiner p. 229; Silva pp. 351–2; only briefly touched by Cranfield p. 97. So also particularly S. Westerholm, *Israel's Law and the Church's Faith. Paul and his Recent Interpreters* (Grand Rapids: Eerdmans, 1988), responded to in my *Jesus, Paul and the Law* pp. 237–41. Otherwise Ziesler: 'The target ... is not Jewish self-righteousness, but Jewish claims to privilege' (p. 125).

neutral or positive. It never carries a negative overtone in and of itself. The negative overtone in 'works' in Paul's theology relates exclusively to the compound, 'works *of the law*'.[30] This should occasion no surprise: it is quite common for a word, even the same word, to have a clearly negative connotation only in certain well defined contexts; in NT writings we may think, for example, of ἐπιθυμία ('desire') and κόσμος ('world'). So here: the negative overtone attaches not to ἐργάζεσθαι, nor to ἔργον, nor even to ἔργον νόμου (2.15), but only to ἔργα νόμου.[31]

I very much doubt, therefore, whether Rom. 4.4–5 is rightly to be understood as accusing Paul's fellow Jews of thinking they could achieve or earn acceptance by God by means of their own efforts and hard work. Since the typical Jewish mind-set was of those who perceived themselves as already within the bounds of God's covenant grace, in that crucial sense there was nothing to be earned! A status to be documented and maintained over against Gentile sinners by works of the law, certainly. And that attitude is not so very far from the attitude of the merit-earner of Professor Cranfield's interpretation. But the two are *not* the same, and the extent of the disagreement between Professor Cranfield and myself shows how far apart they actually are.

2.5 I should perhaps simply add in reference to Rom 9.30–10.4 that Professor Cranfield wholly ignores the careful exegesis I offer of that important section, particularly of 10.2–3.[32] In the light of that passage it seems to me to be quite clear that Paul is striking out against an idea of (Jewish) righteousness as exclusively their own (belonging to Jews and not to Gentiles), to be defended with Maccabean-like 'zeal' – as Paul himself had previously attempted to do (Gal 1.13–14). The ferocity of that persecution (he had attempted to 'destroy' the church) is surely clear enough indication of how deeply these issues ran for Paul.

3. ἔργα νόμου in Galatians

For the sake of completeness I should perhaps add two more comments on the key related passages in Galatians.

---

[30] The full phrase is either explicit (Rom. 3.20, 28; Gal. 2.16; 3.2, 5, 10) or implicit (Rom. 3.27; 4.2, 6; 9.12, 32; 11.6).

[31] Cf. the thought of 'self-love'. The fact that this is generally a negative concept does not carry with it the corollary that either element of the compound is negative when used on its own; and there are cases where 'self-love' can be presented as something relatively positive – as in the case of the command to love one's neighbour as oneself.

[32] Cranfield pp. 97–98; referring to my *Romans* particularly pp. 586–88.

3.1 Gal. 2.16. Whatever may be said about the actual translation of this verse,[33] it is surely clear beyond reasonable dispute: (i) that Paul was responding here to the belief (implicit in the Antioch incident) that faith can and should go hand in hand with works of the law; and (ii) that he does so by posing faith and works of the law in antithesis. All I have been concerned to do is to show how 2.16 can be understood as speaking to these two points. Quite how he gets from one to the other is what stands in dispute.

A main point of criticism of my exegesis has been that Paul uses καί, rather than ἀλλά to join the two main clauses.[34] The only solution I can offer is that Paul uses the former, even though his intention is to contest the shared view enunciated in the first main clause, in order to indicate that he sees his view in continuity with Peter's: the posing of faith and works of the law as an antithesis, rather than as mutually compatible, is the proper or inevitable outworking of the gospel's emphasis on faith. After all, he had already accused Peter of not walking straight in relation to the truth of the gospel (2.14). In other words, Peter's halakhah (works of the law as consistent with and expression of faith in Christ) is (now) to be seen as against the truth of the gospel.

3.2 Gal. 3.10. A fundamental presupposition of Professor Cranfield's whole position is that Paul believed it was impossible to keep the whole law, impossible, that is, for humans to attain true or complete obedience of the law, impossible to avoid falling short of the standard set by God in the law.[35] The claim, however, is usually, and, if anything, more strongly based on Gal. 3.10.[36] I extend my response to this point and this verse simply to note that the understanding of Paul's logic sketched out above (§ 2.2 – in relation to Rom. 2) also gives us a helpful clue for our understanding of Gal. 3.10. What Paul had in mind there too was not human inability to keep the law, but the same problem of Jewish disobedience treated too lightly and discounted by the same confidence that living within the covenant provided complete cover for sin.

a) I believe the talk of 'remaining within everything in the book of the law to do them' (Gal. 3.10 citing Deut. 27.26) has been *mis*understood in terms of total, that is, perfect *obedience.* What Paul had in mind rather was a complete *life-style* – life lived wholly within the covenant, wholly within the law, wholly in terms of its requirements (as also in Gal. 5.3), that is, a mode of living wholly Jewish in

---

[33] Silva finds my response to F.F. Bruce in *Jesus, Paul and the Law* p. 198 'a rather confused comment' (p. 346); but I must confess his response brought me no clarity.

[34] 'We are Jews by nature and not Gentile sinners, knowing that a person is not justified from works of the law but only through faith in Jesus Christ, and we have believed in Christ Jesus, in order that we might be justified from faith in Christ and not from works of the law ...' (Gal. 2.15–16).

[35] See e.g. Cranfield p. 97; so also Schreiner pp. 226–28; Moo p. 215..

[36] See e.g. those cited in my *Jesus, Paul and the Law* p. 234 n.41; also J. Rohde, *Galater* (ThHNT 9; Berlin: Evangelische, 1988) p. 141; Longenecker p. 118.

character. This was the sort of life which Paul had previously led (Gal. 1.13–14). And that life he could call 'blameless' (Phil. 3.6); *not* because he kept the law perfectly; but simply because he lived wholly in the law's terms – including its provisions of sacrifice and atonement for sin.

b) The trouble was that such a self-understanding meant 'trusting in the flesh' (the tie-in between this attitude and the flesh is clear from Rom. 2.28–29, 9.8, and Phil. 3.3–4, as also from Gal. 3.3 and 6.13). Hence we see the bearing of a related verse which does speak of the impossibility of pleasing God (Rom. 8.8). Those thus incapacitated are 'those in the flesh'. But that, in Paul's Christian perspective, included the typical 'Jew' ('trusting in the flesh'). This relates to Gal. 3.10, because the tension in the thought there is closely paralleled by the tension between Rom. 8.7 and 8.8. For if 'those in the flesh' includes Jews, then the train of thought from Rom 8.7 to 8.8 implies that (such) Jews are not, indeed cannot be subject to the law of God. In other words, there is something in the basic Jewish self-understanding which actually prevents them from being (properly) subject to the law of God. Paul expresses this in Gal. 3.10 by indicating that the 'works of the law' mind-set puts those who maintain it under the curse which falls on those who fail to do all that the law requires.

c) Ironically, Paul *does* think that obedience to the law is possible – as Gal. 5.14–15, Rom. 8.4 and 13.8–10 make clear. The difference is the different basis or mind-set – faith (1.5) and love (Gal. 5.6). It is that which Paul sets in contrast to the mind-set he had previously held – characterized by 'works of the law'. In other words, once again the implication is clear that in Paul's perspective, a wrong attitude to the law was preventing his fellow Jews from recognizing that they were indeed in dangerous breach of the law and needed to be shown that the way of fulfilling the law was not in terms of 'works' but through faith from start to finish.

To sum up, the difference between Professor Cranfield's exegesis and mine boils down to two key issues: (1) Did Paul accuse his fellow Jews of seeking to earn salvation by works of the law, or *of seeking to preserve their covenantal privileges as God's righteous ones (over against Gentile sinners) by works of the law?* (2) Did Paul think the law could not be obeyed and that Israel's fault was assuming that it could? Or did he think that Israel was going about obeying the law in the wrong way, *by treating the realm of righteousness as exclusively Jewish territory (marked out by works of the law), and thereby failing to recognize the seriousness of their sin and that they (as much as any Gentile) fell under the law's curse?* It will be clear that I think the latter alternative in each case is much closer to the heart of Paul's gospel and theology.

I am grateful once again to those who have taken up my request for continued dialogue, particularly for the stimulus their response has given me to read again and think through our common heritage with care. May I hope that the dialogue will continue.

Chapter 9

Echoes of Intra-Jewish Polemic in Paul's Letter to the Galatians

No one will need to be reminded that Galatians is one of the most polemical documents in all the Bible. The typically polite thanksgiving of the normal letter opening is replaced by the indignation and fiery anathema of 1.6–9. The Jerusalem Christian leadership is four times referred to with the distancing formula, οἱ δοκοῦντες (2.2, 6, 9), and dismissed with a shrug – 'what they once were makes no difference to me'. The Jerusalem opposition is described with a series of weasel words –'false brothers smuggled in, who sneaked in to spy on our freedom' (2.4). Jerusalem itself is identified with Hagar and dumped in the slavery column in the opposing columns of 4.21–27, and the Galatians are encouraged to throw out the other missionaries as Sarah encouraged Abraham to throw out Hagar and Ishmael, alike expelled from the heritage of Abraham (4.30). The sharpness of polemic poses Christ and circumcision, grace and law as mutually exclusive antitheses (5.2–5), and reaches its climax in the coarse sexual humour of 5.12. And even in the postscript Paul cannot refrain from cheapening the motives of his opponents and denying their integrity (6.12–13).

Such language and tactics are typical of factional polemic the world over. In spirit and tone at least it is not particularly Jewish or Christian.[1] At the same time, there are some elements which seem to echo more specifically intra-Jewish polemic and it is these on which this paper focuses. Peter von der Osten-Sacken has already noted the parallel between 1.6–7 and CD 1.14–17 with its fierce polemic against 'the congregation of traitors' and 'the Scoffer'.[2] But others are still more striking and call for more attention than they have hitherto received. It will suffice to refer to the most noteworthy passage and two others.

---

[1] See e.g. L.T. Johnson, 'The New Testament's Anti-Jewish Slander and the Convention of Ancient Polemic, *JBL* 108 (1989) 419–41.

[2] P. von der Osten-Sacken, *Die Heiligkeit der Tora. Studien zum Gesetz bei Paulus* (München: Kaiser, 1989) 142.

1. Galatians 2.11–17

1.1 Hints of intra-Jewish polemic

The polemical character of the section is clear from the first. To say that Cephas 'stood condemned' (2.11) means, of course, condemned from the perspective of Paul's position: typical of the polemicist is the attempt to prejudice the audience by implying that the view propounded has a universal validity. But the indications of more specifically Jewish character soon begin to appear.

a) 2.12 – Cephas 'separated himself'. Is there here an echo of the nickname by which one of the main 'sects' within contemporary Judaism was commonly designated (Pharisees = 'separated ones')?[3] Pharisees and Essenes were known within Jewish circles as those who separated themselves from others precisely in the matter of table-fellowship, for reasons of purity – even from others who no doubt regarded themselves as Torah faithful, but who were not so regarded by Essenes and Pharisees.[4] Cephas, like these other factions within second Temple Judaism, had now made table-fellowship a test-case of covenant identity and faithfulness, and in concluding that the Gentile believers failed that test (or rather that their company caused *him* to fail that test) had withdrawn from table-fellowship with them. In a verbal exchange between Jews on the subject of table-fellowship such an echo would not have been difficult to hear. We might even paraphrase, 'Cephas played the Pharisee'.

b) 2.12 – 'because he feared those of the circumcision'. The verb here will be at least partly polemical in force: even if Peter was in fact concerned about his personal safety, the reduction of his motives solely to those of fear is a polemical stratagem to discredit the action so described. More remarkable here, however, is the description of those 'feared' as 'of the circumcision'. It is remarkable because Paul can thus describe them in summary fashion by reference to the act and fact of 'circumcision'. Elsewhere Paul can describe Jews at large as 'the circumcision', in contrast to the rest of humanity, characterized simply as 'the uncircumcision' (2.7–8; similarly Rom 2.25–27; 3.30; 4.9–12). This characterization indicates clearly an identity determined by or focused in the act and fact of cir-

---

[3] See e.g. E. Schürer, *The History of the Jewish People in the Age of Jesus Christ*, revised and edited by G. Vermes et al. (Edinburgh: Clark; 1979) 2.396–7; A.J. Saldarini, *Pharisees, Scribes and Sadducees in Palestinian Society* (Edinburgh: Clark, 1988) 215, 220–1. That Paul's use of the same word in 1.15 carries a similar echo has been suggested e.g. by T. Zahn, *Der Brief des Paulus an die Galater* (Leipzig: Deichert, 1905) 61–2 and F. Mussner, *Der Galaterbrief* [HTKNT; 3d ed.; Freiburg: Herder, 1977] 83 n.31).

[4] The point is disputed as to its detail, but the broad picture is hard to dispute. In addition to those cited in the first part of n.2 above, see also e.g. A.F. Segal, *Rebecca's Children. Judaism and Christianity in the Roman World* (Harvard: Harvard University Press, 1986) 124–8; S.J.D. Cohen, *From Maccabees to the Mishnah* (Philadelphia: Westminster, 1987) 119, 129–32, 154–9, 162; and the several contributions by J. Neusner on the subject.

cumcision – hence the metonymy, 'the circumcision', not 'the circumcised' – circumcision providing the fundamental and sufficient principle of classification. And equally clearly it indicates a Jewish perspective: 'the uncircumcision' is hardly a self-designation by Gentiles. But here the term is used by a Jew in reference to another Jew, and must indicate still other Jews distinguished from the likes of Peter and Paul in a way analogous to the distinction between Jew and Gentile. That is to say, they were a faction within Judaism who gave such emphasis to circumcision that they could even be distinguished from other Jews as 'the circumcision'.

c) 2.13 – 'they played the hypocrite'. In Greek the verb meant simply 'to play a part'. But in Jewish use it gained a regularly negative note – 'pretend, deceive' (as in Sir 32.15; 33.2; *Pss. Sol.* 4.20, 22). A particularly poignant parallel is the memory of Eleazar, the Maccabean martyr, who *refused* to pretend to eat pork and food sacrificed to idols as a way of escaping execution (2 Macc 6.21, 24; 4 Macc 6.15, 17).[5] If Paul, in addressing Peter, was looking over his shoulder at the 'group from James', he could well have intended to evoke this classic example of covenant faithfulness. Peter and the other Christian Jews ought to have had the strength of character (to resist the temptation to abandon the truth of the gospel) which Eleazar had shown. Since one would have expected the example of the Maccabean martyrs to be cited by the people from James rather than by Paul, there is at least the suggestion here that Paul was trying to counter the sort of factional argument which in the two hundred years following the Maccabean revolt must regularly have appealed to the example of the Maccabean martyrs.

d) 2.13 – '... their hypocrisy'. The charge is, of course, once again polemical: in polemic a genuine disagreement can easily be represented as hypocrisy by those who see the issues either differently or more intensely. More to the immediate point, Wilckens notes that ὑπόκρισις in diaspora Judaism was used as equivalent to the Hebrew חנף denoting 'a wickedness which alienates from God'.[6] Here too, given the context of bitter denunciation, the overtone may have been present to Paul and his Jewish disputants.

e) 2.14 – 'they were not walking straight towards the truth of the gospel'. The verb (ὀρθοποδεῖν) is *hapax* for this period, but the imagery is obvious and would hardly have been misunderstood. More significant here is the fact that the metaphor, 'walk' = conduct oneself, was typically Jewish (הלך) and atypical of Greek thought. Moreover, the characteristic Jewish use was in commendation of a 'walk in the law/statutes/ordinances/ways of God' (hence 'halakhah').[7] In no doubt deliberate contrast, Paul speaks of a walk towards the truth of the gospel. Evidently he was implying with polemical intent that 'the truth of the gos-

---

[5] See also U. Wilckens, ὑποκρίνομαι, *TDNT* 8.563–5, and H.D. Betz, *Galatians* (Hermeneia; Philadelphia: Fortress, 1979) 109–10.

[6] ὑποκρίνομαι, *TDNT* 8.564.

[7] See e.g. the data illustrated in my *Romans* (WBC 38; Dallas: Word, 1988) 315–6.

pel' provided a different and superior beacon for conduct; but in effect he was engaged in a halakhic dispute.

f) 2.14 – 'how is it that you compel the Gentiles to judaize?' 'To judaize' was a quite familiar expression, in the sense 'to live like a Jew', 'to adopt a distinctively Jewish way of life' – with reference to Gentiles taking up Jewish customs like observance of the sabbath.[8] The polemical note sounds in the verb 'compel'. Judaism at that time was notably uninterested in evangelism, though open to and accepting of Gentile god-fearers and proselytes.[9] The element of compulsion would enter because there were Gentiles who were making claims, or for whom claims were being made, to enter into what generations of Jews had always regarded as their exclusive privileges (in terms of the argument of Galatians, into the direct line of inheritance from Abraham). To safeguard the character of these privileges it was evidently seen as necessary to ensure that such claimants conformed fully to the traditional notes of the covenant people.[10] This Paul regarded as compulsion. There is no doubt an echo of the earlier usage in 2.4, and the implication that Peter was being as coercive, and on an equivalent issue, as the 'false brothers' Peter himself had resisted earlier on in Jerusalem.

All these are at best hints. In themselves they would not be sufficient to demonstrate that Paul was using and echoing characteristic intra-Jewish polemic. But there are clearer indications than these, and when taken together with these the case becomes very strong.

1.2 Echoes of intra-Jewish polemic

a) 2.15. The most obvious of these is the reference in 2.15 to 'gentile sinners'. The word 'sinner' is, of course, characteristic Jewish language – רָשָׁע = 'the one guilty of sin, the wicked'.[11] As regularly in the Psalms (e.g. Pss. 50.16–20; 109.2–7; 119.53, 155), it denoted those who disregarded the law, and whose conduct was condemned by it. This was why it could be used, as here, as more or less synonymous with 'Gentiles' (Ps. 9.17; Tob. 13.6; Jub. 33.23–24; Pss. Sol. 2.1–2; Matt 5.47/ Luke 6.33).[12] For Gentiles were by definition 'law-less', without (outside) the

---

[8] See the data e.g. in my Jesus, Paul and the Law. Studies in Mark and Galatians (London: SPCK/Louisville: Westminster, 1990) 149–50.

[9] See now particularly S. McKnight, A Light Among the Gentiles. Jewish Missionary Activity in the Second Temple Period (Minneapolis: Fortress, 1991); P. Fredriksen, 'Judaism, the Circumcision of Gentiles, and Apocalyptic Hope: Another Look at Galatians 1 and 2', JTS 42 (1991) 532–64, here 537–40.

[10] The classic parallel is, of course, the episode of Izates in Josephus, Ant. 20.38–46.

[11] See e.g. BDB, רָשָׁע.

[12] Cf. K.H. Rengstorf, ἁμαρτωλός, TDNT 1.325–6, 328. This, to the Jew, self-evident association of the words 'gentile' and 'sinner', undermines the attempts of H. Neitzel, 'Zur Interpretation von Galater 2,11–21', TQ 163 (1983) 15–39, 131–49, here 16–30, and A. Suhl, 'Der Galaterbrief – Situation und Argumentation', ANRW II.25.4 (1987) 3067–3134, here 3099–106, to introduce a break between ἐξ ἐθνῶν and ἁμαρτωλοί –'We, of course Jews by nature and not

law, and in consequence their conduct was inevitably in breach of the law (sin-ful).

More to the point here, however, the same epithet was evidently often used in the intra-Jewish factional disputes which seem to have wracked the last two hundred years of second Temple Judaism, at least if our sources from that period are anything to go by. Typically one faction would claim to be 'righteous' and condemn others as 'sinners' (e.g. 1 Macc. 1.34; 2.44, 48; *1 Enoch* 5.4–7; 82.4–5; 1QH 10[=2].8–12; 1QpHab 5.4–8; *Pss. Sol.* 4.8; 13.6–12). Here clearly the usage was polemical. For while 'sinner' still denoted sustained disregard for and breach of the law, the disregard and breach was evidently more often in the eye of the beholder than not. The point is underlined when we recall that the targets of such criticism in the texts just cited include, by general consent, both Sadducean and Pharisaic parties.[13] What was at issue, in other words, was sectarian (or factional) interpretation of the law, halakhic dispute of such intensity that the issues were regarded by the 'righteous' as make or break, as determinative of the others' acceptability or unacceptability to God.

One of these great issues was what can be summed up most simply as the issue of table fellowship – not surprisingly, since a number of concerns regarding clean and unclean foods, eating blood, food contaminated by idolatry, and potentially other purity issues all came to focus in the meal table. We need only recall the way the Maccabean crisis brought such concerns to the fore as tests of covenant loyalty (1 Macc. 1.62–63), and the degree to which the heroes and heroines of the second Temple period were lauded in the popular literature of the time precisely for their refusal to eat 'the food of Gentiles' (Dan. 1.8–16; Tob. 1.10–13; Jdt 10.5; 12.1–20; Add Esth LXX 14.17; *Jos. Asen.* 7.1; 8.5). The clear implication for those who used the vocabulary is that fellow Jews who maintained these standards were 'the righteous'; and that those other Jews who failed to maintain these standards, who failed the test issues posed by table-fellowship, were 'sinners'.

Jesus himself had evidently been caught up in disputes in this area, and came under the critical lash of 'the righteous'. To accuse (the tone is one of accusation and criticism) someone of 'eating with sinners', and of being a 'friend of sinners' (with reference to table-fellowship), as in the traditions of Mark 2.16 and Matt. 11.19/Luke 7.34, was to accuse him of consorting with those regarded by the critics as law-breakers. To be noted once again is the fact that the accusation is factional polemic: those so accused might well have included individuals who

---

stemming from the Gentiles, are nevertheless sinners (as much as them)' (Suhl). In the historical context, the antithesis is much more naturally taken as between 'by nature *Jews*' and 'from Gentiles *sinners*', a contrast of status by reason of origin – Jews by birth, sinners because Gentiles.

[13] See e.g. R.B. Wright, 'Psalms of Solomon', *OTP* 2.642, and those cited in Saldarini, *Pharisees* 279 n.6.

were wholly law-abiding in their own eyes; but because they did not conform to the halakhah of the critics on the sensitive issue of food and purity laws, they were categorized as 'sinners' no less than the much more obviously 'wicked'. The implication is also clear: for Jesus to consort with such people in precisely the area of such halakhic sensitivity (table-fellowship) was to tar himself with the same brush – 'sinner' by association, equally disregarding of important ha-lakhoth.[14]

We need simply recall the evidence of Acts 10–11 that the issue of table-fel-lowship had also been very sharp among the earliest Jerusalem Christians (Acts 10.14; 11.3). Presumably, then, whatever the earlier agreement in Jerusalem amounted to (Gal. 2.6–9), it had not clarified, or at least not clarified sufficiently, questions relating to table-fellowship. Only at Antioch did it become clear to more conservative believers from Jerusalem what was happening – that fellow Jews were sitting light to or actually departing from one of the central traditions of Torah piety, a tradition hallowed by the blood of the martyrs and fully sanc-tioned by the examples of the great heroes and heroines of Israel's history.

This then is the context of the incident at Antioch[15] and fully explains the at-mosphere of suspicion, bitter accusation and savage denunciation. The language ('gentile sinners') is the language of Jews who regarded the law as definitive of righteousness, and who therefore took it for granted that Gentiles 'by nature' were outside the law, out-laws, and therefore 'sinners', unacceptable to God by definition. As such it is hardly likely to have been Paul's own choice of language, given his own much more pro-Gentile stance. Almost certainly, therefore, he is echoing the language of more traditional Jews. And in the case in point (the Antioch incident) that must mean the group from James. In other words, Paul here is probably echoing in ironic fashion the accusation and criticism brought by the James' people against Peter and the other Jewish believers in Antioch: 'How can you, Peter, being a true born Jew, eat with Gentile sinners?'

To be noted once again is the fact that, as in the case of Jesus, the accusation was being brought by Jews against fellow-Jews. Although the language referred to non-Jews ('Gentile sinners'), the issue was still an intra-Jewish one – the issue of covenant loyalty, of Torah piety, of avoiding contamination by the 'sinner'. And since it involved disagreement between Jews on what was and what was not permissible in associating with Gentiles, the issue was in fact one of intra-Jewish

---

[14] For fuller treatment of these and related points I refer to my 'Pharisees, Sinners and Jesus', *Jesus, Paul and the Law* chap. 3; also *The Partings of the Ways between Christianity and Judaism* (London: SCM/Philadelphia: Trinity, 1991) chap. 6. It should perhaps be noted that E.P. San-ders has not yet responded to my critique of his treatment of Jesus and 'the sinners' in his *Jesus and Judaism* (London: SCM, 1985) chap. 6. In contrast, despite criticism on specific points, San-ders agrees with the main thrust of my earlier analysis of the Antioch incident (see below n. 15) in his 'Jewish Association with Gentiles and Galatians 2:11–14', *Studies in Paul and John In Honor of J. Louis Martyn* (ed. R.T. Fortna & B.R. Gaventa; Nashville: Abingdon, 1990) 170–88.

[15] See further my 'The Incident at Antioch (Gal 2:11–18)', *Jesus, Paul and the Law* chap. 6.

factional dispute. The issue and language used was of a piece with similar language and polemic present in such as 1 Maccabees and *Psalms of Solomon*, where 'sinner' can be used both of Gentiles as such, and of other Jews who were regarded by the writers as apostates, but who were actually other Jewish factions. The dispute at Antioch could carry such echoes of intra-Jewish polemic, precisely because it was a further example of the same kind of intra-Jewish polemic which characterized that period.

Finally here we should observe the likelihood that the same language of the group from James is probably echoed again in 2.17 – 'if in seeking to be justified in Christ we find that we too are "sinners" ...'. Evidently the James faction's insistence that the Gentile believers at Antioch were still to be categorized as 'sinners' drew the corollary, obvious to all the Jewish factions represented, that those Jews who consorted with such 'sinners' and thus conducted themselves in ways repugnant to Torah loyalists would find themselves regarded by the Jewish 'righteous' as equally 'sinners'.[16] In which case, Paul points out, the Christ who accepted Gentile (sinners) by faith would have to be described as 'a servant of sin'![17] Impossible!

In short, Paul's use of the term 'sinners' in 2.15 and 17 is best explained as an echo of the language used by the group from James when they successfully persuaded Peter to withdraw and separate himself from the table-fellowship of the Christian Gentiles in Antioch. And the term itself is clearly used with the same polemical thrust as in the intra-Jewish factional polemic of the time.

b) 2.16. A second fairly clear echo of intra-Jewish factional polemic is present in the phrase 'works of the law'. There is no need to recall in detail here how this phrase has traditionally been understood by Christian commentators as a description of human effort and achievement.[18] I have argued the point elsewhere, sufficiently I hope, that the phrase denoted for Paul rather the acts of obedience required by the law of all faithful Jews, all members of the people with whom God had made the covenant of Sinai – the self-understanding and obligation ac-

---

[16] The point is taken by e.g. E.D. Burton, *Galatians* (ICC; Edinburgh: Clark, 1921) 125, 129; H. Feld, '"Christus Diener der Sünde". Zum Auslegung des Streites zwischen Petrus und Paulus', *TQ* 153 (1973) 119–31, here 126; Mussner, *Galaterbrief* 176 n.41; and J. Rohde, *Der Brief des Paulus an die Galater* (THNT 9; Berlin: Evangelische Verlag, 1988) 113. Whereas J. Lambrecht, 'The Line of Thought in Gal 2:14b-21', *NTS* 24 (1977–78) 484–95, here 493; F.F. Bruce, *Commentary on Galatians* (NIGTC; Exeter: Paternoster, 1982) 140–1; and Suhl, 'Galaterbrief' 3108–9, assume too hastily that the issue is simply one of justification by faith in its classic terms.

[17] The possibility that Paul and the Galatians were aware of the tradition of Jesus eating with 'sinners' can by no means be excluded, especially in view of the other possible allusions to Jesus' self-accepted 'servant' role in the same verse (cf. Mark 10.45 pars.; Rom. 15.2–3, 7–8).

[18] E.g. Betz, *Galatians* 117 – 'any and all works as works-of-merit'; R.N. Longenecker, *Galatians* (WBC 41; Dallas: Word, 1990) 86 – 'merit-amassing observance of Torah'; D. Georgi, *Theocracy in Paul's Praxis and Theology* (Minneapolis: Fortress, 1991) 38 – 'social and cultural achievements ... brought about by law – in principle, by any law'.

cepted by practising Jews which E.P. Sanders encapsulated quite effectively in the phrase 'covenantal nomism'.[19]

In the immediate context here it is evident that the phrase had in view the obligations accepted by the group from James and assumed by them to be binding on all Jews – that is, in particular, the food laws and other traditions which gathered round the whole practice of table-fellowship within a Jewish context. What Peter and the other Christian Jews in effect were affirming – that observance of such obligations ('works of the law') was a continuing necessity for them (hence their conduct in 2.12–13) – Paul now emphatically denies (2.16).[20] This is not to say, as I have been understood to say, that by 'works of law' Paul meant only such obligations as the food laws (and circumcision and sabbath observance).[21] It is simply that the larger commitment and sense of obligation to live within the terms laid down by the law, to perform 'works of the law', came to focus in particular test cases like circumcision and food laws (as here).[22]

Here however it is the factional overtones of the phrase which call for most attention. For it is now clear that the closest parallels to the Pauline phrase are to be found in the Qumran literature, in the phrase מעשי התררה, 'deeds of Torah', and others similar to it. Presumably, as with 'works of the law', the Qumran phrase denotes the obligations laid upon the Qumran covenanters by the Torah. What is significant for the present discussion, however, is that these phrases are

---

[19] See my 'The New Perspective on Paul' and 'Works of the Law and the Curse of the Law (Gal 3:10–14) [= ch. 2 and 3 above]', both with additional notes in *Jesus, Paul and the Law* chaps. 7 and 8; also *Romans* 153–5; *Partings* 135–8; and below n. 21. The reference is to E.P. Sanders, *Paul and Palestinian Judaism* (London: SCM, 1977) 75, 420, 544. See also R. Heiligenthal, 'Soziologische Implikationen der paulinischen Rechtfertigungslehre im Galaterbrief am Beispiel der "Werke des Gesetzes"', *Kairos* 26 (1984) 38–53; J. Lambrecht, 'Gesetzesverständnis bei Paulus', *Das Gesetz im Neuen Testament*, (ed. K. Kertelge; Freiburg: Herder, 1986) 88–127, here 114–5; J. Barclay, *Obeying the Truth. A Study of Paul's Ethics in Galatians* (Edinburgh: Clark, 1988; Minneapolis: Fortress, 1991) 78, 82; G.W. Hansen, *Abraham in Galatians. Epistolary and Rhetorical Contexts* (JSNTSup 29; Sheffield: JSOT, 1989) 102–3, 114. In 1968 K. Kertelge was a lone voice in maintaining that 'works of the law' were an expression of 'Jewish consciousness of election' – 'Zur Deutung des Rechtfertigungsbegriffs im Galaterbrief', *BZ* 12 (1968) 211–222, here 215–6, reprinted in his *Grundthemen paulinischer Theologie* (Freiburg: Herder, 1991) 111–22, here 115–6.

[20] However the syntax of 2.16 is construed, Paul's concern was evidently to move the argument from a position where 'works of the law' could be insisted on (as at Antioch) to a position where faith and works would be seen as standing in antithesis. See also my *Jesus, Paul and the Law* 212, and 'Yet Once More – The Works of the Law. A Response', *JSNT* 46 (1992) 114 [= 224–5 above].

[21] As particularly by C.E.B. Cranfield, '"The Works of the Law" in the Epistle to the Romans', *JSNT* 43 (1991) 89–101; D. Moo, *Romans 1–8* (Wycliffe Exegetical Commentary; Chicago: Moody, 1991) 210–11, 214–15; F. Thielman, *From Plight to Solution. A Jewish Framework for Understanding Paul's View of the Law in Galatians and Romans* (Leiden: Brill, 1989) 63.

[22] See now my 'Yet Once More' 100–2 [= 213–15 above]. Contemporary issues which function in the same way to bring to focus larger attitudes and perspectives include women's ordination, inerrancy, and speaking in tongues.

actually used to denote the specific obligations laid on the covenanters by their membership of the (Qumran) covenant, or to be more precise, the interpretations put upon the Torah by the Qumran covenanters which marked them out in their distinctiveness from other Jews and Jewish factions. Thus it is by reference to his 'deeds', his 'deeds with regard to the law' (מעשׂיו בתררה), his 'observance of the law' as understood within the community, that the individual's membership of the covenant was tested (1QS 5.21, 23; 6.18; cf. 4QFlor = 4Q174 1.1–7). Most striking of all is the fact that the recently publicized 4QMMT, entitled מקצת מעשׂי התררה, 'some of the deeds of the Torah', contains a series of distinctive halakhic rulings.[23] 'Deeds or works of the law', then, was evidently itself a factional phrase, embodying both the claim that the conduct therein called for was required by God and the denial that alternative conduct was acceptable to God; or, alternatively expressed, embodying the claim that the group's interpretation of the Torah at disputed points was the correct and only legitimate enactment of what the Torah laid down at these points.

But this is precisely where we find ourselves in the dispute between Paul and Peter, and behind him the James' faction, at Antioch – a dispute over what the law actually required as essential for the Jewish sect of the Nazarene. There is no need to argue that Paul or the group from James were influenced by Qumran usage.[24] It is sufficient that Qumran usage expresses a similar attitude in similar circumstances of halakhic dispute. Whether the phrase was more widely current need not be determined. Either way it remains significant that in just such a context of dispute over the extent and detail of Torah obligation binding on Christian Jews, Paul uses a phrase which was used elsewhere in the Judaism of the time in similar intra-Jewish factional dispute over points of halakhah.

In short, here too we catch a distinct echo of the sort of intra-Jewish factional claims and counter claims which evidently were a feature of this period in second Temple Judaism. What Paul characterizes by this phrase, in other words, is in effect a sectarian interpretation of the obligations laid by the law on members of the covenant people – the attempt to define, too narrowly in Paul's perspective, what membership of the seed of Abraham necessarily involved.

c) 2.14. The third and most interesting echo of intra-Jewish polemic in this section comes in the phrase, 'live like a Gentile' – Paul's actual words to Peter at the confrontation in Antioch, 'If you, a Jew, live like a Gentile and not like a Jew ...'. Two features have proved difficult for generations of commentators. The first is

---

[23] At the time of writing the scroll has not yet been published, but a description of it has already been available in L.H. Schiffman, 'The Temple Scroll and the Systems of Jewish Law of the Second Temple Period', *Temple Scroll Studies* (ed. G.J. Brooke; JSPSup 7; Sheffield: Sheffield Academic Press, 1989) 239–55, here 245–50.

[24] The fact that Paul uses the phrase as self-evident in meaning suggests that it had not been peculiar to the Qumran covenanters.

the present tense of the verb: why does Paul speak as though Peter was still 'living like a Gentile' when by that time Peter had withdrawn from Gentile company? The second is the force of the phrase: does Paul imply that Peter had totally abandoned all characteristic and distinctive Jewish practices?

Some have attempted to explain the present tense by taking it literally as a reference to Peter's continuing conduct at the time Paul spoke to him, after he had abandoned mixed table-fellowship. In particular, Zahn, Kieffer and Howard have suggested that even after withdrawing from table-fellowship Peter had continued to 'live like a Gentile' in other matters.[25] But since the Jewish way of life was a total package in the eyes of conservative Christian Jews, such a compromise would have been most unlikely to satisfy the group from James. The characteristic Jewish perspective at this point is given by the quotation from Deut. 27.26 in Gal. 3.10 and was almost certainly shared by the Christian Jews from Jerusalem, if Matt. 5.18–19 and Jas 2.10 are any guide.

The second puzzling feature, that Peter 'was living like a Gentile', has been seen as a decisive rebuttal of any suggestion that prior to the coming of the James' people, the table-fellowship at Antioch had in fact shown respect for the principal Jewish scruples against, say, eating blood and pork. Against my own earlier thesis at this point the question can be fairly asked: How could even a modest degree of Torah observance of the food laws be described as 'living like a Gentile'?[26] As D.R. Catchpole had put it earlier: 'It would be quite impossible to describe existence under the (apostolic) Decree as living like a Gentile'.[27]

The solution to both difficulties probably lies along the lines of the present thesis: that the language is the language of factional polemic, and that in using it Paul was again echoing what the group from James had said to Peter. The fact is that accusations by one group of Jews against other Jews, that the latters' actions were like those of the Gentiles, were not uncommon within intra-Jewish factional dispute. So the author(s) of *Jubilees* condemn(s) both the sons of Israel who failed to circumcise their sons as 'making themselves like the Gentiles', and also those Jews who used a different calendar to calculate the feast days for 'forgetting the feasts of the covenant and walking in the feasts of the gentiles, after their errors and after their ignorance' (15.33–34; 6.35). And the *Psalms of Solomon* condemn in even stronger terms their opponents (probably Sadducees):

---

[25] Zahn, *Galater* 118; R. Kieffer, *Foi et Justification a Antioche. Interprétation d'un conflit (Ga 2,14–21)* (Paris: Cerf, 1982) 33; G. Howard, *Paul: Crisis in Galatia. A Study in Early Christian Theology* (SNTSMS 35; 2d ed.; Cambridge University, 1990) xxi-xxii.

[26] T. Holtz, 'Der antiochenische Zwischenfall (Galater 2:11–14)', *NTS* 32 (1986) 344–61, here 351–2.

[27] D.R. Catchpole, 'Paul, James and the Apostolic Decree', *NTS* 23 (1976–77) 428–44, here 441. P.C. Böttger, 'Paulus und Petrus in Antiochien. Zum Verständnis von Galater 2.11–21', *NTS* 37 (1991) 77–110, here 80–1, gives up the attempt to understand the phrase in its context at this point (in relation to table-fellowship) and attempts to find a solution most implausibly by reference to 1 Thess. 4:5.

'Their lawless actions surpassed the gentiles before them'; 'there was no sin they left undone in which they did not surpass the gentiles' (1.8; 8.13).[28]

None of this should occasion any surprise. As experience of religious sectarian infighting from all periods of history shows, feelings can run so high over particular test issues, that failure to conform to a sect's interpretation of disputed points can easily result in total and wholesale denunciation of those who hold the 'false' interpretation. Indeed it is characteristic of sectarian polemic generally that when a group's boundaries are threatened, a wholly natural response is to attack those who pose the threat as beyond the pale, as polar opposities, with the aim thereby of reinforcing the group's own identity and boundaries. So, for example, the tendency of the conservative right at all times (whether political or theological) has been to to characterize the whole spectrum of those who disagree with them as far to the left – in current polemics, 'communists' and 'liberals'.

So here, the key to the most plausible solution to the phrase, 'live like a Gentile', probably lies in the recognition that this was *not* the language of objective description, but, once again, the language of inter-Jewish factional dispute. To the traditionalists among the group from James, Peter's action in eating with Gentiles was tantamount to him living like a Gentile: in their perspective Peter had abandoned key distinctives which (in their perspective) should continue to mark out the Jew from the Gentile. In other words, when Paul says, 'If you, a Jew, live like a Gentile and not like a Jew', he was probably deliberately picking up the actual words used by the James' group in their rebuke of Peter, 'How can you, Peter, a Jew, live like a Gentile?'

We may most simply conclude by reading Gal. 2.11–17 with the polemical features italicized and the echoes of the language of the James' group picked out in bold:

> But when Cephas came to Antioch I opposed him to his face, because he stood *condemned*. For before certain individuals came from James, he used to eat with the Gentiles. But when they came, he gradually drew back and *separated himself, fearing* those of the circumcision. And the other Jews also joined with him in *playing the hypocrite*, so that even Barnabas was carried away with *their hypocrisy*. But when I saw that they were *not walking straight* towards the truth of the gospel, I said to Cephas before everyone: 'If **"you being a Jew, live like a Gentile and not like a Jew"**, how is it that you *compel* the Gentiles to judaize?' We are **"Jews by nature"** and not **"Gentile sinners"**, knowing that no human being is justified by **works of the law** but only through faith in Jesus Christ, so we have believed in Christ Jesus, in order that we might

---

[28] We may compare CD 12.8–11 and 13.14–16, where commerce with 'the sons of the Pit' is almost as tightly controlled as commerce with Gentiles.

be justified by faith in Christ and not by **works of the law**, since by **works of the law** shall no flesh be justified. But if in seeking to be justified in Christ we find that we too are **"sinners"**, is then Christ a servant of sin? Surely not.

2. Galatians 4.10

Gal. 2.11–17 provides the fullest echoes of intra-Jewish factional polemic. But two other passages are worthy of note in the same connection. The first is 4.10 – Paul's rebuke to the Galatians for 'observing days and months and special times and years'. Here too insufficient weight has been given to two factors: that Paul clearly has particularly Jewish festivals in mind; and that disagreements regarding the proper observance of such festivals was a regular feature of intra-Jewish factional dispute. The claims can be easily documented.

By 'days' Paul would no doubt mean particularly the Sabbath, but also other special days like the Day of Atonement. The Sabbath was another of the Jewish laws which was seen to mark out Israel as distinctive and to function as a boundary between Jew and Gentile (e.g. Exod. 31.16–17; Deut. 5.15; Isa. 56.6). Indeed, it was probably one of the main 'works of the law' which Paul presumably had had mind earlier (2.16). Already before the Maccabean crisis, at least from Josephus' first century CE perspective, 'violating the sabbath' ranked with 'eating unclean food' as the two chief marks of covenant disloyalty (Josephus, *Ant.* 11 § 346). And the increasingly elaborate halakah attested in *Jubilees* (2.17–33; 50.6–13), in the Damascus document (CD 10.14–11.18) and in the Gospels (Mark 2.23–3:5 pars.), indicates the importance of the Sabbath as a test of covenant righteousness within the factionalism of late second Temple Judaism.[29]

'Months' almost certainly refers to the new moon festival which was part of the Jewish cult (Num. 10.10; 28.11; 2 Kgs 4.23; Ps. 81.3; Ezek. 46.3, 6–7),[30] as the parallel with Col. 2.16 certainly confirms. Since the moon was one of the 'elemental forces' (understood to include the planets – 4.3), a parallel between pagan religious practice[31] at this point and nomistic covenantalism could readily be drawn.[32] The 'special times' were probably the 'appointed feasts' (regularly linked with 'sabbaths and new moons' in 1 Chr. 23.31; 2 Chr. 2.4; 31.3; Neh. 10.33; Isa. 1.13–14; Hos. 2.11), that is, the three pilgrim festivals in particular, presumably called '(special) times', or 'festal seasons' from the regular usage in the Pentateuch (Exod. 13.10; 23.14, 17; 34.23–24; Lev. 23.4; Num. 9.3). Since the degree to which diaspora Judaism observed such feasts is still disputed (almost

---

[29] See further e.g. my *Romans* 805–6.
[30] See G. Delling, μήν, *TDNT* 4:639–41.
[31] Delling 638–9.
[32] See also Bruce, *Galatians* 204.

no one could have made the three times pilgrimage to Jerusalem), this text provides a valuable indication that some sort of observance was maintained in the diaspora (cf. Col. 2.16). More puzzling is the reference of the final item on the list – 'years'. The sabbatical year of Lev. 25.1–7 is unlikely: it would hardly seem to be relevant outside Palestine; though it could possibly have had relevance as part of sectarian dispute (cf. 1QS 10.6–8). But the analogy of 'months' for new moon festivals suggests that annual festivals were in mind, presumably (on the analogy of 'month' denoting 'first of the month') the disputed New Year festival (cf. 1QS 10.6).[33]

Here again it must be noted that, as with the Sabbath, the issue of the right observance of these feasts was a matter of sectarian dispute within the Judaism of the period. This was principally because the calendar by which the dates of these feasts were reckoned (solar or lunar) was not agreed by all parties. Hence the polemical denunciation already noted above: to observe a feast on the wrong date was *not* to observe the feast, but to 'forget the feasts of the covenant and walk in the feasts of the gentiles, after their errors and after their ignorance' (*Jub.* 6.32–35), to commit 'sin like the sinners' (*1 Enoch* 82:4–7; see also 1QS 1.14–15; CD 3.14–15). That such disagreement lies behind the present passage is suggested by such parallels as *Jub.* 2.9 –

The Lord set the sun [solar calendar] as a great sign upon the earth
for days, sabbaths, months, feast (days), years ... and for all the
(appointed) times of the years;

and *1 Enoch* 82:7, 9

True is the matter of the exact computation of that which has been
recorded ... concerning the luminaries, the months, the festivals,
the years and the days. ... These are the orders of the stars which
set in their places seasons, festivals and months.[34]

In view of the *1 Enoch* passage, it is probably also significant that the verb used ('observe') would usually have the force of 'watch closely, observe carefully, scrupulously observe',[35] so that Paul may very well have chosen it in order to evoke the careful calculations of feast dates ('calendar piety')[36] which such disputes entailed.[37] Of particular relevance for us here is the evident integration of 'Torah piety' and 'calendar piety' achieved within such Jewish groups, and the

---

[33] See further e.g. Burton, *Galatians* 234; Rohde, *Galater* 181–2; J. Morgenstern, 'New Year', *IDB* 3.544–6; Schürer, *History* 3.2 (1987) index 'New Year'.

[34] See further H. Schlier, *Der Brief an die Galater* (KEK; 4th ed.; Göttingen: Vandenhoeck, 1965) 204–5; Mussner, *Galaterbrief* 298–301.

[35] J.B. Lightfoot, *Saint Paul's Epistle to the Galatians* (1865; 10th ed. 1890; London: Macmillan) 172; BAGD, παρατηρέω; Schlier, *Galater* 203 n.3.

[36] Mussner, *Galaterbrief* 301.

[37] Josephus however also uses it for observance of sabbath and festival days (*Ant.* 3.91; 11.294; 14.264).

importance of the heavenly bodies in determining the right dates for such Torah observances (Josephus could even claim that the Essenes prayed to the sun – *JW* 2.128). Against such a background Paul's association of the Torah with 'the elemental forces of the world' becomes an inviting and plausible rejoinder on his part: 'under the law' = too dependent on the movements of the heavenly bodies.

Here too, then, as in 2.14–15, we probably have to allow for an element of Jewish factionalism to have been in play in the Galatian crisis.[38] In particular, the proper observance in the diaspora of a festival whose correct timing depended on the actual sighting of the new moon,[39] was likely to add a further twist to the disputes reflected in *1 Enoch* and *Jubilees* (above), even though tradition has it that the responsibility for fixing such dates during the final decades of the second Temple rested with the Sanhedrin (*m. Ros Has.* 2.5–3.1). In other words, Paul was not necessarily confronting a uniform Jewish position on such matters. His was a further alternative (observance not necessary) *within* the spectrum of Jewish opinion, as Paul would have insisted, itself part of the factionalism which marred the latter decades of second Temple Judaism.

If these insights to the climax of Paul's line of argument in 3.19–4.11 are sound, then they also help explain Paul's line of argument through the section. As already indicated, Paul was arguing in effect that for the Gentile Christians in Galatia to put themselves 'under the law' was tantamount to putting themselves back in their old (Gentile) position of slavery under the elemental forces (4.9). In other words, Paul was doing what other Jewish factions of the time did: he was accusing those who disagreed with his understanding of God's purpose and God's law of 'living like Gentiles', that is, in this case, of reverting to their old Gentile status (see above on 2.14).

This in turn enables us to see more clearly the force of Paul's earlier argument in 3.19ff. For there he was arguing in effect that the law functioned in relation to Israel in the role of a heavenly power: Israel was 'under the law', 'under a slave custodian', 'under (slave) stewards'.[40] In Paul's perspective that was essentially a positive role (3.19, 23, 24; 4.1–2).[41] His criticism, however, was that Israel had overemphasized that role: clinging to it when they ought to have been maturing to the fuller inheritance of heirs (4.1–7); and in effect treating the law as a kind of guardian angel which defended and kept Israel separate from the other nations. Here too it would appear, Paul was taking up a traditional Jewish theologoume-

---

[38] Cf. Schlier, *Galater* 205–7; H. Riesenfeld, (παρα)τηρέω, *TDNT* 8.148; Mussner, *Galaterbrief* 301–2; the possibility is dismissed too quickly by Bruce, *Galatians* 205.

[39] T.C.G. Thornton, 'Jewish New Moon Festivals, Galatians 4:3–11 and Colossians 2:16', *JTS* 40 (1989) 97–100.

[40] D.B. Martin, *Slavery as Salvation. The Metaphor of Slavery in Pauline Christianity* (New Haven: Yale, 1990) 15–17, notes that in the Roman Empire as a whole at this time the οἰκονόμοι were usually of servile origin.

[41] See further my *Jesus, Paul and the Law* 262 nn. 41 and 42.

non and turning it to his own account in polemical fashion. Israel was accustomed to the thought that Yahweh had appointed angels over the *other* nations, but had kept Israel for himself (Deut. 32.8–9; Sir. 17.17; *Jub.* 15.31–32; *1 Enoch* 20.5; *Tg. Ps.-J.* on Gen. 11.7–8). Paul's argument is to the effect that Israel's over-evaluation of the law had interposed the law between God and Israel, and, far from distinguishing Israel from the other nations, had simply made Israel like the other nations, as being under a heavenly power which limited and prevented it entering into the full maturity of its sonship to both Abraham and God.[42]

However much individual points in the above may be open to debate, the basic point seems to be sound enough: that the polemical character of the argument of 3.19–4.11, particularly in its climax in 4.10, reflects typical elements of the intra-Jewish factional disputes of the period, and is itself of a piece with such dispute.

3. Galatians 4.17

The other passage on which light can be shed by recognizing the echoes of factional polemic is 4.17 – 'They (the other missionaries opposed to Paul) are zealous over you for no good purpose, but wish to shut you out, in order that you might be zealous over them'. The puzzle comes with the twice repeated verb – ζηλοῦσιν ὑμᾶς ... ἵνα αὐτοὺς ζηλοῦτε. Bauer offers the meanings, 'strive, desire, exert oneself earnestly', and with a personal object, 'be deeply concerned about, court someone's favour', or negatively, 'be filled with jealousy or envy towards someone', and modern translations follow this lead.[43] But the negative tone which the verb conveys in reference to the Torah loyalists in Galatia, and the use of the corresponding noun ('zealot') in 1.14 to characterize the characteristic attitude of the Torah loyalist, which Paul himself had once embraced, suggests the strong possibility that Paul had in mind the same attitude here. We may also note the parallel of Rom. 10.2, with a similar qualification:

Gal. 4.17 – They are zealous over you for no good purpose ...
Rom. 10.2 – They have a zeal for God but not in accordance with knowledge.

It may even be that the language had been used by the other missionaries themselves: in Acts 21.20 'zealot' is used by James in effect in self-definition, just as Paul had used it in self-definition in Gal. 1.14.

In other words, Paul may well have had in view the kind of zeal which characterized the unique relation Israel claimed to exist between Yahweh and his people – Israel's zeal for Yahweh corresponding to Yahweh's own zeal (jeal-

---

[42] For fuller treatment of this much disputed section I must refer to my forthcoming commentary on *Galatians* (Black NT Commentary; London: Black, 1993).
[43] BAGD, ζηλόω. I refer particularly to RSV/NRSV, NEB and REB, NJB, NIV.

ousy) in regard to Israel (Exod. 20.5; 34.14; Deut. 4.24; 5.9; 6.15) – in each case
denoting a burning desire to preserve the uniqueness of that relationship. In
Jewish tradition such zeal for God was best exemplified by Simeon and Levi
(Gen. 34; Judith 9.2–4; *Jub.* 30.5–20), by Phinehas (Num. 25.6–13; Sir. 45.23–24; 1
Macc. 2.54; 4 Macc. 18.12), by Elijah (1 Kgs 19.10, 14, 40; Sir. 48.2; 1 Macc. 2.58),
and by Mattathias, the father of the Maccabean rebellion (1 Macc. 2.19–27; Josephus, *Ant.* 12.270–1). The Maccabean rebels prized highly this 'zeal for the law'
and themselves epitomized it (1 Macc. 2.26, 27, 50, 58; 2 Macc. 4.2), as had Paul
in his persecution of 'the church of God' (Gal. 1.13–14; Phil. 3.6). The common
denominator in each case was unyielding refusal to allow Israel's distinctiveness
as Yahweh's alone to be compromised, whether by intermarriage which
breached Israel's ethnic identity, or by syncretistic influences which diluted Israel's dedication to Yahweh alone and the purity of the cult. It was evidently
such fear of the compromises involved in the spread of the Nazarene teaching to
Gentiles which had provoked Paul's zealot-inspired attempt to stamp out the
Hellenist wing of the new sect.

The suggestion is close to hand, then, that Paul saw the other missionaries in
Galatia as motivated by the same zealot-like concerns to maintain and defend
Jewish covenant prerogatives.[44] The claim made for and by Galatian Gentiles to
full participation in the covenant of Israel, without regard for the distinctive
'works of the law', would be precisely the challenge likely to arouse a Phinehas-
like zeal – a challenge met, in the case of the other missionaries, by the attempt
to eliminate such a breach of covenant boundaries by fully incorporating the
Gentile converts in question.[45] The fact that an intransitive verb is being used
transitively ('to be zealous in relation to') would cause Paul's readers no problem.[46]

The case, however, does not depend on the occurrence of the motif of 'zeal'
alone, and indeed would not be very strong if that was all there was to it, since
other possible meanings of the verb make more immediate sense. But the case
becomes immeasurably stronger as soon as the other clause of the verse is
brought into consideration – 'they wish to shut you out'. At first the objective
seems surprising: was the aim of the other missionaries not precisely the
reverse? – to draw the Galatians more fully *into* the people of Israel through circumcision? The key however is the stated objective: 'to shut out'. Most ignore
this meaning or find it too difficult, and opt instead for the sense 'exclude
you (from Paul and other Gentile Christians)',[47] or 'that you should exclude

---

[44] The possibility is again dismissed too quickly by Bruce, *Galatians* 211.

[45] As A. Oepke, *Der Brief des Paulus an die Galater* (THNT 9; 2d ed.; Berlin: Evangelische
Verlag, 1957) 107 notes, the description rules out the hypothesis that the leaders of the opposition to Paul were Gentiles.

[46] See BDF § 148.

[47] So NJB and NIV, and, e.g., H. Lietzmann, *An die Galater* (HNT 10; 3d ed. 1932; 4th ed.

Paul'.[48] But that involves a less natural use of the metaphor or a more forced sense for the Greek.[49] For the metaphor is clearly that of being shut out or excluded, as from a city or an alliance,[50] and is in fact complementary to that used in 3.23: the law that 'watched over, guarded (the city)' was the law which shut out the aliens.

The metaphor is thus very well suited to describe the typical attitude of the Jewish zealot – that is, the burning desire to defend Israel's distinctiveness by drawing the boundary line sharply and clearly between the people of the covenant so as to exclude those not belonging to Israel; or, in particular, of the Jewish Christian zealot – to exclude all Gentiles other than proselytes from Christ, the Jewish Messiah, and from the eschatological community of his people.[51] It was in fact another way of describing the consequence of the action of Peter and the others at Antioch: by withdrawing from table-fellowship they effectively excluded the Christian Gentiles from the one covenant community (2.11–14). In the Galatian churches, then, the tactic of the other missionaries had clearly been to draw again these firm boundaries as laid down by the Torah, and to point out the (to them) inevitable corollary: that the Gentile converts were still outside them.

Their hope however was not so negative, as in the classic models of such 'zeal'; they were missionaries! Their intention was to raise the barriers between Jew and Gentile 'in order that you might be zealous over them'. That is to say, by demonstrating what membership of the covenant people actually involved ('the works of the law'), they hoped to incite a godly desire for that membership in those whose God-fearing had already shown the seriousness of their wish to be numbered among Abraham's heirs. They hoped to convert the Galatians not simply to Judaism but to Judaism as they understood it. By showing 'zeal for the covenant' themselves, they hoped to spark off an equivalent zeal among the Galatians.[52] Or, more precisely, by showing such zeal with regard to the Galatians, their hope was that the Galatians would come to show a similar zeal with regard to them – so that, apart from anything else, each could share fully in the others' table-fellowship without compromising the other and in a mutually sustaining

---

1971; Tübingen: Mohr) 29; Mussner, *Galaterbrief* 311; R.Y.K. Fung, *The Epistle to the Galatians* (NICNT; Grand Rapids: Eerdmans, 1988) 200; Rohde, *Galater* 188; Longenecker, *Galatians* 194.

[48] Cf. Betz, *Galatians* 230–1.

[49] As Burton, *Galatians* 246 notes.

[50] LSJ, ἐϰϰλείω 2; so RSV/NRSV and NEB.

[51] Cf. Lightfoot, *Galatians* 177; M.-J. Lagrange, *Épitre aux Galates* (EB; 3d ed.; Paris: Gabalda, 1926) 116; P. Bonnard, *L'Épitre de saint Paul aux Galates* (CNT 9; Neuchatel: Delachaux, 1953) 94; Schlier, *Galater* 212–3; J.L. Martyn, 'A Law-Observant Mission to Gentiles: The Background of Galatians', *SJT* 38 (1985) 307–24, here 316. J. Bligh, *Galatians* (London: St Paul, 1969) 388 n.27 suggests an allusion to the imagery of the bridal feast as in Matt. 25.10–12.

[52] Since converts to a religion or movement often put themselves among its most committed and even extreme members the strategy and hope of the other missionaries was quite realistic.

way. This reading gives more weight to Paul's language and recognizes greater point in his charges than most of the current alternatives.

In short, Paul's use of the language of 'zeal' here, and his description of the other missionaries' zeal as aimed at 'excluding' the Galatian believers strongly suggests the strange but powerful mixture of dedication and distrust which is so often a feature of out and out loyalists for their cause, and which was evidently a feature of at least some of the factions within second Temple Judaism. The debate itself, between two groups of Christian Jews (Paul and the other missionaries), was itself part of the intra-Jewish factional arguments on what Israel's unique relation with God meant for relations with non-Jews in particular.

4. Conclusions

The picture then is about as clear as anything can be in exegesis. Particularly in Gal. 2.11–17, where Paul harks back to the incident at Antioch, but at other points too, Paul's argument and appeal reflects the concerns and language of intra-Jewish polemic. At each point the basic concern was the same: a Jewish fear lest the purity of Israel's relationship with God be compromised or adulterated – especially by eating with Gentiles and failure to observe the designated feasts. At each point the response (whether by the group from James or the other missionaries in Galatia) was the same: to reinforce the boundaries between Jew and Gentile, whether by withdrawal from table-fellowship with 'Gentile sinners', or by insistence that Gentile converts to the Jesus movement came fully 'under the law', or by provoking would-be participants in the heritage of Abraham to greater 'zeal' by reinforcing the barriers of exclusion.

To be noted is the fact that these fierce debates were not Jewish versus Christian arguments. They were between Jews, Christian Jews to be sure, but Jews nonetheless – including the disputes which feature in the letter to the Galatians itself, where the real target of Paul's polemic is the other (Jewish) missionaries. And the issues are not (yet) Jewish versus Christian issues. They are about what it means to be a practising Jew, what it means to be an heir of Abraham, what differences the coming of Messiah Jesus has made for Israel's self-understanding and for Jewish relations with Gentiles. These 'echoes of intra-Jewish polemic' are a clear indication of a series of issues still thoroughly within the spectrum of second Temple Judaism, of an awareness that what was at stake was in fact the character and continuity of God's choice of and purpose for Israel.

Of course, the whole question requires more extensive analysis than is possible or appropriate here. In particular, the debate with J.L. Martyn needs to be pursued.[53] For he sees such a line of exegesis as in effect a surrender to the

---

[53] See e.g. his 'Events in Galatia', *Pauline Theology. Volume I: Thessalonians, Philippians,*

theology of the other missionaries (whom he calls 'the Teachers'), whereas the cross has meant for Paul a quantum shift into a wholly new and different perspective (especially 6.14–15). Martyn does indeed give cause for pause at several points (especially Paul's use of 'covenant' theology in Galatians), and it is also true that Paul's argument against maintaining the old boundaries between Jew and Gentile is radically at odds with the attempts of his fellow Christian Jews to maintain them. Nevertheless the fact remains that the whole dispute is entirely in Jewish terms. Moreover, it is clear from chs. 3–4 that the desirability and necessity of sharing in sonship to Abraham and in the blessing of Abraham (3.6–14, 29) was common ground for all parties to the Galatian controversy (whoever introduced the specific topic in the first place). And our findings above do indicate a movement still in process of coming to terms with itself regarding its identity as heirs of the promises to Abraham, where the differences between Christian Jews were of a piece with and the extension of polemical disputes elsewhere among the factions of second Temple Judaism.

It will have been no accident, then, that Paul concludes this his most sustained polemical letter, with a blessing on 'the Israel of God' (6.16), itself a final polemical shot summing up the claim (chs. 3–4) that the Israel of covenant promise is the Israel defined by that promise as including Gentiles as well as Jews.[54] The 'echoes of intra-Jewish polemic in Paul's letter to the Galatians' thus confirm that the fiercest debates within first generation Christianity were among (Christian) Jews conscious of the traditional boundaries marking off Jew from Gentile, over the question of whether or to what extent these boundaries should still be maintained.

Galatians, Philemon, ed. J.M. Bassler (Minneapolis: Fortress, 1991) 160–79. For fuller interaction with Martyn see my *The Theology of Galatians* (Cambridge: Cambridge University Press, 1993).

[54] Cf. Schlier, *Galater* 283; Longenecker, *Galatians* 298–9.

Chapter 10

How New was Paul's Gospel?

The Problem of Continuity and Discontinuity

One of the major issues which has resurfaced in current discussions of Pauline theology is the question of his gospel's newness. Was Paul's gospel in the last analysis simply a re-expression of God's centuries old summons to Israel? Or did it constitute a decisive break with everything that had gone before? The first question suggests what might be called a *heilsgeschichtlich* perspective, where the emphasis is on the line of continuity from Abraham, through Moses, David and the prophets, climaxing in Jesus, and on to Paul – alternatively expressed, the line of promise and fulfilment. In contrast, the second question suggests more of an *apocalyptic* perspective, where the emphasis is on discontinuity between the old and the new, the disruption caused by the inbreaking of the eschatological, the new creation.

The issue has come to focus in recent years as a consequence of two fresh or revitalized tendencies in 20th century Pauline discussion clashing with each other. One is the fairly recent reaction against the typical emphasis of Lutheran theology which poses gospel and law, and so also Christianity and Judaism, in sharp antithesis. Where this emphasis has been given determinative hermeneutical weight the almost inescapable inference has been one of discontinuity between the gospel of Paul and what went before. 'The new perspective on Paul',[1] however, has resulted in a reassessment of Paul's relation with his heritage (as then expressed in Second Temple Judaism), with counter emphasis on the continuity between the two.[2]

The other tendency is also a reaction, in this case against the de-apocalypticizing of Paul's gospel. The apocalyptic/eschatological[3] revolution in NT studies at

---

[1] This was my own attempt to characterise the impact of the work of E.P. Sanders, *Paul and Palestinian Judaism* (London: SCM, 1977), in a lecture under the same title, *BJRL* 65 (1983) 95–122 [=ch. 2 above], slightly revised in my *Jesus, Paul and the Law. Studies in Mark and Galatians* (London: SPCK/Louisville: Westminster, 1990) 183–206 (Additional Notes 206–14).

[2] See e.g. my *The Partings of the Ways between Christianity and Judaism* (London: SCM/Philadelphia: TPI, 1991), with bibliography.

[3] The terms have usually, and regretably, been used interchangeably. I use 'apocalyptic' in the customary sense of most discussions – that is, as embracing the differentiations between 'apocalypse', 'apocalyptic ideas' and 'apocalypticism' which a more analytical discussion would require. See e.g. J.J. Collins, *The Apocalyptic Imagination. An Introduction to the Jewish Matrix*

the turn of the century made its most characteristic impact on Pauline studies in works by A. Fridrichsen and E. Käsemann.[4] But the dominant mood seems to have favoured a downplaying of the apocalyptic/eschatological in favour of an emphasis on 'realized eschatology' or 'fulfilled messianism'.[5] The reaction in this case has been led by J.C. Beker in his assertion that apocalyptic provides the coherent theme of Paul's gospel, translated as it is into the contingent particularities of different human situations.[6] Here, in contrast to the first, the tendency has been to emphasize the discontinuities of the new age which breaks in upon and supercedes the old.

The clash of the two tendencies has been a feature of current discussion on Pauline theology. Representative of the *heilsgeschichtlich* perspective are R.B. Hays and N.T. Wright,[7] who both emphasise the ongoing story of Israel as underlying Paul's teaching. Representative of the apocalyptic perspective are J.L. Martyn, with his emphasis on the 'apocalyptic antinomies in Paul's letter to the Galatians',[8] and J. Bassler who in a recent paper argues that the resurrection of Jesus was for Paul 'an apocalyptic event marking the end of the old age and thus the end of the religious structures that defined the old age'.[9]

The issue is important since on it largely hangs, on the one hand, our understanding of the necessity and character of the Christ event, particularly the cross and resurrection, and on the other, the relation of Christianity to Israel and the religion of the OT. And since these questions have been close to the centre of Dick Longenecker's concerns in NT scholarship, from his original and too much neglected *Paul, Apostle of Liberty*,[10] to his excellent commentary on *Gala-*

---

of Christianity (New York: Crossroad, 1984) ch. 1.

[4] A. Fridrichsen, *The Apostle and his Message* (Uppsala: Lundequistska, 1947); E. Käsemann, 'Primitive Christian Apocalyptic', *New Testament Questions of Today* (London: SCM, 1969) 108–37 (particularly 131–7).

[5] See e.g. J.A. Fitzmyer, *Paul and his Theology. A Brief Sketch* (Englewood Cliffs, NJ: Prentice Hall, 1989) 46–9; R.N.Longenecker, 'The Nature of Paul's Early Eschatology', *NTS* 31 (1985) 85–95, who draws the phrase 'Fulfilled Messianism' from W.D. Davies (86).

[6] J.C. Beker, *Paul the Apostle. The Triumph of God in Life and Thought* (Philadelphia: Fortress, 1980).

[7] R.B. Hays, *The Faith of Jesus Christ: An Investigation of the Narrative Substructure of Galatians 3.1–4.11* (SBLDS 56; Chico, CA: Scholars, 1983); also 'Salvation history: The Theological Structure of Paul's Thought (1 Thessalonians, Philippians and Galatians)', in *Pauline Theology. Vol. 1: Thessalonians, Philippians, Galatians, Philemon*, ed. J. Bassler (Minneapolis: Fortress, 1991) 227–46; N.T. Wright, *The Climax of the Covenant* (Edinburgh: T. & T. Clark, 1991).

[8] J.L. Martyn, 'Apocalyptic Antinomies in Paul's Letter to the Galatians', *NTS* 31 (1985) 410–24. See also his 'Events in Galatia: Modified Covenantal Nomism versus God's Invasion of the Cosmos in the Singular Gospel', in *Pauline Theology. Vol. 1: Thessalonians, Philippians, Galatians, Philemon*, ed. J. Bassler (Minneapolis: Fortress, 1991) 160–79.

[9] J. Bassler, 'The Theology of Rom. 1.18–4.25. A Response to Andrew T. Lincoln', seminar paper at the Theology of Paul's Letters Group at the Society of Biblical Literature annual meeting, at Washington, DC, in November 1993.

[10] (New York: Harper & Row, 1964).

tians,[11] it would seem that the issue is one appropriate for an essay written in his honour.

We begin, naturally, by sketching out the two strands in Paul's statements of his gospel, which seem to be thus pulling in different directions, before going on to investigate whether, and if so how, the two strands can be held together in a single integrated understanding of Paul's theology and gospel. Not surprisingly the issue comes to sharpest focus in Paul's letters to the Galatians and to the Romans.

1. The continuity of the gospel

In many ways this is much the more obvious feature of Paul's gospel, so that it comes as something of a surprise that it should be put under such question. The point can be readily demonstrated even if we maintain quite a narrow focus on the theme of 'gospel' itself.

First, we should note that the term 'gospel' contains in itself an implication of continuity with and fulfilment of earlier hopes. In the debate between Strecker and Stuhlmacher the former has argued that the term was in effect drawn from the usage in the Caesar cult.[12] Were that the case the inference would be that the first Christian 'gospel', properly speaking, was a consequence of the confrontation between the new faith in Jesus and a prominent form of civic religion as the former spread into the wider hellenistic world. The line of dicontinuity would be clear. But Stuhlmacher provides the stronger line of argument[13] when he maintains that the term in earliest Christian thought and reflection was derived from Jesus' own use of Isa. 61.1–2 (Matt. 11.5/Luke 7.22; Luke 4.18; Acts 10.36; cf. Luke 6.20–21/Matt. 5.3–4), a passage which evidently influenced other strands of second Temple Judaism (*Pss. Sol.* 11.1; 1QH 23[= 18].14; 11QMelch 18). It is true that the coining of a singular noun usage ('the gospel') to describe the message about Jesus was itself a new step, but the fact that it was just this word which was chosen clearly reflects an early Christian conviction that their message about Jesus was in fulfilment of and a direct development from the older Isaianic hope of Israel's restoration.

Second, it is equally clear from Rom. 1.16–17 and Gal. 2.14–16 that the content of the gospel, or as Paul puts it in the latter passage, 'the truth of the gospel',

---

[11] (WBC 41; Dallas: Word, 1990).

[12] G. Strecker, 'Das Evangelium Jesu Christi', *Eschaton und Historie. Aufsätze* (Göttingen: Vandenhoeck, 1979) 183–228; also *EDNT* 2.70–4 – 'the primary dependence of the noun (εὐαγγέλιον) on Greek-Hellenistic tradition is evident' (180).

[13] P. Stuhlmacher, *Das paulinische Evangelium* (Göttingen: Vandenhoeck, 1968); also 'The Theme: The Gospel and the Gospels' and 'The Pauline Gospel', in *The Gospel and the Gospels*, ed. P. Stuhlmacher (Grand Rapids: Eerdmans, 1991) 1–25 (especially 19–24) and 149–72 (particularly 160–6 on Isa. 52.7, cited by Paul in Rom. 10.15).

comes to particular focus in 'the righteousness of God from/to faith' (Rom. 1.17), or, alternatively expressed, in a person's being justified through/from faith in Jesus Christ (Gal. 2.16). The point, once again, is that the language and theology of divine righteousness and of being justified (by God) is thoroughly rooted in the same language and expressive of the same theology found particularly in the Psalms and second Isaiah. In both cases the logic of God's covenant faithfulness is that his righteousness consists precisely in his saving and sustaining action on behalf of Israel (Pss. 31.1; 35.24; 51.14; 65.5; 71.2, 15; 98.2; 143.11; Isa. 45.8, 21; 46.13; 51.5, 6, 8; 62.1–2; 63.1, 7). It is thus integral to the gospel for Paul that it is to be understood both as for the Jew first and also as an outworking of the dictum given to Habakkuk (2:4): 'The righteous from faith shall live' (Rom. 1.16–17).[14] That this faith is now to be experienced as 'faith in Christ Jesus' (Gal. 2.16) does, of course, introduce a further and distinctively Christian element,[15] but the very title ('Christ') reminds us that this Christian faith at least began as faith in Jesus as Messiah, that is, in Jesus precisely as fulfilment of Jewish hope, and not as a wrenching away and apart from the hope and heritage of Israel.[16]

Equally notable, thirdly, is the way Paul describes the 'gospel' in his initial reference to it at the beginning of Romans – 'the gospel of God, which was promised beforehand through his prophets in the holy scriptures' (Rom. 1.1–2). The fact that Paul can speak of it as 'the gospel of God' (also Rom. 15.16; 2 Cor. 11.7; 1 Thes. 2.2, 8, 9), and not solely as 'the gospel of Christ/his Son' (Rom. 1.9; 15.19; 1 Cor. 9.12; 2 Cor. 2.12; 9.13; 10.14; Gal. 1.7; Phil. 1.27; 1 Thes. 3.2; 2 Thes. 2.14), contains in itself the same implication of a gospel defined in terms of its continuity with earlier scriptures, since the (usually unspoken) assumption in Paul's theology of God is that this is the one God whom Israel has always confessed (Rom. 3.30; 1 Cor. 8.6). To the same effect we read in the key verse, Rom. 3.21, that 'the righteousness of God has been revealed, as attested by the law and the prophets'. This simply confirms the point already made that the key content of the gospel ('the righteousness of God') was, for Paul, wholly drawn from the categories and theology of 'the law and the prophets'.

---

[14] See further my *Romans* (WBC 38; Dallas: Word, 1988) 40–6.

[15] The point is stronger for those who take the phrase πίστις Χριστοῦ as meaning 'the faith of Jesus' = the faith which Jesus exercised or the faithfulness (to God and his covenant promise) which Jesus displayed and embodied – a view supported by the honorand (see e.g. his *Paul* 150–1); but see below n. 17 and further my 'Once More, *PISTIS CHRISTOU*', *SBL 1991 Seminar Papers*, ed. E.H.Lovering (Atlanta: Scholars, 1991) 730–44.

[16] See particularly N.A. Dahl, 'The Crucified Messiah' and 'The Messiahship of Jesus', in his *The Crucified Messiah and Other Essays* (Minneapolis: Augsburg, 1974) 10–47; reprinted in his *Jesus the Christ. The Historical Origins of Christological Doctrine* (Minneapolis: Fortress, 1991) 15–47. See also my 'How Controversial was Paul's Christology?', in *From Jesus to John. Essays on Jesus and New Testament Christology in Honour of Marinus de Jonge*, ed. M.C. de Boer (JSNTS 84; Sheffield Academic, 1993) 148–67 (here 150–5).

Similarly in Gal. 3.8 Paul can even say that 'the gospel was preached before-hand to Abraham'. The thought is slightly different from the opening of Romans – not just *promised* beforehand (προεπηγγείλατο), but *preached* beforehand (προευηγγελίσατο). In a very real sense for Paul the gospel already existed, or at least was already in effect at the time of Abraham. Of course, Paul is pushing a line: that the gospel consists primarily or essentially in the promise to Abraham that all the nations would be blessed in him (Gen. 12.3; 18.18). But it was of cen-tral importance to Paul that this promise was an integral part of the three-fold promise originally made to Abraham (of seed, land and blessing), the covenant promise on which Israel's own self-understanding was founded. The line of con-tinuity could hardly be clearer.

This reminds us, fourthly, that a key element in Paul's argumentation is that justification by faith was nothing new. On the contrary, for Paul the definitive example of one so justified was Abraham (Rom. 4; Gal. 3). The fact that in the two letters devoted most fully to the exposition of Paul's gospel (Romans and Galatians) essentially the same line of argument is followed presumably should not be taken to indicate a lack of theological inventiveness on Paul's part. Rather it indicates just how crucial the paradigm provided by Abraham was for Paul's understanding of the gospel.

Integral to this argument is the claim that the Gentile believers are as much 'heirs of Abraham' as any Jew. The defining characteristic of Abraham as reci-pient of the promise was his acceptance of it by faith. Consequently the line of descent from Abraham in terms both of sonship and of promise is equally to be defined in terms of faith. The exposition of Gen.15.6 (Gal. 3.6–29) is bracketed precisely by this repeated claim: 'Know then that those of faith,[17] they are Ab-raham's sons ... And if you are Christ's, then are you Abraham's seed, heirs ac-cording to the promise' (Gal. 3.7, 29).[18] Fundamental to the Christian self-understanding expressed by Paul in this chapter, therefore, is the claim to conti-nuity, that unless the gospel can be understood as the fulfilment of the divine purpose which began to be unfolded with Abraham, it cannot be maintained, cannot properly be understood as the gospel of Christ.

The same point is made in the equivalent chapter in Romans, where Paul's language seems to fall over itself as he tries to maintain both the definitive char-acter of faith while also maintaining as strong and as full a line of continuity as possible with the promise to Abraham of seed – 'father of circumcision to those who are not only men of circumcision but who also follow in the footsteps of the faith of our father Abraham which he had in uncircumcision ... in order that the promise might be certain to all the seed, not to the one who is of the law only but

---

[17] The fact that 'those of faith' is a generalising out of the immediately preceding more spe-cific 'Abraham believed God' rules out any suggestion that 'those of faith' = those whose rela-tionship with God was derived from the faithfulness of Jesus Christ (see above n. 15)

[18] See further my *Galatians* (BNTC; London: A. & C. Black, 1993) *ad loc.*

also to the one who is of the faith of Abraham' (Rom. 4.12, 16).[19] The exegetical problems in this passage arise precisely because Paul was attempting to press for such a strong line of continuity between the gospel and the promise to Abraham, so much so that the inevitable question arose: if Gentile believers are seed of Abraham, then what of 'those of the circumcision', whose claim to an unbroken line of descent from Abraham is otherwise so much more clear and direct?

This line of reflection leads in turn, finally, to a reminder that for Paul the continuity of Israel was an integral part of Paul's understanding of the gospel. It is implicit in the much disputed final benediction in Galatians – peace and mercy be 'also on the Israel of God' (Gal. 6.16) – where the most obvious inference is that 'Israel' is understood as defined by the promise to Abraham (and Jacob/Israel), that is, a promise received by faith and including blessings for the nations (Gen. 28.13–14).[20] But even if the meaning and significance of Gal. 6.16 is more open to debate, the position is surely clear enough in Rom. 9–11. There Paul begins by reaffirming the richness of Israel's continuing blessings (9.4–5) and ends with the strongest assertion that the divine purpose for Israel is still in process of unfolding, soon (Paul hoped) to reach its climax (11.25–32). Integral to that hope once again was the understanding that Gentile believers had become participant in these blessings by being engrafted into the olive tree of Israel (11.16–24). To be noted is the fact that Paul was *not* thinking in terms of two separate entities, Israel and the church,[21] which he had to try to hold in balance or awkwardly to integrate, but was thinking only of the one living organism, Israel, in which individuals received and held their place by grace through faith.[22] Here perhaps most clearly of all the integration of 'gospel' and 'Israel' and the line of continuity from Abraham to Gentile believers come to clearest expression. Whether or not *Heilsgeschichte* is the best way to describe this theological assertion may be open to discussion; but certainly a direct continuity of divine saving purpose working in and through history seems to be clearly in view.

To sum up. Other aspects of this line of theological reflection could be opened up, but hopefully enough has been said to put the point beyond dispute. Integral to the gospel for Paul was the line of continuity whose clearest beginning was with Abraham. Not only was Abraham himself the beginning of the gospel and archetypal example of one 'justified by faith', but the gospel itself could only be adequately understood by Paul as the outworking of the promises to Abraham. Indeed, the line of continuity and fulfilment was so central to the gospel that

---

[19] On the difficulties of construing the passage, 4.12 in particular, see my *Romans ad loc.*

[20] See further my *Galatians* 344–6.

[21] It needs to be recalled that at this stage ἐκκλησία in Paul still denoted the local church, or church in an area (see e.g. J. Hainz, *Ekklesia. Strukturen paulinischer Gemeinde-Theologie und Gemeinde-Ordnung* [Regensburg: Pustet, 1972] 229–39, 250–5); the thought of 'the church' as universal, and thus as somehow having superceded 'Israel' had not yet appeared.

[22] See further my *Romans* 520, 539–40.

Paul would have judged the gospel itself to have failed had that line been decisively breached.

2. The discontinuity of the gospel

The element of discontinuity is more difficult to establish – or at least that is how
it appears at first glance. Nevertheless it can be argued strongly that such discontinuity is equally if not more fundamental to Paul's gospel than the element of
continuity.

Central to Paul's gospel is, of course, the death and resurrection of Jesus. It is
striking then that Paul refers to the cross in such apocalyptic terms. Thus already
in one of his earliest letters he can speak of Christ on the cross as the means by
which 'the world has been crucified to me and I to the world', so that what now
counts is 'the new creation' (Gal. 6.14–15). Here indeed, as Martyn points out,
we can speak of 'two different worlds'[23] – the cross functioning as a kind of break
point in history, so that the old creation has been replaced by the new. The same
association of thought underlies the powerful statement in 2 Cor. 5.16–21: at the
heart of the gospel of God's act of reconciliation in and through the death of
Christ is the 'new creation; the old has passed away, behold the new has come'
(5.17). The same thought comes to expression in Paul's talk elsewhere of dying
with Christ. Paul says that he himself 'died to the law' when he was crucified with
Christ (Gal. 2.19). A decisive shift, an eschatological shift through death to life,
has already taken place (Rom. 6.3–6); the old relationships have been broken
and ended by this death, so that a new relationship might take its place (7.4–6).

The same point comes through in Paul's even stronger emphasis on the resurrection of Christ (e.g. Rom. 10.9; 1 Cor. 15.17). For the resurrection of the dead is
itself an apocalyptic category (as expressed typically in such passages as Dan.
12.2; *1 Enoch* 51.1–2; *Apoc. Mos.* 13.3; 28.4; 41.3; 43.2; *2 Bar.* 50.2; Matt. 27.52–
53). To claim that this has already happened in Christ's resurrection, even 'the
resurrection of the dead' (Rom. 1.4 – not just his resurrection from the dead), is
again to claim that the normal course of history has been completely broken; a
wholly new and qualitatively different dimension of reality has come into play
which wholly leaves behind the old. 'Christ having been raised from the dead no
longer dies, death no longer exercises lordship over him' (Rom. 6.9).

Not only is the centre of Paul's gospel apocalyptic in character, but its whole
structure. Thus at the same point in the introduction to Galatians as Rom. 1.3–4
in Romans, Paul again cites what seems to be an established formula, which indicates the framework of theological perspective to which Paul can refer so briefly

---

[23] Martyn, 'Antinomies' 412.

because he took it for granted[24] – Jesus Christ, 'who gave himself for our sins to rescue us from the present evil age' (Gal. 1.4). This is a clear expression of what is generally regarded as the classic apocalyptic belief in the two ages, the present age and the age to come. To be sure, the belief came to full expression only in the later apocalypses *4 Ezra* and *2 Baruch* (*4 Ezra* 6.9; 7.12–13, 50, 113; 8.1; *2 Bar.* 14.13; 15.8; 44.11–15). But it was already implicit in the visions of Dan. 2 and 7, and, more to the point, the apocalyptic doctrine of the two ages is present in the Jesus tradition (Matt. 12.32; Mark 10.30; Luke 20.34–35). What is striking here, however, is not only the confirmation that earliest Christian thought was clearly marked by apocalyptic categories, but, more important, that for the Christian too the present age was marked out as an age of evil, under the thrall of evil powers (so also 1 Cor. 1.20; 2.6, 8; 2 Cor. 4.4; cf. Eph. 5.16). At this point the apocalyptic dualism with which the Pauline gospel is framed is as sharp and as pessimistic as the Qumran talk of 'the time of wickedness' (CD 6.10, 14; 12.23; 1QpHab. 5.7).

Taken with the talk of 'new creation' and 'resurrection' already noted, the conclusion seems hard to avoid: that for Paul the gospel meant not the extension forward in time of the ongoing line of salvation-history, but the breaking of that line, the irruption of a wholly new and different age upon the old; and that the latter (the old age) now has to be seen not as the age of antecedent or proleptic grace, but as the age characterised by evil from which the gospel provides the means of rescue.

Once this apocalyptic framework of Paul's gospel has been grasped, then so many other elements in his theology fall naturally into place. For example, the fact that he describes his 'conversion' in apocalyptic terms as a 'revelation' (Gal. 1.12, 16) – that is, not only as an unveiling of/from heaven, but an unveiling with eschatological significance, which unlocked the mystery of God's purpose hidden until now (cf. the apocalyptic dualism of 2 Cor. 4.4–6). Hence also Paul's use of the characteristically apocalyptic term 'mystery' itself (Dan. 2.18–19, 27–30; 1QS 3.23; 4.18; 1QpHab. 7.5; *1 Enoch* 103.2; 106.19; *2 Enoch* 24.3; *4 Ezra* 10.38; 14.5; Rev. 10.7) to describe his own sense of the eschatologically final revelation and commission which had been given to him (in the undisputed Paulines, explicit only in Rom. 11.25; but implicit also in 1 Cor. 2.7; and central in Col. 1.26–27; 2.2; 4.3; Eph. 1.9; 3.3–4, 9; 'the mystery of the gospel' – 6.19). Hence too the characteristic Pauline understanding of his apostleship to which Fridrichsen drew attention, as an eschatological apostleship (1 Cor. 15.8), last act in the denouement of God's purpose (1 Cor. 4.9; cf. Rom. 13.11–12; 1 Cor. 7.29–31), the means by which the final resurrection will come about (Rom. 11.13–15).

That the apocalyptic framework of Paul's gospel forces the student of Paul's letters to reckon with a very sharp form of discontinuity is clearest in 'the apoca-

---

[24] See e.g. my *Galatians* 34–5.

lyptic antinomies' of Galatians.[25] There, particularly in Gal. 4.21–31, Paul seems to go out of his way to stress the sharpness of distinction and opposition between the covenant of Sinai and the covenant of promise. In this passage the correspondence between the elements in the two columns[26] is not of *heilsgeschichtlich* continuity but of antithetical opposition, with the Jerusalem of apocalyptic vision ('the Jerusalem above') claimed wholly for the Pauline gospel and denied to the inhabitants of earthly Jerusalem, and with the promise claimed exclusively for those, like the Galatian believers, 'born according to the Spirit' (cf. 3.3, 14) and denied to the ethnic descendents of Abraham. The discontinuity could hardly be sharper. Hence the denial of the very term 'gospel' to those for whom that other line of descent from Abraham remained fundamental and of continuing validity in terms of promise (Gal. 1.6–9), where again the language which Paul uses to assert the sole validity of his own gospel is constitutively apocalyptic (1.11): 'to make known' (γνωρίζειν), as of a heavenly mystery (Dan. Th. 2.23, 28–30, 45; 5.7–8, 15–17; etc.; 1QpHab. 7.4–5; 1QH 12.[= 4].27–28; 15[= 7].27; Col. 1.27; Eph. 1.9; 3.3–5, 10; 6.19). Hence too the sharp contrast between the two ages can indeed become a sharp antithesis between life 'in the flesh' and life 'in the (eschatological) Spirit' (Rom. 7.5; 8.9), or between life 'under the law' and life 'under grace' (Rom. 6.14–15; Gal. 3.23–4.7). Here again the apocalyptic perspective of Paul's gospel pushes his formulation into the sharp antithesis from which grew, quite understandably, the sharpness of the antithesis between Christianity and Judaism in subsequent Christian theology.

Here too more could be said to develop the point in greater detail, but hopefully the point is already clear and beyond dispute: that Paul's gospel was fundamentally shaped by an apocalyptic perspective, inevitably so, given the constitutive force of the resurrection and the outpoured Spirit in Christian self-understanding; and that this made inevitable an emphasis on discontinuity be-

---

[25] See Martyn, as in n. 8 above.

[26] On the force of συστοιχεῖ in Gal. 4.25 see my *Galatians* 252. The following table is drawn from 244:

	two covenants	
(first covenant)	(second covenant)	
slave girl	free woman	
gives birth according to flesh	gives birth through promise	
Mount Sinai	(promise)	
bears children into slavery	mother (of the free)	
Hagar	Sarah	
present Jerusalem	the Jerusalem above	
in slavery	free	
wife with few children	abandoned, barren wife with many children	
	two sons	
born according to flesh	born according to Spirit	
persecutes	child of promise	
to be driven out – no inheritance	alone inherits	
born of slave girl	born of free woman	

tween old age and new, where the sense of belonging to the eschatologically new put everything else, including Israel's history, into the old and coloured it with the shades not just of unfulfilled promise, but also of dominance by flesh and evil powers.

3. Squaring the circle

Our conclusion thus far is that both perspectives, both that which can be characterised under the heading of *Heilsgeschichte*, and that which can be characterised under the heading of 'apocalyptic', are present in the Pauline letters. Indeed, not only are they both present, but they are both constitutive of Paul's theology, as expressed particularly in the letters to Rome and Galatia. They are *both* integral to the gospel propounded in these letters.

However, at the same time, it has to be acknowledged that they also seem to run counter to each other – the one proposing a continuity which seems to be broken by the discontinuity presumed by the other, the second implying a radically new start which seems to call in fundamental question what had gone before.

How are we to handle this tension within Paul's theology of the gospel? There are three possible strategies. One is to accept that the tension amounts to a destructive and unresolvable tension and then try to deal with it in those terms. The second attempts to deal with it in what might loosely be called 'rhetorical' terms: the tension is an expression of Paul's apologetic style. The third attempts a resolution in more theological terms: the tension itself is in fact also constitutive of the gospel; both perspectives are together integral to the coherence of Paul's gospel.

3.1 The first strategy suggests as the most obvious deduction that Paul was not a systematic thinker; he was not aware that the two perspectives cut across each other so much; he formulated his theology in an *ad hoc* way, to meet different crises or questions, and would not have been concerned had the degree of contradiction been pointed out to him. This is the solution of E.P. Sanders and H. Räisänen in regard to Paul's treatment of the law in particular.[27] But since Paul's attitude to the law is only the sharpest expression of the tension (contrast, for example, the negative ὑπὸ νόμον of Rom. 6.14–15 and Gal. 3.23, with the positive talk of Christians 'fulfilling' the law in Rom. 8.4 and Gal. 5.14), their conclusion with regard to the law applies more broadly. The conflict in Paul's treatment of the law simply indicates the issue on which the two perspectives come most obviously into conflict.

---

[27] E.P. Sanders, *Paul, the Law and the Jewish People* (Philadelphia: Fortress, 1983); H. Räisänen, *Paul and the Law* (WUNT 29; Tübingen: Mohr, 1983).

This may indeed be a conclusion to which we are in the end forced. But to accept it at the outset would be an exegesis of discourtesy. The more the claim of contradiction and incoherence is pressed, the more we have to wonder whether the claim is well founded, and if so, why Paul himself was not more aware of it. The challenge of discerning the rationale of Paul's gospel in its own first century Jewish/Christian terms may be demanding for 20th century western critics but it should not be lightly dismissed. Sanders may be content to dig out a Paul in his own image, as one who could live quite happily with theological incoherencies. But theologians concerned for the coherence of their own theology are less likely to be persuaded that Paul was any different. And Räisänen should not be surprised that an atomistic exegesis resulted in his discovering an atomistic theology of Paul. Where so little attention was given to the coherence of the movement of thought within individual letters it is hardly surprising that the major finding was of incoherence.

Nor can the problem be resolved by cutting the gordian knot – that is, accepting that the two perspectives are at such odds that the only solution is to deny one or other of the perspectives to Paul himself. Martyn so argues with regard to Galatians: Paul's theology is so through and through apocalyptic that the *heilsgeschichtlich* argument regarding sonship of Abraham can only be explained as being the argument of the Galatian 'teachers', that is, the argument which Paul in effect opposes in his letter.[28] But to read the argument of Gal. 3 in that way, as Paul embracing an argument with which he basically disagreed, is very strained indeed – particularly when in addressing what appears to be the rather different situation in Rome he uses more or less the same argument on his own behalf (Rom. 4). The data and considerations marshalled under § 1 above cannot be so easily sidelined in attempts to restate Paul's gospel. On the other front, it may be possible to demonstrate that Paul has to some extent 'de-apocalypticized' the eschatology of the gospel,[29] not least in shifting some at least of the eschatological significance backward on to the past event of Christ's (first) coming and resurrection; but it is important to recognize that the apocalyptic structure of his gospel remains intact.[30] Paul's gospel can no more be separated from the apocalyptic perspective (§2) than it can from the *heilsgeschtlich* perspective (§1). The tension remains.

3.2   The second strategy is to explore whether the tension can be explained in rhetorical terms. Could it not be that the tension between the salvation-history perspective and the apocalyptic perspective is the product of Paul's apologetic technique or evangelistic strategy?

---

[28] J.L. Martyn, 'A Law-Observant Mission to Gentiles: The Background of Galatians', *SJT* 38 (1985) 307–24; also 'Events in Galatia' in Bassler (above n. 8).

[29] Cf. J. Baumgarten, *Paulus und die Apokalyptik* (Neukirchen: Neukirchener, 1975).

[30] Beker, *Paul* pp. ch.8.

It could be argued, for example, that the two perspectives are simply alternative *metaphorical* ways of conceptualizing the gospel in its larger than individual significance. When Paul attempts to describe the impact of the gospel in other places he regularly makes use of a wide range of vivid metaphors, and these metaphors quite frequently conflict with each other. Thus he can describe conversion by the metaphors both of birth and of adoption (1 Cor. 4.15; Gal. 4.6), both of marriage and engagement (1 Cor. 6.17; 2 Cor. 11.2); effective preaching of the gospel can be equally a sowing, a grafting or a harvesting (1 Cor. 3.6–8; Rom. 11.17–24; 8.23); or the same metaphor (adoption) can be used both for conversion and for the final consummation (Rom. 8.15, 23). In each case the one metaphorical usage runs counter to the other.[31] So perhaps with the metaphors of 'salvation history' and 'apocalyptic'. The point is that with a metaphor one is not attempting precision of definition but offering an elucidating picture whose success as a metaphor may be evocative and emotive rather than definitive. In this case, the one metaphor would emphasize continuity and fulfilment, the other irruption and revelation from on high, but, or so it could be argued, the problem of inconsistency would come more in the metaphorical surplus and not so much in the points being thus emphasized.

Another way of explaining the inconsistency would be to argue that the apocalyptic emphasis comes more with Paul's own self-understanding as to his *personal* role in relation to the gospel, whereas the salvation-history perspective is activated more when he considers the *corporate* dimension of the gospel. Certainly it is noticeable that many of the passages with strong apocalyptic colouring cited in the second section above (§ 2) are in fact passages of self-testimony. Thus, in particular, the revelation was one which Paul himself received (Gal. 1.12, 16); 'I' died to the law and have been crucified with Christ (Gal. 2.19). The idea of the 'new creation' follows directly from Paul's talk of himself as crucified to the world and vice versa (Gal. 6.14–15), just as elsewhere the same thought is bound up with Paul's own sense of commissioning (2 Cor. 5.17–21). Or again, it is Paul's own commission as apostle to the Gentiles which will provide the trigger to the final events of Jewish restoration and endtime resurrection (Rom. 11.13–15); the mystery of God's final purpose was revealed to Paul himself (Rom. 11.25). The difference of perspective could therefore be the difference between Paul's memory of his conversion, as a wrenching, mould shattering, personal apocalypse, and his more reflective understanding of how God's purpose was working out in relation to his people Israel. Alternatively expressed, the tension is the tension in Paul's own self-understanding, as one who was both an Israelite and called to take the gospel to Gentiles.

---

[31] Cf. the range of ecclesiological metaphors in P.S. Minear, *Images of the Church in the New Testament* (Philadelphia: Westminster, 1960).

A third possible solution would be to argue that the different emphases are the result of Paul addressing *different circumstances*. This is a familiar solution to other, similar tensions in Paul. It has proved an effective consideration in the debate about Paul's developing eschatology and the delay of the parousia.[32] More to the point here, Paul himself indicates its potential as a solution with his famous description of his evangelistic strategy (1 Cor. 9.19–23).[33] Could it not be that the apocalyptic/salvation-history tension is of a piece with and even an expression of Paul's readiness to practise what must have appeared to many as self-contradictory life-styles? – life 'under the law' as consistent with the salvation-history perspective, and life 'outside the law' as consistent with the apocalyptic perspective? It might well follow that the apocalyptic perspective was more 'authentically' Pauline, more indicative of Paul's own priorities (cf. Rom. 14.14, 20). But it would also follow that the salvation-history perspective was equally an expression of Paul's personal determination to maintain the continuity between the gospel and its patriarchal and prophetic antecedents, his pastoral concern to support the Jewish members of his churches (cf. Rom. 14.14, 20!). Could the solution to this tension be simply, that where the eschatological significance of Christ's work was being undervalued in favour of the continuity of divine purpose, Paul emphasized the apocalyptic character of the gospel; whereas, where he perceived too strong an emphasis on the discontinuous newness of the gospel he preferred rather to emphasize its salvation-historical continuity with what had gone before? Alternatively expressed, Paul's theology was not like a mathematical point, but more like a plateau, where sometimes it was necessary to speak with one message and tone of voice on one side, and at others with different words and emphases on another. For modern commentators to ask for a greater consistency than that is to ask for a Paul who could not possibly have functioned effectively in the real world.

Any or all of these explanations may well have been factors in the tension evident in Paul's statement and defence of his gospel. But do they solve the problem too lightly? I am well aware that in circles where a more overt literary criticism flourishes an explanation in terms of rhetoric may be judged wholly sufficient. But the primary challenge comes here at the theological level, not solely at the level of the spoken word or of the missionary strategy. The question is whether for Paul the gospel which he preached was 'new' – new in content and character, new in the grace it claimed to embody (Gal. 1.6), new in the power for salvation which it brought to effect (Rom. 1.16) – or was it simply a recycling in different language of old truths and old claims? The question thus posed cannot find satisfaction except with a theological answer.

---

[32] See e.g. C.F.D. Moule, 'The Influence of of Circumstances on the Use of Eschatological Terms', *JTS* 15 (1964), reprinted in his *Essays in New Testament Interpretation* (Cambridge University, 1982) 184–99 – an essay, as I recall, much valued by Dick Longenecker.

[33] Cf. H. Chadwick, 'All Things to All Men (1 Cor. 9.22)', *NTS* 1 (1954–55) 261–75.

3.3   A theological explanation of the tension between the salvation-history and the apocalyptic perspectives of Paul's gospel has to begin by noting that both perspectives were characteristically Jewish. That is to say, the apocalyptic perspective of Paul was part of Paul's own Jewish heritage, part, we may say, of the salvation-history continuity between second Temple Judaism and Christianity. It need hardly be demonstrated that 'apocalyptic',[34] at least so far as it bears upon our discussion, was itself a native growth within second Temple Judaism (the Enoch apocalypses, Daniel, etc.). In other words, it was a perspective to which many Jews before Paul were drawn.

The point, of course, is that such Jews, in embracing an apocalyptic perspective, were not thereby abandoning a salvation-history perspective, they were not denying their heritage as Israelites. On the contrary, an apocalypse was itself a way of reaffirming the continuity of the past with the future as both God's. To be sure, the group whose perspective came to expression in an apocalypse evidently felt itself isolated and under severe threat; it saw itself as the prey of evil powers. The characteristically dualistic pessimism of the apocalyptic perspective with regard to the present age was itself an expression of the pressure under which such groups found themselves.[35] But fundamental to the same perspective was the claim of the apocalyptists, and those whom they represented, to embody *in themselves* the continuity of God's saving purpose from the past into the future. They may have been only a remnant; the rest of Israel may have become apostate; but in themselves at least the line of God's saving purpose was maintained. Moreover, the envisioned future might well reveal that the present blackness was merely temporary and that the age-old pattern of sin, exile and restoration (Deut. 29–30) would again be realised in the salvation of Israel as a whole.[36] In short, an apocalyptic perspective was a way of affirming salvation-history continuity when the faithful were suffering persecution and could see no other way for the covenant and its promises to be sustained.

A classic example of this is the apocalyptic perspective of the Essenes, particularly as we can now gain access to it through the Dead Sea Scrolls.[37] For they regarded themselves as the true Israel, the new covenant people (e.g. 1QS 8.4–9), but also as constantly threatened by the spirit of wickedness (1QS 3.13–4.26), and preparing for the final battle between the sons of light and the sons of darkness (1QM). In the DSS, we may say, *heilsgeschichtlich* and apocalyptic perspectives are well (not fully) integrated and feed into each other. The tension be-

---

[34] Note again n. 3 above.

[35] See further P.D.Hanson, 'Apocalypticism', *IDBSupp* 28–34.

[36] See further the discussion of E.P. Sanders, *Paul and Palestinian Judaism* (London: SCM, 1977) 240–57; also 361, 367–74, 378 (*Jubilees*) and 398–406, 408 (*Psalms of Solomon*).

[37] See e.g. P.D.Hanson, *The People Called. The Growth of Community in the Bible* (San Francisco: Harper & Row, 1986) 364–72.

tween the two perspectives present in a document like 1QpHab is, in effect, sharper than anything we find in Paul.

So too when we turn to Paul. The apocalyptic understanding of the death and resurrection of Christ, which came to Paul in his own personal apocalypse on the Damascus road, did not wholly cut Paul off from his past. Of course, it gave him a fresh perspective on his past as a Pharisee, and he had to redefine his relationship with Judaism (1 Cor. 15.8–9; Gal. 1.13–14), but it did not cause him to renounce his heritage as an Israelite. On the contrary, for Paul the revelation was one which showed him how the ancient promises and hopes were to be fulfilled. It was new in that it focused in Jesus, but the new gospel was also the foretold way of completing the old purpose. In particular, the Damascus road revelation showed Paul how the ancient promises to the patriarchs were to be fulfilled – not just the promise of seed and land, but also the promise of blessing to the nations (Gal. 1.15–16; Gen. 12.3; 18.18). If it took a quantum leap of (apocalyptic) revelation to bring this home to Paul, the revelation was of Jesus as the means by which these promises were to be fulfilled – Jesus as both the content of the new revelation and the hinge of continuity between old and new.

It is relevant to note here that the newness of the revelation to Paul made for tension not only with Paul's ancestral Judaism but also with the first Jerusalem Christians. The underlying issue at this point comes to focus not simply on the relation between Judaism and Christianity, but also on the relation between Jesus and Paul, between the gospel as understood by the first followers of Jesus and the gospel of Paul.[38] The more Jesus himself is recognized to be a Jew of Jews,[39] and the more the first (post-Easter) believers are seen in direct continuity with the pre-Easter Jesus, the more will the salvation-history/apocalyptic tension tend to force Jesus and Paul apart, with catastrophic effects for our evaluation of the relationship of historic 'Christianity' with the one named as its founder (Jesus). But if, in contrast, we accept Paul's assertion that his gospel was continuous with the earliest proclamation of Christ (particularly 1 Cor. 15.1–12), and if we accept that the apocalyptic 'extra' focuses on the 'to the Gentiles' emphasis in Paul's gospel (Gal. 1.15–16),[40] then it becomes necessary to retain the salvation-history/ apocalyptic tension in Paul's gospel without flinching. Indeed, it is precisely the dynamic of this tension which thrust Paul the Jew forth as apostle to the nations, precisely this tension which caused such misunderstandings between Paul and his Christian fellow Jews.

---

[38] See my 'The Relationship between Paul and Jerusalem according to Galatians 1 and 2', *NTS* 28 (1982) 461–78; reprinted in my *Jesus, Paul and the Law* (London: SPCK/Louisville: Westminster, 1990) 108–26.

[39] This is now almost a commonplace in current redefinition of 'the historical Jesus'. See e.g. J.H. Charlesworth, ed., *Jesus' Jewishness. Exploring the Place of Jesus in Early Judaism* (New York: Crossroad, 1991).

[40] See also my *Unity and Diversity in the New Testament* (London: SCM, 1977, ²1990) 66–7.

In short, the degree of integration of the two perspectives (salvation-history and apocalyptic) within pre-Christian Judaism makes one wonder if the tendency to see the two perspectives as mutually exclusive is simply a false reading of Paul by technicians who have too much lost sight of the historical context within which Paul framed and preached his gospel. Certainly we must be careful about defining Pauline Christianity simply as a kind of Judaism (continuity); but equally we must beware of falling into the old trap of thinking that Christianity can only define itself in opposition to Judaism (discontinuity).

3.4 If we now step back from the narrower focus of our discussion thus far, it becomes possible to see our particular issue within a wider theological framework. For the salvation-history/apocalyptic tension in Paul's gospel can be understood as just another expression of a tension which is inescapable in any theistic soteriology. Wherever theology allows for divine intervention into or interaction with the continuities of history and nature, there is bound to be just such a tension.

The tension can come to expression in various ways. It is the tension of cosmos understood as creation, of a creation understood as flawed but still God's and still instrument of his purposes. When a gospel of salvation supervenes upon the story of that creation the tension becomes acute, and human theology has so far found it possible to maintain it as a fruitful tension only by means of myth.

Again, it is the tension of a single people (Israel) chosen for his own out of all the nations by the one God, whose purposes for his creation as a whole are nonetheless good. The tension in the promises to the patriarchs, between particularism (seed and land) and universalism (all the nations) (§1 above), is itself the fundamental expression of that tension. That was why Paul was able to make such effective use of it in holding that the revelation to him was simply of how the ancient promise should be fulfilled, how the ancient tension should be finally resolved. By setting the choice of Israel within the wider purpose of the creator God, the tension between 'particular grace' and 'general grace', between salvation and providence could become fruitful in good news.

Again, it is the tension between tradition and revelation, between the authority claimed for past revelation and the claims of new revelation. This too is a tension which runs through the Christian Bible and beyond; it is not simply the tension between 'Old Testament' and 'New Testament'. It is there already in the reshaping of patriarchal religion by Yahwism.[41] It is there in the impact of the Deuteronomist and of the Ezra reforms on the shape of Israelite religion. It is implicit in the formation of 'Judaism' as such in the Maccabean and post-Maccabean period, though the tension there is more evident in the non-canonical writ-

---

[41] See R.W.L. Moberly, *The Old Testament of the Old Testament* (Minneapolis: Fortress, 1992).

ings of apocrypha and pseudepigrapha (including, of course, the various apocalypses). It is there in the tension between Jesus the Jew, the Jewish eschatological
prophet perceived as the Christ raised from the dead and exalted to Lordship at
God's right hand. It is there, as we have already noted, in the tension between
Paul's gospel to the Gentiles, which is also the gospel of God, the gospel of
Christ, the gospel of those who preach Jesus as the Christ. And it is there in the
subsequent tension between scripture and tradition which has been fruitful of
such controversy within Christianity throughout its history. Of course, for Christians, the tension between Old Testament and New is peculiarly sharp. The revelatory significance of the Christ-event has a fundamental and definitive quality
which makes it stand out from all other claims to revelatory significance. Nonetheless, the fact remains that the revelation of Christ presupposes a continuity
with past (and future) revelation, without which the gospel would not be the gospel of Jesus Christ.

The tension comes to expression not least as the tension integral to the salvation process in Paul's gospel itself. For it is a gospel itself suspended between the
two poles of what has already happened and what is still to happen, between, in
the familiar terms of Pauline studies, the 'already' and the 'not yet'. The Christ
has come, but is yet to come. The Spirit has been given, but only as the beginning
of complete redemption.[42] To put the point more sharply, the apocalyptic rup-
ture with the past is itself ruptured; the aorist indicatives describing entry into
faith have to be accompanied by imperative exhortations and still future
promises (characteristically in Rom. 6–8). Ironically, the eschatological discontinuity has to become an ongoing perspective which makes room for the continuity of individual body, corporate society and fallen cosmos, all conjointly
awaiting the liberation of consummation (Rom. 8.18–23), otherwise it will succumb to millenial revolution or escapist quietism.

It is precisely at this point that the discontinuity between Christianity and its
antecedent Judaism is itself relativized within the more fundamental continuity
– as can be seen most clearly in Gal. 4. There the 'apocalyptic antinomies' are at
their sharpest (4.21–31); there the coming of God's Son is itself indication of eschatological completion and finality (τὸ πλήρωμα τοῦ χρόνου – 4.4). And yet in
that very context the discontinuity is posed precisely as that of the heir who is a
minor in contrast to the adopted son who is already entering into the inheritance
(4.1–7). Moreover, the latter entering in is itself only anticipatory of the complete transformation (4.19), the full inheritance (5.21). The point is, that *both*
Jew and Christian (to use the still somewhat anachronistic distinction) are heirs,
and *both* have not yet entered into the (full) inheritance promised them. The
new beginning can be decisive only as the eschatological completion of the old
hope, but as the eschatological completion it is still incomplete.

---

[42] See e.g. my *Jesus and the Spirit* (London: SCM/Philadelphia: Westminster, 1975) 308–42.

In short, the tension between a *heilsgeschichtlich* and an apocalyptic perspective in Paul's gospel is inescapable, precisely because he took so seriously all these several tensions in the framing of his gospel and theology. It was not that the Damascus road revelation resolved tensions which he had known as a Pharisee and persecutor of the church. Rather it was that the new revelation of Christ introduced that tension, or brought out in a new way and with a new intensity a tension which had always been there in his ancestral religion and in the faith which he had persecuted so vigorously. It is the tension of his gospel simply because it is the tension of his theology, simply because any theology is bound to find itself caught in such a tension.

4. Conclusion

How new then was Paul's gospel? It was new in that it focused on Jesus the Christ. It was new in that it came to sharpest focus in Christ's death and resurrection as providing the decisive salvific key. It was new in that it understood its dynamic (the Spirit) by reference to Christ. It was new in the way it understood the nations at large to be recipients of the blessing now available through Christ.

Moreover, it was new in its claim of something having happened that had never happened before – God active in history in and through a man in a way only foreshadowed but not previously realized. It is new in the claim that in Christ God accomplished his will in a climactic way, without which, from a Christian perspective at least, what had gone before remains incomplete and unfulfilled.

Yet, at the same time and in every case Paul understood the newness as a fresh and final unfolding of ancient promise – new not so much in the 'what' as in the 'how'. Without that ancient promise the new would have been so strange and foreign that it would not have been recognized or preached by Paul as gospel. It was precisely as the revelation of what had been the divine intention from the first that Paul was able to embrace it and to be embraced by it. In short, we may say that it was the continuity in the discontinuity, the apocalyptic climax of the salvation-history which constituted the heart of his gospel.

Chapter 11

Was Paul against the Law?

The Law in Galatians and Romans:
a test-case of text in context

It would hardly be surprising if someone brought up in Protestant Christianity thought of Judaism as the antithesis of Christianity. The impression is rooted deeply in the basic gospel/law dialectic of Lutheran theology, where gospel, not unnaturally, is identified with Christianity, and law, also not unnaturally, is identified with Judaism. Even in the period following the second world war, when Christian conscience had been sensitised by the horror of the Holocaust, Christian scholarship still spoke of pre-Christian Judaism as Spätjudentum, of Jesus as having marked the end of Judaism, of Paul as having been converted from Judaism to Christianity.[1] The inconsistency of talking about first century Judaism as 'late' hardly seems to have dawned on those who so spoke: if *first* century Judaism is *late*, what do we call the last nineteen centuries of Judaism? The doublethink was occasioned, of course, by the idea that Judaism's only role was as precursor to Christianity; now that Christianity had come, Judaism no longer counted for anything.

In the last quarter-century, however, the picture has begun to change rapidly. The term 'late Judaism' no longer appears in scholarly circles; now the same period is usually, and more appropriately called 'early Judaism'. The Jewish reclamation of Jesus has gone apace and many NT specialists now talk of a 'third quest of the historical Jesus', where the quest's distinctive new angle has been to focus on Jesus within the context of his own people, Jesus the Jew.[2] In both these cases the old language has been completely abandoned, its inappropriateness widely recognized.

---

[1] See e.g. the critiques of C. Klein, *Anti-Judaism in Christian Theology* (London: SPCK, 1978), and J.T. Pawlikowski, *Christ in the Light of the Christian-Jewish Dialogue* (New York: Paulist, 1982) ch. 3.

[2] See e.g. D. Hagner, *The Jewish Reclamation of Jesus* (Grand Rapids: Zondervan, 1984); S. Neill & T. Wright, *The Interpretation of the New Testament 1861–1986* (Oxford University, 1988) 379–403; J.H. Charlesworth, ed., *Jesus' Jewishness. Exploring the Place of Jesus in Early Judaism* (New York: Crossroad, 1991); G. Vermes, *The Religion of Jesus the Jew* (London: SCM, 1993).

With Paul, on the other hand, while the same process of reassessment is under way, its outcome is far from clear. It is true that the few lone voices who maintained that Paul's Damascus road experience should be seen as a call rather than a conversion,[3] have been joined by many others. But the idea that Paul had to abandon Judaism in order to become a Christian is still deeply entrenched. And nothing like the Jewish reclamation of Jesus has taken place in the case of Paul; for most Jews, he is still Paul the apostate.[4] Yet, should the tide of reassessment stop short at Paul? Has the relationship between Christianity and Judaism as summed up in the person of Paul been re-examined with sufficient thoroughness? The subject matter is sufficiently important to warrant further investigation.

The issue comes to sharpest focus in the question of the law. The prevailing impression within NT scholarship is still that Paul broke with or abandoned the law when he became a Christian. The text which best sums up what is again a particularly Lutheran perspective is Rom 10:4 – 'Christ is the end of the law ...'.[5] Typical also is the judgment that Paul had persecuted the Hellenists for their breach with the law – an inference drawn largely from a combination of Acts 6.13, Gal. 3.13 and Phil. 3.6 – and was thus converted to what he had persecuted.[6] Particularly vehement is Hans Hübner in his thesis that Paul was uniformly hostile to the law in Galatians, though Hübner also maintains that Paul modified his position somewhat in writing the later Romans.[7] Others prominent in recent discussion are content to find Paul inconsistent in his written views of the law.[8]

Here then is a topic, Paul and the law, where the problem of relating text and context is nicely posed in its complexity. Is the context within which the issue should be weighed that of traditional Lutheran, Gospel/law dialectic? Or should it be the historical context within which Paul himself operated, so far as that may be recovered? Should the issue be handled 'in front of' the text (a hermeneutical exercise), or 'behind' the text (an exegetical exercise)? Again, where two texts seem to be somewhat at odds with each other, should the questions raised be

---

[3] Notably K. Stendahl, 'The Apostle Paul and the Introspective Conscience of the West', *HTR* 56 (1963) 199–215, reprinted in his *Paul Among Jews and Gentiles* (London: SCM/Philadelphia: Fortress, 1977) 84–5.

[4] The issue is sympathetically handled by A. Segal, *Paul the Convert. The Apostolate and Apostasy of Saul the Pharisee* (New Haven: Yale University, 1990).

[5] See e.g. P. Stuhlmacher, '"Das Ende des Gesetzes". Über Ursprung und Ansatz der paulinischen Theologie', *Versöhnung, Gesetz und Gerechtigkeit* (Göttingen: Vandenhoeck, 1981) 166–91.

[6] E.g. S. Kim, *The Origin of Paul's Gospel* (Tübingen: Mohr, 1981); C. Dietzfelbinger, *Die Berufung des Paulus als Ursprung seiner Theologie* (WMANT 58; Neukirchen: Neukirchener, 1985).

[7] H. Hübner, *Law in Paul's Thought* (Edinburgh: T. & T. Clark, 1985).

[8] E.P. Sanders, *Paul, the Law and the Jewish People* (Philadelphia: Fortress 1984/London: SCM, 1985); H. Räisänen, *Paul and the Law* (WUNT; Tübingen: Mohr, 1984/Philadelphia: Fortress, 1986).

handled inter-textually, or inter-contextually, or inter-text-within-contextually? And should a coherence be sought between two texts (Galatians and Romans) by the same author (Paul), or should we moderns be content to make as much sense as we can of each text on its own, lest any linking pattern be of our own devising?

In order to keep the discussion within the confines of a single paper I will limit it to the question posed in the title, Was Paul against the law?, and to the two letters of Paul in which the question of the law is treated most fully (Galatians and Romans). We proceed by examining the way the law is treated in each of the two letters in turn before asking whether and if so how the two treatments hang together coherently.

1. The law in Galatians

1.1 The law as an angelic power

It is easy to draw a very negative picture of the law from Galatians. The impression is strongest in the section Gal. 3.19–4.11. Paul has been speaking of the promise to Abraham, recalling particularly the promises to Abraham in Gen. 12.3 and 7 (Gal. 3.8, 16). The law came 430 years later (at Sinai), but it does not make the earlier promise void. 'For if the inheritance is from law, it is no longer from promise; but to Abraham God gave it freely through promise' (3.18). Since the earlier references to the law had been consistently refutational (2.16, 19, 21; 3.2, 5, 10–13 – 'not from works of the law', 'died to the law', 'by the law no one is justified'), it can be plausibly argued that this further oppositional juxtaposition of law with promise prepares the reader for a thoroughly negative assessment of the law in the verses which follow.

3.19 – 'Why then the law?' To which the answer is given, τῶν παραβάσεων χάριν προσετέθη – 'it was added because of transgressions'. The force of the χάριν is not immediately clear, but a cross (intertextual) reference to Romans (context of Paul's thought) may be said to strengthen the negative tone of the immediately preceding context. The parallel with Rom. 3.20 suggests the sense, 'in order to bring about a knowledge of transgressions', to make sin a conscious act.[9] While the closer parallel with Rom. 5.20 ('the law came in to increase the

---

[9] So M.J. Lagrange, *Galates* (EB; Paris: Gabalda, ²1925) 82; E. de W. Burton, *Galatians* (ICC; Edinburgh: T. & T. Clark, 1921) 188; F. Mussner, *Galaterbrief* (HTKNT; Freiburg: Herder, ³1977) 245–6; R.N. Longenecker, *Galatians* (WBC 41; Dallas: Word, 1990) 138; 'to make wrong-doing a legal offence' (NEB/REB).

trespass') suggests the more negative force, 'in order to bring about transgressions'.[10]

3.19 – 'it was ordered through angels by the hand of an intermediary'. The reference is most obviously to Moses, as most agree.[11] Once again the text sounds fairly innocuous, but the next verse ('Now an intermediary means that there is not just one party; but God is one') indicates clearly enough that the contrast between the law and the promise is being maintained: the promise was given directly by God to Abraham, whereas the law came to Israel at one remove. However, the allusion to 'angels' adds a further complication: does it imply that the law was still more remote from God, with not only Moses but also angels intervening? Or is it, indeed, an attempt to remove the law completely from the domain of God? So some would argue: the clause is 'a categorical denial of the divine origin of the Torah';[12] the law 'is the product of demonic angelic powers'.[13] Here the exegetical rationale is once again the negative tone of the preceding context. And though the sudden sharpness of antagonism and degree of hostility is unexpected, a Christian interpretation of the law as the product of fallen angels can be shown to go back to at least within two generations of Galatians (Barn. 9.4 – 'they erred because an evil angel was misleading them').

After a further contrast between the law and the promise (3.21–22), the more sharply negative tone seems to be resumed. 3.23 – 'before the coming of this faith we were held in custody under the law, confined (ὑπὸ νόμον ἐφρουρούμεθα συγκλειόμενοι) ...'. Here the negative features come thick and fast. The law is treated as though it were a cosmic power, like sin – the ὑπὸ νόμον of 3.23 paralleling the ὑπὸ ἁμαρτίαν of 3.22. In other words, the law itself seems now to be identified with the (evil) angels of 3.19. Moreover, the first verb (ἐφρουρούμεθα) could have a very negative sense, 'held in subjection', and the second (συγκλειόμενοι) strikes the same note, 'confined' or 'imprisoned'. Hence, for example, NIV – 'held prisoners by the law, locked up'.[14]

With this picture in mind it is hardly surprising if the next verse stirs up a similar picture of a rule tyrannous and harsh in character. 3.24 – 'so that the law became our custodian (παιδαγωγός) to Christ'. The image is the familiar one of the slave who conducted a boy to and from school. In such a case, where the word (παιδαγωγός) appears in only one other passage within Paul's letters (and

---

[10] So e.g. BAGD, χάριν 1; H. Schlier, *Galater* (KEK; Göttingen: Vandenhoeck, ⁴1965) 152–4; H.D. Betz, *Galatians* (Hermeneia; Philadelphia: Fortress, 1979) 163 – the phrase 'is to be taken in a wholly negative way'.

[11] Betz 170 notes that 'by the hand of Moses' became almost a formula in the LXX. See further Longenecker 140–3.

[12] J.W. Drane, *Paul: Libertine or Legalist?* (London: SPCK, 1975) 34, 113; similarly T. Zahn, *Galater* (Leipzig: Deichert, 1905) 171; Lagrange 83; R. Bring, *Galater* (Berlin: Lutherisches, 1968) 144–6; R.B. Hays, *The Faith of Jesus Christ* (Chico: Scholars, 1983) 227.

[13] Hübner 24–36.

[14] So also R.Y.K. Fung, *Galatians* (NICNT; Grand Rapids: Eerdmans, 1988) 168.

the NT – 1 Cor. 4.15), and where it clearly alludes to a familiar figure within ancient society, the exegete has little choice but to refer to the context of the times for illumination. In this case what has generally made most impression is the fact that in the literature of the time the παιδαγωγός is a figure often criticised for his abuse of power or is treated as a figure of fun.[15] In consequence, it has been natural to regard the reference here in a strongly negative light,[16] an impression if anything strengthened by the repetition of the phrase, ὑπὸ παιδαγωγόν, in 3.25.

The climax comes in 4.8–10, where Paul seems once again to liken the law to a spiritual power, but now to identify it still more clearly with the gods that are 'no gods' and the 'beggarly elemental forces'. For the Galatians to 'observe days and months and special times and years' was to put themselves back into slavery to such non- or radically inferior beings. To grasp the full train of thought it is again important for the exegete to be aware of such contextual factors as the Jewish attitude to other gods and the widespread belief within the ancient world that human life was influenced by the primal and cosmic forces which shaped and regulated the world as a whole.[17] Also of the fact that 'days, months, special times and years' almost certainly refer to Jewish feasts and festivals.[18] For a Jew to disown the law to such an extent, to lump it together with non-gods and the basic stuff of the cosmos, was an extraordinary turnabout, which alone would seem to make unavaoidable an affirmative answer to the question posed in the title. It looks very much as though Paul was turning wholly against the traditional Jewish belief that God had appointed angels to rule the other nations, but had kept Israel for himself (Deut. 32.15; Sir. 17.17). No! says Paul, in effect, the law has been Israel's angel, and, as in the hostile variation on the older tradition in *Jubilees* 15.31–32, the purpose of this angelic power, of the law, was to lead astray the people over which it ruled. Jewish disdain of the nations has been turned against itself using the law for leverage.

This then is the heart of the case for reading the text of Galatians as a hostile polemic against the law. But is the justification sufficient? Has the context within which the text has been read been too selective and restrictive? In fact an equally, and indeed more persuasive case can be made for reading the same key passages in a much more positive way.

In the case of 3.19a the issue centres on the meaning of χάριν. Here we need to recall that the word is the accusative form of χάρις, 'grace, favour', and that its usual meaning as attested elsewhere in usage of the time is 'for the sake of, on

---

[15] Betz 177.

[16] See e.g. Schlier 168–70; A. Oepke, *Galater* (THNT; Berlin: Evangelische, ³1973) 121–2; Betz 177–8 – 'the pedagogue ... an ugly figure', 'the radical devaluation of the law'.

[17] See further the main commentaries on Galatians, all of which wrestle with the precise reference of these terms, particularly τὰ στοιχεῖα τοῦ κόσμου in 4.3 and 9.

[18] See my *Galatians* (BNTC; London: A. & C. Black, 1993) 227–9.

behalf of, on account of'.[19] This suggests a much more immediately gracious objective for the law than simply 'to make conscious of transgressions', and certainly than 'to provoke transgressions'. It suggests, in fact, the purpose of the law as it was generally recognized within the (OT) scriptures and the Judaism of Paul's time: that is, as a means of dealing with transgressions. In other words, what was probably in mind here was the whole sacrificial cult at whose centre was the provision of means for covering sin and removing guilt, means of atonement. The fact that the law has been set in contrast with promise up to this point in Galatians naturally gives rise to the question, 'Why then the law?' But the flow of thought is equally well served if the answer to the question begins to explain the positive function of the law. Here we might say, then, is a battle of contexts: does it make more sense to read Gal. 3.19a in the light of Rom. 5.20, where the thought is rather different and the key term χάρις has a quite different function, or in the light of the positive, indeed gracious function which the law actually did serve for Israel from Sinai onwards?

As for the angels of 3.19b, it is certainly the case, as already noted, that the phrase strengthens the contrast with the promise, the double phrase, 'through angels' and 'by the hand of an intermediary', heightening the contrast with the immediacy of God's promise given to Abraham. But that said, it has also to be said that the reference itself does not imply that the angels in question were hostile or evil. On the contrary, anyone familiar with Jewish tradition would think most naturally of the well established Jewish belief that angels were indeed associated in the giving of the law (Deut. 33.2 LXX – 'angels from his right hand were with him [the Lord]'; *Jub.* 1.29–2.1; Philo, *Som.* 1.143; Josephus, *Ant.* 15.136; *Apoc. Mos.* preface).[20] And since the motif was also familiar elsewhere in Greek speaking Christianity (Acts 7.38, 53; Heb. 2.2), the most natural inference is that Paul intended the same allusion. In other words, the allusion, while marking a contrast with the promise, certainly did not deny the law was given from God – even if at one or two removes. Here too, we may say, an awareness of the broader context of the time undermines an interpretation dependent on a rather narrow reading of the text.

Similarly with 3.23 and 24. In the former we do well to note that the principal sense of φρουρέω is 'guard, watch over', as in the case of a city garrison (2 Cor. 11.32), or 'to protect, keep', as in the only two other NT uses (Phil. 4.7; 1 Pet. 1.5). That is to say, what Paul had in mind was probably a *protective* custody.[21] Which fits well with the image of the παιδαγωγός in 3.24. For here too the image

---

[19] LSJ, χάρις VI.1.

[20] See further Str-B 3:554–6; T. Callan, 'Pauline Midrash: The Exegetical Background of Gal 3:19b', *JBL* 99 (1980) 549–67.

[21] So Oepke 120; P. Bonnard, *Galates* (CNT; Neuchâtel: Delachaux, 1953) 75; D. Guthrie, *Galatians* (NCB; London: Oliphants, 1969) 108; U. Borse, *Galater* (RNT; Regensburg: Pustet, 1984) 137.

was essentially positive – the slave given the responsible task of protecting his young charge and of instructing him in good manners. Of course the figure of the pedagogue became a butt for many a joke, as has the child's governess and school teacher in subsequent generations. But the essentially positive role is hardly to be thus gainsaid, as recent studies have confirmed.[22] Here again we have to conclude that an awareness of broader usage of language and metaphor, such as Paul could assume on the part of his more literate readers, prevents a reading which can be justified only by ignoring that wider usage and by pushing for a constricted reading of the text.

In short, if indeed Paul was linking the law with angels and thinking of the law itself as a kind of angelic power, it begins to look as though it was the law as a kind of *guardian* angel which Paul had in mind. This provisional conclusion requires further analysis.

1.2 The temporary role of the law as guardian angel

As already noted, there seems to be a predominantly negative thrust in all Paul's early references to the law in Galatians. To be precise, specific reference to the law as such is delayed until 2.16, but then between 2.16 and 3.18 'law' is mentioned fourteen times. The initial references are all to 'works of the law', all in the negative formulation, 'by works of the law' (ἐξ ἔργων νόμου), a phrase which recurs six times in the sequence (2.16; 3.2, 5, 10). The others talk of dying to the law, deny that righteousness and the inheritance comes through the law, set the law and faith in antithesis, and speak of the curse of the law (2.19, 21; 3.11–13, 18). But it is only with 3.19 that the question of the law's actual purpose is addressed. If it is so clear what it was not for, why then was it given? In the flow of Paul's argument the question was inevitable and unavoidable.

Of course, the answer Paul gives in reference to the *function* of the law is contested, as we have seen (§ 1.1). But there can be little dispute that Paul regarded this function as *temporary*. The law was given well after the promise (430 years), and therefore cannot be confused with or understood as part of the promise or render the promise null and void (3.17–18). And it was 'added ... until the coming of the seed to whom the promise was made' (3.19), until faith could be directed to the seed, Jesus Christ.

Before the coming of this faith we were held in custody (ἐφρουρούμεθα)
under the law, confined till the faith which was to come should be
revealed, so that the law became our custodian (παιδαγωγός) to Christ,
in order that we might be justified from faith. But with faith having
come, we are no longer under the custodian (3.23–25).

---

[22] See particularly D.J. Lull, "'The Law was our Pedagogue": A Study in Galatians 3:19–25', *JBL* 105 (1986) 481–98; N.H. Young, 'παιδαγωγός: The Social Setting of a Pauline Metaphor', *NovT* 29 (1987) 150–76.

Notable is the use of the first person plural, which most obviously betrays the perspective of one who thought of himself as a member of Israel, as a Jew.[23] To be sure, it is the perspective of one who recalls an earlier period as one of confinement from which he has now been delivered, the perspective of one who saw himself as having previously been under a custodian slave but who had now reached an age of maturity when the παιδαγωγός was no longer necessary. Whatever debate there may be over the fine print, therefore, the main thrust of this paragraph is surely clear enough: the role of the law as custodian (for Israel) was limited in time; it was a role which had extended from Sinai to the coming of the promised seed and to the proclamation of faith in him.

What this means within the sweep of God's saving purpose is elaborated with a correlated metaphor in 4.1–7. Children of Abraham are heirs of the promise to Abraham (of seed and blessing). But so long as they are under age they are under guardians and stewards, appointed by their father. Only when they reach the appropriate age of maturity do they begin to enter into their inheritance – something achieved (for Gentiles as well) by the coming of Christ and of the Spirit. Since 4.1–7 in effect constitutes a recapitulation of the argument of 3.23–29,[24] the point is clear enough so far as the law is concerned. To be under the law is to be under a custodian (παιδαγωγός), is to be under guardians and stewards (4.2). The law, in other words, has a temporary role for Israel because the coming of Messiah and his Spirit marks the point in time/history at which Israel's transition from childhood to (young) adulthood takes place – the implication being that for the (young) adult the inspiration and monitor of life is now more the Spirit than simply the law (see § 1.3).

It should be noted that in this central metaphor, Israel under the law is again not an essentially negative status. On the contrary, Israel under the law is still heir of the promises to Abraham. The difference is relative – the difference between a son before, including just before reaching his majority, and the brother who has already reached, including just reached his majority. Paul may press the difference here, and more strongly later (4.28–31), but 4.19 shows that he was also conscious of just how relative was the difference: far from having already entered fully into the age of majority as children of Abraham, Gentile believers are still in the womb (4.19)! They too have yet to enter fully into that inheritance (5.21).[25] The contrast between unbelieving Jews (under the law) and believing

---

[23] So W.M. Ramsay, *Galatians* (London: Hodder, 1900) 381; T.L. Donaldson, 'The "Curse of the Law" and the Inclusion of the Gentiles: Galatians 3.13–14', *NTS* 32 (1986) 94–112, here 98; Dunn 197–8; against the majority.

[24] See my *Galatians* 210.

[25] Characteristic of this formulaic usage in the NT epistles is the understanding that the inheritance of the kingdom is still future (Gal. 5.21; 1 Cor. 6.9–10; 15.50; Eph. 5.5; James 2.5); see further my *Galatians* 306–7.

Jews and Gentiles is not at all so sharp as some of the other passages taken alone might suggest.

The conclusion is hard to avoid, then, that for Paul during this interim period the role of the law in relation to Israel was essentially protective. In fact, the picture Paul draws here is very close to that asserted positively in the *Letter of Aristeas:*

In his wisdom the legislator (Moses) . . . surrounded us with unbroken
palisades and iron walls to prevent our mixing with any of the other
peoples in any matter, being thus kept pure in body and soul ...
So, to prevent our being perverted by contact with others or by mixing
with bad influences, he hedged us in on all sides with strict observances connected with meat and drink and touch and hearing and
sight, after the manner of the Law (139, 142).

Indeed, in their different ways, all the main expressions of Judaism at the time of Paul would no doubt have seen themselves as protected by the law, whether from divine wrath on sin or from contamination by impure others, or both. At this point, we may say, Paul's understanding of the law was quintessentially Jewish.

More controversial is my own view that one of the key phrases in the letter, 'works of the law', should be understood within the same context. Still dominant in NT studies is the characteristically Lutheran interpretation of the phrase to mean in effect 'good works achieved by human effort and expressive of human self-assertion'.[26] But in the context of Galatians it is the function of 'works of the law' as distinguishing Jew from Gentile which was probably closest to the top of Paul's mind. Certainly in the first rush of usage (2.16) the context indicates precisely that function, the clear implication of 2.11–18 being that Peter a 'Jew by nature' had 'separated himself' from the Gentile believers at Antioch ('Gentile sinners') on the basis of a theology of 'works of the law'. And this fits with the protective role of the law outlined later in the second half of ch. 3 – 'works of the law' maintaining both Israel's standing within the covenant,[27] and Israel's distinctiveness from others.[28]

Whatever the precise function of this last phrase, however, it is clear that for Paul this function of the law was no longer necessary. Now that the promise that Abraham's blessing would be shared by the nations was achieving eschatological fulfilment, the law in its role of protecting and distinguishing Israel from the nations was at an end. The distinctive marks of the eschatological children of

---

[26] See e.g. those cited on my *Galatians* 135 n. 1.

[27] The attitude described by E.P. Sanders' phrase 'covenantal nomism'; see his *Paul and Palestinian Judaism* (London: SCM, 1977) 75, 180.

[28] See further my 'Works of the Law and the Curse of the Law (Gal. 3.10–14)', in *Jesus, Paul and the Law* (London: SPCK/Louisville: Westminster, 1990) 215–41, here 219–25 [= 125–36 above], 237–41; also 'Yet Once More – "The Works of the Law": A Response', *JSNT* 46 (1992) 99–117 [= ch. 3 above].

Abraham are no longer 'works of the law' but the inclusive markers of Abraham's faith, Christ and his Spirit (3.1–14, 3.22–4.7).

Here again, then, we can see that by setting the text within the context of Jewish thinking of the time, as illuminated by other texts from the period, an exegesis emerges which does fuller justice to the nuances of Paul's argument than a reading of the text as unyieldingly hostile to the law, and which thus focuses the controversial character of Paul's argument more sharply than the straight gospel/law antithesis.

1.3 Otherwise the law still has a positive function

Two important conclusions have thus emerged. The first is that the contrast in Gal. 3 between the promise and the law does not imply a wholly negative attitude to the law. On the contrary, the function of the law outlined in answer to the question, 'Why then the law?' (3.19), is quite positive – the law as given by God as a kind of guardian angel for Israel. The second conclusion is that that role for the law was temporary, to fill the gap between the giving of the promise to Abraham and its fulfilment in the coming of Christ. That is to say, prior to the extension of Abraham's blessing to the nations through his seed, the law had a role to maintain Israel's distinctiveness as heir of the promise, to protect Israel in a hostile world – not to give life (3.21) but to mark out the pattern and way of life for the covenant people (3.12).[29]

It is this twofold conclusion which provides the key to the otherwise puzzling mix of negative and positive comments in Galatians regarding the law. On the negative front it now becomes clear that what Paul was worried about was the possibility of his Gentile converts treating the law as though its role in regard to Israel was permanent, of continuing eschatological validity as well as for the period prior to the coming of Christ. By undertaking 'works of the law' such as the Jewish festivals (4.10) these Gentiles were in effect treating the law as if it were one of their old gods, a power interposed between them and God (4.8–10). By so doing they were failing to appreciate that the time of majority had come, the time of fulfilment (4.1–7). They were longing for the security of the child, always being told by another what to do, whereas they should be rejoicing in the freedom of the greater maturity which the gift of the Spirit brought as Abraham's blessing (3.2–3, 14). To re-erect the law as a bulwark which continued to distinguish and divide (believing) Jews from the (believing) nations was to subordinate the promise to the law and to render Christ's death pointless (2.17–21).[30]

---

[29] On the meaning of and distinction between 3.12 and 3.21 see my *Galatians* 175–6, 192–3.
[30] On the correlation between 2.21 and 3.13–14 see my *Galatians* 147–9 and 176–80.

On the positive side, the point is even clearer. For the temporary function of the law as a protection and bulwark for Israel was evidently not its complete function. And the negative thrust of Paul's argument is directed only against its being too tightly related to Israel as exclusively Israel's. Once that role has been set aside, eschatologically discounted, there is yet more to be said. The law can still be spoken of as having a positive function in the direction of life. This is clearly indicated in 5.14: for Paul 'the whole law' was still an obligation for the believer, Gentile as well as Jew. The difference is that 'the whole law' is not fulfilled by 'works of the law', as in the time before Christ, but in the one word, the well-known, 'You shall love your neighbour as yourself' (Lev. 19.18), a love which is also the fruit of the eschatological Spirit (5.22).[31]

Under the same heading we should also include the reference to 'the law of Christ' (6.2). Presumably in Paul's mind was the loving concern for the other which the Jesus tradition both documented for Jesus' own ministry and also summed up in the love command (as the parallel with Rom. 15.1–8 strongly suggests). But as in 5.14 Paul does not hesitate to describe this attitude and ethos by the same term 'law'. The implication, as in 5.14, is that it is in fact the same law which Paul had in view – the law as lived out and summed up in the life and teaching of Jesus, hence 'the law of Christ'.[32] Perhaps we may further guess that Paul had in mind in particular the Jesus-tradition's emphasis on Jesus eating with 'sinners' (Mark 2.16–17; Matt. 11.19/Luke 7.34), understood by Paul both as an example of Jesus' living out the love command ('the law of Christ'), and as justification for his own stand on 'works of the law' in this letter (2.14–16). If so the inter-contextual links at this point are exceedingly rich. And since they help explain the balance between the negative and positive treatment of the law in Galatians itself they cannot be dismissed as merely speculative.

In short, once the negative thrust of Paul's treatment of the law is clarified and set in the context both of the letter itself and of Judaism at the time of Paul, a coherent theology of the law in Galatians becomes evident. The more negative features of the law relate to its temporary role as a kind of guardian angel for Israel in the period before the coming of Christ. But that role, summed up in the phrase 'works of the law', is complete. What remains is the law understood in the light of the Jesus-tradition, summed up in the love command, and fulfilled by the enabling of the Spirit.

---

[31] Drane 112–3 and Hübner 36–40 are quite unable to make sense of 5.14 in the light of their earlier, too narrowly drawn conclusion that in Galatians Paul rejected the law entirely; see further my *Galatians* 288–92.

[32] See particularly H. Schürmann, '"Das Gesetz des Christus" (Gal 6,2): Jesu Verhalten und Wort als letzgültige sittliche Norm nach Paulus', in *Neues Testament und Kirche*, R. Schnackenburg FS, ed. J. Gnilka (Freiburg: Herder, 1974) 282–300.

2. The law in Romans

In Romans the treatment of the law is fuller. Indeed, the theology of the law is actually the subplot of the letter: it features in every chapter from 2 to 10 inclusive; it forms the main theme in chs. 2 and 7; and the way it is introduced throughout shows that it is the chief counterpoint to the central message of the gospel. Here we have space to draw attention only to the most significant features for a comparison with Galatians.

2.1 The law as yardstick

The most consistently emphasised function of the law in the early chapters is that of a yardstick – making aware of and measuring sin. In each case the reference is in an explanatory clause alluding to a function which was either so familiar or so obvious that it did not require further explanation or justification but could be taken wholly for granted:

... for through the law comes the knowledge of sin (3.20);
   (for) where there is no law there is also no transgression (4.15);
   For until the law, sin was in the world, but sin is not accounted in the
     absence of the law (5.13);
   sin, that it might appear as sin, ... in order that sin through the
     commandment might become utterly sinful (7.13).

The point is obvious and is not disputed in modern discussion either, so it needs little further exposition: one of the chief functions of the law, according to Romans, is to define sin as sin, that is, to indicate the lines and limits of conduct appropriate for an Israelite, as laid down by God, and therefore to make the Israelite aware of what conduct is unacceptable to God and inappropriate within Israel. The Israelite instructed in the law thus knew what conduct should be avoided (3.19), knew the consequences of such conduct (4.15) and knew also how it was to be expunged (3.21). This theology of the law is at the heart of the two lengthier treatments of the law in Romans: it comes to fuller expression in 2.12–16 (the law as the measure of final judgment), and is also the starting point for the trial of the law which begins in 7.7 (see below).

Interestingly enough, this function of the law did not feature in Galatians. This fact presumably helps confirm that it was not the ordinary or basic function of the law which was at issue there, but almost exclusively its function of setting Jew apart from Gentile. In contrast, in Romans, though the Galatians' issue is not absent, what is essayed is a much fuller and more rounded exposition of the law and its functions. Which also strengthens the view that the situation addressed in Rome was of nothing like the same crisis proportions as that which confronted Paul in the churches of Galatia, so that a more measured response was both desirable and possible.[33]

2.2 The law on trial

Despite the theses of Drane and Hübner,[34] it is in Romans rather than Galatians that the more strongly negative note is sounded. Whatever Gal. 3.19 might mean, it is hard to dispute the negative role attributed to the law in Rom. 5.20: 'The law came in to increase the trespass'. The choice of verb (παρεισῆλθεν, 'slipped in, interposed') and the use of the active voice (the law as subject) seems to increase the negative overtone and makes the law appear as a traitorous ally of the oppressive powers, sin and death – a guardian angel (Gal. 3.19), one might say, subverted by the powers of evil.

This is all the more surprising in Romans, since, again in contrast to Galatians, the early treatment of the law in Romans has been on the whole fairly matter of fact and even positive (2.13–15, 25, 27; 3.21, 27b, 31; 4.16). Apart from some indications of an unsatisfactory relation with the law on the part of the Jewish interlocutor in 2.17–29 (but the law is not blamed), the only negative notes are struck by, once again, the repeated phrase 'works of the law' (3.20, 27a, 28) and the contrast with the promise to Abraham (4.13–15). So the more fiercely negative note of 5.20 comes as something of a surprise.

Why Paul introduced such a negative note at this point is only partially clear. It must have been intended at least to heighten the contrast between the two ages of humankind's history outlined in 5.12–21. The age of Adam (Adam to Christ) is pictured as set under the powers of sin and death. Into this grim situation the law was introduced, not as a way of ameliorating the human condition (as in Gal. 3.19), but as an ally of sin and death. Presumably the purpose was at least partly rhetorical: on the one hand to disturb any easy assumption on the part of the earlier Jewish interlocutor that the law protected Israel from the worst effects of sin and death (as implied in Rom. 2.12ff. and Gal. 3.23–24);[35] and on the other to increase the dramatic contrast with the effect of divine grace in and through Christ (5.20–21; 6.14–15). But the effect is still unnerving and leaves a question dangling about the relation of the law to sin and death. No doubt Paul felt able to do this because within a few paragraphs he was going to address this precise question.

Rom 7 (or more precisely 7.7–8.4) thus functions in many ways as a climax to the disturbing questions regarding the law raised by Paul in the preceding chap-

---

[33] On the debates as to the purpose of Romans see particularly K.P. Donfried, ed., *The Romans Debate. Revised and Expanded* (Peabody, Mass.: Hendrickson, 1991); A.J.M. Wedderburn, *The Reasons for Romans* (Edinburgh: T. & T. Clark, 1988).

[34] See nn. 7 and 12 above.

[35] See also my *Romans* (WBC 38; Dallas: Word, 1988) 286.

ters. In 7.7–13 the question is posed explicitly: 'Is the law sin?' Does the link between sin and law put forward in 5.20 amount to an equation of the two? Paul's
answer is immediate: No! And he goes on to explain how it is that sin has made
use of the law's commandment in order to incite transgression and achieve
transgression's consequence of death (7.7–13). Here the blame is clearly transferred to the power of personified sin; the law is not the ally of sin (as 5.20 might
have implied) but its dupe.

A further reason for sin's power, implicit but undeveloped in 7.7–13, is the
weakness of the human condition, the weakness, that is, of the flesh, or to be
more precise, the weakness of the 'I' as flesh. Thus even sin's use of the law to
demonstrate the utter sinfulness of sin (7.13) should not be taken as a criticism
of the law itself: 'we know that the law is spiritual; but I am fleshly, sold under
sin' (7.14). The blame, once again, has to be wholly placed on sin (7.14–17).

With all the actors now introduced (sin, death, law, 'I') the analysis of the
human condition and the role of the law in relation to sin can be clarified and
defended. The key is first of all to recognize that the 'I' itself is divided (7.18–20):
the 'I' as flesh does evil, or to be precise, sin indwelling the 'I' as flesh does evil;
while at the same time the 'I' wishes what is good. This inner division and contradiction of the 'I' is matched, secondly, by an equivalent division and contradiction in the law (7.21–23): the law as used by sin, and the law as indicating the will
of God. And the match is close: the 'I' as willing what is good is the 'I' instructed
by the law of God, 'I' as 'inner man' (7.22), 'I' as mind (7.25); while the 'I' as flesh
remains under the sway of sin, captive to the law as used by sin (in the way explained earlier) (7.23, 25), the law of sin and death (8.2–3).[36]

We need not attempt any further resolution of the much disputed issue regarding the identity of the 'I'.[37] It will suffice to observe that since the argument
of 7.7–8.4 is a defence of the law against the indictment initially posed in 5.20,
the most obvious explanation is to link the split in the 'I' with the division of the
ages outlined in 5.12–21 – the 'I' as flesh, under the power of sin and death as belonging to the age of Adam, and the 'I' as 'inner man' and mind standing for the
human being as intended by God, delighting in the will of God indicated by the
law, though in the event dependent on the enabling of the Spirit to overcome the
weakness of the flesh and to fulfil the requirement of the law (8.4). But whatever

---

[36] This recognition of the split in the law matching the split in the 'I' seems to me to make
much better sense of the sequence of law references in 7.21–8.4 than alternative, still dominant
view which understands the νόμος references in 7.21, 23 and 8.2a in the sense 'principle'; in recent scholarship see J. Ziesler, *Romans* (London: SCM/Philadelphia: TPI, 1989) 197–8, 202; D.
Moo, *Romans 1–8* (Wycliffe Exegetical Commentary; Chicago: Moody, 1991) 490–2, 504–8;
J.A. Fitzmyer, *Romans* (AB 33; New York: Doubleday, 1993) 131; but see also my *Romans* 392–
5, 416–8, with further bibliography.

[37] The most recent fullscale review is by J. Lambrecht, *The Wretched 'I' and its Liberation.
Paul in Romans 7 and 8* (Louvain: Peeters, 1992).

the precise reference of the 'I' it should be clear enough that the defence of the law ends with a very positive emphasis on fulfilment of the law's requirements.

The importance of 7.7–8.4 within the sub-theme of Romans' theology of the law should therefore not be underestimated. It is this passage which above all else shows that Paul was not against the law as such. For it is a skilful defence of the law which 'lets it off the hook'. The charge that the law was sin and functioned as a quasi-heavenly power (like sin and death) was legitimate and indeed invited by the provocative climax to 5.12–21. But now it is clear that for Paul any indictment is against the law only as abused by sin; and in this indictment the weakness of human flesh is equally if not more culpable. But the real culprit is sin. Apart from that, however, the law continues to function as yardstick and measure of God's will; and it is still God's will that its requirements should be fulfilled; he sent his Son and gave his Spirit precisely for that purpose (8.3–4).

The hermeneutical corollary which follows from this is the danger of an atomistic exegesis.[38] In this case Rom. 5.20 taken on its own, or only in the immediate context of 5.12–21, can easily lead to the conclusion that Paul's attitude to the law was thoroughly hostile, as hostile as his attitude to sin and death. But in a letter as well crafted as Romans it is important to take particular texts in the context of the developing argument and rhetoric of the letter as a whole. And elsewhere it is very obvious that part of Paul's technique was to state a radical criticism early on, *not* as his finished conclusion, but as an issue to be dealt with later (particularly 3.1–8). So with 5.20: since it poses an issue which is dealt with only in 7.7–8.4, it cannot be adequately understood except by reference to 7.7–8.4.

2.3 *The continuing positive role of the law*

No one who has grasped the point of 7.7–8.4, therefore, should be surprised at the repeatedly positive role attributed to the law elsewhere, and indeed throughout Romans. Indeed, it is only when the real thrust of Rom. 7, that is as a defence of the law, has been thus grasped, that it becomes possible to make sense of this repeated positive emphasis on the law in Romans. Without the key provided by 7.7–8.4 Paul's theology of the law would remain a riddle, and the argument that that theology was incoherent and contradictory would be hard to counter.

The continuing positive role attributed to the law in Romans can be indicated briefly, without further exposition, since the nub of the argument has already been dealt with:

the doers of the law will be counted righteous (2.13);
circumcision is of benefit if you practise the law (2.25);

---

[38] Räisänen's method of treating *Paul and the Law* illustrates the danger well and thus undermines much of his own exegesis.

... the righteousness of God has been revealed, as attested by the law
   and the prophets (3.21);
boasting has been excluded (not by the law of works but) by the law
   of faith (3.27);
we establish the law (through faith) (3.31);
I rejoice in the law of God, so far as the inner man is concerned (7.22);
the law of the Spirit of life in Christ Jesus has set you free ... (8.2);
God sent his Son ... in order that the requirement of the law might
   be fulfilled in us who walk not in accordance with the flesh but in
   accordance with the Spirit (8.3–4);
theirs is ... the law (9.4);
Israel pursuing the law of righteousness has not reached the law.
   Why so? Because they did so not from faith but as if it was from
   works (9.31–32);
Owe nothing to anyone except to love one another; for he who loves
   the other has fulfilled the law. For the commandment(s are) ...
   summed up in this word, in the command, 'You shall love your
   neighbour as yourself'. Love does no wrong to the neighbour;
   therefore the fulfilment of the law is love (13.8–10).

It is difficult to see how anyone can conclude after such a catena of passages that
Paul had abandoned the law and denied it any continuing role in instructing
those who had believed in Christ. The key is to recognize that Paul's more negative thrust against the law was not directed against the law as such but against
the law as manipulated by sin, against the law regarded as sufficient in itself to
overcome the weakness of the flesh, against the law of works. Once the law had
been freed from that role, and the commandments which served that role and
the way they served that role clearly recognized, then the continuing requirement of the law as expressing the will of God could be re-emphasized. All requirements could be thus manipulated by sin, could become 'works of the law'.
But so long as it was appreciated that all the law's requirements were to be fulfilled through faith and the enabling of the Spirit, and along the lines of the love
command, then the weakness of the flesh could continue to be overcome and the
devices of sin defeated.

The contrast with Galatians is also marked at this point. For in Galatians the
positive emphasis on the continuing role of the law is present, but only briefly,
and the more negative thrust (contrasted with promise, only temporary) pre-
dominates. Whereas here the emphasis is, if anything, the reverse. We may pres-
ume that it was the particular challenge of the other missionaries in Galatia,
seeking to draw the Galatian Gentile believers (back) 'under the law', which
made Paul sound so critical of the law in Galatians. If so, the equally logical deduction here is that in the more reflective mood of Romans Paul was able to
stand back and outline the role of the law within his theology in larger terms of
principle. In that less threatened situation the continuing positive role of the law

for believers (Gentile as well as Jew) could be laid out more dispassionately and effectively.

In short, due regard for the complete sweep of the argument shows Romans to express a wholly coherent understanding of the law, and due regard for the different circumstances with a view to which Galatians and Romans were penned is quite sufficient to explain the different emphases between the letters. The hermeneutical tensions and problems on this theme which have resurfaced in recent debate have arisen primarily because the necessary tasks of setting text within context have been neglected or important historical contextual information has been ignored.

Conclusion

Can we then integrate the treatments of the law in Galatians and Romans into a single coherent theology? I think so. It is possible to speak of 'Paul's theology of the law' on the basis of these two letters – and not as an incoherent theology, with many loose ends and unresolved issues; nor as one which shifted on any point of major significance between the two letters.

Each has its own distinctive features, of course, and it is on these that we have mainly concentrated – Galatians' emphasis on the law's temporary role vis-a-vis Israel as Israel's guardian angel, and Romans' repeated mention of the yardstick function of the law and subtle defence of the law in Rom. 7–8. The other emphasis on the continuing positive role of the law is given different weight in the two letters, but it is present in both. More important for us is the fact that the more distinctive emphases of each letter cohere with each other without any real difficulty. A coherent theology of the law as expressed in the different language and circumstances of the two letters is therefore fairly easy to draw out.

A first common feature is *the God-given character and function of the law*. This is most explicit in Rom. 7's insistence on the law as holy and just and good. But it is evident also in the role of the law as Israel's protector and custodian, a role naturally appointed by God, albeit providing a less immediate relation with God than the promise (Galatians). It is evident also in Romans' stress on the continuing yardstick function of the law and on the law as the measure of final judgment. Paul evidently continued to think of the law as having been given by God to be obeyed, and failure to obey it as provoking serious consequences.

Second, the critique of the law in each letter can now be seen to be more specifically targetted. In Galatians it is against the law's protective function for Israel being maintained as a means to exclude Gentiles as Gentiles from participation in the blessing of Abraham, despite the eschatological fulfilment in Christ and the Spirit. Since Gentiles as Gentiles have also received the Spirit, the law is no longer needed as guardian to protect Jews from them as though they were still 'sinners', still a source of defilement. In Romans it is against the law as used by sin to batten on the weakness of the flesh, to maintain the rule of sin and death as over the age of Adam.

The two critiques are in fact closely related. For in both letters, attempts by other (Christian) Jews to maintain their distinctive privileged standing before God was seen by Paul as a pandering to the flesh, quite as much as 'works of the flesh' (Gal. 3.2–3; 5.19; 6.12–13; Rom. 2.28). And in both letters the criticised attitude is summed up in the phrase 'works of the law' (Gal. 2.16; 3.2, 5, 10; Rom. 3.20, 27–28; 9.32). In Romans the same appreciation of the law is characterised as γράμμα –in effect a focusing of the law on the visible and fleshly, that is, on the ethnic distinction between Jew and Gentile which circumcision in particular indicated (Rom. 2.27–29).

Romans also brings out an aspect of the temporary role of the law not explored in Galatians. For in Galatians the time before and apart from Christ is described not only as the period of Israel from Moses to Christ, but also as 'the present evil age' (Gal. 1.4) and, by implication, the 'old creation' (Gal. 6.15). In Romans this is elaborated as the age of Adam, under the rule of sin and death (Rom. 5.12–21). But whereas in Galatians the role of the law during that period seems to be characterised as something essentially positive (protector, custodian, guardian), in Romans the role of the law in the age of Adam is portrayed as essentially sin's dupe. What we may say, then, is that in Romans Paul shows how the protective role of the law (Galatians) has been perverted by sin and the weakness of the flesh into a negative force preventing the full outworking of the gospel to all who believe. To that extent the 'I' of Romans 7 is Israel,[39] caught between the conflicting roles of the law, the one manipulated by sin to tie Israel in effect more tightly to essentially fleshly concerns, the other awaiting the liberation of the Spirit for its role to be fulfilled. Moreover, since Rom. 10.4 concludes a section criticising Israel for continuing to think of the law of righteousness in terms of works (9.32) and for continuing zealously to defend its special relationship with God (10.2–3), we may further deduce that what Christ marks the end of (10.4) is the temporary role of the law as Israel's protector weakened by the flesh and perverted by sin.

Thirdly, once the danger of the law caught in the nexus of sin and flesh has been fully appreciated, then the continuing positive role of the law can be expressed in its fulness. It still indicates the will of God. God still wants its requirements to be fulfilled. Only those who do the law will be justified. But these requirements are understood now in terms of faith and Spirit and love rather than works of the law – that is, the law fulfilled by trusting in God('s Christ), in walking by the Spirit, in loving the neighbour.

---

[39] Cf. particularly D.J. Moo, 'Israel and Paul in Romans 7:7–12', *NTS* 32 (1986) 122–35.

In formulating a coherent theology of the law as expressed in Galatians and Romans, therefore, it is important, finally, to maintain the proper Pauline dialectic. Not simply between the gospel and the law; that we can now see to be too crude. But between the law as a yardstick of what is good, and the law as the cat-spaw of evil; between the law (as the expresssion) of faith and the law as summed up in works of the law; between the law (as the expression) of the Spirit of life and the law as the tool of sin and death; between the law as showing how the life of faith should be lived through love of the other, and the law always in danger of becoming γράμμα, emphasising the visible marks which distinguish Jew from Gentile. In each case it is the same law – the law, caught like the willing but still fleshly 'I' between the ages, between the competing claims of sin and grace, like the rest of creation awaiting the liberation of the children of God (Rom. 8.19–23).

As a test-case for the most appropriate context(s) within which and in reference to which a Pauline text should be expounded, this study has reaffirmed the importance of reading particular texts within the context of the larger document of which they are part, of illuminating that context from the wider context of the time, and of correlating different texts from the same author inter-text-within-contextually. There are of course other contexts within which and in relation to which Pauline texts dealing with the law will be read, but if we are to speak of Paul's own theology of the law, the former must take precedence. The fact that by doing so we have been able to draw out a coherent theology of the law, which can be attributed to Paul as such, is simply a ratification of the appropriateness of the procedure.

This study is dedicated to Lars Hartman, who I recall first meeting on a railway station many years ago as we both sought to make our way to the annual SNTS meeting. The pleasure of subsequent annual meetings has always been enhanced by his presence. I would have liked to make a contribution more directly related to his own work at points where our various writings have overlapped, but unfortunately I have not yet seen his book on Baptism, nor do I have enough Swedish to do justice to his commentary on Colossians, though I have greatly valued his articles on Colossians. But the theme 'Paul and the Law' was in fact the subject of my lecture at the Exegetical Day at Uppsala in 1985 (full of pleasant memories), to which Lars kindly invited me, and the paper itself was delivered from notes as one of two lectures to the Menighetsfakultetet in Oslo in April 1993, so I hope he will find it sufficiently close, as we might say, theologically as well as geographically, to his own interests. To Lars: *ad multos annos.*

Chapter 12

In Search of Common Ground

1. Introduction

The issues confronting the Symposium,[1] both the agreements and the disagreements, can perhaps best be focused in the question of continuity and discontinuity. The very terms in which the question is posed indicate the extent of the problem and the range of agreement/disagreement. Do we mean continuity/discontinuity between the OT and the NT, or between Israel and the Church, or between the gospel and thc law? The first formulation would presumably attract a strong measure of agreement in such a gathering, since the Christian tradition counts the Jewish scriptures as part of the Christian Bible, a claim in effect dependent on maximising the measure of continuity between the Testaments. Whereas the last evokes the classic Reformation antithesis between law and gospel, where the greater light focused on the latter seems inevitably to cast the former into deeper shadow. And yet the tension between gospel and law in Paul can hardly be understood except against the background of the other two continuities/discontinuities, especially since Torah (law) overlaps to such an extent with scripture (OT) and has been so constitutive of the identity of Israel.

It is this fact, however, which gives us some hope of finding a greater degree of common ground on the issue of Paul and the law. For the issue for us as Neutestamentlers focuses on points of exegesis, and that inevitably means an exegesis which takes historical and social factors of Paul's time as fully into consideration as possible. This was indeed the task the Symposium set itself, as indicated in the programme and in the subjects of the papers. *The common ground we seek, therefore, is not first and foremost agreement among ourselves, but some measure of consensus on what was the common ground between Paul and his fellow Christian Jews with whom he was in dispute.* Or in our present terms, what was the continuity/discontinuity between Paul and his Gentile converts (won by Paul's gospel) on the one hand, and those Jews who, like Paul, had believed in Jesus as the Messiah of Israel on the other? The more clarity we can gain on this point, the greater we may find the common ground to be among ourselves.

---

[1] This paper was my attempt to sum up the results of the Third Durham-Tübingen Research Symposium on Earliest Christianity and Judaism on 'Paul and the Law', held in Durham, September, 1994. The collected papers of the Symposium were published as J.D.G. Dunn, ed., *Paul and the Mosaic Law* (WUNT 89; Tübingen, 1996; Grand Rapids: Eerdmans, 2001).

Two preliminary points should be made which reflect some of the methodological agreement among the participants in the Symposium. The first has already been alluded to: that Paul's principal treatment of the law in his letters was formulated in dialogue and dispute not with non-Christian Jews, but with fellow Christian Jews. This at once cuts the nerve of much of the charge of anti-Judaism laid against Paul, an issue which, somewhat surprisingly, hardly arose within the Symposium. At the same time, it is important to realise that the protests against Paul's gospel in reference to the law arose because so many of Paul's fellow Jewish believers felt their own identity as children of Abraham and their heritage as the people of Israel to be under question or even threat from the success of Paul's mission.

The other is the problem of terminology. At several points in the Symposium we found ourselves stumbling across the problem of language, in particular the unclarity of some key words. On the one hand, there were words used which evidently have (very) different overtones in German and English – for example, 'legalism', 'self-righteousness', 'covenant' and 'political'. Some of the discussions began to run aground because there are what might be called hidden reefs within our different traditions of which those from other traditions were not sufficiently aware. On the other hand, there were key terms within the text on whose scope we were unable to achieve full agreement – for example, 'sin', 'works of the law', 'life' and 'salvation', and their relation to the Torah. Other terms like 'narrative' provoked unexpected responses. Not least of the value of the Symposium was that by spending so much time in each other's company we began to open up these deeper issues and to penetrate below the surface of disputes. We began to appreciate not only the dimensions of the dispute (the 'what'), but also the reasons why alternative views could be held with such conviction and passion (the 'why'). In such circumstances any common ground which can be realised is likely to be the more significant and, hopefully, enable a greater degree of genuine rapprochement than can ever be achieved by a single seminar or a few emollient slogans.[2]

2. The character of the continuity

2.1 It can hardly be disputed that Paul understood his gospel to be thoroughly consistent with and continuous from his heritage as a Jew, the teaching, that is, in Christian terms, of the OT. As hardly needs to be documented or argued (I refer particularly to Romans and Galatians), he draws his understanding of his

---

[2] In what follows I limit footnotes to a minimum, since the primary reference points are the papers presented to the Symposium (but now revised) and the discussion which they evoked. However, to avoid the paper becoming merely an in-house dialogue, I have added a number of explanatory notes with a wider readership in mind.

Hauptmotif, 'the righteousness of God', directly from the Psalms and Second Isaiah.[3] His key texts in the exposition of his gospel are Gen. 15.6 and Hab. 2.4. Abraham is his principal model of the person who has faith, who believes (Gal. 3; Rom. 4). He is desperately concerned to show that the gospel preached to the Gentiles does not contradict God's faithfulness to Israel (Rom. 3.1–8, 21–26; 9–11). Gal. 3.8 in effect sums up the difficult case he had to make in face of Christian Jewish objections: the promise given to Abraham was in fact the *gospel*, precisely because it spoke of the blessing which would come to the *Gentiles*.

The disputes, however, begin when we ask whether the continuity is in effect only between Paul and the OT itself, jumping over, as it were, the intervening period of Second Temple Judaism. So far as righteousness and the law is concerned, do we have to distinguish the biblical treatment from that more characteristic from the Maccabees (or the Exile) onwards? Did the context of Second Temple Judaism for Paul's own training in the law differ decisively from the biblical context? After all, the continuity could hardly be complete or obvious, since so few of Paul's fellow Jews became Christians. And, as we shall remind ourselves more fully later, Paul's critique of the law seems to be more radical than a simple hypothesis of continuity can bear.

In many ways this was the key question confronting the Symposium: how to explain and elucidate Paul's treatment of the law in the light of the understanding of the Torah prevalent in Second Temple Judaism. It was an issue which was unavoidable since it had been posed by 'the new perspective' on Paul, albeit from the opposite side: that the view of God's righteousness in Second Temple Judaism was not as 'legalistic' nor as conducive to 'self-righteousness' as had traditionally been maintained in NT exegesis. From whatever perspective, therefore, whether that of squaring Paul's treatment of the law with his own claims to continuity, or that of reaction against a certain Christian tendency to denigrate the Judaism of Paul's day on this subject, it was essential that the Symposium should begin with an attempt to clarify the understanding of the Torah within Judaism at the time of Paul.

2.2 Hermann Lichtenberger's paper[4] therefore had particular importance as establishing the historical context within Second Temple Judaism for Paul's teaching on the law with reference to which the Symposium's discussion would proceed. His findings could be summed up thus: Although some elements of legalism in Second Temple Judaism cannot be denied, we also cannot conclude that Second Temple Judaism as a whole is to be branded as 'legalistic' (that is, that salvation or life in the world to come is earned by obedience to the Torah).

---

[3] See e.g. my *Romans* (WBC 38; Dallas: Word, 1988) 41 (with bibliography), and P. Stuhlmacher, *Der Brief an die Römer* (NTD; Göttingen: Vandenhoeck, 1989) 31.

[4] H. Lichtenberger, 'Das Tora-Verständnis im Judentum zur Zeit des Paulus. Eine Skizze', in *Paul and the Mosaic Law* 7–23.

The diversity of Second Temple Judaism's teaching on the law can also be summed up in such phrases as: obedience to the Torah is the presupposition of membership of the covenant; or in Lichtenberger's own helpful phrase, 'Weisung zum Leben und Lebens-Weise', that is, not one or other, but both together. The resulting discussion also provided some agreement that while we can speak of salvation in individual and corporate terms in Second Temple Judaism, the question of the individual's status is derivative from membership of the covenant people. Important also was the fact that no one seemed to want to maintain that Second Temple Judaism taught the need for 'perfection' in law-keeping.[5]

Integral to the view of Torah which emerges is the two-fold assertion: (1) That membership of the covenant people is a presupposition (Deuteronomy is addressed to those who are already the people of Israel). Consequently the function of the law (again as archetypically expressed in Deuteronomy) is not to enable 'getting in' to the covenant people nor to make it possible to earn God's acceptance.[6] (2) Obedience to the Torah is a requirement for continuing membership of the covenant, for life within the people, and for gaining a portion in the life of the world to come.[7]

If this is the case, then the question naturally arises: which of these two emphases was Paul reacting against? Or rather, which of these two emphases was Paul's gospel thought to come into conflict with, occasioning the opposition to Paul's gospel from fellow Christian Jews, which is reflected in several of his letters? It could be the first, since a gospel for Gentiles raises the question of whether and how non-Jews 'get in' to the covenant people. It could be the second, since the question of Gentile Christian non-fulfilment of the law raises the question whether and how far obedience to the Torah is still necessary for Christian Jew as well as for (or as distinct from) Christian Gentile. In fact, however, the two emphases would not be easily separable in Jewish self-understanding. It is this fact which causes the confusion in NT exegesis in the first place, since the importance of obedience to the Torah for life (2) can easily be heard as making final acceptance by God conditional on that obedience.

The issue of Paul's attitude to the Torah cannot be resolved, of course, solely by reference to the understanding of the function of the Torah in Second Temple

---

[5] This misunderstanding, however, continues to bedevil the discussion elsewhere, as we see in T.R. Schreiner, *The Law and its Fulfilment: A Pauline Theology of the Law* (Grand Rapids: Baker, 1993) e.g. 71, 181.

[6] The 'getting in' language is drawn from E.P. Sanders, *Paul, the Law, and the Jewish People* (Philadelphia: Fortress, 1983): 'Much of what Paul wrote falls within a framework which I call "getting in and staying in"' (6).

[7] The Symposium needed to give more discussion to the character of this double affirmation. Of particular importance is the obviously deliberate echo of Lev. 18.5 in Ezek. 20.11, 13, 21 – אֲשֶׁר יַעֲשֶׂה אֹתָם הָאָדָם וָחַי בָּהֶם. As the בָּהֶם makes clear, and also the reverse formula in Ezek. 20.25 (לֹא יִהְיוּ בָּהֶם), what is in view is *a way of living* ('he shall live by them'), not life as the reward ('he shall gain life as a result of his obedience').

Judaism. That can only be gleaned from Paul's own writings, and to these the Symposium quickly turned. But it was (and is) important that the debates on the interpretation of Paul's letters remain informed by and in touch with these initial findings.

2.3 Equally if not more crucial for our enterprise was clarification of Paul's attitude to the law in the period covering his conversion up to and including the incident at Antioch (Gal. 1–2). Martin Hengel's paper[8] and the resulting discussion produced a general agreement that Paul's understanding of the law as a Christian was rooted in the Damascus road encounter, that it changed Paul's attitude to the law, and that faith in Jesus was decisive for Paul's gospel and theology from the first. There was significant disagreement, however, over what the change in Paul's attitude amounted to, and on whether and how his attitude to the law developed.

For my own part, the issue of Paul's conversion, of what he was converted from and to, is central, and no clearer answer can be found than that provided by Paul himself in Gal. 1.13–16.[9] (a) What Paul was converted *from* was 'Judaism' (Gal. 1.13–14). Not 'Judaism' as we now define it in contemporary sociological description of Second Temple Judaism. But 'Judaism' as it had been defined in the only other literary uses of the term current at the time of Paul (2 Macc. 2.21; 8.1; 14.38; 4 Macc. 4.26), that is, as the label coined or used to identify the national religion trying to define and defend itself over against the influences of Hellenism (2 Macc. 4.13). That is, 'Judaism' as marked out by loyalty to the laws of God and of their fathers, where the test cases of that loyalty were sabbath and feasts, circumcision, and refusal to eat forbidden flesh (2 Macc. 6). (b) Again, what Paul converted *from* was 'zeal', zeal for these traditions (Gal. 1.14), the zeal that caused him to 'persecute the church of God' (Phil. 3.6; cf. 1 Cor. 15.9),[10] in the tradition of Phinehas and the Maccabees (1 Macc. 2.19–28, 49–64), that is, as the human reflection of the 'jealousy of God' (Exod. 20.4–5; 34.14; Deut. 5.8–9; 6.14–15), in a violent attempt to maintain Israel's set-apartness from Gentiles and their corrupting ways. (c) And again, what Paul was converted *to* was the recognition that the gospel of Jesus had to be taken to the Gentiles (Gal. 1.15–16); that is, he was converted to the beliefs (of the Hellenists) which he had persecuted.

---

[8] M. Hengel, 'Die Stellung des Apostels Paulus zum Gesetz in den unbekannten Jahren zwischen Damaskus und Antiochien', in *Paul and the Mosaic Law* 25–51.

[9] For what follows see more fully my 'Paul's Conversion – A Light to Twentieth Century Disputes', in *Evangelium – Schriftauslegung – Kirche*, P. Stuhlmacher FS, hrsg. J. Ådna et al. (Göttingen: Vandenhoeck, 1997) 77–93 [=ch. 15 below].

[10] The repetition of the phrase shows how deeply rooted it was in Paul's memory. That it probably goes back to the period of Paul's conversion is confirmed by Gal. 1.23 – ὁ διώκων ἡμᾶς.

If this is so, then the change in Paul's understanding of the law, occasioned by his conversion, must be related to his conversion as he understood it. The change in his attitude to the law therefore probably focused on the role of the law as crystallized and reinforced by the Maccabean crisis and as fundamental to the 'Judaism' of the middle Second Temple period thereafter. That is, the law in its role as hedging Israel around and protecting it from outsiders, the law understood as requiring Israel's set-apartness from the Gentiles, the law as consisting of 'pallisades and iron walls to prevent (their) mixing with any of the other peoples in any matter' (in the terms used by the *Letter of Aristeas* 139–42). The issue, in other words, was nothing to do with earning or achieving God's favour, and not even so much about Gentiles 'getting in' to the covenant people. If anything, it would be more accurate to say that the issue was about Jews (Hellenist Christians) breaking down the 'walls' that separated Jew from Gentile. And not necessarily by wholesale abandoning of the law (after all, it was the Hellenist Jewish Christians at Antioch who later sided with Peter in withdrawing from table fellowship with Gentile Christians – Gal. 2.11–14), but by virtue of taking the good news of the (Jewish) Messiah Jesus to the Gentiles in the first place (Acts 11.20).

As for the question of development in Paul's attitude to the law, the issue may be unresolvable. Did Paul see things so clearly from the first, as his account in Gal. 1 indicates? For Paul, as he looked back, the conclusions embodied in Gal. 1 were probably always obvious. But was this hindsight, the product of 'biographical reconstruction'?[11] Was there actual development in his view, or only an unfolding of what was implicit, or not (yet) fully stated at the first? If the above reconstruction of Paul's conversion (drawn from Gal. 1.13–16) is any guide, then the conclusion 'to the Gentiles' seems to have been the immediate reaction to the earlier motivation of the persecutor ('*not* to the Gentiles'). Which would suggest that indeed the reconstruction of Paul's view of the law, at least in respect to its boundary role of separating Jew from Gentile, was formed in Paul's mind as an immediate outcome of his conversion experience.[12]

On the other hand, all the puzzles of the unknown years between Damascus and Antioch remain:[13] When was it that Paul began to engage in extensive missionary work (Gal. 1.17?), and was it directly to Gentiles or only after preaching to his own people (cf. Gal. 5.11), and was it usually (in the first instance at least) directed to the God-fearing and proselyte penumbra round the diaspora synagogue (as Acts indicates)? What actually was achieved at the con-

---

[11] As argued by N. Taylor, *Paul, Antioch and Jerusalem: A Study in Relationships and Authority in Earliest Christianity* (JSNTS 66; Sheffield: JSOT, 1992).

[12] Cf. H. Räisänen, 'Paul's Call Experience and his Later View of the Law', *Jesus, Paul and Torah. Collected Essays* (JSNTS 43; Sheffield: Sheffield Academic, 1992) ch. 1.

[13] For my own views I may refer to my *The Epistle to the Galatians* (BNTC; London: A & C Black/Peabody, Mass.: Hendrickson, 1993).

sultation in Jerusalem so far as the acceptability and Torah obligations of Gentile converts within the church of God were concerned (Gal. 2.1–10)? Why did Peter and the other Christian Jews, including Barnabas, withdraw from table-fellowship with the Gentile Christians in Antioch (Gal. 2.11–14)? Was there an increasing nationalistic pressure upon James and coming from James in Jerusalem? And to what extent, if at all, should we discount Paul's language as rhetoric?

What is clear is that Paul and Peter at Antioch did not share the same understanding of the continuing function of the law; the fact and seriousness of the dispute between the two is no mere rhetorical flourish. The corollaries drawn by each from the Jerusalem agreement were decisively different when the question of continuing table-fellowship between Christian Jew and Christian Gentile arose. Here the issue of continuity is posed as sharply as anywhere. For Peter and all the other Christian Jews evidently concluded that the practice at Antioch prior to the coming of the group from James constituted a breach of continuity, and in the event, an unacceptable breach. The continuity of divine purpose, attested by the grace of God through the ministry of Paul and Barnabas to Gentiles, which had proved decisive in the earlier confrontation (Gal. 2.7–9), was no longer evident or determinative for Peter (contrast Acts 11.2–17), or Barnabas! (contrast Acts 11.23), in the disputed practice at Antioch. And thus we come to a further phase of our discussion.

2.4   The confrontation at Antioch caused Paul to formulate his theological position afresh – Gal. 2.15–16. Had he so formulated it before? If so, had Peter (and Barnabas!) rejected it before? Or did he now so formulate it for the first time, a formulation provoked and shaped by the incident at Antioch itself? The latter would seem to make better sense of the narrative.

As to the meaning of the text itself, what does it tell us of the basic conflict (whether with Peter in particular, or now more generally) over the law as seen by Paul? Here the issues were complicated in the Symposium's discussion, since there was sharp disagreement on the significance of ἁμαρτωλός in 2.15 and 2.17, and on the meaning of πίστις Χριστοῦ in 2.16 and 20. For my own part, it seems most unlikely that ἁμαρτωλός in 2.17 should be read differently from the same word two verses earlier (2.15), where (*pace* Lambrecht)[14] it clearly expresses the factional, nationalistic view which we find elsewhere in Second Temple Judaism (e.g. 1 Macc. 2.44, 48; Pss.Sol. 2.1–2).[15] And I remain unpersuaded by the renewedly popular view that πίστις Χριστοῦ refers to the 'faith(fulness) of Christ'

---

[14] J. Lambrecht, 'Paul's Reasoning in Galatians 2:11–21', in *Paul and the Mosaic Law* 53–74.

[15] See my 'Echoes of Intra-Jewish Polemic in Paul's Letter to the Galatians', *JBL* 112 (1993) 459–77, here 462–5; full discussion in E. Kok, *'The Truth of the Gospel': A Study in Galatians 2.15–21* (Durham PhD, 1993) 207–12.

rather than to 'faith in Christ',[16] though we had insufficient time to enter into that debate at the Symposium itself.

What can be said with more confidence of agreement is that 2.15–16 does reflect, at least in some measure, Paul's arguments at or conclusions from the Antioch incident. In which case the disagreement over the relation between gospel and law as it comes to expression in Gal. 2.15–16 boils down to the question, whether πίστις Χριστοῦ is sufficient in and of itself to secure the full Christian standing of the one who believes and complete acceptability (table-fellowship) between believers. Paul had no doubt that the answer was and should be Yes. Peter and the other Jewish Christians (including Barnabas) were pushed to the conclusion that, for them at any rate, other conditions had to be met – presumably at least the sort of dietary rules which allowed observant Jews elsewhere in the diaspora to share in at least some table-fellowship with Gentile business associates and friends.[17] In 2.16 Paul expresses this policy in terms of πίστις Χριστοῦ plus works of the law, where the 'works of the law' particularly in mind must at minimum have included the rules by which Peter and the others expected the practice of fellowship between Christian Jews and Christian Gentiles to be governed, following the arrival of the group from James.

In other words, the dispute at Antioch and the resulting formulation in Gal. 2.15–16 was occasioned by the 'both-and' outlined above in the description of Second Temple Judaism's understanding of the law (§ 2.2). The 'law-for-life' attitude described there is just the one which Peter and the other Christian Jews were persuaded to return to in Antioch. But for Paul a more fundamental principle had supervened and relativised the other. For Paul πίστις Χριστοῦ had now to be seen as not only a necessary but also the *sufficient* condition for acceptability within the Christian gatherings.

2.5   Which brings us back to the crunch issue. For Peter and the other Christian Jews, πίστις Χριστοῦ was no doubt also an essential prerequisite for those seeking to join the band of Christians in Antioch (as indeed Gal. 2.15–16 indicates – 'we know that ...'). But for them πίστις Χριστοῦ was also wholly consistent with

---

[16] See my 'Once More, *PISTIS CHRISTOU*', *Society of Biblical Literature 1991 Seminar Papers*, ed. E.H. Lovering (Atlanta: Scholars Press, 1991) 730–442; and further below § 3.1. However, I retain the Greek phrase in the text in order that my formulation should facilitate as much consensus as possible, since the issue of how to understand and translate πίστις Χριστοῦ for the most part bears only tangentially on the issue of Paul and the Law.

[17] See particularly S.J.D. Cohen, 'Crossing the Boundary and Becoming a Jew', *HTR* 82 (1989) 13–33; E.P. Sanders, 'Jewish Association with Gentiles and Galatians 2.11–14', in *Studies in Paul and John*, J.L. Martyn FS, ed. R.T. Fortna & B.R. Gaventa (Nashville: Abingdon, 1990) 170–88; Dunn, *Galatians* 119–21. P.F. Esler, 'Sectarianism and the Conflict at Antioch', *The First Christians in their Social World* (London: Routledge, 1994) 52–69, simply dismisses the evidence there cited, attempts to define the ambiguous ἰουδαΐζειν solely from Galatians in complete disregard for its usage elsewhere, and insists that the issue at Antioch must have been precisely the same as that in Galatia.

living as a devout Jew, observing the works of the law (the deeds required by the law).[18] That is to say, Peter and the others were acting on the assumption of continuity between their own religious heritage and the gospel of Christ. It was that continuity which required them to continue to live as good Jews, that is, separated from Gentiles (even Gentile Christians) in table-fellowship at least. The πίστις Χριστοῦ, (and) their believing in Christ, evidently made no difference to that. On the contrary, for them πίστις Χριστοῦ was part of the continuity between Second Temple Judaism and the new movement focused in Jesus the Christ.

Are we then being forced to the conclusion that it was Peter and the other Christian Jews who were much the stronger proponents of continuity between the common Jewish heritage and the new believing in Christ? that they saw no conflict between the gospel and the law? And that Paul in pressing for πίστις Χριστοῦ as the sole determinant of the Christian status of Gentile believers was in fact undermining that continuity? that he saw a much deeper theological issue behind the gospel/works of the law conflict which erupted at Antioch? Evidently it is time to turn to the other side of the continuity-discontinuity motif which we have made the *Leitmotif* in this attempt to search out as much common ground as possible from the Symposium.

3. The problem of discontinuity

3.1 If the problem of discontinuity weakened as some of the older stereotypes of 'late Judaism' and 'legalistic Judaism' dropped away, it seemed to re-emerge again with varied force as the discussion of the Symposium papers progressed.

For example, if πίστις Χριστοῦ does denote 'the faith(fulness) of Christ' (Longenecker)[19], then that itself would strike a strong note of continuity: at the centre of Paul's gospel would be the claim that Jesus himself was faithful, presumably as Abraham had been found faithful in his readiness to offer up Isaac (1 Macc. 2.52; Jas. 2.21–23). My problem with such an exposition is that it would make the πίστις Χριστοῦ phrase in effect continuous and consistent with Jewish faithfulness in doing what the law requires ('the works of the law'). And yet Paul seems to set the two concepts in antithesis, not least in Gal. 2.16. Moreover,

---

[18] F.G. Martinez, *The Dead Sea Scrolls Translated* (Leiden: Brill, 1994) 79, 84 translates the now famous מעשי התורה מקצת from 4QMMT 113 (= 4Q398 fr.2, 2.3) as 'some of the precepts of the Torah' (as also *Discoveries in the Judean Desert Vol. X: Qumran Cave 4 Vol. V: Miqsat Ma'ase Ha-Torah*, ed. E. Qimron & J. Strugnell [Oxford: Clarendon, 1994]). However, at the SBL meeting in Chicago in November 1994, Martinez accepted that his translation was unsatisfactory, and that the phrase should be rendered 'some of the *works* of the Torah'; see further my '4QMMT and Galatians', *NTS* 43 (1997) 147–53 [= ch. 14 below].

[19] B.W. Longenecker, 'Defining the Faithful Character of the Covenant Community: Galatians 2.15–21 and Beyond: A Response to Jan Lambrecht', in *Paul and the Mosaic Law* 75–97.

quite how this faithfulness of Christ would count as decisive in exempting Gentile Christians from showing an equivalent faithfulness is a logic which proponents of the πίστις Χριστοῦ = 'the faith of Christ' thesis need to explain. It seems more likely that πίστις Χριστοῦ should be reckoned on the side of *dis*continuity (cf. Gal. 3.23–24).

Perhaps we could even say that a πίστις Χριστοῦ = 'the faith of Christ' thesis makes better sense of *Peter's* position in the Antioch confrontation, a Christ whose faithfulness warranted the faithful in maintaining their separateness from Gentiles, and thus confirmed Jewish believers in their refusal to eat with Gentile believers. Whereas Paul's position makes better sense if πίστις Χριστοῦ denotes the faith *in* Christ which calls in question the need for the faithfulness practised by Peter and the other Jewish Christians. Again we have to conclude that πίστις Χριστοῦ, as an expression of Paul's own convictions belongs more to the side of discontinuity than of continuity.

A similar issue comes to the fore in the other disagreement already alluded to, over the significance of ἁμαρτωλός in Gal. 2.17. For if it was primarily an issue of factional usage, as seems to be the case in 2.15, of those who counted themselves 'righteous' denying acceptability before God of the 'sinner' who belonged to another faction, or of 'Gentile sinners' generally, then it is primarily an issue of human relationships, and the debate stays within the factional debates which characterise the literature of Second Temple Judaism.[20] A greater degree of continuity can then be postulated, if not with all factions within Second Temple Judaism, at least with the factional spirit of Second Temple Judaism, and particularly in the case of Peter and the other Christian Jews. But if, as Lambrecht argues, the issue in 2.17 is the deeper one of sin as accounted such by God,[21] then the issue is one of relationship between God and human beings, and the dispute has been moved on to a different level. In which case Paul's shift in usage marks a shift from a more containable continuity to a more serious discontinuity.

3.2 Galatians, of course, poses the question of discontinuity in very sharp terms, as recent debate on the letter has underscored. It is not simply a matter of the way the term 'law' itself is used within the letter. In the discussion of Graham Stanton's paper[22] there was general agreement on the negative force attributed to the law in Gal. 3–4, and that the audiences/churches to whom the letter was read could hardly fail to hear the sustained antithesis between law and faith. The

---

[20] See further my 'Pharisees, Sinners, and Jesus', in *The Social World of Formative Christianity and Judaism*, H.C. Kee FS, ed. J. Neusner et al. (Philadelphia: Fortress, 1988) 264–89, reprinted in my *Jesus, Paul and the Law: Studies in Mark and Galatians* (London: SPCK/Louisville: Westminster, 1990) 61–86, here 71–7; and again my 'Echoes of Intra-Jewish Polemic' 462–5 [= 230–3 above].

[21] See above n.14.

[22] G. Stanton, 'The Law of Moses and the Law of Christ – Galatians 3.1–6.2', in *Paul and the Mosaic Law* 99–116.

strength and force of the negative was disputed, but no one could deny that 'under the law' was linked with 'under sin' (3.22–23) and was equated with a slave-like status, indeed with slavery under 'the weak and beggarly elemental forces' (4.3, 8–10).

Even more important for the question of continuity/discontinuity, however, is the apocalyptic context within which the question of the law is raised in Galatians.[23] The note is struck at both beginning and end of the letter: references to 'the present evil age' (1.4) from which believers are delivered, and to the world crucified to Paul and Paul to it (6.14), indicate that 'the revelation of Jesus Christ' (1.12, 16) involved a still more radical shift in Paul's perspective – not simply a passing from 'Judaism' to faith in Messiah Jesus, but from one age to another. And in this schema the law seems to belong to the age now past (Gal. 3.23–26). Hence the sharpness of the antithesis in the allegory of the two wives of Abraham, the two covenants: the law stands with Sinai/Hagar in the opposite/opposed column to Sarah/'the Jerusalem above' (4.22–27), resulting in the very radical command that those of present Jerusalem are to be cast out of their inheritance like Hagar and Ishmael of old (4.28–30). The antithesis between law and Spirit (particularly 3.1–5 and 5.16–23) also reflects a similar eschatological perspective, the Spirit as the power of the age to come over against the law as the power of the age past.

The question which this emphasis poses to the continuity/discontinuity debate is nicely highlighted by reference to the word 'covenant'.[24] For while it is an attractive line of interpretation to argue that Paul saw faith (in Christ) and the Spirit as the fulfilment of the promise to Abraham, and therefore to describe Paul's theology as 'covenant theology', that is not a conclusion which Paul's further argument seems to support. Despite it being an inviting corollary to the argument of 3.15–18, Paul himself does not put 'covenant' and 'law' in antithesis. On the contrary, in the allegory of chapter 4 he speaks of 'two covenants' (4.24); both Sinai/Torah and the promise of a son in accordance with the Spirit are designated as 'covenants', and not as old and new covenant either. 'Covenant' here functions as a neutral term, able to express discontinuity as much as continuity. Despite first appearances, then, Galatians does not validate the designation of Paul's theology of continuity as 'covenant theology'.[25]

---

[23] In recent scholarship the issue has been posed particularly by J.L. Martyn, 'Apocalyptic Antinomies in Paul's Letter to the Galatians', *NTS* 31 (1985) 410–24; also 'Events in Galatia', in *Pauline Theology Volume 1*, ed. J.M. Bassler (Minneapolis: Fortress, 1991) 160–79; for my own debate with Martyn see my *The Theology of Paul's Letter to the Galatians* (Cambridge University, 1993) ch. 3.

[24] I have been influenced here by the thesis of E. Christiansen, *The Covenant and its Ritual Boundaries in Palestinian Judaism and Pauline Christianity* (Durham PhD, 1994) 215–31; similarly Martyn, in *Pauline Theology Volume 1* 179.

[25] To that extent, therefore, N.T. Wright's title, *The Climax of the Covenant* (Edinburgh: T. & T. Clark, 1991), may be misleading as an indication of the *Hauptmotif* of Galatians.

3.3   The same issues were reinforced by Kertelge's paper[26] and the subsequent
discussion on 2 Cor. 3. There can be little question that Spirit and law are being
set in opposition: 3.3, 7 – 'Spirit'/'tablets of stone' (Exod. 32.16; 34.1); 3.6 –
Spirit/γράμμα. Or that Paul had in view two covenants, with the contrast between new and old this time being quite explicit (3.6, 14). Or indeed that the contrast is extended in very radical terms, as between a ministry of death and a ministry of life (Spirit), and again between a ministry of condemnation and a ministry of justification (3.7–9). At the same time, the point was generally taken that
the primary discussion in the chapter was focused on ministry and determined
by the contrast between Moses and Paul.

Here the issue was particularly highlighted by Paul's use of the word 'glory' –
in fact, the key term in the chapter, where it occurs no less than 10 times. Did it
soften the contrast otherwise drawn so sharply? After all, Paul ascribes glory
also to the ministry of Moses (3.7, 9). It is true that he speaks of it as a glory
which faded, was transitory and is now nullified/set aside (3.7, 11, 13, 14 – but
how should the force of καταργέω be rendered?). But it was nevertheless also
the glory of God; in the comparison (3.9–11 – 'how much more', 'the ὑπερ-
βάλλουσα glory') the same heavenly reality stands on both sides. So much so
that Paul is able to use the account of Moses going in to the Lord (Exod. 34.34)
with unveiled face, as a result of which his face reflected the divine glory (Exod.
34.35), as a type of the Jew (or Gentile) of his own day who turned to the Lord,
the Spirit, and who thus beheld the glory of the Lord and likewise began to reflect that glory (3.16–18).

There was thus marked disagreement in the Symposium on the extent to
which Paul could be said to speak of the Torah in 2 Corinthians with any degree
whatsoever of approbation. Not only was the question unresolved as to whether
Paul attributed glory to it and of the significance of that attribution. But the
question of the correlation between Spirit and Torah in 3.3 and 6 became en-
trapped within a sequence of interlinked and disputed issues. Was an echo of Jer.
31.31–33 intended in 3.3 and 6?[27] If so, did Paul think of the 'new covenant' as a
writing of the law upon the heart (Jer. 31.33), and therefore identify the Spirit's
writing upon the human heart (3.3) with the law thus internalised, the circumcision of the heart (Deut. 30.6; Phil. 3.3)? And how to correlate the concept
'Torah/law', which Paul nowhere uses in 2 Corinthians, and the term actually
used here, γράμμα? Which led in turn to questions of the relation between
Torah and γραφή, and between Torah and the νόμος Χριστοῦ of Gal. 6.2. The
problem of getting the right balance between continuity and discontinuity in

---

[26]   K. Kertelge, 'Buchstabe und Geist nach 2 Kor 3', in *Paul and the Mosaic Law* 117–30.

[27]   For a positive response and other bibliography see e.g. V.P. Furnish, *II Corinthians* (AB
32A; New York: Doubleday, 1984) 181, 183–4, 196–7; F. Thielman, *Paul and the Law* (Downers
Grove, Ill.: InterVarsity (1994) 110–1 and n. 32.

Paul's thought seemed to be as intractable here as anywhere in Paul, if not more so.

3.4 The papers and discussions on Romans naturally posed many of the same issues. Out of the session on Romans 2 (Wright)[28] there emerged substantial agreement that the indictment of the 'Jew' (2.17) came within and as part of Paul's indictment of humanity at large (Rom. 2 as following on from Rom. 1.18–32, and leading into 3.1–20); that Paul's indictment embraced both the sense of privilege (2.4, 9–11, 13–16, 17–20, 25) and the actual law-breaking of 'the Jew' (2.1–3, 9, 12–13, 21–27); and that the idea of justification includes both the decisive act of the 'already', but also the still final judgment (2.12–13). But unclarity remains on the degree to which 2.16 (gospel judgment) qualifies or merely restates in another form the judgment spoken of in 2.12–15 (law judgment).[29] And discussion became stuck on the unresolved issue of whether the law-doing Gentile of 2.14, 26–27 was a real or hypothetical figure and whether he was or could (in Paul's view) only be a Christian Gentile.[30]

3.5 With the paper and discussion on Romans 3–4 (Hays)[31] came agreement that we have to speak of several functions of the law, including that of defining Israel as God's people and the importance of works of the law within this framework. There was also agreement on the richness of the concept of the law; it is a unity, not a chameleon; νόμος is also γραφή. But on the continuity/discontinuity question the same issues could not be resolved: how to relate the positive affirmation of Torah/γραφή as a witness to God's way of 'righteousing' (3.21; 4) with a 'righteousing apart from the law' introduced as a new/eschatological development (νυνὶ δέ – 3.21); and how to correlate the νόμος πίστεως of 3.27 with the faith-establishing-law/Torah of 3.31 (a question to which we must return).[32]

Not least of the Symposium's unattained goals was the unresolved question of how to relate the crucial text, 4.4–5,[33] to Paul's on-going argument and particularly to what he says about the law, both the negative and the positive thrust of the preceding verses just alluded to. Fundamental to Paul's gospel of justification is obviously his understanding of God as 'he who justifies the ungodly', including 'him who does not work but believes in' God so understood. But would this come as a total shock and as an unacceptable theological proposition to

---

[28] N.T. Wright, 'The Law in Romans 2', in *Paul and the Mosaic Law* 131–50.

[29] See the helpful discussion by Stuhlmacher, *Römer* 44–6.

[30] In recent years the issue was posed most sharply by C.E.B. Cranfield, *Romans* (ICC; Edinburgh: T. & T. Clark, 1975) 156–7.

[31] R.B. Hays, 'Three Dramatic Roles: The Law in Romans 3–4', in *Paul and the Mosaic Law* 151–64.

[32] See below § 3.7.

[33] Were it necessary to underline the centrality of this text to the debate on Paul and the law, S. Westerholm would have done so firmly enough in his *Israel's Law and the Church's Faith* (Grand Rapids: Eerdmans, 1988); see also Schreiner 51–5, 97–8.

Christian Jews, or Jews at large? How would they or Paul relate it to his understanding of 'the righteousness of God', so completely based as it was on the theological affirmations of the Psalms and Second Isaiah in particular?[34] There was
an interesting debate on the significance of narrative at this point, and on the degree to which we should speak of correspondence more than of continuity (a
synchronic or a diachronic reading of the whole chapter). But the questions with
which the Symposium began remained on the table.

3.6 The paper by Otfried Hofius on Romans 5[35] posed the issue of discontinuity with his customary forcefulness. For in the sharp antithesis between Adam
and Christ, the law/Torah seems to belong wholly on the side of Adam, on the
side of sin and death. The law makes sin accountable and binds the sinner more
firmly to death (5.13–14). Most incriminating of all, 'the law came in to increase
the trespass', establishing all the more firmly sin's reign in death (5.20–21). Here
again we have an apocalyptic or eschatological antithesis: two ages/epochs different in character and effect, the one characterised by law increasing sin reinforcing death, and the other characterised by Christ embodying grace producing
life. And for Paul the new age/epoch of Christ has superceded the old age of law.
Hence Rom. 10.4: 'Christ is the end of the law as a means to righteousness for all
who believe' (10.4).

The discussion here was hampered by failure to achieve agreement on the relation between 'sin' as power and 'sin' as sinful action, and therefore on the relation between sin and death. As ever the precise force of ἐφ' ᾧ in 5.12 remains obscure. More important for the objectives of the Symposium, crucial questions
had to be left hanging. In particular, how far one can generalise from the rhetori-
cally impressed antitheses of Romans 5 and apply the generalisation as an overarching principle elsewhere in Romans.[36] Putting the same point another way,
does Rom. 5.12–21 provide a rounded statement of Paul's view of the law? Is it
only one aspect of the law which Paul had in mind at this point or what might be
described as the essence of the law? How should one relate the shocking assertion of 5.20 to the positive affirmations elsewhere in the letter, not least 3.31.
7.12–13 and 8.4?

3.7 The multiplicity of questions posed by Romans 7 (Hübner)[37] prevented a
full discussion of the passage. It was agreed that Romans 7 was intended by Paul
as a defence of the law, but the Symposium was unable to develop that point of
consensus very far. There was an interesting debate on the question of reading

---

[34] See above n. 3.
[35] O. Hofius, 'Die Adam-Christus-Antithese und das Gesetz: Erwägungen zu Röm 5,12–21',
in *Paul and the Mosaic Law* 165–206.
[36] See further below § 4.5.
[37] H. Hübner, 'Zur Hermeneutik von Röm 7', in *Paul and the Mosaic Law* 207–14.

Romans 7 in context, that is, both in reference to the flow of thought from chapters 5 to 8, and in reference to a Jewish and/or philosophical background. The former has clearly to be acknowledged: if Romans 7 is a defence of the law, it must function as such in relation not least to the negative portrayal of the law which has built up in the preceding chapters and verses. But surprisingly, 7.1–6, with its clear implication of discontinuity between old epoch and new, was not really brought into the discussion, and the relation of 5.20 to 7.7–8.4 was not really followed through. At the same time, setting Romans 7 within a wider philosophical discussion is a reminder that the issue of continuity/discontinuity of Paul's gospel with his Jewish heritage is itself part of a wider and deeper appreciation of the anthropological tension between willing and doing. The discussion, however, became caught up in the old dispute over the extent to which the chapter was retrospective – Paul's Christian view of (his old) life under sin (again implying greater discontinuity), or also of his own life still as a believer (implying greater continuity).[38]

For my own part, two crucial issues do emerge. First, the question cannot be avoided, whether the defence of the law in Romans 7 functions also as a defence against the charge Paul himself brought against the law in 5.20 (and implicitly in 7.6). The argument from 7.7 through to and climaxing in 8.4 surely attempts to get the law 'off the hook' as being not a willing ally of sin but rather sin's (unwitting) tool. Despite all that Paul has said, the law still remains 'the law of God', 'holy and just and good', unveiling the deceitfulness and sinfulness of sin even when being abused by sin (7.7–13), still a delight to the inner self and a proper aspiration for the willing 'I' (7.22, 25). And above all, according to 8.3–4, the purpose of God in sending his Son was 'in order that the requirement of the law might be fulfilled in us who walk ... in accordance with the Spirit' – an astonishing assertion if the law belonged so exclusively to the age of Adam and to the power of sin and death.

The other issue is again the question posed in reference to 3.27 – the meaning of νόμος πίστεως. Here the question becomes the meaning of the similar phrase in 8.2, 'the νόμος of the Spirit of life'. On my view, this phrase shows that Paul can use νόμος very positively – 'the law of the Spirit of life' (8.2) being a summary way of speaking of the law fulfilled in those who walk in accordance with the Spirit (8.4), 8.3–4 functioning, as the γάρ indicates, to explain the logic and force of 8.2. There is for Paul a function of the law apart from its function as the tool of sin and death ('the law of sin and death'). On Räisänen's view, in contrast, νόμος in the phrase 'the νόμος of the Spirit of life' cannot be understood as attributing such a positive role to the law, and so has to be understood as meaning

---

[38] The most recent full treatment is by J. Lambrecht, *The Wretched 'I' and its Liberation: Paul in Romans 7 and 8* (Louvain: Peeters, 1992).

'rule' or 'principle', or, (Räisänen's preference) '(saving) order'.[39] Either way, however, the flexibility of the concept νόμος is considerable, and that must have important implications for Paul's theology of νόμος which the posing of 'law' and 'principle' as *alternatives* may not adequately reflect.

3.8 The discussion of Romans 9–11, initiated by Stephen Westerholm's paper,[40] ran into similar problems. It was helpful to be reminded that the question of the law was part of a much larger issue, though it meant that most of the discussion was on the larger issue rather than on the law![41] A salutary question drew attention to the horizon of Paul's thought: the focal point may be *Israel*, but is not the *horizon* the larger question of the character of God's mercy? Is the issue in Romans 9–11 Israel, or God? Certainly it would appear that this was where the issue of continuity/discontinuity 'bit' most deeply for Paul himself. The implication of continuity in 9.4–5 seems to be decisively countered or qualified by the thematic affirmation of discontinuity of 9.6 ('Not all those descended from Israel are "Israel"'), and by the growing recognition through the three chapters that those now caught in the dark shadow of God's electing purpose seem to be Paul's own Israelite contemporaries. And yet Paul can still conclude that 'all Israel shall be saved' (11.26), in a strong reassertion of continuity in the divine purpose (11.29).

The tensions within and between the chapters were clearly highlighted by Räisänen's response[42] in particular. How typical is the idea of election in Paul's thought? Is it quite the same as his teaching on justification by faith (where does faith come in in the final denouement of 11.26, 31–32)? Do Romans 9–11 contain special pleading? In short, do these chapters reveal the impossibility of Paul holding together both the integrity of his gospel and his despairing belief in the faithfulness of God to Israel? My own answer, that for Paul 'Israel' is *defined* by grace, by divine call (Rom. 9.6–13),[43] is presumably at least a partial answer, but did not succeed in convincing the Symposium as a whole.

But again the Symposium was unable to bring further clarity to the role of the law within this complex area of debate. Does the law belong on the side of the discontinuity, or on the side of continuity? And if Paul's exposition is caught up in irreconcilable inconsistency, is the same true of his understanding of the law within the whole process? Discontinuity seems to be asserted with all vigour in

---

[39] H. Räisänen, 'The "Law" of Faith and the Spirit', *Jesus, Paul and Torah. Collected Essays* (JSNTS 43; Sheffield: Sheffield Academic, 1992) ch. 2; see also Schreiner 35–6; Thielman 183 with 293 n.71, and 200 with 297 n.24 (with further bibliography).

[40] S. Westerholm, 'Paul and the Law in Romans 9–11', in *Paul and the Mosaic Law* 215–37.

[41] In view of its importance in the gospel/law antithesis, more attention should have been given to 10.4 than time or the run of discussion permitted.

[42] H. Räisänen, 'Faith, Works and Election in Romans 9: A Response to Stephen Westerholm', in *Paul and the Mosaic Law* 239–49.

[43] See my *Romans* 539–40.

the famous 10.4, though had Paul wished to denigrate the law as he did in 5.20, one might have expected that he would tie the law in to the process of Israel's hardening, the law as part of their entrapment (11.7–10). In contrast, however, Paul had also affirmed that the law is one of Israel's great privileges (9.4). Moreover, to the surprise of many translators and commentators, Paul can talk of the 'νόμος of righteousness' as a proper goal for Israel to have pursued and which they failed to attain only because they pursued it in the wrong way (9.31–32).[44] And it can hardly be coincidence that his exposition of 'the righteousness which is from faith' used a passage which had affirmed the ease of doing the law (Deut. 30.11–14) and which had already been interpreted of the heavenly wisdom embodied in the Torah (Bar. 3.29–30, 4.1).[45]

We still have the final sessions of the Symposium to review, but the reflections on the discussion of Romans 9–11 provide a particularly appropriate place to make the transition to the final section of this paper, since the passage expresses so clearly the problems and tensions with which the commentator on Paul's theology has to wrestle.

4. Towards common ground?

4.1   The search for common ground in such a controversial area is rendered difficult, some might say impossible, by two factors which came up at different points in the discussions of the Symposium.

The first is whether Paul in fact managed to achieve complete consistency in what is, in effect, his own plea for continuity. The question was posed particularly in the discussions of Romans 2 and (as we have just noted) Romans 9–11. It is partly a problem of how we today 'hear' a text like Romans 2. Should our exegetical assumption necessarily be that Paul's thinking in this chapter was and can be shown today to be consistent with what he wrote elsewhere? One side of that is the problem of recognizing the rhetorical character of what Paul wrote: how to allow most judiciously for an argument slanted to catch the attention of a particular group, for what we might call loud- or soft-peddling in the replaying of a particular theme, for dramatic or stylistic effect in tightly worded passages, and so on? The other side is that our questions may be so much the more determined by issues subsequent to Paul's writing that they are not actually resolvable from what Paul actually says, and may in fact be misleading if it is Paul's theology we wish to uncover. Does our constant search for new analytical or synthetic categories, like 'covenantal nomism' and 'narrative', simply pull the threads of Paul's thought into another pattern of our own designing?

---

[44] RSV/NRSV typify the surprise felt by many commentators when they translate νόμον δικαιοσύνης as 'the righteousness which/that is based on (the) law'.

[45] See further my *Romans* 603–5; Thielman 208–10.

A second problem which emerged with force towards the end of the Symposium is the distinction between Paul's *intention* in his theology and the actual *effect* of his mission. Here the papers and discussion on 1 Corinthians 9 (Barton)[46] and Rom. 14–15 (Barclay)[47] were of particular interest. Not only because they highlighted afresh the importance of the social context and its dynamic for our own understanding of Paul's theology in these passages. But also because they posed the issue of whether Paul's strategy inevitably provoked a *social instability* which was bound to work against his *theological ideal*. Would not Paul's policy as stated in 1 Cor. 9.19–23 inevitably have seemed to lack integrity and to have caused confusion to those whose identity was constituted by their being 'under the law'? And in Romans 14 the appearance of even-handedness is similarly misleading. Paul seemed to be asking more of Gentile believers (who had already shifted from a Gentile frame of reference), but was in fact asking more of Jewish believers (who had not yet shifted from their traditional frame of reference). How could Paul claim both that the law is holy and that nothing is unclean? No doubt he saw behind the two claims a higher logic, but the social reality was that his teaching undermined the social and cultural integrity of the observant Jewish believer.[48]

More fundamental still, by putting circumcision and uncircumcision on the same level of irrelevance (1 Cor. 7.19a, etc.) Paul cut at the root of the identity of those whom he himself called simply 'the circumcision'. Was this the only way for the Christian Jew to go? Could the continuity be maintained only by those who followed Paul's example? In the event, the restructuring of Jewish identity which Paul's gospel called for proved totally unacceptable to the great bulk of his fellow Jews. In other words, the theological question posed by Paul's gospel cannot be resolved solely at the level of ideas and doctrines. And if the social reality of Jewish identity proved an effective stumbling block even among sympathetic Jewish believers, how much less realistic were Paul's hopes regarding Israel as a whole?

The search for common ground, therefore, whether as common ground among present-day interpreters of Paul's writings, or as common ground between Paul himself and his fellow Christian Jews, may be a search for an ideal which Paul himself was unable to achieve and which we today are unable fully to appreciate. Nevertheless, if only out of respect for Paul and for the greatness of his vision, something can and should be said.

---

[46] S.C. Barton, '"All Things to All People": Paul and the Law in the Light of 1 Corinthians 9.19–23', in *Paul and the Mosaic Law* 271–85.

[47] J.M.G. Barclay, '"Do we undermine the Law?": A Study of Romans 14.1–15.6', in *Paul and the Mosaic Law* 287–308.

[48] However, the argument is pushed much too far by F. Watson, *Paul, Judaism and the Gentiles: A Sociological Approach* (SNTSMS 56; Cambridge University, 1986).

4.2   Let us begin with what has usually been regarded as a major expression of Paul's gospel, namely, justification by faith.[49] Although its centrality in Paul's thought has been periodically questioned, it is certainly the teaching of Paul which made the law a problem for Paul's theology, if questions like those posed in Rom. 3.31 ('Do we make the law invalid through faith?') and 7.7 ('Is the law sin?') signal more than 'mere rhetoric'. And it is the doctrine of justification by faith which continues to pose that problem most sharply for contemporary interpreters of Paul. From the Symposium's discussions several threads of agreement can be brought together.

a) The question of justification arises as an issue in Paul's letters within the context of his mission to the Gentiles.[50] The question as posed, particularly in Galatians and Romans, is whether, and if so how, Gentiles may be accounted acceptable to God, whether, and if so how, they may come to share in the blessings of Abraham and of the chosen people. To be noted is the fact that the issue as discussed by Paul is not about whether and how Gentiles might be deemed acceptable to God without reference to father Abraham and his seed – a possible reading of Romans 2, but only if taken in isolation from the rest of the letter. Nor does it matter at this point who first raised the issue of Gentile believers sharing in Abraham's seed and inheritance (Paul himself or other Christian Jewish missionaries in Galatia).[51] The crucial point for us is that this issue is the context in which Paul's major expositions of justification take place.

b) Underlying this specific contingent issue (whether and how Gentiles may be accounted acceptable to God) is the more fundamental theological assertion of divine initiative and human helplessness. This is implicit in the apocalyptic perspective from which Paul views the whole process of God's purpose of salvation; it is not simply a healing and a cleansing which is necessary, but a whole new act of creation, a giving of life to the dead and a calling into existence what had no existence (Rom. 4.17). And it is explicit in the universal indictment of Romans 1–3, as crystallised not least in Rom. 4.4–5.

c) Both aspects are reflected in the term 'sinner'. Partly as a question of Jews regarding Gentiles as outside the people of God ('sinners' – Gal. 2.15); and partly also as the question of actual sin with the consequent liability to condemnation. The way in which the issue is posed in Eph. 2.11–12 may well express a genuinely Pauline synthesis of both aspects: uncircumcised Gentiles were by definition *both* aliens from the commonwealth of Israel, strangers to the covenants

---

[49] We need only recall how Luther, and in this century Bultmann and Käsemann, regarded 'justification by faith' as the fundamental principle of the gospel; see particularly J. Reumann, *Righteousness in the New Testament* (Philadelphia: Fortress/New York: Paulist, 1982).

[50] Here we may say that the arguments of W. Wrede, *Paul* (London: Philip Green, 1907) 122–8, and K. Stendahl, *Paul Among Jews and Gentiles* (Phiadelphia: Fortress, 1976/London: SCM, 1977) particularly 1–7, have carried the day.

[51] This in response to J.L. Martyn, 'A Law-Observant Mission to Gentiles: The Background of Galatians', *SJT* 38 (1985) 307–24.

of promise, *and* separated from Christ, having no hope and without God in the
world.

4.3   The degree of continuity between Paul's gospel of justification and central
emphases not only in the OT but also within Second Temple Judaism can also be
sketched in a broad outline which commands a fair degree of consensus.

a) Characteristic of both Paul and his Jewish heritage is the common recognition that standing with God depends on the initiative of divine grace. Israel's
identity was determined from the first by divine election and call. Deuteronomy
as the classic expression of 'covenantal nomism' starts from the recognition of
Israel's slave status, without any claim on God, at the time of God's choice
(Deut. 5.6; 6.21; 7.6–8; etc). As noted already, Paul's understanding of the δικ-
αιοσύνη Θεοῦ is derived directly from the fundamental theological assertions
on the theme in Israel's scriptures (above n. 3).

b) Equally characteristic of both Paul and his Jewish heritage is the other side
of covenantal nomism – that is, the insistence that certain obligations follow for
those who have been recipients of this grace. Paul insists on the ethical corollary
and consequences of God's choice and acceptance as strongly as the Deuteronomist, with the equal recognition on the part of both that the necessary obedience
has to be from the heart. For Paul as much as Deuteronomy 'righteousness' in effect sums up both sides of covenantal nomism, both the saving action of God and
the obligation of obedience to that righteousness (e.g. Rom. 6.18–19).[52]

c) And Paul would certainly insist that his own commission to preach the gospel to the Gentiles was in fulfilment of Israel's own obligation to be a light to the
Gentiles. He implies as much in Gal. 1.15–16 with its clear echo of Isa. 49.1–6 and
Jer. 1.5, his conversion being understood by him to be wholly in the tradition of
the call and commissioning of Israel's prophets.[53] As Gal. 3.8 also indicates, he
focuses the apologia for his gospel in the third strand of the promise to Abraham: the promise not only of seed and of land, but also of blessing to the nations (Gen. 12.3 etc.). What Israel had not yet fully delivered Paul saw to be his
task, but precisely as the fulfilment of Israel's task.

It is within this continuity that the issue of discontinuity is posed. For what
separates and marks out Paul's theology of grace from that of his Jewish contemporaries is, of course, his sense (in common with other Christian voices of the
NT) that the decisive eschatological climax has already come in the death and
resurrection of Jesus. I say 'within this continuity', since Paul hardly sees the
coming of Christ as a disruption or abandoning of the divine purpose as expressed through Abraham and Israel. If the apocalyptic perspective signals dis-

---

[52] Thielman 238–41 is part of the growing consensus on these first two points; contrast
Schreiner 114–21.

[53] The point is only partially grasped by K.O. Sandnes, *Paul – One of the Prophets?* (WUNT
2.43; Tübingen: Mohr, 1991) 56–69.

continuity it also signals climax. Nevertheless, for all Paul's assertions of continuity here too, the practical effect was that the terms of grace, the basis of acceptance before God, had in his view shifted with the coming of Israel's Messiah.
However much the faith called for was like the faith of Abraham, it was now
faith focused in and through Christ Jesus, a cause of stumbling for the bulk of Israel (Rom. 9.32–33). And the theological/christological discontinuity was mirrored in the sociological discontinuity reflected in Romans 14–15, despite Paul's
continuing ideal (15.7–12).

4.4 It is within this larger theological picture, with its measure of common
ground opened up, and with full recognition of the tensions it contains, that the
question of Paul and the law must be resolved if at all.

We may start with the least controversial point: that there is a spectrum in
Paul's reference to the law, a spectrum running from what sounds a highly positive approbation to what sounds a highly negative condemnation. On the one
hand, in his defence of the law, Paul does not hesitate to describe it as 'holy, just
and good' (Rom. 7.12), a very positive gift of God (Rom. 9.4); the recognition of
such a positive affirmation does not depend, it should be noted, on the disputed
interpretation of the phrase, 'the νόμος of the Spirit of life' later on in the same
section (Rom. 8.2). On the other hand, he clearly speaks of the law as an enslaving power, increasing the trespass and used by sin to bring about death (Gal.
4.1–10; Rom. 5.20; 7.5; 1 Cor. 15.56).[54]

Coordinated with this is the further recognition that for Paul the law has a variety of functions. Three of these call for comment.

The first is the role of the law in disclosure of the will of God, with consequent
awareness or consciousness of sin. Somewhat surprisingly Paul says nothing of
this function in Galatians. And when in Romans he refers to it repeatedly (Rom.
3.20; 4.15; 5.13; 7.13), he does so as to an established axiom which no one would
question and which he therefore did not have to argue for. This function is obviously related to that of condemning sin, as indicated in 4.15, and is thus also the
function referred to in 2.12–13.

This might seem to be the most negative feature of the law – its function in
bringing about divine wrath, in condemning transgression, in cursing the one
who fails to do all that is written in the book of the law (Gal. 3.10). But this is simply part of its God-given purpose, which Paul takes for granted. Certainly at the
heart of Paul's gospel is the claim that Christ brings deliverance from the coming
wrath (Rom. 5.9), that there is no condemnation for those in Christ (Rom. 8.1),
and that Christ has redeemed from the curse of the law (Gal. 3.13). But that is
not entirely a point of discontinuity. The law itself also provided for forgiveness

---

[54] See e.g. Schreiner ch. 3.

and atonement as David attested (Rom. 4.7–8); Abraham was justified by faith long before the coming of Christ. There is continuity here too.

Does this taken-for-grantedness of the law's function in bringing sin to conscious transgression and condemnation give us a clue? Here is a function which the law had from the beginning (5.13; 7.13), and which, for Paul, it evidently still has (3.20; 4.15) and will have in the final judgment, or so the argument of Rom. 2.12–16 seems to indicate. Paul continues to affirm, or rather to assume this function of the law, even in the midst of his more negative comments about the law. However, because this function is part of the common ground which he shared with his fellow (Christian) Jews he saw no need to elaborate it. Whereas, it was the more controversial negative comments for which he had to argue, and as a result of which he had to mount an elaborate (but for us confusing) defence of the law.

The question thus arises whether we have been misled by this imbalance of Paul's exposition. That is to say, has our attention been distracted by the greater emphasis given to the negative function of the law, and have we failed to give sufficient weight to the continuing function of the law in making conscious of and condemning sin, simply because the latter is alluded to so briefly in the midst of other argumentation? In classic treatments the law's role in making conscious of sin and condemning sin leads directly into its role in inciting sin (Rom. 5.20; 7.7–11);[55] but it is only the latter on which Paul mounts his defence of the law (7.7–8.4). Ought not the two functions to be held more distinct in Paul's thought – one affirmed by Paul without question, the other seen by him as an issue calling for a defence of the law?

4.5   A second function of the law, which was generally recognized in the Symposium's discussions, was its role in marking out the people of God. This is indicated for example in Paul's distinction between those who have and 'those who do not have the law' (Rom. 2.12–14), and by his talk of Israel as 'under the law' (as in Gal. 3.23–25)[56] and of the 'Jew' as marked out by his boasting in the law (Rom. 2.23). Paul is obviously critical of this role of the law, a fact which gives rise to several important questions.

a) First, how negative is his criticism of this function of the law? The imagery he uses in Gal. 3.23–4.2 is essentially positive: a protective garrison, the custodian-tutor (παιδαγωγός), the heir under guardians and stewards.[57] The imagery is not far from that used in the *Letter of Aristeas* 139–42 already referred to (§2.3).

---

[55] I am thinking of R. Bultmann, *Theology of the New Testament* Vol. 1 (London: SCM, 1952) 261–8; Cranfield, *Romans* 846–8.

[56] The suggestion of L. Gaston, 'Paul and the Torah', *Paul and the Torah* (Vancouver: University of British Columbia, 1987) 29–30, that Paul used the phrase 'under the law' 'to designate the Gentile situation' is simply incredible.

[57] For detailed exposition I may refer simply to my *Galatians, ad loc.*

b) Second, Paul clearly sees this function of the law as essentially *temporary*, until the coming of Christ and the possibility of faith in him (Gal. 3.22–25; 4.3–7). How much of Paul's negative assessment of the law is focused on this temporary function of the law? And does his criticism amount to a criticism of his fellow Jews for wanting to preserve this function and to remain within the law's protective custody as minors, no better than slaves, when the eschatological moment has come for the transition to full sonship, for the heir to enter his heritage?

Here it needs to be observed that it is when the question shifts to what such an attitude says about Gentile participation in Israel's heritage that the issue of works of the law comes to the fore, as Gal. 2.15–16, Rom. 3.27–30 and Rom. 9.30–32 all indicate: Gal. 2.15–16 – the statement provoked by Christian Jews who will not eat with Christian Gentiles; Rom. 3.27–30 – boasting in works of the law as tantamount to affirming that God is God of Jews only; Rom. 9.30–32 – Gentiles attained raighteousness from faith, but Israel failed to attain the law of righteousness because they pursued it as if it was a matter of works. Is this the primary reason why Paul opposes justification by faith against justification by works? – because justification by works of the law is another way of saying Israel has clung too long to the protective status of the law which set Israel apart from the other nations? Even if that is not the whole answer, it surely must be a significant part of the answer.[58]

Rom. 5.20 also needs to be correlated under this head. For on the one hand it has in view the entry of the law within the processes of human history, that is to Israel's history through Moses (5.13). Its function within the age of Adam is not distinct from its role in relation to Israel (cf. 7.7–13).[59] And on the other hand, as already observed, the defence of the law in 7.7–8.4 must have the charge of 5.20 in view as well, and must therefore serve as Paul's own answer to that charge (above § 3.7). The law in its role as the (unwitting) agent of sin and death is also not distinct from its role in relation to Israel.

c) Third, underlying this more specific issue which so absorbed Paul is the more fundamental issue of human dependence wholly on divine grace. Here the crucial text Rom. 4.4–5 comes centre stage. The issue is of sufficient importance to warrant a separate section.

---

[58] At this point, of course, I am drawing on my own thesis regarding 'works of the law' in Paul, though at this point in a noncontroversial way, I hope. See e.g. my 'Yet Once More – "The Works of the Law": A Response', *JSNT* 46 (1992) 99–117 [= ch. 8 above]; also '4QMMT and Galatians', *NTS* 43 (1997) 147–53 [= ch. 14 below]. That the thesis can be fruitful for Jewish reassessment of Paul is indicated by A.F. Segal, *Paul the Convert: The Apostolate and Apostasy of Saul the Pharisee* (New Haven: Yale University, 1990) particularly 124, and D. Boyarin, *A Radical Jew: Paul and the Politics of Identity* (Berkeley: University of California, 1994) e.g. 52–6.

[59] I am more open than I was in *Romans* 383 to the likelihood that Rom. 7.9–11 includes an allusion to Israel's own fall into sin and death as well as that of humankind at large; see e.g. Thielman 295 n. 15.

4.6 With Rom. 4.4–5 the question has to be posed: however much the preceding exposition (3.27–31) was focused on the relation of Jew and Gentile within the justifying purposes of God, does the issue here not clearly become the impossibility of human endeavour to achieve God's favour and the fundamentally flawed character of the theology which claims otherwise?[60]

The answer is probably Yes! The question is, however, whether such a conclusion runs counter to the theology of the law built up in the preceding paragraphs. Do we have in Rom. 4.4–5 a concept of 'works of the law' at odds with the correlation between 'works of the law' and the issue of Gentile acceptability just noted? Not necessarily so. Here the earlier question, already asked above, also comes into play: would this statement (Rom. 4.4–5) come as a total shock and as an unacceptable theological proposition to Christian Jews, or Jews at large? For my own part, the more probable answer has to be No! And the degree of agreement noted above (§§ 4.2b and 4.3a) points to the same conclusion.

In other words, the proposition of Rom. 4.4–5 was probably *not* at issue between Paul and his fellow Christian Jews (or Jews in general). This was in fact part of the common ground that Paul could take for granted, like his understanding of 'the righteousness of God' (§§ 2.1, 4.3a). That, presumably, is why Paul did not need to argue the point but could simply assert it without argument – because he was confident it would not be disputed by any typically Jewish reader. That is to say, Paul restates the theologoumenon in 4.4–5, not (so much) because it was contested by his fellow (Christian) Jews, but more as a reminder of what they themselves also regarded as fundamental in the establishment of a relationship between God and human beings.

Here we may see a parallel with the argument or repetition of the tactic used a few verses earlier. In Rom. 3.27–30 Paul sets the problem of relating faith and works at once into the context of the issue of Gentiles' acceptability to God, and to resolve the question he appeals to a fundamental Jewish axiom: that God is one (3.29–30). It was precisely because it was a Jewish axiom that Paul appealed to it and could entertain good hope that his argument based on it would have effect on Christian Jews. In like manner in 4.4–5 it makes best sense to assume that Paul repeats the tactic by again appealing to a Jewish axiom and drawing from it a deduction which his fellow Christian Jews could be expected to acknowledge, even when applied to the more contentious question of 'works of the law' as it bore upon the Jew-Gentile issue.

In other words, it should be possible to hold together two conclusions which have been set in contrast. One is that the issue of 'works of the law', like justification, arises in relation to the question whether and how Gentiles can be reckoned acceptable to and by God, since (what Paul refers to as) 'works of the law' served normally to reinforce the separateness of Israel from the other na-

---

[60] See above n. 33.

tions. The second is that Rom. 4.4–5 exposes a more fundamental issue, as Luther rightly saw – the error of thinking that God's acceptance of any person was to be reckoned in terms of God's owing a debt to the latter rather than as an act of divine grace. The only difference is that the latter was probably not in dispute between Paul and other Christian Jews; it was more likely to be common ground, a reassertion as it was of another Jewish axiom. The real issue between Paul and his opponents at this point was how the axiom works out in the continuing Torah obligations of Christian Jews and in their relationships with Gentile Christians. The fundamental theological axiom remains just that; but it was not that which was at issue between Paul and his opponents.

The assertion of Rom. 4.4–5, in other words, is also like the assertion of the first function of the law, as designed to bring about consciousness of sin (§ 4.4). As the former point did not need to be argued, but merely stated as an axiom (like the axiom of Jewish monotheism), so here the point does not need to be argued but merely asserted, as one which no biblically based Jew would wish to dispute. That point of basic agreement having been restated, the issue of how Torah obedience relates to justification, given that God justifies by faith, could be tackled. Or as we might say, the point of continuity having been restated (the basic principle of God's righteousness as justifying grace), the issue of discontinuity could be confronted (what the new manifestation of God's life-giving power in the resurrection meant for Israel's special status before God and under the law).

4.7   Once the focus of Paul's negative critique of the law is thus clarified – as primarily directed against the prolongation or extension of its temporary function vis-a-vis Israel – it becomes easier to recognize a third function of the law which Paul sees as also continuing. This is its function of providing divine direction for life, now distinct from its function in keeping Israel separate from the other nations. That it still has a continuing function is clearly implicit in 1 Cor. 7.19b: 'neither circumcision is anything nor uncircumcision, but keeping the commandments of God'. The challenge of this text was pressed upon us by Peter Tomson's paper.[61] What are 'the commandments of God'? If they are not just the ten commandments, the Torah, then what are they? Did Paul have in mind a different kind of Halakhah, or a different set of 'commandments' (of Christ)? The issue is posed equally by Rom. 13.9, and by the fact that Paul's own paraenesis (Halakhah?) in a passage like Rom. 12.14–21 is so thoroughly impregnated with the paraenesis of Jewish wisdom.[62] And the assertions of such passages as Rom. 3.31, 8.4 and 13.8–10 surely cannot be discounted, or reduced to the love

---

[61] P.J. Tomson, 'Paul's Jewish Background in View of His Law Teaching in 1 Cor 7', in *Paul and the Mosaic Law* 251–70.

[62] For details see my *Romans* 738.

command, however much the love command informs and infuses the way the requirements of the law are to be fulfilled by the believer.[63]

And if this is so, then are we not back once again into a major point of continuity between the Testaments, and with the law itself, in this function at least, as
the bridge? The fact is, as noted above (§§ 2.2, 4.3a, b), that Israel's covenantal
nomism maintains a tension between divine grace and resulting human obligation, and that the tension is remarkably like the tension in Paul's own teaching,
between justification by faith and 'faith working through love' (Gal. 5.6). The
coming of Christ has changed the focus, but the balance of passages like Rom.
8.12–13 and Gal. 6.8, between *Gabe und Aufgabe*, is not so very different from
the balance in Second Temple Judaism's Torah theology, characterised in § 2.2 as
'Weisung zu Leben und Lebens-Weise'. A turn in the ages had indeed taken
place for Paul, but the eschatological tension familiar in Pauline ethics, between
the already and the not-yet, is not so very different from what we find in those
prophets and writers who denounced superficial obedience and looked for obedience from the heart.[64]

5. Conclusion

What can we conclude from all this? If the above lines of reflection are at all
sound, then we do have to recognize a stronger line of continuity between the
function of the law in OT and Second Temple Judaism and a continuing function
for the law into the new age inaugurated by Christ. This is evident both in two of
the law's functions as analysed above: (1) in making conscious of sin, in condemnation of transgression and in final judgment; (2) in providing continuing guidance for conduct and in expressing requirements of God which need to be fulfilled.

As to discontinuity, three things should be said. First, it follows from the discussion above that the gospel-law antithesis is only partially a feature of the continuity-discontinuity discussion. The law has always had the function of condemning transgression (a God-given function), and that function continues for believers. Forgiveness and atonement has always been a necessary desideratum in
consequence of this function of the law, but forgiveness and atonement were

---

[63] Compare and contrast the various wrestlings with the otherwise problematic character of
Paul's conception of Christians 'fulfilling the law' – H. Hübner, *Das Gesetz bei Paulus* (Göttin-
gen: Vandenhoeck, [2]1980) 76–80; J.M.G. Barclay, *Obeying the Truth: A Study of Paul's Ethics in
Galatians* (Edinburgh: T. & T. Clark, 1988) 135–42; Westerholm 201–5; Schreiner ch. 6.

[64] More attention should be given to the observation of M.D. Hooker that 'in many ways, the
pattern which Sanders insists is the basis of Palestinian Judaism fits exactly the Pauline pattern
of Christian experience: God's saving grace evokes man's answering obedience' ('Paul and
"Covenantal Nomism"', *From Adam to Christ: Essays on Paul* [Cambridge University, 1990]
157).

available also before Christ. The discontinuity is the means by which that atonement has now been rendered effective (the death and resurrection of Christ) and the scope of that atonement enlarged (Gentiles as well as Jews). But that the Christ event counts as a denial or rebuke of this function of the law does not follow.

Second, the main thrust of Paul's negative attitude to the law seems to be directed against its function in separating Israel from the other nations. The irony here is that Paul's theological ideal ('Rejoice, O Gentiles, with his people' – Rom. 15.9) seems to have run aground on the social reality of Israel's ethnic and religious identity.

Third, the primary theological issue in the continuity/discontinuity between OT and NT is thus not so much the law, but Christ. Or is even that quite accurate? Jesus is 'Christ' after all precisely as being Israel's Messiah. The problems arose, however, because his coming, and particularly his death and resurrection, seemed to raise the issue of the Gentiles in an unprecedented way, quickly establishing a logic which the Hellenists followed and which Paul first persecuted and then was converted to. Which, perhaps appropriately, brings us back to Paul's conversion, since it was there, in his own mind at least, that the intermingled ingredients of Christology, Israel and the Gentiles, and the law began to ferment in his mind, his mission and his theology.

Chapter 13

'Neither circumcision nor uncircumcision, but ...'

(Gal. 5.2–12; 6.12–16; cf. 1 Cor. 7.7–20)

1. Introduction

The central issue in these passages is obviously circumcision.[1] In the letter to the Galatians Paul opposes those who were trying to persuade his Gentile converts to go beyond (Paul would say, to abandon) his gospel. Up to this point in the letter (5.2), it has not been made clear what it was precisely that these other missionaries[2] wanted of the Galatian believers (beyond the hints of 2.3, 7–9 and 12). Now, however, Paul makes the issue clear beyond doubt. The other missionaries wanted the Galatian Gentile believers to be circumcised. And Paul would have none of it.

What is particularly striking in the two Galatian passages is the sharpness of the contrast Paul draws between circumcision and his own emphases, the out and out antithesis which Paul sets up between circumcision and his gospel. In 5.2–6 *circumcision* is set in antithesis with *Christ:* for the Galatians to be circumcised would mean that they had nullified any benefit Christ brought them; they would be estranged from Christ, fallen away from grace. And in 5.11 and 6.12–14 *circumcision* is set in repeated contrast with the *cross:* circumcision of Gentile believers means denying the scandal of the cross, is a way of avoiding persecution for the cross; circumcision involves a misdirected boasting – in the flesh and not in the cross.[3]

Even such a brief outline is sufficient to indicate that these twin antitheses – circumcision/Christ, circumcision/cross – are shorthand for deeper and larger conflicts. It is not merely a rite (circumcision) which is being set against a person (Christ) or an event (cross). Rather these terms represent larger complexes of belief and praxis. At the same time, it is significant that the larger complexes can

---

[1] In Gal. 5.2–12 and 6.12–16 περιτομή occurs three times and περιτέμνω five times, the highest concentration of both terms in the NT.

[2] I assume (with most) that the 'other missionaries' were Christian Jews probably sent by more conservative Jewish Christian churches. For my own reconstruction of events see my *Galatians* (BNTC; London: A. & C. Black, 1993) 9–19.

[3] For the importance of the repeated circumcision/cross antithesis in what is the conclusion to the letter (6.11–18), see further my *The Theology of Paul's Letter to the Galatians* (Cambridge University, 1993) 28–33.

be summarised in just these terms and that the tensions between the larger complexes come to focus in just these antitheses. It is important for us, then, to clarify as much as possible why and how these terms (circumcision, Christ, cross) could function as they did in Paul's exhortation in these passages and what was at stake here. In particular, we naturally wish to clarify whether Paul was overreacting to the situation in the Galatian churches or had indeed recognized that vital principles were at risk, summed up in just these terms.

The challenges and puzzles confronting us can be summed up in the three 'neither circumcision nor uncircumcision' assertions which seem to function as a kind of Pauline slogan[4] and which form the common link between all three passages of our title:

> Gal. 5.6 – 'in Christ Jesus neither circumcision counts for anything, nor uncircumcision, but faith operating effectively through love';
> Gal. 6.15 – 'neither circumcision counts for anything, nor uncircumcision, but a new creation';
> 1 Cor. 7.19 – 'circumcision is nothing and uncircumcision is nothing, but keeping God's commandments'.

How could Paul make all three assertions? The second seems to imply an apocalyptic discontinuity between old and new, which, if pressed, would assign circumcision and the Judaism it represented to the old creation, now superceded by the new creation represented by Christ, with the cross as the apocalyptic break point between them.[5] But the third seems to imply a kind of *heilsgeschichtlich* continuity between Christ and what went before, a continuity marked by the continuing importance of the commandments and of their being kept, a continuity which evidently runs through the cross.[6] No doubt the different circumstances confronting Paul in Galatia and in Corinth provide sufficient explana-

---

[4] The brevity of the expression does not necessarily imply an already established maxim (H.D. Betz, *Galatians* [Hermeneia; Philadelphia: Fortress, 1979] 319 n.79), far less a Jewish Christian one (R.N. Longenecker, *Galatians* [WBC 41; Dallas: Word, 1990] 296), since it summarizes the distinctive emphasis of the letter. See also n. 64 below.

[5] The emphasis particularly of J.L. Martyn in a number of essays – particularly 'Apocalyptic Antinomies in Paul's Letter to the Galatians', *NTS* 31 (1985) 410–24; and 'Events in Galatia: Modified Covenantal Nomism versus God's Invasion of the Cosmos in the Singular Gospel', in *Pauline Theology Volume 1: Thessalonians, Philippians, Galatians and Philemon*, ed. J.M. Bassler (Minneapolis: Fortress, 1991) 161.

[6] An emphasis well represented in reference to Galatians, in some contrast to Martyn, e.g., by R.B. Hays, *The Faith of Jesus Christ. An Investigation of the Narrative Substructure of Galatians 3.1–4.11* (Chico: Scholars, 1983), and N.T. Wright, *The Climax of the Covenant. Christ and the Law in Pauline Theology* (Edinburgh: T. & T. Clark, 1991). Cf. the earlier controversy between G. Klein, 'Individualgeschichte und Weltgeschichte bei Paulus: Eine Interpretation ihres Verhältnisses im Galaterbrief', *Rekonstruktion und Interpretation* (BEvT 50; München: Chr. Kaiser, 1969) 180–224, and W.G. Kümmel, '"Individualgeschichte" und "Weltgeschichte" in Gal. 2.15–21', in *Christ and Spirit in the New Testament: Essays in Honour of C.F.D. Moule*, ed. B. Lindars & S.S. Smalley (Cambridge University, 1973) 157–73.

tion for such different emphases. But the fact that Paul can speak so positively of keeping the commandments in 1 Corinthians makes one wonder how much of the sharpness of the antitheses drawn in Galatians was the result of rhetorical exaggeration or of short-term alarmist over-reaction.

We must try, first, therefore, to clarify the reasons why circumcision was such a sensitive issue for Paul, why 'circumcision' could sum up and focus the threat he perceived to his Galatian converts, and what were the deeper issues which he saw to be at stake. Second, we need to clarify the force of the other side of the antitheses, and in particular to clarify to what extent for Paul 'Christ' and 'cross' represented a complete break with what had gone before or something more of a realignment within a larger pattern of continuity. The slogans of 5.6 and 6.15 both function as conclusions or corollaries to the antitheses drawn in 5.2–6 and 6.12–15, so we may then be in a position to reach a more adequate understanding of what Paul meant when he said, 'Neither circumcision nor uncircumcision, but ...'.

2. Why was Paul so opposed to the circumcision of the Galatians?

We can best answer this question, first, by reflecting on the importance of circumcision within Judaism, which made circumcision such a focal point and test case whenever any question was raised of Gentiles being accepted as full participants within the Jewish community. Second, we must try to clarify the two principal objections Paul himself raised in the two Galatian passages under consideration.

2.1   Galatians itself does not explain why circumcision was such a crucial concern for the other missionaries. But the reason is obvious, so obvious, indeed, that it does not usually occasion much comment from commentators. It is simply taken for granted that the other missionaries, as Christian Jews, continued to think as Jews and to assume that conversion to Messiah Jesus meant entry into the people of the Messiah, by becoming proselytes, that is, by undergoing circumcision. However, if we are fully to appreciate how it is that circumcision could become such a focal point in the Galatian troubles and be set by Paul in such sharp antithesis to Christ and the cross we need to inquire more deeply into the significance of circumcision for the Judaism of Paul's day.

The basic point is that circumcision was inextricably bound up with Jewish identity, that is, with the identity of the Jews as the people of Israel, the people chosen by God from among all the other nations to be his own. So much so that Paul could identify the Jews as a people simply as 'the circumcision' – not 'the circumcised', but 'the circumcision', ἡ περιτομή, the most distinctive or characteristic feature standing (by metonomy) for the whole. This was already clear in

the references to circumcision in ch. 2: the demand for the circumcision of Titus
was wholly understandable when it was a question of Titus' acceptability to
those identified as 'the circumcision' (2.3, 7, 9); Peter separated himself from the
Gentile believers in 2.12 under pressure from those whose identity or position
was derived from their circumcision (οἱ ἐκ περιτομῆς).[7] The same references
(Gal. 2.7, 9; similarly Rom. 3.30; 4.9; Col. 3.11) remind us that from a Jewish perspective, the rest of the world, the other nations, could be categorised simply as
'the uncircumcision' – again, not 'the uncircumcised', but 'the uncircumcision', ἡ
ἀκροβυστία, the uncut male child's foreskin being sufficient to distinguish Gentile from Jew, the one physical feature standing for all the other nations in all
their diversity.[8]

The fact that the Jews were not the only people to practise circumcision makes
the point all the more forceful. For despite the fact that Egyptians, Arabs and
others also circumcised their male offspring (cf. Jer. 9.25–26; Philo, *Spec. Leg.*
1.2; Josephus, *Ant.* 1.214), circumcision was nevertheless widely regarded as a
distinguishing feature of the Jews, as that which more than anything else marked
them out from all other nations. So, for example, Josephus, *Ant.* 1.192 – God
commanded Abraham to practise circumcision 'to the intent that his posterity
should be kept from mixing with others'; and Tacitus, *Hist.* 5.5.2 – 'They adopted
circumcision to distinguish themselves from other peoples by this difference'.[9]

Why was circumcision such an important identity marker for Jews? Here too
the reason is fairly obvious. Circumcision was important because, in accordance
with the conditions laid down by God when the covenant was first instituted
(Gen. 17.9–14), circumcision was the mark of the covenant, the sign and guarantee of the special relationship between God and the descendants of Abraham, a
seal on God's acceptance of Abraham and his seed (so also Rom. 4.11–12). Not
untypical of the attitude of the day is the description of the covenant given to
Abraham as 'the covenant of circumcision' in the speech attributed to Stephen
in Acts 7.8. The elaboration of the importance of circumcision in *Jub.* 15.25–34 is
only a more extreme expression of the attitude already implicit in Gen. 17: circumcision makes the difference between being a member of the covenant

---

[7] Modern English translations usually fail to catch the force and significance of this phrase in
their translations – 'the circumcision party/faction/group' (RSV/NRSV/NIV), 'the advocates
of circumcision' (NEB), 'the Jews' (REB), 'the circumcised' (NJB). What would be the equivalent translations for οἱ ἐκ πίστεως?

[8] The absence of these terms outside biblical Greek underscores the essentially Jewish perspective which they expressed. The circumcision/uncircumcision (= Jew/Gentile) contrast was
not a Pauline idiosyncracy but came to expression precisely at the point where the first Christian Jews began to break through the boundary between Jew and Gentile, as is indicated by
Acts 11.3 and Gal. 2.7 and 9 (where something like a formal agreement reached at the Jerusalem council may be cited).

[9] See also Petronius, *Satyricon* 102.14; *Fragmenta* 37; and Juvenal, *Sat.* 14.99 (texts in *GLAJJ*
§§ 194, 195, 281, 301).

people and being cut off from the people, the difference almost literally between life and death.

Two centuries before Paul the importance of circumcision as Israel's essential identity marker had been massively reinforced by the Maccabean crisis: for the crisis had been occasioned by the attempt of Israel's Syrian overlords to destroy Israel's distinctiveness, precisely by forbidding circumcision (1 Macc. 1.48, 60–61); and the Maccabean defence of Judaism consequently had included among its first priorities the reassertion of circumcision as indispensable for all Jews (1 Macc. 2.46). Thus, for the great bulk of Jews, the link between 'Jew', 'Judaism' and circumcision was axiomatic; an uncircumcised Jew was virtually a contradiction in terms. And since circumcision was thus so inextricably bound up with the covenant promise to Abraham and his descendants, no one, no Gentile could surely think to have a share in that inheritance without first being circumcised. That this was the theological rationale of the other missionaries in Galatia is hardly to be doubted.[10]

The critical factor in all this is probably that circumcision thus denoted both set-apartness *to God* and set-apartness *from other nations*. Already, therefore, we have vital clues as to why Paul was so opposed to the Galatians being circumcised. It was presumably not so much that he objected to circumcision as the mark of the covenant people: 'the circumcision' in 2.7, 9 is a fairly neutral characterisation; and later on Paul was happy to affirm the 'sign or seal' significance of Abraham's circumcision (Rom. 4.11; cf. Gen. 17.11). The problem probably lay more in the function of circumcision in setting Jew over against Gentile so sharply, that the very affirmation of the importance of 'circumcision' carried with it the corollary that 'uncircumcision' was denied access to covenant grace and life. Separation *to* God of the chosen people had meant separation *from* God of the rest (cf. Eph. 2.12), and in consequence required also separation of circumcision from uncircumcision (cf. Gal. 2.12).[11] Paul himself had previously been inspired by such Phinehas-like zeal to maintain the exclusiveness of Israel's devotion to Yahweh and the boundaries which marked off Israel from the nations (Gal. 1.13–14; Phil. 3.6).[12] But he now saw himself called to be apostle to

---

[10] We need not decide who first introduced the issue of Gentiles sharing in Abraham's inheritance in the Galatian context – whether the other missionaries (cf. particularly C.K. Barrett, 'The Allegory of Abraham, Sarah and Hagar in the Argument of Galatians', *Essays on Paul* [London: SPCK, 1982] 118–31; and J.L. Martyn, 'A Law-Observant Mission to Gentiles: The Background of Galatians', *SJT* 38 [1985] 307–24), or Paul himself. For our present purposes it is enough to know that the question how a Gentile might be counted part of Abraham's seed was central to the dispute between Paul and the other missionaries (Gal. 3–4). The issue of 'the righteous Gentile' as perceived from within Judaism is thus not relevant to the Galatian disputes.

[11] A striking feature of the recently published 4QMMT from Qumran is the first appearance in ancient literature of the language used to denote Peter's 'separation' from other members of the same religious community – 'we have separated ourselves from the multitude of the people' (4QMMT C7); see further my '4QMMT and Galatians', *NTS* 43 (1997) 147–53 [= ch. 14 below].

[12] See further my *Galatians* 55–62, and my 'Paul's Conversion – A Light to Twentieth Cen-

the nations (Gal. 1.15–16; cf. Rom. 11.13) and required by that calling to with-stand Peter's continued policy of separation between Jew and Gentile (Gal. 2.11–14). The reaction in 5.2–12 expresses the same fierce resentment as in 2.11–14 and presumably shares the same motivation.

We may justly infer, therefore, that it was the degree to which circumcision was so closely bound up with Israel's identity, so much an expression of Jewish separation from Gentile, so clearly marking the boundary of covenant grace, which caused Paul to react so strongly to the demand placed upon the Galatian Gentiles by the other missionaries. So much we may deduce simply from the fact that circumcision was such a focal point in the crisis addressed by Paul.

2.2   The first clear reason given for Paul's opposition to the Galatians being cir-cumcised is expressed in 5.2–4. The summary antithesis, circumcision versus Christ, of verse 2, is repeated and elaborated in verses 3–4.[13] Between the brac-keting repetitions of the antithesis – 'Christ will benefit you not at all' (v. 2), and 'you have been estranged from Christ' (v. 4) – comes the illuminating elabora-tion: 'I testify again to everyone who is being circumcised that he is obligated to do the whole law' (v. 3). Paul's first stated reason for his opposition to circumci-sion is that it carried with it obligation to observe the whole law.

The force of Paul's argument here is often confused. Some think that Paul was simply exposing deceitful tactics on the part of the other missionaries – that is, that the 'agitators' in Galatia made circumcision an isolated demand,[14] or played down its consequences,[15] or said nothing of other law-keeping,[16] or presented the issue simply as a matter of 'a few ritual observances'.[17] But such suggestions show too little awareness of the significance of circumcision just demonstrated (§ 2.1). Circumcision was not merely a single act of law-keeping. It was the first act of full covenant membership and obligation.[18] 'Circumcision' could stand metonomically for a whole people precisely because it characterised a people's

---

tury Disputes', in *Evangelium – Schriftauslegung – Kirche*, ed. O. Hofius et al. (Göttingen: Vandenhoeck, 1996) 77–93 [=ch. 15 below].

[13] The πάλιν in 5.3 indicates a repetition of verse 2, not a warning given during his time in Galatia (so most; otherwise E. W. Burton, *Galatians* [ICC; Edinburgh: T. & T. Clark, 1921] 274–5; F. Mussner, *Galaterbrief* [HTK; Freiburg: Herder, ³1977] 347; U. Borse, *Galater* [RNT; Regensburg: Pustet, 1984] 180).

[14] M.-J. Lagrange, *Galates* (EB; Paris: Gabalda, ²1925) 136.

[15] H. Schlier, *Galater* (KEK; Göttingen: Vandenhoeck, ⁴1965) 232.

[16] Burton 274; G.S. Duncan, *Galatians* (Moffatt; London: Hodder, 1934) 155; R. Jewett, 'The Agitators and the Galatian Congregation', *NTS* 17 (1970–71) 198–212 [207]; Mussner 347–8.

[17] H. Lietzmann, *Galater* (HNT; Tübingen: Mohr, ⁴1971) 37.

[18] P. Borgen, 'Observations on the Theme "Paul and Philo"', in *Die Paulinische Literatur und Theologie*, hrsg. S. Pedersen (Aarhus: Aros, 1980) 85–102 [88] = 'Debates on Circumcision in Philo and Paul', *Paul Preaches Circumcision and Pleases Men and Other Essays on Christian Origins* (Trondheim: Tapir, 1983) 15–32 [18].

whole existence, a complete way of life. As Christians today speak of a 'baptismal life', so we could speak here of a 'circumcision life'.

So too for Gentile proselytes. For most Jews the proselyte's act of circumcision naturally entailed also the commitment to 'judaize', to adopt the Jewish way of life as a whole (as in Esther 8.17LXX; Eusebius, *Praep.Evang.* 9.22.5; Josephus, *Ant.* 13.257).[19] For most too, a policy of 'gradualism'[20] would usually have worked up to circumcision as the most challenging demand (for a Greek) rather than taking it as a starting point. The much quoted episode of the conversion of Izates, king of Adiabene, as described by Josephus (*Ant.* 20.34–48) illustrates the point well. The Jewish merchant, Ananias, was willing for Izates to judaize without his being circumcised. Eleazar from Galilee, on the other hand, could not conceive of the adoption of the Jewish way of life without circumcision. All the other Jewish rituals and patterns of behaviour were not sufficient to constitute Izates a Jew, one of God's people. Only circumcision could ensure membership of 'the circumcision', but precisely as the defining act of commitment to the whole, as the climax of a wholly judaized life.

Nor is it likely that Paul reasoned as follows: (1) to accept circumcision, is (2) to accept the need to do the whole law, is (3) to assume that the whole law can be kept, is (4) to make acceptance by God dependent on keeping the whole law = legalism.[21] The reasoning starts well (cf. after all Rom. 2.25), but begins to veer off course in (3). There is no implication here that the logic under attack assumed the possibility (or necessity) of keeping the law in a complete, that is, perfect sense.[22] We know of no such perfectionism within the Judaism of Paul's day, with its insistence on repentance and possibility of atonement.[23] The mistake, as elsewhere, has been to individualize the teaching, as though Paul had in mind simply a sequence of individuals confronting each other, Jews and Gentiles, without any sense of the corporate dimension of a tradition which saw salvation in terms of membership of a people.

What is in view, rather, was the typical Jewish mind-set which understood 'doing the law' as the obligation of those within the covenant people, as that which marked out the covenant people, as the way to live within the covenant

---

[19] We should observe here the proper use of the transliterated term 'judaize' (from ἰουδαΐζειν), as describing the actions of the non-Jew who adopted distinctive Jewish practices or assimilated to the Jewish way of life. The 19th century creation of the term 'Judaizer' to describe the other missionaries (Jewish Christians wishing to make Paul's Gentile converts into full proselytes) unfortunately confuses and obscures the point.

[20] E.P. Sanders, *Paul, the Law, and the Jewish People* (Philadelphia: Fortress, 1983) 29.

[21] See particularly H. Hübner, *Law in Paul's Thought* (Edinburgh: T. & T. Clark, 1984) 18–9, 36–9; F.F. Bruce, *Galatians* (NIGTC; Grand Rapids: Eerdmans/Exeter: Paternoster, 1982) 230–1; J. Rohde, *Galater* (THKNT; Berlin: Evangelische, 1989) 215–6; 'the bookkeeping God of legalism' (Burton 277).

[22] So rightly Sanders, *Law* 27–9.

[23] See further my 'In Search of Common Ground' § 2.2, in *Paul and the Jewish Law*, ed. J.D.G. Dunn (Tübingen: Mohr, 1996) [= 287–9 above].

(3.12).[24] 'To do the whole law' was to adopt a Jewish way of life through and through. In other words, 'the Jewish way of life' was a complete package,[25] though the demand of its integrated wholeness ('works of the law', covenantal nomism) could be focused in a single issue like circumcision and food laws (as here and in 2.11–14). To confuse this with the striving of an individual for (in effect) an attainable sinless perfection is the very denigration of Judaism which has caused so much pain in Jewish and Christian attempts to understand each other.[26]

Evidently it is this total way of life to which Paul refers here. He reminds his would be Gentile judaizers that it is not simply a matter of a single act of circumcision, but a whole way of life, a complete assimilation and absorption of any distinctively Gentile identity into the status of Jewish proselyte.[27] He must have been aware that it was just this completeness of identification with God's people Israel which would have been attractive to many of the Gentiles involved. But presumably he wanted them to be in no doubt that such a degree of assimilation allowed of no continuing residual Gentile identity. More to the point, for them to accept the necessity of circumcision shifted the grounds for their redemption to membership of a people and made their previous commitment to Christ (in baptism) a pointless rite (5.4).[28]

2.3   A second major reason why Paul was opposed to the Galatians being circumcised is given in 6.12–13: those who were trying to compel the Galatians to be circumcised were 'those who want to make a fair showing in the flesh'; 'they want you to be circumcised in order that they might boast in your flesh'.

Here the explication of circumcision as circumcision 'in the flesh' brings further opportunity for clarification of the importance of circumcision as the crucial issue for both the other missionaries and Paul. The significant extra term is 'flesh'. Here too, however, the term has proved strangely misleading for most commentators. Its significance can be ignored, as though Paul was simply pro-

---

[24] Lev. 18. 5, referred to here, has in view primarily a way of living rather than a promise of eternal life – as the earliest commentary on it indicates (Ezek. 20.11, 13, 21, 25); see again my 'In Search of Common Ground' §2.2 n.7 [=288 n. 7 above].

[25] This is the force also of passages like Matt. 5.18–19, James 2.10 and *m. Abot* 4.2. Whether we can speak of an already established rabbinic halakhah, (as P.J. Tomson, *Paul and the Jewish Law. Halakha in the Letters of the Apostle to the Gentiles* [Assen: Van Gorcum, 1990] 88–9), is another question.

[26] See e.g. those cited by E.P. Sanders, *Paul and Palestinian Judaism* (London: SCM, 1977) 5–6, and Longenecker 227.

[27] This is presumably what Paul had in mind when he addresses those 'who are seeking to be justified by the law (ἐν νόμῳ)' (5.4). That is, they were in danger of making their hope of justification dependent either on the fact that they lived within the sphere of the law (ἐν νόμῳ), within the boundaries which separated Jew from Gentile, or on their observing the works of the law which had the same effect (cf. 2.11–16). See further my *Galatians* 267–8.

[28] See further §3 below.

testing against submission to circumcision as such (NEB/REB), or merely thinking in terms of outward appearance (NJB). Indeed, one of the main criticisms to be levelled at modern English translations of Paul's letters is their inability to find a satisfactory way of translating σάρξ, its function as a key term in Paul's theology obscured by a range of circumlocutive phrases.[29] Others make the assumption that Paul must have had in mind here 'flesh' as a moral category: the thought in 6.13 being of boasting in human potential,[30] or in self-achieved merit,[31] or in 'merely human attainments'.[32]

Once again, what has been missed, however, is the significance of circumcision already outlined above (§ 2.1), the importance of circumcision as a, indeed *the* primary physical marker of the covenant people. In the foundational scriptural authorisation for circumcision, it is repeatedly stressed that circumcision is 'in the flesh ...' (Gen. 17.11, 14); 'so shall my covenant be in your flesh an everlasting covenant' (17.13). Here again the point is emphasised in *Jubilees*: 'anyone who is born whose own flesh is not circumcised on the eigth day is not from the sons of the covenant ... (but) from the children of destruction'; those who left their flesh uncircumcised made themselves like the Gentiles, and for them there is no forgiveness (*Jub.* 15.26, 34). In other words, it is precisely the fact that circumcision is visible in the flesh which marked off Israel as distinct and separate from the other nations. This is evidently what Paul had in mind in his several references to circumcision as 'in the flesh' (Rom. 2.28; Phil. 3.3–5; Col. 2.11, 13). The close integration of the religious and ethnic significance of circumcision as circumcision in the flesh is particularly clear in Phil. 3.3–5, as again in Eph. 2.11–12 – 'Gentiles in the flesh', designated as foreskin/uncircumcision by the self-designated 'circumcision in the flesh', and as such 'excluded from the community of Israel, strangers to the covenants of promise, without hope and without God in the world'.[33]

So in 6.12 what we see is the characteristically and distinctively Jewish evaluation of circumcision and of the importance of circumcision as a positive marker of Israel's privileged status in the world. The point is all the more striking here, for who else would regard circumcision as making a good impression 'in the flesh'? In contrast, in normal Greek conversation, talk of making a good impression 'in the flesh' would be taken to refer to the pleasingness of the human body, as, typically, stripped for athletic contest; such 'fair showing in the flesh' is

---

[29] Cf. e.g. in 6.12, REB, 'outwardly in good standing', and NIV, 'a good impression outwardly'.

[30] P. Bonnard, *Galates* (CNT; Neuchâtel: Delachaux, 1953) 129.

[31] As in Betz 318; Bruce 271; R.Y.K. Fung, *Galatians* (NICNT; Grand Rapids: Eerdmans, 1988) 306.

[32] Longenecker 294. But see also H. Räisänen, *Paul and the Law* (Tübingen: Mohr, 1983) 169.

[33] For the significance of 'the flesh' as denoting ethnic descent and identity elsewhere in Paul see also Rom. 4.1; 9.3; 11.14; 1 Cor. 10.18; and here Gal. 4.23, 29.

still evident in the countless statues, part or whole, preserved from the Hellenistic period. Whereas most Greeks would regard circumcision as a form of mutilation (cf. 5.12). The simple fact is that only Jews would regard circumcision as 'making a fair showing in the flesh'. And they did so because it was the public identity marker of their status as God's most favoured nation. That Paul could thus once again sum up the goals of his Galatian opponents in the single objective of having his Galatian converts circumcised confirms the tremendous symbolic power which this one ritual act had for Jews in general.

So too with 6.13 the desire of the other missionaries for the Galatians to be circumcised[34] 'in order that they might boast in your flesh' almost certainly reflects the same typically Jewish sense of identity – both pride in their choice as God's people (as marked by circumcision in the flesh) and genuine desire that those who wished to partake in Israel's covenant blessings should do so by receiving the mark of covenant membership. In the light of what has already been said, the talk of 'boasting' receives most illumination from the similar talk in Rom. 2.17, 23 and 3.27, and again more clearly in Phil. 3.3–5 and Eph. 2.8–12. That is, the boasting in view was almost certainly that of Jews confident in their standing before God as his people (Rom. 2.17; 3.27–29; Phil 3.5; Eph. 2.11–12) and within the law (marked not least by circumcision).[35] In other words, the boasting here in view, 'boasting in the flesh', was boasting in ethnic identity and prerogative, the boast of a 'Jew by nature', confident of acceptance by God, over against the 'Gentile sinner' (cf. Gal. 2.15).[36] In particular, here, it is 'boasting in your flesh', because for Gentiles thus to affirm that their acceptance by God was dependent on their becoming Jews, by taking on the fleshly identification mark of the Jew, was tantamount to affirming the Jewish claims to have a distinctive prerogative

---

[34] Οἱ περιτεμνόμενοι ('those who have themselves circumcised') would seem most naturally to refer to those in the process of being circumcised. That is, Paul may have in mind that group (probably still small) within the Galatian churches who had already succumbed to the propaganda of the other missionaries and who, with the zeal of converts were now trying to persuade others to follow suit (cf. 4.21; see Burton 353 and Lietzmann 44; others cited by Bruce 269; J. Munck, *Paul and the Salvation of Mankind* [London: SCM, 1959] 89 built his thesis that the 'Judaizers' are Paul's own Gentile converts on this verse; similarly L. Gaston, *Paul and the Torah* [Vancouver: University of British Columbia, 1987] 81). The alternative is to suppose that Paul's language is rather loose and that he means simply 'the circumcised' (so NRSV, NJB, NIV), those for whom circumcision is important (e.g. T. Zahn, *Galater* [Leipzig: Deichert, 1905] 280; Mussner 412 n.23; Fung 303; Longenecker 292); or that he uses the middle voice with causative significance (Jewett 202–3; Bruce 270; J.B. Lightfoot, *Galatians* [London: Macmillan, 1865] 222 – 'the advocates of circumcision'); that is, he continues to attack the other missionaries directly. The latter is probably to be preferred.

[35] So also J. Barclay, *Obeying the Truth. A Study of Paul's Ethics in Galatians* (Edinburgh: T. & T. Clark, 1988) 197 n.48.

[36] Wholly implausible is the argument of W. Schmithals, *Paul and the Gnostics* (Nashville: Abingdon, 1972) 55, that what was in view here was a gnostic '*contempt* for the flesh' (my emphasis).

over against the Gentiles.[37] When Gentiles thus subjected *their* flesh to the *Jewish* rite of circumcision, they gave *Jews* grounds to boast in *their* flesh thus subordinated to and incorporated within distinctive Jewish identity.

Here again, therefore, we see that Paul focused the issue antithetically in circumcision primarily because circumcision was so archetypically expressive of Jewish identity as the people of God set apart from the nations. It was because circumcision was such a powerful expression of national identity that Paul was so opposed to it for Gentile converts. National and religious identity had become too inextricably intertwined. The boasting was not simply in God, but in God as God of the Jews only and in effect not also of the Gentiles (cf. Rom. 3.29). It was boasting in the flesh, in physical and ethnic distinctiveness, to which he objected so strongly.

But why did Paul find such pride in ethnic identity, such commitment to a total way of life within the covenant as laid down by the law, so objectionable? Why was it objectionable to him that conversion of Gentiles should be conversion to the wholly different and integrated way of life as now lived by the pioneer people of God's covenant choice? Why should conversion to Christ cease to be simply proselytising to Judaism? Was it simply the reaction of one who was himself a convert going from one extreme to another? Was it simply the attitude of an internationalist opposed to what he perceived to be a more narrowly nationalistic philosophy? Or was there more to it? To answer these questions we must turn to the other side of the antitheses which Paul drew up in these passages.

3. Why were Christ and the cross so antithetical to circumcision?

As with the slogan 'circumcision', we must here first ask why it is that 'Christ' and 'cross' serve as the focal points in the Pauline antithesis with circumcision, and then draw what we can from the elaboration of this side of the antitheses in our two Galatian passages.

3.1 The sharpness of the antitheses (Christ/circumcision, cross/circumcision) can be explained only by recognizing that Christ and cross had become as fundamental and axiomatic for Christian identity as circumcision was for Jewish identity. It was their recognition of Jesus as 'the Christ' which marked out the first followers of Jesus. According to Acts, even before the name 'Christians' had been coined, it was their relation to Jesus which identified them as distinctive: they were followers of 'the way' set out by Jesus (Acts 9.2; 22.4; 24.14), members of the sect of the Nazarene (22.8; 24.5, 14; 26.9), invoking his name in baptism and witness as giving them their *raison d'etre* (3–4). The first appear-

---

[37] Cf. A. Oepke, *Galater* (THKNT; Berlin: Evangelische, ³1973) 202; Rohde 273.

ance of the name 'Christians' (11.26) simply confirms that in the eyes of the
Roman authorities in Antioch[38] they were most distinguishable as 'the Christ
party', 'the Christ faction', the party or faction (among the Jews) gathered round
and loyal to the one known as 'Christ'. It is not unimportant to thus recall that
the Christ-focus of the Pauline gospel was not simply a product of Paul's christophany on the Damascus road and was not dependent on the developed 'in
Christ' theology of Paul himself.

Nor should we forget the significance of the fact that it is this term, 'Christ',
which thus denoted the focus of first Christian commitment and devotion. The
point is, of course, that it was as the one who fulfilled Israel's hope of a Messiah
that Jesus was thus designated, and his followers thus also designated, as distinctive within the wider Judaism of the day. It is the way in which this fulfilled Jewish hope became an axiom, which is not only superimposed on the axiom of circumcision but also supercedes the axiom of circumcision, which is so fascinating
at this point in the evolution of Christian self-understanding. The fact that the
titular significance of the title (the Christ) has so far been lost to sight in Paul's
letters[39] does not weaken the point. Rather it simply indicates that 'Christ' as the
fundamental identity factor for the new movement was already so deeply entrenched and so long established that its use was in a second phase, able to function as a name or identifier in a variety of combinations (Jesus Christ, Christ
Jesus, the Lord Jesus Christ, etc).

Nor, of course, is it an accident that 'cross' functions as the alternative or complement to 'Christ' in the antitheses with 'circumcision'. For it was not the identification of Jesus as the Messiah which made the sect of the Nazarene so problematic within late second Temple Judaism, but the identification of the *crucified*
Jesus as Messiah (cf. 1 Cor. 1.23). The reason for this has already been hinted at
in the letter: the fact of Jesus' crucifixion had facilitated a polemical interpretation of his death in terms of Deut. 21.23 – 'Cursed is everyone who has been
hanged on a tree' (Gal. 3.13).[40] For the covenant conscious (covenant conscien-
tious) Jew, Jesus' crucifixion meant that he had come under the Deuteronomic
curses (Deut. 28–30), and could therefore no longer be counted a participant in
the covenant's blessings, but rather an outcast from the land and the promises,
scattered among the Gentiles, one with the Gentiles in their estrangement from
Israel and Israel's God.[41]

---

[38] It needs to be recalled that Χριστιανοί is a Latinism (*Christiani*), formed like Ἡρῳδιανοί
(*Herodiani*) and *Pompeiani*, and indicating adherents of the person indicated.

[39] But not entirely; see particularly Wright ch. 3. The titular force is still evident at various
points within Galatians itself (1.6–7, 10; 2.20; 3.16, 24, 29; 5.24; 6.2, 12); see my *Galatians* ad loc.

[40] 4QpNah 1.7–8 and 11QT 64.6–13 have shown clearly enough that the application of Deut.
21.23 to crucifixion did not first happen in reference to Jesus; cf. particularly J.A. Fitzmyer,
'Crucifixion in Ancient Palestine, Qumran Literature and the New Testament', *CBQ* 40 (1978)
493–513.

[41] This polemic no doubt also reflected the ambiguity of Jewish sectarian polemic, as illus-

It was evidently this confrontation between a crucified Messiah – Messiah, acceptable, but crucified Messiah, no! – which made the antitheses Paul sets out in Galatians unavoidable. For a crucified Messiah was too much a self-contradiction for the great majority of Torah faithful communities. The other missionaries in effect denied the antithesis by absorbing the thought of a crucified Messiah within an otherwise undisturbed Jewish identity marked out by continuing Torah faithfulness, including, of course, the necessity of circumcision for all members of the Christ sect. In this way, Paul charges them, they attempted to escape persecution for the cross of Christ (6.12),[42] and thus to diminish or avoid the scandal of the cross (cf. 5.11).[43] Paul, however, accepted the logic and force of the Deuteronomic curse and saw Christ's absorption of that curse on the cross as requiring a reassessment both of what Torah faithfulness meant and of covenant identity as defined by separation from Gentiles. Hence the critical function of the proclamation of the cross earlier in the letter (particularly in 2.19–3.1 and 3.13–14) which comes to climactic summary in our passages (5.11; 6.12, 14). The axiom of Christ crucified, Christ and cross, meant that when it came in conflict with the axiom of covenant identity as ethnically defined, circumcision in the flesh, it was the latter which had to be redefined.

3.2   In 5.2–4, as we saw above (§ 2.2), the circumcision side of the Christ/circumcision antithesis was elaborated in 5.3. Somewhat similarly the Christ side of the antithesis is elaborated in 5.4c–5. 'You have been estranged from Christ' is alternatively expressed as 'you have fallen away from grace' (5.4). And the explanation ('for') asserts that the hope of righteousness is dependent on the Spirit and faith (5.5). The key term 'Christ' is thus elaborated by the complementary terms 'grace', 'Spirit' and 'faith'. In each case Paul recalls terms which have played a crucial role in his earlier exposition. In each case he reminds his Galatian converts of a further fundamental feature of their own self-understanding

---

trated most graphically in the DSS – that other Jews belonged to the sons of darkness, but always the hope being cherished that they, with all the sons of Israel, would one day return from exile to the land, from curse to blessing, as promised in Deut. 30.

[42]   The persecution in mind is presumably that also referred to in 4.29 and 5.11; that is, 'persecution' by (some) Jews of Christian Jews, such as Paul both had carried out before his conversion (1.13, 23) and himself experienced (2 Cor. 11.24). The implication is clear enough (despite Mussner's 412 misgivings): if they (the other Jewish missionaries) succeeded in circumcising those Gentiles drawn into the Nazarene movement, they would escape such persecution, presumably because their success in thus drawing these Gentiles fully within the covenant people (as proselytes) removed the reason for the persecution. See further my *Galatians* 336–7.

[43]   To what Paul was referring in 5.11 – 'if I still preach circumcision, why am I still persecuted?' – is much disputed. The most likely explanation is that Paul's willingness to continue a practice of circumcision for Jewish converts, as in the reported case of Timothy (Acts 16.3), and, in circumstances other than those in Galatia, to live himself as one 'under the law' (1 Cor. 9.20–21), brought criticisms of inconsistency from his opponents. See further again my *Galatians* 278–82.

as Christians – viz. what they themselves had experienced as they responded to the gospel preached by Paul.

'Grace' was the term he had used to sum up the experience of conversion, both his own and theirs (1.6, 15), the experience of being grasped by an otherly and effective power without prior condition. It was this same manifestation of divine approval (a sense of divine acceptance and enabling freely granted) which had convinced the Jerusalem apostles that Paul's preaching to Gentiles was divinely sanctioned (2.9), and which made the term 'grace' such an appropriate summary term in Paul's thinking for God's manifest purpose to bestow his blessings on Gentiles apart from the law (2.21). Here the metaphor is a vivid one: those who accept circumcision 'have fallen away (ἐξεπέσατε) from grace' (5.4). Their new life thus far sustained by this grace would be like a withered flower 'falling off' from its stem (cf. Jas 1.11; 1 Pet. 1.24), or like a ship 'failing to hold' the course which leads to safety and falling away into disaster (cf. Acts 27.26, 29). As with Christ, this unconditional experience of divine favour now stood in sharp antithesis to attempts to constrict it within a traditional and characteristically Jewish way of life. So to constrain it was to contradict its character as grace.

'Spirit' is another summary term descriptive of the experience which first brought the Galatians into the Christ movement and which, for Paul, should continue to characterise their life as Christians. This is clear from the second appeal to the Galatians' experience of conversion with which Paul begins the central argument of his letter – 'Was it by works of the law that you received the Spirit or by hearing with faith?' (3.2).[44] So too in 3.14 the reception of the Spirit is the summary of all the blessings promised for the Gentiles through Abraham. In this case, still more clearly than with 'grace', it is evident that Paul was thinking not of a merely rational experience of intellectual persuasion, but of an experience in which the whole person was engaged at a deeply emotive and motivational level as well (cf. e.g. Rom. 5.5; 8.2; 1 Cor. 6.9–11; and earlier Gal. 3.5 and 4.6–7).[45] So here it is the same Spirit which sustains the eagerly awaited[46] hope of righteousness (5.5; cf. Rom. 8.23; 2 Cor. 1.21–22).[47] We should not underplay the

---

[44] C.H. Cosgrove, *The Cross and the Spirit. A Study in the Argument and Theology of Galatians* (Mercer University, 1988) 2, takes 3.1–5 as 'the decisive clue to Paul's view of the "problem at Galatia"'.

[45] See further my *Jesus and the Spirit* (London: SCM/Philadelphia: Westminster, 1975) 201–5.

[46] Note the sense of suppressed excitement in Paul's other uses of the verb (Rom. 8.19, 23, 25; 1 Cor. 1.7; Phil. 3.20).

[47] To be noted here is what we might call 'the future tense' of justification, that Paul saw the Christian life as a matter of justification from start to finish – first accepted, then sustained through life, then finally acquitted in the final judgment (cf. Schlier 233–4; J.A. Ziesler, *The Meaning of Righteousness in Paul* [SNTSMS 20; Cambridge University, 1972] 179–80; K. Kertelge, *'Rechtfertigung' bei Paulus* [Münster: Aschendorff, ²1971] 147–50; Mussner 350–1; Rohde 217; against Fung 224–7, 232–5, who makes uncalled for distinctions and struggles to defend the

fact that it was the reality of their initial and ongoing experience to which Paul appealed at this point. Over against the demand for circumcision he was able to say in effect: Do you not recall the wonder of your experience of God's Spirit? Over against a hope of righteousness dependent on continued performance of the 'works of the law' of covenantal nomism, Paul recalled them to the alternative of a hope of righteousness rooted in their continuing experience of the Spirit. Having been given participation in that which already expresses and gives foretaste of God's full eschatological blessing, what more could circumcision give? 'Are you so foolish? Having begun with the Spirit are you now made complete with the flesh?' (3.3).

The third term simply highlights the other complementary aspect of these initiating experiences to which Paul recalls the Galatians – 'faith'. On their part all that had been involved was 'hearing with faith' (3.2), that is, acceptance of the offer made in the gospel and commitment to the one therein proclaimed. This opening recall to their experience of simply believing had then become the basis of Paul's exposition of the relation between righteousness and faith which runs through the rest of Gal. 3. It is the immediacy of this correlation, of faith and righteousness, which Paul restates in summary in 5.5 – 'by the Spirit, from faith we eagerly await the hope of righteousness'.[48] Here was another term which in principle need not stand in antithesis to a Jewish way of life, to the law – a position which Peter's action in Antioch had attempted to maintain (2.11–16). But events, not least the Antioch incident itself and now the challenge of the other missionaries in Galatia, had conspired to drive the two (faith and works) into antithesis. And in that situation of confrontation Paul was in no doubt that the principle of faith alone as the basis of human acceptability to God must not be compromised in any degree (2.16).

In short, we may say that in elaborating the Christ side of the antithesis with circumcision Paul makes a double emphasis on two givens – as we might say, the objective fact of the cross, and the subjective fact of their experience of believing, and receiving grace and the Spirit. It was presumably the way in which these two so closely dovetailed in Paul's own experience, both of conversion and in preaching, and in the experience of his converts (3.1–5, 13–14; 4.5–7), which gave Paul such confidence in pressing the antithesis as sharply as he did. For anything more to be required as fundamental, without which participation in covenant blessing would not be recognized, was to deny their own experience as well as to nullify the cross.

---

sense, 'the hope of those already accounted righteous'); talk of 'double justification' (see Betz 262 n.87), or 'two distinct justifications' (Cosgrove 150) is also too static.

[48] 'Hope' is here used in the derived sense 'fulfilled hope' – 'the righteousness for which we hope' (NIV), 'hoped-for righteousness' (Burton 279); cf. Tit. 2.13.

3.3   As boasting in the flesh is an elaboration of the circumcision principle
(6.13), so boasting in the cross is the antithetical elaboration of the cross principle (6.14). And the rationale is given epigrammatically: 'the cross of our Lord
Jesus Christ through whom[49] the world has been crucified to me and I to the
world'. The initial point is presumably the same as in 6.12: what the other
missionaries sought to avoid, Paul gloried in. That is, a focusing of the gospel in
the crucified Messiah as alone the sufficient basis for acceptance by God and for
the gift of the Spirit (2.21–3.2; 3.13–14), the very thing which was so disturbing
for those who sought to maintain distinctive Jewish identity, was the very thing
in which Paul boasted.

Paul's thought is still more profound, however. The significance of the cross
was not simply the revaluation of Jewish prerogative over Gentile, for that revaluation meant a revaluation of the whole world and of Paul's relationship to it.
As regularly in Paul, 'the world' denotes the totality of the whole creation
(human as well as non-human) in its distance from God, and as yet unredeemed
state.[50] Here it must be seen as equivalent to 'the present evil age' (1.4; so also
e.g. 1 Cor. 2.6–8 and 2 Cor. 4.4). What Paul meant is that *every* rationale for individual and corporate existence which is independent of God (as in Rom. 1.21–
22), together with its system of beliefs and values and corresponding life-style,
had been condemned and put to death so far as he was concerned; and that he
himself had likewise been rendered inoperative so far as the attractions of such
rationales, belief and value systems and life-styles were concerned. The language is given fuller resonance by modern talk of an individual's 'social world'
or 'world of meaning', but to hear its full resonance, the cosmic and eschatological overtones have to be given full weight.[51]

This is an astonishing leap for Paul to have taken. It certainly fits with the
strong apocalyptic and eschatological perspective which seems to have been a
mark of the earliest Christian communities – tied in, not least, to the understanding of Christ's resurrection and the outpoured Spirit as the 'first-fruits' of the
general resurrection soon to be consummated (Rom. 8.23; 1 Cor. 15.20, 23). Paul
here shared that apocalyptic perspective in that he looked beyond the immediacy of the situation confronting his mission and the Israel of God (6.16) and set
the local or national crisis of Israel's identity within a cosmic framework. Implicit in what he says here is the conviction that his personal apocalypse (1.12,

---

[49] Almost all commentators (and RSV/NRSV, NEB/REB, NIV) translate δι' οὗ as 'through
which', treating 'cross' as the antecedent, even though it is separated from 'through' by the five
words, τοῦ κυρίου ἡμῶν Ἰησοῦ Χριστοῦ. Lightfoot 223 and Lagrange 165, however, observe
that a reference to Christ would more likely have been expressed by 'in whom' or 'with whom'.
NJB and Borse 221 also prefer 'through whom'. But it comes to the same thing, since 'through
whom' must mean 'through the crucified Christ', or 'through Christ on the cross'.

[50] See e.g. Rom. 3.6, 19; 5.12–13; 1 Cor. 1.20–21; 2.12; 6.2; 7.31–34; 2 Cor. 5.19; 7.10; and further H. Sasse, κόσμος, *TDNT* 3.892–3.

[51] Martyn, 'Antinomies' 412–3.

15–16) had a universal significance. That is, what he had recognized to be the case so far as Israel's covenant relation with God was concerned, was true for the world as a whole. No national or ethnic status, or we may add, social or gender status (cf. Gal. 3.28), afforded a determinative basis for or decisive assurance of God's favour. And if this was true for Israel, the chosen people of God, it was true for the world as a whole.

More disturbing, the apocalyptic perspective in effect functioned with an alternative antithesis to the more typical Jewish one. Whereas Israel divided the world into Jew and Gentile, circumcision and uncircumcision (just as the Greek divided the world into Greek and barbarian), the apocalyptic perspective divided time into old age and new age, where old age was ever inferior and oppressed, 'the present evil age' (1.4), in contrast to the fulfilled promise and outpoured Spirit of the new, the 'new creation' (6.15). This is the dark side of the apocalyptic antithesis: the new dawn brightness of the new revelation casts what has preceded into the darkness of night. But in the apocalyptic perspective as expressed by Paul this meant that Israel, 'the present Jerusalem' (4.25), belonged to the old age, itself caught in the toils of evil. The logic of that perspective was that Israel before Christ and apart from Christ had to be painted in the dark hues of the old age: Israel under the law was Israel held under restraint, Israel under age, Israel in slavery to the elemental forces of the world (3.23–4.3). That was why circumcision was such a retrograde step for the Galatians to take: it was not merely the step of affiliation to another group, not merely the step from one ethnic identity to another; it was also a step back into another age, another world, one in which other powers were dominant and whose authority and influence had already been superceded by Christ on the cross (4.8–10).

This is the sharpness and starkness of Paul's alternative antithesis – not just Christ and cross versus circumcision, but new age versus old age still dominated by evil, new creation versus old creation where pride in ethnic identity cloaked a more fundamental dependence on powers other than God. And this is the more fundamental theological reason why Paul so vehemently resisted the other missionaries in their attempts to have the Galatians circumcised. The issue was not just Christ and the cross, not just the reality of the Galatians' own experience of grace, Spirit and faith, but God – God's purpose for humanity as a whole, God's purpose through the onward march of history, God's purpose in revelation and redemption. In turning his face so resolutely against the circumcision of his Galatian converts Paul could not have set the stakes any higher.

4. 'Neither circumcision, nor uncircumcision, but ...'

What then is the force of Paul's repeated 'neither circumcision, nor uncircumcision, but . . .' slogan? Given that it comes at the end (5.6; 6.15) of each the two

paragraphs which elaborate the Christ/circumcision, cross/circumcision antitheses (5.2–6; 6.12–15), why is it that Paul sums up his teaching in this way and
what is it that he wished to convey by the repeated slogan? And what does the
further repetition of the slogan in 1 Cor. 7.19 add to our understanding of Paul's
attitude to circumcision and the law and way of life it encapsulated?

4.1   First we should note the significance of the first part of the formulation –
'neither circumcision, nor uncircumcision'. Despite the thrust of his whole argument in Gal. 5.2–12 Paul does not limit himself to downplaying circumcision
alone. He adds, 'nor uncircumcision'. There are two points worthy of note. (a)
Once again the thought is not limited to the effect of a ritual action or its absence. Once again 'circumcision' and 'uncircumcision' represent, by metonymy,
ethnic identity, a whole corporate and national way of life epitomised by its most
physically visible expression. 'Neither circumcision nor uncircumcision' therefore is not a downplaying of ritual law in favour of moral law, but a denial that
ethnic identity counts for anything with God, a refusal to allow that the uncircumcised state per se disadvantages before God any more than the circumcised
state per se advantages before God. It is a closely complementary thought which
Paul expresses in Gal. 3.28, when he says 'neither Jew nor Greek' – as the elaboration of the slogan in Col. 3.11 indicates: 'no longer Greek and Jew, circumcision
and uncircumcision'.

   (b) At the same time, the perspective implicit in the terms used, circumcision/
uncircumcision, is plainly a Jewish perspective. As already noted, only Jews
would call others 'foreskin' and give significance to the *absence* of circumcision.
Paul therefore speaks as one who comes from within the world-view of Israel,
for whom Christ and the cross meant a break through from that former perspective when circumcision did count and uncircumcision denoted separation from
God's people and from God. This is a fundamental feature of Chritianity and of
Christian identity – that it is not essentially a syncretistic mish-mash, not essentially a form of independent internationalism, not essentially a new religion[52] for
a third race. In its essence Christianity is a form of Israel (or of Judaism) breaking through the boundaries which surrounded Judaism and which were so
clearly expressed in the relative values placed on circumcision and uncircumcision. For Paul, Christianity most truly expressed itself when it affirmed the acceptability of Gentile as Gentile (the uncircumcision) to God, and, as inescapable corollary, denied the necessity of circumcision as the determinative mark
of God's acceptance.

---

[52] Contrast Betz's claim that Paul 'in fact announces the establishment of a new religion'
(320).

4.2   What then of the 'but ...' in the several alternatives Paul puts to the old circumcision/uncircumcision perspective? If world view and way of life are not to be determined by the fact of ethnic identity and distinctiveness, what are they to be determined by?

The first version of the slogan seems fairly anodyne – 'for in Christ Jesus neither circumcision counts for anything (ἰσχύει),[53] nor uncircumcision, but faith operating effectively (ἐνεργουμένη) through love'. The function of the slogan as a conclusion to 5.2–6 is clear: the focal point of Christ as the alternative to circumcision in the Christ/circumcision antithesis is reaffirmed, as is also the emphasis on faith. The sole 'external' ground of acceptance by God is Christ, not a state of circumcision (membership of 'the circumcision'); the sole 'internal' ground of acceptance by God is faith, the simple acceptance of the gospel focused in this Christ and trust in this Christ.

The new term is 'love' (ἀγάπη), the little used word taken over by the first Christians and made their own. It appears here no doubt because it caught another vital facet of the Christ side of the Christ/circumcision antithesis. Ἀγάπη was chosen rather than another love-word because it could express the wholly generous, sacrificial and actively outreaching concern on their behalf shown by God in Christ (2.20). To stand on the Christ side of the Christ/circumcision antithesis meant a life shaped by and expressive of the same love that Christ had manifested on the cross. The love which was the basis of their acceptance by God should also be its expression.[54]

More striking still is the correlation 'faith working through love'.[55] Paul thus makes clear that in the faith/law antithesis he did not intend faith to be understood as simply an attitude of trust, far less as a moment of sheer passivity. He does not allow the Christ/circumcision antithesis to become an oversimplified antithesis between gift and task (*Gabe und Aufgabe*). There is a corollary to faith/conversion just as there is to circumcision/proselytism: there is a life to be lived, a way of life to be walked, a pattern of existence to be pursued, an alternative 'covenantal nomism' if you like. The difference is that where circumcision implied the way of life typical and distinctive of Jews ('judaizing', 'works of the law'), faith implied a life lived out of and through the love embodied on the cross.

---

[53] Ἰσχύω is usually intransitive, in the sense 'be strong, powerful, competent', or in the more closely parallel legal usage 'have force, be valid', or accounting usage 'be worth' (LSJ and MM, ἰσχύω).

[54] See also Mussner 353–4.

[55] The phrase is almost a single concept, faith-through-love, love-energized-faith. A passive rendering, 'faith energized through love', is less likely (see Oepke 158–9; Schlier 235 n. 1; Fung 228–9); still less 'faith energized by God's love' (Duncan 157–8), in view of the elaboration of the thought in 5.13–14. Nor should faith be seen as a beginning and love as an outcome, as though the two were separate – far less faith as theory and love as practice (see Betz 264) – but ongoing faith coming to expression in and through love (Burton 280).

The most striking feature of this redrawn balance between belonging and living is that Paul did not see this as an alternative to law-keeping, but as the fulfilment of what the law was really for. As he indicates only a few verses later: 'the whole law (ὁ πᾶς νόμος) is fulfilled in one word, in the (well known), "You shall love (ἀγαπήσεις) your neighbour as yourself"' (5.14, citing Lev. 19.18). The contrast with 5.3 could hardly have escaped Paul and must surely be deliberate: 'I testify to everyone who is being circumcised that he is obligated to do the whole law (ὅλον τὸν νόμον)'.[56] From what we have already seen it should now be clear what the negative contrast amounts to: not a wholesale disavowal of the law (along with circumcision in particular), not a kind of antinomianism; but a disavowal of the law as the Jewish law, the law as marking out a whole way of life, a corporate identity, the law as distinguishing and separating Jew from Gentile, the law as typified by circumcision. Consequently we can also recognize more clearly what the positive side of the contrast amounts to: not the encouragement of a purely spontaneous, charismatic, law-free ethic;[57] but the encouragement to recognize that love of neighbour, as taught by Christ and as demonstrated by Christ,[58] goes to the heart of the law's purpose, and that the faith-trust in God's love in and through this Christ is the fountain from which that love flows.

So this first form of the 'neither circumcision, nor uncircumcision, but ...' slogan does not amount to a denial of the law as such, but only of that evaluation of the law expressed in the circumcision/uncircumcision categorisation of the world. There is still recognition that membership of Abraham's seed and participation in Abraham's blessing carry with them day-to-day life-shaping obligations. There is still a continuity with the law in its fundamental purpose of showing how the people of God should live. Had Paul not wished to assert such continuity he would certainly have worded 5.14 in quite other terms. The implicit contrast is not between the law and something else, but between different ways of

---

[56] Contrast Hübner's unconvincing attempt to deny that the phrase in 5.14 does not refer to the Mosaic law (36–40). So too J.W. Drane, *Paul: Libertine or Legalist?* (London: SPCK, 1975) 112–3 effectively ignores 5.14 when he argues that 'the devaluation of the Old Testament, and, therefore, the rejection of the law in any sense for the Christian community, was an inevitable outcome of Paul's teaching'. But the 'one word' is obviously from the Mosaic law, the parallel in Rom. 13.9 (not to mention James 2.8) points unmistakeably to the Mosaic law (Barclay 137), and the Matthean parallel to 5.14 uses ὅλος ὁ νόμος as in 5.3 (Matt. 22.39–40). Nor is it likely that Paul intended a clear distinction between 'doing' the law and 'fulfilling' it (as Betz 275; Barclay 139–41; Longenecker 242–3), since elsewhere he can talk of 'doing the law' in a wholly positive sense (Rom. 2.14; cf. Gal. 6.9).

[57] S. Westerholm, *Israel's Law and the Church's Faith* (Grand Rapids: Eerdmans, 1988) ch. 10 leans strongly in this direction.

[58] For the view that Gal. 5.14 does refer back to Jesus' teaching and example see my *Galatians* 291–2, and more fully, 'Jesus Tradition in Paul', in *Studying the Historical Jesus: Evaluations of the State of Current Research*, ed. B. Chilton & C.A. Evans (Leien: Brill, 1994) 155–78.

fulfilling the law, different understandings of what the law was about.[59] The difference is that the appropriate life-style should be determined not by ethnic identity and national heritage (living as Jews do), but by the pattern of Christ, by the daily trust in God through Christ, and by the Spirit inspired and enabled love. Paul's affirmation of his Jewish heritage as well as his restatement of it is underlined by his claim that 'faith operating effectively through love' is a more effective fulfilling of 'the whole law' than a life focused in 'circumcision' ever did.

4.3   The second version of the slogan points in quite a different direction and sharpens all the issues raised at the end of § 3 – 'For neither circumcision counts for anything, nor uncircumcision, but a new creation' (6.15). Paul clearly picks up the thought of the preceding verse ('through whom the world has been crucified to me and I to the world') and expresses it in the still starker language of apocalyptic.[60] As J.L. Martyn in particular has insisted, Paul speaks here in apocalyptic terms of 'two different worlds'.[61] The theological problem is that in so doing he sets the Jewish perspective, represented by the circumcision/uncircumcision distinction, firmly into the old creation, with all the apocalyptic deficit thereby implied. Here too the sharp irony of Paul's critique should not be missed: for Paul the very appraisal of circumcision by which Jews typically saw themselves as marked out *from* the wider world (as special to God) was itself a mark of their belongingness *to* the world, to the old creation in its distance from God and deserving of God's judgment.

Such an assertion raises again the questions posed in the Introduction. Has Paul thereby cut the line of continuity with Israel? Has he totally disowned his people, confining them wholesale (as 'the circumcision') to the old age still in darkness, to a world that does not know God? Has he simply replaced the intolerance of the circumcision/uncircumcision antithesis with that of old creation/new creation, where the slogan, 'neither circumcision nor uncircumcision', could never be complemented with an equivalent slogan, 'neither old creation nor new creation'? Is this in effect the first expression of anti-judaism in

---

[59] This is presumably the point which lies behind the puzzling charges that 'all who rely on works of the law' fail to abide by what has been written in the law (3.10), and that 'those who have themselves circumcised do not themselves keep the law' (6.13) – viz. that an ethnically focused and determined keeping of the law is actually a failure to grasp the law's full purpose and scope; see my *Galatians* ad loc.

[60] Κόσμος is a term Paul confines to the present age, but κτίσις (like αἰών) can also be used for the age to come (cf. Rom. 8.19–22 and 2 Cor. 5.17 – 'new creation'). By 'new creation' he presumably means the world of existence made new, recreated, to serve as a fitting context for God's children (Rom. 8.21; for bibliography see Betz 319 n.79). The word can mean 'creature' (cf. particularly Lietzmann 45), but the contrast with 'world' suggests the larger meaning (cf. Isa. 65.17; 66.22).

[61] Martyn, 'Antinomies' 412; this verse provides the basis for Martyn's exegesis of 4.21–25 and 5.16–17.

the NT which thus roots itself at the heart of Christian self-understanding – the people of Christ having taken over the role of the people of Israel and simply re-expressed the very intolerance to which Paul himself objected so strongly?

The fact that this is the second use of the slogan ('neither circumcision, nor un-circumcision, but ...'), and that the first use of it was deliberately angled to encourage a recognition of the continuity between old and new provided by the love command (§ 4.2), suggests that we have to make allowance for at least a degree of apocalyptic rhetoric (as also in the polemical allegory of 4.21–31). Moreover, we need to recall that apocalyptic was itself a characteristic category within second Temple Judaism. On this point of contrast between old age and new age, Paul was at one with various apocalyptists and Jewish sects who highlighted the epochal importance of what had been revealed to them by disparaging their older heritage and disowning their Jewish contemporaries as still languishing under the Deuteronomic curse (Qumran being the most striking example). Nor should we ignore the fact that Paul himself had earlier made a point of qualifying the sharpness of the apocalyptic antithesis in its effect on his fellow Jews by depicting them as heirs under age, to whom the inheritance still belonged, even though their current state was slave-like in comparison to what it could be (4.1–3).[62]

The only way satisfactorily to resolve the tensions thus exposed between the two uses of the 'neither circumcision, nor uncircumcision, but ...' slogan, therefore, must be to recognize that Paul wished to hold the two together as expressing two sides of the same coin. What solution is it, alternatively, to insist that one must be given priority over the other, that Paul must have maintained an apocalyptic discontinuity which denied all validity (Marcion-like) to Israel's history, or, alternatively, that he must have maintained a thoroughgoing continuity which reduced the apocalyptic language to mere sound and fury signifying nothing? What solution is it to conclude lamely that Paul was simply inconsistent and that no coherent sense can be made out of his various statements on this theme? It must surely be more satisfactory to recognize that Paul saw in the Christ/cross, Spirit/hope, faith/love side of the antithesis both a real continuity with and fulfilment of God's purpose for Israel and in giving the law, and a real discontinuity in that the same features marked both an eschatological climax to what had gone before and a new beginning which fulfilled and transcended the best of Israel's hopes.

---

[62] On the much more positive role attributed to the law by Paul in the section 3.19–4.11 see my *Galatians* ad loc., and more fully 'Was Paul Against the Law? The Law in Galatians and Romans: A Test-Case of Text in Context', in *Texts and Contexts: Biblical Texts in Their Textual and Situational Contexts*, ed. T. Fornberg & D. Hellholm (Oslo: Scandinavian University, 1995) 455–75 [= ch. 11 above].

4.4   This line of exposition seems to be confirmed by Paul's third use of the slogan, 'neither circumcision, nor uncircumcision, but ...' in 1 Cor. 7.19 – 'circumcision is nothing and uncircumcision is nothing, but keeping God's commandments'. The 'neither ... nor' formulation is different, but the first part of the slogan is basically the same – a denial that status as marked out by circumcision or uncircumcision has significance within the community of those being saved. There are, however, two striking features which distinguish this third slogan more clearly from the first two.

The first is that the disavowal of the significance of circumcision or uncircumcision is more even handed. In Galatians Paul disowned an essentially Jewish evaluation of circumcision and of the world as categorized in the light of the significance of the circumcised and uncircumcised states seen from a Jewish perspective. Here what is envisaged is two separate evaluations of the circumcised/uncircumcised states, criticized equally (7.18). The one was that of the Jew who now despised his circumcision, whether for Hellenistic reasons (cf. 1 Macc. 1.15) or as a Christian: he should not seek to remove it. The other was that of the would-be Judaizer familiar to us from Galatians – the Gentile believer attracted by the continuing appeal of Judaism as such, and therefore seeing Christianity as a form of Judaism: he should not seek to be circumcised. The second counsel is wholly of a piece with the more urgent appeal of Galatians. But the first indicates that the situation in Corinth was different.

In fact, even the parallel with Galatians in the second piece of counsel is misleading. The situation Paul envisaged in the Corinthian church was evidently not one where his Gentile converts were being strongly pressurised by Jewish Christians to be circumcised. Otherwise we could have expected a more vigorous and virulent response. Rather Paul brings up the subject under the head of the different portions God has assigned to different believers. He considers that the process and prospect of salvation is not affected by such diversity. Each can remain within the state in which he was first called. He then envisages the possibility that the circumcised man might wish to remove the marks of his circumcision, for reasons unstated; he should feel no need or compulsion to do so. Likewise the uncircumcised man might wish to be circumcised, again for reasons unstated; he too should feel no need or compulsion to do so. Paul evidently envisages possibilities, which no doubt could and did emerge within the melting pot of social and cultural status and religious background which made up the Corinthian church; unlike Galatians, however, he does not confront direct challenges on the issue.[63]

---

[63] This observation, therefore, counts against the view that there was a vigorous Jewish-Christian (Peter?) party within Corinth maintaining policies like those of the other missionaries in Galatia. Those who see an active Peter party behind the scenes in Corinth include J. Weiss, *erste Korintherbrief* (KEK; Göttingen: Vandenhoeck, 1910), T.W. Manson, 'The Corinthian Correspondence (1)', in *Studies in the Gospels and Epistles* (Manchester University, 1962)

The second distinguishing feature is the surprising 'but ...' balancing phrase in this third citation of the slogan (surprising in the light of the Galatian parallels) – 'but keeping God's commandments'. The phrase is quite a typically Jewish one (Sir. 32.23; Wis. 6.18; cf. Matt. 19.17).[64] So it is doubtful whether Paul would have used this form in Galatians: 'fulfilling the whole law' in terms of the love command might be a way of meeting the response that the requirement of circumcision was part of the whole law; but it is difficult to see how 'keeping the commandments' could have avoided that response or have failed to undermine Paul's argument. Here, in addressing the Corinthians, however, he evidently felt that his exhortation was exposed to no such danger. The inference already drawn that there was no active proselytising faction within the Corinthian church is thus confirmed.

However, the possibility of using the final phrase to counter the second half of Paul's advice by reference to Gen. 17 (circumcision commanded by God) was still present.[65] Why does Paul not show any awareness of that danger? Could it be that Paul had made nothing in his Corinthian preaching of the idea of believers as children of Abraham and sharers in his inheritance? A reference like 10.11 (Jewish scriptures 'written down for our instruction'), the reuse of the 'neither Jew nor Greek' slogan in 12.13, and the whole episode of the collection (16.1–4) make that unlikely. Rather we have to conclude from Paul's emphasis on the importance of 'keeping God's commandments' that Paul wanted to insist, in an unthreatening and unthreatened way, on the importance of the Jewish scriptures and law as informative of God's will. The continuity of Christian faith with its Jewish heritage, the responsibility of believers (uncircumcised as well as circumcised) to 'keep God's commandments' had become something axiomatic for Paul.

The deduction to be drawn from the uncontroversial way Paul juxtaposes the two sides of the slogan – a calm indifference to the relative merits of the circumcised and uncircumcised states, and the assumption that what really matters is the 'keeping of the commandments' – is presumably something else, therefore. It is that Paul's converts, in Corinth at least, quickly grasped that 'keeping God's commandments' was not to be taken as simply equivalent to living a Jewish way of life (judaizing) or to taking the step of becoming a proselyte committed to keep the whole law. There was a keeping of the commandments which was different from covenantal nomism, a keeping of the commandments presumably

---

190–209, and C.K. Barrett, 'Christianity at Corinth' and 'Cephas and Corinth', in *Essays on Paul* (London: SPCK, 1982) 1–27 and 28–39.

[64] Hence the suggestion by Weiss and others that the phrase had a Jewish origin; but see W. Schrage, *erste Korinther* (EKK VII/2 = 1 Kor 6.12–11.16; Solothurn & Düsseldorf: Benziger/ Neukirchen: Neukirchener, 1995) 131 n.458.

[65] Cf. e.g. C.K. Barrett, *First Corinthians* (BNTC; London: A. & C. Black, 1968) 169; G.D. Fee, *First Corinthians* (NICNT; Grand Rapids: Eerdmans, 1987) 313.

equivalent to 'faith operating effectively through love (of neighbour)' (Gal. 5.6, 14). This presumably involved a prioritizing of the multitudinous laws of the Torah, presumably in effect a recognition of the continuing force of the moral commandments in the decalogue (cf. Rom. 13.9) and a demotion of commandments regarding circumcision, sacrifice and clean and unclean as matters of indifference (at least as understood literally).[66] The point is, however, that Paul could, without qualification or hesitation, describe such a denationalized understanding of the Torah as 'keeping God's commandments'.

When, finally, we refer back to the Galatians texts, we can learn at least two things from this third use of the 'neither circumcision, nor uncircumcision, but ...' slogan. First, that the sharpness of the antithesis drawn in Galatians did indeed owe a good deal to the rhetoric of apocalyptic, a rhetoric which derived its sharpness from the particular pressure put upon Paul's Galatian converts from the other missionaries. That is not to deny the apocalyptic character of Paul's gospel. But it is to observe the danger of generalising theological principles from the language Paul used in a crisis situation.[67] Second, that even in a situation (Corinth) where the pressures were quite different, Paul was able to affirm both the indifference of circumcision and uncircumcision, and the importance of maintaining the continuity with the earlier phase of God's revelation as expressed in the commandments. Where there was no insistence on a totality of continuity (Christianity simply as unmodified Judaism) Paul continued to take for granted that the continuity was substantial, even in terms of the law.

---

[66] Cf. Schrage 136–7.

[67] That the 'apocalypse' is characteristically 'crisis literature' is a matter of wide consensus by students of the literature; see e.g. J.J. Collins, 'Early Jewish Apoclypticism', *ABD* 1.287.

Chapter 14

4QMMT and Galatians

The occurrence of the phrase מקצת מעשי התורה in 4QMMT had already been exciting comment for some years prior to the official publication of the scroll fragments.[1] In one of the first reflections on the official publication,[2] Martin Abegg has suggested that Paul's use of the same phrase, ἔργα νόμου, in Galatians and Romans (Gal 2.16; 3.2, 5, 10; Rom 3.20, 28) indicates that Paul was 're-butting the theology of documents such as MMT ... that Paul was reacting to the kind of theology espoused by MMT, perhaps even by some Christian converts who were committed to the kind of thinking reflected in MMT'.[3] As we shall see below, Abegg has given some further reasons for seeing a parallel or even connection between the thought of 4QMMT and Paul's argumentation in Galatians in particular, but even he does not seem to have appreciated all the points of possible connection. At this early stage in assessing the significance of 4QMMT for New Testament study ('nothing short of revolutionary', concludes Abegg), it may be of value simply to summarize what these points of possible connection amount to.

Fortunately it is not necessary to become involved in any debate about the reconstruction of 4QMMT. The points of possible connection almost all come in 4Q397 and 4Q398, at what is agreed to be the final section of the composite document, what Qimron and Strugnell designate as an epilogue consisting of 32 lines (Martinez lines 86–118).[4] So we can proceed to the points of comparison without further ado. The sequence of the four main points follows the sequence in MMT.

1. The first point of interest is the self-description of the writer(s) of the scroll: ש[פרשנו מרוב העןם – 'we have separated ourselves from the multitude of the

---

[1] I may refer to my own *Romans* (WBC 38; Dallas: Word, 1988) 154.

[2] E. Qimron & J. Strugnell, *Discoveries in the Judean Desert*, vol. X, *Qumran Cave 4 Vol. V, Miqsat Ma ase Ha-Torah* (Oxford: Clarendon, 1994); the text and translation has been reprinted in *BAR* 20.6 (1994) 56–61.

[3] M. Abegg, 'Paul, "Works of the Law" and MMT', *BAR* 20.6 (1994) 52–5 (here 54).

[4] See Qimron & Strugnell 58–63; *BAR* 20.6, 60–61; F.G. Martinez, *The Dead Sea Scrolls Translated: The Qumran Texts in English* (Leiden: Brill, 1994) 79, 84–5; G. Vermes, *The Dead Sea Scrolls in English*, revised and extended 4th edition (London: Penguin, 1995) 182, includes only the last eight lines; see also R. Eisenman & M. Wise, *The Dead Sea Scrolls Uncovered* (Shaftesbury, Dorset: Element, 1992) 196–200.

people' (Qimron C7; Martinez 92). Qimron reconstructs the next phrase as '[and from all their impurity]'. But even without that reconstruction, it is clear enough from the context, especially when taken in conjunction with the second part of MMT, that the separation was motivated by purity concerns (cf. CD 5–7).[5] פרש of course forms the root from which the name 'Pharisees' is generally derived (פרושים = 'separated ones'), with the implication that they were so called because they tried to separate themselves within or even from the rest of Israel, again with the clear implication that the motivation was purity based.[6] Not least of interest here, however, is that the author(s) of MMT advocate what later sources indicate to have been a Sadducaic halakhah and that the opponents in view sound more like Pharisees.[7] Nevertheless, the usage here to express a clearly sectarian attitude is striking. And the fact that this is the first time the term appears in ancient literature[8] adds immeasurably to the significance of the text.

In this first case the possible point of contact is Paul's description of the action of Peter, followed by the other Jewish Christians, who 'separated himself' (ἀφώριζεν ἑαυτόν) from the Gentile Christians in Antioch, having previously eaten with them (συνήσθιεν). The suggestion that Paul's use of ἀφορίζειν in Galatians echoes his own previous experience of self-separation as a Pharisee is an old one.[9] But the fact that we now have a contemporary text[10] which uses precisely this language to describe a sectarian self-separation from the rest of the larger Jewish religious community[11] for purity reasons, to avoid 'associating/participating with them' (Martinez 93; Qimron C8), gives us an unprecedented and striking parallel. The inference is appropriate that the motivation behind Peter's withdrawal from table-fellowship with Gentile Christians in Antioch (Gal 2.12) was of a similar character and rationale as the withdrawal of the MMT group from their larger community.

2. The second point of comparison is the emphasis on the blessings and curses written in the book of Moses (Qimron C13–22, Martinez 99–108). The allusion is clearly to the famous climax to Deut. 27–30. MMT recalls the curses that have

---

[5] Qimron & Strugnell 142–75.

[6] Cf. E. Schürer, *The History of the Jewish People in the Age of Jesus Christ* (rev. and ed. G. Vermes et al.; Edinburgh: T. & T. Clark, 1979) 2.396–97; cf. e.g. U. Kellermann, ἀφορίζω, *EWNT* 1 (1980) 443.

[7] Qimron & Strugnell 111, 115–7.

[8] Y. Sussmann, 'The History of the Halakha and the Dead Sea Scrolls', Appendix 1 to Qimron & Strugnell 192.

[9] See T. Zahn, *Der Brief des Paulus an die Galater* (Leipzig: Deichert, 1905) 61–2 with reference to Gal. 1.15.

[10] Qimron & Strugnell put the composition of MMT in the period 159–152 BCE (p. 121), but also note that the manuscripts date from about 75 BCE to 50 CE (p. 109); that is, the memory of the 'separation' was being kept alive at Qumran in the contemporary copying of the text.

[11] Abegg 54 thinks that the broken word ה[ע][ס] should read rather ה[ע][דה] (the congregation).

fallen on Israel in the past: 'we know that some of the blessings and the curses have (already) been fulfilled' (Qimron C20). The understanding is obvious that these previously fulfilled blessings and curses await an eschatological completion: '"and it shall come to pass, when all these things [be]fall you" (a clear echo of Deut. 30.1), at the end of days, the blessings and the curses ...' (Qimron C13–14). 'And it is the end of days when those in Israel will return to the law' (וזה הוא אחרית הימים שישובו בישר[אל] לת[]) (Qimron C21–22).[12]

Evidently the authors of MMT shared a more widespread fascination with this section of Deuteronomy as a way of making sense of the ups and downs of Israel's history.[13] Whether this means that they thought they were themselves still in exile – a recently popular line of exegesis[14] – is another question. The authors of CD 1.5–8 clearly thought of themselves as at the end of the process. And the impression given by the MMT passage is that the authors' eschatology was similar to Christian eschatology, in which realised and unrealised, already/not yet, were held in tension. They were confident enough of their own status and acceptance before God (the already), but they still held out the hope that others in Israel would also return to the Lord and to his Torah.[15]

Whatever the finer points of MMT's (and Qumran's) eschatology, the point of significance for us is that this section of MMT indicates a line of self-reflection, or Israel-reflection, on the blessings and curses of Deut. 27–30, which is quite similar to Paul's own Israel-reflection in Gal. 3.8–14. It is true, of course, that the blessing in this case is the blessing promised to and through Abraham (3.8, 9, 14). But anyone familar with the curse language of Deuteronomy would inevitably think of the counterbalancing promise language – a probability which the difficulty of making sense of the Deuteronomic curse language in 3.10 and 13 (Deut. 27.26; 21.23) has caused commentators to forget or neglect. Moreover, in both contexts (Abraham and Deuteronomy) there is an interplay between the ideas of blessing and curse: Gen. 12.3 – 'I will bless those who bless you, and the

---

[12] Qimron translates: 'And this is at the end of days when they will return to Israel'; cf. Martinez 107–8 – 'And this is the end of days, when they go back to Israel for [ever . . .]'. But 'to Israel' is not an obvious translation for [בישר[אל]; 'return to' is classically expressed with אל or ל, and often with the addition, 'in peace' (בשלום). The point was acknowledged by Martinez at the SBL meeting in Chicago in November 1994. The translation in the text is the revised translation he suggested on that occasion, in which he completes the lacuna at the beginning of line 108 (Qimron C22) as לתורה.

[13] See particularly J.M. Scott, '"For as Many as are of Works of the Law are Under a Curse" (Galatians 3.10)', in *Paul and the Scriptures of Israel* (ed. C.A. Evans & J.A. Sanders; JSNTS 83; Sheffield: JSOT, 1993) 187–221 (here 194–213); also 'Paul's Use of Deuteronomic Tradition', *JBL* 112 (1993) 645–65.

[14] N.T. Wright, *The New Testament and the People of God* (London: SPCK, 1992) particularly 268–72; Scott in n. 13 above.

[15] The mistranslation of Qimron and Martinez (initially) – 'to Israel' – may reflect the assumption that the perspective of the writers was as those who wrote from exile. But the better translation – 'in Israel' – points away from that interpretation.

one who curses you I will curse'; Deut. 30.1, 7 – 'When all these things have happened to you, the blessings and the curses ... The Lord your God will put all these curses on your enemies ...'. With considerable subtlety Paul contrives a fresh variation on this interplay, by integrating the Abrahamic blessing into the Deuteronomic pattern of blessing and curse, thereby switching the emphasis from the thought of Gentile cursing to that of Gentile blessing.[16]

In short, at the heart of Paul's exposition is a concern similar to that in 4QMMT: how widely shall the blessing extend. MMT hopes for all Israel to return to (the law) (Qimron C21) and 'for the welfare of Israel (לישראל למוב)' (C31–32). Paul has in mind the blessing to the Gentiles, and perhaps for 'Israel' to be redefined in terms of that blessing (Gal 6.16).[17]

3. The third point of comparison is, of course, the phrase on which most attention has so far focused – מעשי התורה. The closeness of the parallel with Paul's phrase, ἔργα νόμου, has unfortunately been obscured by the translations so far adopted – 'the precepts of the Torah' (Qimron C27; Martinez 113), 'observances of the Law' (Vermes). Eisenman and Wise render the phrase as 'works of the law' (so also Abegg); but the weight of the other translators is likely to count against the Eisenman and Wise version. However, 'deed or act' is the most natural meaning for מעשה,[18] and its appropriateness here is borne out by the various parallels with which we were already familiar in the DSS, particularly 1QH 9[= 1].26 (מעשי הצדקה) –'righteous deeds' [Vermes]; 'works of justice' [Martinez]), 12[= 4].31 (מעשי צדוה) – 'righteous deeds' [Vermes]; 'acts of justice' [Martinez] and 4Q174/Flor. 1.7 (מעשי תורה) – 'works of the Law' [Vermes]; 'the works of the law' [Martinez]) (cf. 1QS 5.21, 23; 6.18; 1QH 14[= 6].9). Indeed, it is noticeable that Qimron and Martinez both translate the same term four lines earlier in MMT (במעשיהמה) as 'their deeds'. And at the SBL meeting in Chicago in November, 1994, Martinez again acknowledged that the printed translation of (his) line 113 was less satisfactory, and that מעשי should after all be rendered 'works of' here too, as elsewhere in the DSS. So the published translation of both Qimron and Martinez should not be allowed to obscure the issue.

It is also quite clear from 4QMMT what was in mind in the phrase, מעשי התורה. The full phrase, מקצת מעשי התורה, clearly refers to the purpose of the document itself: 'We have also written to you some of the works of the Torah which we think are good for you and for your people' (own translation of Qimron C26–

---

[16] Note Qumran's own variation on the blessing/curse language in 1QS 2 and 4Q266; see Eisenman & Wise 197, 215–7.

[17] But the problems of interpreting the reference to 'Israel' in Gal. 6.16 are well known; see e.g. my *Galatians* (BNTC; London: A. & C. Black, 1993) 344–6.

[18] The ambiguity arises because מעשה can signify 'deed' as prescribed deed (hence 'precept') as well as a deed carried out. Qimron & Strugnell 139 n. 41 note that the LXX translates מעשה in Exod. 18.20 as τὰ ἔργα.

27; Martinez 112–113). The allusion back to the beginning of the second section of the text is beyond dispute: 'These are some of our rulings (אלה מקצת דברינו) ... which are . . . the works ([ה]מעשים) ...' (Qimron B1–2; Martinez 3).[19] What then follows is a series of halakhic rulings, chiefly relating to the temple, priesthood, sacrifices and purity, and regularly introduced with the formula, 'we are of the opinion that' (אנחנו חושבים – B8, 29, 36, 37, 42, 55, 73).

The parallel with Galatians is quite striking. As in MMT, the phrase seems to be first used (in Gal. 2.16) as a summary reference to a series of legal/halakhic rulings/practices which have been at the centre of the previous paragraphs – circumcision (2.1–10), and rules governing table-fellowship with Gentiles (2.11–15). It is true that the מעשים of MMT are all highly technical issues, principally related to the cult. Whereas in Galatians the ἔργα νόμου might seem (from a Christian perspective) to focus on much weightier matters.[20] More to the point, however, is the fact that in both cases the rulings and practices (works) have been focal points of dispute within the community, sufficient indeed to cause a separation in the wider community – those following the stricter interpretation separating from those following the less strict practice. This difference between the two texts in what are referred to by the terms (מעשים/ἔργα) may be simply explained by the fact that in the one case it is an intra-Jewish dispute, where the issue of separation hangs on finer points of halakhah, whereas in Galatians the issue was of separation between Jew and Gentile. The principal point of parallel remains the same, however, that מעשי התורה and ἔργα νόμου both seem to refer to 'works of the law' understood as defining a boundary which marks out those of faith/faithfulness from others.

4. Not least striking of the parallels is the one which appears in the penultimate line of 4QMMT.[21] The writer hopes that 'at the end of time, you may rejoice in finding that some of our words/practices are so/true/correct (מקצת דברינו כן). And it shall be reckoned to you for righteousness (ונחשבה לך לצדקה) in doing what is upright and good before him' (Qimron C30–31; Martinez 116–117; Vermes). Clearly in view, on the one hand, are the rulings and practices (works) documented in the previous paragraphs (מקצת דברינו; cf. Qimron B1–2; Martinez 3 cited in § 3 above). Equally clearly in view, on the other hand, is the formulation of Gen 15.6 – 'he (the Lord) reckoned it to him (Abraham) as righteousness (ויחשבה לו צדקה)'. But with the phrase understood as it was understood subsequently in early Judaism, that is, as righteousness reckoned in recognition of covenant faithfulness: Ps 106.31 – Phinehas' action in preventing Israel's de-

---

[19] Qimron & Strugnell 110. This reference back tells against the thesis of Eisenman and Wise that C was a separate document.

[20] The fact that the phrase in Paul is always anarthrous (almost always in the form ἐξ ἔργων νόμου) is comparatively unimportant in view of the similar form in 4Q174/Flor. 1.7.

[21] Noted also by Abegg 55 and Eisenman & Wise 183–5.

filement 'reckoned to him for righteousness (ותחשב לו לצדקה)';[22] 1 Macc 2.52 – 'Was not Abraham found faithful (εὑρέθη πιστός) when tested and it was reckoned to him for righteousness (καὶ ἐλογίσθη αὐτῷ εἰς δικαιοσύνην)?'; and *Jub.* 30.17 – righteousness reckoned to Simeon and Levi for maintaining the purity and apartness of the children of Israel, like Phinehas, by killing the Schechemites. So here, in MMT, the assumption is that 'righteousness is reckoned' to those who are faithful in observing the rulings and following the practices (works) outlined in the earlier paragraphs.

The parallel with Galatians at this point obviously lies in the reference to the same phrase from Gen. 15.6 as used in Gal. 3.6: 'Abraham believed God and it was reckoned to him for righteousness (καὶ ἐλογίσθη αὐτῷ εἰς δικαιοσύνην)'; with the consequence for Paul that 'those who are of faith (οἱ ἐκ πίστεως) are blessed with faithful Abraham (σὺν τῷ πιστῷ Ἀβραάμ)' (3.9). The language is the same – ἐλογίσθη εἰς δικαιοσύνην; in both cases appeal is being made, in effect or explicitly, to Abraham as normative pattern. The difference is that Paul attributes Abraham's being reckoned righteous solely to his faith, whereas in Ps. 106, 1 Macc. 2, *Jub.* 30 and MMT it is attributed to a pattern of behaviour understood by the respective authors, implicitly or explicitly, as demonstrating faithfulness to covenant obligations. More to the present point, the argument in Gal. 3.6–9 is clearly an elaboration of the basic thesis enunciated in 2.16: 'no one is justified from works of law but only through faith in Jesus Christ'.

In other words, Paul is objecting precisely to the sort of understanding and attitude we find expressed in 4QMMT. MMT, in common with other strands of Second Temple Judaism, understood 'righteousness' and 'justification' in relation to and as somehow dependent on מעשי התורה/ἔργα νόμου. The same understanding determined the decision of Peter and the other Jewish Christians to withdraw from table-fellowship with Gentile believers at Antioch. In direct opposition, Paul insisted that πίστις Ἰησοῦ Χριστοῦ alone was sufficient, precisely as 'faith in Jesus Christ' and not as 'faithfulness' to rules and practices which required separation from the unfaithful, of Jew from Gentile.[23]

---

[22] As Abegg observes (55 n), Gen. 15.6 and Ps. 106.31 are the only biblical verses that contain both the verb חשב and the noun צדקה. The implied appeal to Gen. 15.6 carries with it the implication that Phinehas' action was interpreted, like that of Abraham in 1 Macc. 2.52, as an expression of his covenant faithfulness.

[23] Insofar as the contrast between Galatians and 4QMMT implies a contrast between faith and faithfulness (cf. Jas. 2.18–24), it strengthens the case against the currently popular rendering of πίστις Ἰησοῦ Χριστοῦ in Galatians and Romans as 'the faithfulness of Jesus Christ'. Only those who see no contrast between Paul and James on this point could be confident that Paul understood the phrase as indicating Jesus' faithfulness in what he *did*. See further my 'Once More, PISTIS CHRISTOU', in E.E. Johnson & D.M. Hay, eds., *Pauline Theology. Vol.IV: Looking Back, Pressing On* (Atlanta: Georgia, 1997) 61–81, in debate with the preceding paper by R.B. Hays, 'PISTIS and Pauline Christology: What is at Stake?' 35–60.

5. For the sake of completeness we might simply mention one other parallel between 4QMMT and Galatians. I refer to the fact that the first part of MMT is a calendar. This is evidence of a concern, with which we are familiar elsewhere in Second Temple Judaism, to ensure that the observance of the set feasts was in accord with the heavenly calendar – the result being factional dispute between those who calculated the dates of the feasts by the sun and those who calculated by the moon (see particularly *Jub.* 6.32–35; *1 Enoch* 82.4–7; 1QS 1.14–15; CD 3.14–15).[24]

The point of contact here is with Gal. 4.10 – which indicates clearly enough that observance of the set feasts was likewise a concern of those 'troubling' the Galatians.[25] That is to say, observance of the (Jewish) feasts was consistent with the emphasis on 'works of the law' both in MMT and in the teaching of the Galatian (Christian Jewish) missionaries against whom Paul polemicises in Galatians. It is not clear, however, whether further significance for an MMT/Galatians parallel can be drawn at this point.

To sum up, the four or five points of parallel between 4QMMT and Galatians surely give us sufficient grounds for concluding that MMT preserves the sort of theological attitude and halakhic practice which in the event determined the attitude and action of Peter and the other Christian Jews in Antioch (Gal. 2.11–14). I do not mean, of course, that Galatians was written with knowledge of MMT, or that the 'certain from James' (Gal. 2.12) were themselves Qumranites or influenced by Qumran, or anything of the sort. But the weight of the evidence does seem to suggest that MMT preserves a vocabulary and manner of theologising which left its mark on a wider spectrum of Jewish thought and practice, and that it was just this sort of theologising and practice which confronted Paul in Antioch and which he wrote Galatians to counter.[26]

---

[24] 4Q321 tries to correlate the two calendars; see Eisenman & Wise 109–16; Martinez 454–5.

[25] That the Jewish feasts as such were in mind is almost certain; see my *Galatians* 227–9.

[26] I am grateful to my colleagues Robert Hayward and Loren Stuckenbruck for stimulus and comment on this subject and on the first draft of this paper.

Chapter 15

Paul's Conversion:

A Light to Twentieth Century Disputes

The debate occasioned by the so-called 'new perspective on Paul' has included a good deal of misunderstanding and seems often to have generated more heat than light. Peter Stuhlmacher's birthday volume is perhaps an appropriate opportunity to clarify some of these misunderstandings and to do something to reverse the heat/light ratio! At all events this little birthday gift is written with that hope and with heartiest congratulations and best wishes to the one whom our north American cousins no doubt call 'the honoree' and whose writings express so much of what is best in NT scholarship.

A good test passage is 'Paul's conversion', to use the traditional description of the event which transformed Paul from a persecutor of 'the church of God' (Gal. 1.13) into an 'apostle of Christ Jesus'. In recent discussion it has received a fair amount of attention, but in the debate about Paul's attitude to the law and his teaching on justification by faith the significance of Paul's conversion is still more often than not simply taken for granted. In a volume on Paul's gospel, his understanding of his heritage as a Jew and the outworking of both in the church, it is appropriate, therefore, that we ask afresh: What did Paul's conversion contribute to his gospel? How did it change or modify his self-understanding as a Jew? How did it help shape his conception of the church? Or to pose the issue at its simplest: Given that the verb 'to convert' means 'to turn (round)', *from* what did Paul convert and *to* what did he convert?

We can proceed in the obvious way by reviewing the traditional answers to this question, before giving closer attention to the passage which offers most hope of providing us with Paul's own answer but whose resources have surprisingly not been sufficiently exploited hitherto.

1. From what was Paul converted? The traditional views

A variety of answers has been given to this question. In each case some aspect of the whole picture has been grasped, but none seems to be quite adequate in reflecting Paul's own emphases. To cover the full range of nuances we can survey the traditional answers under five headings.

1.1 From Judaism to Christianity

This is an answer often given at the popular level. Its popular rationale is that the word 'conversion' is usually taken to denote a turning from no religion to religion, or from one religion to another. Its theological justification was reinforced by the long time assumption in NT scholarship that Judaism has to be understood theologically simply as the precursor of Christianity. Hence the description of Second Temple Judaism still prevalent only a generation ago as 'Spätjudentum':[1] first century Judaism was 'late Judaism' because its theological significance ended with the coming of Jesus;[2] the old covenant was wholly superceded by the new.[3]

Above all, the strength of this answer lies in Paul's own language in Gal. 1.13–14, the passage we will be devoting close attention to later. There, in the only verses in which he uses the term 'Judaism', he speaks of his 'way of life previously in Judaism' and how he had 'progressed in Judaism beyond many of his contemporaries'. Evidently 'Judaism' describes his former religious practice – a practice which he had now abandoned, and as a direct consequence of his conversion. That surely gives some grounds for the traditional answer: Paul had been converted from this 'Judaism' to Christianity.

The problem is that the answer as usually understood claims too much; in its traditional form it is an overstatement. No NT scholar today would describe Second Temple Judaism as 'late Judaism'. Apart from anything else, such a description, of course, makes it impossible to speak sensibly of the following nineteen centuries of Judaism. Similarly the description that 'Paul converted from Judaism to Christianity' is properly speaking anachronistic nonsense. The term 'Christianity' did not yet exist! It first appears, in our written records anyway, with Ignatius (*Magn.*10; *Rom.* 3.3; *Philad.* 6.1), some eighty years after Paul's conversion.

These linguistic anachronisms are important since they both reflect and highlight a more substantive reappraisal which is now under way of the relationship between the first Christians and their native Judaism. Of course it is not an adequate response to this first answer to say that 'Christianity' did not yet exist as a linguistic phenomenon. The real point is that Jesus and the first Christians were

---

[1] So e.g. still in an early number of the prestigious WUNT series – H. Bietenhard, *Die himmlische Welt im Urchristentum und Spätjudentum* (WUNT 2; Tübingen: Mohr, 1951).

[2] See e.g. L, Goppelt, *Theologie des Neuen Testaments 1. Jesu Wirken in seiner theologischen Bedeutung* (Göttingen: Vandenhoeck, 1975): Jesus 'hebt das Sabbatgebot als solches und damit das Gesetz, die Grundlage des Judentums, auf' (146); '... Jesus tatsächlich das Judentum von der Wurzel her durch Neues aufhebt' (148). See also the criticisms of Pannenberg and Moltmann in J.T. Pawlikowski, *Christ in the Light of the Christian-Jewish Dialogue* (New York: Paulist, 1982) 37–47.

[3] So already in Heb. 8.13. Similarly Barn. 4.6–8; 13–14; Justin *Dial.* e.g. 11.5 and 135.3, 6; Melito, *Peri Pascha* 39–45.

Jews, and remained Jews. 'Jesus the Jew' is now a commonplace among students of 'the historical Jesus', and it forms the principal presupposition of the so-called 'third quest' of the historical Jesus.[4] But Paul too remained a Jew (cf. his own self-description according to Acts 22.3 – 'I am a Jew'); he still described himself in one of his later letters as 'an Israelite' (Rom. 11.1). The fact, which no one would gainsay for the period in which Paul's conversion took place, is that what later became known as 'Christianity' was still a movement *within* Second Temple Judaism, most accurately described at this period as a form of messianic Judaism, its adherents marked out among their fellow Jews by their belief in and beliefs about Jesus.[5]

The upshot is that a simple definition of Paul's conversion as a conversion from Judaism or to Christianity proves to be too simple. A turning from and a turning to there certainly was. But what the *from* and *to* was clearly requires closer analysis and more precise definition.

1.2 From a troubled conscience to peace with God

This is another popular traditional answer. Historically it was based on the assumption that Paul's conversion was a, if not the classic type of conversion, of the same type as the conversions of Augustine and of Luther.[6] Exegetically it was rooted in Paul's 'I' language of Rom. 7, where the traditional assumption was that the spiritual impotence described there was that of Paul in his pre-conversion state; Augustine's use of the language of Rom. 7.22–25 to describe his own pre-conversion wrestlings is a classic example.[7] The popular expression of the view has come in a whole sequence of novelistic biographies of Paul, and no doubt also in countless sermons on his conversion, which have provided vivid descriptions of Paul's wrestlings with his conscience, pricked (cf. Acts 26.14) no doubt by his memory of Stephen's martyrdom and of his own part in it (Acts 7.58; 8.1).

---

[4] See e.g. N.T. Wright's revision of S. Neill, *The Interpretation of the New Testament 1861–1986* (Oxford University 1988) 379–403; B. Witherington, *The Jesus Quest: The Third Search for the Jew of Nazareth* (Downers Grove, IL: InterVarsity, 1995).

[5] The significance of the name 'Christians' which according to Acts 11.26 was first coined at this time is unclear. If Luke's information is accurate, the Latin formation of the name (*Christiani*) suggests that it was coined by the Roman authorities in Antioch. But that need not imply that these 'Christians' were being so designated to distinguish them from the larger category of 'Jews'. On the contrary, the formation simply indicates adherents of Christ, just as the *Herodiani* (Mark 3.6 etc.) denoted adherents of Herod (Herod's party) and *Caesariani* and *Pompeiani* functioned similarly as party names. That is to say, the name may simply indicate that the Roman authorities recognized the 'Christians' to be a distinct faction within the community of Jews (with their numerous Gentile sympathisers – cf. Josephus, *War* 7.44–45) in Antioch.

[6] See e.g. W. James, *The Varieties of Religious Experience* (Glasgow: Collins Fontana, 1960) 176–7, 244–5.

[7] Augustine, *Confessions* 8.5.

This view, however, has also had to be steadily abandoned in the course of the 20th century. The problem is that Paul himself gives no hint that he suffered from a troubled conscience in the period prior to his conversion. Since Kümmel's classic treatment of Rom. 7[8] the idea that Paul's 'I' language describes his own pre-conversion experience has now been generally abandoned. There are still attempts to revive the older view in a modified form,[9] but they have not won much support. Generally reckoned to be much more decisive is the fact that in the two passages where Paul most clearly expresses his own pre-conversion perspective, he does so in terms totally at odds with the 'anguished conscience' hypothesis. In Phil. 3.6 he claims that 'as to righteousness under the law' he had been 'blameless', and this evidently at the very time he had been persecuting the church with zeal. No qualms of conscience prior to the Damascus road encounter recalled here. Similarly in Gal. 1.13–14, the other most explicit allusion to his pre-conversion state of mind, Paul simply recalls his success in maintaining and practising the traditions of his fathers.[10]

Clearly, then, the evangelistic model of Paul's conversion as the anguished soul finding peace with God is too weakly rooted in Paul's own self-testimony for it to carry much weight. It may still be revived using psycho-analytic models to penetrate below his conscious thought and memory – 'the unconscious complex of Christianity broke through into consciousness'.[11] But such speculation becomes increasingly remote from the text, and if the texts themselves yield a more satisfactory answer to our question they should have higher priority.

1.3 From denial to affirmation of Jesus as Messiah

Paul's conversion is portrayed in Acts and recalled by Paul himself as an encounter with the risen Christ (Acts 9, 22, 26; 1 Cor. 9.1; 15.8; Gal. 1.16; cf. 2 Cor. 4.4–6; Phil. 3.7–8). It is natural therefore to conclude that a central feature of the event for Paul was a transformation of his understanding of Jesus, indeed a conversion to the belief about and faith in Christ of those he had been persecuting.

The claim can be given further exegetical reinforcement from 1 Cor. 1.23 and Gal. 3.13. From the former, it can be inferred without strain that when Paul says

---

[8] W.G. Kümmel, *Römer 7 und die Bekehrung des Paulus* (Leipzig: Hinrichs, 1929).

[9] R.H. Gundry, 'The Moral Frustration of Paul Before his Conversion: Sexual Lust in Romans 7.7–25', in *Pauline Studies: Essays Presented to F.F. Bruce*, ed. D.A. Hagner & M.J. Harris (Exeter: Paternoster, 1980) 228–45; G. Theissen, *Psychological Aspects of Pauline Theology* (Edinburgh: T. & T. Clark, 1987) 228–50.

[10] The article by K. Stendahl, 'The Apostle Paul and the Introspective Conscience of the West', *HTR* 56 (1963) 199–215, reprinted in his *Paul Among Jews and Gentiles* (London: SCM, 1977) 78–96, has been particularly influential on this issue.

[11] C.G. Jung, *Contributions to Analytical Psychology* (ET 1945) 257, cited by C.S.C. Williams, *Acts* (BNTC; London: A. & C. Black, 1957) 123; see now also J.G. Gager, 'Some Notes on Paul's Conversion', *NTS* 27 (1981) 697–704.

the proclamation of Christ crucified was 'to Jews a scandal or cause of offence' he was recalling his own attitude as a Jew offended by the claims made for Jesus by his followers. The offence evidently lay in the juxtaposition of the two terms – 'Messiah' and 'crucified'. What the scandal would have consisted of is further illuminated by the second passage: Gal. 3.13 – 'Christ became a curse on our behalf, because it is written, "Cursed is everyone who has been hanged on a tree"', citing Deut. 21.23. Again it is a fair deduction that here Paul was recalling his own application of Deut. 21.23 as a reason for his own previous dismissal and persecution of the view that the crucified Jesus was actually God's Messiah. We know from the DSS that the same Deuteronomic denunciation of the criminal exposed after death ('Cursed is everyone who hangs on a tree') had already been applied to the act of crucifixion (4QpNah. 1.7–8; 11QT 64.6–13). So it is entirely plausible that Paul the persecutor should have used the same reasoning to condemn the Nazarenes' claim that their crucified Jesus was nevertheless Messiah.

If further confirmation is needed we could refer also to 1 Cor. 15.3 and Acts 9.22. In the former, Paul informs or reminds his Corinthian audience that the gospel as he himself first received it began by confessing 'that Christ died for our sins according to the scriptures'. This would have provided Paul with a sufficient theological answer (Christ's death as a sin-offering) to the problem of the crucified Messiah. In the latter, Luke narrates that Paul shortly after his conversion confounded the Damascus Jews by proving that Jesus was the Messiah (Acts 9.22). The justified inference would be that Paul began at once to preach the faith (in Jesus Messiah) to which he had just been converted.

Not surprisingly, then, this has been a well sustained view of the impact of the Damascus road encounter on Paul's own theology. In the 1950s H.G. Wood and Philippe Menoud both expounded the significance of Paul's conversion in these terms.[12] Furthermore, though there has been an understandable reluctance on the part of most scholars lest too much of Paul's christology be read into his conversion, some have not hesitated to find all that was necessary to his full blown christology already present in the Damascus road experience itself.[13] For example, J.A.T. Robinson read Paul's whole theology of the body of Christ into the words from heaven as recorded by Acts – 'Saul, Saul, why do you persecute me?' (Acts 9.5; 22.7; 26.14) – the logic being, of course, that the risen Christ thereby identified himself ('me') with the persecuted church.[14] And more re-

---

[12] H.G. Wood, 'The Conversion of Paul: Its Nature, Antecedents and Consequences', *NTS* 1 (1954–55) 276–82; P.H. Menoud, 'Revelation and Tradition: The Influence of Paul's Conversion on his Theology', *Interpretation* 7 (1953) 131–41.

[13] In speaking of Paul's conversion alternatively as his 'Damascus road experience' I am simply using short-hand convenience; the discussion does not depend on a particular view of the historical value of the Acts accounts as regards the location of Paul's conversion.

[14] J.A.T. Robinson, *The Body* (London: SCM, 1952) 58.

cently Seyoon Kim has built a whole thesis out of the probable echo of the Damascus road encounter contained in 2 Cor. 4.4–6, that Paul would have understood his vision of the exalted Christ more or less from the first in terms of divine Wisdom and the man-like epiphany of both Ezek. 1.26 and Dan. 7.13.[15]

It can hardly be doubted that there is something here. It is hard to see what Paul's conversion (from persecutor to apostle) could have meant had it not at least included a radical 'change of mind' on his part with regard to the first Christian claims regarding Jesus. A christological revelation is clearly indicated in Gal. 1.16 (God revealed his Son in Paul). And Phil. 3.7–8 certainly indicates a complete transformation of life-centre with personal piety now focused in an all absorbing way on Christ. So the basic claim of Wood and Menoud must be right. The more elaborate claims of Robinson and Kim are another matter. At the very least we must allow the likelihood that the more elaborate christology of Paul's letters (first dictated some fifteen years later) is the outworking of reflection over time, no doubt at least including reflection on his Damascus road experience (as 2 Cor. 4.4–6 implies), but no doubt also fed by his increasing knowledge of the Jesus tradition and longer term reading of the scriptures in the light of his new faith in a crucified Christ.[16]

The only weakness of the basic hypothesis is that in his most explicit recollections of his conversion Paul does not mention such a transformation in his beliefs about Jesus (Gal. 1.13–14 and Phil. 3). And in his letters it continues to be a surprising fact that the claim regarding Jesus as Messiah is on the whole uncontentious. As all commentators recognize, 'Christ' had already become a proper name in Paul's writing, having already lost most if not all of its titular force. This can only be because the claim, if contentious once, no longer was so. This in turn may simply be a reflection of the fact that Paul's letters were written to churches for whom the claim was no longer contentious. But if the claim that Jesus was Messiah was indeed at the heart of Paul's earlier persecution and continued to be a major issue between Jews and Christians we would have expected more echoes and indications than we find – echoes such as we find with regard to the law.

Could it be then that the Christian claim that Jesus was Messiah was not quite so contentious after all in Jewish circles? How otherwise could the Jewish believers in Messiah Jesus have been left in Jerusalem as undisturbed as they seem to have been?[17] It was evidently *not* the claim for Jesus' Messiahship which occa-

---

[15] So particularly S. Kim, *The Origin of Paul's Gospel* (WUNT 2.4; Tübingen: Mohr, 1981).

[16] See further my earlier critique of Kim in '"A Light to the Gentiles": The Significance of the Damascus Road Christophany for Paul', in *The Glory of Christ in the New Testament: Studies in Christology in Memory of G. B. Caird*, ed. L.D. Hurst & N.T. Wright (Oxford: Clarenon, 1987) 251–66; reprinted in my *Jesus, Paul and the Law: Studies in Mark and Galatians* (London: SPCK/Louisville: Westminster, 1990) 89–104.

[17] I follow the general consensus that the persecution, which, according to Acts, followed on

sioned the persecution in which Paul was a leading player. References like 1 Cor. 1.23 and Gal. 3.13 may therefore indicate not so much wholesale denunciation of the Christian claim as factional polemic between different Jewish groups and rejection of the Christian claims as unworthy of more widespread acceptance within Judaism. In other words, the claim that the crucified Jesus was Messiah was not in principle objectionable for a Jew to hold; after all many devout and well regarded Jews had themselves been crucified in the past. It was more the Christian claim that other, inded all Jews should also accept this Jesus as Messiah which was likely to have proved offensive.[18]

At all events, although this hypothesis must provide some of the answer to our question, it is far from certain that we have penetrated to what was at the heart of his conversion experience for Paul himself.

1.4 From the law to the gospel

This has been the most consistently maintained answer during the last few decades of scholarly discussion.[19] To be sure it trades to some extent on the sharp antithesis between law and gospel which has been a major motif of most/(all?) strands of Reformation theology, and can quite quickly lapse into the Judaism/ Christianity antithesis (law = Judaism, gospel = Christianity) which we discounted when discussing the first answer above. But it does not depend on posing the law/gospel antithesis so sharply. And, more to the point, it has substantive exegetical grounding in its own right. Above all we may call upon Gal. 2.19–21. Here it can be said fairly confidently that Paul recalls, or at includes a reference to his own conversion: 'I through the law died to the law, that I might live to God ... I do not nullify the grace of God, for if righteousness is through the law, then Christ has died to no purpose'. Most influential, however, as a summary of what Paul concluded from his Damascus road encounter, has been Rom. 10.4: 'Christ is the end of the law'.[20]

---

from Stephen's execution, was directed mainly against the Hellenists, leaving the rest of the Nazarenes largely undisturbed. The consensus has been recently challenged by C.C. Hill, *Hellenists and Hebrews: Reappraising Division within the Earliest Church* (Minneapolis: Fortress, 1992) 32–40; but he ignores or plays down too many of the cumulative arguments which give the consensus position its strength.

[18] See further the question which reflects my own puzzlement on the issue: 'How Controversial was Paul's Christology?', in *From Jesus to Paul: Essays on New Testament Christology in Honour of M. de Jonge*, ed. M.C. De Boer (JSNTS 84; Sheffield: JSOT, 1993) 148–67.

[19] See e.g. U. Wilckens, 'Die Bekehrung des Paulus als religionsgeschichtliches Problem', *Rechtfertigung als Freiheit: Paulusstudien* (Neukirchen: Neukirchener, 1974) 11–32, particularly 15, 18, 23–5; S. Kim, *The Origin of Paul's Gospel* (WUNT 2.4; Tübingen: Mohr, 1981) 3–4 and *passim*; C. Dietzfelbinger, *Die Berufung des Paulus als Ursprung seiner Theologie* (WMANT 58; Neukirchen: Neukirchener, 1985) e.g. 90, 115, 144.

[20] In this instance, of course, particular reference should be made to P. Stuhlmacher, '"Das Ende des Gesetzes". Über Ursprung und Ansatz der paulinischen Theologie', *Versöhnung, Ge-*

Usually as part of the argument it is maintained that Paul persecuted the Hellenists because they had already abandoned the law. This assumes, as I do, that Paul's persecution was directed principally against fellow diaspora rooted, Greek-speaking Jews who had become baptised disciples of Messiah Jesus and to whom Stephen had provided leadership. The exegetical grounding is then provided by Phil. 3.6 – 'as to zeal a persecutor of the church' – since 'zeal' is most naturally understood as 'zeal for the law' (cf. Gal. 1.14 – 'being exceedingly zealous for my ancestral traditions'; Acts 21.20 – 'zealots for the law').[21] The argument then proceeds smoothly: Paul was converted to the position he had persecuted; he abandoned the law like those he had persecuted. If Paul's rationale is wanted it can be readily guessed at: the law had approved the punishment of Jesus by death; but the Damascus road encounter revealed to Paul that God had vindicated this Jesus; therefore 'the law is an ass' and should now be discarded.[22] 'Christ is the end of the law'.

Here again there must be something in this answer. It would be hard to read Gal. 2.21 without such a clear overtone. There are, however, two problems. One is that such traditions we have regarding the Hellenists do not support the view that they had broken with the law.[23] The speech attributed to Stephen in Acts 7 speaks most positively of Moses, describes the law as 'living oracles' and climaxes in the charge that it is Stephen's hearers who have failed to keep the law (Acts 7.20–25, 35–38, 53). The speech's critique of traditional Judaism is directed rather against the temple 'made with hands' (7.47–49). This suggests in turn that the charge brought against Stephen, that he spoke against Moses, against the holy place and the law (6.11, 13–14), is intended by Luke to be understood as directed against the views of the Temple maintained by Stephen in particular or by the (Christian) Hellenists in general. Since the Temple cult and its right ordering stands at the centre of the law and of the customs which Moses handed down, a hostile view of the Temple cult would be regarded as a threat to the law as well. In other words, we cannot conclude from our sources that the Hellenists had broken with the law as a whole, that Paul persecuted them for that reason and that he was converted to that same view. Some greater precision is necessary if we are to do justice to differentiations within our sources.

The second problem is one which has bedevilled assessments of Paul's theology for decades. That is the (for some) remarkably positive view he continues to

---

setz und Gerechtigkeit: Aufsätze zur biblischen Theologie (Göttingen: Vandenhoeck, 1982) 166–91; but see also e.g. Dietzfelbinger 105–6, 118, 125, 145.

[21] See e.g. P.T. O'Brien, *Philippians* (NIGTC; Grand Rapids: Eerdmans, 1991) 375–6 and those cited there.

[22] See e.g. those cited by H. Räisänen, *Paul and the Law* (WUNT 29; Tübingen: Mohr, 1983) 249 n.112.

[23] See e.g. H. Räisänen, 'The "Hellenists": A Bridge between Jesus and Paul?', *Jesus, Paul and Torah: Collected Essays* (JSNTS 43; Sheffield: JSOT, 1992) 177; C.K. Barrett, *Acts 1–14* (ICC; Edinburgh: T. & T. Clark, 1994) 337–8.

maintain in his letters regarding the law. We need only refer to such passages as Rom. 3.31, 8.4, 1 Cor. 7.19 and Gal. 5.14. Someone who speaks as Paul does in these passages cannot be said to have abandoned the law. So whatever Gal. 2.21 and Rom. 10.4 mean they cannot be read as indicating Paul's complete abandonment of the law by anyone who believes in a basic coherence in Paul's view of the law. The issues here, of course, run far beyond the scope of this paper. It must suffice to say, therefore, that Paul's overall teaching on the law must add a further caution in any assessment of the impact of Paul's conversion on his view of the law. That some reassessment of Paul's relation to the law was bound up with his conversion is clear enough from Gal. 2.21. Precisely what it amounted to has still to be clarified.

1.5 From his own righteousness to God's righteousness

For many this is simply a variant of the last answer. But it deserves separate consideration. As an answer it is, of course, drawn from Phil. 3.9 – 'not having my own righteousness which is from the law, but that which is through faith in Christ, the righteousness from God to that faith'. To be fair, Paul presents this as his hope rather than as something already realised at or by his conversion. Nevertheless, righteousness through faith and not from the law is so much at the centre of Paul's gospel, as expounded by Galatians and Rom. 3–4 in particular, that it is at the very least plausible to argue that Paul saw his conversion as a transfer from 'righteousness under the law' (Phil. 3.6) to righteousness through faith in Christ (3.7–9).

The problems arise when 'my own righteousness' (Phil. 3.9) is read as self-achieved righteousness, and the traditional view of Judaism is evoked as teaching that acceptance by God was something to be earned or merited by obedience to the law. Conjointly 'their own righteousness' of Rom. 10.3 is understood in the same way; the boasting of Rom. 2.23 and 3.27 is read as boasting in such self-achieved righteousness; and the 'works of the law' disowned in Gal. 2.16, Rom. 3.20 and elsewhere, are understood as the good works assumed to have been taught by Judaism to be necessary to achieve that righteousness (cf. Rom. 4.4–5).

It is not my intention to re-enter the debate on the exegesis of these passages.[24] That would be impossible here. It must suffice to note the difficulties which bear upon the interpretation of Paul's conversion. One is the difficulty of documenting this view of Judaism from Jewish documentation of the time. Did Judaism teach a self-earned righteousness? The teaching of Deuteronomy is rather that God's election of Israel was in no way on the basis of Israel's merit

---

[24] See my *Romans* (WBC 38; Dallas: Word, 1988) and *Galatians* (BNTC; Lonon: Black, 1993) ad loc.

and that obedience to the law was to be the means of living within the covenant people, not a means to entering it. Likewise the provision of sin-offering and Day of Atonement presumes the recognition of frequent sin, to be dealt with by divine provision of atonement, not by human effort. When Paul claims to be 'blameless' in Phil. 3.6, therefore, the inference to be drawn is not that he was sinless or had maintained perfect obedience, but that he lived within the terms laid down by the law of the covenant, availing himself of the provision of cleansing and atonement when necessary. Nor should we forget that Paul's understanding of God's righteousness, as in Rom. 1.17, seems to be drawn directly from the usage of the OT, the Psalms and Second Isaiah in particular.[25]

There is a similar problem over 'my/their own righteousness' (Phil. 3.9; Rom. 10.3) and 'boasting' (Rom. 2.17, 23; 3.27). In none of the cases cited is it the most natural sense to read '(boasting in) self-achieved righteousness'. In Rom. 10.3 the Greek is more naturally rendered, 'their righteousness' as belonging to them and not to others, that is, Israel's righteousness and as such not accessible to the Gentiles. And in Phil. 3 the reference comes similarly as the climax to a list of what Paul as a Jew could place his confidence in, primarily, it would appear, the priviliges of status as a member of the people of Israel. The same is true of the 'boasting'. The list in Rom. 2.17–20 is self-evidently a list of Israel's privileges. And the argument of 3.27–30 is clearly against a boast which is tantamount to making God the God of Jews only.

It is inappropriate to discuss these particular issues further here, although we may have occasion to allude further to them (and to the issue of 'works of the law') later. My concern at this point is simply to indicate that there are grounds for misgiving over the usual way of evaluating Paul's own assertions about how his understanding of righteousness was transformed by his encounter with Christ. That some transformation in his understanding of righteousness did take place in or as a result of his Damascus road experience I readily affirm on my own part. But whether he conceived it as a turning from his own righteousness, understood as earned by him, to God's righteousness, for the first time conceived as an act of divine grace, is highly questionable. Here too we have cause to wonder whether the traditional interpretations of Paul's conversion have not gone off at something of a tangent and missed aspects of the event more central to Paul himself.

In short, there seems to be at least some grounds for questioning the usual range of interpretations of Paul's conversion. What is most striking of all is that the key testimony of Paul himself has not been examined in sufficient detail. I refer to Gal. 1.13–16, and to that task we now turn.

---

[25] S.K. Williams, 'The "Righteousness of God" in Romans', *JBL* 99 (1980) 241–90; Dunn, *Romans* ad loc.

2. Galatians 1.13–16

It is a surprising fact that the most direct testimony of Paul himself to his conversion has not been paid more attention in discussion of the 'from' and 'to' of his Damascus road experience. For Gal. 1.13–14 gives a clearer insight than any other text to Paul's own attitude and reasoning as 'persecutor of the church'; we note incidentally that 'the persecutor' is Paul's own description in both Gal. 1.13 and Phil. 3.6 and that it was as 'the persecutor' that he was commonly known among the churches of Judea, according to Gal. 1.22–23.[26] Moreover, there is no more explicit statement in Paul's letters as to the divine purpose of the Damascus road encounter than Gal. 1.15–16. There are, in fact, three points which need to be highlighted from these verses if we are to understand the 'from' and 'to' of Paul's conversion in the terms which he himself used. Two of them focus on the 'from', the third on the 'to'.

2.1 From 'Judaism'

Today we are so accustomed to use 'Judaism' as the generic or blanket title for the religion of Jews in the first century CE that we forget just how *un*common it was in that period. We speak of Second Temple Judaism, of 'early Judaism' (just as we used to speak of 'late Judaism'), of 'common Judaism' or diverse 'Judaisms', often forgetting that as an identifying label it seems to have been little used – at least so far as our sources tell us.[27] This raises the important question: To what extent does our twentieth century perception of first century 'Judaism' as expressed in that title reflect the self-understanding of Jews as a whole or of any one or more factions within the Jewish people in particular? There is, evidently, a danger that our attempts to achieve an accurate sociological description of the religion of the land of Israel in the first century CE may fulfil modern sociological criteria at the expense of our ability to enter into the mindset of the Jews thus denoted. I have reflected more fully on this elsewhere.[28] Here it is the consequences for our understanding of what Paul had in mind when he twice spoke of his previous life 'in Judaism' (ἐν τῷ Ἰουδαϊσμῷ) on which we must focus attention.

So far as we can tell, the title 'Judaism' only came into currency in literary sources in 2 Maccabees, which is commonly dated towards the end of the second

---

[26] Gal. 1.23 is 'one of the oldest theological statements of Christianity' – E. Bammel, 'Galater 1.23', *ZNW* 59 (1968) 108–12.

[27] I know of only eight examples of the terms use within and prior to our period (2 Macc. 2.21; 8.1; 14.38 [*bis*]; 4 Macc. 4.26; Gal. 1.13–14; *CIJ* 537).

[28] See my 'Judaism in the Land of Israel in the First Century', in *Judaism in Late Antiquity. Part 2 Historical Syntheses*, ed. J. Neusner (Leien: Brill, 1995) 229–61.

century BCE,[29] that is, about 140 years before Paul's conversion. What is of significance in the four occurrences attested there is that the immediate context gives a clear idea of why the term was coined and what it signified. In each case (2.21; 8.1[*bis*]; 14.38; also 4 Macc. 4.26) 'Judaism' denotes the national religion of the people of Judea, under attack from their Syrian overlords, and become a rallying point for resistence to the Syrians and for maintenance of national identity as the covenant people of the Lord. So we read of the martyr 'accused of Judaism', and of those 'who strove eagerly on behalf of Judaism', 'who continued (faithfully) in Judaism', and who 'had risked body and soul for Judaism'. Alternatively expressed, 'Judaism' as an identifying label clearly received its distinctive emphasis as the antithesis to 'Hellenism' (2 Macc. 4.13).

In other words, the term 'Judaism' seems to have been coined as a means of giving focus to the determination of the Maccabean patriots to defend the distinctive national identity given them by their ancestral religion. It was not simply a neutral description of 'the religion of the Jews'. From its earliest usage it carried overtones of a religious identity shaped and hardened in the fires of persecution, of a religion which identified itself by its determination to maintain its distinctiveness and to remain free from the corruption of other religions and peoples. Wholly understandable is the fact that this confrontation between Judaism and Hellenism came to particular focus in key test cases, particular laws and traditions which the Syrians were determined to suppress and which therefore became the rallying points for the loyalists and the make-or-break points at which the confrontation would be won or lost. In 2 Macc. 6 these are indicated in sequence as the temple and therefore the traditional feasts, circumcision, and eating swine's flesh (cf. particularly 1 Macc. 1.60–63).

It is also relevant to note in the literature which has come down to us from the period following the Maccabean revolt that such determination to remain loyal to covenant God and covenant heritage continued to be a feature of the various Jewish groupings which emerged from that period. The factionalism we overhear between Essene and Pharisee and Sadducee and in other literature of whose authorship we cannot be certain, over issues especially of purity halakhah and calendar (particularly *1 Enoch*1–5, various DSS, *Jubilees*, *Psalms of Solomon* and the *Testament of Moses*) all indicate a widespread passion to maintain faithfulness to the Torah as a primary and dominating concern characteristic of many (most?) Jewish groups of the period. The corollary was a disdain, hostility or even hatred for fellow Jews who followed a different halakhah or different calendar. Among these, Pharisees evidently stood out by their desire to separate themselves, that is, presumably, from their less faithful contemporaries ('Pharisee' is generally understood to have begun as a nickname meaning 'separa-

---

[29] See e.g. T. Fischer in *ABD* 4.441.

tist'),[30] and by their desire to keep the law with scrupulous accuracy and exactness (ἀκρίβεια).[31]

Of course we do not find the term 'Judaism' being used in the self descriptions of such groups – presumably because these confrontations were all internal to the Judaism of the period. The term's function was evidently determined by its antithesis with 'Hellenism', to denote Jewish identity over against other nations and peoples. It is used in this way in the one other occurrence which we can date to this period with some confidence – a funerary description from Italy which praises a woman 'who lived a gracious life in(side) Judaism' (the same phrase as in 2 Macc. 8.1 and Gal. 1.13–14) – Judaism being understood as 'a sort of fenced-off area in which Jewish lives are led'.[32] This accords well with the self-understanding we find particularly in the diaspora document, the *Letter of Aristeas* – 'In his wisdom the legislator (Moses) ... surrounded us with palisades and iron walls to prevent our mixing with any of the other peoples in any matter ... he hedged us in on all sides with strict observances connected with meat and drink ... after the maner of the Law' (139–142). We may say, in other words, that 'Judaism' defined itself by its separation from the wider world and understood the function of the Torah in part at least as reinforcing and protecting that separateness.

The consistency of this picture with the use of 'Judaism' in Gal. 1.13–14 is striking. For Paul's description of his way of life 'in Judaism' is filled out in 1.14 in terms which clearly echo the almost competitive covenant faithfulness which was such a mark of the factionalism of the time. His claim is striking: 'I progressed in Judaism beyond many of my contemporaries among the people ...'. Even while speaking out of the consciousness of conducting his life '(with)in (the protection of) Judaism', he also expresses satisfaction that he had outstripped his less faithful contemporaries. Quite exceptionally, he voices in the same breath the consciousness of separation both *of* Judaism *from the other nations* and *in* Judaism *from other Jews*. And when he continues, '... being exceedingly zealous for my ancestral traditions', it is hard to avoid the conclusion that in these words we hear the authentic voice of the late Second Temple Pharisee, as Paul recalls his pre-conversion understanding of what it meant to live 'in Judaism'.

In short, Gal. 1.13–14 certainly points us to the conclusion that Paul was converted 'from Judaism'. But the 'Judaism' of which he speaks is not the Judaism of modern historical and sociological analysis. It is the 'inside' view of first century Judaism, or rather, of a particular understanding and practice of the ancestral religion of the Jews in the first half of the first century CE. Indeed, it would perhaps be more accurate to speak of Pharisaic Judaism as that from which Paul

---

[30] Schürer 2.395–400.

[31] Josephus, *War* 1.108–9; 2.162; *Life* 191; *Ant.* 20.200–1; Acts 22.3; 26.5.

[32] Y. Amir, 'The Term *Ioudaismos*: A Study in Jewish-Hellenistic Self-Identification', *Immanuel* 14 (1982) 35–6, 39–40.

turned in his conversion. How significant this conclusion is will only become fully apparent in the light of the other two points which emerge from Gal. 1.13–16.

2.2 From 'zeal'

It is an important and too little noted fact that Paul uses the word 'zeal' in both of the passages where he most clearly has in view the impact of his conversion: Gal. 1.14 – 'I progressed in Judaism beyond many of my contemporaries among my people, being exceedingly zealous (ζηλωτής) for my ancestral traditions'; Phil. 3.6 – 'as to the law a Pharisee, as to zeal (ζῆλος) a persecutor of the church'. Now 'zeal' is one of those words which can be used either with a good sense or in a negative sense. And Paul uses it in both – positive, denoting ardour (2 Cor. 7.7; 9.2; 11.2), and negative, as an item in a list of vices, denoting 'jealousy, envy' (Rom. 13.13; 1 Cor. 3.3; 2 Cor. 12.20; Gal. 5.20). But in both our present cases the context points in a particular direction – 'zeal' as a feature of being 'in Judaism', of the competitive factionalism which marked Second Temple Judaism since the Maccabees (Gal. 1.14), of the confidence in Jewish identity which Paul expressed in Phil. 3.4–6.

In this sense we may speak of Jewish zeal as the echo of or response to divine zeal. For deeply rooted in Israel's consciousness of election was the recognition that their God was himself a 'zealot' (ζηλωτής). That Yahweh is 'a jealous God' is firmly stated in Israel's foundation documents – Exod. 20.5; 34.14; Deut. 4.24; 5.9; 6.15 – typically, 'you shall not worship other gods, for I the Lord your God am a jealous God'. In each case the point being made is that Israel should therefore abstain from idolatry or following other gods. God's 'zeal' was expressed in his choice of Israel to be his own and and the conclusion drawn was that Israel should maintain the exclusiveness of its devotion to Yahweh and the distinctiveness of its religion in the face of other nations and religions round about. Israel's 'zeal' for Yahweh and his Torah was a reflection of Yahweh's zeal for Israel.

We also know what this meant in practice. This 'zeal' of Israel was exemplified in Israel's folk memory by a sequence of what we might describe as 'heroes of zeal'. (1) Simeon and Levi who avenged the rape of their sister Dinah by Shechem, son of Hamor, and defended the integrity of the family of the sons of Israel by slaughtering the Shechemites despite their having been circumcised (Gen. 34). The episode is recalled in Judith 9.2–4 – Simeon and Levi 'who burned with zeal for you (Yahweh) and abhorred the pollution of their blood'. Also in *Jubilees* 30, where the lesson drawn is that Israel is holy to the Lord and that it would be a reproach and defilement for any daughter of Israel to be given to a Gentile (30.8–14). In contrast, Levi is remembered for his zeal to do righteousness and judgment and vengeance against all who rose up against Israel (30.18), and their deed is counted as righteousness for Levi and his brother (30.17).

(2) The greatest hero of zeal was Phinehas (Num. 25.6–13), who on seeing an Israelite bring a Midianite woman into his tent, took his spear and pierced them both through, and is remembered in conseqence as being 'zealous for his God' and for thus making atonement for Israel (25.13; Sir. 45.23–24; 1 Macc. 2.54; *4 Macc.* 18.12).

(3) Elijah too is recalled for his zeal (Sir. 48.2–3; 1 Macc. 2.58), presumably not simply for his victory on Mount Carmel when he decisively stopped the drift to syncretistic practices encouraged by Ahab and Jezebel (1 Kings 18), but also for the climax of his victory in the slaughter of the four hundred and fifty prophets of Baal in Wadi Kishon (18.40).

(4) Not least of significance is the fact that the Maccabean revolt is recalled as an expression of that zeal and based on an appeal to such zeal (1 Macc. 2; cf. 2 Macc. 4.2). It began with Mattathias killing both the Syrian officer who tried to force his village to sacrifice swine and/or to idols and the Jew who came forward to do so (2.23–25). 'Thus he burned with zeal for the law, just as Phinehas did against Zimri son of Salut. Then Mattathias cried out in the town with a loud voice, saying, "Let everyone who is zealous for the law and supports the covenant come out with me!"' (2.26–27; Josephus, *Ant.* 12.271). And so began the Maccabean revolt.

There are three striking features of 'zeal' thus understood. First, in each case the zeal was an unconditional commitment to maintain Israel's distinctiveness, to prevent the purity of its covenant set-apartness to God from being adulterated or defiled, to defend its religious and national boundaries. Second, a readiness to do this by force; in each case it is the thoroughgoing commitment expressed precisely in the slaughtering of those who threatened Israel's distinctive covenant status which merited the description 'zeal' or 'zealot'. And third, the fact that this zeal was directed not only against Gentiles who threatened Israel's boundaries, but against fellow Jews too.

It need hardly be said that this must be what Paul had in mind when he speaks of himself as a 'zealot' and of his 'zeal' manifested in persecution of the church (Gal. 1.13–14; Phil. 3.6). First, his zeal for the ancestral traditions was the other side of the coin of his zeal as a persecutor. He would no doubt have understood his zeal as a reflection of God's zeal, a necessary reflection if Israel was to maintain its set-apartness to God. Second, it was certainly expressed in a physically violent way: even though we cannot deduce that the Hellenist Christians whom he persecuted were put to death, it must be significant that he can speak of persecuting the church in excessive measure and of trying to destroy it (Gal. 1.13); the verb used here, πορθεῖν, elsewhere always conveys the idea of material assault, destroying and ravaging cities and territories.[33] And third, as we have al-

---

[33] A sense which P.H. Menoud, 'The Meaning of the Verb *porthein* (Gal. 1.13; Acts 9.12)',

ready noted, his persecution seems to have been directed principally (solely?) against fellow Hellenist Jews. In other words, Paul the persecutor undoubtedly saw himself as a 'zealot' in the tradition of Phinehas and the Maccabees.

From this we gain a surprisingly clear picture of Paul's motivation as a persecutor, but one too little noted in contemporary discussion of Paul's conversion. His motivation was that of earlier heroes of zeal. It was directed against the Hellenist Christians because they were seen to threaten Israel's distinctiveness and boundaries. The deduction is unavoidable that this threat was constituted by the Hellenists taking the gospel of Messiah Jesus to the Gentiles. By opening the door of this particular expression of Jewish religion and tradition to the Gentiles they were in danger of compromising Israel's integrity and purity. By failing to require of such Gentile converts circumcision and the practice of the covenant distinctives on which the Maccabeans had founded 'Judaism', the Hellenists were removing the boundary markers and tearing down the pallisades and iron walls put up by Moses to hedge Israel in on all sides (*Aristeas* 139–42).

It was from *this* zeal, and from 'Judaism' as it called forth this zeal, that Paul converted on the Damascus road.

2.3 To the Gentiles

The other striking feature about Gal. 1.13–16 is that it tells us Paul's understanding of what he had been converted to: 'When it pleased the one who set me apart from my mother's womb, and called me through his grace, to reveal his Son in me, in order that (ἵνα) I might preach him among the Gentiles ...'. The ἵνα clause is most naturally to be taken as a purpose clause: the divine action on the Damascus road was the revealing of God's Son in him (or to him); its purpose was that Paul should preach this Jesus among the Gentiles.

This is one of the most striking points of agrement between Gal. 1.13–16 and the three Acts accounts of Paul's conversion (Acts 9, 22, 16). In the first, Paul, confronted by the christophany, is told to go into Damascus where he will be told what to do (9.6). At the same time Ananias is told to go and minister to Paul because 'he is a chosen instrument of mine to carry my name before the Gentiles ...' (9.15). In Acts 22 Ananias simply tells him that he will be 'a witness (for Christ) to all men' (22.15), and the explicit commission to the Gentiles comes later in Jerusalem, as the climax to the speech (22.21). But in Acts 26 the commission comes directly from the exalted Christ on the Damascus road: 'I have appeared to you for this purpose ... I send you (to the Gentiles) to open their eyes, that they may turn from darkness to light and from the power of Satan to God ...' (26.16–18).

Jesus Christ and the Faith (Pittsburgh: Pickwick, 1978) 47–60 acknowledges but attempts to weaken. See also M. Hengel, *The Pre-Christian Paul* (London: SCM, 1991) 71–2.

Evidently both Luke and Paul understood a commissioning of Paul as apostle (1 Cor. 9.1; 15.8) to the Gentiles to be at the heart of Paul's conversion experience. If we take this testimony seriously we cannot conclude that Paul only reached this conclusion at a later stage. This has certainly been argued: that Paul first turned to the Gentiles after and as a result of his failure to win his fellow Jews to his redirected faith.[34] But the testimony here is plain enough. And we cannot simply discount it as a reading back of a later conclusion, as autobiographical reconstruction.[35] For it fits too well with what we have now gleaned from the rest of Gal. 1.13–16: the conviction that the good news of Jesus Messiah was for the Gentiles is the exact complement to the earlier conviction that Hellenists must be prevented from doing that very thing. If we have understood the rationale of Paul the persecutor aright – and the deductions drawn above make perfect sense both of Paul's language and of its setting in Jewish history – then it also makes perfect sense that Paul found himself persuaded by the very opening to the Gentiles which he had attempted so zealously to suppress. Paul was converted to what he had persecuted. The psychology of the conversion experience is readily recognizable and cannot be easily discounted.

It is of course this self-testimony of Paul himself, regarding what he was converted to, which has raised the question of whether we should speak of a 'conversion' at all. Did Paul so regard it? Did he not rather think of his experience on the Damascus road as a commissioning?[36] The point is strengthened from the clear echoes in Gal. 1.15–16 of the prophetic callings of Jeremiah and the Isaianic Servant.

Jer. 1.5 – Before I formed you in the womb I knew you,
and before you were born I consecrated you;
I appointed you a prophet to the nations.

Isa. 49.1–6 – The Lord called me from the womb,
from the body of my mother he named my name
. . . .
I will give you as a light to the nations,
that my salvation may reach to the end of the earth.

Very striking is not only the clear implication that Paul understood his encounter on the Damascus road as a prophetic call, like that of Jeremiah and the Servant, but like theirs also, as a commissioning 'to the nations'.[37]

---

[34] So particularly F. Watson, *Paul, Judaism and the Gentiles* (SNTSMS 56; Cambridge: CUP, 1986).

[35] Cf. N. Taylor, *Paul, Antioch and Jerusalem* (JSNTS 66; Sheffield: Academic, 1992) ch. 1.

[36] Here again Stendahl has been influential; see particularly his *Paul* 7–23.

[37] K.O. Sandes, *Paul – One of the Prophets?* (WUNT 2.43; Tübingen: Mohr, 1991) rightly recognizes that Paul describes his christophany in the form of a prophetic call (56–9), but fails to bring out the 'to the nations' dimension integral to the call.

We need not engage in further dispute on the point; indeed the dispute (conversion or commissioning) is somewhat artificial. There clearly was a conversion, a turning from and a turning to; and there evidently was that kind of
wrenching, transforming experience which continues to makes Paul's experience a model of conversion experience.[38] But if we take Paul's own testimony
(and that of Acts) seriously we have also to speak of a calling or commissioning.
The point is surely that in Paul's mind they both amounted to the same thing – a
conversion from persecutor to apostle, a conversion from one rather introverted
'sect' within first century Judaism to another more missionary minded 'sect', a
conversion, in other words, at whose heart was the newly implanted conviction
that the time of Abraham's blessing to the nations, of the Servant's light to the
nations, had now come and that he was to be a key figure in bringing about that
blessing and in spreading that light.

Conclusions and corollaries

Rather ambitiously I entitled this paper, 'Paul's Conversion – a light to twentieth
century disputes'. I hope it is now clear how it can serve in that capacity. For if Paul
understood his conversion more or less from the first as conversion *from* a Judaism anxious to preserve its distinctiveness from Gentile corruption, as conversion *from* a zealous determination to defend Israel's Torah defined boundaries,
and as conversion *to* fulfil Israel's eschatological mission to the nations, then that
must tell us something about Paul's subsequently expressed teaching on the law
and on justification by faith as opposed to justification by works of law.

In the light of our findings above, it makes perfect sense to conclude: that the
law became a primary concern for Paul precisely in its boundary defining role
(separating Jew from Gentile); that justification through faith emerged in Paul's
theology as Paul's attempt to explain why and how Gentiles are accepted by
God and should be accepted by their Jewish fellow believers; and that the works
of the law most contentious for Jewish believers were precisely those practices
which had most clearly defined Judaism and most sharply distinguished Jew
from Gentile since the time of the Maccabees (circumcision, food laws and feast
days/sabbath).[39]

---

[38] See now A.F. Segal, *Paul the Convert* (New Haven: Yale University, 1990), particularly ch.
4.

[39] I allude to my several contributions on this theme, in the course of which my views have
become clearer (thanks to critical feed-back): in particular that 'works of the law' do not denote
only circumcision, food laws and sabbath ('works of the law' include all that the law requires);
but that the central issue for Paul posed by 'works of the law' came to focal expression in these
particular laws. See now particularly 'Yet Once More – "The Works of the Law": A Response',
JSNT 46 (1992) 99–117 [=ch. 8 above]; and '4QMMT and Galatians, *NTS* 43 (1997) 147–53
[=ch. 14 above].

It should occasion no surprise, therefore, that this is precisely what we find in Paul's first articulation of these themes, in Gal. 2.15–16, where it is obvious that the theme of justification through faith has to do precisely with the acceptability of Gentiles by Jewish believers on these terms (faith), and where the works of the law particularly in mind were clearly those which had been at issue in Jerusalem (2.1–10 – circumcision) and which had split the community in Antioch (2.11–14 – food laws/table fellowship between Jew and Gentile).

Likewise in Rom. 3.27–31, with another of Paul's clearest assertions of justification by faith (3.28), the problem which for Paul was focused in boasting and works of the law (3.27) is clearly that they encouraged the implication that God is God of Jews only (3.29). That is to say, they were an expression of that same mind-set which Paul himself had shared 'in Judaism' and as a persecutor of the church, the law understood in its function of setting and keeping Israel apart from the nations. And similarly in Rom. 9.30–10.4, it is that same understanding of the law, as focused in works of the law (9.32), which went hand in hand with zeal and with righteousness understood as Israel's alone and not that of the Gentiles (10.2–3), which Paul sets in antithesis to faith. So that when he speaks of Christ as the 'end' of the law, almost certainly he was thinking of the law primarily in its Israel-defining, Judaism-defending boundary role.

To argue such points adequately would, of course, require fuller treatment than can be provided here.[40] Nor does their validity consist in any kind of denial of more traditional Protestant views of justification by faith. At this point the contemporary debate has been plagued by misunderstanding and false 'either-or's. The plea, in other words, is not to do one emphasis down in order to bring another emphasis up. It is rather for recognition of an emphasis which can be too easily lost to sight in expositions of Paul. This is an emphasis which Paul himself evidently saw to be at the heart of his own conversion and fundamental to his apostolic self-understanding. Does it not deserve more emphasis today?

---

[40] I may refer simply to my treatment of these passages in my *Galatians* and *Romans* ad loc.

Chapter 16

Paul and Justification by Faith

1. Introduction

How does Paul's teaching on justification by faith relate to his conversion? The question is an important one for this Colloquium because justification by faith has so often been regarded within both Christian tradition and NT scholarship as the quintessence of Paul's gospel and theology. And precisely because the subject matter is so vital, as touching the raw nerve of personal faith, disagreement in answering the question can easily become fractious and the discussion can run aground on undeclared presumptions or can trigger hidden sensitivities, with disastrous consequences for constructive debate.

The parameters of the disagreement may be sketched out as follows. On the one hand, for a variety of reasons it is logical to assume that Paul's theology of justification was a direct result of his encounter with the living Christ on the Damascus road. At the heart of the logic is the conviction that what Paul *experienced* on the Damascus road was justification by faith, and that his theology of justification was in large part simply the working out of his experience. The key supporting text is Phil. 3.7–9, where the discovery of Christ is linked directly to a new appreciation of what the righteousness of God through faith really means. In the light of that it is natural to link in further key texts like Rom. 4.4–5 and 10.4 as further expressions of what Paul found in his encounter with the risen Christ.[1]

To be noted is the fact that this basic exposition does not require or depend on a more detailed analysis of Paul's internal experience and thought process. It is not necessary, for example, to argue that Paul already had a severe guilt problem before his conversion: the key passages in which Paul refers to the build-up to his conversion (Gal. 1.13–14; Phil. 3.5–6) give no hint of a tortured conscience (over Stephen, or whatever); and Paul never mentions 'repentance' in the context of talk of conversion or justification. Nor does it depend on a detailed account of how Paul's attitude to the law changed in the process (the law con-

---

[1] E.g. P. Stuhlmacher, "'The End of the Law'. On the Origin and Beginnings of Pauline Theology', *Reconciliation, Law and Righteousness: Essays in Biblical Theology* (Philadelphia: Fortress, 1986) 134–54 (particularly 139–41); S. Kim, *The Origin of Paul's Gospel* (Tübingen: J.C.B.Mohr, 1981) 269–311; S. Westerholm, *Israel's Law and the Church's Faith. Paul and his Recent Interpreters* (Grand Rapids: Eerdmans, 1988) *passim*.

demned Christ, God raised Christ, therefore the law is an ass, therefore justification is not by the law). The meaning of Gal. 2.19 ('I through the law died to the law') has of course to be unpacked, but that particular unpacking is not attested by any of Paul's writing on the subject. The traditional exposition of the correlation between Paul's conversion and his teaching on justification does not even depend on building in a text like 1 Tim. 1.15–16 (Paul's conversion = his receiving mercy as 'the foremost of sinners'), whose lack of correlation again with Gal. 1.13–14 and Phil. 3.5–6 leaves its witness problematic as a testimony to how Paul's own self-understanding was transformed by the Damascus road event.

On the other hand, a minority of voices has repeatedly drawn attention to two features of what Paul says on the two subjects (his conversion and justification). The one is that Paul's doctrine of justification through faith seems to arise directly out of and/or within the context of his Gentile mission. It emerges as his answer to the question: how may Gentiles be accounted acceptable to the God of Israel and of Jesus?[2] This is the clear implication of the primary expositions of justification by faith which Paul provides in Galatians 2–3 and Romans 3–4. The other is that the primary significance of his encounter with the risen Christ seems to have been, for Paul, that it commissioned him as missionary/apostle to the Gentiles (Gal. 1.15–16; 1 Cor. 9.1; 15.8–10; cf. Acts 9.15; 22.10; 26.16–18). The echoes of Isa. 42.7, 49.1, 6 and Jer. 1.5 in some of these passages underscores the point that whereas we think most naturally of the Damascus road encounter as a conversion, Paul thought of it more naturally as a prophetic calling.[3]

On this reading of the data, the sequence of Paul's theological re-think consequential on his Damascus road experience is somewhat different. It was not so much: personal experience of acceptance by God (though a sinner), leading to the conclusion that Gentiles could share directly in this same experience for themselves, through faith (alone). It was rather: conviction that God was commissioning him to fulfil Israel's calling (to be a light to the nations), leading to the conclusion (crystallised for him particularly by the Antioch incident in Gal. 2.11–16) that this was possible of realisation only if justification was through faith (alone).

I have attempted to make my own contribution to this debate elsewhere and will endeavour not to repeat myself unnecessarily here.[4] Suffice it to say at this

---

[2] See particularly W. Wrede, *Paul* (London: Philip Green, 1907) 122–8; K. Stendahl, *Paul Among Jews and Gentiles* (Philadelphia: Fortress/London: SCM, 1977) 1–7.

[3] Cf. e.g. J. Knox, *Chapters in a Life of Paul* (1950; Mercer University, 1987/London: SCM, [2]1989) 97–8; Stendahl 7–12; H. Räisänen, 'Paul's Conversion and the Development of his View of the Law', *NTS* 33 (1987) 404–19 (particularly 406–8).

[4] 'Paul's Conversion: A Light to Twentieth Century Disputes', in *Evangelium – Schriftauslegung – Kirche;* P. Stuhlmacher FS; ed. O. Hofius et al. (Göttingen: Vandenhoeck, 1996) 77–93 [= ch. 15 above]; earlier '"A Light to the Gentiles", or "The End of the Law"? The Significance of the Damascus Road Christophany for Paul', *Jesus, Paul and the Law: Studies in Mark and*

point, my emphasis has been on the latter of the two approaches sketched above – principally because it has seemed to me that there were clear expressions of Paul's own summation of the significance of the Damascus road encounter (particularly Gal. 1.13–16) which had been too much ignored by the more traditional view. At the same time I see no reason to dispute – indeed, I wish strongly to affirm on my own account – what the more traditional emphasis highlights and underscores as a theological assertion of fundamental significance, expressed particularly in Rom. 4.4–5, that justification by faith is at the core of Paul's gospel and theology. What is rather at stake in the continuing debate on this subject is to secure a properly rounded and integrated grasp of Paul's teaching, and, in the present case, to clarify so far as possible how much and in what way Paul's conversion contributed to this fundamental element of his faith.

In what follows, therefore, I will attempt to sketch out the heart of Paul's theology of justification, why it was as contentious as it evidently was, and how the particular antithesis, 'justification from faith and not from works', ties back into his conversion.

2. Justification – a fundamental scriptural (Jewish) doctrine

As is well known, discussion of this subject suffers from some terminological problems. I refer not only to the fact that English uses two different words, 'justify', 'righteousness', to translate what are cognate terms in Greek (*dikaioō, dikaiosunē*), thus causing some unavoidable confusion for those who think in English.[5] I refer also to the fact that the underlying Hebrew thought in both cases is different from the Greek. In the typical Greek world view, 'righteousness' is an idea or ideal against which the individual and individual action can be measured. Contemporary English usage reflects this ancient mind set when it continues to use such phrases as, 'Justice must be satisfied'. In contrast, in Hebrew thought 'righteousness' is a more relational concept – 'righteousness' as the meeting of obligations laid upon the individual by the relationship of which he/she is part.[6] A classic example is 1 Sam. 24.17: king Saul was unrighteous, in that he had failed in his duty as king to his subject; David was more righteous because he had refused to lift his hand in violence against the Lord's anointed. A key factor in gaining a secure hold on Paul's teaching on justification, therefore, and one whose ramifications are too little appreciated in much discussion of Paul's teach-

---

Galatians (London: SPCK/Louisville: Westminster, 1990) 89–107; also *The Partings of the Ways between Christianity and Judaism* (London: SCM/Philadelphia: TPI, 1991) 117–39.

[5] The issue is nicely pointed by E.P. Sanders, *Paul* (Oxford University, 1991) 44–7.

[6] See e.g. G. von Rad, *Old Testament Theology* Vol. 1 (Edinburgh: Oliver & Boyd, 1962) 370–6; E.R. Achtemeier, 'Righteousness', *IDB* 4.80–5; K. Kertelge, *'Rechtfertigung' bei Paulus* (Münster: Aschendorff, 1967, [2]1971) 15–24.

ing, is recognition that the thought world which comes to expression in this English term ('justification') is through and through Hebraic/biblical/Jewish in character.

The relevance of this observation begins to become clear when we recall Paul's thematic statement about justification, in Rom. 1.16–17, as 'the righteousness of God ... from faith to faith'. For the righteousness of God, in line with the understanding of 'righteousness' above, denotes God's fulfilment of the obligations he took upon himself in creating humankind and particularly in the calling of Abraham and the choosing of Israel to be his people. Fundamental to this conception of God's righteousness, therefore, is the recognition of the prior initiative of God, both in creation and in election.[7] As Deuteronomy repeatedly points out: it was nothing that Israel was or had done which caused God to choose them as his people, to enter into covenant with them, only his love for them and loyalty to the oath he had promised to the fathers (4.32–40; 6.10–12, 20–23; 7.6–8; etc). It should be equally evident why God's righteousness is repeatedly understood, particularly in the Psalms and second Isaiah, as God's faithfulness to his people, the fulfilment of his covenant obligation as Israel's God in delivering and vindicating Israel, despite Israel's own failure (e.g. Pss. 51.14; 65.5; 71.15; Isa. 46.13; 51.5–8; 62.1–2).

The point here is threefold. First, Paul's teaching on justification is drawn immediately from this Old Testament understanding of God's righteousness; that the language of Romans stems directly from such OT usage is well appreciated and is not in dispute.[8] Second, and fundamental to Jewish self-understanding and covenant theology is this recognition and affirmation that Israel's standing before God was due entirely to the initiative of divine grace; the same point is implicit in a covenant system which provided atonement for sin through repentance and sacrifice. Third, it should be equally clear that this is where Paul derived his emphasis on the initiative of divine grace within his teaching on justification; it did not first emerge for Paul as a reaction against his Pharisaic past or 'judaizing' opponents; it   was simply a restatement of the first principles of his own ancestral faith.

All this needs to be restated against a still prevailing assumption that the Judaism of Paul's day was inherently and thoroughly legalistic, teaching that individuals had to earn acceptance by God by their works of merit. Indeed, it has been a deeply disquieting feature of Christian apologetic, first clearly attested in Ignatius, steadily strengthened since then, and reinforced by Reformation polemic, that Christianity has tended to understand itself in antithesis to Ju-

---

[7] For the emphasis on God's righteousness as Creator see C. Müller, *Gottes Gerechtigkeit und Gottes Volk: Eine Untersuchung zu Römer 9–11* (Göttingen: Vandenhoeck, 1964); P. Stuhlmacher, *Gerechtigkeit Gottes bei Paulus* (Göttingen: Vandenhoeck, 1965) 228–36.

[8] See e.g. S.K. Williams, 'The "Righteousness of God" in Romans', *JBL* 99 (1980) 241–90; J.D.G. Dunn, *Romans* (WBC 38; Dallas: Word, 1988) 40–2.

daism, and to portray Judaism as the polar opposite of Christianity, Christianity as gospel set over against Judaism as law. So it needs to be said clearly here: that justification by faith is at heart a Jewish doctrine; that dependence on divine grace remains a consistent emphasis throughout Jewish thought at least up to the time of Paul (we need take the discussion no further here); and that there is no clear teaching in pre-Pauline Jewish documentation that acceptance by God has to be earned.[9]

There is, of course, an emphasis on the need for Israel's obedience – Israel's law-keeping as its response to God's saving initiative (classically Ex. 20.2ff.), covenant life as ordered and directed by reference to the law (Lev. 18.5). But at its heart that is no different from the Christian/Pauline emphasis that faith also expresses itself in obedience, that faith which does not work through love is not faith (Rom. 1.5; Gal. 5.6).[10] Hence the highly Jewish character of Rom. 2.6–16. There are also questions of definition to be clarified (Who is Israel? What is 'Judaism'?), not to mention the relation to this ancestral faith of the various Jewish sectarian groups and documents which emerged during the two hundred years prior to Paul.[11] But the basic point remains, that God's righteousness in first choosing Israel to be his people, and in sustaining Israel in that covenant relationship, is a theologoumenon fundamental to Jewish religion and identity. The proposition that relationship with God is first and foremost a gift and not something earned, an act of grace and not reward for merit, would be axiomatic to any Jew who took the Torah and the Prophets seriously.[12]

3. From faith – a reaffirmation of the universal outreach of God's grace

The more we stress the continuity between Paul's teaching on justification and Paul's Jewish heritage, the more pressing becomes the question: Why then is Paul's teaching formulated in such a polemical manner (as in Gal. 2.16 and Rom.

---

[9] This recognition is at the heart of 'the new perspective on Paul' inaugurated particularly by E. P. Sanders, *Paul and Palestinian Judaism* (London: SCM, 1977); see my 'The New Perspective on Paul', *BJRL* 65 (1983) 95–122, reprinted in *Jesus, Paul and the Law* 183–214 [= ch. 2 above].

[10] This point was first made effectively by M. D. Hooker, 'Paul and "Covenantal Nomism"', in *Paul and Paulinism: Essays in Honour of C. K. Barrett*, ed. M. D. Hooker & S. G. Wilson (London: SPCK, 1982) 47–56.

[11] I have attempted to clarify these issues particularly in 'Judaism in the Land of Israel in the First Century', in *Judaism in Late Antiquity: Part 2: Historical Syntheses;* ed. J. Neusner (Leiden: Brill, 1995) 229–61.

[12] Hence my strong suspicion (*pace* Westerholm) that Rom. 4.4–5 was neither a controversial nor a polemical statement in Paul's debate with other Christian Jews, but a restatement of a first principle which they would all have espoused; see further my 'In Search of Common Ground' in *Paul and the Mosaic Law*, ed. J. D. G. Dunn (WUNT 89; Tübingen: Mohr Siebeck, 1996) 309–34 (here 321, 331–2) [= ch. 12 above, here 297–9, 308–9].

3.20)? If he was not reacting against his inherited Jewish convictions, if he was not reacting (and precisely as a result of his Damascus road experience) against his own past as a Pharisee, what was he reacting against? If he was not opposing Jewish legalism, at least in the sense of being able to claim salvation as a right, as a wage, rather than a gift, what was he opposing?

In a word the primary answer seems to be not so much Jewish legalism as Jewish *restrictiveness* – the tendency in Judaism to restrict the covenant grace of God, covenant righteousness to Israel. This protest or reaction comes to clear expression repeatedly throughout the argument of Romans.

It is evident, first, in the thematic emphais on 'all': the gospel is for 'all who believe' (1.16); the righteousness of God is 'to all who believe' (3.22); Abraham is father of 'all who believe' (4.11); 'Christ is the *telos* of the law as a means to righteousness for all who believe' (10.4), and so on. 'All' is one of the really key words in Romans (where it occurs 71 times). And as these same references make clear in context, the 'all' consistently means, 'all', Jew as well as Gentile, Gentile as well as Jew. In pressing this point so consistently Paul must have intended to break down the presupposition on the part of his fellow Jews that they were in a privileged position before God over against the non-Jewish nations. This is manifestly the chief thrust of Rom. 2, as the immediately provoked question (3.1) demonstrates: 'What then is the advantage of the Jew?'.[13] Paul insisted on 'all, Gentile as well as Jew', because his Jewish interlocutor or opponents assumed 'Jew and not Gentile'.

That Paul's arguments are directed against Jewish restrictiveness is evident, secondly, in the way Paul immediately draws out the (for him) chief corollary to his central statement of the righteousness of God (3.21–26). For in 3.27–31 the polemical antithesis between the *'law of works'* and the *'law of faith'* (3.27)[14] is elaborated by the antithesis between *'God of Jews only'* and *'God also of Gentiles'* (3.29). It is clear from the run of the argument that the first member of each antithesis go together: 'is boasting excluded through the *law of works*? No! ... otherwise God is *God of Jews alone*'; that is, to affirm the 'law of works' is tantamount to affirming that God is 'God of Jews only'. But that cannot be so, for 'God is one' – Israel's own basic creed (Deut. 6.4); therefore he is 'God of Gentiles also'. Here, it should be noted, the basic antithesis in Paul's formulation of justification – by faith and not by works – is elaborated precisely as: 'Gentiles

---

[13] See further my 'What was the issue between Paul and "Those of the Circumcision"?' in *Paulus und das antike Judentum*, ed. M. Hengel &U. Heckel (WUNT 58; Tübingen: J.C.B. Mohr, 1991) 295–317 [=ch. 5 above]; also 'Yet Once More – "The Works of the Law": A Response', *JSNT* 46 (1992) 99–117 (here 106–9) [=ch. 8 above, here 218–21].

[14] For the view that *nomos* here should be translated 'order' or 'principle' see H. Räisänen, 'Paul's Word-Play on *nomos*: A Linguistic Study', *Jesus, Paul and Torah: Collected Essays* (JSNTS 43; Sheffield Academic, 1992) 69–94; otherwise see my '"The Law of Faith", "the Law of the Spirit" and "the Law of Christ"', in *Theology and Ethics in Paul and his Modern Interpreters*, ed. E.H. Lovering & J.L. Sumney (Nashville: Abingdon, 1996) 62–82.

also and not Jews only'. 'Faith alone' asserts the proposition 'Gentiles also', whereas 'works (of law)' asserts its restrictive counterpart, 'Jews only'.

The passage which most closely echoes this central argument in Romans is 9.30–10.13, the most intense clustering of 'righteousness' terminology in the letter apart from 3.21–4.22. Here we need simply note in passing the same antithesis as in 3.27 between the 'law of works' and the 'law of faith', or, more precisely, between 'the law (of righteousness!)' misunderstood 'as if it was from works' and the same law successfully pursued 'from faith' (9.30–32). But more important at this point is the elaboration of this misunderstanding of righteousness in the second part of the paragraph: 'not knowing the righteousness of God and seeking to establish their own (righteousness), they have not subjected themselves to the righteousness of God' (10.3). This has commonly been understood as a classic statement of Jewish legalism: they thought of righteousness as 'their own' in the sense of a righteousness achieved or accomplished by them.[15] But the Greek sense is clear: 'their own' as denoting something which belonged to them or was peculiar to them; that is, righteousness as Israel's covenant prerogative, the privilege of Jews only and not of Gentiles.[16] Hence, once again, the repeated 'all' – 'for all who believe' (10.4) – and the climax of the paragraph reinforcing the point with repeated strokes: 'For the scripture says, "*Everyone* who believes in him shall not be put to shame". For there is no distinction between Jew and Greek, for the same one is Lord of *all*, rich to *all* who call upon him. For "*everyone* whoever calls upon the name of the Lord shall be saved"' (10.11–13). The restatement of 'the righteousness of God' as a protest against Jewish restrictiveness could hardly be clearer.

More or less the same point has to be made in reference to the passage which has been regarded as the chief basis of the view that Paul's doctrine of justification was the immediate outgrowth and expression of his own experience of grace on the Damascus road – Phil. 3.7–9. The language is strikingly similar to Rom. 10.3: Paul expresses his ardent desire to be found in Christ 'not having my own righteousness which is from the law but that which is through faith in Christ,[17] the righteousness of God to faith' (Phil. 3.9). Here, however, the very personal terms in which Paul describes what was an intensely personal experience (his conversion) may have misled us. For in this case he does not speak of 'their own' righteousness, as in Rom. 10.3, where the corporate dimension of Israel is to the fore. Rather he speaks of 'my own righteousness', and thus may

---

[15] Classically expressed by R. Bultmann, *Theology of the New Testament* (London: SCM, 1952) 1.285; C.E.B. Cranfield, *Romans* (ICC; Edinburgh: T.& T. Clark, 2vols. 1975, 1979) 515.

[16] See those cited and further in my *Romans* 587–8.

[17] It is inappropriate here to go into the renewedly contentious phrase *pistis Christou*, whether it denotes 'faith in Christ', or 'Christ's faith'. I remain convinced of the former rendering; see my 'Once More, *Pistis Christou*', in *SBL Seminar Papers 1991* (Atlanta: Scholars, 1991) 730–44.

have encouraged the individualist suggestion of a personal possession attained and defended by personal effort.[18]

This traditional interpretation, however, has tended to ignore the line of personal confession which builds up to this affirmation of ambition – 3.4–6. The passage is a statement of personal confidence indeed, but the confidence is not primarily, if at all of personal achievement. It is rather, once again, the confidence of Paul as a member of Israel, the covenant people – confident in his ethnic identity, confident in his share in the covenant marked by circumcision, confident that he was living within the terms of the covenant as laid out in the law,[19] confident not least that he was defending the distinctiveness of Israel and its separateness from the nations, like zealous Phinehas and zealous Mattathias of old.[20] That was what he had previously treasured so highly (3.7–8) – his standing before God as a devout member of God's chosen people. As such he had rejoiced in a righteousness which others (non-Jews) knew nothing of; it was 'his', as one who had been 'circumcised the eighth day, of the people of Israel ...'. The thought, in other words, is not essentially different from that of Rom. 10.3, and though Paul does not press the 'all' line (Gentile as well as Jew) in Phil. 3, the thought is just as much of the righteousness of God understood as operating through the openness of faith and no longer restricted as being Israel's sole privilege.

If this line of exposition brings us anywhere near to Paul's thinking on this subject, then we can indeed speak of Paul's doctrine of justification as the immediate expression of his own experience of grace on the Damascus road. But not in the usual terms. For evidently what Paul experienced was not so much his acceptance as one who had previously been without acceptance by God, but primarily *the shattering of his assumption that righteousness before God was Israel's peculiar privilege* and his corollary assumption that those who threatened Israel's set-apartness to God, by preaching Messiah Jesus to Gentiles, had to be persecuted. This reversal is not so clearly mirrored in Phil. 3 where the acceptability of Gentiles to God is not to the fore. But it is clear in the before and after of the parallel passage in Gal. 1.13–16: previously a persecutor *to prevent a gospel for Gentiles* from adulterating or infringing Israel's covenant holiness to God (1.13–14); God's Christ revealed to him (on the Damascus road) *in order that*

---

[18] See e.g. G.F. Hawthorne, *Philippians* (WBC 43; Waco: Word, 1983) 141; P.T. O'Brien, *Commentary on Philippians* (NIGTC; Grand Rapids: Eerdmans, 1991) 394–6.

[19] There may be a deliberate echo of Gen. 17.1 in Phil. 3.6 – 'as to righteousness which is in the law being blameless'. That is, the claim was of one who had lived within the terms of the covenant made with Abraham (covenantal nomism), not as one who never sinned, and not as a matter of personal achievement, but as one who lived a life of dedication (Gal. 1.13–14) and who used the means of atonement and forgiveness provided within the covenant to cover his sins.

[20] On the significance of the term 'zeal' see my *Galatians* (BNTC; London: A. & C. Black, 1993) 60–2; also 'Paul's Conversion' (n. 4 above).

Paul might preach him among the Gentiles (1.15–16).[21] And it is evidently the same theological thrust which drives the exposition of Paul's principal statement of his teaching on justification in Romans – the righteousness of God for 'all', for Gentile as well as Jew and not for Jew only.

As a final observation, we may draw in a point made in passing at the beginning of § 2: that God's righteousness denotes God's fulfilment of the obligations he took upon himself in creating humankind as well as in the calling of Abraham and in the choosing of Israel to be his people. Fundamental here is the recognition that God has a righteousness to fulfil as Creator as well as his righteousness as Israel's covenant God. What Paul is doing in both Galatians and Romans is in effect to go behind the more restricted covenant obligation (to Israel) back to the more basic covenant obligation (to the creation and humankind as a whole). He goes behind Moses to Adam (Rom. 5.12–21); he portrays Abraham as the type of the nations, with no prior covenant to call upon and only his trust in the creator God, 'who gives life to the dead and calls things which have no existence into existence' (4.17); it is the new creation which relativizes both circumcision and uncircumcision (Gal. 6.15). Here is another way in which Paul gets behind Israel's restrictiveness: just as the one God of Gentile as well as of Jew forces the corollary that God justifies each alike through faith (Rom. 3.30); so the confession of God as Creator requires the recognition that God's saving righteousness is open to all humankind, Jew first, but Gentile as well.

This we might say in summary, therefore, is what Paul's conversion brought home to him. It did not teach him of God's grace as though as a Jew he was learning of it for the first time. It did, however, bring home to him that his own typically Jewish attitude had obscured that grace and to a serious degree perverted it. But, once again, not by prompting him to think he had a claim upon God by virtue of his own merits. The error which came home to him on the Damascus road was much more that Israel's claim to a special relationship with God was perverting the more basic insight of God's grace, that as a free grace it was open to all and not restricted in effect to Jews alone and their proselytes. In this way and in this sense Paul rediscovered justification by grace on the Damascus road.

4. And not from works – a rebuke of Jewish (Christian) separateness

The other half of Paul's polemical formulation – 'justification from faith and not from works' – is 'not from works'. We have already touched on some of the key passages in Paul where it appears, but for the sake of completeness we need to

---

[21] See again my *Galatians* 62–8; also 'Paul's Conversion' (n. 4 above).

clarify its meaning and function more fully. This requirement is laid upon us principally because the phrase has been so central to the traditional view of the relation between Paul's conversion and justification which we have been questioning above. In the traditional view, as no one will need reminding, 'justification by works' is understood as shorthand for the conviction that acceptance by God is something which has to be achieved or merited by obedience to the law; that Paul was principally protesting against such a belief depends almost exclusively on a reading of Rom. 4.4–5.[22] But what has been said above should already have been putting various question marks against the traditional view.

The full phrase is, of course, 'works of the law'; it refers to what the law requires. To be noted at once is the fact that we are not talking about any law here. This is an observation of some importance. For the tendency in the traditional view is to push in that direction – to see in Paul's conversion a general revulsion against the thought that any human striving or achievement can be the basis of God's acceptance. But Paul is talking about the Torah, the Jewish law. To be more precise, therefore, we should define 'works of the law' as what the law requires *of Israel as God's people*. Works of the law, in fact, are what we referred to at the end of § 2 – Israel's response to God's grace in first choosing Israel to be his people, the obedience God called for in his people, the way Israel should live as the people of God. This is what E.P. Sanders described as 'covenantal nomism',[23] a phrase regularly echoed in these discussions over the past few years, where both words are important –law as functioning within and in relation to the covenant, law as expression of and safeguard for the covenant, law as indicating Israel's part of the agreement graciously initiated by God.

What has been too much ignored, however, is the way the law, thus understood, came to reinforce the sense of *Israel's privilege*, the law as marking out this people in its set-apartness to God. As God's choice of Israel drew the corollary that God's saving grace was restricted to Israel, so the law's role in defining Israel's holiness to God became also its role in *separating Israel from the nations*. In this way the positive sense of 'works of the law', as equivalent to Paul's talk of the obedience of faith, becomes the more negative sense which we find in Paul – works of the law as not only maintaining Israel's covenant status,[24] but as also protecting Israel's privileged status and restricted prerogative.

It was for this reason that horror of idolatry was so deeply rooted in Israel's psyche. This we might say was the supreme 'work of the law' (Ex. 20.3–6; Deut. 5.7–10), and although avoidance of idolatry does not feature in Paul's references to works of the law (Paul's hostility to idolatry was as implacable as any Jew's), it

---

[22] See again Westerholm.

[23] Sanders, *Paul and Palestinian Judaism* 75, 236; also *Judaism: Practice and Belief 63BCE-66CE* (London: SCM/Philadelphia: TPI, 1992) 262–78, 377–8, 415–7.

[24] This is Sanders' emphasis in his understanding of 'covenantal nomism'; see n.23.

was that 'zeal'/'jealousy' for Israel's special relationship with God which had fuelled his earlier persecuting zeal.[25]

There were, however, other works of the law which from early times marked out Israel's set-apartness to God and separation from the nations. The terms on which *circumcision* was first required of Abraham made circumcision a fundamental identity marker of the people of the covenant (Gen. 17.9–14): failure to circumcise a male child meant exclusion from the covenant and the covenant people. No wonder, then, that Paul in his own time could boil the distinction between Jews and Gentiles down to 'circumcision' and 'uncircumcision' (Rom. 2.25–27; 3.30; 4.9–12; Gal. 2.7–8). Likewise, observance of the *Sabbath* became a touchstone of covenant identity and loyalty (Ex. 31.12–17): since the Sabbath was a sign of Israel's set-apartness, failure to keep the Sabbath law was a capital offence. So, for example, for Isa. 56.6, the mark of Gentile participation in the covenant would be their keeping of the sabbath. In some ways more archetypal still were *the laws of clean and unclean* which marked not only a separation of clean and unclean birds and beasts but also a separation of Israel from the peoples (Lev. 20.22–26) – an association (unclean foods, unclean nations) which, according to Acts 10 was only brought into question in emergent Christianity through Peter's encounter with Cornelius (Acts 10.10–16, 28).

As is well known, the Maccabean crisis reinforced both Israel's sense of distinctiveness and the focus on particular laws as make or break issues in defining and defending Israel's set-apartness. It was the distinguishing features of Israel's religion which the Syrians strove to eliminate, in order to submerge the Judeans within the Hellenistic religious syncretism by which they hoped to unify their declining empire. And, as the Maccabean literature emphasises, it was particularly the practice of circumcision and the laws on clean and unclean which became the focal point of conflict:

> According to the decree, they put to death the women who had their children circumcised, and their families and those who circumcised them; and they hung the infants from their mothers' necks. But many in Israel stood firm and were resolved in their hearts not to eat unclean food. They chose to die rather than to be defiled by food or to profane the holy covenant; and they did die (1 Macc. 1.60–63).

This sense that the law's requirements (the works of the law) had as one of their primary goals the preservation of Israel's covenant distinctiveness and the separation of Israel from the nations is highlighted in the Jewish writings from this period, particularly Jubilees and the Epistle of Aristeas.

> Separate yourself from the nations, And eat not with them, ...
> For their works are unclean, And all their ways are a pollution
> and an abomination and an uncleanness ... (Jub. 22.16).

---

[25] See above n. 20.

In his wisdom the legislator (Moses) ... surrounded us with unbroken
palisades and iron walls to prevent our mixing with any of the other
peoples in any matter ... So, to prevent our being perverted by
contact with others or by mixing with bad influences, he hedged
us in on all sides with strict observances connected with meat and
drink and touch and hearing and sight, after the manner of the
Law (Aristeas 139, 142).

For such a mindset the oracle of Balaam became paradigmatic: Israel, 'a people
dwelling alone, and not reckoning itself among the nations' (Num. 23.9); which
Philo glossed by adding the explanation, 'because in virtue of the distinction of
their peculiar customs they do not mix with others to depart from the ways of
their fathers' (*Life of Moses* 1.278).[26]

Up until recently the actual phrase 'works of the law' was not attested prior to
Paul, which naturally made many commentators wonder whether Paul was
fighting against demons of his own creation. But the growing recognition that
the Qumran sect seem to have used such a phrase (4QFlor. 1.1–7; 1QS 5.20–24;
6.18) has been dramatically reinforced in the last few years by the publication of
one of the most important of the Dead Sea Scrolls – 4QMMT. The document,
Miqsat Ma'aseh Ha-Torah is a letter in which someone, presumably a or even
the leader of the sect, explains to others in Israel the sect's own distinctive halakhah, that is, their own interpretation of various laws which they regard as crucial
to their fulfilment of Israel's obligations under the covenant – in this case rulings
relating chiefly to the temple, priesthood, sacrifices and purity. It is these rulings
which the letter sums up towards the end as 'some of the works of the law', *miqsat ma'aseh ha-Torah*, from which the document has been given its name. More
striking still, the letter makes it clear that these 'works of the law' are the reason
why the sect has 'separated' itself from the rest of Israel, and it is these 'works of
the law' whose practice requires them to maintain that separate existence.[27]

It is against this background that we can make best sense of Paul's use of the
same phrase – 'the works of the law'. First, as a phrase, it does, of course, refer to
all or whatever the law requires, covenantal nomism as a whole. But in a context
where the relationship of Israel with other nations is at issue certain laws would
naturally come more into focus than others; we have instanced circumcision and
food laws in particular. In the Qumran sect the sensitive issues were not those
between Jew and Gentile, but those between Jew and Jew, and so focused on internal disagreements on issues like sacrifice and purity. Elsewhere in the Jewish
literature of the time we are aware of violent disagreement about how to calculate the appropriate feast days, whether by the sun or by the moon. The disagree-

---

[26] See also e.g. P. Ackroyd, *Exile and Restoration. A Study of Hebrew Thought of the Sixth
Century BC* (London: SCM, 1968) 235–7; J. Neusner, *Self-Fulfilling Prophecy. Exile and Return
in the History of Judaism* (Atlanta: Scholars, 1990) 36.

[27] See further my '4QMMT and Galatians', *NTS* 43 (1997) 147–53 [=ch. 14 above].

ment was so sharp that each regarded the other as failing to keep the feast, as observing the feasts of Gentiles and not those of Israel's covenant (Jub. 6.32–35; 1 Enoch 82.4–7).[28] Today we might think of issues like abortion, or women priests, or inerrancy. None of the disputants in such internal controversies would regard the points at issue as the whole of their faith or even as the most important element in their faith. But they have become foci of controversy to such an extent that the status of the opponent's profession as a whole can in fact be called into question.

Second, when we turn to Paul's first use of the phrase, in Gal. 2.16, it is precisely with this sort of issue that we are confronted. Paul clearly uses the phrase to denote the attitudes he has opposed in the preceding verses. The 'false brothers' who tried to secure Gentile Titus's circumcision (2.4) were insisting on works of the law; faith in Christ was insufficient. So too Peter and the other Jewish believers who 'separated' (the same verb as in 4QMMT) themselves from the Gentile believers, presumably because the law required Israel to maintain such separation by observance of various food laws (2.12), were insisting on works of the law; faith alone was insufficient. Hence Paul's attempt to open Peter's eyes to see that 'no human being is justified by works of the law, but only through faith in Jesus Christ', and his repeated insistence in 2.16 that it is faith and not works which is the sole basis of acceptance in Christ and should be likewise for mutual acceptance by those in Christ.

What is of relevance to us here is the way in which this particular formulation, the antithesis between faith and works, seems to emerge from the incident at Antioch (2.11–14). Why had it not emerged earlier? Paul had been converted for perhaps as many as seventeen years. He had been active in missionary work among Gentiles for most of that period. And yet the issue of Jew and Gentile fellowship and integration within the new house groups had not been posed. Even at the Jerusalem consultation, when the issue of circumcision, a primary work of the law, had been resolved, the question of those (other) works which had traditionally marked out Israel's separateness from the nations had not been raised. It looks very much, therefore, as though it took the particular confrontation at Antioch to bring out this fundamental declaration of principle from Paul. What had been thus far a grey area, an issue not perceived, a question not posed, suddenly had the spotlight turned upon it, and Paul, in one of the great defining moments in Christian theology, pronounced what was to become his most memorable and telling principle: no one is justified by works of the law, but only through faith in Christ.

That is not to say, however, that this was a wholly new principle for Paul, first discovered, as it were, in and through the Antioch incident. It would be more accurate to say that the principle was implicit in the 'revelation' made to him on

---

[28] See further my *Partings* 104.

the Damascus road. For that revelation, if we are right, came to focus in the realisation that the God of Israel was also the God of the nations, that the good news of God's Son was not to be restricted to Israel but was also for the Gentiles as freely as for the Jews (Gal. 1.12–16), that (as he later put it) the promise of Abraham was also of blessing for the nations (3.6–14). What his years of initial missionary work, climaxing in the Jerusalem consultation and the Antioch incident, brought home to him were the ramifications of this basic revelation. The controversies which his preaching Christ among the nations were provoking forced him to think through and to articulate in sharper and antithetical terms what that revelation amounted to, what was at stake in the gospel itself. And he summed it up in the classic slogan: justification from faith and not from works.

5. Conclusion

In what sense, then, can we say that Paul's doctrine of 'justification by faith' was part of the impact of Paul's conversion? Not in the sense that Paul as an individual long searching for peace with God at last found peace for his troubled conscience. Not in the sense that he turned there from a legalistic Judaism which had lost all sense and sight of divine grace and found it exclusively in Christ and Christianity. But rather in the sense that on the Damascus road he discovered afresh the roots of his ancestral faith, based in the acknowledgment of God as Creator, rooted in the call of and promise to Abraham, and growing out of God's saving act in the deliverance of the no-people Israel from slavery in Egypt. Rather in the sense that the Damascus road confrontation brought home to him how much his people's and his own preoccupation with maintaining their set-apartness from the nations had become a perversion of that original call and promise and choice, a subversion of the fundamental character of that call and promise and choice as an act of free grace. It was that basic insight (revelation) and the call (to the Gentiles) bound up with it which he sought to implement, and in the success and controversy which ensued it was that basic insight and call which he clarified and crystallised in his most memorable slogan: justification from faith and not from works

Chapter 17

Whatever Happened to 'Works of the Law'?

1. Introduction

As any student of Paul will be well aware, 'works of the law' (*erga nomou*) is a key phrase in Paul's theology. In the two letters which provide the fullest exposition of 'the truth of the gospel' it is the phrase which, more than any other, sums up the alternative to justification *by faith* (Rom. 3.20, 27–28; 9.32; Gal 2.16; 3.2, 5, 10). And if justification by faith is the heart of Paul's gospel, as most still maintain, then 'works of the law' is an important aspect of it, in so far as the negative counterpart or antithesis highlights the positive thrust of Paul's theology of justification, as *by faith* and *not* by works of the law.

And yet, that is the last we hear of the phrase. After Galatians and Romans it seems to disappear from view. It does not recur in the later or deutero-Paulines or in the Fathers even when they sum up the gospel in Pauline-like terms (most strikingly, Eph. 2.8–9; 2 Tim. 1.9; Tit. 3.5–7; 1 Clem. 32.4).[1] Why should that be?

The most obvious solution is that in fact the phrase has not disappeared – or, at least, the point made by the phrase remains the same. What Paul says in Rom 3 and Gal. 2–3 is what is also said in Eph. 2, 2 Tim. 1, Tit. 3 and 1 Clem. 32. Thus, in the early letters we find:

Rom. 3.20 – 'No flesh shall be justified from works of the law (*ex ergōn nomou*) before him (God)';

Gal. 2.16 – 'No person is justified from works of the law (*ex ergōn nomou*), but only through faith (*dia pisteōs*); and we have believed in Christ Jesus, in order that we might be justified from faith in Christ (*ek pisteōs Christou*)[2] and not from works of the law (*ex ergōn nomou*), for from works of the law (*ex ergōn nomou*) shall no flesh be justified'.

Is this any different from the later formulations?

Eph. 2.8–9 – 'For by grace you have been saved through faith (*dia pisteōs*); and that not from yourselves, it is a gift of God; not from works (*ex ergōn*), lest anyone should boast'.

---

[1] Lampe's *Patristic Greek Lexicon* cites only two other relevant passages – Macarius Aegyptius (4th century), *homiliae* 37.9 (Migne 34.756C); and Hesychius Sinaiticus (6th-7th centuries), *temperantia* 1.79 (Migne 93.1504D).

[2] I am not persuaded by the present fashion in English-speaking NT scholarship to read this phrase as a reference to Christ's faith(fulness); see my 'Once More, *PISTIS CHRISTOU*', in E.E. Johnson & D.M. Hay, eds., *Pauline Theology IV* (Atlanta: Scholars, 1997) 61–81; *The Theology of Paul the Apostle* (Grand Rapids: Eerdmans/Edinburgh: T. & T. Clark, 1997) §14.8.

2 Tim. 1.9 – 'He saved us and called us with a holy calling, not in accordance with our works (*kata to erga hēmōn*), but in accordance with his own purpose and grace, which was given to us in Christ Jesus ...'.

Tit. 3.5–7 – 'He saved us not from works in righteousness (*ex ergōn tōn en dikaiosunē*) which we have done, but in accordance with his mercy, through the washing of regeneration ... in order that we might be justified by that grace ...'.

1 Clem. 32.4 – 'We who have been called through his will in Christ Jesus are not justified through ourselves, nor through our wisdom or understanding or piety or the works which we have accomplished (*ergōn hōn kateirgasametha*) in holiness of heart, but through faith, through which the Almighty God has justified everyone from (the beginning of) the age'.

The simplest resolution of our small conundrum would seem to be, then, that when Paul speaks of 'works of the law' he meant 'works which we have done', and that the later writings, despite omitting 'of the law', were in effect repeating just what Paul had said in Romans and Galatians. And this, indeed, is the solution which most hold – or to be precise, which most take for granted. And so had I, until I studied these Pauline letters in close detail. It is my growing dissatisfaction with the consensus solution which lies behind the present paper, dedicated in friendship and respect to Petr Pokorny.

2. 'Works of the law' in the early Pauline literature

My dissatisfaction with the consensus solution can be expressed in three points.

2.1   First is the fact that in the Pauline form, 'works of the law', the latter part of the phrase is crucial to it ('of the law'). What was at stake here for Paul was not the broad category of 'works' or deeds generally, but *the law*, that is, what the law was thought to require of all who claimed participation in the grace of God as covenanted to Abraham and Israel.[3] This is undoubtedly the meaning of the phrase, as recent discussion of the appropriate translation for the same phrase (*ma'ase ha-Torah*) in the recently published Qumran scroll, 4QMMT, has reaffirmed.[4] That is to say, the phrase expresses an obligation seen to be the characteristic and distinctive obligation *of Israel* – to observe the law (obey its com-

---

[3] The fact that in some passages Paul writes simply 'works' and not 'works of the law' does not change the position. On each occasion it is clear enough that he is using the term 'works' as a shorthand for 'works of the law'. Thus in Rom. 4.2, 6, the exposition has been occasioned by the immediately preceding discussion of 'works of the law' (3.27–28); that Abraham was a model for the devout, law-keeping Jew was already taken for granted (e.g. CD 3.2 – Abraham 'was accounted a friend of God because he kept the commandments of God'). And in Rom. 9.11 and 11.6 the discussion is entirely in Jewish terms, where again it could be taken for granted that 'works' referred to 'works of the law', as 9.32 confirms.

[4] See my '4QMMT and Galatians', *NTS* 43 (1997) 147–53, here 150 [= ch. 14 above (342)]. Accordingly, F. Garcia Martinez, *The Dead Sea Scrolls Translated: The Qumran Texts in Eng-*

mandments) which had been given through Moses as an integral part of the covenant which God made with Israel at Sinai. Deuteronomy expresses the theology in clear broad principle as well as in detail (see e.g. Deut. 30.9–10; 32.45–47). The phrase used by E.P. Sanders expresses the basic point effectively – 'covenantal nomism'.[5] That is, the law is predicated upon and is part of the covenant, Israel's obligation in response to the divine grace by which Israel had been chosen in the first place.[6]

The point should have been more obvious than has been the case for generations of commentators on Romans and Galatians. For on each occasion when the phrase 'works of the law' is introduced, the context is Israel's obligations – what Jews, including Jewish Christians, believed to be still their continuing obligation, whatever the coming of Messiah Jesus meant. No one can doubt that 'works of the law' in Gal. 2.16–3.10 have in view the Torah, or that the problem in view was the Jewish (Christian) assumption that it was not possible for Jews to exempt themselves from the obligations (works) of the Torah. The shock of 3.10 is precisely that it placed those who thought they were most faithful in fulfilling the Torah ('as many as are from works of the law')[7] under the covenant curse on those who failed to live by the Torah.

Similarly in Romans. Rom. 3.19–20 stands as the climax and summary of the indictment of 'all the world'. But in order that the universal nature of the indictment might be properly taken on board, it had been necessary to ensure that the 'Jew' of 2.17 recognized that the indictment included him too. 3.19 sums up an indictment stretching from 2.1–3.18 addressed primarily to 'those who are under the law' (3.19). Here too 'works of the law' (3.20) have in view the obligations which the Torah of Israel laid upon Israel. It was precisely Israel's position 'under the law', 'within the law', 'having the law' (2.12, 14), as demonstrated by 'the works of the law', which gave them the security which Paul had attempted to undermine in 2.1–3.18. If the point was not already clear enough, Paul puts it

---

lish has changed the translation of his first edition (Leiden: Brill, 1994) from 'the precepts of the Torah' to 'the works of the Torah' (2nd edition, Leiden: Brill, 1996). For further details see below.

[5] E.P. Sanders, *Paul and Palestinian Judaism* (London: SCM, 1977); he continues to regard the phrase as an appropriate summary of Israel's covenant theology (*Judaism: Practice and Belief 63BCE-66CE* [London: SCM, 1992] 262–78, 377–8, 415–7).

[6] 'Covenantal nomism is the view that one's place in God's plan is established on the basis of the covenant and that the covenant requires as the proper response of man his obedience to its commandments, while providing means of atonement for transgression ... Obedience maintains one's position in the covenant, but it does not earn God's grace as such.' (*Paul and Palestinian Judaism* 75, 420).

[7] The description ('As many as are from works of the law') marks out a particular group of people in contrast to 'those who are from faith' (3.9). In context it most obviously has in view not so much Jews in general as those (principally Jews) who insisted that 'works of the law' are indispensable to participation in the promised blessing of Abraham (here particularly the Jewish Christian 'agitators').

beyond dispute when he recalls the theme in Rom. 9.30–32: it is precisely Israel's mistake that it attempted to 'pursue the law of righteousness'[8] as though that was to be done 'from works'.

The first point to be made, therefore, is that 'works of the law' is a very specific and clearly demarcated phrase. It refers to 'works *of the law*'. And that means not any law or all law, but specifically the Jewish law.[9] In other words, it targets a characteristically and distinctively Jewish attitude. It is this phrase which more than any other makes it clear that Paul's doctrine of justification emerged from a specific context and in response to a particular question: how is it that Gentiles can claim acceptance by Israel's God? how can Gentiles lay claim to Israel's rights and privileges without also taking on Israel's responsibilities as laid down in the Torah?[10]

2.2   We can be more specific. What Paul had particularly in view in the phrase 'works of the law' were the requirements of the law which most clearly marked out Israel as God's covenant people in their set-apartness to God, that is, their separateness from those outside the covenant, above all other nations (Gentiles).

This comes out at once in Gal. 2. The first and in many ways most definitive statement of Paul's theology of justification (Gal. 2.16) is formulated as the immediate conclusion or corollary to the two preceding episodes (2.1–10, 11–14). In these episodes Paul had resisted the attempts of fellow Jews (Jewish Christians) to insist that Gentile believers in Messiah Jesus should be either circumcised (2.3–6) or observe the Jewish food laws (2.12–14).[11] It was just these requirements, or at least such requirements as these, which Paul clearly had in view when he denounced Peter for in effect insisting that 'works of the law' were

---

[8]   To be noted is the positive role attributed to the law here, a point often missed because it is so unexpected on the traditional view; cf. e.g. the translation of RSV – 'Israel who pursued the righteousness which is based on law' (similarly NRSV) – an unjustified paraphrase of the Greek.

[9]   It was established long ago that the presence or absence of the definite article makes no difference: the *nomos* in view is the Torah; see e.g. W. Sanday & A.C. Headlam, *Romans* (ICC; Edinburgh: T. & T. Clark, 1895) 58; E. de W. Burton, *Galatians* (ICC; Edinburgh: T. & T. Clark, 1921) 447–60.

[10]   This was the view championed through the 1960s and 1970s by the lone voice of K. Stendahl; see particularly his *Paul Among Jews and Gentiles* (London: SCM, 1977). 'The new perspective on Paul' has brought this view greater acceptance. Here it is the significance of Stendahl's point which we attempt to bring out.

[11]   To be precise, it was the need of the Jews (Jewish Christians) to observe the food laws which was at issue; but the consequence was that Gentile believers could only continue to have table fellowship with Jewish believers if they in turn observed the same laws, that is 'judaized' (2.14).

still necessary if individuals were to be justified (2.15–16).[12] What is significant here is that these two 'works' (circumcision and food laws) were the very laws which became crucial boundary markers in Israel's attempt to maintain its distinctiveness within the wider Hellenistic world in the Maccabean revolt (1 Macc. 1.60–63).[13] And it is precisely this attitude which comes to expression in Gal. 2.12 – the obligation (works) of the law as requiring Jews to 'separate themselves' from others.

The same point comes out also in Romans. The 'works of the law' (Rom. 3.20) is probably Paul's way of encapsulating the attitude critiqued in 2.17–29 – that is, the evidently characteristic Jewish assumption that the law gave Jews a position of advantage (or superiority) over other nations. This inference is borne out by the way in which Paul reverts to the theme of 'works of the law' in 3.27–31. Two points worthy of note are evident from the train of thought. (1) In 3.27–28 it is obvious that 'works of the law' (3.28) are also a way of understanding the law in terms of works (3.27) – the only way to 'establish the law' (3.31) as by literally doing what it required. This, we recall, was how Paul repeated his critique of Israel in 9.30–32. (2) More to the immediate point, the link between 3.27–28 and 3.29–30 clearly implies that to understand the law in terms of works is tantamount to affirming that God is God of Jews only (3.29); whereas, recognition that God is the God also of Gentiles (as the *Shema* indicates) implies that the law can be established through faith (3.30–31). Here again, works of the law, the law understood in terms of works, function(s) to keep Israel distinct and separate from other nations.

Of interest here is the fact that the recently published 4QMMT uses the phrase in a very similar way.[14] It is 'the works of the Torah', which the letter illustrates (Qimron C26–27; Garcia Martinez 112–3), which explains why the Qumran sect 'separated ourselves from the multitude of the people' (Qimron C7; Garcia Martinez 92). Of course, what is in view here is not separation of Israel from the nations. But it is the same verb (*parash*) which is used in Gal 2.12, and it is the same attitude which both phrases ('works of the law', 'separate oneself') express; that is, the law understood to require a particular pattern of behaviour and ritual, so that failure to observe that pattern was tantamount to breach of the law and of the covenant. It is precisely the function of the law as boundary, as

---

[12] So also e.g. R. Heiligenthal, *Werke als Zeichen* (WUNT 2.9; Tübingen: Mohr, 1983): 'Wenn Paulus von den "Gesetzeswerken" redet, denkt er konkret an Speisegebote und Beschneidung' (133).

[13] I have drawn out the significance of these two sets of laws in particular in several places; see e.g. 'What was the Issue between Paul and "Those of the Circumcision"?', in M. Hengel & U. Heckel, *Paulus und das antike Judentum* (WUNT 58; Tübingen: Mohr, 1991) 295–312, here especially 303–5 [=ch.5 above (161–3)]; *Romans* (WBC 38; Dallas: Word, 1988) 800–2; *Galatians* (BNTC; London: A. & C. Black, 1993) 117–24.

[14] Translations used are E. Qimron, & J. Strugnell, *Miqsat Ma'ase Ha-Torah* (DJD 10.5; Oxford: Clarendon, 1994) and F. Garcia Martinez (n. 4 above).

marking out and protecting the covenant people from the defilement of other peoples, which comes to expression in such use of the phrase, 'works of the law' (cf. particularly *Aristeas* 139, 142; *Jubilees* 22.16). The degree to which the attitude criticized in Galatians is the attitude expressed in 4QMMT confirms that the same mind-set is present in both.[15]

2.3   It follows from all this that in Galatians and Romans 'works of the law' do not signify 'good works' in general. Or to be more precise, when Paul criticizes 'works of the law' he was not attacking an attempt to achieve salvation by one's own efforts.[16]

In the first place, such an interpretation fails to appreciate the theology of covenantal nomism.[17] Even a minimal acquaintance with Deuteronomy, itself the classic statement of covenantal nomism, should have warned later commentators away from the view that the theology of the (Sinaitic) covenant was essentially legalistic; that is, that obedience to the Torah was necessary to gain acceptance by God, or that perfect obedience of the Torah's requirements was necessary to gain admittance to the world to come. On the contrary, the starting point for Deuteronomy's theology is the free choice by God of a slave people, without anything to commend them beyond his own promise to the patriarchs (Deut. 6.20–23; 7.6–8; 8.11–18). The point is expressed in almost Pauline terms in Deut. 9.4–5 -

When the Lord your God thrusts them (the nations of Canaan) out before you, do not say to yourself, 'It is because of my righteousness that the Lord has brought me in to occupy this land'; ... It is not because of your righteousness or the uprightness of your heart that you are going in to occupy their land; but because of the wickedness of these nations the Lord your God is dispossessing them before you, in order to fulfill the promise that the Lord made on oath to your ancestors, to Abraham, to Isaac, and to Jacob (NRSV).

The point should have been more fully appreciated than it has been in the last fifty years, since the Dead Sea Scrolls, precisely as part of their covenantal nomism, express in such Pauline terms their reliance on divine grace and righteousness (1QS 11.11–15; 1QM 11.3–4; 1QH 4[= 12].30–32).

Moreover, the idea that the religion of Israel, or Second Temple Judaism, taught the need for perfect obedience is a kind of wish-fulfilment on the part of generations of Christian interpreters. That is, it most probably emerged as a

---

[15] Not least of interest is the fact that observance of these works of the law is clearly regarded as the ground for being reckoned righteous, where the allusion to Gen. 15.6 is clear (Qimron C30–31; Garcia Martinez 116–7); see further my '4QMMT and Galatians' (above n. 4) here 151–2 [=ch. 14 above (343–4)].

[16] Contra the influential classic study of R. Bultmann, *Theology of the New Testament* [London: SCM, 1952] 1.283 – '"works of the law" ... represent works in general, any and all works as works-of-merit'.

[17] This was Sanders' particular concern in coining the phrase – that is, the phrase itself was intended to embody a criticism of the traditional view that Judaism was inherently legalistic.

necessary presupposition of the hypothesis of Jewish legalism, which has been such a dominant feature of Christian interpretation of Paul's theology of justification.[18] In fact, however, the presupposition lacks any sustaining evidence. On the contrary, the provision of a sacrifical system, of sin-offerings in particular, a provision so fundamental to Israel's covenant, in itself attests a system geared to cope with sin and failure – that is, a system which was not predicated on the need for or possibility of perfect obedience. Nor is there any text from the period which can be readily understood as a statement of Jewish belief that 100% obedience was necessary (contrast 1QH 4[= 12].30–32 and Philo, *Virt.* 177), or for the now very dated Christian view that Pharisees (as typical of Jewish legalism) required accumulated merit to outweigh demerit if inheritance of the world to come was to be ensured.[19]

The relevance of this line of reflection is the too much neglected fact that Paul's doctrine of justification was able to assume the Jewish theology of righteousness as its starting point. It was precisely because Paul drew his concept of divine righteousness (Rom. 1.17) immediately from the scriptures of his people,[20] that he was able to introduce the phrase without explanation. It is covenantal nomism's presupposition that God's righteousness precedes all human response and sustains even recalcitrant Israel as 'saving righteousness' from which Paul's theology of justification also begins. It is hardly likely, then, that the other component of his doctrine – righteousness from faith and not from works of the law – was intended as a rebuttal of that basic axiom of Israel's covenant theology. In other words, 'works of the law' should not be read as an attack on human effort (works) as such; the phrase has a related, but different focus, as indicated above (§ 2.2).

In my view, but the point is more controversial, this insight helps explain a passage usually regarded as confirming the fact of Jewish legalism – Rom. 4.4–5 – 'to him who works the reward is not reckoned as a favour but as a debt; but to him who does not work but believes on him who justifies the ungodly, his faith is "reckoned for righteousness"'.[21] The flaw in the usual exegesis is the assumption that 'he who works for a reward' is a description of a typical Jewish attitude. What it forgets is that Israel's self-understanding was predicated on the recogni-

---

[18] The point is probably most evident in the hidden premise generally assumed for Gal. 3.10; see e.g. H. Hübner, *Law in Paul's Thought* (Edinburgh: T. & T. Clark, 1984) 18–20; T.R. Schreiner, *The Law and its Fulfilment: A Pauline Theology of the Law* (Grand Rapids: Baker, 1993) 60.

[19] That Second Temple Judaism did *not* teach the need for 'perfection' in law-keeping was one of the consensus points in the Durham-Tübingen Symposium on *Paul and the Mosaic Law* (ed. J.D.G. Dunn; WUNT 89; Tübingen: Mohr, 1996) 312 [=288 above].

[20] See e.g. S.K. Williams, 'The "Righteousness of God" in Romans', *JBL* 99 (1980) 241–90.

[21] In recent discussion see particularly S. Westerholm, *Israel's Law and the Church's Faith: Paul and His Recent Interpreters* (Grand Rapids: Eerdmans, 1988), who refers repeatedly to Rom. 4.4–5 on this point.

tion that their Lord was 'a God merciful and gracious, slow to anger, and abounding in steadfast love and faithfulness' (Exod. 34.6); that is, that God's righteousness was reckoned to Israel, as to Abraham, 'as a favour (*kata charin*)'[22] not as a debt. In other words, as in the preceding paragraph (3.30), Paul seems to be citing a theologoumenon which was as much Jewish as Christian in order to draw from it a conclusion which served his more immediate and more restricted debate (regarding the function of works of the law in regard to a gospel for Gentile as well as Jew).

2.4   In short then, (1) it is important for our understanding of Paul's teaching on justification that we observe the complete phrase – works *of the law*. Without the reference to the law the point being made by Paul would be lost. (2) It is equally important that the restricted focus of the phrase be recognized – as a critique of Israel's concern to live out its distinct existence as a people separated to the Lord. (3) Which also means that the phrase should not be regarded as a circumlocution for a legalistic view that acceptance by God had to be earned by good behaviour.

The argument here is nicely summed up in the debate over Paul's critique of 'boasting' (Rom. 3.27). Traditionally this has been understood as boasting in one's own efforts, self-achieved righteousness.[23] But a more obvious reference is to the 'boasting' of Rom. 2.17, 23: it is the only other 'boasting' of which Paul has spoken; and the opening of 3.27 ('Where then is boasting?') is most obviously to be taken as referring to that previously mentioned boasting. In which case it is immediately to the point that the 'boasting' of 2.17, 23 is an expression of Israel's confidence in its covenant status and privilege over against other peoples (Gentiles) (2.17–20).[24] Given the immediate correlation of 'boasting' and 'works of the law' in 3.27, therefore, Paul's critique of 'boasting' simply reinforces the fact that Paul had in view 'works *of the law*', and that his critique of these works was directed against Jewish presumption of privilege and of the need to safeguard that privilege by insisting on the works of the law which sustained their separation from other nations.

---

[22] Although LXX prefered *eleos* to translate the great covenant term *chesed* ('steadfast love'), Paul's characteristic *charis* carries the same force; see further my *Theology of Paul* § 13.2.

[23] 'Sinful self-reliance' (Bultmann, *Theology* 1.242); 'self-glorying' (Hübner, *Law* 116).

[24] The same point is usually missed in regard to Rom. 10.3, where Paul criticizes his fellow Jews for 'seeking to establish their own (*idian*) righteousness'. Here again it is regularly assumed that 'their own' means 'as achieved by them' (Bultmann, *Theology* 1.285; Hübner, *Law* 121, 128–9). But 'their own' (*idian*) properly means 'theirs' and not others, that is, Jewish righteousness not available to Gentiles. See further again my *Theology of Paul* § 14.6b.

3. 'Works' in Ephesians, the Pastorals and 1 Clement

How does this finding reflect on our understanding of the subsequent passages cited above and usually taken as equivalent to the earlier Paul's theology of justification 'from faith and not from works of the law'? The most obvious procedure is to examine each of those cited above in turn.

3.1 Eph. 2.8–9.   Immediately of relevance is the fact that we have here 'faith' and 'works' set in antithesis, and a close association asserted between 'works' and 'boasting'. Equally striking is the fact that in the immediately following context we find expression of a similar Jewish sense of privilege over Gentiles (2.11–12) and a conception of the law as functioning to divide/separate Jew from Gentile (2.14–15). In other words, we seem to have all the same elements which built up into Paul's earlier teaching on justification as 'from faith and not from works of the law'. On the basis of this data it is hardly surprising that some find here a simple restatement of Paul's earlier teaching, with 'works' standing for 'works of the law', and 'boasting' indicating a misplaced confidence in one's own efforts.[25]

Two further features, however, need to be drawn into the discussion. One is that the imagery seems to have moved on from Paul's earlier formulation of the gospel. In particular, we have to note the strong sense of what might be called 'realized eschatology'. I refer to the double fact that both resurrection (and exaltation) with Christ (2.6) and salvation (2.5, 8) are said to have been already accomplished for the believer. Both claims stand in some contrast to the more cautious formulations (eschatological reservation) of key passages like Rom. 6.5–8 and 8.11, where resurrection with Christ, or like Christ's is seen as something belonging to the 'not yet'. More typical of Paul, and, notably, in immediate conjunction with his teaching on justification, is Phil. 3.8–11 – resurrection as the end-point of a life of suffering and increasing conformity to Christ's death. Similarly it is characteristic of the earlier Paul that 'salvation' belongs to the 'not yet', an image of the *completion* of God's redemptive purpose (e.g. Rom 5.9–10).[26] The two points cohere and strengthen the impression that the perspective in this passage (whether that of a post-Pauline disciple or of the late Paul) is different from that of the earlier Paul. What difference might that make to our question?

---

[25] H. Schlier, *Der Brief an die Epheser* (Düsseldorf: Patmos, 1957) 116; M. Barth, *Ephesians* (AB 34; New York: Doubleday, 1974) 244; F. Mußner, *Der Brief an die Epheser* (ÖTKNT; Gütersloh: Gütersloher, 1982) 67; cf. I.H. Marshall, 'Salvation, Grace and Works in the Later Writings of the Pauline Corpus', *NTS* 42 (1996) 339–58 (here 345–7). More careful in formulation is J. Gnilka, *Der Epheserbrief* (HThKNT; Freiburg: Herder, ²1977) 130; P. Pokorny, *Der Brief des Paulus an die Epheser* (ThHNT; Berlin: Evangelische, 1992) 110.

[26] Notable is the contrast with Rom. 8.24: 'we were saved (aorist) *in hope*'; for all the sure confidence of Christian hope, the completion of salvation/redemption is still outstanding (8.23).

The other feature is of more immediate relevance. It is the fact that the talk of 'works' (2.9) does not appear within or as part of the overcoming of the Jew/Gentile divide (2.11–22). On the contrary, there seems to be a deliberate attempt in 2.1–10 to universalize the statement of the gospel. The description of 2.1–2 sounds at first a very Jewish view of Gentiles. But the writer immediately corrects that impression (2.3): 'all of us once so lived'; 'we (Christians, of whatever ethnic origin) were by nature children of wrath, like everyone else'. The point is reinforced when we realize that the writer seems to have pulled apart the elements of the characteristic Jewish perspective of his template (Col. 2.13 – 'dead in transgressions and the uncircumcision of your flesh ...').[27] The first phrase he reuses in Eph. 2.1 ('dead in trangressions'). But the second he incorporates as the beginning of the second part of the chapter – 2.11 ('you were Gentiles in the flesh, those called "uncircumcision" by those called "circumcision" made with hands in the flesh').[28] This indicates a deliberate attempt to separate the perspectives of the two paragraphs (2.1–10, 11–22); in particular, to make 2.1–10 a more universal expression of the gospel, and to give it more specific application to the old Jew/Gentile divide only in the second paragraph (2.11–22).

The appropriate conclusion to draw from this is that Eph. 2.8–9 was *not* intended as a restatement of Paul's teaching on justification 'from faith and not from works of the law'. On the contrary, Eph. 2.8–9 expresses a different perspective. How should we characterize that? Probably as an attempt to restate Israel's own most fundamental theologoumenon (as in Deut. 9.5): that all salvation begins from God's grace and is dependent on God's grace from start to finish. The point of 2.1–10, then, would be that the principle behind Israel's election as God's people was a principle which applied to all. And the point of 2.11–22 would be that in Christ God had demonstrated that what had formally been Israel's unique privilege had now been opened up to all. In other words, Eph. 2.8–9 may have been going back to first principles, rather as Paul himself had done in Rom. 4.4–5 and 9.7–13.

What this means, then, is that Eph. 2.8–9 is not a restatement of justification 'from faith and not from works of the law', but a restatement of the more fundamental theological principle which Paul drew from his heritage and shared with the classic statements of Israel's religion. This also means, on the one hand, that Eph. 2.8–9 cannot be taken as indicating the meaning and point of Paul's

---

[27] The classification of the world into 'uncircumcision/circumcision' (as in Rom. 2.25–27; 3.30; 4.9–12; Gal. 2.7–8; Col. 3.11) is an entirely Jewish perspective. Only Jews regarded circumcision as a positive identity factor (for Greeks it was more like a form of mutilation); and it was certainly not Gentiles who chose to identify themselves as 'uncircumcised foreskin'.

[28] 'Circumcision in the flesh' echoes the classic description of circumcision as marking God's covenant with Israel in Gen. 17.11–14 ('in your flesh' occurs three times); cf. Rom. 2.28; Gal. 6.12–13; Phil. 3.3–5. Here the 'made with hands' (Eph. 2.11) is probably prompted by contrast to the 'made without hands' in Col. 2.11.

earlier formulation; it does not overthrow the conclusions reached in the preceding section; the fact that the passage talks of 'works' and not of 'works of the law' remains of crucial importance for the exegesis of both passages. On the other hand, however, by universalizing the particular concerns of the earlier Paul (2.1–10), and by separating them from these particular concerns (2.11–22), the writer provides one of the classic statements of justification by faith as a universal and fundamental principle which should underlie any realistic religion.

3.2 2 Tim. 1.9; Tit. 3.5.   We can take these two passages together since they share common features and seem to be making the same point. (1) They are both, in effect, 'faithful sayings' – the latter explicitly (3.8a), the former as sharing the characteristics of other 'faithful sayings' (cf. particularly 1 Tim. 1.15). What may be significant here, then, is that they do not express the author's/authors' own fresh perspective, but are cited precisely because they formulate established 'faith', 'truth', 'sound teaching'. (2) They both speak of salvation as an act of God already accomplished (both using 'save' in the aorist tense). That is to say, they share the perspective more of Eph. 2.5, 8 than that of the earlier Paul.

So far as our immediate interest is concerned, it is significant that both formulations, like Eph. 2.8, speak only of 'works', not of 'works of the law'.[29] The phrasing is slightly different (2 Tim. 1.9 – 'not in accordance with our works'; Tit. 3.5 – 'not from works in righteousness which we have done'). But the point is the same. Noteworthy is the emphasis on divine initiative and grace: 'he saved us', 'he called us', 'in accordance with his own purpose and grace', 'given (as a gift) in Christ Jesus', 'before time immemorial' (2 Tim. 1.9); 'the goodness and loving kindness of our Saviour God', 'in accordance with his mercy, he saved us' (Tit. 3.4–5). In other words, here are further examples of what we have already found in Eph. 2.8–9 – that is, a restatement of the more fundamental principle of human acceptability before God, rather than a restatement of Paul's more narrowly directed polemic.[30]

It is equally important to note that the letters reflect a quite different situation and perspective from the polemical context in which Paul first formulated his teaching on justification. There is no hint in the Pastorals that the issue of 'works

---

[29] Where the difference is noted, its significance is not adequately appreciated (see e.g. J.D. Quinn, *The Letter to Titus* [AB 35; New York: Doubleday, 1990] 216). More careful is L. Oberlinner, *Die Pastoralbriefe: Zweiter Timotheusbrief* (HThKNT XI.2/2; Freiburg: Herder, 1995) 38–9.

[30] The addition of 'in righteousness' (Tit. 3.5) may be intended as a still sharper expression of the fundamental principle (cf. L. Oberlinner, *Die Pastoralbriefe: Titusbrief* [(HThKNT XI.2/3; Freiburg: Herder, 1996], citing P. Trummer, *Die Paulustradition der Pastoralbriefe* [Frankfurt, 1978] 187).

of the law' was still a live one. Tit. 1.10 does refer to opponents, 'especially those of the circumcision' – the same phrase as in Acts 11.2 and Gal. 2.12. Like Eph. 2.11, it presumably denotes Jews, since (as already noted) only Jews regarded circumcision as a positive identity marker – or to be more precise, Jewish Christians who still continued to think as Jews, that is, continued to assume that the way for Gentiles to share in Israel's covenant blessings (the Messiah!) was for them to be circumcised (Gen. 17.12–14) and become proselytes. But even less than in Eph. 2.8–9 is there any hint that the formulation of the gospel in Tit. 3.4–7 (or 2 Tim. 1.9–10) was directed against this perspective. In fact there is little indication that such a perspective was active among the Cretan (or Ephesian) churches: other references to Jewish features (the law – 1 Tim. 1.8–9; 'Jewish myths' – Tit. 1.14) provide no support; and 'those of the circumcision' may simply be a formulaic way of referring to Jewish Christians (as in Col. 4.11).

At the same time, the theology of the faithful sayings is that of Israel's covenant. 'Called with a holy calling' (2 Tim. 1.9) is Hebraic in form and echoes Israel's understanding of Israelites as 'called to be saints' (as also particularly in Rom. 1:7 and 8:27–28).[31] Once again the continuity of identity with God's earlier purpose, with Israel as defined by the call of God (cf. Rom. 9:7–11, 24) is implicit. And the use of the term 'mercy' (*eleos*) in Tit. 3.5 is no accident, since it is the normal Greek translation of the strong Jewish term denoting God's 'covenant love, loving kindness' so fundamental to Israel's self-understanding as God's chosen people (Exod. 34:6–7).[32] In other words, once again it is the basic theologoumenon of Israel's self-understanding (a people chosen by God to display his mercy) which is brought to expression in 2 Tim. 1.9 and Tit. 3.5. The gospel is formulated not despite Israel or to contradict Judaism, but by appeal to Israel's most fundamental insight into divine grace.[33] Here too, then, the Pastorals seem to go behind Paul's more polemically formulated critique of 'works of the law' to the more fundamental insight that all human acceptability before God is dependent not on human activity but on divine grace from start to finish.

3.3 1 Clem 32.3–4. With 1 Clement the clear lines marked out in Ephesians and the Pastorals are becoming more blurred. The restatement of the gospel in 32.3–4 certainly strikes the same note as we have heard ringing clearly in the late Paulines; indeed, the assertion that justification is through faith is more explicit than in either of the Pastorals' formulations. The blurring comes in because 1

---

[31] The idea of Israel's 'calling' is prominent in deutero-Isaiah (Isa. 41.8–9; 42.6; 48.12; 49.1; 51.2; 54.6) and the DSS (1QM 3.2; 4.10–11; cf. 14.5; 1QSa 1.27; 2.2, 11; CD 2.11; 4.3–4). More widespread is the thought of Israel as 'saints/holy ones' (e.g. Pss. 16.3; 34.9; Dan. 7.18; 8.24; Tob. 8.15; Wis. 18.9; 1QSb 3.2–4; 1QM 3.5).

[32] See above n. 22. The parallel between 2.11 and 3.4–5 confirms that *eleos* and *charis* were recognized to be near synonyms.

[33] See also Marshall, 'Salvation' 350–1.

Clement, rather like James, finds it necessary to hedge around the more distinctive Pauline statement of justification with a paraenesis whose formulation seems to qualify the forthright statement of justification by faith and not by works. It is not simply that he commends 'good works' and their reward (33–35); the Pastorals did that[34] (as had Paul earlier)[35] without compromising the fundamental statements of the gospel. It is rather that he makes other statements such as, Enoch 'was found righteous in obedience' (9.3), 'because of his faith and hospitality a son was given him (Abraham) in his old age, and in his obedience he offered him as a sacrifice to God on the mountain' (10.7), 'because of her faith and hospitality Rahab the prostitute was saved' (12.1). In the immediately preceding context of 32.3–4 he asks 'Why was our father Abraham blessed?', and answers, 'Was it not because he did righteousness and truth through faith?', referring directly to the offering of Isaac (31.2–3). The echo of James 2.21–25 is strong, itself an echo of the sort of rationale (1 Macc. 2.52) to counter which Paul had probably framed his exposition of Gen. 15.6 in Rom. 4.[36]

In this case, all we can say is that not only has the specific and particular argument of Paul been lost to sight, not least in terms of 'works of the law'. But even the more fundamental gospel principle so clearly formulated in Eph. 2.8–9, 2 Tim. 1.9 and Tit. 3.5 has been compromised even while being reiterated. The perspective is now at two removes from Paul and little further clarification of what Paul himself may have meant can be expected.

4. Conclusions

What may be gleaned from all this?[37]

(1) 'Works of the law' was a formulation of late Second Temple Judaism. It was not a new coinage by Paul, nor did it represent a jaundiced or idiosyncratic view on the part of Paul of Second Temple Judaism. On the contrary, it represented a view characteristic of Second Temple Judaism – the nomistic (not legalistic) attitude of 'covenantal nomism'.

(2) As such, the phrase 'works of the law' was specific to Paul's particular and precisely targetted argument, as directed against the negative consequences for Gentile believers summed up in the phrase.

(3) It was not intended by Paul as an expression of the foundational covenant principle (*covenantal* nomism). Most Jews and many/most Jewish Christians did indeed understood the necessity of 'works of the law' to be derived from the

---

[34] 1 Tim. 2.10; 3.1; 5.10 (twice), 25; 6.18; 2 Tim. 2.21; 3.17; 4.14; Tit. 1.16; 2.7, 14; 3.1, 8, 14.

[35] Rom. 2.6–7; 13.3; 1 Cor. 3.13–15; 2 Cor. 9.8; Col. 1.10; 2 Thes. 2.17.

[36] See my *Romans* 200–1.

[37] Cf. and contrast Marshall, "Salvation" 355–7; hopefully these conclusions will clarify the points of agreement and disagreement with Marshall.

foundational covenant principle (covenantal *nomism*), but in Paul's view the inherent anti-Gentile bias implicit in the phrase constituted a corruption of that principle.

(4) The fundamental principle of justification by grace/loving kindness was also a fundamental principle of Israel's election and covenant, which Paul consciously drew from that source.

(5) Paul takes that principle as given (Rom. 1.17; 4.4–5; Gal. 2.15–16), but it was the later Paulines which gave it clearest statement and classic formulation.

In short, by noting the distinction between the earlier talk of 'works of the law' and the references to 'works' in Eph. 2.9, 2 Tim. 1.9 and Tit. 3.5, we are better able both to identify the particular concern in Paul's use of the former, to recognize the more fundamental principle expressed in the latter, to appreciate that they are not simply the same, and thus to acknowledge the importance of both for a proper appreciation of Pauline theology, not least his theology of the law.

Chapter 18

Jesus the Judge:

Further Thoughts of Paul's Christology and Soteriology

'He shall come in glory to judge the living and the dead'. Thus the familiar words of the Nicene Creed, themselves a slight development of the Apostles Creed: 'from thence (God's right hand) he shall come to judge the living and the dead'. The theme of Jesus as Judge is thus familiar to Christian worshippers if only from countless repetitions of these creeds, as it is also from the rich iconography of Eastern Christianity and the more elaborate confessions of the West. And yet it is a subject which seems to have attracted little close attention in recent christological studies.[1] Why this should be so is an interesting question in itself, but to answer it adequately would involve too much speculation. At this point it may suffice simply to wonder whether thought of Christ's (second) coming (*parousia*) has proved difficult enough to cope with without embracing the fuller picture of judgment by Christ, and whether the problem of reconciling thought of Christ as justifier with Christ as judge has proved a little too confusing.

As a New Testament specialist, it is the NT teaching on the subject which catches the attention. And as one who recently attempted a comprehensive study of Paul's theology, but perhaps did not give enough attention to this aspect of that theology,[2] I take this opportunity, in expressing my appreciation to Gerry O'Collins for all his writings on matters christological, to extend my personal dialogue with him into this difficult area.

I

There is no difficulty in identifying how the idea of final divine judgment entered Christian thought. It was familiar in Greek thought, but particularly prominent in Jewish tradition,[3] and especially in the expectation of 'the day of

---

[1] Including the honoree's *Christology: A Biblical, Historical, and Systematic Study of Jesus* (Oxford: Oxford University, 1995). Even J. Moltmann, *The Coming of God: Christian Eschatology* (London: SCM, 1996) raises the subject only in relation to his discussion of universalism.

[2] J.D.G. Dunn, *The Theology of Paul the Apostle* (Grand Rapids: Eerdmans/Edinburgh: T. & T. Clark, 1998); I thus include myself with those referred to in n.1.

[3] See further *TDNT* 3.933–35; *ABD* 2.82–3.

the Lord' as a day of vengeance and wrath.[4] It is clear that Paul simply took over this eschatological expectation, as the opening chapters of Romans sufficiently indicate: 'we know that the judgment of God is in accordance with truth on those who practise such things' (2.2); 'the day of wrath and of the revelation of the righteous judgment of God' (2.5); 'the day when God is to judge' (2.16); 'all the world become liable to God's judgment' (3.19).

What is striking, however, is the fact that Christ also appears in the judgment scene and even in the role of judge. In Pauline texts this feature is most prominent in 2 Cor. 5.10 ('All of us must appear before the judgment seat of Christ') and 2 Tim. 4.1 ('Christ Jesus who is to judge the living and the dead').[5] Equally striking is the fact that Paul can adapt the OT phrase to speak of 'the day of Christ' (Phil. 1.6, 10; 2.16), 'the day of the Lord (Jesus)' (1 Cor. 1.8; 5.5; 2 Cor. 1.14; 1 Thess. 5.2; 2 Thess. 2.2).[6] The 'day' in view is clearly the day of judgment (Rom. 2.16; 1 Cor. 3.13). Notable also are two other texts which envisage Christ's coming to exercise judgment: 1 Cor. 4.5 – 'Do not pronounce judgment before the time, before the Lord comes, who will bring to light the things now hidden in darkness and will disclose the purposes of the heart'; 2 Thess. 1.7 – 'when the Lord Jesus is revealed from heaven with his mighty angels in flaming fire, inflicting vengeance on those who do not know God and on those who do not obey the gospel of our Lord Jesus. ...'.

Given this data, important questions naturally arise: From where did Paul derive this belief in Jesus as Judge? And what is the significance of this data? To the first question there are two obvious answers.

II

In pre-Christian Jewish thought Yahweh is usually represented as the one who will judge.[7] But the idea that God *delegates* judgment or a share in judgment to another was already quite frequent in the thought of Second Temple Judaism. The notion that God delegated judgment to his representatives on earth (e.g. Judg. 2.16–18; 3.9–10; 2 Chron. 19.6–8) and would call them to account (Ps. 82)

---

[4] E.g. Isa. 13.9, 13; 34.8; Ezek. 7.7–12; Joel 2.1–2; Zeph. 1.7–2.3; 3.8; Mal. 4.1, 5; see also e.g. Dan. 7.9–11; Jub. 5.10–16; 1 Enoch 90.20–27.

[5] Cf. Acts 10.42 – Jesus 'is the one ordained by God as judge of the living and the dead'; 17.31 – God 'has fixed a day on which he will have the world judged in righteousness by a man whom he has appointed'. Rom. 14.10 – 'We shall all stand before the judgment seat of God'; at an early date *theou* was replaced by *Christou*, probably under the influence of 2 Cor. 5.10 (B.M. Metzger, *A Textual Commentary on the Greek New Testament* (London: United Bible Societies, 1975) 531.

[6] See further *ABD* 2.76–7.

[7] R.H. Hiers cites Pss. 58.11; 96.10, 13; Eccl. 11.9; 12.14; Isa. 33.22; Ezek. 11.8–11; Mal. 3.5; T. Ben. 10.8–10; 1 Enoch 91.7 (*ABD* 2.80).

was already old. Similar delegation of judgment was anticipated for God's representatives in the age to come. For example, the Davidic messiah would judge (Isa. 11.3). And the Testament of Levi looks to the Lord to 'raise up a new priest to whom all the words of the Lord will be revealed. And he will execute true judgment on earth for many days' (18.2).

The extension of this line of thought to *final* judgment is not unexpected. Enoch's role in the judgment was a subject of some speculation. Jubilees presents him as the one who was established to 'keep a record of all the deeds of every generation till the day of judgment', who in particular bore witness against the Watchers (Jub. 4.17–24). Similarly in the first book of the Enoch cycle he is described as the 'scribe of righteousness' who carried to the Watchers the heavenly sentence of condemnation (1 Enoch 12–16). In the Testament of Abraham (Recension B), however, Abraham is taken up to heaven and witnesses a judgment scene, where one judges and another brings the charges of sins. He is told by archangel Michael that the judge is Abel. 'And the one who produces (the evidence) is the teacher of heaven and earth and the scribe of righteousness, Enoch. For the Lord sent them[8] here in order that they might record the sins and the righteous deeds of each person' (T. Abr. [B] 11.1–4). What is particularly fascinating here is Michael's further comment: 'It is not Enoch's business to give sentence; rather, the Lord is the one who gives sentence, and it is this one's (Enoch's) task only to write' (B 11.7).[9] It would appear that T. Abr. is attempting to correct or clarify some confusion on the point: there were some who concluded that Enoch would have a share in the final judgment; in response, T. Abr. makes it clear that Enoch's role would be more limited. It is Enoch's role as scribe which is elaborated in 2 Enoch (23.1–5; 40.13; 53.2; 64.5; 68.2).

The fact remains that the Testament of Abraham depicts Abel as 'the judge' (T. Abr. [B] 10). Michael speaks: 'Do you see the judge? This is Abel, who first bore witness, and God brought him here to judge' (B 11.2). Equally interesting is Recension A, where again Abel is depicted as sitting in judgment, as the angel Michael explains. The passage is intriguing and worth quoting at length – T. Abr. [A] 13.3–10[10]:

(Abel) sits here to judge every creature, examining both righteous and sinners, because God has said, "It is not I who judge you, but by man shall every man be judged". For this reason he has committed judgment to him, to judge the world until his own great and glorious coming (*parousia*). And then, righteous Abraham, will follow the final judgment

---

[8] The plural is a puzzle. The context suggests the two in view are Enoch and Abel. But the same context distinguishes Abel's role in judging from Enoch's in recording. Some mss read 'him' instead of 'them'.

[9] Translation by E.P. Sanders in R.H. Charlesworth, *The Old Testament Pseudepigrapha* (London: DLT, 1983) 1.900.

[10] Translation by N. Turner in H.F.D. Sparks, *The Apocryphal Old Testament* (Oxford: Clarendon, 1984) 412; Sparks does not include Recension B.

and retribution, eternal and unchangeable, which no one will be able to dispute. For all men have their origin from the first man; and so by his son they are first judged here. At the second coming (*deutera parousia*) they and every spirit and every creature will be judged by the twelve tribes of Israel. At the third stage they will be judged by the Sovereign God of all; and then at last will the whole process reach its end.

The date of the work is unclear and may be later than Paul, but both recensions are certainly Jewish (rather than Christian) in character:[11] despite talk of 'the second coming' here, there is no Christian input evident (Abel is not presented as a prototype of Jesus); the parousia is presumably that of God himself (cf. Mal. 3.1–2).[12] What is of particular interest at this point is the talk of *three* judgments: one by Abel; one by the twelve tribes of Israel; and a final, final judgment by the Sovereign God.

Certainly earlier than Paul is the fascinating Qumran document which focuses on the mysterious Melchizedek – 11QMelch:

> He (Melchizedek) will, by his strength, judge the holy ones of God (*El*), executing judgment as it is written concerning him in the Songs of David, who said "*Elohim* has taken his place in the divine council; in the midst of the gods (*Elohim*) he holds judgment" (Ps. 82.1). And it was concerning him that he said, "... El will judge the peoples" (Ps. 7.7–8). As for that which he s[aid, "How long will you] judge unjustly and show partiality to the wicked? Selah" (Ps. 82.2), its interpretation concerns Belial and the spirits of his lot [who] rebelled by turning away from the precepts of God to ... And Melchizedek will avenge the vengeance of the judgments of God ... (11QMelch 9–13 Vermes).

Whether Melchizedek is intended to be the equally mysterious figure of Gen. 14.18–20, or possibly a heavenly figure ('King of righteousness'), remains a matter of dispute.[13] What is clear, however is that Ps. 82 is interpreted with reference to this Melchizedek: the (earthly) judges, themselves designated 'gods' in the Psalm itself (82.6 – 'I say, "You are gods [*Elohim*] ..."'), are identified as Satan and the evil angels; and the initial figure ('God', *Elohim*) is identified as Melchizedek. The boldness of the Psalm's own speech ('You are gods'; cf. John 10.34–35) is surpassed by that of its interpretation at Qumran (Melchizedek is the first mentioned *Elohim*). However we interpret the figure Melchizedek, it is clear enough that he is given a role in heavenly judgment; though presumably the final line retains the thought that this role as heavenly judge is delegated by God.

Most stimulating for such reflection were the visions of Dan. 7.9–14. The first vision spoke of 'thrones' (plural) – it always being implied that the occupant of a 'throne' exercised judgment. The indication of a second, empty throne was evidently sufficient to stimulate Rabbi Akiba's suggestion that the second throne

---

[11] Sanders in Charlesworth, *OTP* 1.871–5; Turner in Sparks, *AOT* 393–6.

[12] Sanders in Charlesworth, *OTP* 1.890 n.13a.

[13] See e.g. J.D.G. Dunn, *Christology in the Making* (London: SCM, 2nd edn. 1989) 152–3 and those cited there.

was for the Messiah.[14] Though, according to the visions themselves, the most obvious candidate for the second throne was the man-like figure ('one like a son of man') who came with the clouds of heaven to the Ancient of Days and was given dominion and kingship (Dan. 7.13–14). However, the implication was not actually taken up till the Similitudes of Enoch (1 Enoch 37–71), where the Elect One sits down on the throne of God's glory and judges 'the secret things' and the rebellious angels (1 Enoch 49.4; 55.4; 61.8–9). The Elect One is evidently also the Son of Man (69.27), who is subsequently identified as Enoch (71.14). Again there is the awkward question of dating: but since Daniel's vision seems to have stimulated the writers of 4 Ezra and the Revelation of John in a similar way (4 Ezra 12.32–33; 13.10–11, 37–38; Rev. 1.13–16; 14.14–16) in the aftermath of Jerusalem's destruction (CE 70), it is quite likely that the Similitudes are too late to have influenced Paul.[15] Curiously enough the Synoptic tradition evidences a similar development in regard to talk of the Son of Man. That the Son of Man has a crucial role in the final judgment when he comes in glory is clear enough in its earliest written form (Mark 8.38; 13.26–27), though what that role is is less clear; also that he sits at the right hand of God (Mark 14.62). But nowhere does the earliest written form of the Synoptic tradition speak of the Son of Man exercising judgment from the throne of glory. It is only Matthew which does so (Matt. 19.28; 25.31–32; cf. 16.27 with Mark 8.38/Luke 9.26), and in language which raises the possibility that Matthew's redaction reflects the influence of the Similitudes.[16]

Paul does not show any clear evidence of making use of or being influenced by the Son of Man traditions within earliest Christianity.[17] But that particular possibility is neither here nor there. The idea of a divine agent, whether exalted human or of heavenly origin, having part in God's final judgment seems to have been 'in the air' around the time of Paul's writing. And the use of Ps. 110.1 in reference to Jesus was already well established before Paul: Jesus was the Lord to whom the Lord God had said, 'Sit at my right hand until I make your enemies your footstool'.[18] Such a conviction expressed in such imagery could hardly fail to suggest the corollary: that the risen and exalted Christ would have some share in that eschatological day of judgment.

In view of the Testament of Abraham's conception of a second (stage of) judgment, to be exercised by the twelve tribes of Israel (T. Abr. [A] 13.6), we should also recall that this motif also influenced earliest Christian thought. It presum-

---

[14] *b. Hagigah* 14a; *b. Sanhedrin* 38b.

[15] Dunn, *Christology* 76–8.

[16] Similarly John 5.27 may reflect some influence from the Similitudes (1 Enoch 69.27); see further Dunn, *Christology* 77–8.

[17] Dunn, *Christology* 90–1.

[18] Mark 12.36 pars.; 14.62 pars.; Acts 2.34–35; Rom. 8.34; 1 Cor. 15.25; Eph. 1.20; Col. 3.1; Heb. 1.3, 13; 8.1; 10.12–13; 12.2; 1 Pet. 3.22. For bibliography see Dunn, *Christology* 309 n.45.

ably stemmed from Dan. 7.22: in LXX the text reads, 'He gave judgment to the saints of the Most High'. The idea developed into the thought of Israel being given to judge the Gentiles: 'they (Israel) shall judge all the nations' (Jub. 32.19); 'God will execute the judgment of the nations by the hand of his elect' (1QpHab 5.4); 'they (the righteous) will judge (*krinousin*) (the) Gentiles' (Wisd. 3.8).[19] The Jesus tradition takes up the same motif, with an interesting twist, in what may be the final word in Q: 'Truly I tell you, at the renewal of all things (*palingenesia*), when the Son of Man is seated on his throne of glory, you who have followed me will also sit on twelve thrones, judging the twelve tribes of Israel' (Matt. 19.28/Luke 22.30). And it is the same motif which Paul transfers to the believers in Messiah Jesus (including Gentile believers) in 1 Cor. 6.2: 'Do you not know that the saints will judge the world?' If the thought of sharing in final judgment could be extended to include the saints, how much more natural and compelling would it be to envisage the exalted Jesus as having a determinative part or say in the final judgment.

What emerges from this brief survey are several points of importance for our inquiry. (a) The conception of others sharing in the final judgment was quite commonly entertained, including Israel, or the saints, and exalted heroes of Israel's history. (b) Various roles were envisaged, including those of various courtroom officials: the usher who summons or gathers the participants to the place of judgment; the one who documents or brings the charges; the one who executes the judgment of the court; but also that of the judge himself. (c) All roles, including the last, were characteristically thought of as delegated by God, and so would not be thought to encroach upon the divine prerogative. (d) In at least some cases we probably have to speak of several judgments, and of judgments by saints and exalted ones as subordinate or preliminary (a lower court?) to the final judgment of God.

Against such a background it is easy to see how affirmation of the exalted Lordship of the risen Christ would lead to or include already the implication that this exalted Christ would also have a part in the final judgment of all creation. Something along these lines undoubtedly lies behind Paul's talk of Jesus as Judge.

III

The other source for Paul's theology of Jesus as Judge is presumably his own conception of the process of salvation in terms of courtroom imagery – justification, acquittal. It is hardly necessary to observe that this has been a major subject of scholarly analysis and discussion for several centuries, and I have already

---

[19] Sanders in Charlesworth, *OTP* 1.890 n.13c.

written on it at length.[20] However, it has become evident that in focusing on the subject within the chapter entitled 'The Beginning of Salvation' (in *The Theology of Paul the Apostle*), I may have distracted attention from the fact that the imagery is essentially forensic in character: it is derived from the court room, and not least from the thought of final judgment. When I returned to the subject in #18 of the same book, the focus had changed (to 'the eschatological tension'), so that the comments on the future tense of justification may be overlooked by anyone concerned primarily with the theology of justification.[21] I should rectify the misleading impression here.

The forensic character of the imagery of 'justification' is sufficiently familiar and needs no further exposition.[22] What does need to be stressed, however, is that fundamental to Paul's concept of justification is its *future* orientation. 'Not the hearers of the law are righteous before God, but the doers of the law shall be counted righteous (*dikaiōthēsontai*)' (Rom. 2.13); the context shows clearly that final judgment is in view (2.5–13, 15–16). 'By works of the law shall no flesh be justified/acquitted (*dikaiōthēsetai*) before him' (3.20), where again it is clearly final judgment which is in view. '"God is one", who will justify (*dikaiōsei*) circumcision from faith and uncircumcision through faith' (3.30); once again the universality of the claim looks to its implementation in universal (final) judgment.

The more frequent present tenses should probably be understood as describing the character of God who justifies rather than its timing. God is *ho dikaiōn*, 'the one who justifies' (Rom. 3.26; 4.5; 8.33); hence the present tenses also in 3.24 and 28. The thought is of a divine prerogative which will be most fully demonstrated in the final judgment, as the sequence of argument in 3.4–6 and the context of 8.33 makes plain. Likewise with Paul's occasional use of the noun *dikaiōsis* ('justification, vindication, acquittal'): in both cases the association of the term with resurrection (4.25 – 'he was raised because of our justification') and life (5.18 – 'through the righteous act of one to all men to righteousness of life'/'acquittal that brings life' [BAGD]) suggests that the thought is of the end of the process of salvation (cf. 6.5; 8.11; 11.15).

The mixture of tenses in Gal. 2.16–17 similarly indicates that what may be a present pronouncement will (have to) be ratified by final verdict of acquittal:

We know that no human being is justified (*dikaioutai* – present) by works of the law but only through faith in Jesus Christ, and we have believed in Christ Jesus, in order that we might be justified (*dikaiōthōmen* – aorist) by faith in Christ and not by works of the law, because by works of the law shall no flesh be justified (*dikaiōthēsetai* – future; as in Rom. 3.20). But if in seeking to be justified (*dikaiōthēnai* – aorist) in Christ ...

---

[20] Dunn, *Theology of Paul* #14.

[21] Dunn, *Theology of Paul* 467, 488, 491.

[22] See e.g. J. Reumann, *Righteousness in the New Testament* (Philadelphia: Fortress, 1982) index 'forensic sense of righteousness/justification'.

Similarly with Gal. 3.8, 11 and 24. And in 5.4 the thought is of an aspiration to future justification: 'you who are seeking to be justified (*dikaiousthe*) by the law'. Hence the Christian alternative: 'we (by contrast) by the Spirit, from faith, are awaiting eagerly the hope of righteousness' (5.5); that is, the hope is for 'righteousness', the verdict of God's acquittal, as a still future good.

It is important therefore not to be misled by other aorist uses of the verb, which may seem to imply a verdict already passed, complete and (by implication) irrevocable. Most notably the famous Rom. 5.1: 'Therefore, having been justified (*dikaiōthentes*) from faith ...' (similarly Rom. 4.2; 5.9; 1 Cor. 6.11; Tit. 3.7). Such texts may tempt us to limit the language of justification to the initial stage of the process of salvation, parallel to the washing and setting apart of 1 Cor. 6.11, and with the language of 'salvation' similarly limited to the end product of the process (as Rom. 5.9–10).[23] In fact however, Paul's usage shows that he does think of salvation as a process (as the present tenses of 1 Cor. 1.18; 15.2; 2 Cor. 2.15 confirm – 'those who are being saved'), with 'salvation' as the goal in view (Rom. 5.9–10; 11.26; 13.11; Phil. 1.19; 2.12; 1 Thess. 5.8–9), but also with a present realisation (Rom. 8.24 – 'in terms of hope, we are saved [*esōthēmen*]'). To that extent 'justification' and 'salvation' have a very similar soteriological function in Paul's theology: to indicate a process begun but yet to be completed.[24]

So far as our present inquiry is concerned, the two-stage soteriology (beginning and end, justified already but not yet finally acquitted) is mirrored in the double role of Jesus in the process of justification: justified through faith in Christ; and Jesus the Judge. To affirm that Jesus is also eschatological Judge is to recognize that justification is a process, is not complete in the moment faith is placed in Christ, and that Christ will also signal its completion, while at the same time giving reassurance that the Judge is also the justifier. Something of this is indicated in a text already cited – Rom. 4.25. Paul quotes what is widely recognized to be a variation on a well established early Christian formulation: 'Jesus our Lord who was handed over because of our transgressions and was raised because of our justification'; the two stages of the crucial event (Jesus' death and resurrection) are mirrored in the two aspects/stages of the salvation process. Similarly Rom. 5.10: 'If when we were enemies we were reconciled to God through the death of his Son, how much more, having been reconciled, we shall be saved by his life'. More explicit is Rom. 8.33–34. The scene is the final judgment. Paul asks, in confident assurance: 'Who will bring charges against the elect of God? It is God who justifies. Who is there to condemn? It is Christ (Jesus) who died, rather was raised, who also is at the right hand of God, who also in-

---

[23] Cf. particularly K.P. Donfried, 'Justification and Last Judgment in Paul', *ZNW* 67 (1976) 90–110.

[24] One of the principal emphases in Dunn, *Theology of Paul* #18.

tercedes on our behalf'. Here the two aspects of 4.25 and 5.10 are held together: Jesus' death and resurrection together mean that he is able to plead with God the Judge effectively on behalf of 'the elect of God', and that no prosecutor will be able to overthrow that case.

In short, the conception of Jesus as Judge may stem in part from a double conviction. (a) The whole of human history moves forward inexorably to a final judgment. (b) The saving event of Jesus (death and resurrection) does not eliminate the idea of final judgment or of the need for a final reckoning. Rather, the belief in justification by faith must be integrated into the prior belief in final judgment. That is most simply done by affirming the exalted Christ's role also in that judgment, and the most forceful statement to that effect is the affirmation of Jesus as Judge. In so arguing, of course, I have no wish to suggest that the two 'sources' of the Christian conception of Jesus as Judge were alternatives or independent of each other. On the contrary, they are likely to have interacted and reinforced each other more or less from the first. However, if there is anything in the above arguments, they have important corollaries for our understanding both of Paul's christology and of his soteriology.

IV

The christological corollaries should be already obvious. Two in particular are worthy of further reflection.

First, we need to note that different roles in judgment are attributed to the exalted Jesus in the different texts. 2 Cor. 5.10 and 2 Tim. 4.1 (cited in #I above) have no hesitation in ascribing the role of judge as such to Jesus. Perhaps the same is implicit in the talk of 'the day of Christ', 'the day of the Lord (Jesus)' (also listed in #I above). Similarly, the depiction of the Lord (Jesus) as disclosing the purposes of the heart (1 Cor. 4.5) clearly recalls the description of God as the one who searches the heart (Rom. 8.27)[25] and suggests the picture of the discerning judge. On the other hand, the result of such disclosure is that 'each one will receive commendation from God', God being, presumably, the higher authority. 1 Cor. 3.10–15 somewhat confuses the picture by referring to Christ as the foundation (3.11 – 'that foundation is Jesus Christ'), on which believers must build the superstructure which will be tested in that 'day'. More to the point, Rom. 5.9–10 and 1 Thess. 1.10 seem to envisage Jesus rather as the one who saves or rescues from God's (judicial) wrath. And Rom. 8.33–34 (just cited) seems to envisage Jesus as the defence counsel pleading for the elect before God the Judge. Whether 2 Thess. 1.7 (also cited in #I above) refers to the one who carries out the

---

[25] Cf. e.g. 1 Sam. 16.7; 1 Kings 8.39; Pss. 44.21; 139.1–2, 23; Prov. 15.11.

judgment of the court, or the judge who enacts his own sentence, or indeed is formally independent of courtroom imagery (the avenging angel) is less than clear.

In all this Paul's usage reflects in at least some degree the variety of roles attributed to individuals like Enoch, Melchizedek, Abel, the Elect One/Messiah, and even the saints. What does this tell us? At the very least that there was no clear and widely shared conceptuality of final judgment and of those who were to share in that judgment in the Judaism of Paul's time. Within the fixed conviction of a final divine judgment, it seems to have been widely accepted that there was room enough to envisage others as having share or being given share in that judgment, even in the role of judge itself. In the light of this, Paul's own flexibility of imagery on the same subject, in relation to Jesus' own role as judge, should occasion no surprise.

As I tried to indicate in my *Theology of Paul*, such variety of imagery and role is wholly typical of Paul's christology.[26] He envisages the exalted Christ in very personal terms as exalted Lord and soon to come (on clouds), but also as last Adam and divine Wisdom; but he can also speak of 'Christ in me' and of Christ as a corporate entity, of believers 'in Christ' and functioning as Christ's body. Jesus as Judge obviously belongs with the first group of images. But given the variety of the imagery, we need to remember that it is *imagery* and not attempt to ascribe to it a literalness which would make it impossible to integrate the different roles indicated by the language used. As in other matters[27] Paul was attempting to articulate convictions and hopes which went beyond the limitations of human speech. To attempt on our part to order and integrate these images into a single coherent pattern would probably squeeze them into a mould of our own making. Better to live with the confusion of the imagery in its richness and be content with the basic conviction which comes to expression in such rich diversity. That basic conviction seems to be that Jesus will have a determinative part in the final judgment of God, or even in still less precise terms, that the final judgment of God will be in accord with the gospel of Christ (Rom. 2.16).

Second, it should also be noted that elsewhere in the NT Jesus' role as Judge is explicitly stated to have been appointed by God himself. Acts 10.42; 17.31 – 'he (Jesus) is the one ordained by God as judge of the living and the dead'; 'he (God) has fixed a day on which he will have the world judged in righteousness by a man whom he has appointed, and of this he has given assurance to all by raising him from the dead'. John 5.22, 27 – 'The Father judges no one but has given all judgment to the Son'; 'he (the Father) has given him authority to execute judgment, because he is the Son of Man'. Paul's judgment texts are not so explicit, but the point may well be implicit anyway. This would be all the clearer if the role of Jesus as Judge for Paul follows from his exaltation as Lord, since the influence of

---

[26] Dunn, *Theology of Paul* 314–5, 409–10.

[27] On Paul's metaphors of salvation see again Dunn, *Theology of Paul* 231–2, 328–33.

Ps. 110.1 would likely carry over into the former role: it is in the role as Lord, appointed by God, at God's right hand, that the exalted Jesus exercises judgment. The importance of recognizing the delegated character of Christ's Lordship is certainly in view in Paul's fullest statement on the point – 1 Cor. 15.24–28. Here Ps. 110.1 is alluded to: 'He (Christ) must reign until he has put all his enemies under his feet' (15.25). Which is then glossed by citing Ps. 8.7: 'For he (God) has put all things in subjection under his feet' (15.27).[28] It would hardly strain the thought to include the role of judgment in the rule thus given to the exalted Christ. But Paul then goes on to make clear that the 'all things' subjected to the Lord Christ do not, of course, include the one who put them in subjection to Christ (15.27). Rather, the end comes when Christ returns the royal authority delegated to him (15.24), and when Christ himself is subjected to God, 'in order that God might be all in all' (15.28).

To put what is in effect the same point from another angle, there is no scope for the thought that Jesus as Judge has replaced God, far less usurped God's role. On the contrary, God is still the Judge, as passages like Rom. 2.2–11, 3.6 and 1 Cor. 5.13 show clearly. In Rom. 2.2–11 it is notable that Paul makes a point of reasserting traditional Jewish emphases that God 'will render to each according to his works' (2.6), and that 'there is no partiality with God' (2.11), that is, in his judgment.[29] And in Rom. 3.6 it is obvious that God's righteousness as Judge is the fundamental axiom from which Paul moves out and which he seeks to defend despite the corollaries which might be drawn from Israel's unfaithfulness (3.3–6). Most striking in this context is Rom. 2.16, where Paul describes 'the day when God is to judge the secrets of humankind in accordance with my gospel through Christ Jesus'. As most commentators agree, the 'through Jesus Christ' is to be taken with the verb 'judge': in that final day God will judge 'through Christ Jesus'. A similar balance is maintained in Rom. 8.31–39. It is God who is 'for us', demonstrated by the giving up of his Son (8.31–32). It is God who justifies, and Christ who intercedes at God's right hand (8.33–34). The love from which nothing can separate us is 'the love of God in Christ Jesus our Lord' (8.39).

It need hardly be said that the more explicit talk of Jesus as *Judge* cannot, or should not be taken independently of Paul's overall treatment of these themes. 2 Cor. 5.10 ('the judgment seat of Christ') should not be regarded as contradictory to or inconsistent with Rom. 14.10 ('the judgment seat of God'). Conceivably different judgments, or rather, different stages in the one (final) judgment are in view (if T. Abr. [A] 13 provides any sort of parallel). But even so, Paul would not want the judgment exercised by *Christ* to be conceived of as any other than the judgment of *God*. That judgment is to be exercised by the exalted Jesus is a way

---

[28] The integration of Ps. 110.1 with Ps. 8.7 is a common feature of early Christian apologetic; see again Dunn, *Christology* 108–9.

[29] See further Dunn, *Romans* 85, 88–9.

of saying that the final judgment of God will be in accord with the character of God as revealed in Jesus. The later Pauline text, 2 Tim. 4.1, makes the same point in its own way: the exhortation is made 'in the presence of God and of Christ Jesus, who is to judge the living and the dead ...', where, by implication, Christ Jesus is the one who speaks and acts for God.

There is no difficulty, then, in recognizing that Paul was well able to hold his christology at this point within the monotheistic framework of his overall theology. God is the final judge, but he shares that judgment with Christ (as also with the saints); he judges through Christ; he judges with reference to and in accordance with the gospel of Christ's death and resurrection. This brings us to the soteriological corollary of this line of thought.

V

The soteriological consequences to any recognition of Jesus' role as Judge also deserve some reflection. For, as noted at the beginning, there seems to be some tension with the thought of justification assured through faith in Christ and the thought of Jesus as Judge also of those who believe. Alternatively expressed, how did Paul hold together the image of Jesus as saviour and deliverer from divine wrath, or as counsel for the defence (Rom. 5.9–10; 1 Thess. 1.10; Rom. 8.34), with the image of Jesus as Judge?

Here again, we should note, the problem was not new. It was unavoidably bound up with the twin thoughts of God's election of Israel and of God's role as final judge. A too simple answer was the assumption that all Israel would be saved. This conviction is the starting point for the famous Mishnah Sanhedrin 10 – 'All Israelites have a share in the world to come' (10.1) – although the developed tradition goes on to list the various exceptions. Others attempted to deal with the problem by declaring that only a 'remnant' of Israel would be saved,[30] or by resorting to a sectarian definition of 'the righteous' (e.g. Psalms of Solomon, Qumran). Others again acknowledged God's judgment on Israel, but distinguished that judgment, as the disciplining of a child by its father, from the punishment of condemnation which non-Israelites experienced.[31] But earlier, the classic prophets had repeatedly to remind Israel that Israel too was *not* exempt from divine judgment for its sins.[32]

---

[30] Details in Dunn, *Romans* 573–4, 638, and more fully in *TDNT* 4.196–214 and *IDBS* 735–6.

[31] Particularly again Pss. Sol. 3.4–16; 7.1–10; 8.27–40; 13.4–11; also Wisd. 11.9–10; 12.22; 16.9–10. Paul seems to have had such passages in mind when he speaks of Israel's 'impenitence' and 'hardness of heart' in Rom. 2.5.

[32] E.g. Isa. 1.2–9; 5.1–30; Jer. 2.33–35; 5.1–9; Ezek. 7.2–27; 24.3–14; Hos. 5.11–12; 6.5; Amos 7.4; 8.4–14; Mic. 2.1–4; 3.9–12 (*ABD* 2.80).

It is important to recognize that Paul was deeply troubled by the same problem. He highlights it in Rom. 3.1–6, as an immediate consequence of his conviction that Israel stands under the same condemnation as all humankind (2.1–3.20): what does the acknowledgment of Israel's faith*less*ness to God say about God's faith*ful*ness to Israel (3.3–4) and about God's role as judge (3.5–6)? And Paul's attempt actually to tackle this problem forms the climax of his theological exposition in Romans (Rom. 9–11), where he tries to integrate the older ideas of God's judgment of wrath on Israel (9.22; 11.7–10, 25, 28, 31) and of Israel reduced to a remnant (9.27–29; 11.5) within an overall divine purpose of faithfulness to Israel and of mercy to all (11.28–32).

The problem of marrying the twofold thought of divine election of Israel with divine judgment on Israel can be focused, of course, in the soteriological pattern of Israel's religion. For the pattern begins from the axiom of divine election; but it goes on from that to expect and require obedience to the law provided by the electing God; and it holds out both promises of extended life to those who obey and warnings of fearful consequences for those who fail to obey. Deuteronomy is the archetypal statement of this soteriology. It was this pattern which was heavily criticised by generations of Christian scholarship as 'legalistic' and more recently reassessed by E.P. Sanders in terms of 'covenantal nomism'.[33] The former perspective can certainly be criticised for failing to appreciate the 'covenantal presupposition' of all Israel's law-keeping. Some would reply that the latter perspective should likewise be criticised for an equivalent failure to appreciate the 'conditionality' of the promise of life upon Israel's obedience.[34] However, a potential *rapprochement* between these two alternatives may be given by describing the role of the law in Jewish understanding as 'a way of life and a way to life'.[35] If so, then a greater consensus can be expected on Israel's soteriological pattern as a two-stage soteriology: final salvation dependent *both* on the initial election of Israel *and* on Israel's consequent obedience to that law, to be demonstrated in the final judgment.

What needs to be brought out more clearly now is that this two-stage soteriology is quite closely parallel to Paul's two-stage soteriology outlined above

---

[33] E.P. Sanders, *Paul and Palestinian Judaism: A Comparison of Patterns of Religion* (London: SCM, 1977).

[34] P. Stuhlmacher, '"Christus Jesus ist hier, der gestorben ist, ja vielmehr, der auch auferweckt ist, der zur Rechten Gottes ist und uns vertritt" [Röm 8.34]' in F. Avemarie & H. Lichtenberger, hrsg., *Auferstehung – Resurrection* (WUNT 135; Tübingen: Mohr Siebeck, 2001) 351–61.

[35] F. Avemarie, *Tora und Leben: Untersuchungen zur Heilsbedeutung der Tora in der frühen rabbinischen Literatur* (WUNT; Tübingen: Mohr/Siebeck, 1996); also 'Erwählung und Vergeltung: Zur optionalen Struktur rabbinischen Soteriologie', *NTS* 45 (1999) 108–26. Stuhlmacher's lecture (n. 34) suggests that Avemarie's work provides the possibility of *rapprochement*. 'Weisung zum Leben und Lebens-Weise' was H. Lichtenberger's summary of Avemarie's findings in 'Das Tora-Verstädnis im Judentum zur Zeit des Paulus', in J.D.G. Dunn, ed., *Paul and the Mosaic Law* (Tübingen: Mohr/Siebeck, 1996) 7–23.

(#III). The determinative effect of God's election in Israel's soteriology seems to be more or less precisely equivalent to the determinative effect of Christ's death for the one who believes (e.g. Rom. 6.3–4; 7.4; 8.3) in Paul's soteriology. If so, then the question inevitably arises: whether the second stage in Paul's soteriology is likewise equivalent to the second stage in Israel's soteriology. In other words, is the role of Jesus as executing judgment on believers within Paul's soteriology just the same as the role of God as executing judgment on Israel within Israel's soteriology?

Here the parallel between Rom. 2.2–16 and 2 Cor. 5.10 cannot be ignored. For myself, I would regard Rom. 2.6–16 as a description of God's final judgment which holds valid both before the gospel and under the gospel: the description of God's judgment as 'through Jesus Christ' and 'in accordance with my gospel' (2.16) is continuous with the description of future justification in 2.12–13.[36] The same judgment is in view when Paul speaks in terms of works good and bad (2.6–7, 9–10) as when he speaks of judgment according to the gospel (2.16). Others, however, would regard 2.12–13 as the old terms of final judgment, prior to the gospel, and superceded by the 'But now apart from the law the righteousness of God has been revealed' of 3.21.[37] Yet the terms of 2 Cor. 5.10 seem to echo those of Rom. 2.6–13 to a significant extent: 'all of us must appear before the judgment seat of Christ, in order that each may receive recompense for what has been done in the body, whether good or evil'. Evidently, the gospel did not change Paul's belief that final judgment will be in reference to what one has done, to one's deeds, good or bad. If, then, Jesus is not only counsel for the defence (Rom. 8.34) but also judge (2 Cor. 5.10), what does that say with regard to Paul's soteriology?

1 Cor. 3.10–15 provides a possible answer: Christ is the indestructible foundation; it will be only the superstructure which is tested (to destruction) by the fire of judgment; and even 'if anyone's work is burned up ... he himself will be saved, but so as by fire' (3.15). That however has something of an echo of the special pleading evident in the earlier Jewish distinction between a suffering (of the righteous) which is disciplinary and a suffering (of sinners) which is destructive. Here again, Paul's two-stage soteriology was faced with the same sort of questions as confronted Israel's two-stage soteriology.

My own attempt to clarify Paul's two-stage soteriology focused on the motif of 'eschatological tension' and 'already/not yet' familiar to students of Paul's theology,[38] already referred to above (#III). There again I was struck by the ex-

---

[36] Cf. P. Stuhlmacher, *Paul's Letter to the Romans* (Louisville: Westminster, 1994) 46; he also notes that 'nowhere in his extant letters does (Paul) draw a systematically rounded picture of the final judgment'.

[37] I have in mind particularly a personal conversation with Friedrich Avemarie in September, 1999.

[38] Dunn, *Theology of Paul* #18.

tent to which this Pauline pattern fitted his treatment of Israel in Rom. 9–11: Israel as the chosen of God, but caught between the already and the not yet, between its own (temporary) disobedience and God's final purpose of mercy.[39] In both cases what is in view is a process begun (election, conversion/baptism), but not yet completed, whose completion is not yet evident and has yet to be secured.

Most striking in Paul's treatment are the frequent 'if's which feature in his exhortations to himself and his fellow believers. I cite only the most obvious. 'If (*ei*) you (believers) live in accordance with the flesh, you will certainly die; but if (*ei*) by the Spirit you put to death the deeds of the body, you will live' (Rom. 8.13; cf. Gal. 6.8). 'Heirs of God and heirs together with Christ, provided that (*eiper*) we suffer with him in order that we might also be glorified with him' (Rom. 8.17).[40] 'If God did not spare the natural branches, neither will he spare you ... to you the goodness of God, if (*ean*) you continue in that goodness' (Rom. 11.21–22). 'The gospel ... through which you are being saved, if (*ei*) you hold it firmly ... unless (*ektos ei mē*) you have believed in vain' (1 Cor. 15.2). '(I want) to know him (Christ) and the power of his resurrection and the fellowship of his sufferings, being conformed to his death, if somehow (*ei pōs*) I may attain to the resurrection from the dead' (Phil. 3.10–11).

In the face of such repeated reserve one can only ask whether the Pauline 'if' is not equivalent to the Jewish 'if you obey the law'. 'Conditionality' may not be the best word to describe this note of caution in Paul, but the 'if' certainly should have a place in any attempts to restate his soteriology. And, linked in to the eschatological tension, or eschatological reserve, it is hard to escape the conclusion that Paul both understood salvation to be in some degree at least dependent on continuing perseverance, and allowed the possibility that the process of salvation would not be completed in some/many(?) cases.[41] Of course, the 'if' needs to be held together with the confidence which Paul elsewhere expresses in God completing what he has begun; but a text like Phil. 1.6 needs to be balanced with its parallel in Gal. 3.3, where the confidence of the former is matched by the anxiety of the latter (cf. Gal. 1.6; 5.4); and the assurance of the final scene in Rom. 8.28–39 neither denies nor cancels out the earlier 'if's (8.13, 17). A theoretical solution is to argue that those who do not persevere simply demonstrate that they never began;[42] but that is the solution of the more black and white theologian who wrote 1 John (2.19) and does not reflect the much more nuanced and cautious theology of Paul; nor does it do any justice to the earnestness of his exhortations to his readers on the need to live out their faith to the end. Alterna-

---

[39] Dunn, *Theology of Paul* #19.
[40] See further Dunn, *Theology of Paul* 482–7.
[41] See again Dunn, *Theology of Paul* 497–8.
[42] J.M. Gundry Volf, *Paul and Perseverence: Staying in and Falling Away* (WUNT; Tübingen: Mohr/Siebeck, 1990).

tively, a solution is possible in terms of universalism and a theology of the cross which effects 'the restoration of all things';[43] though a similar universalistic argument in reference to Israel's two-stage soteriology could be mounted on Rom. 11.28–32; and still it is difficult to correlate such universal 'universalism' with passages like Rom. 2.8–9 and 14.15, 1 Cor. 9.27 and 2 Thess. 1.7–9.

In short, it is difficult to avoid seeing Paul's two-stage soteriology as parallel to Israel's two-stage soteriology. This means recognizing a similar degree of assurance resting on God's election in both cases, both able to cry triumphantly in reference to the final judgment, 'Who will bring charges against the elect of God?' (Rom. 8.33). But also a similar note of reserve. The assurance should not become presumption, the fault for which Paul criticised his fellow Jews (Rom. 2.17–29), and against which he warned his fellow believers (11.17–24). Rather it should become the basis and source for living in accordance with the Spirit and thus fulfilling the requirement of the law (8.1–4). For Paul, of course, there were crucial differences between the two, in the effect of Christ's death and resurrection, and in the gift of the Spirit. But the fact that he envisaged Jesus also in the role of eschatological judge should be enough to remind us that a clear note of reserve remained part of his soteriology.

VI

To sum up. Jesus as Judge is a too much neglected feature of earliest Christian theology, and particularly of Pauline theology. The importance of the motif needs, therefore, to be restated.

First, in relation to christology and to Paul's conception of God. On this point we may simply note, that for Paul Christ absorbs all the key roles in final judgment attributed in Second Temple Judaism to other salvific figures, exalted human or heavenly. The role(s) attributed to Jesus in no way infringe the absoluteness of God's prerogative as final Judge as well as initial Creator. But they do express the early Christian conviction that the final judgment would be in accord with the saving event enacted in Jesus' death and resurrection, that the character of God's final judgment would be of a piece with his righteousness and love expressed in and through Jesus. Not only so, but if the language can be pressed, they express the assurance that Jesus himself would be involved in that final reckoning, as agent for and intercessor before God.

Second, in relation to Paul's soteriology. Here the thought of Jesus as Judge underlines the 'not-yet'ness of Paul's soteriology, the 'if's which seem to be inte-

---

[43] Moltmann, *Coming of God* 250–5. Cf. T. Eskola, *Theodicy and Predestination in Pauline Soteriology* (WUNT; Tübingen: Mohr/Siebeck, 1998). Contrast Stuhlmacher: 'For Paul there was no salvation possible in the case of a believer who impugns or repudiates the gospel (Gal. 1.8; 2 Cor. 11.4, 13–15; Phil. 3.18f.)' (*Romans* 47).

gral to his soteriology. Whether the warning that Jesus will be Judge is entirely equivalent to the warnings to Israel of old that the Israel chosen by God is itself liable to judgment for its disobedience, is something which requires further study. And whether there is a degree of provisionality in Paul's understanding of the process of salvation equivalent to the provisionality in Israel's covenantal nomism, is also something that should be further discussed. But, at the very least, no one should take lightly the moral seriousness of Paul's own call for 'the obedience of faith'.

Chapter 19

Noch einmal 'Works of the Law':

The Dialogue Continues

Debating with Heikki Räisänen over issues of Pauline interpretation has been one of the most stimulating and enjoyable experiences of my work on Paul. We have both turned our attention elsewhere since then, but the debates and disputes have continued in the meantime and I hope Heikki will find some pleasure in this brief attempt to re-engage in some of our old dialogue.

The overlap of our interests was quite extensive,[1] but hopefully he will forgive me if I return to a question which became a particular concern of mine and which seems at times to have generated more heat than light – what Paul meant by the phrase 'works of the law'. The ongoing debate has retained a surprising vitality, principally for two reasons, I suppose. One is that what I chanced to describe as 'the new perspective on Paul'[2] has now been around long enough for a new generation of scholars to treat it as one of the more 'established' options, and thus as calling for fresh scrutiny in its turn – just as my own generation, instructed by Sanders[3] and challenged by Räisänen,[4] found it necessary to subject the established 'Lutheran paradigm' to fresh scrutiny. The second is, of course, the publication of the Qumran text 4QMMT, with, at last(!), an example of the very phrase 'the works of the law' in a document nearly contemporaneous with Paul, or at least referring to an attitude to the law which was contemporary with Paul and which was evidently summed up by the same phrase, 'the works of the law'.

Since my earlier formulations on the subject of 'works of the law' in Paul can be included among those which may have generated more heat than light, at least in some circles,[5] it will perhaps not be regarded as too self-indulgent if I

---

[1] As indicated already by the overlap in topics between my *Jesus, Paul and the Law: Studies in Mark and Galatians* (London: SPCK, 1990) and Heikki's *Jesus, Paul and Torah: Collected Essays* (JSNTS 43; Sheffield: JSOT, 1992).

[2] 'The New Perspective on Paul', *BJRL* 65 (1983) 95–122, reprinted in *Jesus, Paul and the Law* 183–206 [=ch. 2 above].

[3] E.P. Sanders, *Paul and Palestinian Judaism* (London: SCM, 1977).

[4] In re-reading Heikki's *Paul and the Law* (WUNT 29; Tübingen: Mohr-Siebeck, 1983) I was delighted to note again the extent of our agreement in his chapter on 'The antithesis between works of the law and faith in Christ' (162–77), though we began to drift apart thereafter (177–91).

begin by explaining how I came to my view of the phrase's reference in Paul. Since I subsequently found the usage of 4QMMT to be supportive of my interpretation of Paul's phrase, it will then be necessary to enter into dialogue with those who have found 4QMMT telling a somewhat different story. It will also be appropriate to reflect a little further on what 'works of the law' and the 'works' by reference to which final judgment will be rendered have to do with each other in Paul's scheme of things.

I

The observation regarding 'works of the law' stemmed from my initial reaction to E. P. Sanders' *Paul and Palestinian Judaism*, as outlined in the 1982 T. W. Manson Memorial Lecture, 'The New Perspective on Paul'. In that lecture I focused on Gal. 2.16, which can certainly be classified as the first extant use of the phrase 'works of the law' in Paul's writings and theology.[6] What struck me then was the fact that Paul introduces the phrase in what is most obviously to be understood as Paul's summing up of the lessons he had learned through the disputes which he has just described, the disputes in Jerusalem on whether Titus should be circumcised (Gal. 2.1–10), and the dispute at Antioch arising from Peter's refusal to eat with Gentile believers (2.11–14). If others prefer to say that Gal. 2.16 represents what Paul had always stood for and what motivated the stands he took at Jerusalem and at Antioch, it makes little difference for the point I am making.[7] For on the present point the outcome is more or less the same: Paul introduced the phrase 'works of the law' to express a key element of the principles on which or for which he had fought to safeguard 'the truth of the gospel' (2.5, 14) at Jerusalem and Antioch.

I stress the importance of thus setting in context Paul's first reference to 'works of the law'. It has been a sound principle of hermeneutics since the Re-

---

[5] For earlier attempts to clarify misunderstandings: Additional Note in *Jesus, Paul and the Law* 206–14; in response to C. E. B. Cranfield, '"The Works of the Law" in the Epistle to the Romans', *JSNT* 43 (1991) 89–101, see my 'Yet Once More – "The Works of the Law": A Response', *JSNT* 46 (1992) 99–117 [=ch. 8 above]; in response to P. Stuhlmacher, *Biblische Theologie des Neuen Testaments 1: Grundlegung von Jesus zu Paulus* (Göttingen: Vandenhoeck & Ruprecht, 1992) 264, see my *The Theology of Paul the Apostle* (Grand Rapids: Eerdmans/Edinburgh: T. & T. Clark, 1998) 358 n.97.

[6] The Additional Note in *Jesus, Paul and the Law* 206–9 already responded to Heikki's response to that lecture, 'Galatians 2.16 and Paul's Break with Judaism', *NTS* 31 (1985) 543–53, reprinted *Jesus, Paul and Torah* 112–26. I still relish his slightly backhanded compliment that 'Dunn comes close to describing Paul's position as Paul himself wished it to be understood' (*Jesus, Paul and Torah* 125). For my more recent exposition see *Theology of Paul* particularly 354–79, bibliography on 335.

[7] Though Räisänen and I agree that Paul's theology regarding 'works of the law' was decisively shaped by the events at Jerusalem and Antioch.

naissance that in order for a text to be properly understood it must first be read in context.[8] But too often still we find that a text like Gal. 2.16 is seized upon, rather like a prize artefact in an early (pre-scientific) archaeological enterprise, regardless of its precisely stratified location (historical context), and plundered for the theological insight it brings to the profundities of Pauline theology understood as timeless verities independent of particular historical circumstances. Paul's central theological affirmations may indeed prove to be so ('timeless verities ...'), in one degree or other. But *the first task is still to read Gal. 2.16 in the sequence of thought which gave rise to its formulation.* The opening hermeneutical gambit has to be the recognition that the phrase 'works of the law' first emerged in what Paul obviously intended as an expression of 'the truth of the gospel' which had come under such threat at Jerusalem and Antioch.

The point, of course, is that the issues in both cases (Jerusalem and Antioch) focused on what religious Jews, at least since the Maccabean resistance, had regarded as fundamental and essential to the practice of their Judaism[9] – viz. circumcision and food laws (I need cite no more than 1 Macc. 1.60–63). Evidently the traditional Jews within the ranks of the believers in Messiah Jesus[10] insisted that these laws continued to be inviolable for all Jews, and that this fact must govern their relations with such Gentiles as also came to belief in this Jesus.[11] It can hardly be accidental, then, that Paul chooses to introduce just this phrase, 'works of the law', in his summing up of what was at stake in these two incidents. The clear implication of 2.16 is that Paul saw the traditionalists as requiring 'works of the law' in addition to faith in Jesus Christ.[12] Which is also to say that in formulating the phrase 'works of the law' he had in mind particularly circumci-

---

[8] Thus Schleiermacher, the father of modern hermeneutics: 'The meaning of each word of a passage must be determined by the context in which it serves' (*Hermeneutics: The Handwritten Manuscripts by F. D. E. Schleiermacher*, ed. H. Kimmerle [ET Missoula, MT: Scholars, 1977] excerpted by from K. Mueller-Vollmer, *The Hermeneutics Reader* [New York: Continuum, 1994] 90).

[9] One of the weaknesses of Räisänen's response to my 'New Perspective' article was that he used 'Judaism' in a too monolithic, undifferentiated way ('Paul's break with Judaism'). We need not go all the way with those who think it more appropriate to speak in terms of many/several Judaisms (plural) for the period. It is enough to note the tension within the terms 'Jew' and 'Judaism' as denoting either an ethnic or a religious identity or both. See further my *Theology of Paul* 347–9; S.J.D. Cohen, *The Beginnings of Jewishness: Boundaries, Varieties, Uncertainties* (Berkeley: University of California, 1999) particularly chs. 3–4.

[10] They must be so described despite Paul describing them dismissively as 'false brothers' (2.4) and allusively as 'some from James' (2.12); but they were certainly regarded in Jerusalem as disciples of Messiah Jesus (cf. 2.15–16).

[11] It is not necessary to achieve sharper resolution in thus referring to the incident at Antioch. What is clear is that the issues focused on the rights and wrongs of Jews eating with Gentiles, as determined by reference to the various food laws which governed the social relations of the meal table.

[12] It will be noted that I remain unpersuaded by the north American fashion to take *pistis Christou* as a reference to 'the faith of Christ'; see *Theology of Paul* 379–85, and further below n.39.

sion and food laws. That is not to say Paul had only these particular laws in mind; some have so read the wording of my 1983 article,[13] but I hope subsequent clarifications have made the point plain.[14] The point, once again, is that these two laws *in particular* had brought the issue summed up in Gal. 2.16 to clarity or at least to focus for Paul. *Whatever else he had in mind when he wrote of 'works of the law' in 2.16, Paul certainly had in mind circumcision and food laws.* I would hope that that observation is beyond reasonable dispute.

The question would then be, why these two in particular? Once again, the immediate context indicates the answer, since the above logic works in reverse. Paul had in mind just these two, because it was precisely these two which were being insisted on as essential in addition to faith in Christ. That is, insisted on as rules which must govern relations between believing Jews and believing Gentiles. It is simply impossible in the context of Galatians 2 to avoid the Jew/Gentile issue. The 'works of the law' which Paul had particularly in mind were rules which, unless embraced by Gentiles, should prevent full acceptance of these Gentiles. In other words, it still seems to me impossible to avoid the strong inference here that the works of the law in view were seen as important by the Jewish traditionalists for what I have called their 'boundary defining function'. They marked out the distinction between the chosen nation and all others (= Gentiles). And by observing these laws, religious Jews maintained the boundary between Israel and the other nations. That is to say, they safeguarded Israel's set-apartness to God, Israel's holy status as God's covenant people.[15]

It is certainly open to exegetes and interpreters to argue out from these basic observations. (1) That 'works of the law' must include all and any laws to which obedience is required as a necessary part of the salvation process. (2) That the principle articulated in Gal. 2.16 is deeper or broader than simply the issue of relations between Jewish and Gentile believers in Messiah Jesus. I would have no quarrel in either case. Where I want to stand firm, however, is in insisting that the context leading up to Gal. 2.16 be given more weight in determining the immediate thrust of 2.16. Moreover, if the reference of 2.16 is deepened or broadened to some more fundamental principle, I also want to insist that the immedi-

---

[13] *BJRL* 65 (1983) 107 = *Jesus, Paul and the Law* 191 [=108 above].

[14] See again n. 5 above. J.C.R. de Roo, 'The Concept of "Works of the Law" in Jewish and Christian Literature', in S.E. Porter & B.W.R. Pearson, eds., *Christian-Jewish Relations Through the Centuries* (JSNTS 192; Sheffield: Sheffield Academic, 2000) 116–47, multiplies the confusion by criticising me for 'reducing the concept of "works of the law" to a mere emphasis on ritual observances' (137). Her '*mere* emphasis' is revealing and fails to appreciate how 'ritual observances' like circumcision and food laws can become make or break test cases of commitment and identity (1 Macc. 1.60–63!); nor do I intend a distinction between ethical and ritual such as she implies (see again my *Theology of Paul* 358–9).

[15] I don't think this point is much in dispute; but the attitude is well illustrated, e.g., by Lev. 20.22–26; Num. 23.9; and the attitude of Peter and the other Jewish believers which had to be overcome in Acts 10 (see again *Theology of Paul* 355–6).

ate reference to relations between Jewish and Gentile believers be not marginalized or lost to sight.

Let me say a little more on the last point. Some have expressed surprise that I could diminish Paul's hostility to the law to a hostility towards an attitude to the law or an attitude encouraged by the law.[16] I accept that 'attitude' is a weak word for what I see to have been at stake. And I see that the term has allowed a too simplistic antithesis between 'attitude' and 'conduct expressive of that attitude'. So let me attempt to make my point more clearly.

My argument is that Paul in or as a result of his conversion reacted particularly against Jewish exclusivism.[17] Not against the fundamental belief in Israel's election as such. But against what had become a more and more dominant feature of Jewish belief in the preceding two hundred years – a zeal for the law which treated other Jews as sinners and apostates in effect, and, in extension of the same zeal, regarded Gentiles as 'beyond the pale'.[18] Paul expresses this in Galatians in describing his conversion as a turning from such zeal to the conviction that he had been called to take the news of God's Son to the Gentiles (1.13–16) – as complete a 180 degree about-turn as one could conceive. My point here is that we should not underestimate the seriousness of the exclusivistic attitude against which Paul now reacted. We have been reminded of just how serious such an attitude can be in the horrors of the Holocaust and more recently in the horrific savagery of the intra-ethnic and inter-ethnic conflicts of former Yugoslavia and Rwanda. It was precisely the same attitude, the same 'zeal' which had inspired Paul himself to 'seek to destroy the church of God' (1.13; Phil. 3.6). The seriousness of an exclusivist attitude to the law is that it leads inexorably to exclusivist conduct. It is a kind of fundamentalism which can only safeguard the correctness of its belief by persecuting those who disagree or by seeking to eliminate (through conversion or otherwise) those who hold divergent views. That sort of exclusivism can produce a complete spectrum of violence, from the most subtle of social pressure to outright force. It was that sort of 'attitude to the law' which Paul came to abhor.[19]

---

[16] Including Räisänen, *Jesus, Paul and Torah* 122.

[17] To avoid misunderstanding I should make it clear that I am *not* posing the old antithesis of Jewish particularism versus Christian universalism; see my 'Was Judaism Particularist or Universalist?', in J. Neusner & A.J. Avery-Peck, eds., *Judaism in Late Antiquity Part Three, Where we Stand: Issues and Debates in Ancient Judaism Vol. Two* (Leiden: Brill, 1999) 57–73.

[18] T.L. Donaldson, *Paul and the Gentiles: Remapping the Apostle's Convictional World* (Minneapolis: Fortress, 1997) argues that prior to his conversion Paul had been interested in attracting proselytes to Judaism (e.g. 78). In my view this gives unjustified weight to a possible interpretation of Gal. 5.11 at the expense of the far weightier considerations which flow from the fact of Paul's 'zeal' as a persecutor (see e.g. my *Theology of Paul* 346–54).

[19] V.M. Smiles, *The Gospel and the Law in Galatia: Paul's Response to Jewish-Christian Separatism and the Threat of Galatian Apostasy* (Collegeville, Minn.: Liturgical, 1998) recognizes that 'Jewish-Christian separatism' was the problem addressed by Paul, but chides me with confusing the 'social function' of the law and its 'theological function'. Instead he somehow finds

Again we do not need to clarify here how soon Paul reached these convictions. Nor whether he entered the confrontations at Jerusalem and Antioch with these convictions already clearly drawn, including any formulation involving 'works of the law'. It should be clear, however, that the crisis for Paul in these confrontations was occasioned by the outworking of the same old exclusivism within the ranks of believers in Messiah Jesus: uncircumcised, unobservant Gentile believers should be 'excluded, regarded as outsiders' (*ekkleiō* – Gal. 4.17). At Jerusalem and Antioch Paul resisted this policy with the same forthrightness as he had enacted it prior to his conversion. And in 2.16 it is that exclusivism which is encapsulated in one degree or other in the phrase 'works of the law'. To Peter he says, or would like to have said in person, 'You must agree that we cannot regard such exclusivist practices as consonant with the gospel; we cannot think that believing Gentiles should either still suffer from such an attitude/ practices or should themselves be expected to order their own conduct accordingly'.

In short, whatever else Gal. 2.16 may mean or may be taken to mean, it certainly was intended to warn against 'works of the law' as constituting or erecting barriers to the free extension of God's grace to Gentiles. The phrase did not include any thought evident on the surface of the argument that 'works of the law' were necessary to gain initial acceptance by God. What Paul objected to was the thought that the law, as expressed particularly in or epitomised by circumcision and food laws, continued to be a *sine qua non* requirement for believing Jews in governing their acceptance of and relations with believing Gentiles, or in a word, that works of the law were necessary in addition to faith in Christ.

II

One of the most forceful challenges to this view of works of the law (*erga nomou*) has been mounted by Michael Bachmann. In a 1993 article he had already argued that 'works of the law' refers to the regulations of the law itself.[20] His most weighty arguments are that references to *erga* elsewhere (as in Jas. 2.14–26) are not relevant, since the Pauline phrase is *erga nomou*, not 'works' of a person. On the analogy of John 6.28–29 ('the work(s) of God') the fuller

---

Galatians contesting 'the law's claims on the entire world' (125–8), which reads into Galatians more than the text can bear.

[20] 'Rechtfertigung und Gestezeswerke bei Paulus', *TZ* 49 (1993) 1–33, reprinted in *Antijudaismus im Galaterbrief: Exegetische Studien zu einem polemischen Schreiben und zur Theologie des Apostels Paulus* (NTOA 40; Freiburg: Universitätsverlag, 1999) 1–31: 'Paulus meint mit dem Ausdruck "Werke des Gesetzes" nicht etwas, was auf der durch das Tun gemäss den Regelungen des Gesetzes markierten Ebene liegt, insbesondere nicht: Gebotserfüllungen, sondern er meint mit dem Syntagma "Werke des Gesetzes" die Regelungen des Gesetzes selber' (14).

phrase should be understood as the works commanded by the law/God, or simply as the commands of the law/God. Moreover, 'works of the law' and 'law' often stand in parallel in Paul (e.g. Rom. 3.21 and 28), implying that by 'works of the law' Paul means nothing other than the regulations of the law.

In a subsequent article Bachmann presses the now famous 4QMMT text into service on behalf of the same thesis.[21] Rather like Gal. 2.16, the key phrase, *ma'ase hatorah*, is used to sum up the case being made in the body of the letter: 'We have also written to you some of the works of the Torah (*miqsat ma'ase hatorah*) which we think are good for you and for your people' (4QMMT C26–27).[22] The allusion back to the beginning of the second/main section of the text is beyond dispute: 'these are some of our rulings (*miqsat debarenu*) ... which are ... the works (*ma'asim*) ...' (B1).[23] What clearly are in view are the intervening content of the letter, the 'series of halakhic rulings, chiefly relating to temple, priesthood, sacrifices and purity'.[24] Bachmann accepts my account on this point, referring particularly to the further summary phrase, 'some of our words/rulings (*miqsat debarenu*)', in C30.[25] His point, however, is, once again, that what is in view is not the '*fulfilment* of these regulations ... but the specific *judgment* of halakhic questions on the part of this "Qumran people"'.[26] The 'works' in question are nothing other than the sect's halakhoth.[27]

The argument has obvious weight. Bachmann cites Qimron and Strugnell as noting the singular *ma'aseh* in Exod. 18.20 in reference to the law, and in Second Temple Jewish writings the 'widespread use of the plural *ma'asim* as a term designating the laws or commandments'.[28] Qimron & Strugnell translate the phrase *ma'ase hatorah* as 'the precepts of the Torah', and Vermes as 'the observances of

---

[21] '4QMMT und Galaterbrief, *ma'ase hatorah* und *ERGA NOMOU*', *ZNW* 89 (1998) 91–113; reprinted in *Antijudaismus* 33–56; in response to my own '4QMMT and Galatians', *NTS* 43 (1997) 147–53.

[22] I follow the verse numbering in E. Qimron & J. Strugnell, *Miqsat Ma'ase Ha-Torah* (*DJD* 10.5; Oxford: Clarendon, 1994), but will refer also to F. García Martínez, *The Dead Sea Scrolls Translated : The Qumran Texts in English* (Leiden: Brill/Grand Rapids: Eerdmans, 1994, ²1996); G. Vermes, *The Complete Dead Sea Scrolls in English* (London: Penguin, 1997).

[23] The various translations fill out the text differently: e.g. García Martínez – 'These are some of our regulations [concerning the law of G]od, which are pa[rt of] the works we [are examining and] they [a]ll relate to [...] and purity'; Vermes –'These are some of our teachings [ ] which are [the] works which w[e think and a]ll of them concern [ ] and the purity of ...'.

[24] Bachmann here quotes my own summary (Dunn, '4QMMT' 150).

[25] In arguing that *ma'ase hatorah* in C27 refers to the deeds of the kings of Israel (C23) and not the preceding halakhic rulings of B, de Roo ('Concept' 142–4) ignores both the bracketing phrases (B1 and C30) and the full sentence (C26–27), 'We have also written to you some of the works of the Torah (*miqsat ma'ase hatorah*) which we think are good for you and for your people', which makes clear the allusion back to the rulings in B.

[26] Bachmann, '4QMMT' 43–4.

[27] Bachmann, '4QMMT' 47.

[28] Bachmann, '4QMMT' 45–6; referring to Qimron & Strugnell, 'Miqsat Ma'ase Ha-Torah' 139.

the Law'. García Martínez initially followed Qimron and Strugnell, but in his second edition changed to 'the works of the Torah'.[29]

My only concern is that Bachmann is driving a wedge between two meanings of *ma'aseh* / *ma'asim* which is quite unjustified. He treats what is in effect a spectrum of meaning as two disconnected and separate meanings. But the root meaning of *'asah* is 'to do, make'. And the only reason why *ma'aseh* can refer to 'precept' is because what is in mind is *the conduct and actions thus prescribed*. It would be more accurate to translate *ma'aseh* as 'prescribed deed', since it is an extended sense of the basic sense 'deed'. Vermes' 'observance' catches the sense quite well, given that 'observance' has more or less the same ambiguity or spectrum of meaning as *ma'aseh*.[30] The point should have been plain from Exod. 18.20: 'teach them the statutes and instructions (*hatoroth*), and make known to them the way they are to go (*yelekhu*) and the things (*hama'ase*) they are to do (*ya'asun*)' (NRSV). The last phrase clearly has in mind 'the deeds prescribed which they are to do'. To drive a wedge between 'precept/prescription' and 'deed (prescribed)', as though the former could be grasped without thought of the latter, puts a distinction between a regulation and its fulfilment which is quite foreign to the thought.[31]

Similarly with 4QMMT. It should surely be self-evident that the writers of 4QMMT were not simply trying to achieve an act of intellectual persuasion, merely to convince the addressees to accept the legitimacy of the halakhic rulings contained in the letter. Here again the term itself, halakhah (from *halakh*, 'to walk'), should be given its proper weight: *halakhoth* refers to rulings on how they are to walk (Exod. 18.20 – *yelekhu*). These 'rulings' indicated how the Torah should be *observed in conduct* in the various matters of disputed practice. What the letter writer(s) wanted was to convince the addressees to follow the sect's halakhoth. So too, the hope held out at the end of the letter is that 'at the end of time, you may rejoice in finding that some of our words/practices (*miqsat debarenu*) are true/correct. And it shall be reckoned to you for righteousness in doing what is upright and good before him' (C30–31). Once again it is important to recall that *dabar* has a spectrum of meaning – 'word, saying, matter (the thing about which one speaks)'. The hope is clearly that those addressed will find that 'some of our words/rulings' are true *by doing them*, by following the sect's halak-

---

[29] I recounted García Martínez's change of mind in Dunn, '4QMMT' 150 [=342 above].

[30] Similarly J.L. Martyn, *Galatians* (AB 33A; New York: Doubleday, 1997), translates *erga nomou* as 'observance of the Law' (ad loc.).

[31] De Roo makes a similar mistake by arguing solely for the sense 'work' or 'deed' in sharp distinction from 'precept' or 'ruling' ('Concept' 138–44); my formulation in *The Partings of the Ways between Christianity and Judaism* (London: SCM, 1991) 136 (cited by de Roo 139) has evidently contributed to the confusion, though the context should have made clear that no antithesis between precept and deed was intended. See also D. Flusser, 'Die Gesetzeswerke in Qumran und bei Paulus', in H. Cancik, et al., eds., *Geschichte – Tradition – Reflexion: Band I Judentum*, M. Hengel FS (Tübingen: Mohr-Siebeck, 1996) 395–403.

hoth.[32] Assuredly the hope was not that those addressed would be 'reckoned righteous' simply by virtue of changing their minds on some disputed points. Only if they did 'what is upright and good before him', that is, by *doing* what the sect commended, could they hope for final vindication.

The point is the same with regard to Paul's use of the phrase, 'works of the law'. How did Paul's opponents understand 'justification by works of the law (*ex ergōn nomou*)'? Surely not simply that justification would be granted on the basis of having the law, the regulations of the law understood as a kind of talisman or amulet. As I noted in commenting on Rom. 2.13, Paul's observation that 'not the hearers of the law are just before God but the doers of the law shall be justified' was one which no scripture-instructed Jew would dispute.[33] At this point, the issue was not *whether* the law should be 'done', but *how* it should be done.[34] My objection to Bachmann is not that he is wrong to affirm that 'works of the law' in Paul can mean the 'regulations of the law'. My objection is rather that he denies that the phrase *also* refers to the implementation of these regulations in daily living. No more than at Qumran would the hope disputed in Gal. 2.16, or Rom. 3.20, 28, be for final vindication on the basis of having been persuaded concerning certain halakhic niceties. The hope was rather that a life lived in accordance with the law (manifesting the works of the law) would be vindicated by God.

Bachmann makes a good deal of the much puzzled-over Gal. 3.10.[35] The puzzle is how Paul can regard those who are 'from works of the law' (*ex ergōn nomou*) as 'under a curse'. It is the usual interpretation of 'works of the law', as referring to *performance* of the law, which causes the problem, since scripture explicitly pronounces the curse on all who *fail* to perform the law (3.10b). In contrast, Bachmann thinks that to understand 'works of the law' as referring only to the regulations of the law resolves the puzzle: those who define themselves by reference to such regulations can be said to be under the curse precisely by virtue of their *failure* to fulfil these regulations. I might respond by pointing out that such quite traditional reasoning imports a consideration which is not present in the text: the logic that it is impossible for anyone to fulfil the law (therefore all are under the curse) has to be imported into the text. But that is another issue which I cannot enter into here.[36]

---

[32] Qimron & Strugnell translate 'some our practices' (C30).

[33] *Romans* (WBC 38; Dallas: Word, 1988) 97; see again Flusser, 'Gesetzeswerke'.

[34] Paul sees faith, the Spirit and love as the key to the 'how' (Rom 3:31; 8:4; 13:8–10; Gal 5:14); see further my *Theology of Paul* ch. 8; see also C. Burchard, 'Nicht aus Werken des Gesetzes, sondern aus Glauben an Jesus Christus – seit wann?', in H. Cancik, et al., eds., *Geschichte – Tradition – Reflexion: Band III Frühes Christentum*, M. Hengel FS (Tübingen: Mohr-Siebeck, 1996) 405–15.

[35] Bachmann, '4QMMT' 53–5, referring back to the fuller exposition of 'Rechtfertigung' 23–6.

[36] See already my *Galatians* (BNTC; London: A. & C. Black, 1993) 170–4; *Theology of Paul* 361–2.

The only point I need to make here is the same point already made above. I agree that *hosoi ex ergōn nomou* can be well explicated as 'those who define themselves by reference to the *erga nomou*'. But that must mean that they define themselves in terms of their *obedience* to the law. What sense does it make to envisage Jews who defined themselves by reference to the law of circumcision but who excluded thereby the affirmation that they themselves had, of course, been circumcised? When Paul categorizes Jews as 'the circumcision (*he peritomē*)'[37] he hardly refers to an intellectual appreciation of the rite's significance as distinguished from the performance of the rite itself. The phrase does indeed denote those who defined themselves by reference to *erga nomou*. But it must mean those who defined themselves over against others (Gentiles, and other Jews?) in terms of the halakhoth by which they lived. This is the basis for my own interpretation of Gal. 3.10, which understands Paul to mean that the very act and life-style of defining oneself over against others in a condemnatory and dismissive (exclusive) way is itself a failure to live out what the book of the law envisaged (cf. Rom. 9.31–32).[38] But here again to pursue that debate would take us too far from our present, necessarily circumscribed task.

In short, Bachmann's attempt to resolve the issue of what Paul meant by 'the works of the law' must be judged as misconceived. Not because he has advocated an inadmissable sense for the term. Not at all. But because he has thought it possible to distinguish and separate this sense ('the regulations of the law') from the sense of obeying these regulations ('doing what the law requires'). Paul in turn assuredly did not understand those *ek pisteōs* as those who cherished a particular opinion about Christ.[39] *Hoi ek pisteōs* were those who expressed and lived out of faith, as had Abraham before them (Rom. 4.16; Gal. 3.7–9), and who could therefore be defined in terms of that faith.

III

A different critique has been offered by Tom Wright – basically that the parallel argued between Paul's use of *erga nomou* and 4QMMT C27 is disproportionate.[40] (1) 'MMT defines one group of Jews over against the rest. The "works"

---

[37] Rom 2:26–27; 3:30; 4:9; Gal 2:7–9; Col 3:11.

[38] See again n. 36 above.

[39] Here I am tempted to point out the parallel between Bachmann's interpretation of *erga nomou* and the popular 'faith of Christ' interpretation of *pistis Christou*. In both cases what would be in view was the means to salvation (regulations, Christ' faithfulness), but not its implementation (deeds, faith). In contrast, my own view is that in the one case what is in view is not simply the halakhah but its observance seen as necessary, in the other not simply a saving Christ but the means by which that saving act becomes effectual in individual cases.

[40] N.T. Wright, 'Paul and Qumran', *Bible Review* 14/5 (1998) 18, 54; Wright's original, working title was '4QMMT and Paul: What Sort of "Works"?'.

which Paul opposes, however, define all Jews and proselytes over against the gentile or pagan world'. (2) MMT is concerned with 'highly tuned postbiblical regulations' regarding animal foetuses, banning the blind and lame from the Temple, the purity or otherwise of streams of liquid, and such like; whereas Paul is concerned with 'the biblical marks of Jewish identity (circumcision, sabbath, food laws)'. (3) MMT's regulations refer to the Jerusalem Temple and its purity. But neither Paul nor his opponents mention the Temple itself, or the purity codes required for its operation. The two situations are related 'only very obliquely'.

All of which distinguishing detail is quite correct. But Wright nevertheless misses the fuller and more fundamental parallel involved. That parallel is indicated not only by the phrase 'works of the law', but by two of the other points of contact between MMT and Galatians to which I had directed attention.[41] (1) The writers of MMT remind the addressees that 'we have separated ourselves from the multitude of the people [and from all their impurity]' (Qimron & Strugnell C7).[42] The letter itself is obviously intended at least in some measure to provide an explanation of why they had thus 'separated' themselves. The verb used is precisely equivalent to the verb used by Paul to describe the action of Peter, followed by the other Jewish believers, who 'separated himself (*aphōrizen heauton*)' from the Gentile believers in Antioch, having previously eaten with them (Gal. 2.12–13). The point is that the attitude behind both 'separations' is the same. It is true that the Qumranites 'separated' themselves from the rest of Israel, whereas Peter and the other Jewish believers 'separated' themselves from the Gentile believers. But in each case the primary concern on the part of the 'separatists' was their own purity: they 'separated' because they feared the defilement which would be contracted by associating with those who did not maintain the same degree of purity.[43] In short, the motivation and theological rationale were the same in MMT and Antioch: that it was necessary for Torah-true, covenant-loyal Jews to separate themselves from impurity, whether the impurity of apostate Jews or the impurity of Gentiles. That is what Paul objected to.

---

[41] Dunn. '4QMMT' 147–8, 151–2 [= 339–40, 343–4 above].

[42] Whether Qimron & Strugnell's completion of the lacuna is correct or not, the overall concern of MMT with purity issues is hardly disputable.

[43] The point probably needs to be repeated that the laws of clean and unclean were both essentially purity concerns, and reflected precisely the separation of Israel from the nations (Lev. 20.24–26; Acts 10.14–15, 28). Since purity was an issue correlated directly with the Temple (to be pure enough to take part in the Temple ritual) it is worth noting that such purity concerns were evidently a factor determining table fellowship not only within the land of Israel (Pharisees and Jesus as 'eating with taxcollectors and sinners') but also beyond beyond (Romans 14). See further my *Partings* 107–13, 130–4; also *Romans* 818–9, 825–6; and the discussion of purity concerns among the Diaspora in E.P. Sanders, *Jewish Law from Jesus to the Mishnah* (London: SCM, 1990) 258–71.

(2) The parallel extends to the idea of righteousness as dependent on observing such regulations: 'This will be "reckoned to you for righteousness" in doing what is upright and good before him' (C31), with the same echo of Gen. 15.6 which was central to Paul's reasoning on the subject (Gal. 3.6; Rom. 4.3–22). Clearly the letter writer(s) believed that those who followed Qumran's halakhoth would be 'reckoned righteous'; that is, they would be 'reckoned righteous by reference to their *ma'ase hatorah*', or, in the term used by Paul, they would be 'justified *ex ergōn nomou*'. In both cases, that is to say, what was seen to be at stake by the separatists was their own righteousness/justification; their own righteousness/justification would somehow be imperilled by association with those who did not so understand and practise the Torah, that is, by the impurity of these others. And, once again, it is precisely that attitude and praxis to which Paul objects.

Wright in fact is very much on target when he indicates that what was at stake in one case was self-definition, and in the other self-identity. For in each case the integrity of their own identity (as Israel, as believers) was understood to be put at risk by association with the non-observant (other Jews, Gentiles). By the same token, the observance of the Torah (halakhoth, food laws) was vital to that self-definition, to maintaining that identity. What has proved so interesting about 4QMMT at this point is that it has used the very same phrase, 'the works of the law', in the very same way as does Paul in characterising the attitude of Peter, and with the very same implication that such 'works of the law' were deemed by the observant to be necessary bulwarks to sustain and preserve their self-definition, their identity.[44]

I press the point simply to underscore the way in which it strengthens my basic thesis about 'works of the law'. Despite Wright, the parallel between MMT and Galatians is close and significant. Not because the specific issues/rulings/halakhoth/ practices in view were the same. But because the *attitude and concerns* expressed in the phrase 'works of the law' were the same. The writers of MMT used the phrase to indicate those halakhoth and practices which were of such importance for them as to necessitate their separation from the rest of the people.[45]

---

[44] De Roo misses the common element ('works' which require 'separation') which makes appropriate talk of works as identity factors and boundary defining in both cases; in the context of Galatians we can speak more specifically of Jewish or national identity markers ('Concept' 126–7); my 'Works of the Law and the Curse of the Law (Galatians 3.10–14)', *NTS* 31 (1985) 523–42, reprinted in *Jesus, Paul and the Law* 215–36 [= ch. 3 above]), in which I first drew attention to 'the social function of the law', was, of course, written before 4QMMT became widely known.

[45] The earlier complaint about failure to read a text in context (above n. 8) applies also to MMT's reference to 'works of the law'. E.g., in disputing my view B. Witherington, *Grace in Galatia: A Commentary on Paul's Letter to the Galatians* (Grand Rapids: Eerdmans, 1998) 176–7, ignores both the obvious inference that 'some works of the law', 'some of our rulings/practices' (C27, 30) refer back to the rulings laid out in the letter, and that these constituted a dividing line of separation from the rest of the people. T.R. Schreiner, *Romans* (Grand Rapids:

Paul used the phrase to describe the Torah-faithful practices which Peter and the other Jewish believers regarded as of such importance as to necessitate their separation from the rest of the believers in Messiah Jesus. Both sets of separatists were making such 'works of the law' essential to being reckoned righteous by God. Not, to say it again, because these 'works of the law' were thought somehow to achieve an initial acceptability to God, but because such 'works of the law' enforced and enacted separation from others of Israel or others of faith.[46] Whereas for Paul, faith alone, faith in Christ, was the sole ground of acceptance by God and for social fellowship with others who shared that faith.

IV

There is one further aspect which deserves some attention. The current debate regarding 'works of the law' in Paul has been carried forward without sufficient regard to the fact that the key word, 'works (*erga*)', appears elsewhere in other passages where justification/acquittal is in view. I refer, of course, to the fact that Paul envisages the final judgment as being determined with reference to the 'works' of those being judged. God 'will render to each according to his works', whether good or evil (Rom. 2.6). The 'work' of each will be tested by fire (1 Cor. 3.13–15). 'We must all appear before the judgment seat of Christ, in order that each may receive recompense for what he has done in the body, whether good or evil' (2 Cor. 5.10). Bachmann, of course, defuses the issue by making a sharp distinction between such humanly wrought 'works' and the 'works (= regulations) of the law'.[47] And Wright recognizes the importance of the eschatological aspect to the discussion, though he pursues it in his own characteristic way.[48] But the issue cannot be avoided either way. The issue is this: if 'works of the law' are indeed the deeds prescribed by the law, then how does Paul relate them to the 'works' by reference to which final judgment shall be rendered?

The issue, of course, is all the sharper for those who understand 'works of the law' to refer to the whole range of conduct required by the law. For then Paul's various statements on the subject of 'works' seem to fall into complete confusion. He certainly denies that justification/acquittal is 'from works (of the law)'. But then, on the one hand, he asserts that the law is fulfilled in the command for

---

Baker, 1998) 173 ignores the context altogether. H.-J. Eckstein, *Verheißung und Gesetz: Eine exegetische Untersuchung zu Galater 2.15–4.7* (WUNT 86; Tübingen: Mohr-Siebeck, 1996) does not even mention 4QMMT!

[46] See now also M.A. Abegg, '4QMMT C 27, 31 and "Works Righteousness"'. *Dead Sea Discoveries* 6 (1999) 139–47.

[47] Bachmann, 'Rechtfertigung' 14–19.

[48] 'Towering over these issues is MMT's *biblical eschatology* (something ignored by scholars so far), and the way this relates to its "works of the law" on the one hand and to Paul's "works" on the other' (Wright).

neighbour love (Gal. 5.14), and that believers who 'love their neighbour' do in fact fulfil the law (Rom. 13.8, 10); are those who 'love their neighbour' *not* doing 'the work(s) of the law'? Moreover, he affirms that final judgment/acquittal is 'in accordance with works'; presumably love of neighbour is the sort of 'work(s)' which will survive the fiery test and by reference to which acquittal will be recorded.

Ironically, we encounter here a feature of Paul's theology which seems, to the surprise of some, very similar to the theology of his Jewish contemporaries: that judgment will be according to works. Christian scholarship generally has been so anxious to mark out the difference and distance between Paul and Second Temple Judaism on the issue of justification that we have neglected this point of similarity.[49] But the future emphasis in Paul's teaching on justification must not be neglected. For example, as already noted, the thought of Rom. 2.13 is no different from the traditional emphases of Second Temple Judaism: it is 'the doers of the law (who) shall be justified'. And when in Gal. 5.5 Paul talks of 'awaiting the hope of righteousness', that can hardly be different from the hope of future acquittal, of being accounted righteous at the final judgment.[50] The logic here cannot be escaped by arguing that reference to the gospel in Rom. 2.16 changes the picture of 2.13, or that the 'but now' of 3.21 signals a change in the terms of judgment, so that it will no longer be 'in terms of works'. For we have already noted that Paul paints the same picture of final judgment on work, on actions done in the body, for believers too (1 Cor. 3.13–15; 2 Cor. 5.10). The extent to which Paul has simply taken over and integrated into his own theology the traditional Jewish understanding of final judgment as 'according to works' cannot be escaped and should not be ignored.[51]

---

[49] The charge should not be laid at Sanders' door since he emphasized the importance of 'staying in' in his definitions of 'covenantal nomism': 'the covenant requires as the proper response of man his obedience to its commandments ...'; 'obedience maintains one position in the covenant ...'; 'righteousness in Judaism is a term which implies the maintenance of status among the group of the elect' (*Paul and Palestinian Judaism* 75, 420, 544). My own treatment in *Theology of Paul* may have encouraged such an inference, since I treated 'justification by faith' solely in terms of the beginning of the process of salvation (ch. 14), and the issue of final justification 'according to works' was likely to be lost sight of in ch. 18.

[50] The future tenses of *dikaioō* should not be ignored here – Rom. 2.13 (note the context, 2.5–13, 15–16); 3.20, 30; God's role as justifier, *ho dikaiōn* (3.26; 4.5; 8.33) will be most fully demonstrated in final judgment (3.4–6; 8.33); salvation likewise is not fully achieved until the end (5.9–10; 11.26; 13.11; Phil. 1.19; 2.12; 1 Thess. 5.8–9).

[51] F. Avemarie, *Tora und Leben: Untersuchungen zur Heilsbedeutung der Tora in der frühen rabbinischen Literatur* (WUNT; Tübingen: Mohr/Siebeck, 1996), also 'Erwählung und Vergeltung: Zur optionalen Struktur rabbinischen Soteriologie', *NTS* 45 (1999) 108–26, stresses this aspect in describing the 'structure of rabbinic soteriology', as a correction or qualification of Sanders' 'covenantal nomism'. But it is also necessary to note how similar is the 'structure of Pauline soteriology' at this point. I have developed the point in 'Jesus the Judge: Further Thoughts on Paul's Christology and Soteriology', in D. Kendall & S.T. Davis, eds., *The Convergence of Theology*, G. O'Collins FS (New York: Paulist, 2001) 34–54 [= ch. 18 above]. See now

The upshot is further confirmation that in denying that justification is *ex ergōn nomou*, Paul cannot have intended to discourage his readers from doing 'good works', since he certainly also believed that judgment would have reference to just such 'good (deeds/works)' done during life (Rom. 2.7, 10; 2 Cor. 5.10). What then was being denied in Gal. 2.16? The answer seems to have two parts. (1) The first obviously lies in the antithesis between faith and works of the law. Paul asserts that faith alone is necessary. Any attempt to require more than faith is unacceptable to Paul, denies 'the truth of the gospel'. That, however, as we have now seen, does not mean that believers are not expected to produce any 'works'. It must simply mean that the works to be tested in the final judgment are works which are themselves the expression of that faith, works, if you like, *ek pisteōs*,[52] or as Paul himself puts it, 'faith working through love' (Gal. 5.6). It is the failure of Peter to appreciate that faith remains the single constant, while 'works' as the expression of that faith are variable and cannot be narrowly prescribed, which Paul condemns. Alternatively, we might say, Paul insists that the grace which first established the covenant with Israel remains the single determinant of membership of the covenant (Rom. 11.6), even though he expects that grace to fructify in the fruit of good character and relationships (Gal. 5.22–23).

(2) The second part of the answer lies in the recognition, once again, that 'the works of the law' must be rather more circumscribed than is usually assumed. There are 'works of the law' which provide no basis for justification, and 'works' by reference to which final judgment shall be reached. Paul cannot have the same 'works' in view in both cases. What is so wrong about 'the works of the law' of Gal. 2.16? Evidently that they have proved antithetical to the openness of faith, to the claim that a Gentile's faith alone is sufficient ground for full acceptance, not least at the meal table, by believing Jews. Once again, then, we are driven by the logic of Paul's wider thought to the conclusion that by 'works of the law' Paul had in mind that obedience to the precepts of the law which was deemed still necessary for believing Jews, particularly at the point where it meant treating believing Gentiles as outside the community of salvation.

If he has persevered thus far I can well imagine Heikki giving a wry smile at this point (if not well before). There are surely more important issues for biblical scholarship and theology than to pursue such finer exegetical points at such length. My only defence is that the issue 'not from works of the law' was evi-

---

K.L. Yinger, *Paul, Judaism and Judgment According to Deeds* (SNTSMS 105; Cambridge: Cambridge University, 1999). Cf. P. Stuhlmacher, *Der Brief an die Römer* (NTD 6; Göttingen: Vandenhoeck & Ruprecht, 1989): 'Die Paulusbriefe bieten keinen Anlaß, diese Vorstellungswelt als "vorchristlich" oder "bloß jüdisch" abzutun. Der Apostel hat sie nicht als Widerspruch zu seiner Rechtfertigungsverkündigung empfunden, vielmehr sein Evangelium in eben diesem Erwartungshorizont entfaltet' (44). De Roo resorts to the old polemical categories by insisting on describing 'works of the law' as 'meritorious' ('Concept' 145–7).

[52] It will readily be recognized that I have in mind the old Protestant tag that 'works are the fruit, not the root of faith'.

dently important for Paul. And since Paul has been such a creative force in Christian theology, it is well worth while persevering in an attempt to ensure that nuances which were important for Paul when he first drew the phrase into his theology are not lost to sight. But such a defence simply invites a widening of our dialogue beyond what is appropriate here. Next time perhaps. *Ad multos annos*, Heikki.

Chapter 20

Did Paul have a covenant theology?

Reflections on Romans 9.4 and 11.27

I

The motif of 'covenant' plays a rather puzzling role in Paul's theology. The problem is not simply that Paul uses the term relatively infrequently,[1] but that his usage seems to be more reactive than expressive of his own cutting edge reflection, and that consequently it is difficult to derive a coherent 'covenant theology' from the passages where the term occurs. The tension is already reflected in the two principal streams of the Reformation which both drew their theological inspiration from Paul: is 'covenant' a means of expressing continuity between Old Testament and New (with Calvin)? or does it succumb to the antithesis between law and gospel (*new* covenant) so paradigmatic for Lutheran theology? And the problem is enhanced by the hundred years of debate in Old Testament scholarship as to whether the covenant is a late (Deuteronomic) concept (Wellhausen) or fundamental to Israel's self-consciousness more or less from the beginning (particularly Eichrodt), each giving scope either to the Lutheran antithesis or to Calvin's continuity in its own way. Or to put the issue in terms more directly applicable to our present concerns: against what within his heritage did Paul react? on what within his heritage was Paul drawing? And where does the idea or theology of 'covenant' fit in? – as part of that against which Paul reacted, or as part of that upon which he drew?

In the wake of E.P. Sanders' critique of the traditional portrayal of the Judaism against which Paul reacted and his restatement of second Temple Judaism in terms of 'covenantal nomism',[2] the pendulum has swung again in favour of an emphasis on continuity. And in this reassessment 'covenant' has usually been taken as a motif of continuity. For example, Tom Wright could entitle his collection of studies on Paul's theology, *The Climax of the Covenant*.[3] And David Kaylor has entitled his study of Romans *Paul's Covenant Community*.[4] 'Covenant'

---

[1] Rom. 9.4; 11.27; 1 Cor. 11.25; 2 Cor. 3.6, 14; Gal. 3.15, 17; 4.24; also Eph. 2.12.

[2] E.P. Sanders, *Paul and Palestinian Judaism* (London: SCM, 1977) 75, 420, 544.

[3] N.T. Wright, *The Climax of the Covenant: Christ and the Law in Pauline Theology* (Edinburgh: T. & T. Clark, 1991).

[4] D. Kaylor, *Paul's Covenant Community: Jew and Gentile in Romans* (Atlanta: John Knox, 1988).

likewise became a leading term in my own statement of 'the new perspective on Paul'.[5] Further reflection, however, has raised the question for me as to whether the category is being used too casually in descriptions of Paul's theology and in a way that fails to bring out with sufficient clarity the ambivalence of his usage, as reflecting also the ambivalence of his attitude to his ancestral religion.[6] Particularly striking are the two Romans references which seem to be at some remove from the characteristic contrast of 'old covenant' and 'new covenant' so familiar to Christian theology. How to understand them in relation to or as part of a Pauline 'covenant theology'?

II

From one perspective there can be little doubt that Paul's theology may justifiably be described as 'covenant theology'. In this line of thought 'covenant' denotes the fundamental character of Israel's religion, emphasizing particularly a people chosen by divine initiative and sustained by divine *chesed*. And it is just this emphasis which Paul's gospel brings to fresh focus: the God who created the cosmos and made free choice of Israel is the God of Paul's theology;[7] the central term ('righteousness') in his most characteristic teaching (justification by faith), draws directly on Israel's covenant theology as expressed most clearly by the Psalmist and Second Isaiah.[8] It is precisely this recognition of the extent to which Paul's gospel presupposes these fundamental features of Israel's covenant religion which has marked out 'the new perspective on Paul'.

It is all the more surprising, then, that the concept itself seems to play so little part in Paul's theology. The more fundamental the concept in describing the manner of divine grace, the more we might have expected Paul to make it central to his own exposition. But he did not do so. Why not?

A likely explanation soon offers itself. For the covenant theology to which Paul was undoubtedly indebted is never formulated within Paul's scriptures in terms of what we may call the Calvinist abstraction of the 'covenant of grace'. It always appears within more specific contexts and in more concrete terms. And it is when these different facets of covenant theology are brought into juxtaposi-

---

[5] J.D.G. Dunn, *Romans* (WBC 38; Dallas: Word, 1988) lxviii. See also W.L. Lane, 'Covenant: The Key to Paul's Conflict with Corinth', *TynB* 33 (1982) 3–29; W.J. Webb, *Returning Home: New Covenant and Second Exodus as the Context for 2 Corinthians 6.14–7.1* (JSNTS 85; Sheffield: JSOT, 1993).

[6] This line of reflection was stimulated particularly by the research of E.J. Christiansen, *The Covenant in Judaism and Paul: A Study of Ritual Boundaries as Identity Markers* (Leiden: Brill, 1995).

[7] For fuller exposition see my *The Theology of Paul the Apostle* (Grand Rapids: Eerdmans/ Edinburgh: T. & T. Clark, 1998) § 2.

[8] See again my *Theology* § 14.2.

tion that the questions and problems begin to mount, as the history of discussion of the subject has shown. For example, how to relate the concept itself to what are usually described as different covenants – the covenants with Noah, with Abraham and the patriarchs, with Moses at Sinai, with Phinehas, with David, and so on? Given the spectrum, from the universal perspective of the Noah covenant[9] to the particularism of the Phinehas covenant,[10] how should each be related to the others? Is one of them to be regarded as more definitive (Sinai?) than the others? Is Deuteronomy to be regarded as the paradigmatic statement of Israel's covenant theology? Was there a shift in emphasis from the model of an unconditional royal grant, the promissory covenant, to that of a more conditional suzerain-vassal treaty, the obligatory covenant,[11] or as we might say from the religion of Israel to early Judaism? How does the 'new covenant' prophesied by Jeremiah (Jer. 31.31–34) relate to its predecessors? Above all, is there a single 'covenant theology' which embraces all these different facets, or only a sequence of shifting emphases and tensions?

Self evidently we cannot hope to discuss all these questions here, but the issues which they pose obviously impact upon any 'covenant theology' affirmed by Paul. Was he himself working with an abstracted theology of covenant, or did he simply seize on one strand or make only one emphasis his own? Is the election of a particular people, the nation of Israel, such a prominent theme within the covenant theology of the Hebrew Bible, also a feature of Paul's own theology or a stumbling block for it?[12] Is his use of the concept arbitrary, an idiosyncratic development of the concrete covenant theology which he inherited, or can it be regarded as an appropriate outworking of the scriptural theme?

It is important to bear such questions in mind as we approach the passages where Paul speaks of 'covenant', otherwise we may hear them with ears too preconditioned by the traditional 'new testament'/'old testament' Christian perspective, by previous debates on the theme, and by the more casual talk of 'covenant' which has been a feature of recent discussion. Since our goal is to make best sense of the two Romans references, our obvious procedure is to work up to them through the earlier Pauline references. We proceed, then, by examining

---

[9] The universal aspect of the Noah covenant is emphasized in the contexts where the term itself (*bᵉrith/ diathēkē*) occurs (Gen. 6.18; 9.9–17), though Gen. 9.4–6, the basis for the subsequent Noahide Laws which rabbinic Jews regarded as applicable to non-Jews, does not use the term and implies conditions to the covenant.

[10] Num. 25.6–13; Sir. 45.23–24; 1 Macc. 2.54; Pseudo-Philo 46–48; Phinehas was the great paradigm for the Zealots (see M. Hengel, *The Zealots: Investigations into the Jewish Freedom Movement in the Period from Herod I until 70 AD* (1961; [2]1976; Edinburgh: T. & T. Clark, 1989) 149–77.

[11] See e.g. M. Weinfeld, *TDOT* 2.265–76.

[12] It is notable, for example, that whereas those who make much of Paul's covenant theology tend naturally to speak in terms of 'the people of God', Paul himself only uses the term 'people' (*laos*) in scriptural quotations (Rom. 9.25, 26; 10.21; 11.1–2; 15.10, 11; 1 Cor. 10.7; 14.21; 2 Cor. 6.16).

Paul's usage in what may be regarded as the most probable chronological sequence.[13]

III

Galatians. Paul uses the term 'covenant' (*diathēkē*) in two passages in Galatians – 3.15, 17 and 4.24.

1. *Gal. 3.15–17* – [15]Even a human *diathēkē* once ratified, no one sets aside or adds to. [16]But the promises were spoken to Abraham and to his "seed". It does not say, and to his "seeds", as to many, but as to one: "and to your seed" – who is Christ. [17]My point is this: a *diathēkē* ratified beforehand by God, the law which came four hundred and thirty years later does not make void so as to render the promise ineffective (*katargēsai*).

The point of immediate note is that Paul here uses the term *diathēkē* (the usual word for 'covenant') primarily because *diathēkē* also means 'will, testament' and so allows an effective wordplay.[14] Of course central to the wordplay is the fact that a human will or testament is unilateral: what it determines or disposes (within its own competence) no one else can alter.[15] So the wordplay reinforces the unilateralness of the divine initiative in the commitment God made to Abraham, and to that extent it serves to reinforce a fundamental feature of 'covenant theology'. Nevertheless it would be a mistake to conclude that Paul had in mind the Abrahamic *covenant* as such.[16] Rather he sees the promise to Abraham as a kind of *will* or *testament* – hence the formulation of 3.17 as 'a will ratified by God' rather than 'the covenant made with Abraham'.

The key term in the passage is actually 'promise' (8 times in 3.14–29).[17] That is the term which provides the cutting edge of Paul's exposition in ch. 3. That is the term which carries the contrast with *nomos*,[18] as the sequence 3.17–22 clearly in-

---

[13] Many reckon that Galatians was chronologically adjacent to Romans, that is, after the Corinthian letters. My own view is spelt out in my *Galatians* (BNTC; London: A. & C. Black, 1993); but the issue is largely irrelevant to the present concerns.

[14] On the various translations of *diathēkē* offered by commentators, see Christiansen, *Covenant* 235–6.

[15] For the nuances necessary in the assertion see R.N. Longenecker, *Galatians* (WBC 41; Dallas: Word, 1991) 128–30.

[16] It may be of relevance to recall that the term *bᵉrith/ diathēkē* does not occur in the unconditional promise of Gen. 12.1–3. The term occurs for the first time in reference to Abraham in Gen. 15.18 and is prominent in Gen. 17.1–21 (11 times) – notably (and ominously?) with particular emphasis on circumcision as a condition (17.9–14).

[17] The text Paul had in mind (3.16) was presumably the repeated promise of Gen. 13.15, 17 LXX; 15.18; 17.8; 24.7.

[18] In contrast, no doubt, to the other missionaries in Galatia who would assume that the law was simply the outworking of the promise, as the 'covenant' language of Genesis actually suggested (n. 16) (so particularly J.L. Martyn, *Galatians* [AB 33A; New York: Doubelday, 1997] 337; also 'The Abrahamic Covenant, Christ, and the Church', *Theological Issues in the Letters of Paul* [Edinburgh: T. & T. Clark, 1997] 161–75 [here 165–7]); see also n. 19 below.

dicates: in 3.17 the *diathēkē* is simply the carrier of the promise.[19] Had *diathēkē* = 'covenant' been more central to his exposition of Abraham it would almost certainly have reappeared with some prominence in Paul's reworking of the same theme (the exposition of Gen. 15.6) in Rom. 4. But there too it is the theme of 'promise' which carries the heavy theological freight (Rom. 4.13–21) and the term *diathēkē* does not even appear.

The fact, then, that Paul chose to build his theological argument round the theme of 'promise', despite the term 'covenant' being close to hand and actually in use within the immediate context of his argument, must tell us something about Paul's theology. That theology is better described as 'promise theology' rather than 'covenant theology'. Moreover, we note that 'covenant' is not used for the other partner in the contrast (the law); indeed on a strict reading of the wordplay, the law was not a *diathēkē*.[20] But such an inference would be as perverse as the conclusion that Paul wanted to refer to the Abrahamic *covenant* as such. On the contrary, he was evidently not thinking of covenants (properly speaking) at all, whether the covenant with Abraham or the covenant with Moses. 'Covenant' as such was neither a leading nor an organising category in his thought at this point. Quite probably it was precisely the close link between covenant and circumcision (above n. 16) which made 'covenant' too dangerous a category for Paul, too much locked into a covenant of circumision mindset. By contrast, the recent neologism 'promise' (above n. 19) evoked no such negative overtones. Which also means that the features and emphases which some have tried to reinforce within Paul's theology by categorizing them as 'covenant theology' may have been categorized misleadingly, with misleading consequences for our understanding of Paul's 'covenant theology'. But we should hesitate to draw out further possible corollaries before the other Pauline references to 'covenant' have been drawn into the discussion.

2. *Gal. 4.24–26* – [24]Such things [Abraham's two sons, one by a slave girl, the other by a free woman, the one born in accordance with the flesh, the other born through promise] are to be interpreted allegorically. For these women are two covenants; one from Mount Sinai gives birth into slavery – such is Hagar. [25]This Hagar-Sinai ... belongs to the same

---

[19] Again it may be important to recall that the term 'promise' had no equivalent in Hebrew and was a fairly recent coinage in Greek. That does not at all illegitimize Paul's usage here; though it is noticeable that when the term does begin to feature in Jewish theology it is much more integrated with the law (2 Macc. 2.17–18; Pss. Sol. 12.6; *Sib. Or.* 3.768–9) a tendency which Paul seems deliberately to cut across; see further my *Romans* 212.

[20] In the imagery which Paul uses the law at best could be regarded as a codicil; despite the usage of the Torah, Paul did not seem to think of circumcision (above n.16) or the law (Exod. 19.5; 24.7–8; 31.16; 34.28; Lev. 26.15; Deut. 4.13, 23; 5.2–3; 7.9, 12; etc.) as potentially a superceding will/covenant. E. Grässer links the treatment here too quickly into the discussion of 'new covenant' and 'old covenant' ('Der Alte Bund im Neuen', *Der Alte Bund im Neuen* [WUNT 35; Tübingen: Mohr, 1985] 68).

column as the present Jerusalem, for she is in slavery with her children. [26]But the Jerusalem above is free; such is our mother.

The point of immediate note in this case is the fact that Paul speaks explicitly of
'two covenants'. The passage seems to invite the conclusion that Paul thus recognized two of what have regularly been designated as 'covenants' within the
Hebrew Bible – the covenant with Abraham and the covenant made on Sinai.
And of course Paul does explicitly identify the first covenant as the 'one from
Mount Sinai' (4.24). The way is then open for an exegesis which contrasts old
covenant/law with new covenant/promise and we at once find ourselves back in
a classic formulation of law/gospel covenant theology.

One problem with this is that covenant is used on both sides of the contrast.
Slave Hagar-Sinai is as much to be identified with 'covenant' as free Sarah. In
which case 'covenant' cannot be used to distinguish a theology of promise, of
grace and gospel, from a theology of law. This covenant theology embraces both.

The observation is important since it also relates back to the previous passage
(3.15–18). There the inference was certainly possible that Paul wanted to
reserve the language of 'covenant' for the promise to Abraham; by implication,
the law given through Moses was a different category, or at best (or worst) an un-
authorized codicil. But if in this case the later covenant (Sarah's freeborn child)
is now to be regarded as superceding or taking higher priority than the earlier
(Hagar's slaveborn child), that would throw the previous argument into total
confusion. For in 3.17 Paul argued the precise reverse – that the prior promise
could not be annulled by the later law. This line of reflection strengthens the previous conclusion that the imagery of 'covenant' is incidental in the earlier argument, and it strongly suggests that the language of 'covenant' is not central to the
argument in ch. 4. In neither passage is Paul attempting to develop a covenant
theology as such.

More to the point, the primary category in this case is not covenant or law
(Sinai), or gospel, but relation to Abraham (the two wives) and particularly descent from Abraham (the two sons). That was the category which the other
(Jewish Christian) missionaries had evidently introduced to the Galatians,[21]
with the corollary that (in their view) the Galatians were claiming sonship from
Abraham illegitimately. To be more precise, the primary category is the sonship
of Isaac, for the promise came to effect only through him. There was in fact no
covenant made with Hagar or Ishmael (Gen. 17.18–21 is quite explicit on the
point); and none of the parties in the Galatian churches was interested in claiming sonship of Abraham through Ishmael.[22] The problem was that both sides

---

[21] C.K. Barrett, 'The Allegory of Abraham, Sarah, and Hagar in the Argument of Galatians', *Essays on Paul* (London: SPCK, 1982) 154–70; Martyn, *Galatians* 302–6.

[22] Martyn, *Galatians* 436: 'Nothing is clearer in those stories than the singularity of the covenant God made with Abraham and the passing down of that covenant through Isaac and not
through Ishmael. There is, thus, no Hagar covenant'.

were laying claim to the determinative sonship, sonship through Isaac. And the theological problem which Paul's treatment leaves with us is that in responding to the other missionaries' attempt to exclude the Gentile Galatian believers from that sonship Paul himself seems to exclude his fellow native born Jews: the category of Ishmael actually means not another covenant but exclusion from the determinative covenant relationship.[23]

In short, there was really only one covenant in question – the covenant of sonship as promised to Abraham (Gen. 17.19–21). What Paul describes as two covenants for the purpose of his argument here are in effect two different ways of understanding the one covenant promise of God to Abraham regarding seed. As with the category 'Jerusalem', where Paul refracts the one category of 'Jerusalem' into two contrasting columns (4.25–26), so here Paul refracts the one category of 'covenant' into the two contrasting columns.[24] 'Covenant' is part of the common ground, not part of the argument. The issue is not 'covenant' set in antithesis against some other category (for example, law); nor is it properly speaking 'new' covenant set against 'old' covenant (despite the explicit reference to Sinai).[25] It is the issue of how the one covenant with and through Abraham is to be understood and realized.

Here again, then, we see Paul taking up a category which lay conveniently to hand as a means of developing the difficult argument he has to make in order to counter the more obvious claim of his opponents, that sonship to Abraham is secured through natural descent. His usage reflects the traditional Jewish emphasis both on the promises made to the patriarchs and on the covenant made at Sinai. And in the immediate context Paul was certainly concerned to prevent his readers from putting themselves 'under the law' (4.21; 5.1). But the idea of 'covenant' as such and an explicitly 'covenant theology' is not at the forefront of his argument. And the casualness of his usage here, cutting across his earlier usage a few paragraphs earlier as it does, simply confirms that 'covenant' was not a major theological category for Paul's own theologizing.[26]

---

[23] The surprising turning of the tables is reinforced by Paul's use of the harsh words of Sarah in Gen. 21.9 , 'Throw out the slave girl and her son; for the son of the slave girl will never inherit with the son of the free woman' (Gal. 4.30).

[24] Cf. Martyn, *Galatians* 447–57 = 'The Covenants of Hagar and Sarah', *Theological Issues* 194–204.

[25] Christiansen, *Covenant* 243–4; against the traditional exegesis in such terms (as e.g. by H.D. Betz, *Galatians* [Hermeneia; Philadelphia: Fortress, 1979] 243–4; Longenecker, *Galatians* 211) which may divert the point of the 'allegory' too quickly into another discussion; cf. Grässer, who transposes Paul's context-specific polemical antithesis into an enduring theological antithesis: 'Es fehlt in Gal. 4.21ff. jede Anspielung auf Jer. 31.31ff! Nicht die Vollendung des Alten Bundes im Neuen ist das Thema des Paulus. Es geht vielmehr darum, daß der Alte Bund im Gegenüber zum Neuen gleichsam seine *Nichtigkeit* zeigt ... *diametralen Gegensatz* von *Alten* und *Neuen Bund*' ('Alte Bund' 74, 76). Contrast H. Merklein, 'Der (neue) Bund als Thema der paulinischen Theologie', *ThQ* 176 (1996) 290–308, here 302–3.

[26] Cf. D. Lührmann, *Die Brief an die Galater* (ZB; Zürich: TVZ, 1978, [2]1988) 79; Grässer,

IV

Corinthians. Somewhat curiously, the two Corinthians passages are the only two within the Pauline corpus to use the concept of the 'new covenant' (1 Cor. 11.25; 2 Cor. 3.6), as also the contrasting talk of 'old covenant' (2 Cor 3.14). This is all the more striking since of the four *Hauptbriefe* it is Galatians and Romans who are most immediately and fully concerned with what elsewhere would be described as the relation between the old covenant and the new. The fact that talk of 'new covenant' is confined to the Corinthian letters may therefore be significant.

We need not spend too much time with the first reference – the words remembered as spoken by Jesus in inaugurating the Lord's Supper:

3. *1 Cor. 11.25* – Likewise also the cup after dinner, saying, "This cup is the new covenant in my blood. Do this, as often as you drink it, in remembrance of me".

The point of interest here is that the phrase ('the new covenant') appears only in a quotation. Paul was familiar with the Lukan version of the 'words of institution' (Luke 22.20)[27] in which the emphasis falls on the cup as a symbol and expression of the new covenant rather than on the blood (Matt. 26.28/Mark 14.24). That is to say, the tradition with which Paul was familiar, and which he no doubt celebrated regularly, portrayed the death of Jesus as the sacrifice (cf. Exod. 24.8) which established a new covenant, or the new covenant (Jer. 31.31), between God and the followers of the Christ Jesus.[28]

It presumably is significant, therefore, that Paul nowhere else makes this link. He nowhere speaks of the Lord's Supper in covenant terms. That might seem a small matter since he says so little about the Lord's Supper as such (1 Cor. 11.17–32). But it could have provided a point of substance and leverage in his contrast between participation in Christ and partnership with idols, between 'the cup of the Lord' and 'the cup of demons' (1 Cor. 10.14–22). Did not the fact that the table of the Lord was a covenant meal give it an extra weight, which should have underlined the exclusiveness of the commitment to the Lord which the Lord's Supper expressed? Did the idea of 'new covenant' not underline the outmodedness of the old ways?[29] But Paul brings in the thought of 'new covenant' merely as part of the tradition authorizing the meal and not as an item of his own theologizing.

'Alte Bund' 56, 77.

[27] On the much discussed issue of the form of and echoes in the Lukan text see, e.g., J. A. Fitzmyer, *Luke* (AB 28; New York: Doubleday, 1985) 1386–95.

[28] Once again, Grässer, 'Alte Bund' 119–21, questions any allusion in the talk of 'new covenant' to Jer. 31.31–34.

[29] In contrast, Paul parallels 'the table of the Lord' with 'Israel *kata sarka*' eating the sacrifices of the table as 'partners of the altar' (1 Cor. 10.18).

The same point emerges when we think of the other passages where Paul speaks of the death of Jesus. In most cases the imagery is of sacrifice, but of sacrifice for sin,[30] not covenant sacrifice. Here again the link between Christ's death and thought of the new covenant is not one which is central to Paul's theologizing about Christ's death, itself so fundamental to his theology. Here again, in other words, we have confirmation that 'covenant' was not a primary category for Paul, and even that the link between his gospel and the idea of the 'new covenant' lay somewhat on the periphery of his thought.

But does the picture change with the second Corinthians reference?

4. *2 Cor. 3.5–14* – [15]... our qualification (as ministers) is from God, [6]who also qualified us as ministers of a new covenant, not of letter but of Spirit; for the letter kills, but the Spirit makes alive. [7]But if the ministry of death carved in letters of stone came with glory, so that the children of Israel were unable to gaze on the face of Moses, because the glory of his face was being set aside (*katargoumenēn*), [8]how much more will the ministry of the Spirit be with glory ... [11]For if what is being set aside (*katargoumenon*) is through glory, how much more shall what remains be with glory. ... [13]Moses put a veil over his face to prevent the children of Israel gazing at the end of what was being set aside (*katargoumenou*). [14]But their minds were hardened. For, up to the present day the same veil remains unlifted over the reading of the old covenant, because in Christ it is set aside (*katargeitai*).

Here we seem to have a clear exposition of what is usually regarded as the normal Christian covenant theology, that is, of the contrast between old covenant and new. The old covenant is evidently related to Moses and the law, the new covenant to the life-giving Spirit claimed by the first Christians. The contrast is heightened by correlating the old covenant/new covenant antithesis with the further antitheses, death/life (3.6–7) and condemnation/saving righteousness (3.9). Most striking of all is the use of *katargeō*, a popular term with Paul, to indicate the current status (in Paul's eyes) of the old covenant. Unfortunately the force of the verb is not entirely clear, but central to its usage is the sense 'make ineffective, abolish, set aside'; so the implication is that in some sense the old covenant has been made ineffective, abolished, set aside in favour of the new (3.11, 13).[31] That is as close as Paul comes to the more emphatic language of He-

---

[30] See my *Theology of Paul* §§ 9.2–3.

[31] It is noticeable that the same verb (*katargeomai*) seems to have different referents within the scope of a few verses. The first refers to the glory on Moses' face (3.8); see e.g. M.E. Thrall's comments (*2 Corinthians* Vol. 1 [ICC; Edinburgh: T. & T. Clark, 1994] 243–4) which conclude with the relevant note: 'It is essential to note that the participle of *katargeomai* here specifically refers to the radiance on Moses' face, and is to be understood within the context of what is said to have happened at Sinai. If Paul were alluding to the eventual abolition of the Mosaic covenant, the participle would have been attached to *diakonia*, not to *doxa*. Moreover, his argument in this chapter is concerned as much with the personal agents of the two covenants as with the covenants themselves in the abstract'; for a critique of RSV's inadequate rendering 'fading (away)', see S.J. Hafemann, *Paul, Moses, and the History of Israel* (WUNT 81; Tübingen: Mohr, 1995) 301–9. The same verb in 3.11 and 13 refers probably to 'the entire ministry of the old covenant symbolized by Moses' (V.P. Furnish, *2 Corinthians* [AB 32A; New York: Doubleday,

brews: 'In saying "new (covenant)" he has declared old/rendered obsolete (*pe-palaiōken*) the first (covenant); and what has become obsolete (*palaioumenon*) and growing old is close to disappearing' (Heb. 8.13). The language certainly seems, at first glance, to support a fairly straightforward supersessionist covenant theology.

Yet the issue is more complex. For one thing, 'covenant' is, once again, not the primary category. That is 'ministry' – the key concept which links 2 Corinthians 3 to its context (4.1; cf. 2.14–17)[32] – and the question of 'sufficiency/competence' for ministry.[33] The contrast is between two kinds of ministry – that represented by Moses and that represented by Paul himself. Moreover, it is noticeable that the contrast between the two does not arise immediately out of the preceding discussion. From this we may deduce that the reason why Paul introduced the contrast here was because those engaged in the other ministry which he contrasts with his own (2.14–3.1) were making so much of Moses as precedent and norm. Quite likely, indeed, it was these other ministers[34] who referred to the immediacy of Moses' authorisation as a spokesman for God, presumably documented by the account of Moses coming down from Mount Sinai, his face all aglow ('because he had been talking with God') as 'he gave them in commandment all that the Lord had spoken with him on Mount Sinai' (Exod. 34.29–35).[35]

The importance of this conclusion is that it gives us the probable reason why Paul introduced talk both of 'covenant' and of the contrast between two covenants. It was because the text at issue (Exodus 34) spoke of covenant (Exod. 34.10, 12, 15, 27–28) that Paul took up the term (2 Cor. 3.6); the words that Moses spoke (his ministry) were 'the words of the covenant' (Exod. 34.28). Paul also picked up Exodus 34's identification of the covenant with 'stone (*lithinos*) tablets' (Exod. 34.1, 4, 28–29); hence the same phrase in 2 Cor. 3.3. It was presumably this characterisation of the Moses/Sinai covenant which triggered off the contrast for which Paul was looking. For it must have prompted both the contrasts which he echoes in 2 Cor. 3.3 and 3.6: the contrast between the 'stone (*lithinos*) heart' and the 'fleshly heart' = 'new spirit'/'my (God's) Spirit' of Ezek. 11.19 and 36.26–27; and the contrast between the Exodus/Sinai covenant and the 'new covenant' = God's law written on their hearts of Jer. 31.31–34.[36] In

---

1984] 205), or 'the Mosaic covenant in general' (Thrall, *2 Corinthians* 1.252–3, 257). Whereas in 3.14 the same term probably refers to the veil (cf. Thrall, *2 Corinthians* 1.264–6).

[32] *Diakoneō* – 2 Cor. 3.3; *diakonia* – 2 Cor. 3.7, 8, 9(2); 4.1; *diakonos* – 2 Cor. 3.6.

[33] *Hikanos* – 2 Cor. 2.16; 3.5; *hikanotēs* – 3.5; *hikanoō* – 3.6.

[34] Alluded to in 2.17 and 3.1. Note the parallel: 'not as so many' (2.17), 'not as some' (3.1); 'not just as Moses' (3.13).

[35] Cf. particularly D. Georgi, *The Opponents of Paul in Second Corinthians* (1964; Philadelphia: Fortress, 1986) ch. 3. The debate Georgi occasioned is reviewed briefly by Thrall, *2 Corinthians* 1.238–9, 246–8.

[36] It is hard to doubt that an allusion to Jer 31.31–34 was intended; see e.g. my *Theology of Paul* 147, with other bibliography in n. 103.

other words, Paul seems to have introduced the talk of covenant and the contrast of new covenant/old covenant not because it was a primary feature of his own theology and gospel, but because it was a way of countering a glorification of Moses' ministry which sought to denigrate his own.

In addition we may note features to which attention has been drawn elsewhere.[37] In the first place, the contrast between the two covenants is not so sharp as might at first appear. Paul acknowledges the claim presumably made by the other ministers that Moses' ministry was one of 'glory' (2 Cor. 3.7–11). To counter the other ministers he infers that this glory is now being set aside – assuming that the glow on Moses' face was not permanent.[38] But he then goes on to treat Moses' going into the presence of the Lord (Exod. 34.34) as still a type of Christian conversion (2 Cor. 3.16);[39] the unveiled face of Moses reflecting the glory of the Lord can still serve as the archetype of believers being transformed into the same image from glory to glory (2 Cor. 3.18).

Secondly, the ambivalence in regard to what is being/has been 'set aside' (the glory, the Mosaic covenant in general, the veil covering the face of those who belong to the old covenant – see above n. 31) should be a warning to us that Paul's view of what it is of the old covenant which is passé is more nuanced that we generally recognize.

Thirdly, we should recall that the promise of the 'new covenant' in Jer. 31.31–34 was not of a different covenant so far as the law was concerned. On the contrary, the promise is of the law to be 'written on their hearts' – that is, of the more effective keeping of the law for which the Deuteronomists had always looked.[40] Here is not implied a simple contrast between gospel and law, or Spirit and law.[41]

This ties in, fourthly, with a recognition that the word 'law' is never used in the passage. What Paul places on the passé side of the antithesis is 'letter', *gramma*. The point is that *gramma* is not simply a synonym for 'law', *nomos*. The term *gramma* focuses rather on the law as written, visible to sight in the written letter. This no doubt related in Paul's mind to Israel's inability to understand Moses

---

[37] I refer to my *Theology of Paul* 148–9.

[38] Paul evidently read the idea into the text.

[39] See my *Theology of Paul* 326 and n. 40, 421–2.

[40] Deut. 10.16; Jer. 4.4; 9.25–26; Ezek. 44.9; 1QpHab. 11.13; 1QS 5.5; 1QH 10(formerly 2).18–19; 21(formerly 18).20; Philo, *Spec. Leg.* 1.305.

[41] Cf. the Qumran community which regarded itself as already entered into 'the new covenant' (CD 6.19; 8.21; 19.33–34; 20.12) and its more rigorous halakhah as given by the Spirit (1QH 20[formerly 12].11–12). It is precisely because Jer. 31.31–34 does *not* set new covenant and law in antithesis that Grässer doubts the allusion to Jeremiah's 'new covenant' ('Alte Bund' 81). J. Murphy-O'Connor can even argue that 'Paul is not making a distinction between the Old and New Covenant, but between two types of New Covenant, one that he perceives as being characterized by Letter and the other by Spirit' ('A Ministry Beyond the Letter [2 Cor. 3.1–6]', in L. De Lorenzi, ed., *Paolo Ministro del Nuovo Testamento [2 Co 2.14–4.6]* [Roma: Abbazia di S. Paolo, 1987] 105–29 (here 116–7).

properly, that is, to grasp the temporary nature of the epoch[42] (and therefore) of the ministry represented by Moses and regarded as still valid by the other ministers (3.15–16). Presumably it is this shortfall in understanding which gave the 'letter' its killing character, in contrast to the writing of the Spirit in the human heart (3.3, 6–7).[43] *Gramma*, in other words, is the law, the Torah, misunderstood as to scope and continuing relevance. The 'old covenant' here is not law, but *gramma*, the law misunderstood. The 'new covenant', in contrast, is the law in its divine intention, the law written in the heart, as Jeremiah promised, the Spirit operating in the fleshly heart, as Ezekiel predicted.[44]

In short, once again we see that talk of covenant is not central to Paul's theologizing,[45] nor a point of distinctiveness within second Temple Judaism. Consequently, any conclusion that 2 Corinthians 3 implies a strong gospel/law antithesis in Paul's theology is at best premature and probably misconceived.

V

Romans. And so we reach the last of the 'covenant' references in the undisputed Paulines.[46] How do the two references in Romans fit with our findings so far? What light do our findings so far shed upon the covenant references in what was undoubtedly Paul's most elaborate and carefully worked-out statement of his theology?

5. *Rom. 9.3–5* – ... my kinsmen in terms of the flesh, [4]inasmuch as they are Israelites: theirs is the adoption, the glory and the covenants, the law, the service and the promises; [5]theirs are the fathers and from them came the Christ insofar as the flesh is concerned.

---

[42] See further my *Theology of Paul* §6.4–5.

[43] If there is no life for the law to regulate then its primary function becomes one of condemnation (see again my *Theology of Paul* §§6.6 and 6.3).

[44] Cf. Merklein, 'Der (neue) Bund' 294; and particularly Christiansen, *Covenant* 253–9, who argues that '"new" is that which brings the potential of the "old" into existence by adding a new christological and pneumatological dimension' (259), and Hafemann, *Paul* 156–73, who argues that 'the letter/Spirit contrast is between *the Law itself without the Spirit* ... and *the Law with the Spirit*' (171 his emphasis). See also S.J. Hafemann, 'The "Temple of the Spirit" as the Inaugural Fulfilment of the New Covenant within the Corinthian Correspondence', *Ex Auditu* 12 (1996) 29–42 (here 32–3, 36–9). In contrast, Grässer, in simply identifying the point here with that of Gal. 4.21–31 ('Alte Bund' 84, 95), misses the nuances which distinguish the two passages.

[45] Despite Hafemann, 'Temple of the Spirit' 34.

[46] The only other reference in the Pauline corpus is Eph. 2.12, whose plural ('the covenants of promise') provides an immediate comparison with Rom 9.4. It is noteworthy that there too 'covenant' describes Jewish privilege and is not developed as a specific theme of Ephesians.

Two features catch the eye immediately. One is the plural usage ('covenants'). Does this mean that Paul had in view the sequence of covenants mentioned at the beginning – with Abraham (Genesis 15, 17), with Israel at Mount Sinai (Exod. 19.5–6), in the plains of Moab (Deuteronomy 29–31), and at Mounts Ebal and Gerizim (Josh. 8.30–35), with Phinehas (Num. 25.12–13; Sir. 45.24; 1 Macc. 2.54) and with David (2 Sam. 23.5; Jer. 33.21)?[47] More likely, the thought was of the covenant as first given to Abraham and then renewed with Isaac and Jacob – the covenant(s) with the fathers.[48] Another possibility, not least in view of the two passages from Corinthians, is that he was referring to the two covenants, old and new, since the latter as well as the former had been given to Israel.

The second feature to catch the eye is precisely this fact, that this reference to 'covenants' appears in a list of the blessings given to Israel. At the same time, it is evident that the blessings listed are those into which believers in Jesus Messiah, Gentiles as well as Jews, had been entering. This was implicit from the first in Paul's letter to Rome, in the designation of Gentile believers as 'beloved of God, called as saints' (Rom. 1.7), an implication reinforced in the preceding paragraph – 'saints', 'those who love God', 'the called', 'firstborn', 'God's elect' (8.27–33) – all of them terms drawn from traditional epithets for Israel.[49] And the inclusion in the list of 9.4 of key words like 'adoption', 'glory' and 'promise', so important in the preceding argument,[50] reinforces the point still more. These blessings are Israel's blessings in which Gentile believers have been given part. They have not been transferred from Israel to some other body. Gentiles have not been given a share in them at Israel's expense.

By obvious implication the same applies in the case of the 'covenants' of 9.4. The covenant(s) in view here are Israel's, and continue to be Israel's.[51] The Gentile believers have been given a share in Israel's covenant blessings.[52] There is no thought that Gentile believers have superseded Israel, that Israel has forfeited these covenants, or that a new covenant excludes Israel. For Gentile believers to have received a share in the covenants means that they have been given to share in Israel. The observation ties in to a further point which is often mistaken: that

---

[47] C.E.B. Cranfield, *Romans* (ICC; Edinburgh: T. & T. Clark, vol. 2 1979) 462; D.J. Moo, *Romans* (NICNT; Grand Rapids: Eerdmans, 1996) 563. See also J.A. Fitzmyer, *Romans* (AB 33; New York: Doubleday, 1993) 546. Christiansen, *Covenant* 220–5, argues vigorously for the reading *diathēkē* (singular).

[48] Deut. 4.31; 7.12; Wisd. Sol. 18.22 (plural); 2 Macc. 8.15 (plural); *Pss. Sol.* 9.10; CD 6.2; 8.18; 1QM 13.7; 14.8; *Test. Mos.* 4.5; Ps-Philo 10.2 (plural); 13.10 (plural); 19.2.

[49] Documentation in my *Romans* 19–20, 481–2, 485 and 502.

[50] 'Adoption' – 8.15, 23; 9.4; 'glory' – 5.2; 8.18, 21; 'promise' – 4.13–14, 16, 20.

[51] It is equally noticeable that Paul uses the correlative concept of 'election' almost exclusively in Rom. 9–11 (*eklogē* – 9.11; 11.5, 7, 28; elsewhere only 1 Thes. 1.4; though note also *eklektos* – Rom. 8.33; 16.13; Col. 3.12; *eklegomai* – 1 Cor. 1.27–28).

[52] It is worth noting that Paul does not attempt to distance talk of 'covenants' from 'the giving of the law', the very next item in the list (9.4), nor does he attempt to deny the latter's continuing relevance for Gentile believers.

ch. 9–11 are not about Israel and another entity, the church; the sole entity in view is Israel itself, the definition of Israel and membership of Israel, who and how the branches of the olive tree of Israel (11.17–24) are constituted.[53]

This finding confirms our earlier hesitation about speaking of a covenant theolgy as something which distinguished Paul's theology from that of his Jewish contemporaries, or distinguished a Christian theology as Christian. On the contrary, it is precisely as a Jew, or more precisely as an Israelite (11.1) that Paul speaks here. And as such he affirms the continuing blessings of Israel, including not least the covenant(s) which believers now benefit from as first of all Israel's and as continuing to belong to Israel. Here is a covenant theology indeed, but one at some remove from the traditional terms of Christian supersessionist theology.

6. *Rom. 11.25–27* – [25]I do not want you to be unaware, brothers, of this mystery, lest you be wise in your own estimation, that a hardening in part has come over Israel, until the full number of the Gentiles has come in; [26]and so all Israel shall be saved, as it is written: "Out of Zion will come the deliverer; he will turn away ungodliness from Jacob. [27]And this will be my covenant with them, when I take away their sins".

In some ways this is the most distinctive of all Paul's covenant references. For one thing, it is the only 'covenant' reference in Paul which appears in and as a scriptural citation.[54] More to the point, it seems to envisage an *ad hoc* covenant, 'covenant' as a way of speaking about God's proposed dealings with his people, and not any of the covenants normally designated as such.[55] On a little closer inspection, however, it becomes evident that the talk of covenant on which Paul draws here (Isa. 59.20–21) itself presupposes the more familiar covenant talk. Isa. 59.21 goes on to speak of teaching given to children and children's children, which naturally recalls the exhortation attached to the Sinai covenant (Deut. 4.9–10; 6.6–7). The variation which Paul incorporates into the final line of his quotation ('when I take away their sins'),[56] is probably intended as an echo of Jer. 31.34 ('I will forgive their iniquity and remember their sin no more'). And it may be no coincidence that Isa. 59.21 refers to God's spirit upon them, which sounds very like the equivalent promise of Ezek. 36.27 ('I will put my spirit within you').

Two important points emerge from these observations. First, all the elements just mentioned are intended to ensure effective keeping of the covenant – by careful instruction, by the law written on the heart, by the new spirit within. Second, the promise of the new covenant explicit in the allusion to Jer. 31.31–34 is

---

[53] See further my *Theology of Paul* § 19 particularly § 19.2.

[54] Grässer, 'Alte Bund' 22.

[55] But such a usage was familiar enough in the OT, particularly in Second Isaiah (Isa. 42.6; 49.8; 55.3; 59.21; 61.8).

[56] The last line of the quotation seems to be drawn from (or modelled on) Isa. 27.9 – thus the consensus (see further my *Romans* 682–4).

that the law written on the heart will be a more effective way of keeping the law, that is a more effective way of fulfilling covenant obligation; similarly Ezek 36.27 ('I will put my spirit within you and make you careful to observe my ordinances'). In other words, the covenant envisaged in Isa. 59.21 is a variation of the new covenant of Jer. 31.33, and both are better described as renewals of the Sinai covenant or indeed as the promise of a more effective implementation of the earlier covenant by divine initiative.[57]

More important still, the promise is explicitly to Israel: its fulfilment is what will constitute the eschatological salvation of 'all Israel' (Rom. 11.26). The inference drawn from Rom. 9.4 is thus confirmed: the covenant in view is still Israel's. Israel's promised salvation is not to be brought about by a switch to a covenant other than that already given to them and reaffirmed to them.[58]

This obvious conclusion has posed such a puzzle to traditional Christian covenant theology that many have been encouraged to resolve the puzzle by splitting Paul's covenant theology into two covenants: a covenant with Israel which endures, and the new covenant which is Christianity's means of salvation; Israel will be saved in terms of its own covenant, whereas Christians will be saved by gospel grace through faith.[59] But that cannot be right. It would run counter to Paul's universal assumption elsewhere that the gospel is the eschatological unfolding of the saving righteousness of God, not least in the thematic statement of Romans itself (Rom. 1.16–17). In Paul's perspective the 'redeemer out of Zion' could hardly be other than Christ.[60] Which is also to say that the effective covenant in view in Isa. 59.21 can hardly be different from the 'new covenant' of 1 Cor. 11.25 and 2 Cor. 3.6. In other words, it is the same covenant which is in view – not two covenants, not a Jewish covenant different from a Christian covenant, but one and the same. The covenant in terms of which relationship with God is established for Christians is the covenant given to Israel, whose more effective implementation was looked forward to by Jeremiah and Ezekiel.[61]

A striking feature thus emerges from this most Pauline of Paul's letters: that Paul does not speak of the 'covenant' in Rom. 1–8, but only in Rom. 9–11; that the only two covenant references in Romans are to the covenant(s) with Israel;

---

[57] D. Zeller, *Der Brief an die Römer* (RNT; Regensburg: Pustet, 1985) 199, notes the association of forgiveness of sins and covenant renewal in *Jub.*22.14–15; *Pss. Sol.* 18.5; and Qumran. See also Moo, *Romans* 729.

[58] Cf. Merklein, 'Der (neue) Bund' 306; Christiansen, *Covenant* 226–7. Grässer, 'Alte Bund' 18–19, disputes the link/equation between the covenant of 9.4 and that of 11.27, despite recognizing that 9.4 could include a reference to Jer. 31.31, 33.

[59] See those cited in my *Romans* 683 and *Theology of Paul* 528 n.138, with further discussion there.

[60] Despite the suggestion of some that 'the deliverer' in view was Yahweh (e.g. C.D. Stanley, '"The Redeemer Will Come *ek Sion*": Romans 11.26–27', in C.A. Evans & J.A. Sanders, eds., *Paul and the Scriptures of Israel* (JSNTS 83; Sheffield: JSOT, 1993) 118–42 (here 137–8).

[61] Once again in dispute with Grässer, 'Alte Bund' 24–5.

that Paul uses the concept of covenant in Romans only when talking about his own people. Which is also further confirmation that Paul does not make use of 'covenant' terminology as a major building block of his own theology as apostle to the Gentiles.[62] Or to be more precise, he does not use 'covenant' language except to reinforce what was evidently an important claim for him, that Gentiles who believe in Jesus Christ are accepted by God on no other terms than the covenant with the fathers, the promise of Isaac and the call of Jacob (9.7–12) .

VI

What may we say in conclusion? Does Paul have a covenant theology?

1. Paul's use of the term 'covenant' is surprisingly casual when we consider the weight of significance subsequent theology invested in it. He drew it in because it provided a word-play in Gal. 3, and in Gal. 4 because a view of Abraham's sonship was being argued which ran counter to his gospel. In the Corinthian correspondence he twice speaks of the 'new covenant': in the one case because it was given to him in the tradition of the Last Supper, but without making any more of it on his own account; and in the other case probably to counter a reading of Moses' ministry which was being used to diminish his own. Finally in Romans he used the term twice, both references within his exposition of Israel, but never in the earlier exposition of his gospel. In other words, the theme of 'covenant' was not a central or major category within his own theologizing.

2. In every case the reference is determined by Israel's scriptures and focuses on a central aspect of Israel's self-identity and hope: the promise to Abraham of seed; the new covenant promise of Jeremiah, that is, the promise of a more effective implementation of Israel's covenant; the covenants of and with Israel, including the promised covenant of eschatological salvation. It is important to appreciate that Paul's talk of covenant is restricted within these themes. He did not use it to develop a theology of a different covenant for Christians. Even his talk of 'new covenant' is much more nuanced than is usually recognized. And in his single most important letter (Romans) the only covenant in view is the covenant(s) with Israel. The consequences for Israel's identity within Paul's theology are of exceeding importance, and the consequences for Christian identity as essentially sharers in Israel's identity are still more profound.

3. If, then, we are to speak of Paul's 'covenant theology', it must be not just in terms of Paul taking over the categories of Israel's covenant and applying them to Christians, but in terms of Paul affirming Israel's covenant, and doing so in terms which Israel could recognize. It must be in terms of believers, Jew first but also Gentile, being given share in the covenant relationship of God with Israel.

---

[62] Covenant is not a category of changed identity (Christiansen, *Covenant* 232).

Where that heritage was disputed, as its terms certainly were between Paul and other missionaries, it was a dispute within that heritage, not dissimilar in terms and claims to the dispute between the Qumran new covenanters and the rest of Israel. The dispute was not over the fact of the covenant, or that it was Israel's covenant, or that it was open to Gentiles. The dispute was rather over its terms and timing, of how sonship to Abraham was determined and sustained, of how Moses functioned as a paradigm of ministry, and of how its eschatological promise would be implemented. Paul's covenant theology is an in-house contribution to Israel's understanding of itself as God's covenant people.

Chapter 21

Paul and the Torah:

The role and function of the Law in the theology of
Paul the Apostle

There is nothing quite so complex in Paul's theology as the role and function which he attributes to the law. In my *Theology of Paul the Apostle* I found it necessary to devote three different sections to analysing what Paul writes on the subject.[1] And there have been several weighty treatments of the theme over the past decade or so.[2] It is not possible, therefore, to do adequate justice to the subject in the space of a single paper. Rather than take time to remind you of the outlines of the older debate or to review some of the most recent contributions, it seems more sensible for me to attempt a brief overview of Paul's own treatment of the subject. My hope is that either through footnotes or in discussion I can pick up neglected issues, clarify obscure arguments and respond to alternative views critical of my own. I will focus on the four *Hauptbriefe*, treating them in what is probably their chronological order – Galatians, 1 and 2 Corinthians and Romans.

1. Nomos as 'the law'

My starting point is that *when Paul wrote of the law (*nomos*) he almost always intended his readers to think particularly of the law of Moses, the Torah.*

1.1   So far as *Galatians* is concerned, there is a clear consensus that Paul was addressing churches almost persuaded by other Jewish missionaries to accept circumcision (2.2–4, 14; 5.2–4, 11–12; 6.12–16). That is, they were being urged as Gentile converts to accept the obligations laid upon the Israel of God in the Torah, to accept the Jewish way of life (to 'judaize').[3] So when Paul used the

---

[1] *The Theology of Paul the Apostle* (Grand Rapids: Eerdmans, 1998) ##6, 14, 23.

[2] For bibliography see particularly J.D.G. Dunn, ed., *Paul and the Mosaic Law* (WUNT 89; Tübingen: Mohr Siebeck) 1996; V. Koperski, *What are they saying about Paul and the Law?* (New York: Paulist, 2001).

[3] I use 'judaize' in its ancient sense – 'to follow a Jewish way of life' (see my *Galatians* [BNTC; London: A. & C. Black, 1993] 129); the contemporary sense of 'judaizer' = a Jew or

term 'law' for the first time in the letter ('works of law' – 2.16) there could be
little doubt that he was referring to what the law of Moses required. His reference to the coming of the law in 3.17 could refer to nothing other than the giving of the law at Sinai (cf. 4.25). And his challenge in 4.21 to those who wanted to
be 'under law' (*hupo nomon*) was clearly directed to those of his Galatian converts who were being convinced that they should become full proselytes by accepting the obligations of Israel under the law.[4]

In *1 Corinthians* Paul again speaks of those 'under law' (9.20), evidently referring to the typical and distinctive Jewish life-style, and appeals to 'the law' on
several occasions (9.8–9; 14.21, 34). Evidently, even though he was addressing a
very mixed congregation, he could take it for granted that his audiences would
hear the term 'law' as a reference to the Jewish Torah.[5]

In *2 Corinthians* Paul never mentions 'law' as such. But it is very noticeable
that his lengthy self-defence in chs. 1–3 climaxes in a contrast between his own
ministry and that of Moses, between the 'new covenant' and that written on 'tablets of stone' (3.3–11), where allusion to Exod. 31.18 and 32.15 can hardly be
doubted.[6] Evidently the role and law of Moses provided an important foil in his
theologizing.

Romans can be described as Paul's 'law-book', at least in the sense that *nomos*
occurs there more than in any other NT writing. And once again it should occasion more surprise than it does that in writing to unknown, largely Gentile churches, Paul could initially refer to 'law' without further explanation (2.12). The
assumption presumably was that the thrust of his argument, already implicitly in
dialogue with a characteristically Jewish interlocutor (2.1–11),[7] would leave no
doubt that he was referring primarily to the Torah. And even if the point was not
immediately obvious for some, the continuation of the exposition would soon
have removed any doubt on the matter: the 'Jew' 'rests on *nomos*' and 'boasts in
nomos', but has to be challenged by reference to the ten commandments as to
whether he does indeed 'practise *nomos*' (2.17–27); the Jewish law is clearly in
view. Similarly Paul sums up his slashing indictment (1.18–3.18), climaxing in the
fearsome catalogue of judgmental texts, drawn principally from the Psalms

---

Christian Jewish missionary trying to persuade Gentile Christian converts to become proselytes, is a 19th century adaptation.

[4] See further on 5.3 my *Galatians* 265–7.

[5] The reference to the law as 'the power of sin' in 1 Cor. 15.56 presumably has in mind both
the law's effect in stimulating sin ('the law of sin') and its role in condemning sin to death (as in
Rom. 1.32); see further below #4; my *Theology of Paul* 159; A.C. Thiselton, *1 Corinthians*
(NIGTC; Grand Rapids: Eerdmans, 2000) 1303.

[6] There is a substantial consensus that Paul intended an allusion to the new covenant
promised in Jer. 31.31 (sample bibliography in my *Theology of Paul* 147 n.103).

[7] That 2.1 is addressed to a Jewish interlocutor, subsequently identified explicitly (2.17), is
again the consensus view; see again my *Theology of Paul* 115 n.67; to which add D. Moo, *Romans* (NICNT; Grand Rapids: Eerdmans, 1996) 128–30.

(3.10–18), by observing that what 'the law' says it says to those 'within the law' (*en tō nomō*), that is, presumably, those who regarded the Psalms as part of their people's holy writings.

Likewise ch. 5 envisages a time before *nomos*, and a time when '*nomos* came in' (5.13, 20), presumably thinking of the time when the law was given at Sinai (as in Gal. 3.17). Ch. 7 begins with an appeal to those who know *nomos* (7.1), where most agree that Paul had the Jewish law in mind, in this case regarding the legal status of the wife in relation to her husband.[8] And an intensive section on *nomos, ho nomos*, begins by identifying this law as forbidding people to covet, the tenth commandment of the decalogue (7.7; Exod. 20.17), and by insisting that 'the law' is 'holy' (7.12) – undoubtedly referring to the law of Moses.

In short, it is clear enough that when Paul referred to 'law' or 'the law' he assumed that his readers would think first and foremost of the Torah. The presence or absence of the definite article seems to make little or no difference. We certainly cannot deduce that the anarthrous *nomos* means something like 'the principle of law' and that only *ho nomos*, 'the law', refers to the Mosaic law.[9]

1.2　Some qualifications or clarifications are in order, however.

For one thing Paul can use *nomos* in a *narrow* sense, more or less synonymous with 'the commandment', as in Rom. 7.7–12. More to the point, he can see the law as summed up or focused in a single commandment like 'You shall not covet' (7.7), or in the requirement of circumcision (Gal. 5.3), or in the word, 'You shall love your neighbour as yourself' (5.14; Rom. 13.9).

At the same time, he can use *nomos* in a *broader* sense, to include what lies in the narrative material in the Pentateuch (Rom. 4 as elaboration of 3.31; Gal. 4.22–30 as exposition of 4.21). In Rom 3.10–19, 'what the law says' refers to the catalogue of texts just cited, none of which come from the Pentateuch. And in 1 Cor. 14.21 the passage cited from 'the law' is from Isa. 28.11–12. In other words, there is some flexibility in Paul's talk of 'law/the law', though the predominant weight lies in the middle of the range of usage, denoting first and foremost the law of Moses.

Some wish to press this flexibility in Paul's use of *nomos* still further. They find it difficult to envisage Paul linking 'the law' with the highly positive motifs of his theology, 'faith', 'Spirit' and 'Christ' – (1) 'the law of faith' (Rom. 3.27), (2) 'the law of the Spirit' (8.2) and (3) 'the law of Christ' (Gal. 6.2). For them it makes more sense to understand Paul using *nomos* in the sense of 'principle' or 'rule' rather than in the more specific sense of 'law'/'Jewish law'.[10] That is certainly a very possible usage for *nomos* at the time of Paul, as Heikki Räisänen in

---

[8] See further my *Romans* (WBC 38; Dallas: Word, 1988) 359–60; Moo, *Romans* 411–2; T.R. Schreiner, *Romans* (Grand Rapids: Baker, 1998) 346–7.

[9] See further my *Theology of Paul* 131–3.

[10] This is the larger consensus, well illustrated by Moo, *Romans* 247–50.

particular has shown.[11] The only trouble is that in each case the context shows that Paul is thinking in terms of the Mosaic law as such.

The case can be made briefly. (1) In Rom. 3.27–31 we have an *inclusio* where 'the *nomos of faith*' (3.27) is spelled out as the law 'established' *through faith* (3.31), where, clearly the Pentateuch is in view.[12] (2) Rom. 8.2 is the climax to an argument where Paul has defended the law by depicting it as a tool used by sin (7.13–23) – hence 'the *nomos* of sin' (7.23; 8.2). The implication is hardly distant that a different power could use this essentially holy, good and spiritual law (7.12–14) in a positive way – hence 'the *nomos* of the Spirit' (8.2). That the same law is in mind in this latter phrase is indicated by the end-point of the argument: 'the law of the Spirit of life' has in view the objective 'that the requirement of the law might be fulfilled' in those who walk 'in accordance with the Spirit' (8.4). Obviously the term *nomos* is being used flexibly, but the crucial point is that 'the law of the Spirit' enables the believer to fulfil the law.[13] And (3) in Gal. 6.2 'the law of Christ' is best understood as taking up the thought of 5.14: the law summed up in the commandment to 'love your neighbour as yourself' (Lev. 19.18) is equally summed up by Christ's teaching and life as a living out of the love command.[14] It has been too little noticed that the command to 'love the neighbour' is equally portrayed as summing up and fulfilling the whole law in Rom. 13.8–10, and equally echoed by reference to Jesus' example in 'pleasing' the neighbour (15.1–3).[15]

The argument should not be narrowly conceived here as though *nomos* always referred to the law of Moses as such, the specific commands contained in the legal sections of the Pentateuch. It is clear enough that Paul could and did

---

[11] H. Räisänen, 'Paul's Word-Play on nomos: A Linguistic Study', *Jesus, Paul and Torah: Collected Essays* (JSNTS 43; Sheffield: Sheffield Academic, 1992) 69–94. Räisänen's essays (also 'The "Law" of Faith and the Spirit', *Jesus, Paul and Torah* 48–68) have been particularly influential.

[12] Moo insists that Paul has 'fully separated "faith" from the law of Moses' (*Romans* 248), but his subsequent exposition of 3.31 (252–5) stands in some tension with this argument. The tension is resolved by noting that the negative thrust in 3.27–28 is directed not against the law as such but against 'works of the law'. That would still raise the question in 3.31a (since works of the law are what the law requires), but the distinction allows both the negative assertion of 3.27–28 and the positive assertion of 3.31 (see further #5 below). See further my *Theology of Paul* 638–9; also P. Stuhlmacher, *Romans* (Louisville: WJK,1994) 66–7; Schreiner, *Romans* 201–2.

[13] See my *Theology of Paul* 645–7; Schreiner, *Romans* 399–400 (both with further bibliography); at the Toronto SBL meeting (November 2002) J.L. Martyn, 'Deliverance from Illusion', advocated the same view, though without referring to 8.4.

[14] That Jesus' teaching on the subject (Mark 12.28–31 pars.) is in view is most likely: explicit references to Lev. 19.18 are lacking in Jewish literature prior to Jesus, and such allusions as there are give it no particular prominence (see my *Romans* 778–80; *Theology of Paul* 655–6). See also B.W. Longenecker, *The Triumph of Abraham's God: The Transformation of Identity in Galatians* (Edinburgh: T. & T. Clark, 1998) 85–7, with further bibliography in n.27.

[15] Paul speaks of the 'neighbour' on only three occasions – Gal. 5.14; Rom. 13.9–10; 15.2. That he was thinking of the command to love 'the neighbour' when he wrote 15.2 is therefore very probable.

use *nomos* more loosely than that. What I am more confident of is that central to his range of usage for *nomos* was the meaning, *nomos/ho nomos* = the Torah. *For Paul the primary and normative reference was to the law of Moses*, however loose or more extended any particular usage might be. If this insight is true to the mind of Paul it may have further corollaries or ramifications in what follows.

2. The law in Galatians

If indeed *nomos* = the law of Moses in Paul's letters, then that is also to say that *the primary function of 'the law' for Paul must have been as 'the law of Israel'*, or to be more accurate, *the law for Israel*. This function of the law Paul spells out most clearly in his letter to the churches in Galatia.

In Gal. 3.19 Paul explicitly asks: 'Why then the law?' Previously in the letter the law has been presented in rather negative terms: something to which Paul himself had died (2.19), not the means to righteousness (2.21; 3.11), not 'of faith' (3.12), effecting a curse (3.10, 13), somehow antithetical to the promise and inheritance of Abraham (3.17–18). So well might he ask the question: in that case, 'why the law?'

Paul's answer to that question has been much debated. But the short answer seems to be that the law was given for two pre-eminent reasons: (1) to protect Israel (3.23–24), (2) until the promise could be fulfilled in Christ (3.19, 22, 23–26, 29).

2.1   The protective role of the law is most clearly indicated in 3.23–24: 'before the coming of faith we (Jews/Israel) were held in custody under the law, confined till the faith which was to come should be revealed, so that the law became our custodian to Christ ...'. The verb translated 'held in custody' has a more positive role than is usually recognized. Its principal sense is to 'guard, watch over, protect'.[16] So what seems to be envisaged is what we would now describe as a *protective* rather than a punitive custody.[17] The image is elaborated by depicting the law as a *paidagōgos*, the household slave who conducted the boy of the household to and from school, and whose responsibility typically included guarding the boy, instructing him in good manners and disciplining him when necessary. The image is essentially positive.[18] That we are on the right lines with

---

[16] See my *Galatians* 197–8.

[17] 'Confined' (3.22, 23) has a more obviously negative sense; but both here and in Rom. 11.32 (Paul's only other use of the term) the confinement is temporary and has in view a longer-term positive outcome within the purpose of God.

[18] See my *Theology of Paul* 141–2 (with further bibliography); also B. Witherington, *Grace in Galatia: A Commentary on Paul's Letter to the Galatians* (Grand Rapids: Eerdmans, 1998) 262–6; otherwise J.L. Martyn, *Galatians* (AB 33A; New York: Doubelday, 1997) 363.

this interpretation is confirmed by Paul's return to the imagery of the under-age heir, under the authority of guardians and stewards, as depicting the status of Israel prior to the coming of faith (4.1–2). In other words, the role attributed to the law in this passage is that of protecting Israel in the immaturity of its youth from the enticements and entanglements, particularly the idolatry, impurity and lower moral standards of the wider Gentile world.

If we ask for further detail on how the law carried out this function, then the best clues are given in the first part of Paul's answer to the question, 'Why the law?' (3.19). The immediate response is that the law 'was added for the sake of transgressions' (3.19). This could mean, 'in order to make clear what constituted transgression' – an early formulation of the function repeatedly attributed to the law in the later Romans.[19] That is, in terms of the image of the immature child needing to be instructed and trained, the law's function was to provide clear guidelines to direct the child and boundaries to prevent him veering from the correct path.[20] The phrase 'for the sake of (*charin*) transgressions' may be intended to indicate a still more positive role: in order to deal with transgressions; that is, referring to the provision made through the law for repentance and atonement.[21]

The second clue is the denial to the law of any role of giving life: had the law been able to give life (*dunamenos zōopoiēsai*) then righteousness would be from the law (3.21). This affirmation, we should note, is Paul's response to the question whether the law is against the promises of God. 'Of course not!', says Paul; 'for had the law been given which was able to make alive, then righteousness certainly would be from the law' (3.21). The denial is clear: the law is not antithetical to the promise. The further implication is that the promise and the law operate on different levels: the *promise* could be said to give life,[22] but not the law; it is from the promise's life-giving function that righteousness comes. What then is the function of the law? The obvious short answer is that the law is given for the lesser but still positive function of ordering the life given by the promise; it does not *give* life, it *regulates* life. This would certainly accord with the role of the law as characteristically set out in Israel's pre-eminent book of the covenant (Deuteronomy), and with its role as summarized in Lev. 18.5 – the law as providing the rules by which Israel should live (Gal. 3.11).[23] Perhaps more to the point here,

---

[19] So still Martyn, *Galatians* 354–5; see below 457–8.

[20] The common view that 'for the sake of transgressions' means in order to increase = produce transgression, a wholly negative role (see those cited in my *Theology of Paul* 139 n.57) hardly squares with the positive role of protective custody described a few verses later.

[21] See further my *Galatians* 188–90; and *Theology of Paul* 139.

[22] Paul almost puts his thought in these terms in Rom 4.16–18; of course, the life-giver proper is the one who makes the promise (references in *Theology of Paul* 154 n.130).

[23] The standard understanding of Lev. 18.5, as inculcating a life lived by doing the commandments, is indicated by Ezek. 20.5–26 (the earliest commentary on Lev. 18.5); as confirmed by Deut. 30.15–20; Prov. 3.1–2; 6.23; Neh. 9.29; Bar. 4.1; 1QS 4.6–8; CD 3.15–17; *Pss. Sol.* 14.2–3;

that function, indicated already in 3.11 and implied by contrast in 3.21, fits best with the role of the law as protector and custodian about to be elaborated in 3.23–24.

So once again we find a very tight focus on the law of Israel, the Torah. What is interesting for us, however, is the way in which Paul further plays variations on this basic idea of the law's protective role in relation to Israel. For the image shifts little by little from that of 'custodian' (*paidagōgos*) (3.23–25), through that of 'guardians and stewards' (4.1), to that of 'elemental forces' (*stoicheia*) (4.3, 9). And the status of those 'under' these figures likewise shifts little by little: from boy of school age ('under the *paidagōgos*' – 3.25), to the heir who is a child (*nē-pios*) ('under guardians and stewards' – 4.2), and who though an heir 'is no different from a slave' (4.1), to the condition of enslavement 'under the *stoicheia*' (4.3, 9). Notable is the fact that by the end of the transition Paul can in effect equate the law with the *stoicheia*: to accept circumcision and the rest of the works of the law insisted on by the other Jewish missionaries was equivalent to turning back and becoming enslaved once again to 'the weak and beggarly elemental forces' (4.9). In other words, the role of the law in its capacity as protector and guardian of Israel is closely similar to that of the *stoicheia* popularly thought to determine the destiny of individuals and nations.[24] The law, we might say, functioned for Paul somewhat as Israel's guardian angel. Along the lines of Deut. 32.8–9, God had appointed guardian angels for each of the nations but had kept Israel for himself.[25] Paul may have elaborated that thought in 3.19–20 in the light of Deut. 33.2–4,[26] to the effect that the law thus given was the means by which God exercised the guardianship over Israel which he had reserved for himself.

If we are on the right lines here, it becomes again clear that Paul did not hesitate to treat *nomos* in a quite flexible or expansive way. The focus on the Torah of Israel remains firm. But he could both narrow and broaden that focus. He narrowed it by limiting its role in Gal. 3–4 to that of protecting and probably of regulating Israel's life. But he also broadened it by setting that narrower role against the cosmic perspective of God's purpose for the nations as a whole and not just for Israel. Within that broader sweep, this role of the law can be likened to that

---

Ep. Arist. 127; Philo, *Cong.* 86–87; *LAB* 23.10; 4 Ezra 7.21; *m. Abot* 2.7; 'the law of life' (Sir. 17.11; 45.5; 4 Ezra 14.30); 'the commandments of life' (Bar. 3.9). The thought seems to have emerged (in Qumran?) that the length of life thus promised could be expressed in terms of (acquiring) 'eternal life' (1QS 4.7 – 'plentiful peace in a long life ... eternal enjoyment with endless life'; CD 3.20 – he 'will acquire eternal life'; 7.6 – 'they shall live a thousand generations'); see again *m. Abot* 2.7. The thought of resurrection to eternal life (Dan. 12.2; 2 Macc. 7.9; cf. 4 Macc. 15.3) does not appear to be so directly connected with Lev. 18.5. S.J. Gathercole, *Where is Boasting? Early Jewish Soteriology and Paul's Response in Romans 1–5* (Grand Rapids: Eerdmans, 2002) 66–7, 100–02, treats the senses 'way of life'/'way to life' too antithetically.

[24] Details in *Theology of Paul* 107–8; Longenecker, *Triumph* 127–8.

[25] A familiar interpretation of Deut 32.8–9 (LXX); Sir. 17.17; *Jub.* 15.31–32; *1 Enoch* 20.5; *Targ. Ps. Jon.* on Gen. 11.7–8.

[26] 'The Lord came from Sinai ... and with him were myriads of holy ones ...' (REB).

of a guardian angel, equivalent to the protective, directive role of the angels appointed as rulers over the other nations. Here we are not far from the idea of the Torah as embodying a cosmic law, as a particular expression of a divine order to which all nations are subject. The irony is that the angelic rulers of other nations can be corrupted to the level of enslaving *stoicheia* (cf. *Jub.* 15.31–32; Barn. 9.4), and that if other nations try to put themselves under the rule of the law, Israel's guardian angel, it is tantamount to treating the law as one of the *stoicheia* and to accepting a status of slavery under the law.

2.2   It is even clearer that Paul regarded this function of the Torah, in protecting Israel, as *limited in time*. Paul makes the point repeatedly: the law 'was added for the sake of transgressions, until the coming of the seed' (3.19); its protective role was in force 'before the coming of this faith ...; we were confined till the faith which was to come should be revealed' (3.23); 'but with faith having come, we are no longer under the custodian' (3.25); the child heir 'is under guardians and stewards, until the time set by the father' (4.2); 'when the fullness of the time came, God sent his son ... born under the law, in order that he might redeem those under the law ...' (4.4–5).

Evidently the protective function of the law vis-à-vis Israel was intended by the divine law-giver as *a temporary measure*. That function was limited to the period before the coming of Christ. But with the coming of Christ and the new possibility of faith[27] which his coming opened up, the need for that protective role had ceased. That status of protection, 'under the law', 'under guardians', was necessary for the heir only so long as the heir was a child. But Christ's coming marked the transition to maturity for the people of God's purpose, when they could begin to enter into the full inheritance (as actualized and attested by the Spirit) (4.5–7). So *there was no longer need for the law in its role as protector and regulator of the immature child*. And to want to live life wholly regulated by the law was to want to go back to that immaturity and to its slave-equivalent status (4.1, 9).

Here again, then, we see how Paul could treat the law in both a restrictive and a much wider sense. The law as focused in circumcision was the law in its distinguishing and protecting Israel mode. That role was passé. At the same time, Paul could also say later that the law as focused in the love command (5.14) was still highly relevant; and as summed up and lived out by Christ, 'the law of Christ' (6.2), it still carried obligations for believers.

On the other hand he could set the law within the cosmic sweep of God's purpose for creation. Christ's coming, we might say, marked a cosmic shift in the

---

[27] I remain unconvinced by the currently popular view that 'the coming of faith' in 3.23, 25 refers to 'the faithfulness of Christ'; the coming of faith in Christ, as the possibility opened up by the coming of Christ, so typified the new age for Paul that he could speak of it simply as the coming of faith; for the vigorous debate on the subject see further my *Theology of Paul* 379–85.

ages, from 'the present evil age' of 1.4 to the 'new creation' of 6.15. Within that
universal sweep, the role of the law can be seen as not merely equivalent to
angelic rule over other nations, but as having a firm and positive purpose in relation to Israel and in preparation for the 'fullness of time'. In short, the particularist role of the law as Israel's protector can be seen within a larger framework,
both spatial and temporal, set on both a cosmic and a salvation-history scale.

In the light of this analysis it becomes clearer what Paul's objection to the law
amounts to, or more precisely what his objection to Gentile converts putting
themselves under the law amounts to. The problem was Israel's failure to see
that with the coming of Christ everything had changed. The coming of Christ
had ended the need for the law's role as protector of Israel from the Gentiles.
The positive role previously played by the law in regard to Israel had been superseded by Christ; the maturity marked by the coming of the Spirit meant that the
period of restrictive childhood has been left behind (4.6–7). How then could
those who had experienced this freedom want to go back to the comparative
slavery of a life restricted by law and circumcision to those of 'fleshly' descent
from Abraham (4.8–11; 4.21–5.1)? Instead, life could and should now be lived
under the guidance of the Spirit, faith working through love, life of a different
quality than life under the law, under the *stoicheia* (ch. 5). What had been positive in the law's function during the pre-Christ, pre-faith epoch was not thereby
lost. In the new cosmic and salvation-historical framework, that positive role
had been superseded by Christ, was now focused in the love command and could
be summed up as 'the law of Christ'.

In short, the law was inevitably to be seen as Israel's law first and foremost.
But if the law was regarded as the law for Israel alone, as securing righteousness
for Jews alone, then it was effete and worse than useless. Only as summed up in
the love command, as interpreted and lived out by Christ, did it still have a role.

3. The law in Corinthians

The few relevant references in Corinthians *confirm both the negative and the
positive attitudes to the law documented in Galatians.*

3.1 In *2 Corinthians 3* we see a similar contrast to that which dominated Galatians 3–4. In Galatians Paul posed a sharp contrast between promise and law, the
law in its relation to Israel as a temporary function until the time came for the
fulfilment of the promise in Christ. To attempt to extend that function to Gentiles was to impose on these Gentiles a form of slavery. In 2 Corinthians 3 the
contrast is rather one between old and new covenant.[28] But the sense of an es-

---

[28] It is worth noting that the contrast old/new covenant is lacking in Galatians (cf. 3.15, 17;

chatological shift is the same: the old Mosaic covenant has been superseded by the new one promised by the prophets.[29] And quite similar too is the contrast between a much more limited benefit (only Moses experienced the glory, a fading glory at that – 3.13) and a more open benefit ('we all with unveiled faces' continue to experience a transforming glory – 3.18).

At the same time, the contrast seems much sharper: between a 'written code' (*gramma*) that kills, and the Spirit that gives life (3.6); between a ministry of death and of condemnation, and the ministry of the Spirit and of righteousness (3.7, 9). But we should note that the ministry of Moses was one of 'glory' (3.7–11), albeit a lesser glory now set aside. And Moses' going into the presence of the Lord (Exod. 34.34) is presented as a type of Christian conversion (2 Cor. 3.6).[30] More to the immediate point, the fact that Paul uses *gramma* and not *nomos* should be given more weight than is usually the case. The point is that *gramma* is not simply a synonym for *nomos*. It focuses rather on the law as written, visible to sight in the written letter. *Gramma* is not the law *per se*, but the law in its obvious aspect, the old covenant in its most immediate reference as the covenant with Israel.[31]

In other words, the contrast between Spirit and letter is very close to that between promise and law. The law here to which Paul in effect objects is not the law as such, but the law in a more limited characterisation as *gramma*, that is, the law as focused in the commandments which marked out the covenant as Israel's, the law as focused in circumcision (Rom. 2.28–29). When the law is read in such a restrictive way, Paul says, it is deadly in its outworking.

3.2   In 1 Cor. 7.19, however, we see the other side of Paul's treatment of the law. For he makes the astonishing assertion that 'Circumcision is nothing and uncircumcision is nothing, but keeping God's commandments'. It should be clear at once that *only someone who worked with a differentiated concept of God's law/commandment could make such a distinction*. Paul would not need to be told that circumcision was one of 'God's commandments'. He would be fully aware that such a statement would be self-contradictory to a devout Jew. If nothing else made it clear, at least 1 Cor. 7.19 should make it clear that Paul *both* devalued (aspects of) the law *and* regarded (aspects of) the law as still an obligation on his converts.[32]

4.24); see further my contribution to S.E. Porter & J.C.R. de Roo, eds., *The Concept of the Covenant in the Second Temple Period* (Leiden: Brill, 2003) 287–307 [= ch. 20 above].

[29] See above n.6.

[30] See further my '2 Corinthians 3.17 – "The Lord is the Spirit"', *JTS* 21 (1970) 309–20; reprinted in *The Christ and the Spirit, Vol. 1 Christology* (Grand Rapids: Eerdmans, 1998) 115–25.

[31] The point is even clearer in Rom. 2.28–29 (see my *Romans* 123–5).

[32] Cf. W. Schrage, *1 Korinther* (EKK 7/2; Düsseldorf: Benziger, 1995): 'Das Ende des Gesetzes als Heilsweg (Röm 10,4) impliziert nicht sein Ende als Lebensweisung' (136).

The obvious solution to the conundrum he thus poses is fairly straightforward. For the contrast 'Neither circumcision, nor uncircumcision, but ...' is one which Paul had used already, twice in Galatians (5.6; 6.15); it is evidently the same contrast that he echoes in 1 Cor. 7.19.[33] We can deduce, therefore, that the negative side of the contrast echoes the emphasis Paul made in Galatians: in each case he was warning against the claim made by his fellow (believing) Jews that identification with Israel (becoming a proselyte) by means of circumcision was essential to sharing the inheritance and blessing of Abraham. The positive side of the contrasts is presumably correlated similarly, though with different emphases in accordance with the different situations addressed. In Galatians, where the threat of another gospel was critical, Paul insisted that faith working through love rendered circumcision unnecessary, that the 'new creation' rendered circumcision passé. In 1 Corinthians, where the threat was different, Paul had no qualms in emphasising the importance of keeping God's commandments – so long as it was sufficiently clear that the commandment which marked out Israel from the rest of the nations could be regarded with indifference *without thereby diminishing the importance of keeping God's commandments.*

Here again, then, it is evident that Paul worked with a differentiated concept of *nomos*, that he had different attitudes to the law of Israel, depending on what aspect or function of the law was in view. The key seems to be the law in its connection with Israel, as the law of Israel. Where that central aspect of the law was overemphasized, in an exclusive, outward manner (the case in point being circumcision), Paul would have none of it. But the law seen as the law/commandments of God, differentiated from and not restricted to the law defining Israel, was still expressive of God's will for humankind.

4. The law in Romans

In his letter to the Romans Paul develops his view of the law, or probably more accurately, he articulates aspects of his understanding of the role of the Torah which he had not brought out (so clearly) before.

4.1   First, he affirms that *a centrally important role of the law is to serve as a measure of sin*: that is, to define sin, to make sinners conscious of their sin, and to provide a yardstick by which sin would be judged. 3.20 – 'through the law comes the knowledge of sin'; 4.15 – 'where there is no law there is also no transgression'; 5.13 – 'sin is not accounted in the absence of law'; 7.13 – 'in order that

---

[33] See further my '"Neither Circumcision Nor Uncircumcision, but ..." (Gal. 5.2–12; 6.12–16; cf. 1 Cor. 7.17–20)', in A. Vanhoye, ed., *La Foi Agissant par l'Amour (Galates 4.12–6.16)* (Rome: Abbaye de S. Paul, 1996) 79–110 [=ch. 13 above].

sin through the commandment might become utterly sinful'. This role may have
been hinted at in Gal. 3.19; but the role only becomes explicit in the later Romans. His repeated reference to this role in Romans hardly implies that he had
just thought of it(!). Rather Paul may have brought this function of the law to the
fore, since the continuing relevance of the law was being questioned in some
Christian circles, and since his own interpretation of the role of the law within
God's purpose could easily be heard as a rejection of the law, as will become
clear shortly.

It is this role of the law, as a measure of sin, to which he gives prominence in
the initial indictment of 1.18–3.20. The role is explicit in ch. 2, especially 2.12–16.
At first it seems that the judgmental function of the law is relevant only to Israel:
'as many as have sinned without the law shall also perish without the law; and as
many as have sinned within the law shall be condemned through the law' (2.12).
The Torah is, after all, the law of Israel (#2). But Paul has already appealed to a
wider (universal) awareness of 'the just decree of God' (1.32),[34] and he goes on
to envisage Gentiles who 'do by nature what the law requires', who demonstrate
the business of the law written in their hearts', and who 'keep the requirements
of the law' (2.14–15, 26). So again he was thinking of God's *nomos* as focused in
the Torah, but as not limited to the Torah or restricted within the Torah. If those
who do not know the Torah nevertheless know God's just decree and do God's
nomos, then *nomos* is not simply identical with Torah.[35] Human obligation before God is most fully expressed in the law of Israel, but is not simply co-exten-
sive with the Torah and can be known and responded to apart from the Torah.
The law, even as the law of Israel, transcends Israel.

This has particular relevance to the climax of the indictment in 3.19–20. Paul's
point is that the law holds all people accountable before God. But as Israel's law
pre-eminently, it is Israel who finds itself especially addressed by the words of
condemnation in the law. Here again Paul holds in tension thought of the law as
peculiarly Israel's, but also as providing a measure by which all humankind will
be measured.

4.2   The second role of the law which comes into sharp focus in Romans is *the
way the law is used and abused by the power of sin to incite desire/lust and to produce what is contrary to God's will*. The initial statement of the theme sounds
harshly accusatory of the law: 'the law came in to increase the trespass' (5.20).
This could be another restatement of the first theme: the law in making conscious of sin, makes more sin; or in making aware of sin makes the sin seem all
the more heinous. But when Paul returns to the theme foreshadowed in 5.20, it

---

[34] This 'knowing' (1.32) obviously harks back to the 'knowing' of 1.19, 21, 28.

[35] On the debated issue whether Paul was referring the concept of an 'unwritten law', and on
the recent emergence of the concept of 'conscience' see my *Romans* 99–102.

becomes clear that what he had in mind was the role of the law as an agent in stir-ring up sinful passions (7.5).[36] That he seems to be accusing the law of being an *instrument* and not simply a *measure* of sin is clearly implicit in the inference which Paul sees to be logical: that the law itself is sin (7.7)?! But having prompted his audience to face this possibility Paul immediately denies it, and launches into what is a vigorous defence of the law (7.7–25). The fault lies not in the law but in the weakness of flesh and the power of sin (ab)using the law to stir up desire/lust for the 'forbidden fruit'.[37]

It is this 'unwilling agent' role of the law which Paul sums up in the phrase 'law of sin' (7.23, 25; 8.2), to which reference has already been made (#1.2). It is anal-ogous to the role of the law in Galatians, when the law intended as Israel's pro-tector begins to function in regard to Gentile converts too much like one of the *stoicheia* to which they had formerly been enslaved (#2.2). And as in Galatians, the law is being set against a cosmic backcloth – not merely a code of require-ments laid on Israel by Israel's God, but capable of playing a role on a larger stage and in the heart of humankind. We might even say that as behind individ-ual sins lies (the power of) Sin, so behind the Torah lies the higher principle of God's will. At any rate, the Torah functions not simply as measure of right and wrong but can be manipulated by other powers – sadly the power of Sin, but also the power of the Spirit (8.2). In all this the law remains the expression and measure of God's will, and fulfilment of its just requirement remains the goal of those who walk 'according to the Spirit' (8.4).

4.3   The many faces of the law thus brought variously into focus become most clearly visible in 9.30–10.12. On the one hand, Paul speaks of the law in relation to Israel in most positive terms. The law was a goal to be pursued by Israel, 'the law of righteousness' (9.31).[38] Paul presumably was thinking of the law's func-tion as a standard and measure of God's will for Israel. Israel did not reach the law (9.31), but that did not diminish the role of Israel's law as God-given and as expressive of God's will. Here the thought is consistent with the idea in Gala-tians of the law functioning as Israel's protective guardian (#2.1). But as in Gala-tians, the coming of Christ and of the need for faith in Christ marked the close of that phase (9.33–10.4).[39] In consequence the more limited role of the law, in pro-viding guidance for Israel's life (10.5),[40] was also at an end.

---

[36] Presumably, since the law is thought of as given specifically to Israel, the sinful passions in-clude the strange mixture of national pride and self-indulgence indicted in 2.17–24 (see below 461–2).

[37] The echo of Gen. 3.13 in Rom. 7.11 puts the allusion to the primeval story of Adam be-yond doubt (see my *Romans* 384, and earlier 379–81; *Theology of Paul* 98–100).

[38] On the misunderstanding of the phrase see my *Romans* 581; J.A. Fitzmyer, *Romans* (AB 33; New York: Doubleday, 1993) 578.

[39] In Rom. 10.4 *telos* can mean both 'end' and 'fulfilment', but a fulfilment which brings to an end a former role (my *Romans* 589; Moo, *Romans* 636–42).

At this point Paul makes one of his boldest interpretative moves. For in 10.6–10 he cites Deut. 30.11–14 as an expression of 'the righteousness of faith', as distinct from the righteousness from the law expressed in 10.5/Lev. 18.5. But Deuteronomy 30 is the climax of 'the book of the law' (Deuteronomy), the classic statement of 'covenantal nomism'.[41] Its whole point was to urge that obedience to the law was entirely possible for Israel: 'the commandment is not too hard for you; ... the word is in your mouth and in your heart, so that you can do it' (Deut. 30.11, 14). In almost any Jewish line of exposition, Lev. 18.5 and Deut. 30.11–14 would be heard as speaking with one voice. But Paul lights on an interpretation of the Deuteronomy passage already current in Jewish circles which sees the law of which it speaks as an expression of a more universal wisdom or good.[42] And he takes the passage as referring to what he regarded as a more transcendent expression of God's will than the law seen (merely) as the Torah of Israel. The 'commandment/word' of which Deuteronomy speaks is 'the word of faith, which we preach' (Rom. 10.8). Here, as with 'the law of Christ' (Gal. 6.2), and 'the law of the Spirit' (Rom. 8.2), the law could be seen as an expression of saving righteousness, as gospel! The thought is very similar to that of Rom. 3.27 ('the law of faith'): the law as the expression of faith. This is what makes 10.6–10 a real inclusio with 9.31: the law was the law of righteousness for Israel, but Israel did not reach it because they did not pursue it 'from faith' (9.32); however, the law heard as the word of faith (10.8) is a means to righteousness to all who believe (10.4, 9–10).

In short, once again we see that the law could be conceived narrowly, focused too exclusively on Israel and on what Israel must do. For Paul that was of a piece with the law betrayed by the weakness of the flesh and abused by the distortions of the sinful passions. But the law transposed out of that restrictive and restricting perspective, the law as invoking faith and used by the Spirit for life, continued to serve as the measure of God's will and judgment.

5. The works of the law

The most striking result of this initial probe is the tremendous flexibility in Paul's talk of the Torah. Let us recap. (1) By *nomos* Paul almost always means

---

[40] It is not by chance that Paul cites Lev. 18.5 (see above n.23) in both Gal. 3.11 and Rom. 10.5, and in a way which plays down the role of the law in ordering life in some contrast to justification by faith.

[41] The phrase made popular by E.P. Sanders, *Paul and Palestinian Judaism* (London: SCM, 1977) as an attempt to replace the more traditional view of Judaism as narrowly legalistic with one which indicated better the balance between Israel's sense of election (covenant) and consequent obligation to obedience (nomism).

[42] Bar. 3.39–40; Philo, *Post.* 84–85; cf. *Targ. Neof.* on Deut. 30.11–14 (details in my *Romans* 603–5).

the law per se, Israel's Torah. But the reference can be narrow, to a particular commandment; or it can be broader – to scripture at large, or the will and wisdom of God expressed through scripture. (2) As *the law of Israel*, it can be seen as focused in a particular commandment (circumcision, love command), or as a kind of guardian angel protecting Israel. Both roles can be either negative or positive: an enslaving power, when its protective role is clung to beyond due time; *gramma*, as interpreting the commandments of God too exclusively and restrictively in relation to Israel, and thus preventing their wider and continuing applicability from being fully recognized. (3) As *the measure of sin*, the law of God is most clearly spelled out in the Torah, but is also more widely known. (4) Though expressing God's will, the law can be used and is abused by *the power of sin*. But it can also be used by *the Spirit*, and remains *a goal to be aimed at*. Israel missed that goal, failing to see that it could only be achieved through *faith*; the gospel by bringing God's fuller wisdom to expression in the word of faith made it possible for Gentiles to attain that goal.

In all this we have almost entirely ignored one of the key phrases used by Paul – the 'works of the law'. I have left discussion of the phrase till this point since its meaning and significance are more easily grasped once the broader picture of the role of the law is clear. To tackle it too soon can easily distort that larger picture. What then does Paul mean when he speaks of 'works of law'?

5.1   The phrase *erga nomou* is used by Paul only in Galatians and Romans.[43] These of course are the two letters in which Paul addresses most fully the issue of how it is that believers from nations other than Israel can claim a share in the promise and inheritance of Abraham. So we can assume that by the phrase 'works of the law' Paul had in mind specifically the law of Israel and what the Torah demands of Israel. This is borne out by the regular talk in the Hebrew Bible of the obligation on Israel to 'do' the law.[44] Hence the phrase, 'deeds or works of the law', what the law requires of the people of the law. If 'covenantal nomism' describes, however inadequately, the balance in Jewish soteriology between a people chosen by grace and the obligation laid upon that people to obey the Torah,[45] then 'works of the law' denote that obligation within the framework of God's covenant with Israel. Anticipating a little, we could define 'works of the

---

[43] Gal. 2.16 (3 times); 3.2, 5, 10; Rom. 3.20, 28; *erga* without *nomou* but probably implied (4.2, 6; 9.12, 32; 11.6).

[44] Particularly in Deuteronomy – Deut. 27.26; 28.58; 29.28; 31.12; 32.46; see further Gathercole, *Where is Boasting?* 92–3.

[45] D. A. Carson, P. T. O'Brien & M. A. Seifrid, ed., *Justification and Variegated Nomism. Volume I: The Complexities of Second Temple Judaism* (WUNT 140; Tübingen: Mohr Siebeck, 2001) test the applicability of the phrase across the spectrum of Second Temple writing. Carson interprets the findings negatively (543–8), but the findings actually confirm that most of the writings examined did insist on a balance between the two emphases. F. Avemarie, *Tora und Leben: Untersuchungen zur Heilsbedeutung der Tora in der frühen rabbinischen Literatur*

law' more fully as *what members of the covenant must do in order to attest their membership, to live their life as God's people, to secure acquittal in the final judgment, and* (when thought of life beyond death emerges) *to ensure participation in the life of the age to come.*[46] The thought, it should be noted, is not so much of meriting a reward as of attaining an inheritance already promised.[47]

If that is a fair summary of where the debate on 'works of the law' now stands, then we might well ask what Paul was objecting to when he denied so emphatically that 'no one is/will be justified from works of the law' (Gal. 2.16; Rom. 3.20)?

5.2 A clue is given in what seems to be the earliest attested use of the phrase itself – that is, in the now famous 4QMMT, a letter written by a or the leading figure in the Qumran sect to explain to others in Israel the sect's distinctive halakhah. It is clear from the context that the phrase *miqsat ma'ase ha-torah* (113/ C27),[48] 'some of the works of the law', refers to the sect's interpretation of various laws relating to the temple, priesthood, sacrifices and purity (3–5/B1– 2).[49] The sect evidently regarded their differences of interpretation as sufficient reason to 'separate' itself from the rest of Israel (92/C7).[50] The letter itself ends by urging the recipients to follow the sect's halakhah, assuring them that if they do so it will be counted to them for righteousness (116–118/C30–32). What is of interest here is the same phenomenon that we have found in Paul's wider talk of the law. That is, the letter-writer no doubt thought of *ma'ase ha-torah* as 'the works of the law' in general, all that the doings that the law required of Israel. But the specific reference is narrower, to a number of specific laws as inter-

---

(WUNT; Tübingen: Mohr Siebeck, 1996), justly warns against looking for consistency in this balance in rabbinic texts.

[46] In my work I have emphasized particularly the first two of this fourfold aim, principally because they had been neglected; see my *Theology of Paul* 354–9 (bibliography on 335; add 'Noch einmal "Works of the Law": The Dialogue Continues', in I. Dunderberg, et al., eds., *Fair Play: Diversity and Conflicts in Early Christianity*, H. Räisänen FS (Leiden: Brill, 2002) 273–90 [=ch. 19 above]. Gathercole, *Where is Boasting?*, properly emphasizes the last two of this fourfold aim, though see n.23 above.

[47] One of the features of the Carson et al., eds. *Justification* volume is the regular denial by contributors that merit was the basis of Israel's continuing relationship with God (9, 29, 41–42, 218, 222, 238, 324, 331, 353, 396–7); for the thought we should compare rather Paul's own concern to attain the prize (1 Cor. 9.24–27; Phil. 3.14).

[48] References are to the translation by F.G. Martinez, *The Dead Sea Scrolls Translated* (Leiden: Brill, ²1996) 77–79, and the critical text by E. Qimron & J. Strugnell, *Miqsat Ma'ase Ha-Torah* (DJD 10.5; Oxford: Clarendon, 1994).

[49] The sequence of halakhoth is introduced thus: 'These are some of our rulings ... which are ... the works ...'(3–5/B1–2); and individual rulings that follow are regularly introduced by the formula, 'we are of the opinion that' (11, 32, 39, 40, 45, 58, 76/B8, 29, 36, 37, 42, 55, 73).

[50] The verb used, *parash*, is clearly attested in this sense for the first time in ancient literature; an echo of the Pharisees' defining characteristic (*parushim* = 'separated ones') would hardly be lost on Paul.

preted by the sect. The general principle that Israel must do what the law requires (the works of the law) came to focus in the halakhic rulings which distinguished the sect from the rest of Israel and caused them to separate from the rest of Israel on the grounds that the rest of Israel was failing in the works of the law. Unless the rest of Israel did these works of the law they would not be 'reckoned righteous' at the end of time.

So the thought is of final vindication. But it is not so much of meriting that acquittal. It is more the thought of securing an acquittal assured only to those who followed the Qumran halakhah – an exclusive righteousness rather than an earned righteousness.

5.3 The parallel with Paul's earliest use of the phrase in *Galatians* is astonishing.[51] For Paul first talks of 'the works of the law' (Gal. 2.16) in the wake of describing his response to two attempts by Jewish believers to coerce Gentiles into adopting Jewish practice – circumcision (2.1–10) and food laws, which otherwise would prevent Jew eating with Gentile (2.11–14). Insistence on the latter by Peter and the other Jewish believers in Antioch had been sufficient ground for them to '*separate*' (2.12) from the Gentile believers (the same word used by the Qumran sect). In taking his response further in the letter itself, Paul draws from these episodes the general principle, repeated for emphasis, that 'no one is/will be justified from works of the law' (2.16). And a few verses later he goes on to point out that it was from his faith that *righteousness was reckoned* to Abraham (3.6 – echoing the same text, Gen. 15.6, as the Qumran letter).

All this suggests that Paul was using 'works of the law' in a way similar to the only other known use of the period. That is, he was thinking of the general principle (Israel's obligation to do the law), but of the general principle in its application to particular issues. As the Qumran halakhic rulings were controversial within Israel, so Paul regarded the Jewish Christian rulings on circumcision and table-fellowship with Gentiles as controversial in the same way. Qumran insisted that observance of its halakhic rulings, these works of the law, was necessary for final justification. Similarly in Paul's view, his opponents, by insisting that Gentile believers must accept circumcision and observe the laws of clean and unclean, were making justification with God dependent on works of the law.[52] Here again the thought is of exclusive justification (those who failed thus to 'do' the law would not be justified) rather than of justification merited.

A question may help further clarify Paul's thought. Would he have said the same about other commandments, about the Torah's forbidding of *idolatry* or *porneia*, for example? Not entirely, for his warnings against both show how

---

[51] See my '4QMMT and Galatians', *NTS* 43 (1997) 147–53 [= ch. 14 above].

[52] Witheringon, *Grace in Galatia* 176–7 confuses the parallel; in both cases it was '*some* of the works of the law' which posed the more fundamental issue.

traditional Paul could be.[53] He would not have seen avoidance of both as grounds for salvation, though he probably feared that practice of either put salvation at peril. But he probably would not have spoken of them as 'works of the law'. In other words, the negative denunciation of 'works of the law' should not be taken as a denunciation of doing the law in general. There was a principle at stake for Paul: that acceptance of the gospel depends only on faith. But the particular focus of the negative thrust of the general principle is against the insistence that certain laws had to be observed if justification was to be secure. In view of our earlier findings regarding Paul's flexible use of *nomos*, this ambiguity in his talk of 'works of the law' should occasion little surprise.

The use of a more general principle in more specific application probably explains the other occurrences of the phrase, 'works of the law' in Galatians. Paul reminds his Galatian converts that they received the Spirit without any of the requirements being insisted on by his Jewish missionary opponents (3.2, 5). And his reference to 'as many as are of works of the law' in 3.10 presumably refers to the same opponents.[54] We can also probably fairly deduce that when, in the line of argument running from 2.11–21, Paul talks of his having died to the law (2.19), it is this aspect of the law which he had in mind – that is, the assumption of his fellow Jewish believers that all believers had to take on the distinctively Jewish way of life; *that* was the law to which he had died.[55] And since the flesh is so much bound up with circumcision (3.3; 4.23; 6.12–13), it may not be straining Paul's thought too far to suggest that in this sense 'works of the flesh' (5.19) are in Paul's scheme of things not so far distant from 'works of the law'.[56]

The suggestion lies near to hand, then, that with this phrase Paul had in view the same Jewish exclusiveness and insistence on a works of the law mind-set which he subsequently attacked by arguing that the law's role as guardian protector of Israel had been ended by the coming of Christ (#2). To insist on works of the law was to return to the under-age slavery of an inheritance restricted to the law-ful heirs of Abraham.

5.4   With *Romans* Paul was able to step back a little and to press the fundamental principle that justification is by faith alone and not by doing what the law lays down. But the focus of the phrase 'works of the law' still remains fairly tight on Jewish understanding of what the law requires, as unacceptable to the gospel. Rom. 3.20 makes the same universal announcement as Gal. 2.16. But again we

---

[53] See my *Theology of Paul* 32–3, 121–3, 690–2, 702–5.

[54] See my *Galatians* 170–4; *Theology of Paul* 361–2; and further J. R. Wisdom, *Blessing for the Nations and the Curse of the Law: Paul's Citation of Genesis and Deuteronomy in Gal. 3.8–10* (WUNT 2.133; Tübingen: Mohr Siebeck, 2001).

[55] See my *Galatians* 143; Longenecker, *Triumph* 111–3.

[56] In *Theology of Paul* 68–70 I observe that Paul often uses 'flesh' when referring to Jewish emphasis on ethnic identity.

notice that Paul's words are directed particularly to those '(with)in the law' (3.19). And since 3.19–20 sums up Paul's indictment (1.18–3.20), he presumably had in mind his indictment of Jewish presumption in 2.17–29 in particular. That is to say, 'works of the law' hardly describe Jewish assumption of privilege over other nations (2.17–20), but the same presumption is probably present in Jewish insistence on works of the law – that Gentile believers should do the law, including not least the sort of distinctive Jewish practices to the fore in Galatians.[57] The same implication is present a few verses later in the second reference to 'works of the law' (3.28), since the line of argument makes clear that insistence on works of the law is tantamount to saying that God is God of the Jews alone (3.27–29).[58] Whatever else 'works of the law' signify, then, they attest or are particularly exemplified in Jewish insistence that the laws which set Israel apart from the nations have to be maintained.

In 4.4–5 Paul draws out the general principle which he regarded as at stake in all this: that God's way of justifying is not like a contract between employer and employee, specifying work to be done and reward to be paid; for God justifies the ungodly and reckons faith for righteousness. It is unclear whether he was accusing his Jewish interlocutors of such a contractual misunderstanding, or affirming a basic principle at the heart of Israel's concept of election.[59] Be that as it may, the kind of work in mind is once again circumcision in particular, as the sequel makes clear (4.9–12). As with *nomos*, the phrase *erga* (*nomou*) is used by Paul with both broader and narrower reference. The logic, then, is to deny that faithful obedience of the law as characterized by circumcision is sufficient to attest righteousness or to secure final justification.

In the remaining references we see the same features. In 9.12 and 11.6 it is the more sweeping principle in view: by divine call, not of works; by grace, not of works.[60] But in 9.32 the criticism is of Israel having failed to reach the law of righteousness because they sought it 'not from faith but as from works'. Here again we note the implication that the law of righteousness could have been reached if pursued 'from faith'. And the equal implication that because Israel pursued the law in terms of works, works of the law, it failed to reach righteousness. Again the thought is of Israel's law as opposed to the gospel because it was regarded as *Israel's* law; the righteousness thought to be established by works of the law as

---

[57] My reading of 3.20 in the light of 2.17–29 is one of the more controversial interpretations in my *Romans* 153–5. For critique see particularly Moo, *Romans* 206–17; but he does not take sufficiently seriously that the point of 3.19–20 is to include Jews within the general indictment of all flesh; or that the summary of 3.19–20 focuses on works of the law rather than breaches of the law (as in 2.21–27).

[58] See the fuller statement in *Theology of Paul* 363–4.

[59] The consensus view is that Paul was attacking a theology of works-righteousness prominent in the Judaism of his time (e.g. S. Westerholm, *Israel's Law and the Church's Faith* [Grand Rapids: Eerdmans, 1988] ch. 8; Moo, *Romans* 263–5).

[60] Moo, *Romans* 582–3, 678.

Israel's righteousness (its own and not open to others – 10.3); final justification as attainable only for those who obeyed the law as currently understood by most Jews. It is the fact that works were so bound up with being Israel and with denying righteousness to those who only believed that they had proved so calamitous.[61]

5.5   A necessary final reflection is on the fact that Paul does not condemn 'works' as such. On the contrary, he encourages good work (2 Cor. 9.8; Col. 1.10). He assumes that final judgment will be 'according to works', and that good work will be rewarded with glory, honour and eternal life (Rom. 2.6–7; 2 Cor. 5.10). In the same connection he does not hesitate to speak of 'reward' (1 Cor. 3.8, 14). Here again 'works' are being conceived more generally; but since the principle of judgment 'according to works' is thoroughly Jewish (Ps. 62.12; Prov. 24.12), and since many good works will be enactments of 'loving your neighbour as yourself' (Lev. 19.18), we can speak of 'works *of the law*' without forcing the sense.

Earlier I asked whether Paul would have regarded abstinence from idolatry and *porneia* as 'works of the law' and suggested that he would have avoided using that phrase for such obedience to the law. But we should note both that Paul continued to call for such obedience, and that such obedience could be described as doing the law, as examples of the sort of obedience that the law called for, examples, in other words, of 'works of the law' defined broadly as what the law requires. It is not the case that Paul distinguished walking by the Spirit from that sort of obedience to the law. It is not the case that justification by faith dispensed with that sort of obedience. Evidently, then, *Paul's differentiated view of the law could hold together both the affirmation that final justification will* not *be 'from works of the law' and the thought that final judgment* will *be according to 'works (of the law)'*. In other words, Paul's concept of works as necessarily to be performed by believers and as forming the basis for final judgment was little different from that commonly held in the Judaism of his day.[62]

We are therefore driven to a twofold conclusion in regard to Paul's theology of 'works': (1) *the principle of justification by faith does not exclude the obligation to works, even works of the law*; and (2) *when Paul denies that justification depends on works of the law he had a more limited target in mind, particularly his fellow Jewish believers' insistence that the practices which traditionally defined Is-*

---

[61] For criticism see again Moo, *Romans* 622–7, particularly n.49; but he reads the connection of thought between the criticisms of 9.32 and 10.3 differently (634–6 n.24), and does not recognize in 10.3 the echo of the attitude expressed in 1 Macc. 2.27 (see my *Romans* 588).

[62] Cf. Stuhlmacher, *Romans* 45–7; and particularly K.L. Yinger, *Paul, Judaism and Judgment According to Deeds* (SNTSMS 105; Cambridge: Cambridge University, 1999) who recognizes that Second Temple Judaism and Paul share a similar tension at this point.

rael must continue to be practised by all those wanting to claim descent from Abraham.

Conclusion.

(1) *Nomos* for Paul was not a narrowly constricted term. It functions in his theology more as a spectrum. At the centre of the spectrum is the law of Moses, the law which specified how God wanted his people Israel to live.

(2) That role for the law could be and was interpreted in a too narrow way – as not only protecting Israel, but as defining Israel, as *gramma*. Equally as seriously, it could be and was used and abused by sin to incite selfish and narrowly nationalistic passions.

(3) The need for the former role and the excuse for the latter role were ended by the coming of Christ and of his Spirit. To continue to give scope to that function of the law was to do the works of the flesh, to insist on works of the law as necessary for salvation.

(4) But the law could also be read in a way that transcended Israel's particularity, as expressing the will and wisdom of God for but also beyond Israel. Heard as the word of faith, and inciting to deeper trust rather than to sinful passion, it could be the instrument of the Spirit. It remained as ever the measure of God's will and judgment, but not in a narrow or restrictive way, rather as exemplified by Christ and capable of fulfilment by those who walk by the Spirit.

Chapter 22

Philippians 3.2-14 and the New Perspective on Paul

1. Introduction

The debate occasioned by 'the new perspective' on Paul has focused mainly on Paul's letters to the Galatians and the Romans. This is due in large part to two factors. One is the fact that Paul hardly uses the verb 'justify *(dikaioō)*' outside these two letters;[1] consequently Romans and Galatians have provided the main warrants for the doctrine of justification by faith, the key feature of 'the old perspective' on Paul. The other is the fact that these two letters focus so strongly on the terms of Gentile acceptability to God (and to Jews); consequently they also provide the main warrants for the new perspective's insistence that integral to and a primary motivation for Paul's formulation of the doctrine of justification was his commission to preach the gospel to Gentiles and his defence of that gospel.

Philippians 3 has not been given such focused attention.[2] This is unfortunate since it provides the resources for rapprochement between old and new perspectives. Or, better, it enables us to move beyond the tendency to polarise the different emphases in the debate into some kind of either-or, and to recognize the importance of holding together what might otherwise be seen as disparate and even inconsistent strands of Paul's theology.

The precise function of Phil. 3.2-16 within the letter to the Philippians is a matter of some continuing dispute.[3] But there is a general agreement that for some reason or other, with the abrupt warning to 'Beware of the dogs,

---

[1] *Dikaioō* — Romans 15; Galatians 8; elsewhere 1 Cor. 4.4; 6.11; also 1 Tim. 3.16; Tit. 3.7; and cf. Jas. 2.21, 24-25.

[2] As noted by D. Marguerat, 'Paul et la Loi: le retournement (Philippiens 3,2–4,1)', in A. Dettwiler, et al., eds., *Paul, une théologie en construction* (Genève: Labor et Fides, 2004) 251-75 (here 254). It was Marguerat's paper (particularly 270-1) at the Lausanne consultation on 'Paul and the Law' (March, 2003) which made me realize more clearly both that Phil. 3 had been too much neglected in the current debate on Paul and the law and that it was a major resource for moving the debate beyond the impasse in which it was in danger of becoming stuck.

[3] See e.g. U. Schnelle, *The History and Theology of the New Testament Writings* (1994; ET with additional material, London: SCM, 1998) 135-8; R. E. Brown, *An Introduction to the New Testament* (New York: Doubleday, 1997) 496-8; and further Marguerat, 'Paul et la Loi' 254-9.

beware of the evil workers, beware of the mutilation' (3.2), Paul turns to address a challenge to his mission very similar to the challenge he confronted
in his letter to the Galatians. The challenge is usually attributed to those misleadingly described as 'Judaizers',[4] that is, to Christian Jews[5] who sought to
complete Paul's missionary work by ensuring that his converts had 'gone all
the way' by accepting circumcision and the full status of proselytes. Such a
concern was clearly what motivated the 'agitators' or 'teachers'[6] in Galatia.
The directly relevant extra-biblical model is that of King Izates of Adiabene,
who desired to convert to Judaism (Josephus, *Ant.* 20.38). He was initially
told that he could practise the religion of the Jews without being circumcised
(*Ant.* 20.41-42). But he was then firmly counselled by one, Eleazar, 'who had
the reputation for being exceedingly strict *(akribēs)* in regard to the ancestral laws', that circumcision was indispensable (*Ant.* 20.43-45). Presumably it
was the same or a very similar concern that is referred to in Matt. 23.15. According to Acts 15.5, there was a Pharisaic wing of the earliest Christian
movement which demanded circumcision of Gentile converts (cf. Gal. 2.3-4).
So, whatever the precise details of the situation envisaged in Philippi, or, alternatively, of the relation of Phil. 3.2-16 to the rest of the letter, it is clear
enough that the passage in view is closely parallel to Paul's defence of his
law-free gospel in the Gentile mission. It therefore deserves as close attention as has been devoted to the equally fiery Galatians and the more reflective Romans on the subject.

I shall proceed in the most straightforward way by working through the passage in sequence.

2. Phil. 3.2-4

The opening verses make it clear that some sort of clash between Christian
and Jewish identity is what provoked the sequence beginning in 3.2. In calling
his opponents 'dogs', 'evil-workers' and 'mutilation',[7] Paul seems to turn a typ-

---

[4] Misleading, because the verb *ioudaizein,* from which the term in effect has been derived,
actually means 'to live like a Jew'; that is, it refers to *non-Jews* living like Jews, *not* to Jews ex-
horting Gentiles to do so (see above 174).

[5] But perhaps Jews and not Christian Jews; see K.-W. Niebuhr, *Heidenapostel aus Israel:
die jüdische Identität des Paulus nach ihrer Darstellung in seinen Briefen* ((WUNT 62;
Tübingen: Mohr Siebeck, 1992) 88-92.

[6] The latter is the preferred designation of J. L. Martyn, *Galatians* (AB 33A; New York:
Doubleday, 1997) 18.

[7] Most agree that all three terms refer to the same group. '. . . the recurrence of the defi-
nite article in the three clauses — 'the dogs, the evil workers, the concision — shows that St
Paul is alluding to a well-known and well-marked party in or out of the Church' (J. B.
Lightfoot, *Saint Paul's Epistle to the Philippians* [London: Macmillan, 1868, [4]1878] 143).

ical Jewish attitude to Gentiles against his Jewish opponents[8] and to adopt a rather crude parody of their values.[9] 'Dogs' probably denotes a Jewish denigration of Gentiles, deemed incapable of distinguishing between pure and impure, clean and unclean (cf. Matt. 7.6; 15.26-27; Rev. 22.15), 'those who, from the imagined superiority of their Jewish status and practice, reject fellowship with Gentile Christians whose indifference to the purity laws makes them like dogs'.[10] 'Evil-workers' may be a play on the Jewish Christian insistence on 'works of the law' which triggered off Paul's earlier virulent attack on such 'Judaizers' (Gal. 2.11-18; cf. 2 Cor. 11.13 — 'deceitful workers').[11] And 'mutilation' *(katatomē)*[12] is obviously a play on circumcision; 'in other words, circumcision that is not of the heart[13] is no better than ritual pagan laceration'.[14]

Whether all three epithets can be pressed quite so much as here suggested, in the clash of identities it was obviously the significance of circumcision which was chiefly at issue: '*we* are the circumcision' (3.3). Even more striking is the repeated reference to the 'flesh' *(en sarki)*: 'we do not have confidence *in the flesh*, although I too have (grounds for) confidence *in the flesh*. If anyone else thinks to have confidence *in the flesh*, I have more' (3.3-4). Paul was evidently confronted by a number of people (3.2) who regarded themselves as 'the circumcision', no doubt on the grounds that they had fulfilled the obligation rooted in Gen. 17.9-14: they had been 'circumcised in the flesh'; they had met one of the key requirements for maintaining their status as participants in the covenant made with Abraham and his descendants (17.13-14).[15]

Moreover, Paul's assertion that '*we* are the circumcision' echoes his own

---

[8] Rather as he does in the catena of Rom. 3.10-18; see my *Romans* (WBC 38; Dallas: Word, 1988) 149-51.

[9] '. . . inversions of Jewish boasts' (P. T. O'Brien, *Commentary on Philippians* [NIGTC; Grand Rapids: Eerdmans, 1991] 354); 'epithets that "turn the tables" on them (G. D. Fee, *Paul's Letter to the Philippians* [NICNT; Grand Rapids: Eerdmans, 1995] 295).

[10] M. N. Bockmuehl, *The Epistle to the Philippians* (BNTC; London: A. & C. Black, 1997) 185-7; similarly O'Brien, *Philippians* 354-5. Note the reading of the episode of the Syro-Phoenician woman in *Clem. Hom.* 2.19 (cited by Lightfoot, *Philippians* 143).

[11] G. F. Hawthorne, *Philippians* (WBC 43; Waco: Word, 1983) 125; Bockmuehl, *Philippians* 187-9. The likelihood that Paul intended such an allusion is strengthened by the almost immediate reference to 'boasting': whereas the typical 'Jew' 'boasted' in God as Israel's God and in the law and the works of the law (Rom. 2.17, 23; 3.27-29) — not 'boasting based on self-trust' (O'Brien, *Philippians* 362) — Paul the Christian boasted in Christ Jesus (Phil. 3.3).

[12] *Katatomē* appears only here in the NT. BDAG render it 'mutilation, cutting in pieces' and draw the obvious deduction that a word-play with *peritomē* ('circumcision') is intended, 'probably to denote those for whom circumcision results in (spiritual) destruction' (528).

[13] See below n. 17.

[14] Bockmuehl, *Philippians* 189; following Lightfoot, *Philippians* 144; '. . . only marginally more subtle than that expressed some years earlier in Gal. 5.12' (Bockmuehl).

[15] On the importance of circumcision for Second Temple Judaism and as an issue posed by Paul's Gentile mission see further above ch. 5.

characterisation of Jews in general as 'the circumcision' (Rom. 3.30; Gal. 2.8-9), including his fellow Jews who opposed his law-free Gentile mission (Gal. 2.12). Circumcision was evidently regarded as a distinctively Jewish rite, so distinctive as to define Jewish identity as 'the circumcision'.[16] So established was this metonymy for Paul (one aspect standing for the whole), that he could introduce the subject by the word-play, *katatomē* for *peritomē*, 'mutilation' for 'circumcision', and take it for granted that the word-play, and its implicit devaluation of circumcision would be immediately recognized. Again the point to be noted is that he does not say 'the mutilated', just as he does not say 'the circumcised'. As the Jews in view could be identified simply as 'the circumcision', so Paul's opinion of their urging of circumcision on his converts is summed up in his dismissal of them and their arguments by defining them as 'the mutilation'. As we might say of those we believe to be advocating a disastrous policy, 'They are disasters', so Paul's judgment on the Jewish missionaries' advocacy of circumcision for Gentile believers is summed up in the dismissive epithet, 'the mutilation'.

Noteworthy is the fact that Paul found it necessary to contest circumcision as a crucial identity marker or at least that understanding of the identity marker. He does not deny that circumcision was indeed an essential identifying badge marking out the covenant member. Rather, it was evidently important for him to claim that identifying badge for his own largely Gentile mission. Yes, circumcision is important, a *sine qua non* of the covenant people of God. But the real circumcision is the work of the Spirit enabling acceptable worship of God (3.3); the real circumcision is of the heart! Here Paul takes up the longstanding recognition that circumcision 'in the flesh' was inadequate without an inward circumcision, a recognition deeply rooted in Jewish religious thought.[17] But instead of denying that the very concept of circumcision was passé, Paul insists that he was moved by the same concerns as the Deuteronomist and Jeremiah for the covenant people. What really mattered was that *inward* circumcision; the theology is obviously that of Rom. 2.28-29.[18] Paul's claim is that that priority had been achieved in and through the Spirit's work in and upon his converts. And he does not hesitate to draw the corollary that the higher priority having been achieved (circumcision of the heart), the lower priority (circumcision in the flesh) is thereby rendered redundant.

In contrast, the intention of the people referred to in 3.2 was clearly to deny participation in God's covenant to any other than those who had been circumcised in the flesh. Paul therefore chose to spike their main gun by claiming the identity marker of circumcision for his own mission's success. The fact that

---

[16] Rom. 2.26-27; 3.30; 4.9; Gal. 2.7-9; Eph. 2.11.

[17] Deut. 10.16; 30.6; Jer. 4.4; 9.25-26; Ezek. 44.7, 9; Jub. 1.23; 1QpHab 11.13; 1QS 5.5; 1QH 10(= 2).18; 23?(= 18).20; Phil, *Spec. Leg.* 1.305.

[18] See further my *Romans* 123-5.

Gentiles as well as Jews were worshipping God by the Spirit was sufficient proof for Paul that they had received that inward circumcision,[19] that they could now properly be called 'the circumcision'. The point, once again, is that Paul thought it important to maintain the *continuity of identity* with Abraham's descendants ('the circumcision'). It was not enough that his Gentile converts had been able to worship God fully and freely. He did not want to boast in Jesus as founder of a new religion, discrete and distinct from his (and Jesus') native Judaism. The issue of continuity was of primary importance, and in terms of the key Jewish identity marker, circumcision.[20]

This claim could be read in supersessionist terms: *we* (Christians) are the circumcision; you (Jews) are no longer God's people. That may be how it has been read through most of Christianity's history.[21] But it is an unjustified reading nonetheless. Paul's point is rather that the coming of Jesus Messiah, and of the Spirit into the hearts of those who believed in this Jesus, had fulfilled Israel's hope for the age to come. It is fulfilled hope that he had in mind, not superseded hope. It is continuity with his Jewish forbears that he sought to maintain, not to provoke disruption. He was as opposed to Gentile pride vis-à-vis Jews as he was opposed to Jewish pride vis-à-vis Gentiles (Rom. 2.17-24; 11.17-24).

Which brings us back to the key point for this essay: that the starting point for one of Paul's most expressive statements on justification (or more precisely, righteousness from God as distinct from righteousness from the law) was the Jew/Gentile issue. Jewish missionaries were evidently insisting that Paul's converts be circumcised if they wanted to claim a share in the blessings of the covenant with Abraham. Paul was evidently insisting that that is what his gospel was about — the fact that Gentiles could share in these blessings through faith in Christ and without circumcision in the flesh. He was insisting that those who received the Spirit were 'the circumcision' to whom the covenant had been promised. All this was evidently bound up in Paul's mind with his theology of justification. The corollary is that Paul's teaching on justification may indeed be more bound up with the Jew/Gentile issue than has traditionally been recognized.

---

[19] This was the victory that Paul had achieved at the Jerusalem consultation (Gal. 2.7-9; cf. Acts 15.7-11) and built on in Gal. 3.1-5, indeed 3.1-14.

[20] Cf. F. Thielman, *Paul and the Law: A Contextual Approach* (Downers Grove: InterVarsity, 1994): 'Even within a passage that claims that the Mosaic law is "loss" and "rubbish" [sic], then, the law continues to provide the pattern for the boundaries that demarcate the people of God' (155).

[21] Cf. O'Brien: Paul's point 'is that "the circumcision" should not be applied to Israel at all. . . . It is this title and all that it means which no longer apply to Israel *kata sarka*' (*Philippians* 358).

3. Phil. 3.4-5a

If reflection on 3.2-4 shows how important the new perspective on Paul may be for our better understanding of his gospel of justification, the point is reinforced by what Paul goes on to say about his own experience. 'If anyone else thinks to have confidence in the flesh, I have more: circumcised on the eighth day; (a member) of the people of Israel; (a member) of the tribe of Benjamin . . .' (3.4-5). Here clearly is an expression of 'confidence' *(pepoithēsis)* before God;[22] and confidence 'in the flesh' — that is, not in human strength or worldly achievement, but in the advantages about to be listed.[23] The confidence was confidence (or pride) in status, status as a member of the covenant people Israel, the physical descendants ('in the flesh') of Abraham, and as heirs of the covenant promises made to and through Abraham (as confirmed by circumcision 'in the flesh'). Paul ticks off his qualifications, his ground for confidence, in what can quickly be seen to form a sevenfold list. We begin with the first three.

a) First item on his list — 'circumcised on the eighth day'. The echo of Gen. 17.12 is obvious: 'every male among you shall be circumcised when he is eight days old'. One might have expected that Paul would start with the second item (birth as an Israelite), as chronologically prior and more fundamental. But he begins with circumcision: presumably because it was the primary point at issue with the interlopers into the Philippian church; but also, no doubt, because circumcision was not merely a rite of entry for the Gentile proselyte, but a (if not the) defining characteristic of the member of the covenant people,[24] and thus also a 'sign of distinctiveness over against a non-Jewish environment'.[25] Circumcision, it should be recalled, was not a rite of entry into the covenant for the descendant of Abraham; that was given with his descent from Abraham. Circumcision was rather the first act of covenant-keeping by the new-born member of the covenant people. To use the terms introduced by E. P. Sanders, circumcision on the eighth day was the first act in 'maintaining' the new-born Jew's standing within the covenant, the first enactment of a covenantal nomistic life.

b) Second item on the list — '(a member) of the people of Israel' — of direct descent from Abraham, Isaac and Jacob, not a proselyte. Here, clearly, the ground of Paul's confidence before God was his *ethnic identity;* he was an Israelite, belonging to that people which God had chosen for himself out of all the nations (Deut. 32.8-9). He lays out in more detail in Rom. 9.4-5 the grounds of an Israelite's confidence before God: God had given them 'the adoption, the

---

[22] As in Phil. 1.14; 2.24; also 2 Cor. 1.9; 2 Thess. 3.4; Eph. 3.12.

[23] J. Gnilka, *Der Philipperbrief* (HTKNT 10.3; Freiburg: Herder, ²1976) 187.

[24] See again #2 above.

[25] Niebuhr, *Heidenapostel* 105; see further ch. 5 above.

glory and the covenants, the law, the service and the promises . . .'. It was such signs of divine favour, of God's election of Israel to be his peculiar people, which gave the Israelite this confidence before God. Here too, as with circumcision, Paul shows himself unwilling to abandon this prized title of divine choice; he continued to think of himself as an Israelite' (Rom. 11.1; 2 Cor. 11.22). Still as a believer in Jesus Messiah he did not denounce his ethnic heritage but saw his gospel as in direct continuity with it and even affirmation of it.[26]

c) Third item on the list — '(a member) of the tribe of Benjamin'. It is of interest that Paul knew his tribal identity and that it was a matter of pride for him, a further ground for his confidence before God. Of Jacob's twelve sons only Benjamin had been born in the promised land (Gen. 35.16-18), and only the tribe of Benjamin had remained faithful to Judah and the house of David when the kingdom split after the death of Solomon.[27] Here the point to be noted is that, once again, it was *something given* him with his birth, not something achieved or merited by him. As with his ethnic identity as an Israelite, so with his tribal identity as a Benjaminite, it was the fact that he was a beneficiary of God's prevenient choice of Israel that gave him confidence. His confidence at this point is simply that of someone who belonged to the chosen people, who began his life as a member of one of the continuing tribes of Israel.

The confidence expressed thus far is clearly in ethnic terms. The implication, of course, is that those *not* circumcised, *not* of the people of Israel, could *not* share the same confidence. The other implication, the more negative side of the same coin, was that the non-Israelite was disadvantaged before God, was indeed a subject of God's wrath rather than of his mercy; Paul highlights the one in Rom. 2.17-24 and wrestles with the other in Rom. 9–11 (particularly 9.13-24; 11.7-12, 25-31). It was the same reasoning, as a mission of mercy, which urged forward the other missionaries to bring willing Gentiles within Israel as proselytes. Paul in effect recognizes the theology behind that mission. It was one which would work very well in his own case. But he will soon make it clear that he has abandoned that theology (Phil. 3.7-8). The point to be noted, however, in the debate occasioned by the new perspective on Paul, is that what he objects to thus far is *confidence in ethnic identity,* confidence in the fact of belonging to Israel, the covenant people of God, confidence in having been circumcised and thus, even as an eight-day old, having been faithful to that covenant. In speaking of Jewish confidence before God he did not turn first to thoughts of self-achievement and merit-earning deeds. Rather, it was pride in

---

[26] See further on Romans 9–11 and my *Romans* 526-8, 538-40, 681-6; also my *Theology of Paul the Apostle* (Grand Rapids: Eerdmans/Edinburgh: T&T Clark, 1998) #19.

[27] Lightfoot, *Philippians* 146-7; Hawthorne, *Philippians* 132-3; O'Brien, *Philippians* 370-1; Bockmuehl, *Philippians* 196; the possibility is certainly strong that Paul (Saul of Tarsus) had been named after the first king of Israel (Saul).

ethnic identity, of the Israelite over against the other, of Jew over against Gentile, against which he registered his first protest in setting out to express afresh what the gospel of divine righteousness now meant to him.[28]

It is the strength of the new perspective that it has brought this aspect of Paul's gospel and theology to the fore again.

4. Phil. 3.5b-6

d) The fourth item on Paul's listing of his grounds for confidence before God reads 'a Hebrew of the Hebrews'. 'The name "Hebrew" was conventionally associated with traditionalism or conservatism'.[29] The intensification of the claim — 'a Hebrew of the Hebrews' — rather than just 'I am a Hebrew' (as in 2 Cor. 11.2), must reflect Paul's early determination to maintain his ethnic identity. Indeed, not merely to maintain it, but to identify himself more completely with the ancient origins and character of his people.[30] There is something of a fundamentalist evaluation of origins here: original is best; only original is truly authentic; getting back to the roots, to the beginnings, as the way to remain most true to one's heritage.

It is at this point that we begin to see a transition in the seven-fold list, at the central item in the seven-fold list. For though 'a Hebrew' is a linguistic identity, almost as much 'given' as the ethnic identity 'Israelite', language is not entirely a given, and has to be learned. More to the point, 'a Hebrew of the Hebrews' indicates a deliberate choice to maintain and strengthen that linguistic identity, much as a Welshman might today affirm his identity by refusing to function except in Welsh. Here is an attitude and enactment which goes beyond the normal dimensions of covenantal nomism and indicates that the pre-Christian Paul deliberately set himself on that course.

---

[28] Although they clearly recognize the difference between the former and latter members of the list, O'Brien and Fee tend to underplay the ethnic character of the former, particularly when the former sums up the list as 'religious accomplishments' (*Philippians* 365), and the latter sums up the grounds for 'confidence in the flesh' as having 'grounds for boasting before God on the basis of human achievement, the ultimate "self-centered" expression of life' (*Philippians* 303, 323). Similarly T. Laato, *Paulus und das Judentum: Anthropologische Erwägungen* (Helsinki: Abo, 1991): 'Das *pepoithenai en sarki* bedeutet nichts anderes als das Selbstvertrauen des Menschen'; 'das Sich-Rühmen der Selbstgerechtigkeit' (259, 263). Also T. R. Schreiner, *Paul, Apostle of God's Glory in Christ* (Downers Grove, IL: InterVarsity, 2001): 'The problem was a fixation on his own accomplishments and righteousness. He was devoted to the law as a means to buttress his own ego and his own glory' (123). C. G. Kruse, *Paul, the Law and Justification* (Leicester: Apollos, 1996) is more balanced (257-8).

[29] G. Harvey, *The True Israel: Uses of the Names Jew, Hebrew and Israel in Ancient Jewish Literature and Early Christian Literature* (AGAJU 35; Leiden: Brill, 1996) 146.

[30] So most; see e.g. Gnilka, *Philipperbrief* 189-90; 'a kind of climax of the different elements of his Jewish identity' (Niebuhr, *Heidenapostel* 106-8).

The list of grounds for Paul's pre-Christian confidence before God continues: 'as to the law, a Pharisee; as to zeal, a persecutor of the church; as to righteousness which is in the law, blameless' (3.5-6). The transition from items of ethnic identity becomes steadily more marked.

e) The fifth item on the list, 'as to the law, a Pharisee', takes us further down the same path. For a Jew to be a Pharisee was not a given; it was a matter of choice. The Pharisees, in terms used by both Acts and Josephus, were a Jewish 'sect' (Acts 15.5; 26.5; Josephus, *War* 2.162; *Ant.* 13.171, 288; 20.191, 197). Paul must have chosen to join or to number himself with that sect. More specifically, to have become a Pharisee the younger Saul must have chosen to come to Jerusalem (if he was not already there).[31] If already in Jerusalem, he must have put himself under a Pharisaic teacher; the picture of Acts 22.3 is completely plausible.

The point, and the reason why Paul makes the point, is that the Pharisees were particularly devout in their devotion to the Torah. They were known for their scrupulousness *(akribeia)* in observing the requirements of the law.[32] Their very name, originally a nickname (?), 'Pharisees', 'the separated ones',[33] indicates a commitment to maintain the holiness of the people of God, as uncontaminated by impurity as possible. The theological logic was expressed in the strictness of their table-fellowship and in the criticism of Jesus' table-fellowship with 'sinners' which the Jesus tradition attributes to them (Mark 2.15-16; Matt. 11.19; Luke 15.2). The same theological logic evidently lay behind the 'separation' of the Jewish believers in Antioch from their Gentile fellow-believers in Gal. 2.11-14.[34] Paul, in other words, clearly implies that he knew that logic 'from inside'; he had himself formerly lived by the same logic.

And the point for the present debate is that a Pharisaic observance of the law is not simply to be described as typical 'covenantal nomism'. The Pharisees no doubt did regard the way they lived and conducted themselves as required of them as faithful members of the covenant people. But the very fact that they are identified as a sect within Second Temple Judaism indicates that they were not typical of Second Temple Judaism, or of the covenantal nomism of Second Temple Judaism. It was not enough for Paul to identify himself as an Israelite; he goes further. As confession of himself as 'a Hebrew of the Hebrews' inten-

---

[31] Jerusalem was the only obvious place where Paul could have trained as a Pharisee, as M. Hengel, *The Pre-Christian Paul* (London: SCM, 1991) has convincingly argued; similarly Niebuhr, *Heidenapostel* 55-7.

[32] *Akribeia* — Acts 22.3; 26.5; Josephus, *War* 1.108-9; 2.162; *Ant.* 20.200-201; *Life* 191.

[33] *Pᵉrushim*, from *parash*, 'to separate'; see E. Schürer, *The History of the Jewish People in the Age of Jesus Christ* (revised and edited by G. Vermes & F. Millar; 4 vols; Edinburgh: T&T Clark, 1973-87) 2.396-7; S. J. D. Cohen, *From the Maccabees to the Mishnah* (Philadelphia: Westminster, 1987) 162; A. J. Saldarini, *Pharisees, Scribes and Sadducees in Palestinian Society* (Edinburgh: T&T Clark, 1988) 220-5.

[34] See above ch. 1 #2.3.

sified the more widespread status of 'Hebrew', so confession of himself as a 'Pharisee' marks a deliberate choice to go beyond the law observance of 'common Judaism', and a belief in the necessity of doing so.

Here, in other words, we move beyond question of confidence in ethnic identity to confidence in the extra commitment he had chosen to make by becoming a Pharisee.

f) Sixth item in the list recounting the grounds of Paul's pre-Christian confidence before God — 'as to zeal, a persecutor of the church'. Here we see a further intensification; Paul evidently intended the latter half of the list to steadily ratchet up his grounds for confidence. The term 'zeal' clearly indicates something still further beyond what most Jews saw to be their obligations under the law. It was not simply that he had been 'zealous for the ancestral traditions' (Gal. 1.14); that went with being a Pharisee. But his zeal was of an extreme type, impelling him to act with violence against those he perceived to be in breach of the law: he had persecuted the church and attempted to destroy it (Gal. 1.13). Perhaps like the Maccabees before him and the Zealots after him, his hero had been Phinehas, whose violent action against a flagrant disregard for the law had made him a model of devoted zeal (Num. 25.6-13; Ps. 106.28-31; Sir. 45.23-24; 1 Macc. 2.26, 54; 4 Macc. 18.12).

Here again, then, is something well beyond confidence in ethnic status. At the same time, however, we should note that the zeal of a Phinehas was not a concern for personal standing with God. It was much more provoked by concern to maintain and protect Israel's identity as a people set apart to God, a concern, in other words, for Israel's holiness over against other nations.[35] It was a breach of this barrier which inspired Phinehas' zeal (Num. 25.6-8; Ps. 106.28-29), as it did also Elijah's in his destruction of the prophets of Baal (1 Kgs. 18.40; 1 Macc. 2.58), as it did the Maccabees in their readiness to kill Hellenizing Jews as well as Syrians (1 Macc. 2.23-24).[36] That Paul's zeal was expressed in willingness to 'destroy' fellow Jews suggests to me that a large part of his persecuting zeal was motivated by the same concern to maintain and protect Israel's holiness against incursions from 'Gentile sinners' (Gal. 2.15).[37]

---

[35] Reflecting Yahweh's own 'zeal/jealousy' in insisting that Israel must not worship any other gods but remain dedicated to him alone (Ex. 20.5; 34.14; Deut. 4.23-24; 5.9; 6.14-15; 32.21). E. Reuter notes that the relationship between Yahweh and his worshippers 'is characterized by an intolerant demand for exclusivity: it is Yahweh's will "to be the only God for Israel, and . . . he is not disposed to share his claim for worship and love with any other divine power"' (*qn'*, *TDOT* 13.54, citing G. von Rad, *OT Theology* 1.208). Hengel does not give this dimension sufficient recognition (*pre-Christian Paul* 84).

[36] 'Sinners and lawless men' in 1 Macc. 1.34; 2.44, 48 certainly included those whom the Maccabees regarded as apostate Jews, Israelites who had abandoned the law; see further my 'Pharisees, Sinners and Jesus', *Jesus, Paul and the Law* (London: SPCK/Louisville: Westminster John Knox, 1990) 61-86 (here 74).

[37] See further ch. 15 above; similarly Bockmuehl, *Philippians* 199-200.

If I am on the right lines, then it means that we cannot set this sixth item wholly over against the first three, for this zeal is indeed an intensification, but an intensification of the same pride in ethnic identity with its negative corollary of disdain for other nations.[38] In all these cases, concern for the standing of the people before God was the primary motivation.

g) Seventh and final item on the list — 'as to righteousness which is in the law, blameless'. This should almost certainly be read as an expression of the confidence of one who saw himself as living before God in accordance with the requirements of God's law. The law set a pattern for living, and the pre-Christian Paul claimed to live in accordance with that pattern.[39] I doubt if the term *amemptos*, 'blameless', should be understood as equivalent to 'sinless', that is, never having breached any commandment in the slightest degree.[40] For the terms of covenant law included demand for repentance and provision of sacrifice and atonement for sin.[41] So to live in accordance with the law must have included availing oneself of the ritual and cultic provisions of the law when impurity and sin blighted the covenant life.[42] Such I imagine to be the character and quality of life attributed to Zechariah and Elizabeth in Luke 1.6.[43] And Paul presumably did not envisage his own converts as sinless when he spoke in the same terms ('blameless') in Phil. 2.15 and 1 Thess. 2.10 and 3.13. This pattern of law-directed living is quite well caught in Sanders' phrase 'covenantal nomism'.[44]

---

[38] *Pace* S. Kim, *Paul and the New Perspective* (WUNT 140; Tübingen: Mohr Siebeck, 2002), who insists on categorizing the last three items under the heading of 'personal achievement' (76-7).

[39] S. Westerholm, *Perspectives Old and New on Paul* (Grand Rapids: Eerdmans, 2004) comments wryly: Paul 'did not suffer from poor self-esteem, nor was his conscience of an introspective, troubled sort' (403).

[40] '*Amemptos* should not be pressed to mean that Paul completely [ful]filled the law or entirely avoided transgressions' (O'Brien, *Philippians* 380); Lightfoot paraphrases the claim, 'I omitted no observance however trivial' (*Philippians* 148).

[41] This is one of the important points that E. P. Sanders, *Paul and Palestinian Judaism* (London: SCM, 1977) brought to our attention; see also his *Judaism: Practice and Belief 63 BCE–66 CE* (London: SCM, 1992) especially 107-10, 271-2. Kim ripostes: 'Doesn't Phil 3:2-6 rather carry the connotation that he tried to keep the commandments of the law as perfectly as possible so as to need to repent as little as possible? If so, in Phil 3:2-6 Paul is not very much conscious of the atonement provisions'. But he recognizes that in the DSS, talk of perfection could go hand in hand with confession of inadequacy and failure, and suggests an analogy between Paul the Pharisee and the Qumran covenanters at this point (*Paul and the New Perspective* 149-50).

[42] Cf. Thielman: 'he probably means that he observed the commandments as conscientiously as possible and that when he transgressed them he used the means prescribed in the law itself to atone for his sin' (*Paul and the Law* 155).

[43] See already my *Theology of Paul* 349-50.

[44] '. . . not an assertion of sinlessness, but of complete compliance with Torah interpreted in covenantal terms, through which forgiveness and cleansing were available' (M. A. Seifrid, *Justification by Faith: The Origin and Development of a Central Pauline Theme* [NovTSupp

At the same time, we have to recall the degree of intensification that Paul evidently intended in his listing of his pre-Christian grounds for confidence before God. This suggests that the more illuminating parallel with Paul's thought at this point is the similar climax of Gal. 1.13-14. There Paul remembers how 'I progressed in Judaism beyond many of my contemporaries among my people, being exceedingly zealous for my ancestral traditions' (Gal. 1.14). Here we are back with the zealous Pharisee going *beyond* the life style of common Judaism. Here indeed we see an element of *competitiveness,* of a pre-Christian Paul seeking to *outdo* his contemporaries in his zealous devotion to and application of the more scrupulous halakhoth of the Pharisees, outdoing even many of his fellow-Pharisees, not least, once again in his persecution of the church. This is now well beyond confidence in ethnic status.[45] There is at least an element of self-achievement and of pride in self-achievement in both Gal. 1.14 and by implication in Phil. 3.6.[46]

In short, if the first half of the list of Paul's pre-Christian grounds for confidence before God gives substance to the insight and emphasis of the new perspective, then it could equally be said that the second half of the list gives as much substance to the emphasis of the old perspective.

68; Leiden: Brill, 1992] 174. 'The Law as a way of life was widely thought to be feasible and practical: for most faithful Jews it would have been absurd to think that God had given a revelation that could not in fact be lived out. In this respect, too, Paul does not say he was "sinless", merely that he was upright and blameless by the standards he was following' (Bockmuehl, *Philippians* 202). Similarly N. T. Wright, 'Romans', *The New Interpreter's Bible* Vol. 10 (Nashville: Abingdon, 2002) 461. Is it better, then, to speak of righteousness 'attained' and 'achieved' (Kim, *Paul and the New Perspective* 77-8), or of righteousness lived out and exemplified?

[45] '. . . an achievement which set him apart from other Jews' (M. A. Seifrid, *Christ, or Righteousness: Paul's Theology of Justification* (Downers Grove, IL: InterVarsity, 2000) 27. I did not give enough weight to this in my 'Paul and Justification by Faith', in *The Road from Damascus: The Impact of Paul's Conversion on His Life, Thought, and Ministry,* ed. R. N. Longenecker (Grand Rapids: Eerdmans, 1997) 85-101 (here 93-4) [= ch. 16 above (373-5)].

[46] I thus qualify my earlier argument that the last three items on Paul's list 'cannot be considered "self-achieved"' (*Theology of Paul* 370) where I was more concerned not to lose sight of 'righteousness' as covenant practice rather than a goal still to be 'achieved'. Most recent commentators recognize the need to be aware of the full scope of the list in 3.5-6 and the integrated character of the 'inherited privileges' and 'personal achievements', using the terms of P. T. O'Brien, 'Was Paul Converted?', in D. A. Carson, et al., eds., *Justification and Variegated Nomism. Vol. 2: The Paradoxes of Paul* (Tübingen: Mohr Siebeck, 2004) 361-91 (here 372-3); privileges of birth and active practice of the law (Marguerat, 'Paul et la Loi' 266); I. H. Marshall, *New Testament Theology* (Downers Grove, IL: InterVarsity, 2004) 446-7. The sort of exegesis to which I was objecting is well exemplified by Marguerat's quotation (260) from G. Bornkamm, *Paul* (London: Hodder & Stoughton, 1971): 'Paul's example of the prisoner of sin is this very Jew jealous for the Law. Under the illusion that he is devout, in his quest of righteousness he fancies that the hopelessly barred access to God is open, or imagines that he can open it by his works' (123).

5. Phil. 3.7-9

Verse 7 marks the volte-face, the conversion of Saul the Pharisee to become Paul the Christian. The first striking feature is the intensity of this turn-around. 'What was *gain* to me, these things I have come to regard as *loss* on account of the Christ. More than that, I regard everything as *loss* on account of the surpassing value of knowing Christ Jesus my Lord. On account of him I *have suffered the loss* of everything, and I regard it as *garbage,* in order that I might gain Christ, and be found in him, not having my own righteousness which is from the law, but that which is through faith in Christ, the righteousness from God on the basis of faith . . .'. Paul does not deny the benefit of his previous situation: it had been 'gain', something of advantage to him — he uses the same word *(kerdos)* in 1.21, in affirming that death would be to his own advantage; in renouncing that previous 'gain' he had 'suffered loss', with the implication which *zēmioō* has of undergoing hardship or suffering in consequence.[47] It was tantamount to losing *everything* — another reminder that his life as a zealous Pharisee had been all-consuming; it had meant everything to him.

But now he counts it as 'garbage', as of no more value than 'excrement' *(ta skubala).*[48] The impact of Jesus the Christ[49] had been so overwhelming for him that it completely relativized every other set of revealed and traditional values by which he had hitherto lived. The completeness of reversal of values could hardly be expressed more sharply. Even so, however, it need not mean that Paul now denied all value to these things he had previously counted as so important. That is unlikely in view of his attempt to retain the value of circumcision indicated by Deuteronomy and Jeremiah (3.3), his affirmation of circumcision's continuing value in Rom. 3.1-2, as of Israel's continuing blessings (Rom. 9.4-5), and his own status as an Israelite (Rom. 11.1; 2 Cor. 11.22). *The sharpness of the contrast is not so much to denigrate what he had previously counted as gain, as to enhance to the highest degree the value he now attributes to Christ, to the knowledge of Christ, and to the prospect of gaining Christ.*

It is to be noted that what Paul turned his back on was not simply the competitiveness of his former life as indicated by the last four items of his former grounds for confidence (Phil. 3.5b-6). It was not simply that he now eschewed the need to strive to outdo his fellow Jews and Pharisees (Gal. 1.14). He evidently had in mind also the first three items of his confidence list — the status of covenant membership, given him by birth and affirmed by his eighth-day circumcision (Phil. 3.5a). That too had been gain for him, a ground of confidence before God. It is the *whole* package which he saw now to be lacking in the very

---

[47] BDAG 428.

[48] BDAG 932.

[49] The definite article in 3.7 retains the force of the discovery that Jesus, despite having been crucified, really was the Messiah/Christ of Jewish hope.

advantage for which he had previously prized it — the covenantal nomism which regarded the non-circumcised, the non-Israel as constitutionally unable to have such confidence before God, as well as the intensified covenantal nomism of the blameless Pharisee; the zeal which persecuted fellow Jews who seemed to threaten Israel's set-apartness from the (other) nations, as well as the zeal for the traditions of the fathers in which he outstripped his contemporaries (Gal. 1.14).

It follows also that when Paul speaks of 'my righteousness which is from the law' (Phil. 3.9) he was probably not thinking of righteousness as something achieved by him. Without getting into the debates reviewed earlier,[50] 'righteousness' may be defined as a status or activity in conformity with or bringing to effect what God counts as right. That includes God's election of Israel and his requirement of circumcision for the male children of Israel, as much as it includes the Pharisee's heightened prescription for what is required if the covenant people's righteousness is to be maintained. The qualification of 'righteousness' as '*my* righteousness' at this point should not mislead us.[51] It refers to the same set of values that Paul had previously claimed for himself (3.5-6), '*I* more' (3.4), and had affirmed to have been 'gain *to me*' (3.7) — that is, the advantages which Saul the Pharisee had enjoyed as a circumcised Israelite, as well as the competitive advantage he had gained over his contemporaries.[52]

The contrast is twofold: between 'my righteousness' and 'that (righteousness) which is through faith in Christ . . . on the basis of faith';[53] and between the righteousness which is 'from the law' *(tēn ek nomou)* and the righteousness which is 'from God' *(tēn ek theou).*[54]

---

[50] See above 68-9.

[51] As O'Brien is in danger of being ('Was Paul Converted?' 373).

[52] Cf. 203 n. 36 above. R. H. Gundry, 'Grace, Works, and Staying Saved in Paul', *Biblica* 66 (1985) 1-38, sees only 'the attitudinal sin of self-righteousness' in the list (13-14). O'Brien prefers to emphasise only the latter: '*dikaiosunē* describes Paul's own moral achievement. . . . *Emēn dikaiosunēn* was nothing other than self-righteousness' (*Philippians* 394-5). Kim fails to appreciate the degree to which Paul identified himself with Israel's heritage and covenanted status — 'a human righteousness, a righteousness achieved by human beings . . . this human (i.e., fleshly) quality, and not a nationalistic quality' (*Paul and the New Perspective* 77-9).

[53] There is no need to engage in the currently familiar debate about the force of *pistis Christou* ('faith in Christ', or 'the faithfulness of Christ') since the second 'faith' is certainly that of the believer, as O'Brien (*Philippians* 400) and Bockmuehl (*Philippians* 211-3), who both prefer the sense 'the faithfulness of Christ', agree. It should be noted, however, that repetition for rhetorical effect ('beware' × 3; 'confidence in the flesh' × 3; 'loss' × 3; 'on account of . . . Christ' × 3; 'attain' × 3) is a feature of the passage.

[54] M. Theobald, 'Paulus und Polykarp an die Philipper. Schlaglichter auf die frühe Rezeption des Basissatzes von der Rechtfertigung', in M. Bachmann, ed., *Lutherische und Neue Paulusperspektive* (WUNT 182; Tübingen: Mohr Siebeck, 2005) 349-88, in effect reminds us that the 'my' should not be understood in some universal individual terms, the 'my' of modern individualism; the 'my' is rather that of one who had known himself, his personal identity, as a member of a people, Israel (358-61, further 361-9).

The first contrast sets in antithesis the righteous status and covenant faithfulness that Paul could claim as an Israelite, a Hebrew of the Hebrews, a zealous Pharisee, and righteousness understood as an acceptability before God given only through or on the basis of faith. This is a central axiom of Paul's gospel elsewhere — that God's saving outreach is to *all* who believe, Gentile as much as Jew (Rom. 1.16-17), and that this central insight must not be adulterated or compromised by any attempt to insist that believers must live as Jews (Gal. 2.14-16). Here again it misses the mark to see the former righteousness as something earned or achieved.[55] Paul's point is rather that faith alone is the basis for an effectively right relationship with God — the trust in God and the reliance on God which Abraham had so exemplified in regard to the promise of an heir (Rom. 4.16-21) as the medium through which, on the basis of which, out of which life should be lived (Rom. 14.23).[56] Anything which detracted from or diminished or obscured that fundamental religious insight Paul was opposed to. And that included *both* the confidence in birth and religious tradition, *and* the confidence arising from being a superlative practitioner of that tradition.

The second contrast sets in antithesis 'righteousness from the law' and 'righteousness from God'. Again it is obvious that by the former Paul clearly had in mind the confidence list of 3.4-6. The righteousness was what he had enjoyed as a Jew and as a faithful Jew, a status derived from being a member of the people to whom God had given the law, and a status maintained by his Pharisaic commitment to live (more) righteously as a member of the righteous people of God. Here again to see 'righteousness from the law' as self-achieved righteousness is to ignore the context of Paul's previous confidence. 'Righteousness from the law' must denote rather a standing before God understood to be derived 'from the law', that is, from being a member of the people of the Torah, the people marked out by the law of Moses, and from the practice, the zealous practice of that law.[57]

In contrast Paul sets 'righteousness from God', God's drawing of a person into relationship with himself and affirming that person as righteous. By setting the two understandings of righteousness in contrast, Paul presumably would not have intended to imply that the law was not from God, or that Is-

---

[55] Cf. N. T. Wright, *What Saint Paul Really Said* (Grand Rapids: Eerdmans, 1997): 'That which he is refusing in the first half of verse 9 is not a moralistic or self-help righteousness, but the status of orthodox Jewish covenant membership' (124).

[56] 'Faith is not to be taken as an achievement. . . . The pronouncing of justification is God's act alone, and faith is not detached from grace, but is encompassed by it' (Gnilka, *Philipperbrief* 194).

[57] Seifrid suggests that the seventh item in the list, 'as to righteousness which is in the law blameless', 'is most likely a summary of all these benefits', that is, those listed in 3.5-6; 'my righteousness' of 3.9 is not 'a righteousness gained by his own efforts', though the preconversion Paul had 'attached salvific value to obedience' (*Justification* 173-5).

rael had not been God's chosen people; his affirmation to the contrary else-where is clear enough (Rom. 7.12; 9–11). Just as he had not intended to deny the value of circumcision or that being an Israelite was 'gain', despite the overwhelmingly superior value of knowing Christ (Rom. 3.1-2). The contrast is probably that of Gal. 3.19–4.7: the law had had a valuable but inferior role in the relationship between God and Israel compared to the relationship of faith.[58] The contrast is between the *immediacy* of relation with God through faith (as in Rom. 5.2) and the interposition of the law seen as mediating that relation. That the law did continue to play a role in that relation in at least some degree Paul continued to affirm.[59] What he objected to, then, here as elsewhere, was the assumption that the law in its full scope still had an essen-tial mediating role even for those who already experienced the full relation with God through faith. To be content with a righteousness mediated 'from the law' when the righteousness 'from God' was available directly to faith was bad enough. But to insist that believers who already rejoiced in the righ-teousness from God had necessarily to submit to the righteousness from the law was to threaten if not to destroy God's righteousness. Paul no doubt puts the contrast with rhetorical exaggeration (3.7-8), but also because his own ex-perience had made such a revolution in his understanding of how divine righ-teousness functioned, and not least because he saw now how corrupting of the essential insight of the gospel (Rom. 1.16-17) would be a return to his old way of thinking.

6. Phil. 3.7-11

The most striking feature of the fuller passage (3.7-11) is the centrality of Christ. It was clearly Paul's discovery of Christ, of the significance of Jesus the Christ, that both brought him to a complete reassessment of his previous grounds of confidence before God, and resulted in Christ assuming that cen-tral place in his revised soteriology. Noticeable, but insufficiently noticed is the variety of ways he expresses this new-found centrality of Christ.

He uses the phrase *dia* + accusative no fewer than three times in vss. 7-8: 'on account of the Christ'; 'on account of the surpassing value of knowing Christ Jesus my Lord'; 'on account of him'. For Paul to use *dia* + accusative in relation to Christ is unusual enough;[60] much more typical of his thought is *dia* + geni-

---

[58] See above ch. 1 #3.3(7).

[59] See further my *Theology of Paul* #23. See also, e.g., P. J. Tomson, *Paul and the Jewish Law: Halakha in the Letters of the Apostle to the Gentiles* (CRINT 3.1; Assen/Maastricht: Van Gorcum, 1990); B. S. Rosner, *Paul, Scripture and Ethics: A Study of 1 Corinthians 5–7* (Leiden: Brill, 1994).

[60] Elsewhere only 1 Cor. 4.10; *dia Iēsoun* (2 Cor. 4.5, 11).

tive ('through Christ').[61] But to use *dia* + accusative so intensively in these verses cannot but indicate that Paul was making a point which he saw to be important in this context. The formulation is used each time as a way of expressing the re-evaluation which his conversion had brought about: 'these things I have come to regard as loss *on account of the Christ*'; 'I regard everything as loss *on account of the surpassing value of knowing Christ Jesus my Lord*';[62] '*on account of him* I have suffered the loss of everything'. The formulation, then, was evidently Paul's way of referring to and highlighting what it was that had caused him to regard his previous grounds of confidence as so much rubbish. It was the light of Christ which threw everything else into shadow. That presumably included his recognition that Jesus was indeed *the Christ*, and that he had been exalted as *Lord*. But it no doubt included or came to include also an appreciation of the significance of Jesus' death. The phrase suggests a reference to something done outside of himself *(extra nos)*, whereas *dia* + genitive suggested more of an engagement of God with the individual and vice-versa through the medium of Christ. So the first new ground of Paul's confidence before God was what Christ had done, particularly in his death and resurrection.

The 'on account of Christ' formulation is complemented with Paul's familiar 'in Christ' formulation — in vs. 9, but already also in vs. 3. This denotes a much more intimate relation to Christ and to what Christ had done — a reference not simply to what Christ had done quite apart from Paul, but to something equivalent to physical location within Christ. That is, not simply a locating of oneself *by reference to* Christ's life, death and resurrection, but a personal involvement *within* the continuing reality of Christ, the risen and exalted Christ.[63] The same note of personal relationship is struck by his talk of 'the *knowledge* of Christ Jesus my Lord', with its overtone of intimate personal relationship with the one known.[64] In vs. 10, indeed, 'to *know* him (Christ)' is set by Paul as perhaps the chief outcome and goal of his reversal of values,[65] an aspect to which we must return.

What is of particular note in the present discussion is the way Paul combines the thought of 'having the righteousness from God' with the 'in him': 'in order that I might gain Christ and *be found in him*, not having my own righteousness which is from the law, but that which is through faith in Christ, *the righteousness from God* on the basis of faith'. These were evidently *two inter-*

---

[61] Rom. 1.5, 8; 2.16; 5.1, 9, 11, 17-18, 21; 7.25; 8.37; 16.27; 1 Cor. 15.57; 2 Cor. 1.20; etc. See further my *Theology of Paul* 406.

[62] *To huperechon* ('surpassing value') of course further heightens the contrast with what had been 'gain' (3.7) and now was valued as no more than 'garbage' (3.8).

[63] On the significance of Paul's 'in Christ' language see again my *Theology of Paul* #15.2.

[64] O'Brien, *Philippians* 388-9 and Bockmuehl, *Philippians* 205-6, who *inter alia* note that this is the only time within his extant letters that Paul uses the expression 'my Lord'.

[65] '"To know Christ", therefore, is the ultimate goal toward which the apostle sets the course of his life' (Hawthorne, *Philippians* 143).

locked strands in Paul's soteriology — what has been referred to as his participationist language and his forensic terminology. Assuming that the forward look is to the final judgment ('that I might be found in him . . .'), it was
evidently important to Paul that his hope should be expressed not simply in
forensic terms — as though his hope rested entirely and exclusively on what
Christ had done on his behalf ('on account of Christ'). His hope rested also
on his being found to be 'in Christ'. We could even press the point by observing that the 'in him' was the basis of his hope of having 'the righteousness
from God'; *it was only as being 'in Christ' that his hope to be recognized by
God as righteous could be realised;* just as we should add, *it was only as having
'the righteousness from God' that his hope to be found 'in Christ' would be
realised.*[66]

This prompts further recognition on our part of the 'not yet' implicit in
Paul's formulation through these verses: 'in order that I might gain Christ, and
be found in him'; 'to know him and the power of his resurrection and the fellowship of his sufferings, being conformed to his death, if somehow I may attain to the resurrection from the dead'. The 'on account of Christ' no doubt refers, perhaps entirely, to what had been done in the past. The 'in Christ'
elsewhere certainly refers to Paul's present situation, and the 'gaining' of
Christ and 'being found in him' he would surely regard as already at least begun as from his conversion; after all, he had already affirmed, 'For me living is
Christ' (1.21; cf. Gal. 2.20). That Paul already 'knew' Christ and enjoyed some
share in Christ's risen life he would presumably affirm also, at least in some
measure (Rom. 6.4; 7.6; 8.2). But the main thrust of vss. 10-11 is clearly to describe an aspiration: to know Christ and the power of his resurrection (still
more); to be (steadily more and more) conformed to his death; with the final
hope of arriving where Christ had already arrived, the resurrection from the
dead.[67]

Here again Paul's christological soteriology qualifies and clarifies his language of justification. However much he already enjoyed 'the righteousness
from God', that was neither a complete nor a final description of the process of
salvation. However much emphasis he placed on the decisiveness of what
Christ had done on the cross and already in his own life (Rom. 6.3-4; 7.4-6; 8.1-
2), Paul did not think of that as the whole story or as a story whose ending had
already been achieved or secured. If the 'in Christ' indicated in shorthand

---

[66] Gnilka cites Stuhlmacher as noting that 'for Paul "the juridical and mystical teachings
on redemption" may not be separated' (*Philipperbrief* 195); cf. O'Brien, *Philippians* 393, 415-
7. Gnilka also observes that 'the being in Christ is grounded in the *dikaiosunē theou* (195),
and O'Brien rightly objects to any suggestion that the 'righteousness' language is somehow
strange to the context (416-7), though it remains true that the climax of 3.8d-11 is in
'participationist' terms; cf. Fee, *Philippians* 314, 326, 337.

[67] Cf. O'Brien, *Philippians* 391-2, 402, 411.

Paul's hope to be found (in the final judgment) as having the righteousness from God, vv. 10-11 spell out more clearly how the 'in Christ' brought about and secured that end.

Particularly striking is the clear assertion that that process was one of growing conformity to Christ. The power of Christ's resurrection might already be in evidence in Paul's life and through his mission. But Christ's sufferings had still to be shared. Paul had yet to be fully conformed to Christ's death. He would not share fully in the resurrection from the dead except at the climax and end of his life (Rom. 8.11; 2 Cor. 4.16–5.5) or at the parousia (1 Cor. 15.50-52). That is, he would not be fully conformed to Christ's resurrection as well as to his death until his own death or 'the last trumpet' (Rom. 6.5; 1 Cor. 15.49; Phil. 3.20-21). Integral to the thought here is that *a personal transformation was necessary,* and that it would come about only 'in Christ' and 'through Christ' (*dia* + genitive) and 'with Christ'.[68] It was not simply a matter of a judicial verdict already given, provisionally (or even finally), or yet to be given (but sure to be given 'on account of Christ') at the last judgment. The forensic metaphor of justification was inadequate on its own to describe the scope and character of the process of salvation, both the already and the not yet. It had to be complemented by an understanding of a process of transformation to become like Christ in his suffering and death as a necessary stage on the way to resurrection like Christ's.[69] To make the point again: the effectiveness of the death of Christ to which Paul refers here is not its function as an atoning sacrifice; that past event in itself did not encompass all that had to happen in regard to the believer. The full saving effect of Christ's death was its effect in transforming the believer to share ever more fully in that death, that is, what Paul refers to elsewhere as the dying off/wasting away of 'our outward man *(ho exō hēmōn anthrōpos)*' (2 Cor. 4.16).[70]

If all this is so, it has a very important corollary for the debates occasioned by the new perspective. The lesson to be learned is that Paul's understanding of salvation cannot adequately be appreciated solely or even principally in terms of justification, as though, for example, it could be affirmed solely in terms of an 'alien righteousness' imputed to the believer, or in terms of the effectiveness of the cross as atonement — indispensable and crucial though these be. Equally fundamental to Paul's understanding, and in his own mind fully integrated with his understanding of how God's righteousness operates,

---

[68] A striking feature of Paul's soteriology, too little noticed, is his distinctive and characteristic *sun-* formulations ('with' Christ); listed in my *Theology of Paul* 402-3 n. 63.

[69] Marguerat, 'Paul et la Loi' 271-2, exemplifies a contemporary trend to see 3.7-11 in parallel to 2.6-11; I would press beyond to see the two aspects of 3.4-6 in parallel to the two aspects of 2.6.

[70] See further my *Theology of Paul* #18 (especially #18.5), and earlier *Jesus and the Spirit* (London: SCM, 1975) #55.

was his understanding of a process of being 'in Christ' (participation, if you like), but also a process of becoming more deeply 'in(to) Christ', or becoming more fully conformed to the image of God in Christ.

7. Phil. 3.12-14

The texts and translations make a paragraph break between vss. 11 and 12, understandably so, since vs. 11 formed such a climax to the sequence 3.7-11, and because 3.12-16 takes the thought forward with a quite different imagery. At the same time, however, the opening of the new paragraph is clearly intended to take up and clarify the previous affirmation. 'Not that I have already obtained or already reached the goal *(teteleiōmai)*'[71] — that is, the goal envisaged in 3.9-11 (not just 'the resurrection from the dead', but the 'whole package'). The point was important for Paul, for he repeats it for emphasis: 'I do not reckon myself to have attained it' (3.13). The double denial suggests that Paul feared the thrust of what he had just asserted might be misunderstood, perhaps was being misunderstood. That is, the force of the 'not yet' aspiration Paul held out in 3.9-11 might be critically weakened by those who put more weight on the 'already' accomplishment of cross and conversion. Whatever his precise train of thought, Paul hurried to disallow and to dismiss emphatically any such diminishing of the force of the 'not yet' end to the process of salvation. For God's purpose of saving righteousness to be completed there was much still to be done. Paul expresses himself in personal terms (3.12-14), but it is clear that his message was for all (3.15-16).

The striking feature in this case is *the intensity of focus and personal effort* which Paul envisages as necessary if the goal described in 3.9-11 is to be accomplished. As elsewhere, he depicts the course of his life as a Christian as a foot race, such as would have been run at the various national and international games held round the Aegean (cf. particularly 1 Cor. 9.24-27).[72] 'I pursue/press on *(diōkō)* so that by all means *(ei kai)* I might attain it *(katalabō)*' — that is, the prize mentioned in vs. 14 (as again in 1 Cor. 9.24). 'The one thing I

---

[71] There may be a backward glance here to his old attitude, since the claim to be 'perfect' featured in Second Temple Judaism, in the praise of heroes of the past, like Noah (Sir. 44.17) and in assurance among the Qumran covenanters that they were 'perfect' in their understanding and observance of Torah (1QS 1.8; 2.2; 3.9-11; 8.18; 9.8-9, 19); see further S. J. Gathercole, *Where is Boasting? Early Jewish Soteriology and Paul's Response in Romans 1–5* (Grand Rapids: Eerdmans, 2002) 182-90. But we should also note that according to Col. 1.28, Paul himself hoped to present his converts *teleios* ('complete', 'mature', 'perfect') in Christ, and that here he immediately addresses himself to 'as many as are *teleioi* (3.15)!

[72] No one doubts the allusion to such games; details in J. R. C. Couslan, 'Athletics', in C. A. Evans & S. E. Porter, eds., *Dictionary of New Testament Background* (Downers Grove, IL: InterVarsity, 2000) 140-2.

do *(hen de)*'; we might even translate, 'The only thing I am concerned about', 'My single aim' (Phil. 3.12).[73] And what is that? '. . . forgetting what lies behind (not only the *skubala* of 3.5-6) and exerting myself to the uttermost *(ep-ekteinomenos)*, I pursue/press on toward the goal *(kata skopon)* for the prize *(brabeion)* of the upward call of God in Christ Jesus' (3.13-14).

The point Paul evidently wanted to make is clear beyond dispute. He did not think of salvation as something already completed. He did not think that every-thing towards that goal was already done for him or required no participation or effort from him. He did not hesitate to use an image of intense personal exer-tion, with the suggestion that without such exertion he might otherwise fail to reach the finishing line of the race to which he was committed — as again most explicitly in 1 Cor. 9.27: '. . . lest having preached to others I myself become dis-qualified *(adokimos)*'. He did not hesitate to speak of salvation/eternal life/life in the age to come[74] as a 'prize' to be won. The 'prize', of course, would be of a piece with 'the resurrection from the dead' (Phil. 3.11), where, noticeably, he ex-pressed a similar reservation — 'if somehow I might attain to the resurrection from the dead' — the 'if somehow' indicating 'a degree of contingency', which, however, as Bockmuehl observes, is 'often underrated by commentators'.[75] The humility expressed here is also part of the contrast Paul saw between his old 'confidence' and his faith in Christ.[76]

If this clearly important emphasis of Paul could be correlated with later dis-putes and terms, it would be fascinating to hear Paul's own response to those who thought such language and imagery to be too much open to a semi-Pelagian interpretation or to be in danger of undermining the righteousness from God as an 'alien righteousness'. Here again we note that the climax to be attained is 'the upward call of God in Christ Jesus'. The call is God's. The me-dium of its effectiveness is Christ Jesus. To affirm, at the same time and in the same breath, that the dedicated effort of the believer was also necessary was evidently neither inconsistent with nor a threat to the God-givenness and the Christ-centredness of the end result.

There is a lesson here for all parties to the ongoing debate occasioned by the new perspective on Paul and concerning Paul's teaching on justification by faith and participation in Christ.

---

[73] 'The single-mindedness of the athlete for whom nothing else counts' (Bockmuehl, *Philippians* 222).

[74] Whether 'the upward call' was the initial 'call' of conversion, or the summons 'on high' (discussion in O'Brien, *Philippians* 430-3) 'the prize' itself is evidently the final act in the process of salvation here dramatized as a life-long race.

[75] Bockmuehl, *Philippians* 217. 'The Apostle states not a positive assurance but a modest hope' (Lightfoot, *Philippians* 151). Otherwise O'Brien, *Philippians* 412-3.

[76] Gnilka, *Philipperbrief* 197.

8. Conclusion

What does Phil. 3.2-16 contribute to the current debate on the new perspective on Paul? Much in every way.

(1) The passage confirms that a central problem, which found its resolution in Paul's understanding of how God's righteousness worked, was Jewish confidence in their ethnic identity as Israel, the people of God, the people of the Torah, 'the circumcision'. The implication is fairly obvious that such reliance on ethnic identity carried with it the corollary that Gentiles, 'the uncircumcision' as such, were debarred from the benefits of God's covenant with Israel. To ensure that the separation between Jew and Gentile was properly maintained may very well have been a major motivation of Paul's persecuting zeal.

(2) The passage also confirms that the pre-Christian Paul placed great reliance on the fact that he conformed to the law and was faithful to God's covenant with Israel in a superlative degree. His discovery of God's righteousness, as a gift given directly to and through faith, was a discovery that 'my righteousness' as a devout and zealous Jew, a righteousness understood in terms of living wholly in accordance with the law, was in comparison a valueless and entirely unsatisfactory understanding of the righteousness required by God.

(3) The passage further indicates that for Paul participation in Christ was a fundamental expression of his new understanding of salvation. It was what Christ had done and Christ himself as the medium of his acceptance by and relationship with God which made all the difference. His righteousness from God and his being in Christ were two sides of the same coin, fully integrated in his own understanding of God's saving righteousness. Any attempt to play off one against another or to play up one over the other would have almost certainly have been sharply contested by Paul himself.

(4) Still clearer is Paul's emphasis that salvation was an ongoing process and that the goal of salvation (being found in him having the righteousness from God, knowing him, complete conformity to his death, the resurrection from the dead, the prize of the upward calling) was still to be attained. Two features of this hope should not be ignored. (a) The goal would only be achieved by Paul's being conformed to Jesus' death in order that he might share fully also in his resurrection. That a personal transformation is envisaged and not simply an affirmation of status is clearly implied. (b) Paul did not hesitate to emphasise the personal commitment and supreme effort required if the goal was to be reached, or to describe the goal as a 'prize' to be awarded to the one who successfully completed the course.

In these four emphases we may see important emphases which should be borne in mind in the ongoing debate on the new perspective on Paul.

Publication Credits

1. *The New Perspective on Paul: whence, what, whither?*

2. *The New Perspective on Paul*
   from *BJRL* 65 (1983) 95–122, reprinted in *Jesus, Paul and the Law: Studies in Mark and Galatians* (London: SPCK, 1990)183–214.

3. *Works of the Law and the Curse of the Law (Gal. 3.10–14)*
   from *NTS* 31 (1985) 523–42, reprinted in *Jesus, Paul and the Law* 215–41.

4. *The New Perspective on Paul: Paul and the Law*
   from J.D.G. Dunn, *Romans* (WBC 38; Dallas: Word, 1988) lxiv–lxxii, reprinted in K.P. Donfried, ed., *The Romans Debate* (Peabody, MA: Hendrickson, 1991) 299–308 = 'Die neue Paulus-Perspektive. Paulus und das Gesetz', *KuI* 11 (1996) 34–45.

5. *What was the Issue between Paul and "Those of the Circumcision"?*
   from M. Hengel & U. Heckel, hrsg., *Paulus und das antike Judentum* (1988 Tübingen-Durham Research Symposium) (Tübingen: Mohr Siebeck, 1991) 295–312.

6. *The Theology of Galatians: The Issue of Covenantal Nomism*
   from J.M. Bassler, ed., *Pauline Theology Vol. 1: Thessalonians, Philippians, Galatians, Philemon* (Minneapolis: Fortress, 1991) 125–46; a slightly expanded version in *Jesus, Paul and the Law* 242–64.

7. *The Justice of God: A Renewed Perspective on Justification by Faith*
   (The Henton Davies Lecture, Oxford 1991), *JTS* 43 (1992) 1–22.

8. *Yet Once More – "The Works of the Law": A Response*
   from *JSNT* 46 (1992) 99–117.

9. *Echoes of Intra-Jewish Polemic in Paul's Letter to the Galatians*
   from *JBL* 112 (1993) 459–77.

10. *How New was Paul's Gospel? The Problem of Continuity and Discontinuity*
    from L.A. Jervis & P. Richardson, eds., *Gospel in Paul: Studies on Corinthians, Galatians and Romans for Richard N. Longenecker* (JSNTS 108; Sheffield: Sheffield Academic, 1994) 367–88.

11. Was Paul against the Law? The Law in Galatians and Romans: A Test-Case of Text in Context
from T. Fornberg & D. Hellholm, eds., *Texts and Contexts: Biblical Texts in Their Textual and Situational Contexts*, L. Hartman FS (Oslo: Scandinavian University Press, 1995) 455–75.

12. In Search of Common Ground
from J.D.G. Dunn, ed., *Paul and the Mosaic Law* (WUNT 89; Tübingen: Mohr Siebeck, 1996; Grand Rapids: Eerdmans, 2001) 309–34.

13. "Neither Circumcision Nor Uncircumcision, but ..." (Gal. 5.2–12; 6.12–16; cf. 1 Cor. 7.17–20)
from A. Vanhoye, ed., *La Foi Agissant par l'Amour (Galates 4.12–6.16)* (Rome: Abbaye de S. Paul, 1996) 79–110.

14. 4QMMT and Galatians
from *NTS* 43 (1997) 147–53.

15. Paul's Conversion – A Light to Twentieth Century Disputes
from J. Ådna et al. eds., *Evangelium – Schriftauslegung – Kirche*, P. Stuhlmacher FS (Göttingen: Vandenhoeck & Ruprecht, 1997) 77–93.

16. Paul and Justification by Faith
from R.N. Longenecker, ed., *The Road from Damascus: The Impact of Paul's Conversion on His Life, Thought, and Ministry* (Grand Rapids: Eerdmans, 1997) 85–101.

17. Whatever Happened to "Works of the Law"?
from J. Kerkovsky et al., eds., *Epitoayto*, P. Pokorny FS (Praha: Mlyn, 1998) 107–20.

18. Jesus the Judge: Further Thoughts on Paul's Christology and Soteriology
from D. Kendall & S.T. Davis, eds., *The Convergence of Theology*, G. O'Collins FS (New York: Paulist, 2001) 34–54.

19. Noch einmal "Works of the Law": The Dialogue Continues
revised from I. Dunderberg & C. Tuckett, eds., *Fair Play: Diversity and Conflicts in Early Christianity*, H. Räisänen FS (Leiden: Brill, 2002) 273–90.

20. Did Paul have a Covenant Theology? Reflections on Romans 9.4 and 11.27
from S.E. Porter & J.C.R. de Roo, eds., *The Concept of the Covenant in the Second Temple Period* (Leiden: Brill, 2003) 287–307; also in S.E. McGinn, ed., *Celebrating Romans: Template for Pauline Theology*, R. Jewett FS (Grand Rapids: Eerdmans, 2004) 3–19.

21. Paul and the Torah
English version of 'Paul et la Torah: le rôle et la fonction de la Loi dans la théologie de Paul l'apôtre', in A.Dettwiler, J.-D.Kaestli & D.Marguerat, eds., *Paul, une théologie en construction* (Genève: Labor et Fides, 2004) 227–49.

22. Philippians 3.2–14 and the New Perspective on Paul

Bibliography

Abegg, M. G., '4QMMT C 27, 31 and "Works Righteousness"', *DSD* 6 (1999) 139-47.

———, 'Paul and James on the Law in Light of the Dead Sea Scrolls', in J. J. Collins & C. A. Evans, eds., *Christian Beginnings and the Dead Sea Scrolls* (Grand Rapids: Baker Academic, 2006) 63-74.

Alexander, P. S., 'Torah and Salvation in Tannaitic Literature', in D. A. Carson, et al. eds., *Justification and Variegated Nomism. Vol. 1: The Complexities of Second Temple Judaism* (WUNT 2.140; Tübingen: Mohr Siebeck, 2001) 261-301.

Aune, D. E., ed., *Rereading Paul Together: Protestant and Catholic Perspectives on Justification* (Grand Rapids: Baker Academic, 2006).

Avemarie, F., *Tora und Leben: Untersuchungen zur Heilsbedeutung der Tora in der frühen rabbinischen Literatur* (TSAJ 55; Tübingen: Mohr Siebeck, 1996).

———, 'Bund als Gabe und Recht', in Avemarie & Lichtenberger, eds., *Bund und Tora* 163-216.

———, 'Erwählung und Vergeltung. Zur optionalen Struktur rabbinischer Soteriologie', *NTS* 45 (1999), 108-126.

———, 'Die Werke des Gesetzes im Spiegel des Jakobusbriefs: A Very Old Perspective on Paul', *ZTK* 98 (2001) 282-309.

———, 'Die Wiederkehr der Werke', *Jahrbuch für evangelikale Theologie* 19 (2005) 123-38.

———, 'The Tension between God's Command and Israel's Obedience as Reflected in the Early Rabbinic Literature', in Barclay & Gathercole, eds., *Divine and Human Agency in Paul* 50-70.

Avemarie, F., & Lichtenberger, H., eds., *Bund und Tora: Zur theologischen Begriffsgeschichte in alttestamentlicher, frühjüdischer und urchristlicher Tradition* (WUNT 92; Tübingen: Mohr Siebeck, 1996).

Bachmann, M., *Sünder oder Übertreter: Studien zur Argumentation in Gal 2,15ff.* (WUNT 59; Tübingen: Mohr Siebeck, 1992).

———, 'Rechtfertigung und Gesetzeswerke bei Paulus', *TZ* 49 (1993) 1-33, reprinted in *Antijudaismus im Galaterbrief: Exegetische Studien zu einem polemischen Schreiben und zur Theologie des Apostels Paulus* (NTOA 40; Freiburg: Universitätsverlag, 1999) 1-31.

———, '4QMMT und Galaterbrief, *ma'ase hatorah* und ERGA NOMOU', *ZNW* 89 (1998) 91-113, reprinted in *Antijudaismus im Galaterbrief* 33-56.

———, 'Keil oder Mikroskop? Zur jüngeren Diskussion um den Ausdruck "'Werke' des Gesetzes"', in Bachmann, ed., *Lutherische und Neue Paulusperspektive* 69-134.

———, 'J. D. G. Dunn und die Neue Paulusperspektive', *TZ* 63 (2007) 25-43.

Bachmann, M., ed., *Lutherische und Neue Paulusperspektive* (WUNT 182; Tübingen: Mohr Siebeck, 2005).

Barclay, J. M. G., 'Paul and the Law: Observations on Some Recent Debates', *Themelios* 12 (1986-87) 5-15.

———, *Obeying the Truth: A Study of Paul's Ethics in Galatians* (Edinburgh: T&T Clark, 1988).

————, ' "Neither Jew Nor Greek": Multiculturalism and the New Perspective on Paul', in M. G. Brett, ed., *Ethnicity and the Bible* (Leiden: Brill, 1996) 197-214.

Barclay, J. M. G. & Gathercole, S., eds., *Divine and Human Agency in Paul and his Cultural Environment* (LNTS 335; London: T&T Clark, 2006).

Barrett, C. K., 'Christocentricity at Antioch', in C. Landmesser, et al., eds., *Jesus Christus als die Mitte der Schrift*, O. Hofius FS (Berlin: de Gruyter, 1997) 323-39; reprinted in Barrett, *On Paul: Essays on his Life, Work and Influence in the Early Church* (London: T&T Clark, 2003) 37-54.

Bassler, J. M., *Navigating Paul: An Introduction to Key Theological Concepts* (Louisville: Westminster John Knox, 2007).

Becker, J., *Paul: Apostle to the Gentiles* (Louisville: John Knox, 1993).

Beker, J. C., *Paul the Apostle: the Triumph of God in Life and Thought* (Philadelphia: Fortress, 1980).

Bell, R. H., *No One Seeks for God: An Exegetical and Theological Study of Romans 1.18– 3.20* (WUNT 106; Tübingen: Mohr Siebeck, 1998).

Bergmeier, R., *Das Gesetz im Römerbrief und andere Studien zum Neuen Testament* (WUNT 121; Tübingen: Mohr Siebeck, 2000) 31-102.

————, 'Vom Tun der Tora', in Bachmann, ed., *Lutherische und Neue Paulusperspektive* 161-81.

Bird, M. F., *The Saving Righteousness of God: Studies on Paul, Justification and the New Perspective* (Milton Keynes: Paternoster, 2007).

Blocher, H., 'Justification of the Ungodly *(Sola Fide):* Theological Reflections', in D. A. Carson, et al., eds., *Justification and Variegated Nomism. Vol. 2: The Paradoxes of Paul* (Tübingen: Mohr Siebeck, 2004) 465-500.

Bockmuehl, M., 'Antioch and James the Just', in B. Chilton & C. A. Evans, eds., *James the Just and Christian Origins* (NovTSup 98; Leiden: Brill, 1999) 155-98.

Boers, H., *The Justification of the Gentiles: Paul's Letters to the Galatians and Romans* (Peabody, MA: Hendrickson, 1994).

Bornkamm, G., *Paul* (London: Hodder & Stoughton, 1971).

Bovon, F., 'The New Person and the Law According to the Apostle Paul', *New Testament Traditions and Apocryphal Narratives* (Allison Park: Pickwick, 1995) 15-25.

Bruce, F. F., *Paul: Apostle of the Free Spirit* (Exeter: Paternoster, 1977).

————, 'Paul and the Law in Recent Research', in B. Lindars, ed., *Law and Religion* (Cambridge: James Clarke, 1988) 115-25.

Burchard, C., 'Nicht aus Werken des Gesetzes gerecht, sondern aus Glauben an Jesus Christus — seit wann?', in H. Lichtenberger, ed., *Geschichte — Tradition — Reflexion: Vol. 3, Frühes Christentum*, M. Hengel FS (Tübingen: Mohr Siebeck, 1996) 405-15.

Byrne, B., 'Living Out the Righteousness of God: The Contribution of Rom 6:1–8:13 to an Understanding of Paul's Ethical Presuppositions', *CBQ* 43 (1981) 557-81.

————, 'The Problem of *Nomos* and the Relationship with Judaism in Romans', *CBQ* 62 (2000) 294-309.

————, 'Interpreting Romans Theologically in a Post-"New Perspective" Perspective', *HTR* 94 (2001) 227-42.

————, 'Interpreting Romans: The New Perspective and Beyond', *Interpretation* 58 (2004) 241-52.

Cairus, A. E., 'Works-Righteousness in the Biblical Narrative of Josephus', *ExpT* 115 (2003-04) 257-9.

Calvert-Koyzis, N., *Paul, Monotheism and the People of God: The Significance of Abraham Traditions for Early Judaism and Christianity* (JSNTS 273; London: T&T Clark International, 2004).

Campbell, D. A., *The Quest for Paul's Gospel: A Suggested Strategy* (JSNTS 274; London: T&T Clark, 2005).

Campbell, W. S., *Paul's Gospel in an Intercultural Context: Jew and Gentile in the Letter to the Romans* (Frankfurt: Peter Lang, 1991).

Carson, D. A., *Divine Sovereignty and Human Responsibility* (Atlanta, GA: John Knox, 1981).

——, 'Mystery and Fulfilment: Towards a More Comprehensive Paradigm of Paul's Understanding of the Old and the New', in Carson et al., *Justification and Variegated Nomism Vol. 2* 393-436.

Carson, D. A., ed., *Right With God: Justification in the Bible and the World* (Carlisle: Paternoster, 1992).

Carson, D. A., and Moo, D. J., *An Introduction to the New Testament* (Grand Rapids: Zondervan, 2nd edition, 2005).

Carson, D. A., O'Brien, P. T., and Seifrid, M. A., eds., *Justification and Variegated Nomism. Vol. 1: The Complexities of Second Temple Judaism* (WUNT 2.140; Tübingen: Mohr Siebeck; Grand Rapids, MI: Baker, 2001).

——, *Justification and Variegated Nomism. Vol. 2: The Paradoxes of Paul* (Tübingen: Mohr Siebeck, 2004).

Corley, B., 'Interpreting Paul's Conversion — Then and Now', in Longenecker, *The Road to Damascus* 1-17.

Cosgrove, C. H., 'Justification in Paul: A Linguistic and Theological Reflection', *JBL* 106 (1987) 653-70.

Cook, E. M., 'Covenantal Nomism in the Psalms Targum', in S. E. Porter & J. C. R. de Roo, eds., *The Concept of the Covenant in the Second Temple Period* (SSJSup 71; Leiden: Brill, 2003) 203-20.

Cranfield, C. E. B., 'Paul and the Law', *SJT* 17 (1964) 43-68.

——, ' "The Works of the Law" in the Epistle to the Romans', *JSNT* 43 (1991) 89-101, reprinted in Cranfield, *On Romans and Other New Testament Essays* (Edinburgh: T&T Clark, 1998) 1-14.

Cranford, M., 'The Possibility of Perfect Obedience: Paul and an Implied Premise in Galatians 3:10 and 5:3', *NovT* 36 (1994) 242-58.

——, 'Abraham in Romans 4: The Father of All Who Believe', *NTS* 41 (1995) 71-88.

Crossley, J. G., *The Date of Mark's Gospel: Insight from the Law in Earliest Christianity* (JSNTS 266; London: T&T Clark International, 2004) 141-54.

Dahl, N., 'The Doctrine of Justification: Its Social Function and Implications' (1964), *Studies in Paul* (Minneapolis: Augsburg, 1977) 95-120.

Das, A. A., 'Another Look at *ean mē* in Galatians 2:16', *JBL* 119 (2000) 529-39.

——, *Paul, the Law, and the Covenant* (Peabody, MA: Hendrickson, 2001).

——, *Paul and the Jews* (Peabody, MA; Hendrickson, 2003).

Davies, G. N., *Faith and Obedience in Romans: A Study of Romans 1–4* (JSNTS 39; Sheffield: JSOT, 1990).

Davies, W. D., *Paul and Rabbinic Judaism* (Philadelphia: Fortress, [4]1981).

——, 'Paul and the People of Israel', *NTS* 24 (1977-78) 4-39, reprinted in his *Jewish and Pauline Studies* (London: SPCK, 1984) 123-52.

——, 'Paul and the Law: Reflections on Pitfalls in Interpretation', in M. D. Hooker & S. G. Wilson, eds., *Paul and Paulinism*, C. K. Barrett FS (London: SPCK, 1982) 4-16.

Dettwiler, A., Kaestli, J.-D., & Marguerat, D., eds., *Paul, une théologie en construction* (Genève: Labor et Fides, 2004).

Donaldson, T. L., 'The "Curse of the Law" and the Inclusion of the Gentiles: Galatians 3.13-14', *NTS* 32 (1986) 94-112.

————, *Paul and the Gentiles: Remapping the Apostle's Convictional World* (Minneapolis: Fortress, 1997).

Donfried, K. P., 'Justification and Last Judgment in Paul', *ZNW* 67 (1976) 90-110, reprinted in his *Paul, Thessalonica and Early Christianity* (London: T&T Clark, 2002) 253-78, with further reflection, 'Justification and Last Judgment in Paul — Twenty-Five Years Later' (279-92).

Drane, J. W., *Paul: Libertine or Legalist?* (London: SPCK, 1975).

Dunn, J. D. G., 'The Relationship between Paul and Jerusalem according to Galatians 1 and 2', *NTS* 28 (1982) 461-78, reprinted in *Jesus, Paul and the Law: Studies in Mark and Galatians* (London: SPCK; Louisville: Westminster John Knox, 1990) 108-26.

————, 'The Incident at Antioch (Gal. 2.11-18)', *JSNT* 18 (1983) 3-57, reprinted in *Jesus, Paul and the Law* 129-74, and in M. D. Nanos, ed., *The Galatians Debate* (Peabody, MA: Hendrickson, 2002) 199-234.

————, '"Righteousness from the Law" and "Righteousness from Faith": Paul's Interpretation of Scripture in Rom. 10.1-10', in G. F. Hawthorne & O. Betz, eds., *Tradition and Interpretation in the New Testament*. E. E. Ellis FS (Grand Rapids: Eerdmans/Tübingen: J. C. B. Mohr, 1987) 216-28.

————, 'Pharisees, Sinners, and Jesus', in J. Neusner, et al., eds., *The Social World of Formative Christianity and Judaism,* H. C. Kee FS (Philadelphia: Fortress, 1988) 264-89, reprinted in *Jesus, Paul and the Law* 61-86.

————, 'The Theology of Galatians', *Jesus, Paul and the Law* 242-64.

————, 'Paul and "Covenantal Nomism"', in Dunn, *The Partings of the Ways between Christianity and Judaism* (London: SCM/Philadelphia: TPI, 1991) 117-39.

————, *A Commentary on the Epistle to the Galatians* (BNTC; London: Black, 1993).

————, *The Theology of Paul's Letter to the Galatians* (Cambridge: Cambridge University, 1993).

————, 'Should Paul Once Again Oppose Peter to his Face?', *The Heythrop Journal* 34 (1993) 58-65.

————, 'Anti-Semitism in the Deutero-Pauline Letters' in C. A. Evans & D. A. Hagner, eds., *Anti-Semitism and Early Christianity: Issues of Polemic and Faith* (Minneapolis: Fortress, 1993) 151-65.

————, (with A. M. Suggate) *The Justice of God. A Fresh Look at the Old Doctrine of Justification by Faith* (Carlisle: Paternoster, 1993/Grand Rapids: Eerdmans, 1994).

————, 'Deutero-Pauline Letters', in J. Barclay & J. Sweet, eds., *Early Christian Thought in its Jewish Context* (Cambridge: Cambridge University, 1996) 130-44.

————, '"The Law of Faith", "the Law of the Spirit" and "the Law of Christ"', in E. H. Lovering & J. L. Sumney, eds., *Theology and Ethics in Paul and his Interpreters,* V. P. Furnish FS (Nashville: Abingdon, 1996) 62-82.

————, 'Two Covenants or One? The Interdependence of Jewish and Christian Identity', in H. Lichtenberger, ed., *Geschichte — Tradition — Reflexion,* M. Hengel FS (Tübingen: J. C. B. Mohr, 1996) 97-122.

————, 'Jesus and Factionalism in Early Judaism', in J. H. Charlesworth & L. L. Johns, eds., *Hillel and Jesus: Comparisons of Two Major Religious Leaders* (Minneapolis: Fortress, 1997) 156-75.

————, *The Theology of Paul the Apostle* (Grand Rapids: Eerdmans, 1998).

————, 'Whatever Happened to Exegesis? In Response to the Reviews by R. B. Matlock and D. A. Campbell', *JSNT* 72 (1998) 113-20.

————, 'Paul: Apostate or Apostle of Israel?', *ZNW* 89 (1998) 256-271.

————, 'Who Did Paul Think He Was? A Study of Jewish Christian Identity', *NTS* 45 (1999) 174-93.

————, 'The Jew Paul and his Meaning for Israel', in U. Schnelle & T. Söding, eds., *Paulinische Christologie: Exegetische Beiträge*, H. Hübner FS (Göttingen: Vandenhoeck & Ruprecht, 2000) 32-46.

————, 'A Response to Peter Stuhlmacher', in F. Avemarie & H. Lichtenberger, eds., *Auferstehung — Resurrection* (WUNT 135; Tübingen: Mohr Siebeck, 2001) 363-8.

————, 'The Narrative Approach to Paul: Whose Story?', in B. W. Longenecker, ed., *Narrative Dynamics in Paul: A Critical Assessment* (Louisville/London: Westminster John Knox, 2002) 217-30.

————, 'The Dialogue Progresses', in Bachmann, ed., *Lutherische und Neue Paulusperspektive* 389-430.

Dunn, J. D. G., ed., *Paul and the Mosaic Law* (WUNT 89; Tübingen: J. C. B. Mohr, 1996; Grand Rapids: Eerdmans, 2001).

Eckstein, H. J., *Verheissung und Gesetz: Eine exegetische Untersuchung zu Galater 2,15–4,7* (WUNT 86; Tübingen: Mohr Siebeck, 1996).

Ego, B., 'Abraham als Urbild der Toratreue Israels. Traditionsgeschichtliche Überlegungen zu einem Aspekt des biblischen Abrahambildes', in Avemarie & Lichtenberger, eds., *Bund und Tora* 25-40.

Elliott, M. A., *The Survivors of Israel: A Reconsideration of the Theology of Pre-Christian Judaism* (Grand Rapids: Eerdmans, 2000).

Elliott, N., *The Rhetoric of Romans: Argumentative Constraint and Strategy and Paul's Dialogue with Judaism* (JSNTS 45; Sheffield: Sheffield Academic, 1990).

Eskola, T., 'Paul, Predestination and "Covenantal Normism": Re-assessing Paul and Palestinian Judaism', *JSJ* 28 (1997) 390-41.

————, *Theodicy and Predestination in Pauline Soteriology* (WUNT 2.100; Tübingen: Mohr Siebeck, 1998).

————, *'Avodat Israel* and the "Works of the Law" in Paul', in T. Eskola & E. Junkkaala, eds., *From the Ancient Sites of Israel: Essays on Archaeology, History and Theology* (Helsinki: Theological Institute of Finland, 1998) 175-97.

Esler, P. F., 'Making and Breaking an Agreement Mediterranean Style: A New Reading of Galatians 2:1-14', *BibInt* 3 (1995) 285-314.

————, *Galatians* (London: Routledge, 1998).

————, *Conflict and Identity in Romans: The Social Setting of Paul's Letter* (Minneapolis: Fortress, 2003).

Fitzmyer, J. A., *Romans* (AB 33; New York: Doubleday, 1993) 131-5.

————, 'Paul's Jewish Background and the Deeds of the Law', *According to Paul: Studies in the Theology of the Apostle* (New York: Paulist, 1993) 18-35.

Frankemölle, H., 'Völker-Verheissung (Gen 12–18) und Sinai-Tora im Römerbrief. Das "Dazwischen" (Röm 5,20) als hermeneutischer Parameter für eine lutherische oder nichtlutherische Paulus-Auslegung', in Bachmann, ed., *Lutherische und Neue Paulusperspektive* 275-307.

Flusser, D., 'The Dead Sea Sect and Pre-Pauline Christianity' (1958), *Judaism and the Origins of Christianity* (Jerusalem: Hebrew University, 1988) 23-74.

————, 'Die Gesetzeswerke in Qumran und bei Paulus', in H. Cancik et al., eds., *Geschichte — Tradition — Reflexion. Vol. 1: Judentum*, M. Hengel FS (Tübingen: Mohr Siebeck, 1996) 395-403.

Gager, J. G., *Reinventing Paul* (New York: Oxford University, 2000).

Garlington, D. B., *'The Obedience of Faith': A Pauline Phrase in Historical Context* (WUNT 2.38; Tübingen: Mohr, 1991).

————, *Faith, Obedience and Perseverance: Aspects of Paul's Letter to the Romans* (WUNT 79; Tübingen: Mohr, 1994).

————, *An Exposition of Galatians: A New Perspective/Reformational Reading* (Eugene, OR: Wipf & Stock, 2002, ²2004).

————, *In Defense of the New Perspective on Paul: Essays and Reviews* (Eugene, OR: Wipf & Stock, 2005).

Gaston, L., 'Paul and the Torah', in A. T. Davies, ed., *Antisemitism and the Foundations of Christianity* (New York: Paulist, 1979) 48-71, reprinted in *Paul and the Torah* (Vancouver: University of British Columbia, 1987) 15-34.

Gathercole, S. J., *Where Is Boasting? Early Jewish Soteriology and Paul's Response in Romans 1–5* (Grand Rapids, MI: Eerdmans, 2002).

————, 'A Law unto Themselves: The Gentiles in Romans 2.14-15 Revisited', *JSNT* 85 (2002) 27-49.

————, 'Torah, Life, and Salvation: Leviticus 18.5 in Early Judaism and the New Testament', in C. A. Evans, ed., *From Prophecy to Testament: The Function of the Old Testament in the New* (Peabody, MA: Hendrickson, 2004) 126-45.

————, 'Justified by Faith, Justified by his Blood: The Evidence of Romans 3:21–4:25', in Carson, et al., *Justification and Variegated Nomism Vol. 2* 147-84.

————, 'The Petrine and Pauline *Sola Fide* in Galatians 2', in Bachmann, ed., *Lutherische und Neue Paulusperspektive* 309-27.

Gatiss, L., 'Justified Hesitation? J. D. G. Dunn vs. The Protestant Doctrine of Justification', *Churchman* 115/1 (2001) 29-48.

George, T., 'Modernizing Luther, Domesticating Paul: Another Perspective', in Carson et al., *Justification and Variegated Nomism Vol. 2* 437-63.

Gorman, M. J., *Cruciformity: Paul's Narrative Spirituality of the Cross* (Grand Rapids: Eerdmans, 2001).

Grindheim, S., *The Crux of Election: Paul's Critique of the Jewish Confidence in the Election of Israel* (WUNT 2.202; Tübingen: Mohr Siebeck, 2005).

Gundry, R. H., 'Grace, Works and Staying Saved in Paul', *Biblica* 66 (1985) 1-38.

————, 'The Nonimputation of Christ's Righteousness', in Husbands & Trier, *Justification* 17-45.

Haacker, K., 'Paulus und das Judentum im Galaterbrief', in E. Brocke & J. Sein, eds., *Gottes Augapfel: Beiträge zur Erneuerung des Verhältnisses von Christen und Juden* (Neukirchen-Vluyn: Neukirchener, 1986) 95-111.

————, 'Der "Antinomismus" des Paulus im Kontext antiker Gesetzestheorie', in H. Lichtenberger, ed., *Geschichte – Tradition – Reflexion. Band III: Frühes Christentum,* M. Hengel FS (Tübingen: Mohr Siebeck, 1996) 387-404.

————, *Der Brief des Paulus an die Römer* (ThHK 6; Leipzig: Evangelische, 1999) 39-42.

————, 'Verdienste und Grenzen der "neuen Perspektive" der Paulus-Auslegung', in Bachmann, ed., *Lutherische und Neue Paulusperspektive* 1-15.

————, 'Merits and Limits of the "New Perspective on the Apostle Paul"', in S.-W. Son, ed., *History and Exegesis,* E. E. Ellis FS (New York: T&T Clark, 2006) 275-89.

Hafemann, S. J., *Paul, Moses, and the History of Israel* (WUNT 81; Tübingen: Mohr Siebeck, 1995).

Hagner, D. A., 'Paul and Judaism. The Jewish Matrix of Early Christianity: Issues in the Current Debate', *BBR* 3 (1993) 111-30.

————, 'Paul and Judaism: Testing the New Perspective', in P. Stuhlmacher, *Revisiting Paul's Doctrine of Justification: A Challenge to the New Perspective* (Downers Grove, IL: InterVarsity, 2001) 75-105.

Hahn, F., 'Das Gesetzesverständnis im Römer- and Galaterbrief', *ZNW* 67 (1976) 29-63.

————, *Theologie des Neuen Testaments* (Tübingen: Mohr Siebeck, 2002).

Hansen, G. W., *Abraham in Galatians: Epistolary and Rhetorical Contexts* (JSNTS 29; Sheffield: Sheffield Academic, 1989).

Hartman, L., Bundesideologie in und hinter einigen paulinischen Texten', in S. Pedersen, ed., *Paulinische Literatur und Theologie* (Göttingen: Vandenhoeck & Ruprecht, 1980) 103-18.

Hays, R. B., *The Faith of Jesus Christ: The Narrative Substructure of Galatians 3:1–4:11* (Grand Rapids: Eerdmans, 1983, ²2002).

———, 'Three Dramatic Roles: The Law in Romans 3–4', in Dunn ed., *Paul and the Mosaic Law* 151-64.

Heiligenthal, R., *Werke als Zeichen: Untersuchungen zur Bedeutung der menschlichen Taten im Frühjudentum, Neuen Testament und Frühchristentum* (WUNT 2.9; Tübingen: Mohr, 1983).

Hengel, M., *The Pre-Christian Paul* (London: SCM/Philadelphia: TPI, 1991).

———, 'The Attitude of Paul to the Law in the Unknown Years between Damascus and Antioch', in Dunn, ed., *Paul and the Mosaic Law* 25-51 = 'The Stance of the Apostle Paul Toward the Law in the Unknown Years Between Damascus and Antioch', in Carson, et al., *Justification and Variegated Nomism Vol. 2* 75-103.

Hengel, M. & Schwemer, A. M., *Paul Between Damascus and Antioch* (London: SCM, 1997).

Hofius, O., 'Das Gesetz des Mose und das Gesetz Christi', *Paulusstudien* (WUNT 51; Tübingen: Mohr Siebeck, 1989, ²1994) 50-74.

———, 'Gesetz und Evangelium nach 2. Korinther 3' (1989), *Paulusstudien* 75-120.

———, '"Rechtfertigung des Gottlosen" als Thema biblischer Theologie' (1987), *Paulusstudien* 121-47.

———, 'Zur Auslegung von Römer 9,30-33' (1993), *Paulusstudien II* (WUNT 143; Tübingen: Mohr Siebeck, 2002) 155-66.

Holland, T., *Contours of Pauline Theology* (Fearn, Ross-shire: Mentor, 2004).

Hong, I.-G., *The Law in Galatians* (JSNTS 81; Sheffield: JSOT Press, 1993).

Hooker, M. D., 'Paul and "Covenantal Nomism"', in M. D. Hooker & S. G. Wilson, eds., *Paul and Paulinism*, C. K. Barrett FS (London: SPCK, 1982) 47-56, reprinted in Hooker, *From Adam to Christ: Essays on Paul* (Cambridge: Cambridge University, 1990) 155-64.

Horn, F. W., 'Der Verzicht auf die Beschneidung im frühen Christentum', *NTS* 42 (1996) 479-505.

———, 'Juden und Heiden. Aspekte der Verhältnisbestimmung in den paulinischen Briefen. Ein Gespräch mit Krister Stendahl', in Bachmann, ed., *Lutherische und Neue Paulusperspektive* 17-39.

Howard, G. E., 'Christ the End of the Law: The Meaning of Romans 10:4', *JBL* 88 (1969) 331-7.

———, *Crisis in Galatia* (SNTSMS 35; Cambridge: Cambridge University, 1979).

Hübner, H., *Law in Paul's Thought* (ET of first edition; Edinburgh: T&T Clark, 1984).

———, 'Pauli theologiae proprium', *NTS* 26 (1980) 445-73.

———, 'Was heist bei Paulus "Werke des Gesetzes"?', in E. Grässer & O. Merk, eds., *Glaube und Eschatologie*, W. G. Kümmel FS (Tübingen: Mohr Siebeck, 1985) 123-33.

Husbands, H. & Trier, D. J., eds., *Justification: What's at Stake in the Current Debates* (Downers Grove, IL: InterVarsity Press, 2004).

Kaiser, W. C., 'Leviticus 18:5 and Paul: "Do This and You Shall Live" (Eternally?)', *JETS* 14 (1971) 19-28.

Käsemann, E., '"The Righteousness of God" in Paul', *New Testament Questions of Today* (London: SCM, 1969) 168-82.

Kertelge, K., *"Rechtfertigung" bei Paulus: Studien zur Struktur und zum Bedeutungsgehalt des paulinischen Rechtfertigungsbegriffs* (Münster: Aschendorff, 1967).

———, 'Zur Deutung des Rechtfertigungsbegriffs im Galaterbrief', *BZ* 12 (1968) 211-222, reprinted in his *Grundthemen paulinischer Theologie* (Freiburg: Herder, 1991) 111-22.

———, 'Gesetz und Freiheit im Galaterbrief', *NTS* 30 (1984) 382-94, reprinted in *Grundthemen* 184-96.

———, 'Rechtfertigung aus Glauben und Gericht nach den Werken bei Paulus' (1989), *Grundthemen* 130-47.

Kim, S., *The Origin of Paul's Gospel* (WUNT 2.4; Tübingen: Mohr Siebeck, 1981/Grand Rapids: Eerdmans, 1982).

———, *Paul and the New Perspective: Second Thoughts on the Origin of Paul's Gospel* (Grand Rapids, MI: Eerdmans, 2001).

Klein, G., 'Ein Sturmzentrum der Paulusforschung', *VuF* 33 (1988) 40-56.

Kok, E. H., *The Truth of the Gospel: A Study in Galatians 2:15-21* (Hong Kong: Alliance Bible Seminary, 2000).

Koperski, V., *What are They Saying about Paul and the Law?* (Mahweh, NJ: Paulist, 2001).

Kraus, W., 'Gottes Gerechtigkeit und Gottes Volk. Ökumenisch-ekklesiologische Aspekte der New Perspective on Paul', in Bachmann, ed., *Lutherische und Neue Paulusperspektive* 329-47.

Kruse, C., *Paul, the Law and Justification* (Leicester: Apollos, 1996; Peabody, MA: Hendrickson, 1997).

Kuss, O., *Paulus: die Rolle des Apostels in der theologischen Entwicklung der Urkirche* (Regensburg: Pustet, 1971).

Kuula, K., *The Law, the Covenant and God's Plan: Vol. 1. Paul's Polemical Treatment of the Law in Galatians* (Göttingen: Vandenhoeck & Ruprecht, 1999).

———, *The Law, the Covenant and God's Plan: Vol. 2. Paul's Treatment of the Law and Israel in Romans* (Göttingen: Vandenhoeck & Ruprecht, 2003).

Laato, T., *Paul and Judaism: An Anthropological Approach* (Atlanta: Scholars, 1995).

———, 'Paul's Anthropological Considerations: Two Problems', in Carson, et al., *Justification and Variegated Nomism Vol. 2* 343-59.

Lambrecht, J., 'Gesetzesverständnis bei Paulus', in K. Kertelge, hrsg., *Das Gesetz im Neuen Testament* (Freiburg: Herder, 1986) 88-127.

———, 'Paul's Reasoning in Galatians 2:11-21', in Dunn, ed., *Paul and the Mosaic Law* 53-74.

Lambrecht, J. & Thompson, R. W., *Justification by Faith: The Implications of Romans 3:27-31* (Wilmington: Glazier, 1989).

Lichtenberger, H., *Studien zum Menschenbild in Texten der Qumrangemeinde* (Göttingen: Vandenhoeck & Ruprecht, 1980).

———, 'Paulus und das Gesetz', in M. Hengel & U. Heckel, eds., *Paulus und das antike Judentum* (WUNT 58; Tübingen: Mohr, 1991) 361-78.

———, 'The Understanding of the Torah in the Judaism of Paul's Day: A Sketch', in Dunn, ed., *Paul and the Mosaic Law* 7-23.

Liebers, R., *Das Gesetz als Evangelium: Untersuchungen zur Gesetzeskritik des Paulus* (Zürich: Theologischer, 1989).

Limbeck, M., *Die Ordnung des Heils: Untersuchungen zum Gesetzesverständnis des Frühjudentums* (Düsseldorf: Patmos, 1971).

Lincoln, A. T., 'From Wrath to Justification: Tradition, Gospel and Audience in the Theology of Romans', in D. M. Hay & E. E. Johnson, eds., *Pauline Theology, Volume III: Romans* (Minneapolis: Fortress, 1995) 130-59.

Lincoln A. T. & Wedderburn, A. J. M., *The Theology of the Later Pauline Letters* (Cambridge: Cambridge University, 1993).

Lohse, E., *Paulus* (München: C. H. Beck, 1996).

———, 'Theologie der Rechtfertigung im kritischen Disput: zu einigen neueren Perspektiven in der Interpretation der Theologie des Apostels Paulus', *Göttingische Gelehrte Anziegen* 249 (1997) 66-81.

———, *Der Brief an die Römer* (KEK; Göttingen: Vandenhoeck & Ruprecht, 2003) 126-7, 140-5.

Longenecker, B. W., *Eschatology and Covenant: A Comparison of 4 Ezra and Romans 1–11* (JSNTS 57; Sheffield: JSOT, 1991).

———, 'Contours of Covenant Theology in the Post-Conversion Paul', in R. N. Longenecker, ed., *The Road from Damascus: The Impact of Paul's Conversion on His Life, Thought, and Ministry* (Grand Rapids: Eerdmans, 1997) 125-46.

———, *The Triumph of Abraham's God* (Edinburgh: T&T Clark, 1998).

———, 'On Critiquing the "New Perspective" on Paul: A Case Study', *ZNW* 96 (2005) 263-71.

Longenecker, R. N., *Galatians* (WBC 41; Dallas: Word, 1990).

Longenecker, R. N., ed., *The Road to Damascus: The Impact of Paul's Conversion on His Life, Thought, and Ministry* (Grand Rapids: Eerdmans, 1997).

McGrath, A., *Iustitia Dei: A History of the Christian Doctrine of Justification* (Cambridge: Cambridge University, 1986, [2]1998).

Macleod, D., 'The New Perspective: Paul, Luther and Judaism', *Scottish Bulletin of Evangelical Theology* 22 (2004) 4-31.

Marguerat, D., 'Paul et la Loi: le retournement (Philippiens 3,2–4,1)', in A. Dettwiler, et al., eds., *Paul, une théologie en construction* (Genève: Labor et Fides, 2004) 251-75.

Marshall, I. H., 'Salvation, Grace and Works in the Later Writings in the Pauline Corpus' *NTS* 42 (1996), 339–58.

———, *New Testament Theology* (Downers Grove, IL: InterVarsity, 2004).

Martyn, J. L., *Galatians* (AB 33A; New York: Doubleday, 1997).

———, 'God's Way of Making Right What is Wrong', *Theological Issues in the Letters of Paul* (Edinburgh: T&T Clark, 1997) 151-56.

Matera, F. J., 'Galatians in Perspective: Cutting a New Path through Old Territory', *Interpretation* 54 (2000) 233-45.

Matlock, R. B., 'Almost Cultural Studies? Reflections on the "New Perspective" on Paul', in J. C. Exum & S. D. Moore, eds., *Biblical/Cultural Studies: The Third Sheffield Colloquium* (JSOTS 266; Sheffield: Sheffield Academic, 1998) 433-59.

———, 'A Future for Paul?', in *Auguries: The Jubilee Volume of the Sheffield Department of Biblical Studies* (JSOTS 269; Sheffield: Sheffield Academic, 1998) 144-83.

———, 'Sins of the Flesh and Suspicious Minds: Dunn's New Theology of Paul', *JSNT* 72 (1998) 67-90.

Merklein, H., '"Nicht aus Werken des Gesetzes . . .": Eine Auslegung von Gal 2,15-21' (1993), *Studien zu Jesus und Paulus II* (WUNT 105; Tübingen: Mohr Siebeck, 1998) 303-15.

Mijoga, H. B. P., *The Pauline Notion of Deeds of the Law* (San Francisco: International Scholars Publications, 1999).

Moo, D., '"Law", "Works of the Law", and Legalism on Paul', *WTJ* 45 (1983) 73-100.

———, 'Paul and the Law in the Last Ten Years', *SJT* 49 (1987) 287-307.

———, 'Paul, "Works of the Law", and First-Century Judaism', in Moo, *The Epistle to the Romans* (NICNT; Grand Rapids: Eerdmans, 1996) 211-7.

————, 'Israel and the Law in Romans 5-11: Interaction with the New Perspective', in Carson, et al., *Justification and Variegated Nomism Vol. 2* 185-216.

Moule, C. F. D., 'Jesus, Paul and Judaism', in G. F. Hawthorne & O. Betz, eds., *Tradition and Interpretation in the New Testament*, E. E. Ellis FS (Tübingen: Mohr Siebeck/Grand Rapids: Eerdmans, 1987) 43-52.

Müller, H. M., '"Evangelium latuit in lege": Luthers Kreuzespredigt als Schlüssel seiner Bibelhermeneutik', in Landmesser, et al., eds., *Jesus Christus als die Mitte der Schrift*, O. Hofius FS (BZNW 86; Berlin: de Gruyter, 1997) 101-26.

Nanos, M. D., *The Mystery of Romans: The Jewish Context of Paul's Letter.* Minneapolis: Fortress, 1996).

Nanos, M. D., ed., *The Galatians Debate* (Peabody, MA: Hendrickson, 2002).

Niebuhr, K.-W., 'Die paulinische Rechtfertigungslehre in der gegenwärtigen exegetischen Diskussion', in Söding ed., *Worum geht es in der Rechtertigungslehre* 106-30.

O'Brien, P. T., 'Justification in Paul and Some Crucial Issues in the Last Two Decades', in D. A. Carson, ed., *Right with God: Justification in the Bible and the World* (Carlisle: Paternoster, 1992) 69-95.

————, 'Was Paul a Covenantal Nomist?', in Carson, et al., *Justification and Variegated Nomism Vol. 2* 249-96.

————, 'Was Paul Converted?', in Carson et al,. *Justification and Variegated Nomism Vol. 2* 361-91.

Oden, T. C., *The Justification Reader* (Grand Rapids: Eerdmans, 2002).

Oropeza, B. J., *Paul and Apostasy: Eschatology, Perseverance, and Falling Away in the Corinthian Congregation* (WUNT 2.115; Tübingen: Mohr Siebeck, 2000).

S. E. Porter, 'Was Paul a Good Jew? Fundamental Issues in a Current Debate', in S. E. Porter & B. W. R. Pearson, eds., *Christian-Jewish Relations through the Centuries* (JSNTS 192; Sheffield: Sheffield Academic, 2000) 148-74.

Quarles, C. L., 'The New Perspective and Means of Atonement in Jewish Literature of the Second Temple Period', *Criswell Theological Review* 2.2 (2005) 39-56.

Rainbow, P. A., *The Way of Salvation: The Role of Christian Obedience in Justification* (Milton Keynes: Paternoster, 2005).

Räisänen, H., 'Legalism and Salvation by the Law: Paul's Portrayal of the Jewish Religion as a Historical and Theological Problem', in S. Pedersen, hrsg., *Die Paulinische Literatur und Theologie* (Göttingen: Vandenhoeck & Ruprecht, 1980) 63-83.

————, *Paul and the Law* (WUNT 29; Tübingen: Mohr, 1983).

————, 'Galatians 2.16 and Paul's Break with Judaism', *NTS* 31 (1985) 543-53, reprinted in Räisänen, *Jesus, Paul and Torah: Collected Essays* (JSNTS 43; Sheffield: Sheffield Academic, 1992) 112-26.

————, 'Paul's Call Experience and his Later View of the Law', *Jesus, Paul and Torah* 15-47.

Rapa, R. K., *The Meaning of "Works of the Law" in Galatians and Romans* (New York: Peter Lang, 2001).

Reed, S. A., 'The Role of Food as Related to Covenant in Qumran Literature', in S. E. Porter & J. C. R. de Roo, eds., *The Concept of the Covenant in the Second Temple Period* (SSJSup 71; Leiden: Brill, 2003) 129-64.

Reinmuth, E., *Geist und Gesetz: Studien zu Voraussetzungen und Inhalt der paulinischen Paränese* (Berlin: Evangelische, 1985).

Rengstorf, K. H., *Das Paulusbild in der neueren deutschen Forschung* (Darmstadt: Wissenschaftliche Buchgesellschaft, 1964).

Reymond, R. L., *Paul: Missionary Theologian* (Fearn: Mentor, 2000).

Ridderbos, H., *Paul: An Outline of his Theology* (Grand Rapids: Eerdmans, 1975).

Roloff, J., 'Die lutherische Rechtfertigungslehre und ihre biblische Grundlage', in W. Kraus & K.-W. Niebuhr, hg., *Frühjudentum und Neues Testament im Horizont Biblischer Theologie* (WUNT 162; Tübingen: Mohr Siebeck, 2003) 275-300.

Roo, J. C. R. de, 'The Concept of "Works of the Law" in Jewish and Christian Literature', in S. E. Porter & B. W. R. Pearson, eds., *Christian-Jewish Relations Through the Centuries* (JSNTS 192; Sheffield: Sheffield Academic, 2000) 116-47.

——, 'God's Covenant with the Forefathers', in S. E. Porter & J. C. R. de Roo, eds., *The Concept of the Covenant in the Second Temple Period* (SSJSup 71; Leiden: Brill, 2003) 191-202.

——, *'The Works of the Law' at Qumran and in Paul* (NTM 13; Sheffield: Phoenix, 2007).

Sanders, E. P., 'On the Question of Fulfilling the Law in Paul and Rabbinic Judaism', in C. K. Barrett, et al., eds., *Donum Gentilicium*, D. Daube FS (Oxford: Clarendon, 1978) 103-26.

——, *Paul and Palestinian Judaism* (London: SCM, 1977).

——, *Paul, the Law and the Jewish People* (Philadelphia: Fortress, 1983).

——, *Paul* (Oxford: Oxford University, 1991).

Schäfer, R., *Paulus bis zum Apostelkonzil* (WUNT 2.179; Tübingen: Mohr Siebeck, 2004).

Schlier, H., *Grundzüge einer paulinischen Theologie* (Freiburg: Herder, 1978).

Schnelle, U., *Apostle Paul: His Life and Theology* (Grand Rapids: Baker Academic, 2005).

Schreiner, T. R., 'The Abolition and Fulfilment of the Law in Paul', *JSNT* 35 (1989) 47-74.

——, '"Works of Law" in Paul', *NovT* 33 (1991) 214-44.

——, *The Law and Its Fulfilment: A Pauline Theology of Law* (Grand Rapids: Baker, 1993).

——, *Romans* (BECNT; Grand Rapids: Baker, 1998).

——, *Paul, Apostle of God's Glory in Christ: A Pauline Theology* (Downers Grove, IL: IVP, 2001).

Seifrid, M. A., *Justification by Faith: The Origin and Development of a Central Pauline Theme* (NovTSupp 68; Leiden: Brill, 1992).

——, 'Blind Alleys in the Controversy over the Paul of History', *TynBul* 45 (1994) 73-95.

——, 'The "New Perspective on Paul" and its Problems', *Themelios* 25.2 (2000) 4-18.

——, *Christ, our Righteousness: Paul's Theology of Justification* (Downers Grove, IL: InterVarsity, 2000).

——, 'Righteousness Language in the Hebrew Scriptures and Early Judaism', in D. A. Carson, et al. eds., *Justification and Variegated Nomism. Vol. 1: The Complexities of Second Temple Judaism* (WUNT 2.140; Tübingen: Mohr Siebeck, 2001) 415-42.

——, 'Paul's Use of Righteousness Language Against its Hellenistic Background', in Carson et al., *Justification and Variegated Nomism Vol. 2* 39-74.

——, 'Unrighteous by Faith: Apostolic Proclamation in Romans 1:18–3:20', in Carson, et al., *Justification and Variegated Nomism Vol. 2* 106-45.

Silva, M., 'The Law and Christianity: Dunn's New Synthesis', *WTJ* 53 (1991) 339-53.

——, 'Faith Versus Works of Law in Galatians', in Carson, et al., *Justification and Variegated Nomism Vol. 2* 217-48.

Sloan, R. B., 'Paul and the Law: Why the Law Cannot Save', *NovT* 33 (1991) 35-60.

Smiles, V. M., *The Gospel and the Law in Galatia: Paul's Response to Jewish-Christian Separatism and the Threat of Galatian Apostasy* (Collegeville: Liturgical, Glazier, 1998).

Smith, J. E., 'The New Perspective on Paul: A Select and Annotated Bibliography', *Criswell Theological Review* 2.2 (2005) 91-111.

Smith, R., 'Justification in "The New Perspective" on Paul', *Reformed Theological Review* 58 (1999) 16-30.

———, 'A Critique of the New Perspective on Justification', *Reformed Theological Review* 58 (1999) 98-112.

———, *Justification and Eschatology: A Dialogue with 'The New Perspective on Paul'*, *Reformed Theological Review* Supplement Series #1 (2001).

Snodgrass, K. R., 'Justification by Grace — to the Doers: An Analysis of the Place of Romans 2 in the Theology of Paul', *NTS* 32 (1986) 72-93.

———, 'Spheres of Influence: A Possible Solution to the Problem of Paul and the Law', *JSNT* 32 (1988) 93-113.

Söding, T., ed., *Worum geht es in der Rechtfertigungslehre: das biblische Fundament der "Gemeinsamen Erklärung" von katholischer Kirche und lutherischem Weltbund* (Freiburg: Herder, 1999).

———, 'Die Rechtfertigung der Sünder und die Sünden der Gerechtfertigen', in T. Schneider & G. Wenz, eds., *Gerecht und Sünder zugleich? Ökumenische Klärungen* (Freiburg: Herder, 2001) 30-81.

Stanley, A. P., *Did Jesus Teach Salvation by Works? The Role of Works in Salvation in the Synoptic Gospels* (Eugene, OR: Pickwick, 2006).

Stendahl, K., 'The Apostle Paul and the Introspective Conscience of the West', *HTR* 56 (1963) 199-215.

———, *Paul Among Jews and Gentiles* (London: SCM, 1976).

Stolle, V., *Luther und Paulus. Die exegetischen und hermeneutischen Grundlagen der lutherischen Rechtfertigungslehre im Paulinismus Luthers* (Leipzig: Evangelische, 2002).

———, 'Nomos zwischen Tora und Lex. Der paulinische Gesetzesbegriff und seine Interpretation durch Luther in der zweiten Disputation gegen die Antinomer vom 12. Januar 1538', in Bachmann, ed., *Lutherische und Neue Paulusperspektive* 41-67.

Stowers, S. K., *A Rereading of Romans* (New Haven: Yale University, 1994).

Strecker, C., 'Paulus aus einer "neuen Perspektive": der Paradigmenwechsel in der jüngeren Paulusforschung', *Kirche und Israel* 11 (1996) 3-18.

Strecker, G., *Theology of the New Testament* (New York; de Gruyter, 2000).

Stuhlmacher, P., 'The Law as a Topic of Biblical Theology', *Reconciliation, Law and Righteousness: Essays in Biblical Theology* (Philadelphia: Fortress, 1986) 110-33.

———, *Biblische Theologie des Neuen Testaments. Band 1: Grundlegung von Jesus zu Paulus* (Göttingen: Vandenhoeck & Ruprecht, 1992).

———, 'Christus Jesus ist hier, der gestorben ist, ja vielmehr, der auch auferweckt ist, der zur Rechten Gottes ist und uns vertritt', in F. Avemarie & H. Lichtenberger, eds., *Auferstehung — Resurrection* (WUNT 135; Tübingen: Mohr Siebeck, 2001) 351-61.

———, *Revisiting Paul's Doctrine of Justification: A Challenge to the New Perspective* (Downers Grove, IL: InterVarsity, 2001).

Synofzik, E., *Die Gerichts- und Vergeltungsaussagen bei Paulus: Eine traditionsgeschichtliche Untersuchung* (Göttingen: Vandenhoeck & Ruprecht, 1977).

Talbert, C. H., 'Paul, Judaism, and the Revisionists', *CBQ* 63 (2001) 1-22.

Thielman, F., *From Plight to Solution: A Jewish Framework for Understanding Paul's View of the Law in Galatians and Romans* (NovTSupp; Leiden: Brill, 1989).

———, 'The Coherence of Paul's View of the Law: The Evidence of First Corinthians', *NTS* 38 (1992) 235-53.

———, *Paul and the Law: A Contextual Approach* (Downers Grove, IL.: InterVarsity, 1994).

———, 'Paul as Jewish Christian Theologian: The Theology of Paul in the Magnum Opus of James D. G. Dunn', *Perspectives in Religious Studies* 25 (1998) 381-7.

Theobald, M., 'Der Kanon von der Rechtfertigung (Gal 2,16; Röm 3,28)', *Studien zum Römerbrief* (WUNT 136; Tübingen: Mohr Siebeck, 2001) 164-225.

——, 'Paulus und Polykarp an die Philipper. Schlaglichter auf die frühe Rezeption des Basissatzes von der Rechtfertigung', in Bachmann, ed., *Lutherische und Neue Paulusperspektive* 349-88.

Thompson, M. B., *The New Perspective on Paul* (Cambridge: Grove Books, 2002).

Thurén, L., *Derhetorizing Paul: A Dynamic Perspective on Pauline Theology and the Law* (Tübingen: Mohr Siebeck, 2000).

Tomson, P. J., *Paul and the Jewish Law: Halakha in the Letters of the Apostle to the Gentiles* (CRINT III/1; Assen/Maastricht: Van Gorcum, 1990).

——, 'Paul's Jewish Background in View of His Law Teaching in 1 Cor 7', in Dunn, ed., *Paul and the Mosaic Law* 251-70.

——, '"Die Täter des Gesetzes werden gerechtfertigt werden" (Röm 2,13). Zu einer adäquaten Perspektive für den Römerbrief', in Bachmann, ed., *Lutherische und Neue Paulusperspektive* 183-221.

Tyson, J. B., '"Works of the Law" in Galatians', *JBL* 92 (1973) 423-31.

VanLandingham, C., *Judgment and Justification in Early Judaism and the Apostle Paul* (Peabody, MA: Hendrickson, 2006).

Wander, B., *Gottesfürchtige und Sympathisanten: Studien zum heidnischen Umfeld von Diasporasynagogen* (WUNT 104; Tübingen: Mohr Siebeck, 1998).

Waters, G. P., *Justification and the New Perspectives on Paul* (Phillipsburg, NJ: Presbyterian & Reformed, 2004).

Watson, F., *Paul, Judaism and the Gentiles: A Sociological Approach* (SNTSMS 56; Cambridge: Cambridge University, 1986).

——, 'The Triune Divine Identity: Reflections on Pauline God Language, in Disagreement with J. D. G. Dunn', *JSNT* 80 (2000) 99-124.

——, *Paul and the Hermeneutics of Faith* (London: T&T Clark International, 2004).

——, 'Constructing an Antithesis: Pauline and Other Jewish Perspectives on Divine and Human Agency', in Barclay & Gathercole, eds., *Divine and Human Agency in Paul* 99-116.

Watson, N. M., 'Justified by Faith: Judged by Works — An Antinomy?', *NTS* 29 (1983) 202-21.

Wedderburn, A. J. M., 'Paul and the Law', *SJT* 38 (1985) 613-22.

——, 'Eine neuere Paulusperspektive?', in E.-M. Becker & P. Pilhofer, eds., *Biographie und Persönlichkeit des Paulus* (WUNT 187; Tübingen: Mohr Siebeck, 2006) 46-64.

Wendel, F., *Calvin: The Origins and Development of his Religious Thought* (1950; ET London: Collins Fontana, 1965).

Westerholm, S., 'Letter and Spirit: The Foundation of Pauline Ethics', *NTS* 30 (1984) 229-48.

——, 'On Fulfilling the Whole Law (Gal. 5.14)', *SEÅ* 51-52 (1986-87) 229-37.

——, *Israel's Law and the Church's Faith: Paul and His Recent Interpreters* (Grand Rapids: Eerdmans, 1988).

——, 'Paul and the Law in Romans 9–11', in Dunn ed., *Paul and the Mosaic Law* 215-37.

——, 'Sinai as Viewed from Damascus: Paul's Reevaluation of the Mosaic Law', in R. N. Longenecker, ed., *The Road from Damascus: The Impact of Paul's Conversion on His Life, Thought, and Ministry* (Grand Rapids: Eerdmans, 1997) 147-65.

——, *Perspectives Old and New on Paul: The "Lutheran" Paul and His Critics* (Grand Rapids: Eerdmans, 2004).

——, 'The Righteousness of the Law and the Righteousness of Faith in Romans', *Interpretation* 58 (2004) 253-64.

————, 'The "New Perspective" at Twenty-Five', in Carson et al., *Justification and Variegated Nomism Vol. 2* 1-38.

————, 'Paul's Anthropological "Pessimism" in its Jewish Context', in Barclay & Gathercole, eds., *Divine and Human Agency in Paul* 71-98.

Wilckens, U., 'Was heisst bei Paulus: "Aus Werken des Gesetzes wird kein Mensch gerecht"?' (1969), *Rechtfertigung als Freiheit: Paulusstudien* (Neukirchen-Vluyn: Neukirchener, 1974) 77-109.

————, 'Zur Entwicklung des paulinischen Gesetzesverständnis', *NTS* 28 (1982) 154-90.

Williams, S. K., 'The "Righteousness of God" in Romans', *JBL* 99 (1980) 241-90.

Winninge, M., *Sinners and the Righteous: A Comparative Study of the Psalms of Solomon and Paul's Letters* (CBNTS 26; Stockholm: Almqvist & Wiksell, 1995).

Wintle, B. C., 'Justification in Pauline Thought', in D. A. Carson, ed., *Right With God: Justification in the Bible and the World* (Carlisle: Paternoster, 1992) 51-68.

Wischmeyer, O., ed., *Paulus: Leben — Umwelt — Werk — Briefe* (Tübingen: Francke, 2006) 35-43.

Wisdom, J. R., *Blessing for the Nations and the Curse of the Law: Paul's Citation of Genesis and Deuteronomy in Gal. 3.8-10* (WUNT 2.133; Tübingen: Mohr Siebeck, 2001).

Witherington, B., *Grace in Galatia: A Commentary on Paul's Letter to the Galatians* (Edinburgh: T&T Clark, 1998).

Wolter, M., 'Eine neue paulinische Perspektive', *ZNT* 14.7 (2004) 2-9.

Wright, N. T., 'The Paul of History and the Apostle of Faith', *TynBul* 29 (1978) 61-88.

————, *The Climax of the Covenant* (Edinburgh: T&T Clark, 1991).

————, *The New Testament and the People of God* (London: SPCK, 1992).

————, 'Romans and the Theology of Paul', in D. M. Hay & E. E. Johnson, eds., *Pauline Theology, Volume III: Romans* (Minneapolis: Fortress, 1995) 30-67.

————, *What St. Paul Really Said: Was Paul of Tarsus the Real Founder of Christianity?* (Grand Rapids: Wm. B. Eerdmans, 1997).

————, 'A Fresh Perspective on Paul?', *BJRL* 83 (2001) 21-39.

————, 'The Law in Romans 2', in Dunn, ed., *Paul and the Mosaic Law* 131-50.

————, 'The Letter to the Romans', *NIB* 10 (2002) 395-770.

————, 'Redemption from the New Perspective? Towards a Multi-Layered Pauline Theology of the Cross', in S. T. Davis, et al., eds., *The Redemption: An Interdisciplinary Symposium on Christ as Redeemer* (Oxford: Oxford University, 2004) 69-100.

————, '4QMMT and Paul: Justification, "Works", and Eschatology', in S.-W. Son, ed., *History and Exegesis*, E. E. Ellis FS (New York: T&T Clark, 2006) 104-32.

————, *Paul: Fresh Perspectives* (London: SPCK, 2005).

Yarbrough, R. W., 'Paul and Salvation History', in Carson, et al., *Justification and Variegated Nomism Vol. 2* 297-342.

Yinger, K. L., *Paul, Judaism, and Judgment According to Deeds* (SNTSMS 105; Cambridge: Cambridge University 1999).

Zahl, P. F. M., *Die Rechtfertigungslehre Ernst Käsemanns* (Stuttgart: Calwer, 1996).

————, 'Mistakes of the New Perspective on Paul', *Themelios* 27/1 (Autumn 2001) 5-11.

Zeller, D., 'Zur neueren Diskussion über das Gesetz bei Paulus', *ThPh* 62 (1987) 477-99.

Ziesler, J., *The Meaning of Righteousness in Paul* (SNTSMS 20; Cambridge: Cambridge University, 1972).

————, 'Justification by Faith in the Light of the "New Perspective" on Paul', *Theology* 94 (1991) 189-94.

Modern Authors Index

Subject Index

Biblical and Ancient Texts Index

**JEWISH
PSEUDEPIGRAPHA
JOSEPHUS, PHILO**